HUMAN RESOURCE MANAGEMENT

Strategies for Managing a Diverse and Global Workforce

Sixth Edition

Michael R. Carrell

Northern Kentucky University

Norbert F. Elbert

Saginaw Valley State University

Robert D. Hatfield

Morehead State University

The Dryden Press
A Division of Harcourt College Publishers

Fort Worth Philadelphia San Diego New York Orlando Austin San Antonio Toronto
Montreal London Sydney Tokyo

Publisher	Michael Roche
Acquisitions Editor	John Weimeister
Marketing Strategist	Lisé Johnson
Development Editor	Tracy Morse
Project Editor	Rebecca Dodson
Production Manager	Angela Urquhart
Art Director	Garry Harman
Picture and Literary Rights Editor	Linda Blundell

ISBN: 0-03-026161-9

Library of Congress Catalog Card Number: 99-74021

Address for Domestic Orders

The Dryden Press, 6277 Sea Harbor Drive, Orlando, FL 32887-6777

800-782-4479

Address for International Orders

International Customer Service

The Dryden Press, 6277 Sea Harbor Drive, Orlando, FL 32887-6777

407-345-3800

(fax) 407-345-4060

(e-mail) hbintl@harcourtbrace.com

Address for Editorial Correspondence

The Dryden Press, 301 Commerce Street, Suite 3700, Fort Worth, TX 76102

Web Site Address

http://www.hbcollege.com

0 1 2 3 4 5 6 7 8 9   032   9 8 7 6 5 4 3 2

Printed in the United States of America

The Dryden Press

Harcourt College Publishers

THE DRYDEN PRESS SERIES IN MANAGEMENT

GOLD
EXPLORING ORGANIZATIONAL BEHAVIOR: READINGS, CASES, EXPERIENCES

GREENHAUS AND CALLANAN
CAREER MANAGEMENT
Second Edition

HARRIS
HUMAN RESOURCE MANAGEMENT
Second Edition

HIGGINS AND VINCZE
STRATEGIC MANAGEMENT: TEXT AND CASES
Fifth Edition

HODGETTS
MODERN HUMAN RELATIONS AT WORK
Sixth Edition

HODGETTS AND KROECK
PERSONNEL AND HUMAN RESOURCE MANAGEMENT

HODGETTS AND KURATKO
EFFECTIVE SMALL BUSINESS MANAGEMENT
Sixth Edition

HOLLEY AND JENNINGS
THE LABOR RELATIONS PROCESS
Sixth Edition

HOLT
INTERNATIONAL MANAGEMENT: TEXT AND CASES

JAUCH AND COLTRIN
THE MANAGERIAL EXPERIENCE: CASES AND EXERCISES
Sixth Edition

KINDLER AND GINSBURG
STRATEGIC & INTERPERSONAL SKILL BUILDING

KIRKPATRICK AND LEWIS
EFFECTIVE SUPERVISION: PREPARING FOR THE 21ST CENTURY

KURATKO AND HODGETTS
ENTREPRENEURSHIP: A CONTEMPORARY APPROACH
Fourth Edition

KURATKO AND WELSCH
ENTREPRENEURIAL STRATEGY: TEXT AND CASES

LENGNICK-HALL, CYNTHIA, AND HARTMAN
EXPERIENCING QUALITY

LEWIS
IO ENTERPRISES SIMULATION

LONG AND ARNOLD
THE POWER OF ENVIRONMENTAL PARTNERSHIPS

MORGAN
MANAGING FOR SUCCESS

RYAN, ECKERT, AND RAY
SMALL BUSINESS: AN ENTREPRENEUR'S PLAN
Fourth Edition

SANDBURG
CAREER DESIGN SOFTWARE

VECCHIO
ORGANIZATIONAL BEHAVIOR
Third Edition

WALTON
CORPORATE ENCOUNTERS: LAW, ETHICS, AND THE BUSINESS ENVIRONMENT

WEISS
BUSINESS ETHICS: A STAKEHOLDER AND ISSUES MANAGEMENT APPROACH
Second Edition

ZIKMUND
BUSINESS RESEARCH METHODS
Fifth Edition

MICHAEL R. CARRELL

Dr. Carrell is dean of the College of Business at Northern Kentucky University, located in the greater Cincinnati area. He received his doctorate from the University of Kentucky, and MBA and B.A. in Economics from the University of Louisville. Most of his professional career has been spent in the Louisville area and has included positions as a personnel director and labor negotiator. In addition, he was elected to the City of Louisville Board of Aldermen for five terms, and served as President of the Board and Mayor Pro-tem for three terms.

Dr. Carrell has held academic positions at California State University, Bakersfield; The University of Nebraska–Omaha, Marshall University, Morehead State University, and the University of Louisville. He has authored over 50 scholarly works in some of the leading management and human resource journals including *The Academy of Management Journal, The Academy of Management Review, Organizational Behavior and Human Performance, Personnel Journal, The Personnel Administrator, HR Magazine, Labor Law Journal, Business Forum, Personnel, The Journal of Accountancy and Training,* and *Public Personnel Management.* Other textbooks published by Dr. Carrell are in the fields of collective bargaining and labor relations, organizational behavior, and negotiations. During his academic career he has received awards for both outstanding research and teaching.

NORBERT F. ELBERT

Dr. Elbert holds the Harvey Randall Wickes Chair of International Business at Saginaw Valley State University in Michigan. He received his doctorate from the University of Kentucky and his MBA and BS in Management from the University of Louisville. He has taught at Marshall University, Ball State University, Northern Arizona University, University of Denver, Bellarmine College, and

SVSU. He was awarded a Fulbright Scholar to Hungary and has been a visiting professor to several Central and Eastern European institutions, including Janos Pannonius University in Pecs, Hungary, the International Management Center in Budapest, the Czechoslovak Management Center in Prague, and the Romanian Institute of Management in Bucharest. He has authored over two dozen scholarly publications in such journals as the *Journal of Management Education, Journal of Experimental Education, Health Care Management Review, Decision Sciences, Journal of Marketing Research, Personnel,* and the *Academy of Management Journal.* Dr. Elbert is also the co-author of other professional books including the first post-socialist human resource management textbook published in Hungary. While he has received many honors, most recently he was nominated to receive an Honorary Degree from Janos Pannonius University in Hungary.

ROBERT D. HATFIELD

Dr. Hatfield has spent his entire 25 year career focused upon Human Resources. He was a Manager of Industrial Relations for a Fortune 500 company, working out of Kansas City and Louisville for 10 years. It is this professional and practical background which shapes his viewpoint as an author. For the past 15 years he has been in demand as a management consultant, guest speaker, trainer, labor arbitrator, and mediator. During that time he also taught HR full-time at the University of Louisville, Bellarmine College, West Virginia State College, and Morehead State University.

Dr. Hatfield received his Ph.D. in HR and Organizational Behavior from Indiana University and his Juris Doctor (focusing upon HR and labor law) from the University of Louisville. He has published scholarly articles and cases in the fields of training, employment discrimination, and international management. He has also served as the advisor for college SHRM chapters.

ARCHIE AND MYRTLE CARRELL, A PERSON COULD NOT ASK FOR MORE LOVING, SUPPORTING AND DEDICATED PARENTS.

—M.R.C.

TO BARB, MY BEST FRIEND AND "SOUL-MATE".

—N.F.E.

TO THE LOVES OF MY LIFE AND JOYS OF MY HEART: MY TWO REDHEADS— MELANIE AND MICHAEL FITZPATRICK HATFIELD. ETERNAL THANKS TO MY WONDERFUL AND WISE PARENTS, BOB AND NORMA HATFIELD.

—R.D.H.

"There is nothing permanent except change." This sounds like Bill Gates describing the momentous changes in technology, or the President discussing the "shrinking" of the world by global trade. Instead, the often cited quote is from Heraclitus, a philosopher from Ephesis who died in 480 B.C. Indeed, change has been a constant during every generation. The business world in 2000 certainly has changed since the last turn of the century.

The changes in business reflect the changes in the greater society over these years. For good or ill the following trends may be observed in the U.S.: the government and the regulation of people and business grows; sensitivities concerning inequities at work heighten; inclination to sue (hoping to "hit the jackpot") increases; lawsuits cause employers to react and overreact with strictness; connections among and between businesses and nations become more obvious and meaningful; immigration continues to change the demography and culture of the work force in this nation created by immigration; educational levels improve; more information is available but employees profess to understand less; and it is a wonderful yet scary time in history to be starting a career. These and other influences have a huge impact upon what is important today in management and Human Resources (HR).

In this sixth edition of this book, we attempt to address and incorporate those facts and competencies with which modern managers need to be knowledgeable. Many of the traditional functions of Human Resources (HR) are today incorporated into the job descriptions of line managers and teams as a result of restructuring and employee empowerment. So, we write this book not just for future HR managers, but primarily for future managers and team members who must now know HR.

We are proud that the fifth edition of our book outsold the previous two editions. We thank our adopters and the tens of thousands of students who value our book. We believe that our easy readability, lively and controversial examples, and straightforward approach accounts for our book's increasing popularity. By integrating global and strategic issues we believe that this book integrates well with other business and management courses. There are some caution lights out there for anyone dedicated to trying to set or explain important HR policies.

Thomas Stewart sparked a fierce debate with his *Fortune* article, "Taking on the Last Bureaucracy," in which he said, "Nothing is more dangerous than a group of (HR) people trained in the art of monitoring compliance with rules, fluent in a language that does not include a word for 'customer,' and who have time on their hands and are looking for something to do." Stewart drew great attention to this perception of HR in the 1990s, and he had this advice, "Why not blow the sucker (HR) up? I don't mean improve HR. . . . I mean abolish it. Deep six it. Rub it out; eliminate, toss, obliterate, nuke it, . . . force it to walk the plank, turn it into road kill." Well before these comments employers started outsourcing functions and integrating traditional HR tasks into teams or management. HR must make sure Stewart's characterization is incorrect. HR must become a strategic partner in organizations and be more concerned with issues like firm performance. We use many strategic terms to help students grasp this needed change.

In *Human Resource Champions*, HR futurist and analyst Dave Ulrich uses the term "frou-frou" to describe the "cute" and "faddish" HR trends which come and go and do not add long-term value to an organization. Although we probably mention the latest fads, we try to focus instead upon the essential functions and roles that management needs to master to add value to employees, investors, customers, and the organization itself.

Will Rogers once said, "It's not what we don't know that gets us into trouble; it's what we do know that isn't so." We are bombarded by the news, which we forget is, by definition, only about the odd and unusual—"man bites dog." We often confuse the oddball (news) with the common. For example, employers are so frightened about being sued over giving out references that they have almost stopped helping each other screen applicants. I have seen so much news about defamation suits against employers that I assumed they are common. Instead, it turns out that an HR manager is much more likely to get leprosy than be sued over a reference. According to a 1999 study, only twelve such defamation suits were filed, and only four won by plaintiffs over an entire recent ten year period. I call this error the "Dan Rather error"—assuming the odd is important. Employers, and authors, must avoid the "Dan Rather error" when setting or understanding solid HR policies. We have tried.

CONTENT HIGHLIGHTS

Attempting at avoiding those pitfalls and in the spirit of continuous improvement, this sixth edition is a major revision and update.

Chapter 2: "Going global" may be a cliche, but the HR implications are significant. This completely revised chapter examines whether HR strategies that work in the U.S. will be as effective in Europe or Asia (and vice versus). How does HR help build cooperative relationships in a multicultural world? A unique nation-by-nation HR comparison of major global competitors is included by our International Business Chair author.

Chapter 3 is an entire chapter sharply focused upon defining and managing workforce diversity. Companion Chapter 4 introduces employment legislation in an easy to understand format and includes coverage of the landmark Supreme Court 1998 sexual harassment rulings and other new cases.

Chapters 5 and 6 have new material on the dramatic changes occurring in the global corporations and the effects on the design of work. New job analysis and design approaches are discussed and their relationship to motivation, retention, and performance—written to relate well with Organizational Behavior and Strategy courses. There are updates on work place flexibility, telecommuting, the office environment, and the contingent workforce.

Chapter 7 includes coverage of electronic and other nontraditional employee recruiting methods. Companion Chapter 8 on selection includes new behavioral interview questions and reference checking techniques.

Chapter 9 fully discusses 360-degree feedback, portfolio approaches, and team reviews along with the traditional Performance Appraisal material. The fierce conflict in managerial philosophies on the topic of PAs is also exposed.

Chapter 10 now includes discussion of learning styles and adult learning and provides a simple five-step training model to help future managers manage training. Companion Chapter 11 identifies special problems women and other minorities have in moving in to upper management; examines the "glass ceiling" debate; and identifies the changes managers should expect as the baby boomers, busters, Gen X, and Gen Y employees progress through their careers.

Chapters 12 and 13 discuss multiple and creative compensation options—like team-based reward systems—as alternatives to traditional pay strategies. There is a future-focused discussion of medical and retirement packages along with latest innovations in benefits—like concierge and spiritual benefits at work. The importance of fit between business strategy and total compensation is stressed.

Chapters 14 and 15 include the latest safety and labor updates and an exposé of the worker replacement issue in the UPS strike of 1997 and the historic 1997–99 UAW-GM agreement.

Chapter 16 includes helpful discipline and counseling tools like the "hot stove rule" and a reformulated discussion of the changing at-will doctrine. Recent cases and, as always, *HR in the News* boxes keep the student updated and stimulated. Old chapters on HRIS and Problem Solving (like absenteeism and turnover) have been cut and central portions integrated into other appropriate chapters.

A Resource Appendix has been added to give students tools for doing class projects and writing papers. There is helpful guidance on how to do research and handy listings of HR-related associations and publications. Useful Web sites are printed inside the book's covers.

Individual and group exercises are included at the end of each chapter and cases are available after each section. Hundreds of new articles, mostly from 1998 and 1999 have been added. A new Web site extends the text—making it continuously current and relevant. As always, we as authors make ourselves available to instructors, and, through the Web, to students.

Heraclitus also said, "Nothing is; everything is becoming. . . Upon those who step into the same rivers flow other and yet other waters." Everything changes and we have done our best to reflect those dramatic change forces and identify those changes managers and HR professionals must know. Finally, Heraclitus said, "It is the thunderbolt that steers the course of all things." Who knows what the next thunderbolt will be in this world?

PEDAGOGICAL FEATURES AND SUPPLEMENTS

Each chapter opens with a list of behavioral learning objectives to present an overview and create focus. In addition, each chapter contains several features designed to enhance excitement and student learning.

① *HR in the News,* a unique feature to this text, contains a brief new or analysis article to help the student see the application of text material and/or create lively discussion.

② Summary Points help refocus and refresh the text material.

③ Key Terms and Concepts include much of the unique management and HR vocabularies.

④ Review and Discussion Questions stimulate classroom or study discussion and reinforce key chapter concepts.

⑤ Case Studies at the end of each chapter facilitate a teaching-by-case approach and to provide detailed examples of text concepts.

⑥ Two Experiential Exercises at the end of each chapter—one is for individuals and the other is for teams. This allows for multiple uses, including in-class team building, skills enhancement, and distance learning opportunities.

Ancillary Package   To supplement the text, several ancillary items have been developed to aid the instructor. The *Instructor's Manual/Test Bank/Transparency Masters* help the instructor use the text most effectively. The IM provides a wealth of supplementary information for enriching lectures such as learning objectives, lecture outlines and notes, and transparency masters. The Test Bank includes approximately 900 test questions and features a range of problems to test students' knowledge, as well as containing separate answer sections for test-making facility. The test items include true/false, multiple choice, and essay questions.

The Computerized Test Bank also facilitates test construction. *ExaMaster 99* is a cross-platform program available on CD-ROM that works with the latest versions of Macintosh, Windows, and Windows NT operating systems. *ExaMaster 99* includes online testing capabilities, a grade book, and much more. It contains all questions from the Test Bank and is available to all adopters.

CD-ROM PowerPoint Presentation Software   This innovative PowerPoint package provides colorful slides to reinforce material found in the text. The CD-ROM has been prepared in a Power Point format to be easily supplemented by instructors who wish to introduce additional materials into their lecture presentations.

Video Package   This video package has been prepared to provide a relevant and interesting visual teaching tool for the classroom. Each video segment is relevant to chapter material and gives students the opportunity to apply what they are learning to real-world companies such as JCPenney, Harley Davidson, AFSCME, McDonald's, and University National Bank. The video material enables instructors to better illustrate text concepts to students.

Human Resource Management Web Site   Visit the Dryden Web site at **http://www.harcourtcollege.com** for the latest support material. The site contains a wealth of Internet resources specific to the topic areas of this textbook. These resources include relevant links to publications, data and resources, information on careers, national and international business news, internet exercises, company profiles, time-management aids, and much more.

ACKNOWLEDGMENTS

We would like to thank the following people for their support and direct assistance on this edition. First, we want to thank Executive Editor and excellent developer John Weimeister at Dryden/Harcourt College Publishing for supporting this project. Tracy Morse, Ellen Hostetler, and the other great people at Fort Worth have been more helpful and easier to work with than I thought possible. Also, Lisé Johnson and Marcia Masenda have been very helpful to we "new guys" on Dryden's book list.

Thanks also to Gary Clark, Hong Park, Dean Paul Uselding, Academic VP Robert Yien, and President Eric Gilbertson, all from Saginaw Valley State University; Jozsef Poor, Ferenc Farkas, and Zsuzsanna Karoliny all from Janos Pannonius University in Pecs, Hungary; and Jason Schweizer at Houston Energy.

We also want to acknowledge the support of Extended Campus Librarian Gary Austin, Management and Marketing Chair Peggy Osborne, Interim Dean Bob Albert, Vice President Michael Moore, and President Ronald Eaglin, all of Morehead State University; People-Soft guru Mike Bedell at California State University, Bakersfield; and my training mentor Tim Baldwin at Indiana University.

On behalf of thousands of former management students at the University of Louisville, a personal friend and great teacher, we thank Robert Myers for his many years of outstanding teaching.

We thank our colleagues, support staff, students, families and each other for "mutual aid and protection" as we worked on this long and continuous project. Most of all, we thank the thousands of readers and instructors who choose our book for the fun and work it takes to explore an HR course.

MICHAEL R. CARRELL

NORBERT F. ELBERT

ROBERT D. HATFIELD

PART

V

EMPLOYEE RELATIONS   **399**

Contents

P A R T

II

ATTRACTING HUMAN
RESOURCES   **99**

CHAPTER 7

PART IV

RETAINING HUMAN RESOURCES 309

CHAPTER 12
COMPENSATION SYSTEMS   311

PART
V

PART 1

THE ENVIRONMENT FOR HUMAN RESOURCES

CHAPTER 1

THE FOUNDATION AND CHALLENGES OF HUMAN RESOURCE MANAGEMENT

CHAPTER OUTLINE

HR IN THE NEWS

PAYING ATTENTION TO THE HEARTS, MINDS, AND LIVES OF PEOPLE

In their book, *Making It in America: Proven Paths to Success from 50 Top Companies* (Simon & Schuster), Jerry Jasinowski and Robert Hamrin argue that employee empowerment is the most widespread and proven way to be a winner in today's harshly competitive corporate environment.

"Workers," they write, "are the ones who make modern manufacturing work. They are the ones who must take full advantage of today's sophisticated and expensive machines. They are the ones who know best where the key problems and most promising opportunities lie."

Dana Corporation, an automotive components manufacturer based in Toledo, Ohio, has created a culture where empowerment has become a reality. "Dana believes people must have a sense of purpose, that people want to be involved, and that people want to do a good job," explains Gary Corrigan, director of corporate communication.

WWW.DANA.COM

Because of this belief, the company has implemented a number of HRM strategies that encourage and recognize individual contributions. These HRM strategies include a commitment to 40 hours of education per employee per year; an internal promotion policy, in which the people who help create the company's success share in the rewards; a suggestion system in which each employee is encouraged to submit two ideas per month (the company strives for 80 percent implementation of those ideas); a decentralized organizational structure that supports individual responsibility; a retirement program that encourages employees to stay with the company; and a stock purchase program that encourages eligible employees to own a share of the company (currently 40 percent of eligible employees participate).

The Dana style of management reinforces the belief that its employees are the true experts when it comes to their specific tasks, and the company looks to its people to be "experts of their own 25 square-foot area," Corrigan adds.

Source: Adapted from Shari Caudron, "The Only Way to Stay Ahead," *Industry Week* 247 (August 17, 1998): 98–101.

CHAPTER OBJECTIVES

1 To recognize the importance of environmental forces in the management of people, the design of work, and the organization's capacity to compete effectively.

2 To trace the history of personnel/human resource management.

3 To define the connection between successful companies and strategic human resource management.

4 To understand the organizational structure of the typical human resource department.

5 To describe the major functions and roles of the human resource department.

6 To identify the major issues and challenges faced by HR professionals today.

7 To describe the career opportunities within the human resource field.

The traditional corporation is becoming a thing of the past. Efficiency and economies of scale, two dominant 20th-century themes, have been replaced by new values: teamwork over individualism, global markets over domestic ones, and customer-driven focus over short-run profits. Only fluid, flexible highly adaptive organizations, like the Dana Corporation highlighted in the opening *HR in the News,* will thrive in the fast-paced global economy.[1]

For HR professionals, one thing is certain: Traditional personnel approaches that were conceived in cultures emphasizing command and control are giving way to new approaches characterized by greater employee commitment, cooperation, and communication. Companies with rigid structures will be swept away.[2] By contrast, companies like the Dana Corporation are empowering employees, letting workers manage everything from budgets to inventory control, often without direct oversight from top management.

Has there really been that much change in the way employees need to be managed? In short, yes. For example, the issue of workplace flexibility has emerged in response to the needs of today's companies and the diversity of its employees. Before the 1980s, standardization was the norm in personnel administration. Consistency and conformity were once hallmarks of management policy. Today, developing the capacity for flexibility is considered a vital component of the company's corporate human resource strategy.[3]

What makes an organization effective? Is it the land, buildings, capital, patents, and technology it owns? An organization's tangible assets are certainly important factors in its success, but managers today recognize that an organization's people—its HR—are its most critical assets. How should this critical human resource be managed? What are effective HR policies and practices? Which methods of HR management can lead to maximum productivity, quality, and customer satisfaction? The answers to questions such as these, and many more, are the focus of this book. Without question, the successful management of an organization's human resources—its people—is an exciting, fluid, and challenging field.

HUMAN RESOURCES: PAST AND PRESENT

Modern HR management is radically different from personnel management of decades ago. Since the turn of the century, the managerial philosophy that has defined the personnel function has undergone significant changes. In the last 80 years, both the scientific management approach and the human relations approach have appeared and declined; today what has popularly become known as the human resource approach has emerged.

SCIENTIFIC MANAGEMENT

The technique of **scientific management** was the first radical change in what most owners and managers of the early 1900s generally considered the most effective means of managing employees—constant supervision and threats of the loss of their jobs (similar to that of Dickens's Ebenezer Scrooge). Before the advent of scientific management, all employees were considered equally productive, and if their productivity did not measure up, they deserved to be quickly terminated. The founders of the scientific management movement believed differently. Instead of simply relying on the use of fear and intimidation, Frederick Taylor, Frank and Lillian Gilbreth, and Henry Gantt believed that managers should take a scientific and objective approach in studying how work can be most efficiently designed.

Taylor, the "father of scientific management," and the others employed data collection and analysis methods often found in research laboratories at that time. He emphasized the study of the motions required for each job, the tools utilized, and the time required for each task. Then, based on scientific data instead of a boss's subjective judgment, fair performance standards for each job could be determined. Scientific management principles spread quickly, generally with success. However, the movement's treatment of the worker—someone motivated solely by money—led to problems.

Frederick Taylor declared that "one of the very first requirements for a man who is fit to handle pig iron as a regular occupation is that he shall be so stupid and so phlegmatic that he more nearly resembles in his mental makeup the ox than any other type."[4] Taylor's oft-quoted comment underscores a widespread managerial attitude of the early 20th century: Along with raw materials, capital, and machinery, the employee is simply another factor of production. As such, the scientific management approach resulted in work methods and techniques that showed great concern for employee output but little concern for employee satisfaction. Typically, the one best way to do the job was highly specialized and routine, involving little mental effort and few opportunities to make decisions or use judgment. Proponents of scientific management are quick to point out that the average turn-of-the-century worker had little formal education and few skills or abilities that could be applied to organizational problems.

Taylor created the *differential piece-rate system,* whereby workers would receive a higher rate of pay per piece produced after the daily output standard had been achieved. Workers who produced output above the standard would receive additional incentive pay. At the time, all employees were generally given the same daily or weekly wage, regardless of their individual efforts.

The personnel departments of large manufacturing companies during the early years of the century had the traditional responsibilities of recruiting, selection, training, and health and safety. But the main focus of their activities was the implementation of scientific management techniques. For example, the personnel staff conducted time-and-motion studies and fatigue studies, performed job analyses, prepared job specifications, and created wage incentive programs.[5]

It was during this period that employers began to view workers as something more than machines. Personnel managers began developing a set of practices that set the stage for continuing study and investment in the role of effective human resource management.

HUMAN RELATIONS

During the 1930s and 1940s, with impetus provided by the classic Hawthorne studies, management's attention shifted from scientific management to **human relations.** The Hawthorne studies demonstrated that employee productivity was affected not only by the way the job was designed and the manner in which employees were rewarded economically, but also by certain social and psychological factors.[6] Hawthorne researchers Elton Mayo and F. J. Roethlisberger provided new insight derived from studies that linked improved productivity to management philosophies emphasizing employee communications, cooperation, and involvement.[7]

It was asserted that treating employees with dignity would both enhance employee satisfaction and enable the achievement of higher productivity. The research led to the widespread implementation of behavioral science techniques in industry, including supervisory training programs that emphasized support and concern for the workers. The personnel staff was primarily responsible for designing and implementing such programs.

The shift to human relations was also influenced by the growing strength of unions during the period. Unions began challenging the fairness and validity of Taylor's scientific management theories.

The rise of unionism did compel many employers to improve their personnel programs (that is, employee relations) in an effort to keep unions out. Although unionization led to an erosion of labor–management relations

in some firms, in many other companies it resulted in greater acceptance of the principles of human relations.

The human relations approach was no doubt instrumental in improving the working environment of many workers, but it achieved only minimal success in increasing worker output and enhancing job satisfaction. The lackluster performance of the approach is attributable to the following:

- The approach was based on an oversimplified concept of human behavior in an organizational setting. The notion that "a happy worker is a hard worker"—generally presented to management as an untested hypothesis—is now recognized to be valid for only part of the workforce.
- The approach failed to consider the concept of individual differences. Each worker is a unique and complex person with different wants, needs, and values. What motivates one worker may not motivate another; being happy or feeling good may have little or no impact on the productivity of certain employees.
- The approach failed to recognize the need both for job structure and for accountability. It largely neglected the importance of procedures, standards, and work rules in guiding employees toward the goals of the organization.
- The approach failed to recognize that good human relations are but one of many conditions necessary to sustain a high level of employee motivation. For instance, productivity may also be improved using workplace flexibility, teams, career development programs, empowerment programs, and selection and placement systems that successfully match the employee with the job.

The human relations approach fell out of favor with management during the 1950s and 1960s and is considered passé today. Good feelings are necessary but certainly not sufficient to ensure peak levels of employee satisfaction and productivity.

HUMAN RESOURCES (HR)

The emerging trend in **human resource (HR) management** is clearly toward the adoption of the human resource approach, through which organizations benefit in two significant ways: an increase in organizational effectiveness and the satisfaction of each employee's needs. Rather than addressing organizational goals and employee needs as separate and exclusive, the human resources approach holds that organizational goals and human needs are mutual and compatible: One set need not be gained at the expense of the other.

FIGURE 1–1   HUMAN RESOURCE APPROACH

EMPLOYEE

Leads to

HIGHER
Employee Motivation
and Applied Ability

GREATER
Quality, Quantity
of Work

Leads to   Leads to

GREATER
Employee Rewards,
Recognition

HIGHER
Organization
Productivity, Profits

ORGANIZATION   Leads to

Personnel and human relations managers were now responsible for motivating people and helping their organizations navigate a maze of regulations, executive orders, and court decisions. Over time, the nature of work changed. Self-fulfillment became a primary concern, and employees wanted jobs that were challenging and interesting.

A number of principles provide the basis for a human resources approach:

- Employees are investments that will, if effectively managed and developed, provide long-term rewards to the organization in the form of greater productivity.
- Policies, programs, and practices must be created that satisfy both the economic and emotional needs of employees.
- A working environment must be created in which employees are encouraged to develop and utilize their skills to the maximum extent.
- HR programs and practices must be implemented with the goal of balancing the needs and meeting the goals, of both the organization and the employee. As Figure 1–1 indicates, this can be achieved through a circular process in which the organization and employees enable each other to meet their goals.

HUMAN RESOURCES TODAY

In contrast to the attitudes of the early 20th century—when workers were no more valuable than a piece of

machinery—the prevailing notion today is that the firm's people are its most important asset. Despite these widely held beliefs, many organizational decisions suggest a relatively low priority on both the human resources of the firm and the Human Resource department.[8] For example, when organizations require cost cutting, they look first to reductions in training or downsizing. Even when executives value the firm's people, they may not value the HR department.[9]

The fault often can be found with the fact few HR professionals can explain, in economic terms, how a firm's people can provide sustainable competitive advantages and the role the HR function plays in this process.[10] Their past success has hinged on being "policy police" by ensuring that proper policies and procedures exist and by advising managers on what they can and cannot do. Some critics even claim HR blocks progress and should be kept out of key business decisions because they bring "nothing to the table."[11] Viewing HR as a barrier, some companies are doing away with the department altogether and delegating the attracting, retaining, and motivating aspects to operational managers.[12]

To avoid that fate, HR professionals must chart roles that include early and active involvement in key strategic business decisions. They must become partners—including sharing accountability—with the operational side of the business.

How to avoid extinction and earn a place at the table as a strategic partner is the most important challenge facing HR professionals today. There are many suggestions, but it all comes down to understanding and managing the important interaction of technology, workflow, organizational strategies, and most importantly, people. In the new age of technology and rapid product innovation, unleashing the minds and creative souls of tomorrow's workforce is the factor most likely to propel businesses and the HR profession into the future.[13]

HUMAN RESOURCES TOMORROW: CHALLENGES

Knowledge is a factor of production potentially greater than the traditional triad of land, labor, or capital. It falls to human resource professionals to capture critical intellectual capital, codify it, and transfer it to others. In short it is HR's challenge to provide a blueprint of how to put knowledge to work as a source of competitive advantage.[14]

Knowledge derives from information as information derives from data. If information is to become knowledge, people must do virtually all the work. The fact is that, while it's true that an organization's knowledge has always been critical to its competitive success, up to now it wasn't so much in need of explicit management.[15] Knowledge flowed naturally, informally, at a level sufficient to fuel a marketplace advantage. Over the past decade, HR professionals' task was simple—attract, retain, and motivate good people. Certainly nothing was said or expected about creating work environments that encourage interconnecting people, knowledge, and markets.

Things have changed. Today, HR professionals who leave critical intellectual capital to its own devices put themselves in severe jeopardy. At best, this extremely valuable asset remains underleveraged, isolated in pockets of the organization, trapped in individual minds and local venues.[16]

It's become almost a cliché to talk about the accelerating pace of change in the business environment: Every commentator on any business trend pays homage to it. But undeniably, today's organization seems to experience evolutionary change faster and revolutionary change more frequently. This has made it imperative for firms to manage knowledge actively.[17]

In a relatively stable business environment, an organization's people tend to stay and naturally become highly knowledgeable over time. Tacitly, they absorb and socialize knowledge about the company's products and services, its markets, customers, competitors, and suppliers—and once gained, that knowledge sustains

them indefinitely.[18] Knowledge becomes embedded in the firm's routines and culture. New recruits learn from old hands purely by working alongside them, and exposure and seasoning is a far more important learning mechanism than training. In such an environment, it is safe to assume that sufficient knowledge and capabilities exist in the organization, or that incremental learning occurs fast enough, to deal with most contingencies.[19]

The next century will bring rapid change, meaning quicker knowledge obsolescence and a need to scale new learning curves in unnaturally compressed timeframes. Every week in a typical company brings news of some emerging market, some hot technology, some unexpected form of competition—but the company must have a knowledge base to take advantage of them.[20]

STRATEGIC HUMAN RESOURCE MANAGEMENT

In a fast-paced global economy, change is the norm. Environmental factors—social, technological, legal, skill shortages, balancing work/family issues, and others—can only mean that long-term planning is risky, but absolutely essential. How do organizations make decisions about their future in this complex, rapidly changing world? The process is called **strategic planning.** It involves making those decisions that define the overall mission, determining the most effective utilization of its resources, and crafting and executing the strategy in ways that produce the intended results.

Business strategy is management's game plan.[21] Without one, management would have no road map to follow and no action plan to produce the desired results. Strategic human resource management activities address a variety of "people issues" relevant to business strategy.

If one views human resources as any firm's most valuable asset, then it is logical that the most important task becomes finding and keeping the people who will contribute value to the firm's bottom line. Identifying the type of people needed should only be done after defining desired business results, as shown in Figure 1–2. Once the results are clearly defined, the next step is to identify the business strategies that will achieve the desired results. From there, it becomes easier to identify the kind of employees—skills, competencies, experiences, and so on—needed to implement the strategy.

A software firm, for example, needs software designers who think creatively and who are in tune with the needs of particular markets. The same firm needs

FIGURE 1–2   BUSINESS RESULTS DRIVE PERSONNEL REQUIREMENTS

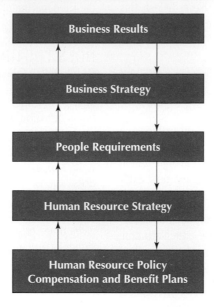

technically proficient, detail-oriented programmers to make the creative designs work on computers, and software marketing specialists to promote their products in a highly competitive market.

Understanding the kind of people the firm needs to find and keep takes an organization one step closer to determining an effective human resource strategy. The strategy should identify how one finds such people, what is necessary to keep them, and how to help them achieve their individual objectives. The HR strategy is then applied in practice and influences the design and administration of other HR programs and functions such as compensation and benefit plans.

The flow of information and influence, as illustrated in Figure 1–2, functions in reverse as well, with HR policies and plans affecting HR strategy, which in turn affects personnel requirements, and so on. This chain of influence can have a negative impact if HR policies and plans are badly out of alignment with the firm's business strategies and objectives.

Successful firms have at least one commonality. They have developed a strategy for developing and maintaining superiority in critical technical and organizational skills. Wal-Mart's competitive advantage, for example, is to offer lower prices and better services than its rivals. It can accomplish this feat by having a better distribution system (building within easy driving distance of warehouses), information management systems (transmitting point-of-sale data by satellite to suppliers), good supplier relations (no hassles and quick payment, access to satellite communication system, authority to reorder automatically based on sales), and good customer service (for example, greeting customers as they enter the store).

WWW.WAL-MART.COM

Wal-Mart refuses to leave to chance the development of critical skills that will give them a competitive edge. Identifying the mix of talents and skills needed to achieve desired results, and matching that mix to what is currently available, is a big part of strategic HR planning. Each HR function (training, recruitment, performance appraisal, and so on) can then be examined to consider how it supports the strategic thrust. Any gap between desired and existing human resource skills, knowledge, and abilities (SKA) necessitates the adoption of changes in HR policies and practices, such as hiring people with needed skills, creating new training programs, and so on.

Well-conceived HR strategies are an important basis for competition. How important depends entirely on the industry and on the extent to which people play a vital role in the success of the business. The bigger the role, the greater the potential payoff for having well-conceived HR strategies for maximizing talents. While this philosophy applies to most industries, there are situations in which success or failure is governed by market and financial forces that have little to do with human resources. Low-skill manufacturing, for example, may not depend on people's creative juices as much as on low wages. Nevertheless, this book rests on the premise that effective strategic HR management is a powerful competitive weapon.

HUMAN RESOURCE FUNCTIONS

Because the **human resource function** within each organization is unique to that organization, the activities included in the HR department will vary from organization to organization. Among the activities that are most likely to be assigned exclusively to the HR department are:

1 Compensation and benefits issues, such as insurance administration, wage and salary administration, unemployment compensation, pension plans, vacation/leave processing, and flexible benefits accounts.

2 Employee services such as outplacement services, employee assistance plans, health and wellness programs, savings plans, and relocation services.

3 Affirmative action and equal employment opportunity compliance and record keeping.

4 Job analysis programs.

5 Preemployment testing, including drug testing.

6 Attitude surveys (research).

In addition, the HR department is likely to carry out some activities jointly with other departments in the organization, including interviewing, productivity/motivation programs, training and development, career planning, disciplinary procedures, and performance appraisals. Each of these functions are discussed in more detail later.

HR DEPARTMENT ROLES

The primary task of the HR department is to ensure that the organization's human resources are utilized and managed as effectively as possible. HR administrators help design and implement policies and programs that enhance human abilities and improve the organization's overall effectiveness. Top executives have learned—sometimes the hard way—that inattention to personnel relations and neglect of HR programs are often causes of poor labor–management relations, excessive absenteeism and turnover, lawsuits charging discrimination, and substandard productivity. More and more, leaders of

public and private organizations recognize that *people* are the organization's primary resource and acknowledge the HR department's role in developing that resource.

DOES THE HR FUNCTION AFFECT THE SUCCESS OF AN ORGANIZATION?

Managers, owners, and even college professors sometimes question whether the HR department can really affect the financial success of an organization. Without a doubt, organizations wishing to remain competitive in today's rapidly changing global marketplace need to address the issue of achieving productivity through their employees. The question that is often asked, however, is how important the HR function is in that achievement, given other critical factors such as the leadership provided by top management, product superiority, customer service, and research and development.

The importance of the HR function in the organization's efforts to achieve financial success is solidly supported. The top 100 rapid-growth companies as identified by *Inc.* magazine were included in a study of twelve HR practices. The results indicated a strong relationship between HR practices and bottom-line profits. A second finding was that company size, measured by number of employees, did not affect the results: Companies of all sizes were equally affected. The results generally indicated that more successful companies engaged in more HR practices than did less successful companies. Successful rapid-growth companies were generally able to use the HR function to solve problems and achieve success in the following ways:[22]

- Having the HR directors report directly to the president.
- Placing a major company emphasis on employee recruitment, selection, and training.
- Using team building and creating an environment of rapid decision making at lower levels.
- Communicating key company performance objectives through all programs and linking them to goals at all levels.
- Including HR planning as part of management's strategic planning.

Throughout this book, you will find many of these points repeated and discussed in detail. Employers who have successfully integrated the HR function into the top level of management and strategic planning, and who have placed a strong emphasis on employee recruitment, selection, motivation, and team building, can expect greater employee productivity and thus greater overall company success.

To acquire and retain employees, HR administrators perform five critical roles: Create and implement policy, maintain communication, offer advice, provide services, and control personnel programs and procedures. Let us examine the multiple roles of the personnel staff more fully.

HR POLICIES

HR policies are guides to management's thinking, and they help management achieve the organization's HR objectives. Policies also help define acceptable and unacceptable behavior and establish the organization's position on an issue. Top HR officials—the vice-president or the HR department heads—are generally responsible for policy making. In critical HR matters, such as equal employment or management development, the policies may be drafted by an HR committee for approval by the chief executive officer. HR committees generally include members from both line and staff departments. A *line function* is one that is directly related to the achievement of an organization's goals. In a typical manufacturing enterprise, line functions include production and sales. In a university, teaching is a line function and the faculty members are line personnel. *Staff* generally refers to a department that provides specialized services for the entire organization. Staff departments normally include engineering, research and development, purchasing, quality control, legal, finance, and HR. Line managers not only bring experience to the HR committee but are also more likely to support the policies they help create.

To be maximally effective, HR policies should be in writing and should be communicated to all employees. To ensure that employees are familiar with HR policies, many organizations—particularly large firms and government agencies—publish an HR policy manual. Each manager receives a copy of the manual, with instructions to review it in detail with all new employees. Updates of the manual may be posted on bulletin boards, and supervisors may be required to discuss policy revisions with their employees. A well-written and well-used policy manual can be a valuable aid not only in orienting new employees to the workplace but also in settling differences between supervisors and subordinates.

CRITICAL POLICY ISSUES

Most of the critical issues facing HR management are included in four broad areas: employee influence, staffing flow, reward systems, and work systems. Each of these areas must be addressed regardless of the industry, size of the firm, or types of employees involved. By developing critical HR policies with those four areas in mind, decision makers can create HR programs in a unified and systematic manner rather than by accident or by gut reaction to problems and pressures. Such decisions involve choices, and choices are most effectively made through planned policies and practices.[23]

Employee Influence   With the increasing popularity of worker participation, more and more organizations are developing policies that define the scope and breadth of employee influence in managing the organization. Such policies specify the degree of authority and responsibility that are delegated to employees and employee groups, and the way in which those relationships (for example, self-managed workgroups) may most effectively be institutionalized. Policies defining the degree of employee influence deal with such diverse matters as organizational goals, compensation, working conditions, career advancement, and job design.

Staffing Flow   Attention must be paid to the task of ensuring that **staffing flow**—the management of people into, through, and out of the organization—meets the organization's long-term requirements for the number and kinds of human resources. Decisions about selection, promotion, job security, career development and advancement, fair treatment, and termination must be made in light of profits, growth, and other critical organizational goals.

Reward Systems   The objectives of reward systems include the attraction, motivation, and retention of employees at all organizational levels. The accomplishment of these objectives forces management to consider a number of critical policy issues: Should pay incentives reward individual or group behavior? Should profits or reductions in operating costs be shared by employees? If so, how? Should employees be involved in the design and administration of the pay system? What is the most effective mix of pay and nonpay rewards to motivate performance? Answers to these questions will define a critical aspect of the employee–employer relationship.

Work Systems   Work systems are concerned with the design of work: how tasks and technologies are defined and arranged, the quantity and kinds of decisions that people make, and the extent to which quality of work life is an important organizational goal. Policy decisions that affect work systems include the kinds of manufacturing and office technologies implemented and the way in which labor is divided.

COMMUNICATION ROLE

All business organizations depend on communication. Communication is the glue that binds various elements, coordinates activities, allows people to work together, and produces results. It is more important today—given current trends—because companies are larger than ever, and more mergers and acquisitions are on the way. Departments within a company may be spread throughout the country or even throughout the world. Trends in management style—away from the strictly authoritarian and toward the more collaborative—also make communication more important than ever.

Often it is the HR staff who plays a pivotal role in the design and maintenance of good companywide communication flows to and from all employees. HR communication efforts, of course, can occur in a variety of ways. Downward communication methods, from management to employees, include orientation sessions, bulletin boards, newsletters, and employee handbooks. Upward communication methods usually include suggestion programs, complaint procedures, electronic mail, attitude surveys, and open-door meetings.

- **New Employee Orientation.** Consider the impression made on new employees during their first few days and weeks in a company. The HR staff is usually the first contact employees have when they come on board. First impressions are usually the most important. How HR comes across in terms of defining the employee's role, explaining critical policies, procedures and rules, as well as benefits regarding vacations, health, and so on, can set the tone for encouraging future participation and involvement.
- **Bulletin Boards.** Communications of a general nature, including official notices of policy changes, and personal employee news such as marriages or births may be posted on an employee bulletin board or by e-mail.
- **Communication Meetings.** Top management can hold open meetings with small groups of employees to answer questions and provide an opportunity for employees to raise questions of interest to them. These regular meetings may also be used to present special issues such as a new health insurance program. If such meetings are held regularly and employees develop a sense that management has a sincere interest in their concerns, they can provide an excellent source of upward communication.

- **Newsletters.** The widespread use of computers and newsletter software programs has made the employee newsletter a popular communication technique. A company may use the company newsletter to explain and promote organizational and industry-wide changes.
- **Employee Handbooks.** A well-written, up-to-date handbook can address important policies, procedures, and rules that apply to employees, such as wage and benefits information, general personnel policies concerning vacation, sick leave, insurance, and so on. In addition, the company's history and philosophy are usually included.
- **Complaint Procedures.** A critical communication need is to provide employees with a comfortable and effective means for bringing problems or complaints to management. Organizations are becoming more sensitive to employees' complaints about supervisors, jobs, and organizations. A few organizations have developed whistle-blowing procedures for addressing illegal or unethical acts before they reach the point where outside investigators are brought in. To encourage more employees to speak up without fearing retaliation from their supervisors or management, many organizations are adopting systems that protect the individual's identity. One popular system involves appointing an ombudsman, who investigates reported complaints.
- **Electronic Mail.** Almost unheard of a decade ago, e-mail is quickly becoming the method of choice for rapid, informal, and accessible intercompany communication. Employees can be linked together either through a local electronic mail system or connected to outside systems such as the Internet for communicating over great distances.
- **Surveys.** The employee survey is the most widely used research technique among HR professionals. The most common surveys include the wage survey and the job satisfaction survey. The job satisfaction survey is often referred to as an *attitude* or *morale* survey. It may either be developed internally or prepared by an outside consulting firm. Survey results communicate information upward, telling management how employees view their jobs, work conditions, management and supervision, and so on.
- **Open-door Meetings.** A popular management practice and an excellent upward communication technique is the open-door policy. Usually at a specified time each week or month, a manager's door is open to any employee who has a suggestion, question, or complaint. If over time the manager makes employees feel comfortable using this process and

each action receives a follow-up investigation (often by the HR office), this technique can effectively open lines of communication between employees and management.

ADVICE AND SERVICES

Over the past several decades, management has become increasingly complex. A restrictive legal environment, sophisticated technologies, a restive labor force, and demands by various societal groups for more socially responsible activities are a few of the pressures felt by managers. To cope with complex issues, managers often turn to staff experts for advice and counsel. Some questions that personnel staff members may be asked to answer include the following:

- How do I deal with an employee who I suspect is on drugs?
- How do I meet my equal employment goals without raising cries of "reverse discrimination"?
- How do I tell a high-achieving employee that the budget will not allow a merit increase this year?
- How do I counsel a manager who is suffering a midcareer crisis?
- How do I deal with an employee who has been with the company for 25 years but now can no longer perform effectively?
- How can I increase employee morale?

In theory, advice from the HR staff may be accepted or rejected. Line managers who think the advice is not sound have the prerogative to disregard it. Of course, the rejection of staff advice will be inversely proportional to the confidence a manager has in staff experts. Thus, all staff members have an obligation to ensure that their advice is sound, objective, fair, and will contribute to the goals of the organization.

An unexpected problem can occur in an organization when line managers rely heavily on the advice of HR specialists and transfer the major responsibility for dealing with people issues from themselves to the HR department. This is counterproductive because everyday people problems should generally be solved by the organization's supervisors. It is, in fact, a critical aspect of their job. A survey of supervisors at Roy Rogers, a division of Marriott Corporation, indicated the supervisors believed that almost 60 percent of unwanted turnover by managers who reported to them was caused by factors beyond their control. Yet they believed that the HR department was almost three times more responsible for the causes of the turnover.

They cited human resources as responsible for recruiting, training, and locating employees—all frequent causes of turnover. One supervisor even held the HR function responsible for his own poor supervision practices: "Human resources doesn't train us to manage properly!"[24]

Of course, supervisors who are generally responsible for many decisions affecting their employees should be the first to identify unmet needs or problems and, perhaps with assistance from the HR department, find a solution. The daily involvement with employees must be the responsibility of line managers, yet the HR department should be able to give them advice and assistance in meeting the needs of their employees.

CONTROL FUNCTIONS

Like the quality control department in many manufacturing concerns, the HR department performs important control functions for the management of human resources. For example, a written policy on equal employment opportunity is ineffectual unless executives are aware of the policy and adhere to it. HR administrators are responsible for monitoring personnel goals and guidelines to ensure their achievement. Common control activities include the following:

- Collection and analysis of hiring, selection, placement, and promotion data to ensure that equal employment opportunity laws and policies are being observed.
- Analysis of performance appraisal records to determine if appraisals are being conducted in an effective and unbiased manner.
- Analysis of statistics on absenteeism, grievances, and accidents to determine where problems are most critical and what may be done to reduce them.

Because of the nature of these activities, HR staff members generally possess the authority necessary to carry out control functions. In theory, line managers and other leaders must cooperate with those HR officials, but the latter must ensure that decision makers fully understand all HR policies, procedures, and standards so that resentment and conflict are not created when control activities are performed. Further, HR administrators should be tactful when putting pressure on managers to conform to guidelines. Harmonious relationships between the HR department and other organizational units will ensure compliance with guidelines, with a minimum of stress to the organization.

STRUCTURE OF THE HUMAN RESOURCE DEPARTMENT

The HR department normally contains clerical (support), professional, and managerial jobs. Clerical employees include clerks, typists, receptionists, and lower-level administrative assistants. Professional employees are specialists in fields such as counseling, benefits, employee development, employee testing, and labor relations. They often possess college degrees in business administration and may have concentrated their studies in HR. Lower-level employees are occasionally promoted to professional positions and are given both on- and off-the-job training for their new roles. The managers oversee the clerical and professional employees and coordinate the organization's personnel activities. Top HR managers formulate personnel policies and create important personnel programs.

The HR department in medium-sized to large companies contains individual work groups organized by function. An HR manager heads each group, providing leadership to the professional and clerical employees. The HR department may be headed by a vice-president of human resources who reports to the president. An example of the HR structure for a medium-sized or large organization is shown in Figure 1–3.

Large corporations generally have divisions in many states and foreign countries. Each division is usually run independently as a decentralized profit center. Division managers have their own staff services, such as engineering, accounting, finance, legal, and HR. The corporate HR staff, however, generally creates major HR policies and programs for recruiting, management development, equal employment opportunity, and wages and salaries. Divisional HR managers put the policies into operation so that there is consistency across all divisions. Each HR manager has some flexibility in his or her division's program.[25] No doubt, the average day in the HR profession is never dull.

The responsibility for performing the HR function does not reside only in the HR department; all managers at all levels of the organization share in that responsibility. For example, the branch manager of a bank will normally interview job applicants, orient new employees, train and develop new and current employees, evaluate employee performance, and so on. In most organizations, particularly larger ones, the HR staff designs HR policies and procedures, and the operating managers implement them. On occasion, line managers help design HR policies, and HR staffers help implement them. But the primary responsibility for implementation of HR policies and procedures rests with those who are responsible for day-to-day supervision of subordinates.

CURRENT ISSUES AND CHALLENGES

There are several major challenges HR professionals must help their companies confront. Furthermore, most of these challenges are external—a part of the environment—and beyond the control of any single person.

GLOBALIZATION

Globalization has arrived, but what does it really mean? Selling products or providing a service abroad would seem to apply, but is not the complete story. What it really implies is that all organizations, whether domestic or international, will need to become more global in their outlook, if not their operations. The real challenge is not so much being able to compete effectively in the global marketplace, but rather in creating a "global mindset" in managers, employees, and HR professionals.

Robert Reich, the former U.S. secretary of labor, made the following comment:

> We are living through a transformation that will rearrange the politics and economics of the coming century. There will be no national products or technologies, no national corporations, no national industries. There will no longer be national economies. All that will remain rooted within national borders are the people who comprise a nation. "American" corporations and "American" industries are ceasing to exist in any form that can meaningfully be distinguished from the rest of the global economy.[26]

For HR professionals, the challenge is developing a global corporate culture that is aligned with—and supportive of—a new global strategy and structure. It means creating an organization whose people are adept at exchanging ideas, knowledge, and processes across borders; people who are absolutely free of the "not-invented-here" syndrome and who can work in a multicultural environment.[27] The world leaders in aligning global strategy, structure, and culture are such companies as Ford, General Electric, Toyota, 3M, Shell, and Motorola.

WWW.FORD.COM

WWW.GE.COM

WWW.TOYOTA.COM

FIGURE 1–3 ORGANIZATIONAL STRUCTURE OF AN HR DEPARTMENT

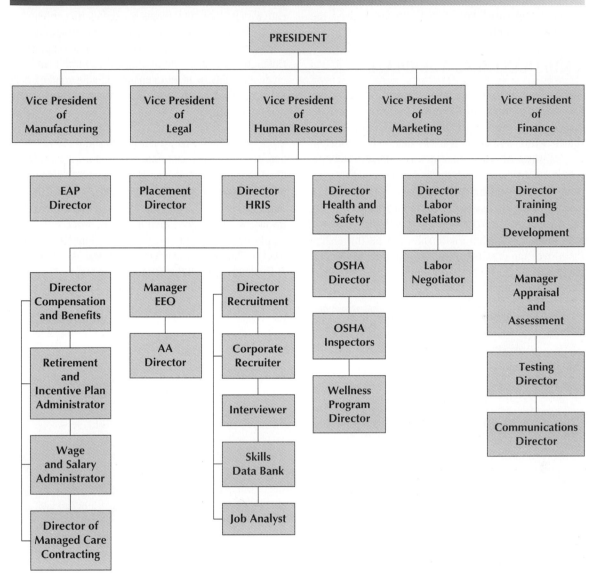

Abbreviations: AA, Affirmative Action; EAP, Employee Assistance Program; HRIS, Human Resource Information System; OSHA, Occupational Safety and Health Administration

Global businesses that were once organized along geographic lines are increasingly reorienting themselves according to markets, or products, or processes—or all of the above in complex matrices. Within organizations, people in widely dispersed locations combine efforts on **virtual teams.**

In their simplest forms, virtual teams are formerly integrated organizations which have outsourced parts of their operations. Amazon.com is an example. It is the Internet-based bookstore that has no physical storefronts and owns no inventory, but orchestrates promotion, selling, and delivery of over 1 million titles. The competitive advantage for a company such as Amazon.com, depends on harnessing the creativity of its people and then leveraging new ideas into useful products and services.

The increasing numbers of cross-border mergers and acquisitions, such as the Daimler–Chrysler merger in 1998, present a whole new set of issues for HR professionals as the accompanying *HR in the News* suggests. Merging corporate cultures is tough enough, but when there are also national cultures involved, the challenge is daunting.

A MULTICULTURAL WORKPLACE

Globalization also means the creation, organization, and management of **multicultural teams**—groups that represent diversity in functional capabilities, experience levels, and cultural backgrounds. **Diversity** in the American workplace and multiculturalism in international enterprises both engender the need to compare, contrast, and understand cultural differences in a new way, a way that does not attempt to make everyone alike but recognizes differences as a plus. Diversity—both domestic and international—will be the engine that drives the creativity of the corporation of the 21st century.[28]

Training and development strategies are needed, teaching people how to lead, work with, and communicate with multicultural teams is needed. HR professionals are expected to design and deliver programs that build crosscultural competencies in their employees. Competencies needed within multicultural teams include an ability to adapt to change, handle conflict, deal with complexity, and learn sensitivity to other people and their cultures.

THE IMPACT OF GOVERNMENT

The HR profession has always been known for the major role it plays in keeping the company out of trouble. The massive number of federal, state, and local laws that involve worker safety, health, wages, work rules, and employee equal rights require a full-time HR effort in most medium—and all large—firms. Making things even more confusing are the variety of decisions and rulings

HR IN THE NEWS

"IF MARRIAGES ARE MADE IN HEAVEN —CROSS-BORDER MERGERS ARE MADE IN. . . ."

As Asia's economic troubles force more corporate takeovers and mergers, a new study warns those unions often entail hidden human costs and difficulties.

"Even the most successful mergers and acquisitions often stumble over people issues," says Hewitt Associates LLC, an international human-resource consulting firm.

Of the 42 local and foreign-owned companies operating in the Asian-Pacific region that took part in the study, 65 percent had participated in a merger, acquisition, or formation of a joint venture within the past two years.

Nearly half those companies said they incurred unanticipated costs while implementing their respective transactions. What's more, companies in the Asian-Pacific region reported a higher incidence of unanticipated costs than did those surveyed in Canada, Europe, Latin America, and the United States.

Among the pitfalls were additional charges associated with staff turnover because managers either didn't communicate effectively with employees, or employees were unhappy with the way the company was going to be run. Other issues that loom large in such transactions are problems associated with integrating organizational cultures and melding human-resource programs such as benefits.

While these deals may look good on paper, the bottom line is that changes in management, policies, and programs can be very threatening to employees in both organizations. To win over skeptical employees, define the unspoken "rules of the road" for the combined organization.

Hewitt also cautions that another potentially costly trouble spot in cross-border transactions is determining national cultural issues, or traits, from national business practice. For instance, a China-bound American company unfamiliar with the local scene should get professional help to separate "what's the way things are done because that's the way this business has been run," and "the way things are done because this is the way people are."

SOURCE: "Mergers Entail Human Costs, a Study Shows," *Dow Jones Newswires,* December 21, 1998.

made by the courts. Unfortunately, the role of government and the courts is not going to get any smaller.

Personnel decisions related to hiring, disciplining, promoting, and discharging employees are subject to very complex rules. Mistakes and failures usually result in costly litigation. For the most part, HR departments have performed this role diligently and professionally by creating internal systems for ensuring compliance with laws and regulations. Sexual harassment, gender, and race discrimination are areas that currently occupy HR professionals, and that is likely to continue. The future appears to be more of the same—increased complexity on the legal front and more regulations for HR professionals to learn.

SKILLS SHORTAGES

The effects of globalization, rapid technological changes, and record employment levels have created a skills shortage. Finding and keeping highly skilled workers, especially information technology workers, is becoming a serious challenge for American employers. According to the Information Technology Association of America, there are already 190,000 unfilled high-tech jobs. A net increase of 1 million such jobs are expected to be created over the coming decade.[29] Labor shortages are widespread and include both skilled and unskilled jobs.

Keeping up with changing technology is a challenge every skilled worker is facing. **Technology** is a global phenomenon, and employers whose people are better trained, educated, and skilled are better able to compete. For example, AlliedSignal Inc. invests two percent of payroll annually on workforce development. To stay competitive, every worker is required to have 40 hours of company-paid, job-related training per year. Training is a core competence at AlliedSignal and the reason they were selected as one of *Industry Week*'s 100 Best-Managed Companies.[30]

More **training** is needed. In fact, companies in the United States are spending more money than ever on training, but the dollar figure has not kept pace with the number of people in the workforce. Universities and colleges are not the answer either. The need for computer programmers is so critical, for example, firms are contracting with commercial enterprises to provide needed instruction.

It is not just the manager and skilled employees who will need to stay on the cutting technological edge; the HR professional must be there as well. Maybe it was not a major issue a decade ago, but HR professionals must be competent with sophisticated HR information systems, telecommunications, research methodology, the Internet, and, to some extent, the firm's core technologies.

QUALITY IMPROVEMENT

The idea of continuous improvement and the quest for zero defects is now widely accepted. Most people understand that in today's global marketplace, only those companies able to deliver what customers want, at the price they are willing to pay, survive.

The approach most often practiced in North America, and in Europe, is called **Total Quality Management (TQM).** TQM involves continuously examining and improving every process that leads to a final product or service—including HR programs and functions. Technical training programs, for example, are reviewed in terms of whether they add value to the end product.

Quality issues will not go away. The pressure to improve processes, reduce mistakes, control costs, and identify new distinctive capabilities will only continue to mount.

WORK AND FAMILY BALANCE

The **changing workforce,** whose needs and expectations range from Generation X to Baby Boomers, pose many daunting challenges. American lifestyles are varied, unique, and constantly changing. Flexible work arrangements are becoming more and more accepted. Better and cheaper technology is available, facilitating a wider array of flexible work options.

The increase in these types of programs stems from the skills shortage described earlier. Consider that "inflexibility" increases turnover and reduces productivity in a group that companies can ill afford to lose: young, committed professionals with management experience, according to one study.[31]

A survey also reported that of 500 women seeking flexible work arrangements, 64 percent of them had quit or were planning to quit their jobs because of a lack of flexibility.[32] What's more, younger women were more assertive in their hunt for flexibility than baby boomers.

Research into the payoff of nontraditional work assignments is proliferating as employers try to determine if giving employees flexibility in their work schedules is worth the perceived trouble (see *HR in the News:* "Two Careers, One Marriage . . ."). More workers are pressuring their employers for help in balancing work and home, as traditional families in which only one parent works become more unusual. Such traditional households represent only 17 percent of working families, compared with about 63 percent in 1950.[33]

More employers are making flexibility an explicit part of their recruiting efforts. Bosses are also making

HR IN THE NEWS

TWO CAREERS, ONE MARRIAGE: MAKING IT WORK IN THE WORKPLACE

As two-career couples take over the workplace—and there's no doubt that they've booted out the traditional wife-at-home family—the thing they want most from employers is not child care centers or telecommuting options. Their big wish wouldn't cost very much and could be provided by even the smallest of companies.

What dual-career duos crave most is simple flexibility, according to a study by Catalyst, a New York nonprofit research and consulting firm. These couples say their greatest need is an informal freedom to arrive late, leave early, or work at home when family needs make it necessary.

But as easy as that sounds, it could require an overhaul of corporate culture, something notoriously difficult to pull off. Working couples "are telling companies loud and clear that simply adding benefits or isolated programs is not enough," says the report. "They are looking for work environments which are flexible and allow them the control they need to tailor their own schedules and career futures. A culture that supports those requirements can only be created from the top," it says.

Traditional families in which the father works and the mother stays at home with one or more children represent only about 17 percent of working families, compared with about 63 percent in 1950, according to U.S. Census Bureau figures. Dual-worker couples head up 43 percent of families in the workforce, up from about 20 percent in 1950.

SOURCE: Sheila Wellington, CEO. "Two Careers, One Marriage: Making It Work in the Workplace," *Catalyst* (New York, 1998).

---

special efforts to retain workers, too. When it is obvious a talented employee has to leave, perhaps because of a spouse relocating to another region, telecommuting is explored.

Employers also are finding their "new contract" with workers—the one that says there is no such thing as a guaranteed job—comes with a rider attached that says that workers are taking charge of their work style. They're saying, "I'll get your job done, I'll do everything I promised, I'll keep my end of our new bargain. But I'll do it on my terms," says Sue Shellenbarger.[34]

The challenge for HR professionals is to meet the needs of this changing workforce. David Ulrich goes so far as to recommend "flex everything," because the firm, in a highly competitive industry, cannot afford to lose workers to rigid rules and schedules.[35]

DECLINE OF WORKER LOYALTY

No matter what you call it—outsourcing or downsizing—as corporations trim costs and the nation shifts from a manufacturing economy to a service economy, companies are laying off employees at a pace reminiscent of that of the Great Depression. Among them are such giants as IBM, Kodak, and Procter & Gamble, whose former guarantees of job security are only memories. These massive layoffs are not happening in the United States alone; more than half of Europe's largest corporations plan to cut their workforces as global competition and high wages take their toll. The financial and economic crisis in Asia is also taking a toll.[36]

Companies cite many reasons for cutting payrolls: plant and store closings, cost-cutting measures, restructuring, slowdowns in military and commercial aircraft programs, and acquisitions.[37] And it isn't just low-skilled or unskilled workers who are being let go. Layoffs are happening just as often to people once thought to have very marketable skills.

If this trend isn't depressing enough, consider what some experts are predicting. Doomsayers are convinced that companies will continue to let people go because, unlike earlier downsizing periods in which employers simply wanted to cut costs until business picked up, today an operation that does not create value is permanently squeezed out.[38]

As to the issue of loyalty, there is clearly a trend toward workers being less loyal to employers than in the past. The results are understandable, considering that 42 percent of those surveyed had already experienced corporate restructuring, downsizing, or unacceptable

HR IN THE NEWS

WHATEVER HAPPENED TO WORKER LOYALTY, UPS WANTS TO KNOW

WWW.UPS.COM

As the head of a company which saw its ties to customers and employees strained by last year's contentious 15-day strike with the Teamsters, James Kelly has good reason to ruminate on the topic of loyalty.

"We've gone from an era in which a decent percentage of American workers had the option of building a lifelong career with a single company to a period where employees consider themselves free agents, and companies hire and lay off with abandon," Kelly said.

Kelly, who directs the country's third largest employer, said the fundamental contract between companies and their employees has changed. He added that loyalty in the modern workplace requires both a responsible employer and a flexible employee bonded by mutual self-interest.

He defined a responsible employer as one who takes a long-term view of employment and matches workers with jobs suited to their specific talents, while keeping a careful eye on the bottom line.

"A long-term view of employment doesn't mean employers guarantee jobs for life," Kelly explained, "or fail to fire underperforming employees, or disregard shareholders and profits. It just means that employers do their best to keep employees who are performing well in their jobs and that employers use layoffs only as a last resort."

Kelly described UPS's attempts to become a responsible employer by implementing extensive education and job retraining program. Last year, they spent more than $300 million on internal education.

SOURCE: Adapted from: "UPS Chief Decries Decline of Company, Worker Loyalty," *The Plain Dealer* (December 2, 1998): 2C.

job relocations.[39] Even more discouraging, 20 percent of the sample perceived they were currently extremely vulnerable to being fired.

It is understandable why so many workers, both employed and unemployed, are less loyal today. Many feel hurt, and far too many have a sense of betrayal by their employers. One result is that there are predictions of more strikes such as the one at UPS in 1997 (see *HR in the News:* "Whatever Happened to Worker Loyalty, UPS Wants to Know"). However, despite these anxieties about their employers, workers continue to express high commitment to their jobs. The typical American worker takes pride in, and personal responsibility for, his or her work.

HUMAN RESOURCE CAREER OPPORTUNITIES

Students often ask: What are the best strategies for entering HR careers? Can someone with no HR work experience enter the profession? What are the most important skills HR people need in order to succeed? Serious students are asking these questions much ear-

lier in their educations, and wisely so, given the increasingly tighter prospects for meaningful employment.

Despite the gloomy job projections for employment overall, the future still holds numerous opportunities for students who seek careers in HR management. However, it will demand diligent preparation.

HR professionals consider academic preparation a necessity. Years ago, this was not always the case. HR staff members were often selected largely because of their personalities; those with people-oriented traits were preferred. Certainly, liking people is important, but it does little to describe the skills and knowledge of the modern HR professional.

The future HR professional will almost certainly be expected to hold a college degree. A recent survey of HR managers concluded that the most preferred academic background was business administration, followed by the social sciences (communication and psychology), humanities (art, English, history), education, and science.[40] As to whether it is better to pursue a master's degree (without experience), the evidence seems to suggest that it depends on the position being sought. If the HR job opening requires detailed technical knowledge or skills that a particular graduate degree can provide, such as a master's degree in

FIGURE 1–4   WHAT RECRUITERS ARE LOOKING FOR

MOST IMPORTANT SKILLS NEEDED

SKILL	FREQUENCY	SKILL	FREQUENCY
Communication skills	79	Flexible/resilient	16
Interpersonal skills	65	Leadership	13
Analytical skills	35	HR law knowledge	12
Listening skills	34	Interviewing/selection skills	11
Organizational skills	25	Practical experience	9
HR knowledge	23	Action oriented	9
General business knowledge	22	Innovative thinking	8
Planning skills	22	Group dynamics	8
Management skills	20	Problem solving	8
Good judgment/common sense	18		

SOURCE: T. Bergman, "Preparing to Enter and Succeed in Human Resource Management," *SAM Advanced Management Journal* (Winter 1992): 37.

compensation systems, then probably it would be an advantage.

Useful HR-related academic courses include organizational behavior and change, training and development, employee selection, labor–management relations, and compensation. While successful academic work is a big plus, recruiters also look for applicants who can demonstrate the specific skills identified in Figure 1–4. The ability to communicate and work with people will open up a lot of opportunities.

Can skills such as those in Figure 1–4 be acquired through academic preparation? Certainly; for example, active participation (that is, demonstrated by holding a leadership position) in campus organizations, such as student government, is an excellent strategy for preparing to enter the HR profession.

While technical knowledge and critical communication and interpersonal skills can be acquired through academic preparation, other competencies such as organizational and management skills are best developed outside the classroom.[41] Students who work off campus, either part-time or full-time, rather than thinking of this situation as a limitation, should reframe it and use it to acquire the critical skills. Many recruiters consider a student's work experience a plus, especially if it shows increasing levels of responsibility and initiative. Job experience, such as assistant manager of a fast-food restaurant, can be an excellent strategy for demonstrating many HR skill competencies.

Perhaps the most prevalent strategy for entering and succeeding in the HR profession is networking. The results of surveys of Society for Human Resource Management (SHRM) members suggest that HR managers depend on their networks for referrals and internal transfers to fill HR management openings. Otherwise, entry-level positions are filled about half the time by applicants coming through college placement services. Executive HR openings are frequently filled through search firms.

The trend is clearly toward staffing entry-level HR positions with internal applicants before going outside. For example, Toyota's Georgetown, Kentucky, facility prefers that new employees first prove themselves on the operational side of the business, such as the assembly line, before being selected for specific staff assignments.

Another strategy for entering the HR profession is to obtain work experience in a specific industry. HR internships are one way of gaining valuable experience of this type. That experience, plus the contacts made through it, may provide the edge for gaining entry into HR. While an attractive resumé is always an advantage, it would appear that professional contacts and networks are important—some experts argue that they are the most important—strategies for finding an HR job in a tight labor market.

A practical strategy for building an HR network is through the local SHRM. There are hundreds of SHRMs throughout North America. Many universities and colleges have SHRM-sponsored student chapters. The link between student chapters and SHRMs is strong. Students often attend monthly meetings with HR professionals and are included in major functions. The SHRM is an excellent place to begin networking. SHRM also sponsors an accreditation program to certify professional competency. Students who pass the Personnel Accreditation Institute exams and who then work in the HR field for two years will be designated as Professional in Human Resources (PHR). There is also a Senior Professional in Human Resources (SPHR) designation. For those already working in the HR field, accreditation is becoming one method for rising to the top.

SUMMARY POINTS

- Strategic HR activities address a broad range of issues relevant to the successful implementation of operational plans. The more critical HR is to an organization's success, the more important strategic planning becomes.

- The management of people has seen three distinct approaches since the turn of the century: scientific management, human relations, and human resources. The trend has been toward the human resources approach, whereby two complementary goals are sought: increased organizational effectiveness and the satisfaction of individual employee needs. HR policies and programs strive to achieve both goals.

- A number of critical issues face HR managers and administrators today. Hiring and motivating today's changing work force is a major HR challenge. Innovative HR programs must meet the needs of a diverse labor force while enabling the corporation to compete successfully in a global economy.

- HR managers and administrators play a number of roles in achieving effective HR management. These include creating HR policies, offering advice to line managers, providing services (for example, recruiting, training, and research), and controlling activities to ensure that employment legislation and HR policies are being followed. Also, it is usually HR's responsibility to design and maintain effective companywide communication flows.

- Free trade and globalization are putting most firms in fiercely competitive markets where factors for success depend on the quality of HR. The scope of HR functions has broadened to include attracting, training, and motivating a heterogeneous workforce from a variety of cultures. Management styles, selection, appraisal, training, and reward systems need to be reevaluated in terms of the local culture if the company is to operate effectively. International HR managers are faced with the challenge of balancing corporate long-term HR policies and practices with the workforce needs of their international subsidiaries.

CASE STUDY

FAMILY FEUD

It was Friday evening and Tom Bennett's turn to prepare the family meal. He had not given this task much thought; actually, he didn't want to think about it all, and only at the last moment decided to grill some hamburgers. "Keep it simple" was his motto—a decision his family appreciated too. Tom took off early in order to squeeze in some time with his kids and to meet with their teachers.

Tom and his wife, Margie Vintner (she kept her maiden name), were a successful dual-career couple, living in Denver for the past five years with their two children—Jacob, nine, and Emily, seven. By most measures, the couple had achieved the American dream—a healthy income, a beautiful home, vacations in the mountains for skiing, and a housekeeper. Normally, a housekeeper would help with the cooking tonight, but the family is without one at the moment, thus the need for Tom to prepare the evening meal.

What was unusual about this couple is that Tom and Margie were both in the HR profession at separate companies in the Denver area. Margie worked at one of the banks downtown, and Tom worked with one of the airlines based in the city. Although both jobs required long hours and some travel (more in the case of Tom), Margie's job had recently become more intense since her bank was recently acquired by National Bank Corporation (NBC) in San Francisco. It was during their graduate school days, back in New York, that the couple met and married.

The couple often found themselves discussing work-related issues at home. Tom worked in the benefits area, and Margie's job was in employee relations. The fact that they shared the same profession has presented few problems. Each partner always gave the other morale support, and on more than a few occasions, one partner would provide the other with specific, useful professional, assistance. Margie's superior had even bragged to top management that they were getting two professionals for the price of one. Ironically, while it was their mutual interest in the profession that initially brought them together, recently it had become a source of tension. Tonight would be no exception.

Continued.

CASE STUDY—con't

Margie, in an afternoon phone conversation with Tom, announced that she had something important to tell him this evening. Tom had become increasingly ambivalent and didn't really like surprises, so his anxiety level was a bit higher than normal as he flipped the hamburgers and watched Margie slowly walk onto the deck, carrying two glasses of wine. Tom winced. Margie normally drank only on special occasions or when she was angry about something. Which one would it be tonight?

"Hi, Tom. How did it go for you and the kids today?" Margie's tone lacked genuineness—a bad sign, Tom concluded correctly.

Tom gave her a quick summary of the kids' day as he accepted a glass of wine. He mentioned Jacob's invitation (pleading was more accurate) to attend his Little League game in the morning and Emily's school play next Monday afternoon. It was the latter that sparked Margie's attention.

"They never consider the parents who work during the day and who have schedules to maintain," she replied. "It's frustrating that the schools are dragging their heels on moving into the 21st century with regard to single parents or dual-career couples."

There she goes again, thought Tom. She hasn't been home more than ten minutes, and she's already knocking the system. For the past couple of years, the two had had a friendly debate over many HR issues, but none had raised more passion than the role of the corporation in resolving work–family conflicts.

Margie was an advocate for businesses taking a more activist stance on behalf of workers with family duties. Doing nothing, which is what she believed traditional businesses like hers practice, can only lead to loss of the best talent.

Tom came from the traditional school of thought. He hesitated when it came to breaching the traditional wall between work and family. Employers had no business involving themselves more deeply in workers' family lives. The corporate culture should be values neutral, not pro-family. Emphasis should stay on what companies do best—creating jobs—and avoid opening the Pandora's box of raised expectations, employer liability, invasion of privacy, and even accusations of unfairness that work–family programs could cause. Tom was also afraid that expensive programs would hurt a company's global competitiveness–a situation that he saw occurring in the airline industry. In fact, his particular airline was already looking at ways to cut such core benefits as health insurance and pensions.

Margie's comments also triggered memories of his conversation at lunch that day with a group of airline employees who had complained to management about the airline's new policy on flexible hours. He gave Margie a quick account.

"They presented a senior manager with a list of grievances," he said, "including complaints that childless employees are expected to work more hours than their counterparts who have children. Some resented having to forfeit more weekends. One person even accused Jane Busby of using her children as a convenient copout. The jealousy is much more serious than you can imagine."

Margie conceded that change was a problem, but one that could and must be overcome. "Companies say they want to be family friendly; some may actually mean it." She paused for effect. "But the way they do business runs contrary to it."

"Tom, certainly you agree that there is a push for balance between work and home," Margie continued, "even at the cost of lost promotions and pay. But the reality is that respect for the individual in most companies is biased against certain people. People are managed very, very rigidly. The traditional system still puts much more emphasis on **face time** at the office instead of results. And people who can achieve results, but in nonconventional ways, are constantly having roadblocks put in their way between doing their best at work and taking care of their families."

"And Tom, the prevailing corporate culture in most businesses is far from values neutral. If anything, it reflects the traditional family structures of the 1950s: a wife who cares for the children at home while the husband goes off to work. Top management has a hard time sympathizing with work–family conflicts because it is male dominated and rarely has them. And whether you want to believe it or not, Tom, there is a glass ceiling, and I think it is getting thicker—not thinner."

"I think that's bogus," Tom rebutted. "You've been watching too many *Current Affair* and *Oprah Winfrey* shows. Yes, I agree that some managers demand long hours and seven-day workweeks. But that is because those jobs cannot be restructured, and it is so impractical to permit the kind of flexibility you're touting. I shouldn't need to remind you that my own company and industry are downsizing; our managers are under intense pressures, much of it from huge waves of change. Expecting them to be flexible when reducing staff is just not realistic. And besides, there is no proof that these programs help the bottom line."

"Okay, Tom." Margie accepted the challenge. "Where's the research that says that taking a client out for an expensive dinner and entertainment has a payoff—or memberships in the country club, for that matter?"

"You're applying a double standard," she said. "Work–family programs are being held to higher standards. Everyone knows that these programs increase our ability to attract, retain, and motivate skilled employees. But getting management to sign on is next to impossible. Which, by the way, hit home for me today."

Margie then proceeded to tell Tom that she had learned that the new owner of her bank, NBC, had offered the recently vacated vice-president for HR position to Larry Wellington, not her. It would have meant a much higher salary, more responsibility, and a move to San Francisco.

Although Tom and Margie had discussed relocation before, and had agreed to consider it should it be offered to either of

CASE STUDY—con't

them, it was a sensitive topic because it raised the ultimate work–family conflict: Whose career is more important? And tonight, Tom wisely concluded, was not the night to tackle *that* issue.

"Larry is a competent guy," Margie added, bringing Tom back to the immediate topic, "but I cannot help but think that when it came down to it, Larry got the job because there is another double standard operating as well. Tom, who is most likely to succeed in *your* company? Honestly, isn't it the person who can transfer at a moment's notice or who puts in the most face time at the office? Larry is single, I'm not. Isn't it the person with the least number of things to keep him or her from moving around, from being available at a moment's notice, from working any hours—all things that don't really have a valid business rationale?"

Tom understood that Margie's questions were rhetorical. He also understood why Margie was on edge and uncharacteristically embittered. Margie's comments did stir his own conscience, leaving him to wonder: Is Margie right? Is management's concern for work–family issues all talk, no action? And is the entire structure of work biased in favor of those who can come in early, leave late, and travel at a moment's notice instead of those who are most effective?

QUESTIONS

1 Even though both Margie and Tom are HR professionals, their views about what companies should do about easing work–family conflicts are quite different. Describe their differences. What do you think is the source of their differences?

2 Work–family proponents cite a number of barriers in the workplace that prohibit employees who want to maintain a balance between work and family from achieving their goals. Describe the barriers. What is the price of corporate inaction in failing to address these employees' personal and family needs?

3 Tom raised the issues that family support programs may have a negative side effect: resentment among childless workers. Is this true, and if so, what solution would you recommend?

4 What evidence is available that work–family conflict causes workplace problems? Do you agree or disagree with Tom's claim that these programs do not help the bottom line? Is Margie's response ("Everyone knows that these programs increase . . .") a sufficient answer for top management? What effect will corporate inaction have on employee morale and productivity?

EXPERIENTIAL EXERCISES

1. SOURCES OF PERSONNEL/HR INFORMATION

PURPOSE

To learn how to research a personnel/HR topic and to gain practice in researching personnel-related issues in the library.

TASK

A number of topics related to the field of personnel/HR management follow. Choose a topic of interest to you (or your instructor may assign a topic for you to research). After you have chosen a topic, do the following:

1 Find at least six recent references (or more, depending on your instructor's wishes) that pertain to your topic. Do not use a reference (for example, *Personnel Journal*) more than once.

2 For each reference, indicate the title of the book, journal, and so on; the title of the journal article (if applicable); the author's name; and the publisher and publication date. In addition, indicate how you located each reference (for example, *Business Periodicals Index*).

3 Write a one-paragraph abstract for each source (if your source is a book review at least one important chapter and write an abstract for that chapter).

PERSONNEL/HR TOPICS

- Absenteeism: Causes and Cures
- Age Discrimination in Industry
- Americans with Disabilities Act of 1990
- Profit Sharing
- Recruiting Problems and Issues
- Sexual Harassment: How to Prevent and Control It
- Social Security: Is It Failing?
- Stress: What Causes It, How to Reduce It
- Test Validation Techniques
- Assessment Centers: How Effective?
- Benefit Plans (Flexible)
- Career Opportunities in Personnel/HR Resource Management
- Child-Care Programs
- Collective Bargaining Issues in Current Negotiations
- Compensation: Problems and Issues
- Disciplinary Methods and Techniques

EXPERIENTIAL EXERCISE—cont'd

- Drug Usage and Testing
- Dual-Career Couples
- Employee Rehabilitation Programs
- Employee Stock Option Plans (ESOPs)
- Employment at Will
- Executive Compensation Techniques
- Flextime Programs
- Grievance Procedures (Union and Nonunion Employers)
- Health Care Cost Containment Methods
- Immigration Reform Act of 1986: Is It Working?
- Incentive Compensation Systems
- Job Enrichment: Successes and Failures
- Labor Relations: Current Trends and Issues

- Management by Objectives (MBO)
- Negligent Hiring
- Occupational Safety and Health Act (OSHA): How Effective?
- Employee Orientation Programs
- Outplacement Programs for Managerial and Non-managerial Personnel
- Part-time Employees
- Polygraph and Honesty Testing
- Turnover: Causes and Cures
- Union–Management Relations: Current Trends and Issues
- Wellness Programs
- Women and Work: Problems and Perspectives
- Workforce Diversity

2. PREDICTING WORK IN THE YEAR 2025

PURPOSE

To understand the potential influence of trends and changes occurring in North America that will influence the design and implementation of HR management practices.

TIME

Thirty minutes of class time

PROCEDURES

This exercise should be done in groups of four to five students. The year 2025 is not far away. One prediction seems certain to occur: The next century promises to bring even more rapid advances in technology, more intense global competition, and increased pressures on workers to be more productive. Review each of the trends that are predicted to occur and list ideas about the impact of each on major HR management functions: global strategic planning, job design, recruitment and selection, performance appraisal, training and development, career planning, compensation and benefits, health and safety, and labor relations.

Each group will then present its ideas to the class.

TRENDS   IMPACT ON HRM

❶ The average company will become smaller, employing fewer people.

❷ The traditional hierarchical organization will give way to a variety of other structures.

❸ Business will shift from producing or manufacturing to providing a service.

❹ Work itself will be redefined: constant learning, more high-order thinking, less nine-to-five work.

❺ Increasing numbers of dual-career and single-parent families.

❻ More technicians, professionals, and specialists than manufacturing workers.

KEY TERMS AND CONCEPTS

Changing workforce
Diversity
Face time
Globalization
Human relations
Human resource functions

Human resource management
Human resource policies
Knowledge
Multicultural teams
Staffing flow
Scientific management

KEY TERMS AND CONCEPTS—cont'd

Strategic planning
Technology
Total Quality Management

Training
Virtual teams

REVIEW QUESTIONS

1. How do scientific management, human relations, and human resources approaches to managing people differ? Why is the human resources approach considered by many to be better than the traditional ways of managing people?

2. What are the traditional personnel functions performed by almost every HR department? Describe the different roles performed by HR managers. What HR functions and roles are performed by all managers, line as well as staff?

3. Describe the variety of ways top management might communicate important information to its employees.

Which communication methods are effective for passing information from employees to managers?

4. What are the most critical challenges facing HR professionals today? What changes in society and within organizations have been instrumental in reshaping the HR role?

5. Describe the forces that make up the global environment.

6. What is the career outlook for those who wish to enter the HR field? What is a good strategy for students with no experience who want to break into the field?

DISCUSSION QUESTIONS

1. One often hears that the scientific management approach is still widely used in manufacturing and other forms of unskilled or semiskilled work. Why might this be so? Will scientific management principles still be used in the year 2025? Explain.

2. Why did the human relations approach decline in popularity? How important are good human relations? What else must a good manager do in addition to practicing good human relations?

3. The question of government interference in private enterprise has long been a hot topic for businesspeople. In general, have equal employment opportunity laws

been good or bad for business? Good or bad for women or minorities? Do you feel that more equal employment opportunity legislation will be enacted in the coming decade?

4. Much more professionalism is demanded from HR officials today than in the past. Why is this so?

5. What types of HR programs are needed to attract, retain, and motivate today's culturally diverse workforce?

6. Much has been said about global competition. What will it mean to managers and HR professionals in the decades to come in terms of HR functions, roles, and policies?

ENDNOTES

Chapter 1

1. Michael Hammer and James Champy, *Reengineering the Corporation* (New York: HarperBusiness, 1993), 7–14.

2. *Business Week/Reinventing America* (Special Issue 1992): 60–63.

3. Sue Shellenbarger, "Work-Force Study Finds Loyalty Is Weak, Divisions of Race and Gender Are Deep," *Wall Street Journal* (September 4, 1993): B1.

4. Frederick W. Taylor, *Scientific Management* (New York: Harper & Brothers, 1947), 45–46.

5. For a description of personnel functions and activities undertaken by large companies during the scientific management era, see Ordway Tead and Henry C. Metcalf, *Personnel Administration* (New York: McGraw-Hill, 1920).

6. For a detailed description of the Hawthorne studies, see F. J. Roethlisberger and W. J. Dickson, *Management and the Worker* (Cambridge, MA: Harvard University Press, 1939).

7. Not all researchers agree that changes in employee behavior were caused by changes in the work environment. For an alternative explanation, see H. M. Parsons, "What

Happened at Hawthorne?" *Science* (March 8, 1974): 922–32.

8. J. Barney and P. Wright, "On Becoming a Strategic Partner: The Role of Human Resources in Gaining a Competitive Advantage," *Human Resource Management* 37, no. 1 (Spring 1998): 31–46.

9. Ibid., 31

10. Ibid., 31–32

11. C. Metzler, "Charting a New Role as Strategic Business Partners," *HRMagazine* (SHRM Fiftieth Anniversary, 1998): 69–70.

12. Ibid.

13. M. Losey, "HR Comes of Age," *HRMagazine* (SHRM Fiftieth Anniversary, 1998): 40–53.

14. T. Davenport and L. Prusak, *Working Knowledge* (Boston: Harvard Business School Press, 1998), 1–24.

15. Ibid., 12.

16. Ibid., 2–6.

17. Ibid., 25–51.

18. Ibid., 88–97.

19. Ibid., 107–119.

20. Ibid., 161–169.

21. A. Thompson and A. Strickland, *Strategic Management, 6th ed.* (Boston: Irwin, 1992), 2–6.

22. Michael Alvert, "HR Profit Power," *Personnel* 67, no. 2 (February 1990): 47–49.

23. This discussion is taken from M. Beer, B. Spector, P. Lawrence, D.

Mills, and R. Walton, "Managing Human Assets," *Personnel Administrator* (January 1985): 60–69.

24. Barbara Whitaker Shimko, "All Managers Are the HR Managers," *Human Resource Magazine* 35, no. 1 (January 1990): 67–70.

25. Linda Thornburg, "Madelyn Jennings Wins Excellence Award," *HR News* (July 15, 1990): 12.

26. Robert Reich, *The Work of Nations: Preparing Ourselves for Twenty-First Century Capitalism* (New York: Alfred A. Knopf, 1991)

27. R. Maruca, "The Right Way to Go Global: An Interview with Whirlpool CEO David Whitwam," *Harvard Business Review* (March–April 1994): 135–145.

28. S. Rhinesmith, *A Manager's Guide to Globalization*, 2d ed. (Chicago: Irwin Professional Publishing, 1996), 157.

29. S. Overman, "Strategy," *Hrfocus* (New York: American Management Association, 1998), Article #9985.

30. S. Caudron, "The Only Way to Stay Ahead," *Industry Week* (August 8, 1998): 98–101.

31. N. Brooks, "Balancing Act: Inflexible Companies May Pay a Steep Price in Employees and Productivity," *Los Angeles Times* (September 6, 1998): D-5.

32. Ibid.

33. Ibid.

34. S. Shellenbarger, "More Corporations Are Using Flexibility to Lure Employees," *Wall Street Journal*, (September 17, 1997): B-1.

35. S. Overman, "Strategy."

36. Fred R. Bleakley, "Over Half of Europe's Big Firms Are Planning Work Force Cuts," *Wall Street Journal* (September 21, 1993): A19.

37. Louis S. Richman, "When Will the Layoffs End?" *Fortune* (September 20, 1993): 54–56.

38. Ibid., 56

39. For more information, see Sue Shellenbarger, "Work-Force Study Finds Loyalty Is Weak, Divisions of Race and Gender Are Deep," *Wall Street Journal* (September 4, 1993): B1. Note: The Families and Work Institute, a nonprofit New York research and consulting company, surveyed a national sample of 2958 workers about their work attitudes and personal lives.

40. T. J. Bergmann, M. J. Close, and T. Will, "Preparing to Enter and Succeed in Human Resource Management," *SAM Advanced Management Journal* (Winter 1992): 36–40.

41. T. J. Bergmann and M. J. Close, "Entry Level Human Resource Positions: What Is the Employer Looking For?" *Personnel Journal* 66, no. 1 (January 1987): 124–125, and "Preparing for Entry Level Human Resource Management Positions," *Personnel Journal* 29, no. 4 (April 1984): 95–100.

CHAPTER 2

A GLOBAL PERSPECTIVE OF HUMAN RESOURCES

CHAPTER OUTLINE

CHAPTER OBJECTIVES

1 To learn what globalization is, and what it will mean in the management of human resources.

2 To learn how culture, both national and corporate, can influence HR management strategies.

3 To build cooperative relationships across a multicultural world.

4 To recognize that multicultural differences present an opportunity that can lead to creative and synergistic results.

5 To understand some of the regional and cultural differences in labor conditions.

6 To understand the differences within HRM systems across several advanced nations and transitioning economies.

GOING GLOBAL

Is business becoming more global? Consider these facts:

- More than 100,000 U.S. companies are engaged in a global venture.
- U.S. multinational corporations employ over 7 million people—outside the U.S.
- U.S. multinationals employ over 18 million people in the United States—representing about 20 percent of the workforce.
- Foreign corporations employ 3 million Americans.[1]

Markets today know no borders. The very concept of domestic business has disappeared. Modern organizations no longer have any place to hide—national boundaries are not the sanctuaries they once were. Businesses do not have the luxury of focusing on their own little world. They must adopt a global perspective.

As companies rush to become global, more human resource professionals are being asked to navigate through the white-water rapids of a multicultural workplace, complex markets, and new global competitors. Beneath the turbulent water are the hidden challenges of lost talent, inequities, and the unknown. The signals, the warnings, are often not seen or heard until it is too late, and the damage is done. Moreover, navigating one river successfully is no guarantee of success on another just as one new global business experience rarely resembles another.[2]

NEW TERMINOLOGY

There is a great deal of talk today about exactly what it means to be global. For most people, it means doing business in other countries. That could involve exporting, licensing, and distribution agreements or foreign sourcing of technology, capital, facilities, labor, and materials. The general public can live with this definition, but for those interested in learning the language of international business, it is confusing.

Even among businesspeople the term global corporation is often used interchangeably with *multinational*

HR IN THE NEWS

CROSS-BORDER MERGER RESULTS IN HEADACHES FOR A DRUG COMPANY

As everyone knows, Swedes take off the entire month of July for vacation, and Italians take off August. Everyone in *Europe* knows, that is, but apparently hardly anyone in Kalamazoo, Michigan, does.

So it was that after the merger of two drug companies—Upjohn and Pharmacia of Sweden, with operations in Italy—things got a bit confused. American executives scheduled meetings throughout the summer, only to cancel many because their colleagues were basking at the beach.

WWW.UPJOHN.COM

Few observers anticipated what an obstacle culture would pose. The average American who gets off the plane and takes a cab into Stockholm is struck by the similarities. Most Swedes speak English and enjoy the same lifestyle as Americans. It was a short honeymoon.

Work rules became a point of contention. At Upjohn, a buttoned-up company known for its strict HR policies, all workers were tested for drug and alcohol abuse; at Pharmacia's Italian business center, waiters poured wine freely every afternoon in the company dining room.

Management styles and HRM systems were very different, too. Italy became the most volatile. Italy's laws and unions made layoffs difficult.

In the end, Pharmacia and Upjohn says, it will meld the different cultures and systems and get on with its growth plans. There is little doubt the many cultural mix-ups that have strained managers at the merged company did teach one painful lesson: Though globalization is the biggest buzzword in business, *going global* is a lot tougher than it looks.

SOURCE: R. Frank and T. Burton, "Side Effects: Cross-Border Merger Results in Headaches for a Drug Company," *Wall Street Journal* February 4, 1997: A-1, A-12.

corporation (MNC) to describe a business with overseas operations. Other knowledgeable people define a global firm as one that attempts to standardize operations—"one size fits all"—but that responds to national market differences when necessary.[3] The term *transnational* is suitably applied for this type of global corporation. Procter & Gamble—with manufacturing operations in 70 countries and its products sold in over 140 countries—truly is a transnational corporation.

We define globalization with a slightly different twist. *Globalization* is the process of efficiently utilizing worldwide assets (land, labor, capital, and knowledge) against competitors employing a *multicultural* workforce.

HR IMPLICATIONS FROM GLOBALIZATION

Corporations such as Procter & Gamble locate production facilities all over the world to gain the benefits of lower-cost labor and better-educated workers. Improvements in technology, telecommunications, and teleconferencing have made it possible for transnational project teams to meld ideas from different cultures. Human talent is leveraged wherever it can be found— from *home* country nationals to *host* country nationals or perhaps *third* country nationals (see Table 2–1).

WWW.PG.COM

There is more free flow of people as well as ideas. Promotion to the executive rank won't necessarily depend on what nationality or gender one happens to be, because talent will prevail—it has to if corporations are to compete successfully in a global market place. MNCs may still send their *expatriates* abroad, but the huge expense means fewer of them will go. Rather, local (host country) people will be recruited and trained to run overseas operations. For HR professionals and top managers it means company mission, HRM system, infrastructure, and compensation strategy must be inextricably intertwined.

Globalization means that companies are challenged to deliver products in a consistent manner to areas of the world that for many managers have been nothing more than names on a map. With new and more demanding customers asking for speedy and responsive service, companies are finding new ways to decentralize authority and responsibility.

Increasing demand for quality products and services means new forms of cooperation and new cross-functional coordination to allow global organizations to meet the needs of internal and external customers. Newly emerging markets are demanding new partnerships and joint ventures with people who have unfamiliar ways of doing business and different views of the world and their relationships with foreigners.

CREATING A "SUSTAINABLE" COMPETITIVE ADVANTAGE

It is now clear that global change will be a way of life in the 21st century. The increased complexity of a global business environment makes it necessary for multinational firms to utilize all organizational capabilities such as speed, responsiveness, agility, learning capacity, and employee competence. Winning companies will be those that are able to "turn strategy into action quickly; to manage processes intelligently and efficiently; to maximize employee contribution and commitment; and to create conditions for seamless change."[4]

As the HR function is one means of gaining competitive advantage, two questions arise: What can MNCs do to create a "sustainable" competitive advantage? And should MNCs adapt HRM systems to fit local workforce needs, or adopt a "one size fits all" strategy.[5]

Three types of resources are capable of contributing to a firm's competitive advantage: (1) physical (land, capital, technology); (2) organizational (structure, processes); and, (3) human (knowledge, skills).[6] While physical and organizational resources may lead to a competitive advantage, the success is usually temporary. Competitors quickly re-create "winning" conditions, recapturing lost markets.

The only thing that will distinguish one competitor from another is the quality of its workforce. Specifically what people know, how they use what they know, and how fast they can learn something new, simplistic as it sounds, is critical intellectual capital. How to attract, develop, and retain that kind of talent becomes an even greater challenge internationally— and, it all falls under the responsibility of the HR function.[7]

Strategies for achieving a competitive advantage are described in detail elsewhere.[8] The focus here is turned to the second question: "Can one size fit all?" Will HR strategies that work in one country, for example the United States, be effective in China? Or, using a specific example, can pay-for-performance schemes, popular in the United States and United Kingdom, be effective in France?

These are not just issues for North American companies either. It works both ways. Quality circles are widely used and effective in Japan, for example, yet continue to meet with resistance in North America.[9]

TABLE 2–1 GLOSSARY FOR 21ST CENTURY BUSINESS

Co-determination:	A system in which representatives of labor participate in the management of a company. It is a legal right of employees and unions to participate in relevant organizational decision making. Germany, Sweden, and other northern European countries follow co-determination.
Culture:	The pervasive and shared beliefs, norms, and values that guide the everyday life of a group.
Ethnocentric:	All aspects of HRM for managers and technical workers tend to follow the parent organization's home country HRM practices.
Euro:	The name of the single currency that will replace national currencies of European countries which become part of the economic and monetary union.
Expatriate:	Employee who comes from a country different than that in which he or she is working.
GATT:	General Agreement on Tariffs and Trade reduces the average worldwide tariff on manufactured goods.
Geocentric:	Hiring and promoting employees because of their abilities without reference to their nationality or race.
Globalization:	MNCs engaged in the process of efficiently utilizing worldwide assets against competitors employing a multicultural workforce.
Home country:	The country in which the parent company's headquarters is located.
Host country nationals (HCNs):	Workers native to the country hosting a subsidiary (plant, sales unit, etc.).
Joint venture:	A cooperative effort among multiple organizations that share a common interest in a business enterprise or undertaking.
Multinational (MNC):	An organization consisting of a parent company in one country that owns relatively autonomous subsidiaries in other countries.
NAFTA:	North American Free Trade Agreement links the United States, Canada, and Mexico in an economic bloc that allows a freer exchange of goods and services.
Open market economies:	Economies characterized by a market sector relatively free of government control.
Polycentric:	A firm treats each country separately, allowing for local culture, staffing, developing, and compensating all human resource activities.
Repatriation:	Employees returning to their home countries and reconnecting with their home organization.
Strategic alliances:	Partnerships between competitors, customers, or suppliers that may take various forms.
Third country nationals (TCNs):	Workers who come from neither the host nor home country.
Transnational:	An organization that attempts to achieve economies of scale through global integration of its functional areas while at the same time being highly responsive to different local environments.
Wholly owned subsidiary:	Owning a foreign subsidiary outright—no partners.
Works council:	A directive issued by the EU in 1995 requiring all firms with more than 1,000 employees to set up a consultative mechanism if at least 150 of the firm's employees are located in two or more member states. The objective is to improve information flow and worker participation in all relevant business decisions.

ENVIRONMENTAL IMPACT ON HR MANAGEMENT SYSTEMS

There are many forces operating in the environment which influence the design and implementation of various HRM systems. As Figure 2–1 depicts, the obvious forces include legal, political, and economic systems. Economic systems in place reflect how large a role government plays in the marketplace. HRM systems in China, for example, are highly influenced by the communist government. Legal and political traditions, such as co-determination (discussed later), directly have an impact on the essence of every medium and large firm in northern Europe.

Global corporations tend to pay a great deal of attention to local conditions such as laws, regulations, and the economic system in place, but less attention is given to the local labor traditions and culture. Lincoln Electric, for example, was not successful internationally due to its lack of understanding of multicultural differences in expectations regarding compensation policies and practices.[10] Their experience is not unique.[11]

Too many "global" organizations do not believe in the saying, "When in Rome, do as the Romans do."[12] Perhaps firms overlook these forces or, more likely, they understand them but choose to ignore them. The evidence, thus far, clearly indicates that global firms—specifically their HRM systems—must be sensitive and alert to the local environment, especially the culture. Companies must adapt their business and HR practices to other parts of the world, rather than merely transplanting American ways.

THE IMPACT OF CULTURE

Many companies overestimate the probable effect of cultural differences. For example, whenever a global company introduces a new product, strategy, or operating procedure, several managers are sure to declare, "It won't work in my territory."

Sometimes they are right. But often they are merely saying the safest thing when they feel neither ownership of, nor confidence in, the strategy devised by corporate headquarters. Other times, the same companies underestimate the importance of local cultures. They assume a strategy, product, or approach that succeeds in one culture will work in all cultures.

Culture is real. It affects everything we do as people and organizations, and all managers must understand how to make the best of what it can offer. Culture is a business issue that affects products, strategy, operating procedures, and people. It is laden with assumptions about barriers and opportunities—real or perceived—about what managers think can or cannot be done.

WHAT IS CULTURE?

Culture is defined as the shaping of the mind that distinguishes the members of one group or category of people from those of another.[13] It is expressed as the

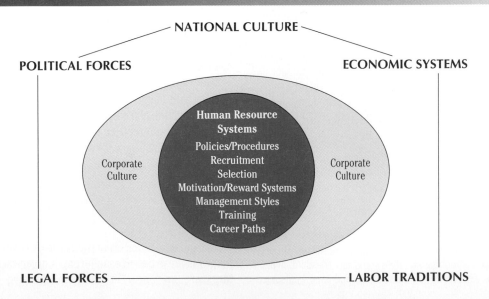

FIGURE 2–1 ENVIRONMENTAL FORCES

NATIONAL CULTURE

POLITICAL FORCES

ECONOMIC SYSTEMS

Corporate Culture

Human Resource Systems

Policies/Procedures
Recruitment
Selection
Motivation/Reward Systems
Management Styles
Training
Career Paths

Corporate Culture

LEGAL FORCES

LABOR TRADITIONS

collective values, norms, traditions, myths, and institutions that are characteristic among members of a group. Culture defines people, context, human relationships, and leadership—virtually every aspect of business.[14]

People who share the same culture need not be constantly mindful of the implication of their behavior. They can predict, accurately, the reactions of those with whom they interact. The codes for interpreting the environment, attaching values and priorities to that information, classifying behavior as acceptable or not, and recognizing social rank are all passed from one generation to the next through the cultural process.[15]

Interpersonal conflict is often the result of tensions brought about from cultural conflicts. In the United States, cultural clashes are expressed in racism and gender gaps. At societal levels, ethnic tensions, religious conflict, racial friction, and linguistic differences across regions and countries have led to wars. At the corporate level, the costs of intergroup cultural conflicts are higher turnover, absenteeism, low morale and productivity, and litigation.[16]

Culture is complex. Researchers have identified five key areas that demonstrate cross-cultural differences.[17]

Human Nature: How much trust can we place in "other" people? How much we trust co-workers or subordinates to carry through with a project?

Relationships: What are the differences in building and maintaining relationships (family, work, church, state, and so on)?

Nature: What is the relationship to our environment: harmony versus mastery?

Time: Where is the temporal focus of life: from "time is money" to no language regarding time?

Activity: How do people live their lives: from live to work to work to live?

Simple ways in which the world is viewed and how the world shapes people can have significant impact on determining personal priorities, family relationships, communication and motivation styles, and management success. One story often cited illustrates how far apart peoples' views of the world can be.

On a sea voyage, you are traveling with your wife, your child, and your mother. The ship develops problems and starts to sink. Of your family, you are the only one who can swim and you can only save one other individual. Who would you save?

This question was posed to a group of men in Asia and the United States. In the United States, more than 60 percent of those responding said they would save the child, 40 percent would choose to save the wife, and none would have saved the mother. In the Asian countries, 100 percent said they would save the mother. Their rationale? You can always remarry and have more children—but you cannot have another mother.

When doing business overseas, Americans can't rely only on American values and behavior patterns. What is good in one place ("Father is getting about the age where he probably would be happier in the senior citizens home in Arizona") is scandalous in another ("Look at how they treat older people in this country—it's awful.").[18]

Another common misunderstanding that occurs between Americans and others in the world is that between an individualist perspective and that of a collectivist perspective.[19] In the United States, performance appraisals reflect an individual's success whereas in most other parts of the world, individuals are defined by the group they are in.

BUILDING CROSS-CULTURAL COMPETENCE

It is perfectly normal to think one's own culture is superior. Yet consider that it also implies other cultures are inferior, which is an ethnocentric way of thinking. Simply being aware that people are prone to ethnocentrism is important. Usually people don't even think about culture until they step outside their comfort zone.

What are a few key cross-cultural competencies? The ability to deal with *ambiguity* is one. Most people in North America are slowly becoming accustomed to the day-to-day ambiguities and uncertainties that work, family, and society create. Another success factor—for individuals and firms—is the ability to *adapt to change.* Change is overwhelming, inescapable, and challenging. Dealing with *complexity* is also important. The most important skill, however, is the ability to *empathize* and see issues from another person's point of view.

Although a person can never truly claim total identification with someone of a different culture, one can question, listen, and respond. These are competencies that demonstrate respect and sensitivity.

ALIGNING CORPORATE CULTURE WITH A MULTICULTURAL WORKFORCE

Global and domestic corporations are discovering traditional business practices inherent in organizational cultures are no longer in-sync with changing realities.

Certainly, corporate culture can lead to a competitive advantage, yet over time it can also limit success by being culturally bound. Failing to tap into talented people who happen to be different, for example, can lead to a costly loss of human potential.

One common problem in a multicultural world is attempting to treat everyone the same way. That is often a mistake. What will succeed is working to create an equitable environment? Creating an organizational culture of equitable HRM systems and activities that maximize each employee's potential is considered a business imperative.

"Corporations must create a culture of inclusion that leverage the talents of every individual and engage every employee," says Bill Tate, a GM HR director. "Accessing talent is a bottom-line business necessity."[20]

Corporate cultures are sometimes blind to their exclusion of others. The people within are often not aware of the consequences of such a system. The HRM role is to continually remind key stakeholders that the world is pluralistic and not to get stuck in an "us versus them" perspective. It is about recognizing how the organization limits people and then designing HR strategies for building on multiculturalism and eliminating barriers. Aligning corporate culture with a multicultural world helps to overcome the inherent limitations placed on people and to fully leverage intellectual capital.

MULTICULTURAL TEAMS

Understanding differences across cultures is important but hardly sufficient. Today, the accent is on developing multicultural teams. An increasing number of people are working with foreign colleagues. It is a serious mistake to assume that because there may be a few common interests within the mixed group that the methods for achieving those interests are the same too. The merger of Upjohn and Pharmacia described earlier (HR in the News: "Cross-Border Merger Results in Headaches for a Drug Company") depicted major differences between the way business is conducted and how human resources are managed.

The role of the boss; how meetings are conducted; how decisions are made; and how employees are selected, motivated, and compensated are some of the basic elements of management which vary from country to country. Misunderstanding cultural and managerial differences are bound to lead to problems and conflict.

When conflict occurs, it is helpful to check the deep cultural assumptions that are in place, find common ground, and from there begin generating solutions. An ability to recognize strengths that different cultures can bring to the team and how they can be used effectively are competencies HR professionals need to encourage and reward. Conflict can be thought of as an opportunity for creative tension leading to better decision making, more creative ideas, solutions to problems, and improved communication and interpersonal relationships.

LEVERAGING A MULTICULTURAL WORKFORCE

Leveraging a multicultural workforce means assuring everyone is included in all aspects of the organization. This can only be done by reducing the barriers which prevent people from fully using their talents for the firm.

The process begins at the top. If the rhetoric for inclusion is vague—and the leaders' actions don't match the words—the effort will fail, because nothing else will matter. The important thing is ensuring an organization has addressed systemic actions for creating an inclusive environment capable of leveraging its talent of all kinds and at all levels.[21]

As shown in Figure 2–2, managers have four basic strategies for selecting an approach to multicultural situations. In all cross-cultural situations, managers must create a balance between continuing to work in their own way—that is, the way they manage in their home country—and adapting to the ways of other cultures.[22] The HR in the News: "Multicultural Reciprocity" illustrates the synergistic power of multicultural teams.

HRM STRATEGIES: CROSS-NATIONAL COMPARISONS

How do different countries manage their people? How do they balance the needs of workers and employers in order to compete in dynamic, global markets? Are human resource systems different around the world and, if so, are there such things as "best practices" that are transferable? Will HR strategies that succeed in North America hold true in Asia or Europe? Or, do the variations across cultures necessitate the deployment of customized HRM systems devoted to the idiosyncrasies of local labor markets?

This section will examine the human resource management systems of four important trading partners of the United States, including Japan, France, Germany, the United Kingdom, plus the systems in emerging markets of Mexico, Eastern Europe, and China. Indeed, this knowledge will contribute to better strategic decisions on doing business in other countries because, in some

FIGURE 2–2   MULTICULTURAL ADAPTATION MODEL

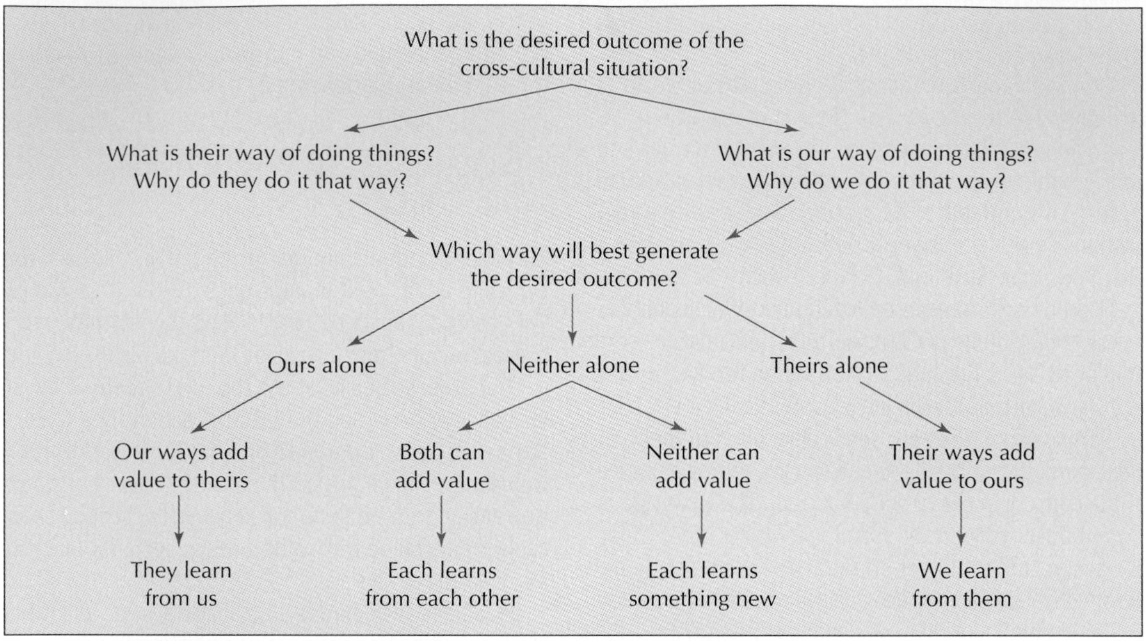

SOURCE: Lisa Hoecklin, *Managing Cultural Differences* (Reading, MA: Addison-Wesley, 1995), 81.

instances, less adaptation will be required between home and overseas human resource activities.

JAPAN

The Japanese Business Environment   Although the country has been in an economic slump, don't count the Japanese out. The country has few natural resources, but this limitation has served to pressure the government and various industries to concentrate on building a competent workforce. One of Japan's competitive advantages is the investment its companies make in the development of human resources. This competitive advantage derives not from the amount spent on training, but the methods. The United States, for example, spends a larger proportion of its Gross National Product (GNP) on education than Japan.[23]

Development   Japanese organizations invest in their people to a greater extent than most other nations, and much more of it is spent on workers compared to managers. In their U.S. facilities, Japanese auto companies train workers 370 hours per year (versus 380 hours at home), compared to 46 hours for U.S. auto plants and 173 hours for European plants.[24] All em-

ployees, beginning with an extensive orientation that could last up to two months, are thoroughly grounded in the organization's corporate culture. Initial emphasis is placed on building teamwork and problem solving, but over time the approach tends to create a workforce that is loyal, flexible, and adaptable to rapidly changing technology.[25]

Labor Unions   In Japan, worker participation is usually in the form of enterprise unions rather than on an industry or trade basis. Unions are company based. Occupational membership in the unions is quite broad and includes supervisors. In the past, as much as 90 percent of eligible employees joined; that proportion has been declining in recent years.[26] Unions are most concerned with wages which are set during the spring labor offensive known as *shunto*. The negotiations are between the enterprise union and its firm, but guidelines are established by agreements negotiated by union industrial federations and employer groups.[27]

Japanese enterprise unions are an integral part of the company—both having mutual interest in the successful performance of the firm. Unlike the United States and the United Kingdom, the relationship between management and labor is not adversarial.

HR IN THE NEWS

MULTICULTURAL RECIPROCITY

While in Japan, a New York–based investment banker had his notion of working in teams challenged. For him, teaming meant working individually then bringing individual tasks back to the group. In Japan, this didn't work. In his experience, the Japanese valued collaterality and mutuality in every one of the tasks of the work that was done.

At first, he thought it was a waste of time, but he discovered that their idea of team presented the opportunity to develop relationships. He found knowledge was not placed in individual silos, but transferred among the group. In turn, he had recommended that at some point during deal construction when they ran into a problem, they take 30 minutes individually to think about it, then bring it back to the table. When they returned, the team found many new ideas on how to structure the deal. Taking the time to share and reciprocate on some team practices helped land a $65 million deal for the company.

SOURCE: A. Duran, President, The Duran Group, Roundtable Discussion, December 14, 1998.

HR IN THE NEWS

IS LIFETIME EMPLOYMENT A LUXURY EVEN THE JAPANESE CANNOT AFFORD?

Japan's floundering economy has crossed another humiliating milestone: Its official unemployment rate is as high as America's for the first time since the end of World War II: Both countries reported jobless rates of 4.4 percent in November, 1998.

Japan's famous commitment to lifetime employment is still prevalent, but it appears to be contributing to the country's ongoing economic problems. Companies that cannot fire workers when times turn bad are reluctant to hire in the first place.

Today, there is a growing sense in Japan that jobs must be destroyed if new ones are to be created. Still, Japanese advocates for maintaining employment guarantees point to the culture of frequent firings in the United States and how it has fostered an unnerving sense of insecurity among workers. More importantly, the critics charge, it has meant meager wage and benefit gains for many people too afraid to demand more.

The contrasting history of unemployment reflects the evolution of two different forms of capitalism. Americans are more willing to embrace the unpredictable fluctuations of markets. The Japanese corporate leadership has been less concerned about pleasing shareholders and more concerned about pleasing "other" stakeholders, such as suppliers, borrowers, communities, and—most important—workers.

Still, while layoffs remain officially taboo, many employers have resorted to de facto firings. Hoya Corporation, a Tokyo optic-glass maker, shed about a third of its workforce through an early-retirement program. Those who refused to leave faced a 30 percent pay cut.

Embracing American-style labor flexibility isn't necessarily desirable. But it surely looks inevitable.

SOURCE: Adapted from Yumiko Ono and Jacob Schlesinger, "Sign of Changed Times: Japan's Jobless Rate Rises to the U.S. Level," *Wall Street Journal* (December 28, 1998): A-1 and A-8.

The Japanese labor–management partnership encourages faster, accurate communication, fewer grievances and strikes, and speedier organizational decision making.[28]

Staffing Flow
A normal practice is to begin recruiting certain university applicants well before the time they actually begin employment. Firms compete on general reputation, getting to recruits first, and contacts with instructors.[29] Most employees are hired at entry levels and usually are not hired for specific positions. They are hired for their general knowledge and usually are extensively screened.

When economic times are bad, as they have been recently, firms will often rely more on temporary and part-time workers who are not promised employment security. As of 1992, part-time employment accounted for more than 16 percent of the labor force while temporary workers accounted for another 12 percent.[30] Should these numbers continue to grow, it would reduce the influence of unions since neither group is heavily unionized.[31]

Job hopping is increasing, but given the seniority-based promotion and rewards systems that are characteristic of larger Japanese firms, it is doubtful experienced workers will be doing it much. Most mid-career job hopping is to lower status small- and medium-sized firms or to foreign firms operating in Japan, neither of which offer the traditional Japanese employment system.[32]

Taking a cue from the United States, job descriptions are also being developed to provide a basis for performance evaluation.[33] Seniority still remains important in many firms, however. A new president of Pharmacia Biotech K.K. complained that the promotion system of the company had produced hardworking but uncreative executives compensated "more by seniority than output."[34]

The Japanese concept of performance varies from that of the West and includes not only the achievement of actual results but the expenditure of good faith effort. Job duties are generally broader and more ambiguous than in North America. New employees are expected to learn by doing rather than from a written description, and they are expected to do anything. The national culture encourages a sense of collectivity and precludes a strong identification with occupational expertise; for example, employees do not see themselves in terms of their skills, such as marketer or HR management professional, but rather as a Toyota or Mitsubishi family member.

WWW.MITSUBISHI.COM

Reward Systems
The compensation system begins with a monthly salary based on level of education attainment (but not job assignment). Salary increases usually take place every twelve months, and this progression is usually based on seniority. An annual base-up of salaries takes place during the spring wage offensive of the unions. Workers can usually expect a slow wage progression until the age of 35; but from the ages of 40 to 45, the rate increases and continues rise until the wage earner reaches an age in the early 50s when wage progression either slows down or stops.[35]

Skill-based pay is another component used in many Japanese firms.[36] It is similar to pay-for-knowledge systems used in the United States and is a strong incentive for learning more complex tasks. Other salary components include monthly allowances that can amount to 20 percent of monthly pay and overtime pay that can amount to approximately 10 percent of compensation. Monthly allowances cover health insurance, pensions, social security, and unemployment insurance. Twice yearly bonuses can constitute as much as an extra 33 percent of annual compensation.[37]

Compensation is not considered a measure of personal worth, as in the United States. Salary increases and promotions are generally automatic and result from time on the job, not necessarily exceptional performance. There does appear to be a movement away from the seniority system. While bonuses are common, the principal motivators are interesting assignments, training opportunities, and eventual promotion to a higher grade or managerial position.

The use of performance appraisals is widespread in Japan, but it has a different meaning in Japan then the United States.[38] Rather than based solely on work results, other elements enter into the measure including educational attainment, communication skills, cooperativeness, and sense of responsibility. While performance-based systems are beginning to surface, Japanese companies continue to attach considerable importance to age and length of service when considering promotions to senior-level positions.[39]

Japanese companies provide various fringe benefits, including transportation allowances, housing subsidies, meals at work, family allowances, and use of company-owned recreational facilities. There is evidence that the generous benefits offered create high job satisfaction and company commitment in Japanese firms and are used more to tie workers to firms than producing higher job performance.[40] Health insurance is available either through a company-sponsored plan or by a national health insurance program. There is also a national pension program that covers all employees when they reach the age of 65.

Status differentials between managers and workers are rare. Symbols of privilege such as executive dining rooms and stock options are avoided. There is no such term as "blue collar" worker among Japan's "non-diverse" workforce; rather, workers are thought of as colleagues or associates. Salary differentials of CEOs to the average worker are much lower in Japan than in the United States. Data from a 1992 study showed the average American CEO is paid 160 times as much as the average worker, compared to 20 times in Japan.[41] Moreover, Japanese CEOs are the first to take drastic cuts in salaries, bonuses, and perks, contrasted to American customs.[42]

Is Japanese-Style HRM Exportable The question of transferability of Japanese HRM practices to the United States and other countries needs to be addressed. Japanese global companies are firmly established in the United States and have achieved great success, but is their U.S. success a function of superior human resource management practices or cutting-edge manufacturing techniques?

The answer to both would appear to be yes. The Japanese adapt their HR management systems, such as team building, to the host culture. Combined with a cutting-edge technology, such as flexible manufacturing, Japanese companies become formidable competitors. The HR practices in place at Toyota USA, for example, are not the same ones that would be found in Japan (see accompanying *HR in the News*). At home, the Japanese culture encourages HR systems that support lifetime employment, seniority-based promotions, housing allowances, consensus decision making, and enterprise unionism. A North American environment simply would not support cloned Japanese HR systems. Quality circles—a popular Japanese activity—is not entirely effective in North America.[43] However, specific HR activities and strategies such as employee empowerment and state-of-the-art training are transferable to most foreign operations.

HR IN THE NEWS

TOYOTA USA'S STAFFING STRATEGY: A CORE COMPETENCY

Toyota USA has a large operation employing more than 8,000 people in its Georgetown, Kentucky operations. The manager is Japanese, as are most of the top management staff. The HR management philosophy is built around one pervasive theme: the Toyota Production System. Toyota wanted only people who could work on teams, who were willing to be flexible in the performance of their tasks, and who would be loyal to the company. These are common characteristics in Japanese workers, but finding such people in Kentucky posed a challenge.

Toyota received over 100,000 applications for 3,000 jobs. Over half were rejected because they failed to meet basic education and experience requirements. Many others failed to pass the battery of tests covering such areas as manual dexterity, job skills, and technical knowledge. Worker attitudes toward unionization were also measured because Toyota wanted to avoid encouraging an adversarial attitude between labor and management.

Having screened out thousands of applicants, Toyota wasn't through yet. They created an organizational simulation that eliminated hundreds of applicants. Next they created a mock production line and had the applicants perform assembly-line work. Only one of every twenty applicants managed to pass this hurdle, and those that did were interviewed to determine their fit into the Toyota corporate culture. Finally, the interview survivors were asked to take a physical examination and drug test and, if they passed both, were then hired.

Toyota spent over $13,000 per person actually hired; the time between an applicant's initial application and the offer to join the Toyota family could stretch out to two years. Clearly, time was on Toyota's side.

The Toyota staffing strategy is considered world class. Other foreign auto manufacturers, such as BMW and Mercedes/Chrysler, have patterned their own selection methods after that of Toyota USA.

SOURCE: Adapted from: R. Griffin and M. Pustay, *International Business, 2d ed.* (Reading, MA: Addison-Wesley, 1999), 729–730.

WESTERN EUROPE

Western Europe is an area with great diversity among national cultures. Three of the dominant cultures—the British, French, and German—are as different from each other as Americans are from Mexicans. National culture, labor traditions, government, and economic philosophy need to be understood by multinational corporations hoping to do business in Europe. Certainly human resource systems are created by top management, but it is also true that these systems are shaped by local history and government policies.

The Euro   The countries of Europe have been moving toward greater economic integration at various levels for many years. The creation of a single euro zone—with one currency and uniform interest rates—is one of the factors that is contributing to a significant shift in how businesses operate in Europe. It is anticipated that large- and medium-sized companies will be forced to revisit their supply chain and vendor relations, financial operations, marketing and pricing strategies, and *human resources philosophies*.

Much has been written about the business implications of the euro, but most of the focus to date has been on financial and systems implications. However, the creation of the euro zone will also have far-reaching compensation, benefits, and human resource implications for large employers. These include both tactical issues around the process of converting currencies and more strategic issues such as compensation strategy, recruiting, and benefit strategy.

The euro will make it possible for employees in different countries to compare their pay.[44] This means that employers will need to reconsider their approach to communicating salary structure and philosophy. It is likely cost-of-living differences may also converge over time. Although there are many remaining barriers to uniform pension rules across the European Union (EU), the euro will give employers the opportunity to consolidate different pension systems. Critical changes in HR strategy will probably not be needed as the result of a new currency per se, but instead will be needed as companies face new competitive challenges and develop new business strategies.

Although efforts toward a common currency suggest a convergence of business practices, markets, and government, for the moment significant differences remain in how people are managed. Three of our largest trading partners—France, Germany, and the United Kingdom—have different HRM systems reflecting different cultures, laws, labor traditions, and economic systems.

FRANCE

The French Business Environment
Like Japan, France is classified as a high-context culture. That is, important information is transmitted in nonverbal or indirect ways. Communication is less dependent upon what is actually said then on how or when it is said. French attitudes toward time are different as well. People and relationships are always more important than meeting schedules.[47]

The "social partners"—labor, management, and the government—are an integral part of the business environment in France. The government mandates a legal framework on relevant issues, and labor and management negotiate the details of its implementation into everyday business life.

Development
Employee training and development is a high priority among the social partners with the government providing financial and technical assistance for the unemployed or for those industries where jobs have become obsolete. The most prestigious educational institutions, known as the "grandes écoles," prepare many of the country's top CEOs and government leaders. Although there is some change taking place, these institutions have taught management as a state of mind rather than a set of techniques. In fact, France is often called the Japan of Europe because what Japan achieves through consensus, France achieves through a core of like-minded people.[46]

Labor Unions
French unions are unique, even in Europe, because their orientation is political rather than social or economic. Various types of collective bargaining forms the basis of the relationship between employees and employers at almost all levels, from industry-wide agreements negotiated between the national unions and employer associations to plant-level agreements negotiated between a works council and the plant manager.

Despite the large role unions play in French society, labor unrest is higher than in the United States. Part of the reason may be that French workers tend to believe they have little economic mobility, thus making more demands on business and government. Certainly when compared to the United States, France has a more rigid class structure.[47] The French, and other European societies, have long traditions of cradle-to-grave social welfare entitlements and support the notion of a "just wage" even when market forces drive down the cost of labor.

In Paris recently, jobless protesters stormed the agency that oversees the French stock market, demanding a Christmas bonus and better unemployment aid from the government. French train conductors, feeling overworked, went on strike. Paris bus drivers went on strike, too, to protest having to drive through bad neighborhoods. And, French journalists went on strike to protest a plan to strip them of a special tax deduction. The French solution to unemployment: Shorten the work-week from 39 hours to 35 hours and give the left-over hours to the jobless.[48]

Staffing Flow

Recruitment and selection methods and laws are not very different from those of the United States. For example, certain protected groups (for example, the disabled, veterans) are given employment preferences. Surprisingly few restrictions or limitations exist in terms of what the interviewer may ask of job applicants.

Most new employees are hired on a probationary basis, subject to collective bargaining agreements. Dismissing an employee in the private sector is not very different from the practice in the United States. Usually ample justification must be provided and strict procedural steps followed. Discharging a worker in the public sector is much more difficult.[49] Downsizing and restructuring is becoming more prevalent, and again, special procedures must be followed.

Reward Systems

Individual performance appraisals and peer evaluations do not occur regularly. Furthermore, goal-setting and management by objectives are management techniques not widely accepted in France. Job security and leisure time are more important to the French than to North Americans as a whole.[50]

It would be a mistake to assume that the French are not productive or hard workers. They take great pride in their work. Quality of life is simply more important to the typical French person than working overtime for extra compensation might be to an American worker. The separation between loyalty to an employer and loyalty to family and/or other nonwork interests is wide.[51] Quality of life is evident in the lengthy vacations—5 weeks minimum—and in the leisurely attitudes employers have toward mixing business and pleasure at the office.

GERMANY

The German Business Environment

Germany has the largest population of any country in the European Union. There is a lot of diversity in this large country, thus many of the generalizations about Germans do not hold true in every region. For example, German workers have a reputation for hard work, but the truth is that the German worker is not at work often. The law requires a full 30 days of paid vacation—not to mention paid holidays. In addition, the labor cost is the highest in the world.[52]

Stereotypes that appear to hold some truth include the methodical planning practiced by managers and workers alike. Business decisions do take longer when compared to the United States, but that is usually the result of German workers examining every possibility. As for communication style, Germans generally say what they mean, which is characteristic of low-context cultures. There are very few nonverbal cues to watch for, unlike the French and Japanese. Other general characteristics include strict punctuality, seriousness, and proper use of people's title and surname (that is, first names are rarely used).[53]

Development

Labor, management, and government put great emphasis on training, especially vocational. An extensive apprenticeship program is available to qualified youths. Over 65 percent of a given age group enters vocational education either through full-time study in vocational schools or through a dual system providing for part-time study and in-plant training.[54] There is probably no other advanced economy in which so many workers are prepared to work in industry.[55]

Promotion from within is the prevalent method for developing managers in Germany. Managers and professional technicians are expected to be university graduates; however, their education is heavily slanted toward engineering and other specialized fields. Desirable management and leadership qualities, from the German perspective, are superior technical skills and communication skills. Americans, of course, would rather have leaders who are charismatic and confident.[56] Performance appraisals are an accepted HR practice and usually very formal. They are conducted in private and seldom involve input from peers or anyone other than the manager.[57]

In comparison with the United Kingdom and France, Germany has the lowest proportion of staff to line workers. This suggests that German firms have fewer layers of management and larger spans of control, and/or line workers who are willing and able to perform staff work.[58]

Labor Unions

The German constitution guarantees employees the right to organize. Unions are organized by industry; craft unions do not exist. The largest union is IGM (Industrial Union of Metal Workers) which is responsible for the auto industry, steel, machine tools, ship building, aerospace, and the electrical engineering industry.[59] No single industry dominates union policy. IGM usually sets the pattern in negotiations for all unions.

The unions' objectives are higher wages, fewer working hours, and longer vacations. The unions, as a whole, have negotiated extremely generous benefit packages, including six weeks of vacation and a 35-hour work week. Furthermore, although Germany does not provide a lifetime employment guarantee, there are strict rules for termination of labor contracts, making dismissal of unproductive workers difficult.

Unlike many other advanced nations, German unions have maintained a stable presence in their society. During the period from 1970 to 1988, they grew to 34 percent of the workforce.[60] Clearly, the unions have made a positive difference for German workers.

Staffing Flow

A characteristic unique to Germany is the legally defined role of labor in all business decisions. The arrangement is called *co-determination*. Employees are given certain rights and obligations in relation to the employer and, as a group, are given the right to participate in matters concerning plant operations. Co-determination is implemented through the creation of *works councils*.[61] Every business, except the smallest, is expected to have a works council that represents the employees, addresses complaints, and ensures input into business decisions relevant to labor.

Work councils only focus on co-determined areas of decision making. Size of workforce, compensation systems, selection systems, job design, training, restructuring, and termination are examples where management and the works council share formal authority.

On balance, management under co-determination still retains a substantial amount of power, but by having to take the works councils perspective into consideration, the relationship of human resource planning to business planning has increased considerably. In practice, works councils have immense legal power but generally do not need to use it. It would appear that the interests of the workers are more closely aligned to the firm's goals due to the continuous interaction of workers and managers without creating substantial inflexibility for management.

Reward Systems

Since around 90 percent of all German industrial employees are covered by collective bargaining agreements, pay-for-performance plans are rare. Although individual performance is not monetarily rewarded, most large firms do rely on profit-sharing plans.[62] Mandatory pensions, unemployment insurance, health insurance, maternity benefits, six weeks of vacation, and a 35-hour maximum work week are only a few of the fringe beneits provided by law. Hourly pay is extremely high—Germany has the highest hourly labor costs in the world[63]—so it would appear logical to conclude that workers are motivated by both money and fringe benefits.

UNITED KINGDOM

The British Business Environment

In recent decades, the industrial structure of the United Kingdom has been undergoing a substantial transition. It has always been an extremely open economy, but following World War II, the government began nationalizing key industries—only to reverse itself during the 1980s. It now appears the country is moving forward and will continue to be a major force in the global arena. The United Kingdom is one of the major trading partners of the United States and a primary source for foreign direct investment.[64] The UK has been the primary European location for the Japanese auto industry and the Asian electronics industry.

Citizens of the United Kingdom include the English, Scots, Welsh, and the Northern Irish, but the group as a whole is called British. The English class system continues to exist. Despite many societal changes, people still tend to stay within the same class into which they were born. Still, the British love tradition and show distaste for change. Also, like the Germans, the British operate in a low-context communication culture with people saying exactly what they mean.[65]

Development

Surprisingly, managers are less likely to be university graduates or to have been technically trained when compared to other advanced nations.[66] One possible reason is that managerial positions in industry hold lower status than careers in law, medicine, finance, and civil service.[67] In-house management training is also viewed more as a cost rather than an investment in people. One study reported that only 40 percent of UK corporations have training budgets at all.[68]

Performance appraisals are common. One estimate is that 85 percent of UK businesses have implemented some form of employee evaluation.[69]

Labor Unions

The collective bargaining process in the United Kingdom is similar to the United States in that both are based on an adversarial relationship between labor and management. Collective bargaining is also less regulated by legal frameworks, but rather determined by custom and practice. Labor–management contracts seldom have legal status. Union membership has been declining, and fell from 53 percent to 40 percent of the labor force from 1979 to 1990.[70]

Collective bargaining is conducted at both industry and company levels. A typical agreement reflects an understanding between the parties at a given time. If conditions change, a new understanding is required. Agreements cover wages (or minimum rates), job classification, pay for overtime and shift work, the standard workweek (37 hours), and procedures for settling disputes and changing the agreement. Also, as in the United States, HR activities such as downsizing, selection, training, and promotions are primarily shaped by firms, with or without help of unions.

Staffing Flow

Typically, recruitment is performed through word-of-mouth and newspaper advertising. Selection methods are old-fashioned with a near total reliance on the application form to pre-select candidates and on the interview, supported by references, to make the final decision. Testing and assessment centers are rarely used.[71]

Equal employment opportunity laws exist, but there are no age-discrimination laws and age preferences often appear in newspaper ads. Part-time female workers are an important source of flexible labor and comprise about 23 percent of the workforce. Temporary workers represent about 8 percent of the workforce.[72] Both groups are usually paid less and receive lower benefits.

Employers in the United Kingdom, unlike continental Europe, have a great deal of freedom from government interference when downsizing organizations or terminating employees. Downsized workers do receive a modest severance package, as required by law.[73]

Neither management nor unions have enthusiastically embraced work design strategies such as team building or quality circles. Management perceives empowering employees as a threat to their autonomy, whereas unions have other priorities, such as pay rates, job security, and involvement in management decision making.[74]

Historically in the United Kingdom, factories were designed with production workers doing repetitive, highly specialized tasks. British first-line supervisors, unlike those in Germany, have a management style that emphasizes consideration and support rather than the task content. Production workers, on the other hand, tend to have greater influence over job design, task allocation, and even input on determining the number of workers needed.[75]

Reward Systems

Historically, pay is a function of job classifications in which the employees are paid the same rate for the same job description. It is no coincidence that such a system is strongly supported by unions. Movement up the grade is often based on time-on-job considerations. Status differentials between blue- and white-collar workers are substantial.

Over the past few years, pay-for-performance plans have appeared but are still far fewer than those found in the United States. Profit-sharing schemes appear to be more popular than pay for performance.[76]

Fringe benefits are generous, and most are provided by the government—including a national health care program. Vacations are somewhat below the norm of western Europe, averaging 22 working days per year.

HR MANAGEMENT CHALLENGES IN TRANSITION ECONOMIES

If there were a defining moment in the lives of post–World War II baby-boomers, it occurred for many in November, 1989, the day the Berlin Wall fell. The disintegration of the Soviet Union created huge untapped markets and opportunities for the West. The transition to open markets, however, has not been easy.

Communism left countries ill-prepared for instituting market reforms. Central planning created millions of unproductive workers, obsolete factories, a devastated infrastructure, double-digit unemployment, and runaway inflation.

Central European countries such as Hungary, Poland, and the Czech Republic have made tremendous progress. For Eastern European countries, such as Russia, Ukraine, Bulgaria, and Rumania, progress is much slower. China is another story. Technically, it is still a communist country, but market reforms have started and appear to most experts as significant steps in the direction of becoming more open and freer.

CHINA

Because human systems have been neglected, the role of HR is particularly critical in leading state-owned, formerly state-owned and now privatized organizations, and newly acquired organizations to profitability. In open market systems, employees and management look to HR professionals for leadership. This is not a tradition in transition economies.

The personnel director in a government-controlled enterprise was often closely linked to the Communist Party. The party wanted to maintain a political voice in the company and used the personnel title to give it legitimacy.[77]

Clearly, a centralized plan depended on workers who would cooperate. Promotions were awarded on the basis of party loyalty and connections. Management training was neither available nor respected.[78] Unfortunately, the most talented people were discouraged from taking risks. Instead, they spent their working lives as paper pushers or fixers. Under communism, making connections, networking, and depending on relationships for favors were refined and valued skills.

China, the most populous country in the world, and the oldest as well, is changing with breathtaking speed. Doing business in China is not for the faint of heart. One of the most serious obstacles to overcome is corruption. Bribery and payoffs are a part of doing business.

Staffing and motivating workers in a transition economy can be a major challenge. Oftentimes, the labor market is controlled by the government, as in the case of China, Cuba, and some central Asian countries. The government may insist that if a foreign company purchases an existing factory, the workforce must remain intact.

Foreign employers will probably have no trouble attracting unskilled workers willing to work for low wages, but they should also be prepared to guarantee lifelong employment, housing allowances, maternity leave, pensions for current employees as well as cash payments for those who have already retired. In China, for example, the foreign owner must reimburse the state for hiring "already trained" recruits.

When it becomes necessary to discharge an employee, stringent rules must be followed. A worker who feels "grieved" will go to the labor grievance board, which usually rules in the worker's favor. Most employers provide generous severance packages in the hope of avoiding untimely and costly legal hassles.

MEXICO

Events are moving rapidly in Mexico. With a growing, dynamic economy, Mexicans spend more per person on U.S. goods than either the Europeans or Japanese.[79]

The Mexican economy had resembled an Asian model more than a Western one. Historically, it was a top-down, centrally planned economy in which the president and a single political party had immense control. Today, it is

HR IN THE NEWS

WORKERS, WORKERS EVERYWHERE

One American couple, Lucy and Saul Randell, have been in China since 1996 and own a small mail-order company. They pay triple wages for an average worker and as much as six times average wages for good performers, even then they have a hard time keeping them.

Zhang Lu, the Randells' accountant, was a good one. She left a government job and accepted the Randells' offer that was ten times her old salary. Is she happy with her move? Not quite.

"I was overwhelmed with the amount of work and responsibility here," she says. "I couldn't believe one person had to do all this."

At her old government job, expectations were so low that a full day's work was required only about twice a month. She has since gone back to her old government job.

After more than 40 years of Communism, workers have forgotten what it is like to work hard. "They're not ambitious because all jobs are dead-end, and all work is treated the same," Saul explains. "Climbing the ladder and going places are not in the vocabulary."

The biggest challenge for private Western employers is competing with the idea of the iron rice bowl— the belief that the government will care for its workers forever.

"We can't get a lot of people out of the state companies," he says, "because they're afraid we'll go under or they'll be fired."

SOURCE: *Wall Street Journal*, Asian Edition (December 11, 1998): B6.

also undergoing a major transition to becoming an open-market economy. Membership in NAFTA guarantees this move to a full market system will continue.

The business environment in Mexico can be characterized as *machismo*. Unlike U.S. culture, which discourages authoritarian leadership styles, there is little risk of antagonizing Mexican subordinates. Most Latin Americans respect powerful people and prefer leaders who demonstrate a "strong man" image.[80]

The Mexican labor market is immense, with approximately 10 million skilled and semi-skilled workers.[81] The workforce is young and open to new ideas.[82]

There are 300,000 Mexicans who work in 1,500 manufacturing plants along the U.S.–Mexican border.[83] The working arrangement is called *maquiladora*, a Mexican term for production sharing. Initially created to take advantage of plentiful labor and low wages, both countries offer tax incentives to encourage manufacturers to assemble products in Mexico, then ship them to the United States and Canada.

The Mexican Constitution guarantees many worker rights. The right to unionize is a constitutional right. On the other hand, interest in unionizing varies from region to region. The main concern for industrial unions has been the improvement of working conditions. Since maquiladoras usually provide benefits above those required by law, employee interest in organizing is minimal unless the region has a strong historical union tradition.

Labor unions are growing and represent about 25 percent of Mexico's labor force. Historically, Mexican unions were not aggressive, but that appears to be changing as well. The relationship between labor and government is positive. The relationship between labor and management, while not as adversarial as in the United States, is still intense and can be combative at times.[85]

Staffing strategies appear similar to North American processes. Word-of-mouth and local newspaper advertising is common for blue-collar positions. Managerial positions are recruited internally, if possible, or by employment agencies when internal candidates are unavailable or inappropriate. Dismissing employees is only possible "with cause," specifically identified by law. Although there are no unemployment benefits, laid-off workers are legally entitled from three to six months' severance pay.[85]

Reward systems are evolving rapidly, and becoming more like those used in North America. Wages are much lower than in the United States but increasing quickly along with the Mexican economy. Employee incentives, particularly profit sharing, is becoming the most popular monetary incentive.[86] Individual pay-for-performance incentives, given the Mexican orientation toward collectiv-

ity, are not popular. One exception to this is the traditional expectation of a Christmas bonus.

What is popular for attracting workers is the fringe benefit package an employer offers. Company allowances for housing, lunch, availability of in-house training, tuition reimbursement, paid vacations, and pensions are particularly attractive and also effective at retaining Mexican workers.[87]

CONVERGENCE OR DIVERGENCE?

The forces that shaped the human resource management system of the advanced nations examined here varied widely, producing an array of HRM activities. For each country, the HRM systems were congruent with the social, political, and economic context in which they evolved. Although the HR evolution began long ago for each nation, it accelerated with international competition. We opened the chapter asking the question: Is global competition gradually creating one way of doing business and, if so, does that suggest that the activities and strategies used to attract, retain, and motivate superior performance are converging?

Proponents insist on spreading one corporate culture so that, for example, employees in Taiwan are treated the same as employees in Germany or the United States. They argue that companies in the United States and United Kingdom have begun to develop a more collectivist orientation in the treatment of employees, while firms in Japan and Germany are beginning to adapt more individualistic employee practices.[88] Certainly there are many Japanese HR activities that have been applied successfully in the United States and elsewhere as noted with Toyota USA. American management development techniques are being used in Europe and Asia with great success, as well.

Nevertheless, overwhelming evidence points the other way. What is philosophically desirable is often, in practice, difficult—if not impossible—to achieve for many reasons, ranging from cultural values to different tax and dismissal laws. Although organizations are becoming more similar in how they go about conducting business, the behavior of people within distinct cultures will continue to be unique.[89] The design of HRM activities and strategies is best done at the local level because the differences are too great. It is a myth, critics argue, to think that HRM systems can be beyond nationality in their design and operation.[90]

Most MNCs must find a balance between imposing one international corporate culture and respecting local cultures. Finding this balance is perhaps the most difficult part of articulating an international HR strategy.

SUMMARY POINTS

- Markets know no borders. Domestic businesses will face increasing competition from foreign competitors. Foreign corporations have invested heavily in the United States and employ over 30 million Americans. Globalization is a fact of life for everyone.

- New terminology has evolved. Expatriates are going abroad, expected to adapt to other cultures, and then be repatriated upon their return. Multicultural work teams will become common, thanks to the technology of teleconferencing. Transnational corporations will have manufacturing facilities in one country, research and development in another, and markets in a third country.

- The only true sustained source of competitive advantage that firms can employ is their people. Specifically, developing their people and what they know, how they use what they know, and how fast they can learn something new. The question was raised: Can HR strategies and systems used in the development of people in one country be effective in another?

- If the United States is to operate effectively at a global level, its global managers need to recognize that there are different ways of thinking, perceiving, behaving, managing, and doing business. The forces that influence doing business and the type of HRM systems in each country are legal, political, economic, labor, and cultural.

- Culture is defined as the shaping of the mind that distinguishes the members of one group from those of another. It defines people, context, assumptions, relationships, and leadership. Understanding the different cultures in an organization is critical to building a corporate culture of inclusion. A corporate culture that is in alignment with national culture is necessary in order to attract, retain, and motivate the workforce.

- Cross-cultural competency is needed by anyone who interacts with people in a multicultural setting. Specific competencies that are critical include an ability to handle ambiguous situations, adapt to change, deal with complexity, and have empathy toward others. Conflict resolu-

tion skills are needed, too, for checking the deep cultural assumptions in place, finding common ground, and generating solutions.

- Japanese corporations have some of the most sophisticated HRM systems in the world. Many of their HR activities are the envy of the world. But whether they can be transferred to other countries and cultures is debatable given the strong linkage some of these HR practices have with Japanese culture. Quality circles, for example, are neither popular nor effective in the United States.

- Three western European countries, France, Germany, and the United Kingdom, are major trading partners of the United States. Like Japan, they have made large foreign direct investments in the United States, employing millions of people. Their HRM systems are older and, in many ways, more sophisticated than those in the United States. France is a country in which the people put great emphasis on quality of life. HR systems in France reflect this. Government plays a large role in guaranteeing the balance between work and family. Germany, surprising to some, offers to workers the most generous compensation and benefits package of any advanced country. It is also a country that has legislated a formal role for labor in organizational decision making. Co-determination, operationalized through works councils, presents the largest difference between North American and European attitudes toward labor. Of the three, the United Kingdom is most similar to the United States in terms of collective bargaining, work flow, development, and reward systems.

- Transition economies present special challenges in the design and implementation of HRM systems. Central and Eastern European countries have made the most advancements, patterning many of their HR systems along the lines of advanced nations. Mexico, in particular is making great progress. China is making progress, as well, but the large role of government in controlling[91] the emerging private sector makes real advancement in HR systems problematic.

CASE STUDY

HOW DOES JAPANESE MANAGEMENT PLAY IN HUNGARY?

After a difficult start, industrial relations have settled down at Suzuki of Hungary, a car factory run by Suzuki of Japan at Esztergom in northern Hungary. Suzuki founded the plant in April 1991 and sent some of its staff to Japan for training courses. Many of them reacted coolly to the Japanese approach to work. Discontent festered when Suzuki imposed a smoking ban in most areas of the factory.

Relations have improved since then, and Japanese management and Hungarian employees are now working well together—although the Hungarians appear to be making all the compromises.

Says Szabolcs Foldvari, chairman of the workers' council at the plant: "We are having to adopt the Japanese way of thinking about work on the production line. We have to concentrate

CASE STUDY—cont'd

HOW DOES JAPANESE MANAGEMENT PLAY IN HUNGARY?

on making good cars. So it is not only about technology but a way of thinking, an emphasis on quality. The Japanese think it most important that everybody moves continuously."

Nine of Suzuki's 600 employees sit on the workers' council, but the employees are not represented by trade unions. Says Foldvari: "By Hungarian law, we have the opportunity to join any trade union. We have not decided whether we want one. The workers' council functions like a trade union." However, about one hundred workers have joined the iron and metalworkers union.

Workers on the production line find the speed quicker than anything they have ever experienced. Clerical staff have also had to change their work habits to comply with the practices of their owners. Says Bela Baka, an assistant manager in the maintenance and utilities division: "It's working rather well, with no big problems. It was strange at first, working in such big, open offices. It was quite noisy, but now people are used to it. Before, we were used to having small offices with just two or three people."

Work hours are dictated by Hungarian labor law—eight hours per day. Overtime is paid at one and one-half times the hourly rate. Wages average Ft 23,000 ($251) a month, close to the Hungarian average, but they vary each week and are determined by several factors. A basic salary is supplemented by additional payments based on a worker's attendance rate and productivity, as determined by a complicated formula. In addition, workers are assessed by their managers every six

months and can receive a discretionary increase as a result of that appraisal.

The workers' council generally meets every month, but it can meet at short notice to deal with an emergency. Management attends if the problem is relevant to them. The last meeting concerned the way workers are able to buy cheaper cars from the factory. A plan devised by managers allows employees a 10 percent discount from cost, with 20–50 percent paid in a lump sum and four years to pay off the balance.

However, workers are not very happy with this arrangement. Says Foldvari: "It takes up a large part of our wages. In the future, I think we will have more meetings about this issue."

QUESTIONS

1. Describe the changes taking place that reflect Japanese management practices. Would American automotive companies such as Ford or GM do things differently? Explain.

2. What are the chances of a trade union being established in the factory? What is the Japanese strategy regarding unions?

3. Based on the information presented, what approach is Suzuki's management taking with its Hungarian factory—ethnocentric, polycentric, or geocentric? Explain.

4. What do the Hungarian workers seem most interested in? What other incentives might the Suzuki management use?

EXPERIENTIAL EXERCISES

1. WORKING ABROAD

PURPOSE

This exercise is intended to familiarize students with the concept of *culture*. Teams will gather information on what life would be like in a different country and culture and examine the need for administration and coordination of HR systems throughout global organizations.

TASK

Students will be grouped into teams. Each team should select a country, preferably a non-English-speaking one, and gather materials on what life would be like if one were transferred for a three-year assignment. Assume that the spouse and two children, ages nine and fifteen, would accompany their parents.

Each team will present oral reports, including maps, to the class. The project will involve some outside work. The instructor will tell each team how much time is allotted.

1. Using the criteria identified here, what are the differences between your national culture and the one to which you will be moving?

Criteria:

Relation to nature: (1) domination over nature, (2) harmony with nature, (3) submission to nature

Time: (1) emphasis on the future, (2) concentration on the present, (3) preoccupation with the past

Relationships: (1) individualistic, (2) group, (3) hierarchical (for example, as in the Middle East)

Space: (1) private, with emphasis on barriers and closed doors; (2) public, open, frequent touching, physically close

Important nonverbal communication signals (facial expressions, gestures, and so on)

Humor (what is considered funny and what is thought odd behavior)

E X P E R I E N T I A L   E X P E R C I S E S — c o n t ' d

2 What type of economic system is practiced (free market, socialism, and so on)? Explain the relationship between government and business: Does the government control land, labor, and capital? What role does the government have in maintaining the welfare of its citizens, particularly the aged, unemployed, and minorities? What is the role of men and women? Are there differences in the way women are treated at work?

3 What is the role of religion and education in the daily life of citizens? Does religion affect the type of government and the everyday work life? Is education encouraged? If so, explain why. Compare their educational system to yours; what are the differences? How are foreigners treated?

4 Identify important indicators of personal success (for example, salary, title, power). Is a particular type of management style expected? How are rewards given (for example, individual monetary reward, group recognition)? How are poor performers disciplined?

5 Assume that your company has decided to organize a subsidiary in this country. What philosophical approach would your team recommend: ethnocentric, polycentric, or geocentric? How much control should the home office exercise in establishing important HR policies, procedures, and systems (hiring, compensation, evaluation, training and career paths, and so on)? Which HR systems ought to be decentralized?

2. Performance Appraisal across Cultures

PURPOSE

This exercise is designed to illustrate how one particular HR function is performed in different countries. The function is performance appraisal, and the countries are the United States, Saudi Arabia, and Japan.

TASK

Experts have noted that one important cross-cultural communication distinction is *context.* Cultures that have high-context communications emphasize the environment in which the information is conveyed; that is, the meaning comes less from the words that are used and more from the physical context. The Spanish, Chinese, Japanese, and Saudi Arabians put extensive effort into interpreting what is not said—nonverbal communication or body language, silences and pauses, and relationships and empathy. North American cultures engage in low-context communications.

The emphasis is on sending and receiving accurate, articulate messages.

Global managers are expected to evaluate people and situations, just as domestic managers are. However, how individual performance information is observed, gathered, described, communicated, and evaluated depends largely on the underlying assumptions prevalent in the local culture. Performance appraisal is a routine function performed universally by every global company. But the why, when, what, and how of performance appraisal will vary. Test your cross-cultural knowledge of three cultures and the performance appraisal process.

Your task is to match each culture (United States, Saudi Arabia, and Japan) to the performance appraisal dimensions. For each of the ten dimensions, select the alternative that best matches your impression of how performance appraisal is handled in the United States, Japan, and Saudi Arabia. Every alternative matches one of the three countries, although some practices are shared across cultures.

Cultural Variations: Performance Appraisal

1. The objective or purpose of performance appraisal is
   a. Direction of the company/employee development.
   b. Placement.
   c. Evaluation of past performance and development for the future.
2. Who conducts appraisal?
   a. Immediate superior.
   b. Manager several levels above the employee who is very familiar with the employee's personal situation.
   c. Mentor and immediate superior, both of whom know the employee well.
3. Where does the authority of the appraiser come from?
   a. Reputation (prestige is determined by nationality, age, sex, family, tribe, title, education).
   b. Presumed by superior's position or title.
   c. Respect accorded by the employee to the superior.

(continued).

EXPERIENTIAL EXERCISE—cont'd

4. How often are appraisals performed?
   a. Once per year or periodically.
   b. Once per year.
   c. Developmental appraisal as often as once per month; evaluative appraisal at much longer intervals, sometimes of several years.

5. Assumptions behind the appraisal process:
   a. Connections are important; who you know is more important than what you did.
   b. Superior's subjective performance appraisal is acceptable because the employee trusts the process.
   c. Objective appraisal is fair; subjective appraisal is a problem.

6. Manner of communicating and feedback:
   a. Formalities are observed, and any criticism is subtle and given verbally.
   b. Criticism is direct, given in writing, and based on authenticated, objective facts.
   c. Criticism is subtle and never written.

7. Most popular motivators:
   a. Internal excellence.
   b. Money and promotion.
   c. Loyalty to management or the desire to become a group leader or manager.

8. Praise is*
   a. Given individually.
   b. Given to entire group.

9. Rebuttals (rejection or appeal):*
   a. Would rebut appraisal.
   b. Would rarely rebut appraisal.

10. If a problem arises in the office, it is handled by
   a. Asking the superior for advice.
   b. Learning to depend on yourself to solve the problem.
   c. Requesting an office meeting, politely mentioning that there may be a problem, and patiently discussing alternative methods for solving it.

*Two cultures share the same practice

REVIEW QUESTIONS

1 What is so important about globalization, and why should someone who never expects to go abroad be concerned?

2 How does a company achieve a sustainable competitive advantage?

3 Most everyone has heard the phrase "When in Rome, do as the Romans do." It was stated in the chapter that many global firms do not believe this is true. Why? What arguments would you use to convince them that the statement is true?

4 Define *culture*. How might national culture influence the effectiveness of HR management practices?

5 What is an ethnocentric perspective?

6 Identify the competencies needed to be an effective manager in a multicultural environment.

7 Describe a method of conflict resolution when dealing with multicultural misunderstandings.

8 How does the Japanese culture as well as the legal, political, labor, and economic forces there influence the type of HRM systems in Japan?

9 Compare French, German, and British cultures in relationship to their typical HR systems. What are the differences? Similarities?

10 What steps are the advanced nations of the United States, Canada, Western Europe, and Japan taking to help the emerging transition economies (Mexico, China, Central and Eastern Europe)?

DISCUSSION QUESTIONS

1 Global corporations, through their HR professionals, have been leading major change efforts to streamline production processes and improve quality. One such industry is the auto industry. Innovative methods such as lean manufacturing processes, low inventory, just-in-time parts delivery, flexible teams of workers, *kaizen* (or continuous improvement), total quality management, and reengineering have been implemented with great fanfare. Will these methods work in the former Soviet-bloc nations? Explain your reasoning.

2 Assume that you are in charge of global HR management for a large transnational automotive corporation. Your company has decided, after much deliberation, to begin operations in Moscow, but the corporation is having difficulty deciding whether to begin fresh (new factory, new employees, and so on) or to acquire the large state-owned enterprise that produces the Lada car. You have had preliminary discussions and negotiations with the Russian State Property Agency (SPA) and with officials at the Lada facility. One person who has been very friendly and helpful was your Russian personnel counterpart. However, you have just learned that he was previously a high-level official in the Communist Party. This is causing you to be apprehensive. The SPA is eager to sell, and you suspect that the factory can be purchased for a bargain-basement price. You know that converting an old factory—and an existing workforce—to an efficient, modern operation is a major undertaking. Your top management is waiting for your recommendations before deciding. Should you be concerned about this person's former affiliation with the Communist Party? What are some of the advantages and disadvantages of acquiring an existing facility versus starting a new operation? What would you do?

3 Americans have been hearing a lot about maquiladoras operating along the U.S.–Mexican border. What advantages did they have before the passage of NAFTA? Now that NAFTA has passed, will HR practices in Mexico begin to resemble those of the United States?

4 How do Japanese HR management practices, policies, and systems differ when managing a factory in Japan versus managing American workers at a Japanese-owned facility in the United States? Which method best describes the Japanese approach at the Toyota manufacturing facility in Georgetown, Kentucky: ethnocentric, polycentric, or geocentric?

5 Describe the relationship of western European labor unions with government and business. How does it differ from the U.S. and Japanese relationships?

6 Toyota USA's selection process at its Georgetown, Kentucky operation is considered world class. Other companies, such as BMW and Mercedes/Chrysler, have patterned their own selection processes in South Carolina and Alabama based on the Toyota USA approach. Discuss whether Ford and General Motors should also adopt Toyota USA's staffing model.

7 In Germany, the concept of co-determination with the implementation of works councils has resulted in workers who are more committed to their company and, arguably, better firm performance (that is, quality, profitability, service). Discuss whether and how the co-determination concept could be transferred to North America.

ENDNOTES

Chapter 2

1. J. Laabs, "HR Pioneers Explore the Road Less Traveled," *Personnel Journal* (February 1996): 70–72, 74, 77–78.

2. Ibid., 72.

3. C. Bartlett and S. Ghoshal, *Managing across Borders: The Transnational Solution* (Boston: Harvard Business School Press, 1989), 24–56.

4. Dave Ulrich, "A New Mandate for Human Resource," *Harvard Business Review* (January–February, 1998): 124.

5. R. Schuler and N. Rogovsky, "Understanding Compensation Practice Variations across Firms: The Impact of National Culture," *Journal of International Business Studies* 22, no. 3, (1998): 159–178.

6. Ibid., 159–160.

7. Laabs, 70–72.

8. G. Hamel and C.K. Prahalad, "Strategic Intent," *Harvard Business Review* 67, no. 3 (1989): 63–76.

9. K. Newman and S. Nollen, "Culture and Congruence: The Fit between Management Practices and National Culture," *Journal of International Business Studies* 27, no. 4 (1996): 754.

10. Schuler and Rogovsky, 163.

11. B. Punnet and D. Ricks, *International Business* (Boston: PWS-Kent, 1992), 5–31.

12. Newman and Nollen, 754.

13. Geert Hofstede, "Cultural Dimensions in People Management," in V. Pucik, V., N. Tichy, and C. Barnett, "Culture and Congruence," (eds.) *Globalizing Management* (New York: John Wiley, 1992), 139.

14. Fons Trompenaars, *Riding the Waves of Culture: Understanding Diversity in Global Business* (Dallas, TX: Irwin Professional Publishing, 1994), 12–34.

15. G.W. Scully, *Multiculturalism and Economic Growth,* NCPA Policy Report No. 196 (August 1995), ISBN # 1-56808-061-1.

16. Ibid.

17. F. Kluckhohn and F. Strodbeck, *Variations in Value Orientations* (Evanston, IL.: Row, Peterson, 1961) and N. Adler, *International Dimensions of Organizational Behavior* (Cincinnati, OH: South-Western College Publishing, 1997), 19.

18. J. McCaffrey and C. Hafner, "When Two Cultures Collide: Doing Business Overseas," *Training and Development Journal* (October 1985): 26.

19. Geert Hofstede, *Culture's Consequences: International Differences in Work-Related Values* (Beverly Hills, CA: Sage, 1980), 25–28.

20. Advertisement, *Business Week* (December 14, 1998).

21. S. Covey, *Tearing Down Walls: Managing Change and Dismantling Barriers to Better Team and Organizational Performance* (Salt Lake City, UT: Covey Leadership Center, Inc., 1997).

22. N. Adler, *International Dimensions of Organizational Behavior,* 3d ed. (Cincinnati, OH: South-Western College Publishing, 1997), 60–61.

23. M. Hashimoto, *The Japanese Labor Market in a Comparative Perspective with the United States* (Kalamazoo, MI: W. E. Upjohn Institute, 1990), 11.

24. J. Womack, D. Jones, and D. Roos, *The Machine that Changed the World* (New York: Harper Perennial, 1990), 85.

25. K. Lindberg, "The Intricacies of Training and Development in Japan," *Human Resource Development Quarterly,* no. 2, (1991): 101–114.

26. T. Tsuru and J. Rebitzer, "The Limits of Enterprise Unionism: Prospects of Continuing Union Decline in Japan," *British Journal of Industrial Relations* 33, no. 3, (1995): 459–492.

27. Ibid., 475.

28. Hashimoto, *Japanese Labor Market,* 63.

29. Ibid., 26–31

30. S. Houseman and M. Osawa, "U.S. Labor Gets Flexible and Japan Joins the Club," *Business Week* (January 15, 1996): 22.

31. M. Morishima, "Part-Time Employment as a Response to Internal Labor Market Constraints." Paper presented at the Academy of Management Meetings, August 8, 1995, Vancouver, British Columbia.

32. J. Lubin, "Japanese Are Doing More Job Hopping, " *The Wall Street Journal* (November 18, 1991): B1, B5.

33. Y. Takahashi, "Human Resource Management in Japan," In R. Pieper, (ed.) *Human Resource Management: An International Comparison* (Berlin, NY: Walter de Gruyter, 1990), 211–232.

34. J. Schlesinger, M. Williams, and C. Forman, "Japan Inc., Wracked by Recession, Takes Stock of Its Methods," *The Wall Street Journal* (September 29, 1993): A-1, A-10.

35. R. Ballon, *The Salary System and Foreign Firms. Bulletin No. 133* (Tokyo: Sophia University, 1990).

36. M. Morishima, "The Japanese Human Resource Management System: A Learning Bureaucracy," In L. Moore and P. Jennings (eds.) *Human Resource Management on the Pacific Rim* (Berlin/New York: Walter de Gruyter, 1995), 119–150.

37. Hashimoto, *Japanese Labor Market,* 83.

38. K. Endo, "*Satei* (Personal Assessment) and Interworker Competition in Japanese Firms," *Industrial Relations* 33, no. 1 (1994): 70–82.

39. Ibid., 81.

40. J. Lincoln and A. Kalleberg, *Culture, Control, and Commitment* (Cambridge: Cambridge, England: University Press, 1990), 243–244.

41. Y. Tsurumi, "If Americans were Chinese . . ." *Pacific Basin Quarterly* 19 (Fall 1992): 13–19.

42. Ibid., 15.

43. Endo, "*Satei* (Personal Assessment)," 73.

44. K. L. Miller, "Why Central Europe Loves the Euro," *Business Week,* (August 7, 1998): 74.

45. T. Morrison and W. Conaway, *The International Guide to Doing Business in the European Union* (New York: Macmillan Spectrum, 1997), 120–138.

46. P. Harris and R. Moran, *Managing Cultural Differences,* 3d ed. (Houston: Gulf Publishing, 1991), 345–346.

47. Andre Laurent, "The Cultural Diversity of Western Conceptions of Management," *International Studies of Management and Organization* 13, no. 1–2 (Spring–Summer, 1983): 75–96.

48. Jeff Bailey, "Joy to the World: Despite Everything, America Still Embraces a Culture of Optimism," *The Wall Street Journal* (December 22, 1998): A-1.

49. Harris and Moran, *Managing Cultural Differences,* 348.

50. Jean-Louis Barsouz and Peter Lawrence, "The Making of a French Manager," *Harvard Business Review* (July–August, 1991): 58–67.

51. Morrison and Conaway, *International Guide,* 135.

52. U.S. Bureau of Labor Statistics, 1998.

53. Morrison and Conaway, *International Guide,* 153.

54. C. Lane, *Management and Labour in Europe* (Aldershot, England: Edward Elgar, 1989), 63.

55. Ibid., 66.

56. Harris and Moran, *Managing Cultural Differences,* 477.

57. Ibid., 478.

58. P. Lawrence, "Management Development in Europe: A Study in Cultural Contrast," In M. Mendenhall and G. Odou, (eds.), *Readings and Cases in International Human Resource Management.* 2d ed. (Cincinnati, OH: Southwestern College Publishing, 1995), 248–262.

59. F. Furstenberg, "Recent Trends in Collective Bargaining in the Federal Republic of Germany," *International Labour Review* (September–October, 1984): 615–630.

60. Morrison and Conaway, *International Guide,* 317.

61. Harris and Moran, *Managing Cultural Differences,* 465–475.

62. C. Brewster, A. Hegewisch, and L. Mayne, "Trends in European HRM: Signs of Convergence?" In Paul Kirbride, *Human Resource Management in Europe* (London: Routledge, 1994), 116–118.

63. U.S. Bureau of Labor Statistics, 1998.

64. R. Stevenson, "Smitten by Britain, Business Rushes In," *The New York Times* (October 15, 1995): 3–1.

65. Terri Morrison, Wayne Conaway, and George Borden, *Kiss, Bow or Shake Hands* (Holbrook, MA: Adams Media Corporation, 1994), 109–114.

66. M. Porter, *The Competitive Advantage of Nations* (New York: The Free Press, 1990), 489.

67. G. Bamber and E. Snape, "Industrial Relations in Britain," In M. Roomkin (ed.), *Managers as Employees: An International Comparison of the Changing Character of Managerial Employment* (New York: Oxford University Press, 1989), 17–49.

68. H. Rainbird, "Continuing Training," In K. Sisson (ed.), *Personnel Management* (Oxford, United Kingdom: Basil Blackwell, 1994), 334–364.

69. G. Randell, "Employee Appraisal," In K. Sisson (ed.), *Personnel Management,* 221–252.

70. P. Beaumont and R. Harris, "Union De-recognition and Declining Union Density in Britain," *Industrial and Labor Relations Review* 48, no. 3, (1995): 389–402.

71. T. Watson, "Recruitment and Selection," In K. Sisson (ed.), *Personnel Management,* 185–220.

72. C. Lane, "Industrial Change in Europe: The Pursuit of Flexible Specialization in Britain and West Germany," *Work, Employment and Society* 2, no. 2 (1988): 141–168.

73. Ibid., 155.

74. D. Buchanan, "Principles and Practice in Work Design," In K. Sisson (ed.) *Personnel Management in Britain* (Oxford, United Kingdom: Basil Blackwell, 1989), 78–100.

75. E. Lorenz, "Trust and the Flexible Firm: International Comparisons," *Industrial Relations* 31, no. 3 (1992), 455–472.

76. N. Millward, M. Stevens, D. Smart, and W. Hawes, *Workplace Industrial Relations in Transition* (Aldershot, England: Dartmouth, 1992), 262–263.

77. J. Pearce, "From Socialism to Capitalism: The Effects of Hungarian Human Resource Practices," *Academy of Management Executive* 5, no. 4 (1991): 75–88.

78. N.F. Elbert, "Reflection on Life Outside the HRM Mainstream: One Year's Experience in Hungary," *Academy of Management Annual Meeting,* Atlanta, GA, August 13, 1993.

79. "The Mexican Worker," *Business Week* (April 19, 1993): 84–92.

80. Harris and Moran, *Managing Cultural Differences,* 375.

81. "The Mexican Worker," 85.

82. Ibid., 86.

83. Ibid., 85.

84. Ibid., 90.

85. S. Lefler, *Doing Business in Mexico* (Dallas, TX: Southern Methodist University, 1988), 46.

86. "The Mexican Worker," 91.

87. Ibid., 89.

88. I. Nonaka, "Self-renewal of the Japanese Firm and the Human Resource Strategy," *Human Resource Management* 27, no. 1 (1988): 45–62.

89. N. Adler, 96–120.

90. Ibid., 63.

91. J. Laabs, "Why HR Can't Win Today," *Workforce* 775 (1998): 62–74.

CHAPTER 3

WORKFORCE DIVERSITY

CHAPTER OUTLINE

CHAPTER OBJECTIVES

1 To understand the impact the diversification of the American labor force is having on the workplace.

2 To learn the value of a diversified workforce that mirrors the population.

3 To clearly define diversity.

4 To understand how diversity programs can impact the bottom line.

5 To describe the differences between stereotypes and prejudices.

6 To recognize the processes of assimilation and valuing diversity.

7 To identity successful diversity management programs.

8 To understand the need for awareness programs.

WORKFORCE DIVERSITY

AN HR CHALLENGE FOR
A NEW CENTURY

It's the '90s, and the United States is experiencing an enormous challenge. The demographics of its workforce has changed dramatically, and the turn of the century heralds a revolution in the way work will be done in America.

Sound familiar? With the recent advent of *cultural diversity* as an HR concept, it should. But the "'90s" just referred to are not the 1990s, they're the 1890s. Before the turn of the last century, America faced the challenge of converting from an agrarian to an industrial nation and the challenge of accepting and accommodating over 20 million immigrants who had come to this country during the half-century after the Civil War.[1] At first, these immigrants were primarily western European—Irish, Scandinavian, English, and German. Soon, however, word spread of the opportunities for work and religious freedom, and masses of immigrants came from Italy, Poland, Austria, Hungary, and Russia. From all of these countries, groups migrated to escape direct and persistent discrimination in their native lands.[2] This second wave of immigrant workers from southern and eastern Europe also came about because of America's need for cheap, plentiful labor to fill the factories and mines that multiplied during the Industrial Revolution.

Through World War I, the Depression, and World War II, America's production continued, and after World War II it flourished. Unlike Europe and Japan, the United States emerged from World War II with its industrial base intact. The production system was geared to turn out standard, assembly-line products in high volume. For the United States, it was a seller's market. There were plenty of customers, domestically and internationally, ready to absorb our goods.

But while the United States continued to organize and produce in the same way for most of the 20th century, other countries were rebuilding, using the technology of the 21st century in that rebirth. Their postwar recovery was slow and, out of necessity, was designed to supplant the United States as the main producer of goods worldwide. This buildup of industry in sync with the latest technology during the last quarter of this century placed the United States at a competitive disadvantage. The need to meet this global competition and to utilize new technology has made U.S. companies reassess their most important asset—their workforce.

In this chapter, we will examine the American workforce as a diverse workforce, how the diversity came about, and the legal environment that affects the way employers interact with this new workforce. We will explore approaches to managing workforce diversity and

HR IN THE NEWS

CIGNA CORPORATION DIRECTOR RESIGNS OVER LACK OF DIVERSITY

In a move that "shook the clubby world of corporate directors," Frank S. Jones resigned from the Cigna Corporation board of directors. A 21-year veteran of the board, Mr. Jones, a black director, said the reason for his departure was:

> There are people of color in the ranks of our company who feel a severe estrangement and devaluation in their working lives—lives which should otherwise be filled with promise, pride and hope.

. . . and . . .

> I cannot remain in a position of fiduciary responsibility . . . when I find myself so at odds with the company's unwillingness—an unwillingness which could bring, ultimately, company liability—to . . . [enhance] diversity within Cigna.

WWW.CIGNA.COM

Mr. Jones's action was rare in the corporate world; usually minority directors (6 percent of the board members) use their influence to support diversity programs.

SOURCE: Joann Leblin, "Cigna Directors Diversity Challenge Hits A Dead End," *The Wall Street Journal* (June 15, 1998): Sec. B, p. 1.

review real-life programs by employers on the leading edge of diversity training.

DEFINING DIVERSITY

In 1987, the Hudson Institute, funded by the U.S. Department of Labor, released the study **Workforce 2000: Work and Workers for the 21st Century.** The predictions of that study startled corporate America. While probably not the first indication of a changing American workforce, the study certainly brought the future composition of America's workforce into clear and dramatic focus. Almost overnight the HR field began to view the recruitment, selection, and management of the increasingly diverse workforce as a key issue in long-term survival.

The study predicted that the homogeneous workforce, long composed of, and led by, white males born in America, was rapidly changing (Figure 3–1). New entrants into the labor force by the year 2000 would consist of only 15 percent native white males. Women (white

and of color) would make up 61 percent of the new workers, and people of color (including women of color) would provide 29 percent of the *new* century's beginning work force. Coupled with the changing faces of the workforce will be a reduction in the numbers of new entrants. In the 1970s, when baby boomers were still joining the employment lines, the labor force grew by 2.9 percent a year. Growth of about 1 percent a year was realized in the 1990s.[3] Ironically, a new wave of immigrants into the American workforce is a part of the solution to the shrinking labor pool, just as it had been in the late 1890s.

To meet the challenge of the 21st century, American businesses must have access to the best and brightest employees. The workforce must be willing and able to provide the skills and commitment necessary to compete in the world economy. They must be trained in new technologies, sometimes two or three times during their careers, just to stay even.

Leaders must emerge from the workforce to motivate and direct the workplace. As in the past, these leaders must be able to understand the organization's

FIGURE 3–1 THE WORKFORCE 2000

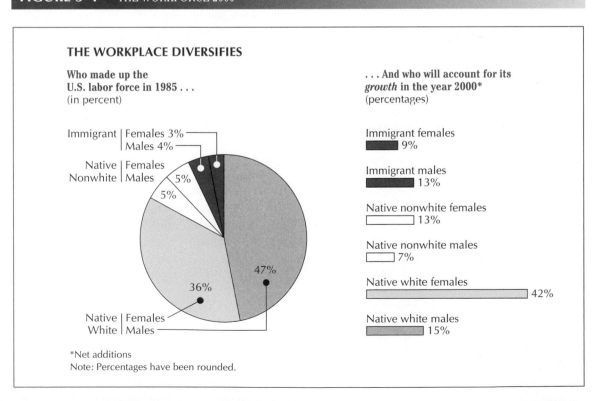

THE WORKPLACE DIVERSIFIES

Who made up the U.S. labor force in 1985 . . . (in percent)

Immigrant | Females 3%
           | Males 4%

Native | Females
Nonwhite | Males — 5%

5%

Native | Females — 36%
White | Males — 47%

. . . And who will account for its *growth* in the year 2000* (percentages)

Immigrant females — 9%

Immigrant males — 13%

Native nonwhite females — 13%

Native nonwhite males — 7%

Native white females — 42%

Native white males — 15%

*Net additions
Note: Percentages have been rounded.

SOURCE: *Workforce 2000: Work and Workers for the 21st Century* (New York City) The Hudson Institute, (1987).

TABLE 3–1	CHANGES IN THE YEAR 2000 AND BEYOND
Technological	By the year 2015, 1 million Americans will be over the age of 100.
Productivity	28 million American workers work out of their homes.
Globalization	Successful executives need a working knowledge of four languages.
Organization	Management layers compress from an average of twelve to an average of six.
Competition	Workers shift careers more frequently, some as often as every five years.
People	Companies discover that their employees are their biggest asset, and diverse individuals make critical professional contributions to the workplace.

and the employees' needs and see that both are met. Table 3–1 gives examples of just some of the changes that can be expected in the workplace in the year 2000 and beyond.

If American business is to succeed, it must recognize the emergence of the diversified workforce and find the means to harness its energies, talents, and differences for tomorrow's challenges. The major groups that provide diversity in the workforce will now be considered. Not all business leaders have moved to develop diversity programs, sometimes leading to top-level disagreements (See *HR in the News:* "Cigna Corporation Director Resigns.")

RACIAL AND ETHNIC GROUPS

Currently, racial and ethnic groups—people of color—make up one-fourth of America's population. If current trends in immigration and birth rates continue, by the year 2050 these groups will outnumber whites in the general population. More specifically, African Americans now comprise 11 percent of the labor force and are projected to reach 12 percent by 2000. Hispanics make up 7 percent of the workforce today and will be 10 percent by the year 2000 if they contribute the projected 23 percent of new workforce entrants by that date. Three percent of the workforce now consists of Asian Americans, Pacific Islanders, and Native Americans. By 2000 these Asian/American groups will represent 4 percent of the workforce.[4] Some argue that Asian Americans are a "model minority" due to their cultural assimilation, high levels of education, wealth, and employment. This belief is particularly held for descendants from China, Japan, and Korea. Critics of the model minority note Asian Americans, as a group, are bimodal: One group is generally highly educated and wealthy, while a second group is concentrated in low-paying jobs and often faces workplace obstacles.[5]

Immigrants who contribute to this increase in the proportion of people of color are generally underrepresented in the growth occupations, which require technical skills and education. They are overrepresented in slow-growing or declining occupations such as farm and factory work. Since they are protected against employment discrimination, which is discussed later in the chapter, these underrepresented groups present great recruitment opportunities and challenges to the HR professional.

WOMEN

Women are expected to provide almost two-thirds of the 15 million new entrants into the job market by the year 2000. The availability of women will likely offset the decline in the number of younger male workers. But female workers are still not utilized in top management positions by many employers. Also, women are concentrated in occupations that have been seen as female occupations and that pay less than traditionally male occupations.

OLDER WORKERS

Of the 26 million people in the United States who are 65 years or older, 4 million are still in the workforce. In the year 2000, the average age of America's worker will be 39 years, up from the 1990 average of 36 years.[6]

AMERICANS WITH DISABILITIES

Depending on the definition used, the U.S. Department of Health and Human Services has estimated that the number of Americans with one or more disabilities could be as high as 43 million. Approximately 21 million are able to work, but fewer than 6 million have jobs. That leaves 15 million, or nearly 72 percent of this population, unemployed.[7]

SEXUAL/AFFECTIONAL ORIENTATION

The famous Kinsey Report on sexual attitudes guessed that 10 percent of the population is homosexual. Research indicates that about 4 percent of U.S. men and 2 percent of women are gay. If these estimates are correct, then between 2 and 10 percent of the men and women in the workforce are gay and may constitute a greater percentage of the workforce than some other minorities.[8]

EXACTLY WHAT IS DIVERSITY?

The change in the demographic structure of the U.S. workforce mirrors the diversity of the U.S. population as a whole. This diverse customer base and the increased importance of globalization for U.S. industry will challenge organizations to appeal to a diversified marketplace. The challenge of recruiting, selecting, and managing a diverse workforce involves more than complying with federal and state employment laws; it is necessary for organizational survival. The technological revolution that replaces unskilled laborers with machines is changing the way companies design work in America. More skilled workers demand a more receptive environment. Companies that want to succeed in the 21st century must form pluralistic organizations.[9]

The term **diversity** is not contained in the *Workforce 2000* report or any law; instead, it grew out of academic and popular press usage. Every individual is unique. At the same time, every individual shares biological and environmental characteristics with any number of others. *Diversity* in the workplace can be generally defined as recognition of the groups of peo-ple who share such common traits. These traits—the properties and characteristics that constitute a whole person—both unite and divide us. In the HR field and in U.S. organizations, however, the term *diversity* has three major working definitions:[10]

- The "politically correct" term for equal employment opportunity/affirmative action.
- The recruitment and selection of racial and ethnic minorities and women.
- The management of individuals from different cultures sharing a broad range of common traits.

The first of these definitions represents a very narrow view of diversity and is more likely to be found in organizations without formal diversity policies or programs. The second definition reflects the reality that many diversity programs focus on employment law concerns. The third definition is the broadest and is likely to be used in organizations with diversity programs that include many of the activities in Figure 3–2.

FIGURE 3–2   PRIMARY AND SECONDARY DIMENSIONS OF DIVERSITY

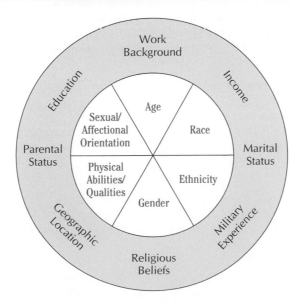

SOURCE: Marilyn Loden and Judy B. Rosener, *Workforce America* (Homewood, IL: Business One-Irwin, 1991), 20.

Primary dimensions are those human differences that are inborn and that exert a major impact on us. Age, ethnicity, gender, race, physical abilities/qualities, and perhaps, sexual/affectional orientation are primary dimensions at the core of individual identities. All of us view the world and experience the world through the filter of these dimensions.

Secondary dimensions are more mutable and can be changed, discarded, or modified throughout our lives. Secondary dimensions add depth and individuality to our lives. Education, geographic location, income, marital status, military experience, religion, work experience, and parental status are examples of secondary dimensions. One can view the primary and secondary dimensions as a circle, as shown in Figure 3–2, with the primary dimensions at the center and the secondary dimensions on the outside ring.

People are grouped and identified most often, and certainly in any initial encounter, by the primary dimensions that are most readily observed: age, gender, race, and physical abilities/qualities. Many of us live in homogeneous communities, or at least in communities far less diverse than our society as a whole. Therefore, our entry into the workplace may be our first encounter with a diverse population.

In a national survey of U.S. organizations of all types and sizes, employers were asked about diversity issues. In response to the question "What is meant by 'diversity' to decision makers in your organization?" the characteristics of diversity were ranked as shown in Table 3–2.

Some employers further volunteered the additional characteristics of language, education, and sexual preference as also constituting diversity. The survey confirmed the recognition of HR officials of the primary dimensions of diversity.

STEREOTYPES AND PREJUDICES

A **stereotype** is a fixed, distorted generalization about members of a group. Stereotyping that stems from the primary dimensions of diversity—race, gender, age, physical abilities/qualities, or sexual orientation—assigns incomplete, exaggerated, or distorted qualities to members of this group.

As human beings, we process information by using learned knowledge. A child whose fingers are burned when touching a stove learns not to touch the stove again. Such generalizations about the world around us are arrived at through logic, experience, and available facts.

Stereotyping is not generalization. A stereotype usually comes from outside sources, not individual experiences. A belief is formed early in life by contact with our parents, teachers, neighbors, and contemporaries. It might be stated that "A woman's place is in the *home.*" In itself, such a statement may not threaten a woman's right to equal employment. Nonetheless, it becomes a stereotype when exaggerated beliefs about a woman's ability to function in the workplace are told and retold and begin to be believed. A stereotype requires that the exaggerated beliefs about a group be sustained by selective perception and/or selective forgetting of facts and experiences inconsistent with the stereotype. All the years of experience each of us have had with women teachers, for example, are suddenly forgotten when one questions a woman's ability to succeed.

Stereotyping negates people's individuality and limits their potential. To a great extent, people perform

TABLE 3–2	CHARACTERISTICS OF DIVERSITY (INCLUDED IN EMPLOYER DEFINITIONS)			
RANK	CHARACTERISTIC	PERCENTAGE YES	PERCENTAGE NO	PERCENTAGE UNCERTAIN
1	Race	94.1%	4.2%	1.7%
2	Culture	86.3	8.4	5.3
3	Gender	84.5	11.6	3.9
4	National origin	83.6	11.4	5.0
5	Age	70.6	24.7	4.7
6	Religion	57.5	34.6	7.9
7	Physical abilities	56.0	20.4	23.6
8	Regional origin	36.9	48.4	14.7

SOURCE: Michael R. Carrell and Everett E. Mann, "Defining Workforce Diversity Programs and Practices in Organizations," *Labor Law Journal* 12 (December 1993).

according to the expectations placed on them. If the stereotype is that the person is not competent, then he or she may not perform competently.

Clinging to negative stereotypes about people different from ourselves results in prejudice. **Prejudice** consists of processing our stereotypes in such a way as to reinforce one's own sense of superiority to the members of that group. Stereotyping and prejudice against diverse groups have been institutionalized in the workplace. Therefore, one function of the organization is to recognize and eradicate both stereotyping and prejudice.

ASSIMILATION

In the past, the workplace response to an influx of people who are different was assimilation. **Assimilation** assumed that the dominant group's performance and style were superior to those of persons who are not in the dominant group. This assumption devalued diversity in the organization and reinforced the value of homogeneity. "The problem with measuring everyone against that white male standard," says Gerald Adolph, a management consultant and principal at Booz, Allen, and Hamilton, "is that you set up a sizable portion of your workforce for failure."[11]

Organizations may contend that assimilation is a proper response to diversity. Some companies believe they have been successful because the homogeneous ideal—a Lee Iacocca or a Ross Perot—made them succeed due to their tough, no-compromise, macho approach to management. They believe that if diverse employees conform to those traits, they too will be successful.

But for companies that value diversity, assimilation is not the ideal. The basis for assimilation is bias. Pressuring diverse employees to conform diminishes them as individuals. In trying to gain acceptance by the dominant group, they may lose touch with their own cultural backgrounds. An example is a woman manager who has been told to be more assertive and is accused later of being pushy and unfeminine.

When diversity is not valued, the diverse employee's accomplishments may not be noted and mistakes may be magnified. African–American managers often complain that they are expected to prove themselves before getting a promotion, while white managers are promoted on the basis of their potential.[12] There are few role models for diverse employees, and to a great extent, those diverse employees who have assumed positions of authority in an organization do not have the clout of white male authority figures. Women and mi-

nority managers find themselves frozen in middle management positions or advancing only in staff positions.[13]

Finally, the energy and effort used by diverse employees to assimilate drains them of enthusiasm for reaching the goals of the organization. More and more diverse people are giving up the struggle to succeed in corporations and creating their own businesses. Between 1974 and 1984, women started their own businesses at six times the rate of men. Companies like Corning Glass Works, in an effort to stem the flow of women and minorities, have had to devise specific programs to retain a diverse workforce.[14]

Pushing assimilation does not benefit the dominant workforce group either. It reinforces the bias that spawns this approach, and it perpetrates stereotyping and prejudice in the workplace. Companies whose workforce cannot adapt to the new century will not survive. And if the organization fails, the current dominant group will find itself jobless, along with fellow diverse employees. With the breakup of AT&T in 1984, the eliminating of more than 100,000 employees caused some white men to rethink their biases. They became pragmatic when they realized that it was going to take everyone, people of color and women included, to keep the corporation functional.[15]

VALUING DIVERSITY

The first step in getting an organization to value diversity is to acknowledge the fundamental difference between valuing diversity, on the one hand, and equal employment opportunities and/or affirmative action, on the other. As stated earlier, equal employment opportunity is a legal approach to workplace discrimination. It is against the law to deny a person a job or a job advantage because of race, gender, age, or other primary characteristics. Affirmative action is a response to underutilization of protected groups in various job categories in which a business attempts to attract and advance people from such groups because of their failure to do so in the past due to discrimination. Valuing diversity moves past both of these concepts and results in management designed to reap the benefits that a diverse workforce offers.[16]

Unfortunately, for some companies, managing diversity is still seen as part of its affirmative action/equal employment opportunity policies. Equal employment opportunity and affirmative action, however, are government initiated, legally driven efforts to change—from a quantitative standpoint—the makeup of a company's workforce. From their inception, the emphasis was on numbers and assimilation. By contrast, valuing diversity is a company-specific, necessity-driven effort to change—from a qualitative standpoint—the utilization of the company's workforce. From its inception, the emphasis was on performance by individuals as individuals. In an organization that values diversity, managing diversity becomes a substitute for assimilation.

An excellent example of such an organization is Kinney Shoes. John Kozlowski, senior vice-present of human resources of Kinney Shoes, believes that serving a diverse customer base requires a diverse workforce. He also believes that compliance with equal employment laws is not enough. "When we say equal employment opportunity is a good business practice, but all we do is compliance, we demean it," Kozlowski says. In a proactive approach to diversity, Kozlowski created Kinney's Office of Fair Employment Practice, which is not part of their human resource EEO/AA compliance arm. Through education of their managers, Kinney is trying to instill within the corporate culture the best hiring and management practices so that the *best* candidates for hiring or promoting are identified, regardless of race, culture, or gender. The program used by Kinney includes an 8-hour "Valuing Diversity" seminar for executives and store managers which focuses on managing persons from different cultural backgrounds. Through a number of problem-solving situations, the training teaches the managers how different persons react to the same workplace situation. One example is to show how a Native American is embarrassed by public praise from a supervisor, while a white American is honored.[17]

MANAGING DIVERSITY

An organization must be clear about its motivation in **managing diversity.** Being in compliance with equal opportunity laws is not enough. The organization must recognize the business necessity of having a diverse workforce and tapping the potential of that workforce.

Typically, such motivation is articulated in the organization's mission statement or strategic plan. Figure 3–3 is a vision statement of U.S. West, a corporate leader in diversifying its workforce. The effect of diversity may depend, however, on the type of organization. Diversity will likely be least beneficial, research shows, in organizations that employ "routine technology" with stable environments, a high dependance on written rules and repetition of tasks. Organizations with a dependance on flexibility in terms of structure and rapid response to change are more likely to benefit from diversity programs.[18]

There may be considerable benefits to be gained by managing diversity and considerable costs for not doing so. Organizations that cannot change will be faced with higher employee turnover and higher recruitment and training costs. Employee conflicts that may result in sabotage or high absenteeism can be expected. Misunderstandings can lead to expensive discrimination litigation.[19]

Potential benefits for an organization that successfully manages diversity include the following:

- **Bottom Line**   Companies that experienced high absenteeism and job turnover rates in diverse employee populations have found that frustration over career growth and cultural conflict with the dominant white male culture were most often the cause of employee unrest. As these populations grow within the workforce, companies that satisfy their diverse needs will have a competitive advantage. Merrill Lynch, for example, developed a strategy to leverage its diversity within its workforce to capture a large portion of a specific segment of the marketplace on Wall Street. Merrill Lynch credits its large representation of women and minorities for the successful development and implementation of the market plan.[20]

WWW.MERRILLLYNCH.COM

- **Getting the Best Person for the Job**   For many organizations, diversity is a question of HR and the ability to attract the best employees in a predominantly female, nonwhite workforce. Some employers are already having difficulty in recruitment. A survey of 645 HR professionals conducted as a follow-up to the *Workforce 2000* report found that 55 percent of

FIGURE 3–3   U.S. WEST'S DIVERSITY VISION STATEMENT

Our culture will be devoid of racism, sexism, and all other forms of discrimination: Equal opportunity will maximize the contributions of all individuals to the profitability of the business.

the respondents cited problems in hiring entry-level secretaries and 53 percent had difficulty hiring entry-level professionals.[21]

- *Retention*   The ability to retain top employees of all backgrounds is the reason most cited by employers for initiating diversity training programs.[22]
- *Valuing the Diverse Customer*   Diversity in the workforce mirrors the diversity in the consumer market. The organizations that know how to manage a diverse workforce will be able to sell to a diverse customer base. Low profitability in inner-city markets gave Avon Corporation the motivation to adopt diversity. Those markets are now among their most profitable.[23] U.S. West realized that its English-speaking employees were not communicating with a large proportion of its customer base in the southwestern part of the United States—Spanish-speaking Hispanics. Because of its groundbreaking approach to diversity, the company now boasts that people of color constitute 13 percent of its man-

agers.[24] U.S. companies cannot ignore the need to compete in a global market. With the diversity of the general population to rely on, companies in the United States should have a competitive edge if it manages that diversity (Table 3–3).

- *Understanding That Innovation Means Profits*   To compete in the 21st century, companies will have to be creative, innovative, and flexible. Studies have shown that heterogeneous groups have more creativity and better problem-solving skills than homogeneous groups. The broader, richer base of experience provided by people with diverse backgrounds improves problem solving and decision making. While complete diversity might be disruptive and complete homogeneity unstimulating, cohesive groups of diverse people provide an increased number of alternative ideas that are then subjected to a high level of critical analysis, resulting in a much better product.[25] As organizations become more flexible in their basic employment practices in order to respond to the

---

TABLE 3–3   COMPETITIVE ADVANTAGES OF CULTURAL DIVERSITY

1. Cost argument	As organizations become more diverse, the cost of a poor job in integrating workers will increase. Those who handle this well will thus create cost advantages over those who don't.
2. Resource	Companies develop reputations on favorability as prospective employers for women and ethnic minorities. Those with the reputation for managing diversity will win the competition for the best personnel. As the labor pool shrinks and changes composition, this edge will become increasingly important.
3. Marketing argument	For multinational organizations, the insight and cultural sensitivity that members with roots in other countries bring to the marketing effort should improve these efforts in important ways. The same rationale applies to marketing in subpopulations within domestic operations.
4. Creativity argument	Diversity of perspectives and less emphasis on conformity to norms of the past (which characterize the modern approach to management of diversity) should improve the level of creativity.
5. Problem-solving	Heterogeneity in decision and problem-solving groups potentially produces better decisions through a wider range of perspectives and more thorough critical analysis of issues.
6. System flexibility argument	An implication of the multicultural model for managing diversity is that the system will become less determinant, less standardized, and therefore more fluid. The increased fluidity should create greater flexibility to react to environmental changes (that is, reactions should be faster and at less cost).

SOURCE: Reprinted with permission from Taylor H. Cox and Stacy Blake, "Managing Cultural Diversity: Implications for Organizational Competitiveness," *Academy of Management Executive* 5, no. 3 (March 1991): 47.

changing workforce, they become more flexible in their practices. This flexibility can be seen in a company like Levi Strauss. This San Francisco–based apparel manufacturer developed a mission statement whose goal was to create a company that supported employees balancing their work and personal lives. In reaching this goal, it experimented with telecommuting and flexible work schedules, job sharing, and part-time work, programs unheard of in the garment industry.[26]

DIVERSITY PROGRAMS

When the first **diversity programs** were initiated in the late 1980s, they mostly were created to meet federal and state laws. While satisfying legal requirements remains a

goal of today's programs, they have grown in scope. By 1998 more than one-third of all U.S. employers reported having a program and another one-third just starting one. The primary objective of the programs is to meet or gain an edge over competitors. New ones have also been initiated because others have realized cost advantages (such as reducing turnover), the ability to attract and retain good employees, and the greater need to be effective in the global marketplace—which requires a more diverse workforce.[27] Some model diversity programs have been reported at Kinney Shoes, U.S. West, UNUM Life Insurance Company, and Gannett Corporation, publisher of USA Today. (See *HR in the News:* "Diversity at *USA Today*").

The first decade of diversity programs produced some successes and some failures. Most U.S. employers

HR IN THE NEWS

DIVERSITY AT *USA TODAY*

Gannett Corporation may well have the granddaddy of diversity programs. The media conglomerate first embarked on managing diversity in 1980.

The publisher of *USA Today* and many small-town papers, as well as the owner of numerous radio and television stations, Gannett wanted to be an industry leader in minority recruitment and retention. It also saw a need to better mirror its audience in terms of the composition of its workforce. Finally, Gannett wanted not only to publish all the news, but to act as a force for change in communities in which it was based, and it saw a diverse workforce as the means toward that end.

WWW.GANNETT.COM

After 16 years, the Arlington, Virginia, firm succeeded in diversifying its employee ranks. Total minority employment was 12 percent in 1980; by 1996, 26 percent. In terms of managerial positions, minorities took up 9 percent of the job slots when Gannett began focusing on diversity. At the end of 1996 that figure had jumped to 21 percent. The company has also worked to diversify its board of directors. "Thirty-one percent of our board is minority . . . you have to diversify the ranks of people that run the business," says Jose Berrios, vice president of diversity and personnel.

While minority recruitment was first emphasized by Gannett, the media company has expanded into career advancement training. "We now handle diversity across the board," Berrios says. "We're training and developing up through the management pipeline." The company also publishes an in-house newsletter devoted to the topic and sponsors noon seminars, for example, on different cultural communications techniques, how communication between members of different genders works, and so on. These lunchtime workshops are open to all employees. In addition, some of Gannett's regional locations have set up mentoring programs for minorities; but "the newspaper, TV station, or radio station, have done this on their own. There is not a formal company-wide mentoring program," Berrios says.

According to the diversity manager, what has made Gannett's program work is the fact that it is closely aligned with overall business aims. "You have to understand the business tie-in," Berrios says. "It's not just an HR program, it's a business objective." Finally, like any other business venture, a company needs to have goals for a diversity program and the ability to measure results. "You have to have accountability to make it work," Berrios says. "After 16 years, our program is a part of the culture. It's part of everything that we do."

SOURCE: Jenny McCune, "Diversity Training—A Competitive Weapon," *Management Review* 85, no. 6 (June 1996): 25–30.

developed programs with the policies/activities listed in Figure 3–4. In particular, the awareness and valuing-diversity training programs have not met with great success. In fact, a national survey of HR professionals found that only 32 percent of companies rated their training programs as a success, 50 percent were neutral, and 18 percent rated them as unsuccessful. The possible reasons for their lack of success include: (1) no follow-up activities after the initial training; (2) few or no incen-

tives for managers to increase the diversity of their workgroups; and (3) top management's view of diversity as an HR issue, not as a key to the organization's long-term success.[28] Furthermore, attitudes toward diversity within organizations depend on the people being asked. HR professionals are generally positive about diversity and recognize the need for a diverse workforce. Line managers are generally more skeptical and believe that diversity has made their jobs more difficult. Top managers'

FIGURE 3–4   ORGANIZATIONS PROVIDING BROAD DIVERSITY INITIATIVES

MANAGING DIVERSITY POLICIES/PROGRAMS

POLICY/PROGRAM	PERCENTAGE POLICY EXISTS	PERCENTAGE BELIEVE THEY NEED TO DO MORE
Awareness and Valuing Diversity		
Discussion groups to promote tolerance and understanding	49.9%	75.1%
Diversity training for supervisors	38.0	74.5
Efforts to change corporate culture to value differences	37.0	61.4
Team building for diverse groups that must work together	35.3	68.8
Diversity task force to recommend policy changes where needed	34.6	44.9
Holding managers accountable for increasing diversity in the managerial ranks	32.7	65.5
Educational Initiatives		
Incentives for younger workers to complete their education	65.6	72.7
Basic education classes (reading, math)	29.8	57.1
Classes in English for non-English-speaking employees	21.4	64.8
Career Support		
Minority internships	58.5	62.2
Networking among minority groups	41.7	70.3
Programs to steer women and minorities into "pivotal" jobs—key positions critical to rapid advancement	25.7	61.8
Specific goals to diversify middle and upper management	27.7	57.1
Accommodating Special Needs		
Scheduled days off to accommodate religious preferences	58.2	40.5
Policies to hire retirees for temporary assignments	45.1	51.6
Daycare arrangements or benefits	24.5	48.8
Work-at-home arrangements	19.5	32.7
Job redesign to accommodate disabled employees	17.3	49.4
Translation of written materials (manuals, newsletters) into several languages	12.6	21.0

SOURCE: Benson Rose and Kay Lovelace, "Piecing Together the Diversity Puzzle," *HR Magazine* 36 (June 1991): 56–59.

attitudes fall between those of HR professionals and line managers (Figure 3–5).

A careful analysis of successful diversity programs noted that they included the process stages identified in Figure 3–6. The first and critical stage involves top management committing to make diversity part of the culture of the organization. This requires direct involvement of key leaders and the incorporation of diversity into mission and philosophy statements. The second stage usually includes specific needs—such as training and quantitative goals for each organizational level. The critical factor of this stage is the reward system—people usually do what is rewarded, and don't take seriously that which is not rewarded in the performance-appraisal process. The third stage involves the sensitization of the entire workforce to the diversity goals/policies of top management, usually achieved by education and training programs. The last

---

FIGURE 3–5   THE EFFECT OF TRAINING PROGRAMS ON MANAGERS' ATTITUDES

ATTITUDES TOWARD DIVERSITY MANAGEMENT

FAVORABLE ATTITUDES	HR VIEW	LINE MGRS' VIEW	TOP MGRS' VIEW
Diversity programs help companies project a positive public image	62.6	33.9	54.8
Diversity management is no longer a choice for us: Our employees are too diverse to ignore this issue	61.5	20.3	35.3
A more diverse workforce will better enable us to serve our clients and customers	60.0	21.0	40.8
In our industry, diverse organizations will be more successful and innovative	58.8	16.8	37.3
Diversity programs are socially desirable activities	50.3	17.8	34.7
Without a diversity program, we risk losing some of the best employees in our company or industry	40.8	11.7	25.9
Diversity programs are necessary because there are still a lot of insensitive or discriminatory employment behaviors	25.0	11.3	24.8
UNFAVORABLE ATTITUDES			
Greater workforce diversity has made the manager's job more difficult	41.1	65.1	46.9
Valuing diversity is a "politically correct" term for affirmative action	25.8	28.8	26.7
Special treatment for various subgroups of workers reinforces negative stereotypes of these groups	23.3	43.0	29.3
Diversity programs are motivated primarily by a desire to comply with regulations and avoid costly lawsuits	18.1	42.7	34.1
Greater workforce diversity increases the cost of doing business	11.6	26.1	23.7
Overall, the costs of a more diverse workforce outweigh the potential benefits	10.9	15.3	15.4
As diversity increases among employees, group cohesiveness typically decreases	9.5	22.2	13.4
Greater workforce diversity leads to more employee grievances	9.3	29.1	18.9
The existence of a diverse workforce makes it more difficult to uphold performance standards	6.6	20.9	12.9
Diversity management programs are just a passing fad	6.5	20.5	17.0
Diversity training programs discriminate against white males	5.8	26.6	14.0

SOURCE: "1993 SHRM/CCH Survey," *Human Resources Management* (Washington, DC: CCH, Inc., May 26, 1993): 10

FIGURE 3–6   THE DIVERSITY MANAGEMENT PROCESS

STAGE 1	2	3	4
FOUNDATIONS	POLICY CONSIDERATIONS	SENSITIZATION	PROGRAMS DESIGNED TO ADDRESS SPECIFIC DIVERSITY INITIATIVES
• Top Management Conviction	• Identify Organization-Specific Diversity Goals	• Increase Awareness through Educational Efforts	
• Active Top Management Support	• Establish Meaningful Diversity Goals	• Train as an "Activating Event"	
• Organizational Mission and Philosophy Statements	• Reinforce Diversity Commitments through Appraisal and Reward System		
	• Time		

SOURCE: Charles R. Stower and Lori A. Russell-Chapin, "Creating A Culture of Diversity Management: Moving from Awareness to Action," *Business Forum* (Spring–Fall 1997): 6–12.

stage is the development of specific programs, such as minority internships, where needed.[29]

DIVERSITY AWARENESS TRAINING

Education begins the process of cultural change within an organization that has the motivation and the requisite leadership to change attitudes. The first group to undergo this training should be top management. General manager and employee training should soon follow, focusing primarily on stereotyping and the dimensions of diversity. Education in managing diversity as a resource is ongoing and will be unique to each organization's needs. And, awareness training alone usually does not produce results, but when combined with a total program (Figure 3–6)—and when diverse leaders are hired—then employers can attract diversity.[30]

Awareness training seeks to motivate employees to recognize the worth and dignity of everyone in the workplace and to treat them with respect. It also seeks to diminish the negative impact of individual prejudices by getting each person to *accept responsibility for the problem.* Role playing and/or listing commonly held stereotypes are two methods trainers use to get employees to see themselves through their fellow workers' eyes. Unlearning biases is a long-term process. Individuals must be willing to reevaluate and reprogram many deeply held beliefs. Awareness is the first step.

Diversity training takes various forms. It may involve encounter-type retreats or quiet consciousness-raising sessions. Following are some exercises that may be used in diversity training:

1 *Values Clarification*   A checklist of values—like punctuality, honesty, acceptance, and financial success—is prioritized by all individuals in terms of their own preference and how they believe the organization ranks the values. The group then discusses the differences and similarities in the priorities.

2 *Perceptual Differences*   The participants are asked to give a precise percentage definition of such as *always, frequently,* and *almost always.* This exercise uncovers the imprecise communication that may exist in the workplace.

3 *Problem-solving Case Studies*   The participants are given a partial description of a job applicant and are told to come up with a complete profile. Depending on the limited facts given, the profile may uncover any number of biases when the group completes the picture. For example, one group was told to profile a woman who was returning to the workforce and was responsible for two children. The group profiled her as a recently divorced woman who had stopped working to raise her children. The group leader pointed out that she may in fact have been out of the workforce completing her education and that she may be married.

4 *Exploring Cultural Assumptions*   The participants can openly explore assumptions that one group may make about another. For example, at one such awareness session, there was a lively discussion on whether or not it was ever acceptable for women—or men, for that matter—to cry in the workplace.

5 *Personalizing the Experience*   The awareness trainer may try to make everyone aware of their own uniqueness and of the possibility that they can be different. One trainer had the group members describe the first time they became aware that there were people different from themselves—in color, in gender, perhaps in religion, or in economic status. By doing this, even white males can experience the difference that surround them.

At a labor–management legal seminar attended by an equal number of male and female professionals, a luncheon speaker warned the audience of the impact of diversity in the workforce by saying, "I'm sorry to say this, but by the year 2000, the workforce will be made up of nearly 50 percent women." There were audible objections by a number of the women present and embarrassed looks by the men. The speaker seemed totally unaware of the impact of this statement on the audience.

This incident points to the powerful role language plays in reinforcing stereotypes and in dividing workers in the workforce. While the message sent by the speaker was that U.S. companies were not prepared for *Workforce 2000* and had to become prepared, the message received was that a workforce made up of more than 50 percent women was something to be sorry about.

Language sensitivity and guidelines for appropriate language help managers value a diverse workforce. Some rules would seem to be so obvious as to not need repeating, but unfortunately they do.

- Don't tell jokes directed at a group of people stereotyped because of their primary or secondary characteristics.
- Use metaphors and analogies from diverse sources and diverse disciplines, like the arts and sciences, as well as sports.
- Avoid terms that devalue people—*crippled, boy, girl*—or that spotlight differences—*black doctor, old supervisor.*
- Be aware of, and sensitive to, the preferences of members of diverse groups regarding titles or terminology. *People of color* seems to be the most acceptable reference for those who have been called minorities. *Physically disabled* is the current term used most often to refer to differently abled people.

Table 3–4 contains a list of appropriate words used to communicate in a diverse environment.

TRAINING BACKLASH

Awareness training may, however, cause a **backlash** among some employees. In the 1990s diversity training came into the mainstream of the U.S. workplace. About 65 percent of medium and large U. S. employers have conducted some form of diversity training program. The programs generally consist of 1–2 day classroom sessions involving lectures, film, and role playing. The objectives of the program are to increase employees' sensitivity toward others and inform them of organizational diversity policies. The programs have not always succeeded in changing employee attitudes and behaviors toward others. In fact, in some cases they have produced a backlash and resulted in employees feeling more polarized than before the training.

A good example of diversity training backlash occurred at the Washington State Ferry System in Seattle. All 1,500 employees of the ferry system were required to participate in day-long seminars. It was intended to provide "shock therapy" or a "cultural boot camp" for the deckhands, seamen, captains, and mates. One year later, as intended, the training did produce some workplace changes—the girlie calendars were taken down and some female and black workers reported that they were treated with greater respect. However, a "huge backlash" of anger and polarization was the most significant result, according to one of the program's supporters. The training increased tension among groups of workers. One supervisor summarized this result: "We used to all be just ferry workers, but now everyone's divided up into little groups: blacks, women, gays, even white males." The training also failed to achieve a primary objective—reduction of sexual harassment and racial incidents. Instead the number increased.[31]

Some critics of diversity-training programs believe the ferry system experience is similar to that of other organizations. They believe it is futile to try and change attitudes by forcing people to sit in all-day seminars or giving them lists of forbidden words. While participants may agree with the goals of such training, they often find the process condescending, especially when white-collar trainers try to tell blue-collar workers how to behave and talk. One backhoe operator in Portland, Oregon, may have summed up the situation with his comment: "Let's face it—I'm a middle-aged guy, and my mind is made up. Sitting in a classroom all day isn't going to change me one iota."[32]

What's the solution for organizations trying to improve their diversity environment? According to some managers: hiring a diverse workforce, enforcing policies and laws on discrimination, and leaders setting the right example.

TABLE 3–4   APPROPRIATE DIVERSITY TERMS

WHEN REFERRING TO:	USE:	INSTEAD OF:
Women	Women	Girls, ladies, gals, females
Black people	African Americans, Caribbean Americans, black people, people of color	Negroes, minorities
Asian people	Asian Americans, Japanese, Koreans, Pakistanis, and so on; differentiate between foreign nationals and American born; people of color	Minorities
Pacific Islanders	Pacific Islanders, Polynesians, Maoris, and so on; use island name (for example, Cook Islanders, Hawaiians); people of color	Asians, minorities
American Indians	American Indians, Native Americans, name of tribe (for example, Navajo, Iroquois), people of color	Minorities
People of Hispano-Latin American origin	Latinas/Latinos, Chicanas/Chicanos; use country of national origin (for example, Cubanos, Puerto Ricans, Chileans); people of color, Hispanics	Minorities Spanish–surnamed
Gay men and lesbians	Gay men, lesbians	Homosexuals
Differently abled people	Differently abled, developmentally disabled, physically disabled, physically challenged	Handicapped, crippled
White people	European Americans; use country of national origin (for example, Irish Americans, Polish Americans); white people	Anglos, WASPS
Older/younger adults	Older adults, elderly, younger people, younger adults	Geriatrics, kids, yuppies

SOURCE: Marilyn Loden and Judy Rosener, *Workforce America! Managing Employee Diversity as a Vital Resource* (Homewood, IL: Business One Irwin, 1991), 85–90.

HR IN THE NEWS

TEXACO'S $175 MILLION MISTAKE

Like the Rodney King beating and the Mark Fuhrman tapes at the O.J. Simpson hearing, the tape which contained top Texaco Corporation officials making derogatory comments about blacks and other minorities shocked most white Americans. The tape was also critical evidence in a discrimination case which led to Texaco's payment of a record $175 million. The suit was a class-action case brought by 1,400 black professionals and middle-managers at Texaco who claimed they were denied promotions because of their race. The case, and especially the tape of Texaco officials making racial slurs, led to a boycott of Texaco products by the National Urban League and NAACP. The publicity and boycott led Texaco to agree to the $175 million settlement and a new diversity program.

WWW.TEXACO.COM

SOURCE: Shari Caudron, "Don't Make Texaco's $175 Million Mistake," *Workforce* (March 1997): 58–66.

SUMMARY POINTS

- The very term *workforce diversity* only rose to prominence after the 1987 Hudson Institute report which noted that the U.S. labor force of the year 2000 would be very different than that of 1950 or even 1970. Yet past terms such as "melting pot" also noted that the American workforce had undergone similar changes in past years.

- In the 1990s, however, American employers began realizing that well-designed diversity programs could provide many organizational benefits including attracting and retaining top people, managing a diversified workforce, relating to more customers, and expanding global opera-

tions. The primary reason for most early programs—complying with federal and state regulations—still remains an objective at such programs as well. Some employers stung by poor management practices and/or lawsuits filed by employees, have initiated diversity programs to help change their culture. (See *HR in the News*: "Texaco's $175 Million Mistake".)

- Diversity awareness programs have caused a backlash by some employees, but overall have been successful in creating employee sensitivity. Overall diversity programs represent a new HR focus and are experiencing rapid change.

CASE STUDY

TEXAS SOUND CO.

Texas Sound manufactures automotive radio/tape deck components. It has relocated from Detroit where its workforce of around 950 people had been unionized and consisted predominately of white, male native-born Americans. Its facility in Detroit had become obsolete and noncompetitive. In order to supply parts to a new Japanese–American automobile manufacturer, it has relocated to a state-of-the-art facility in south Texas that was partially financed through a state economics development program. Texas, as a "right-to-work" state has few unions. Although Texas Sound's employees were offered jobs at the new facility, very few outside of management made the move.

The federal government assisted Texas Sound in making the move by agreeing to prepare local workers for the company's needs.

Technical training programs began a year or so before the company relocated, and the workforce Texas Sound found upon its move was prepared for the jobs offered. The management employees who relocated with the company did not receive any additional training nor did any management policies change.

With all of the government involvement, the diversity of the workforce would have been assured even if the demographics of the area had not dictated a high percentage of Hispanic and female employees.

Texas Sound began production with high hopes and even higher expectations that its new modernized plant and superiorly trained workforce would ensure that it could supply its customers with quality products at competitive prices. However, from the beginning the company was plagued with a high rate of turnover among the newly trained workforce. Departing employees, mostly women and Hispanics, found the transplanted managers too difficult. They were very rigid when it came to work rules. Seldom, if ever, did they praise or encourage the workers. Many of the workers had been led to believe during their training that they would have oppor-

tunities to vary their work experience in the new plant; but most managers placed the workers at one location and refused to discuss changes. The managers' experiences with a unionized workforce and rigid contract terms carried over into this workplace.

Within a year the following conversation between the company's president and the director of personnel was recorded:

Director of Personnel: The turnover rate for our production employees this year has been overwhelming. I cannot train new employees fast enough to replace them. We've got to do something fast. The overtime costs alone are causing every department major budget problems. None of our projections for employee costs are coming out close.

President: Certainly we anticipated a shakedown time during this first year. I'm disappointed that we've lost so many new employees, but I would expect this next year to be different.

Director of Personnel: I don't think so. Even our recruitment of new employees seems to be in trouble. Disgruntled employees have spread the word that we're not the company to work for in the community. I think some of our managers have displayed less than respectful attitudes toward some of our Hispanic employees. There's no overt discrimination, but there's certainly an undercurrent that I don't like.

President: I don't understand. This community has a high unemployment rate; are you telling me we can't find people willing to work for us? I don't believe it.

Director of Personnel: There is high unemployment, but the better trained applicant is going elsewhere. That year of government-sponsored training before we got here prepared our first wave of employees. From now on we have to train them if we can't retain our employees. I just don't think we've got the money to continually train a turnover workforce.

President: OK. What are you going to do about it?

QUESTIONS

1. If you were the director of personnel, how would you convince the company president that the problem could not be solved by the personnel department alone?

2. Could Texas Sound have avoided this crisis? How?

3. Design a step-by-step diversity program for Texas Sound that could help retain the trained work force.

SOURCE: M.R. Carrell, D.F. Jannings, C. Heavrin, *Fundamentals of Organization Behavior* (Upper Saddle River, N.J.: Prentice-Hall, 1997): 308–309. Used by permission.

EXPERIENTIAL EXERCISES

1. DIVERSITY TRAINING AUDIT

PURPOSE

To learn about diversity training programs currently being conducted

TASK

Step 1: Divide the class into pairs of students and assign each pair the task of locating an employer (private or public) which has recently conducted a diversity training program.

Step 2: Each pair should conduct an audit of the program, concluding (1) the purpose(s), (2) specific objectives, and (3) measures of success.

Step 3: Each pair should present the audit, and, if possible report on an "awareness" exercise which was utilized in the training.

2. EXPLORING DIFFERENCES

PURPOSE

To explore differences in personal values among diverse coworkers.

TASK

Step 1: Divide into small groups that are diversified as much as possible by gender, race, age, and so on. Complete *as a group,* the following "Personal Values Inventory." Consensus must be reached on a "yes" or "no" answer, with *no* change in the numbered statements.

Step 2: The instructor will ask each group to report its answers and lead a discussion of them.

YES	NO	DO YOU BELIEVE THAT . . .

1. It is acceptable for women to cry at work

2. It is okay for men to cry at work

3. It is okay for women to leave work early to coach Little League

4. It is okay for men to leave early to coach Little League

5. The company should provide day care

6. Women and minorities should change for the organization's needs

7. The organization should change for the needs of women and minorities

8. A woman or minority could become the CEO of the organization within the next ten years

9. Women have a higher absentee rate than men

10. There are some jobs or markets in which women and minorities cannot be effective

11. There are jobs in your area that women and minorities cannot perform

12. There are many women or minorities who can effectively take over your job

13. The organization should provide separate programs for special groups

14. Minorities will always have primary loyalty to their group, not to the company

15. Our society is suffering because women are not at home

16. Men should alter their careers to raise children

17. Native dress and behaviors should affect advancement for minorities

18. Intelligence is ethnically based (that is, blacks are less intelligent, Japanese are more intelligent)

EXPERIENTIAL EXERCISES—cont'd

19. Children from different backgrounds should be educated together

20. Certain groups can handle certain jobs more effectively

21. All people have a right to live in any place of their choice

22. Integrated neighborhoods are beneficial

23. Socializing with people of other cultures is appropriate

24. Business associates should socialize

25. We should have private (exclusive) clubs that restrict women and minorities

26. Women and minorities want to socialize with majority males

27. Minorities should be sponsored to join your most intimate circles

28. You should try to avoid putting minority men and majority women into social and travel situations for their own good

29. Interracial dating/marriage is acceptable

30. You would accept an interracial marriage in your family

KEY TERMS AND CONCEPTS

Assimilation
Awareness training
Diversity
Diversity programs
Managing diversity

Prejudice
Primary/Secondary dimensions of diversity
Training backlash
Stereotype
Workforce 2000

REVIEW QUESTIONS

1. How did the workforce diversity in the 1890s compare with that of the 1990s?

2. Why are most U.S. employers offering or developing diversity programs?

3. How can an employer best recruit and retain a diverse workforce?

4. What are the major reasons managers should value diversity?

5. Should new employees be assimilated into the organization's culture?

6. What are the keys to developing a successful diversity program?

7. How can a diverse workforce add to the "bottom line"?

8. What are the primary and secondary dimension of diversity?

DISCUSSION QUESTIONS

1. Can the stereotypes of senior workers be changed by awareness training?

2. Should an employer develop a diversity program to meet legal requirements?

3. In some cases diversity training has caused a backlash among some workers. Should such training be conducted?

4. The globalization of many markets and workforce diversity are two concepts which have received a great deal of interest in recent years. How are they related?

5. Are American companies ahead or behind those of other industrial nations in the area of workforce diversity?

ENDNOTES

Chapter 3

1 Ralph K. Andrist, ed., *The American Heritage History of the Confident Years* (New York: American Heritage, 1991), 306.

2. Alistair Cooke, *America* (New York: Alfred A. Knopf, 1973), 273–288.

3. Beverly Geber, "Managing Diversity," *Training* 27 (July 1990): 23–30.

4. The Hudson Institute, *Workforce 2000: Work and Workers for the Twenty-First Century* (New York: 1987).

5. Cliff Cheng, "Are Asian-American Employees a Model Minority or Just A Minority?" *The Journal of Applied Behavioral Science* 33, no. 3 (September 1997): 277–290.

6. Sami M. Abbasi and Kenneth W. Hollman, "Managing Cultural Diversity: The Challenge of the 90s," *Records Management Quarterly* (July 1991): 24–32.

7. Wayne E. Barlow, "Act to Accommodate the Disabled," *Personnel Journal* (November 1991): 119.

8. George K. Kronenberger, "Out of the Closet," *Personnel Journal* (June 1991): 40–44.

9. Linda Thornburg, "What's Wrong with Workforce 2000," *HR Magazine* (August 1991): 38.

10. Michael R. Carrell and Everett E. Mann, "Defining Workforce Diversity Programs and Practices in Organizations," *Labor Law Journal* 12 (December 1993): 755–765.

11. Lennie Copeland, "Learning to Manage a Multicultural Workforce," *Training* (May 1988): 51.

12. Floyd Dickens, Jr., and Jacqueline Dickens, *The Black Manager* (New York: AMACOM, 1991), 96–97.

13. Ann M. Morrison and Mary Ann Von Glinow, "Women and Minorities in Management," *American Psychologist* 45, no. 20 (February 1990): 200–208.

14. Ann Morrison and Carol Hymowitz, "One Firm's Bid to Keep Blacks, Women," *Wall Street Journal,* Marketplace Section (June 21, 1993): 201.

15. Charlene Marmer Solomon, "Are White Males Being Left Out?" *Personnel Journal* (November 1991): 88–94.

16. Copeland, "Learning to Manage," 49–56.

17. Joyce E. Santora, "Kinney Shoe Steps into Diversity," *Personnel Journal* 70 (September 1991): 72–77.

18. Bilaye R. Benibo, "A Technology Contingency Framework for Workforce Diversity," *Advanced Management Journal* 62, no. 2 (Spring 1997): 28–32.

19. Marilyn Loden and Judy B. Rosener, *Workforce America! Managing Employee Diversity As a Vital Resource* (Homewood, IL: Business One Irwin, 1991), 12.

20. John M. Iannuzzi, "Reaping Diversity's Competitive Rewards," *Business Forum* (Spring–Fall 1997): 4–5.

21. Jerry Beilinson, "Workforce 2000: Already Here?" *Personnel* (October 1990): 3–4.

22. Cassandra Hayes, "Employee Retention," *Black Enterprise* 25, no. 1 (January 1995): 59.

23. Taylor Cox and Stacy Blake, "Managing Cultural Diversity: Implications for Organizational Competitiveness," *Academy of Management Executive* 5, no. 3 (March 1991): 53.

24. Shari Caudron, "U.S. West Finds Strength in Diversity," *Personnel Journal* (March 1992): 40–44.

25. Cox and Blake, "Managing Cultural Diversity," 51.

26. Charlene Marmer Solomon, "24-Hour Employees," *Personnel Journal* (August 1991): 61–62.

27. Jenny McCune, "Diversity Training: A Competitive Weapon," *Management Review* 85, no. 6 (June 1996): 25–30.

28. "1993 SHRM/CCH Survey," *Human Resources Management* (Washington, D.C.: CCH, Inc., May 26, 1993), 1–12.

29. Charles R. Stoner and Lori A. Russell-Chapin, "Creating a Culture of Diversity Management: Moving from Awareness to Action," *Business Forum* (Spring–Fall 1997): 6–12.

30. Karen Hildebrand, "Use Leadership Training to Increase Diversity," *HR Magazine* 41, no. 8 (August 1996): 53.

31. "Sensitivity Class Causes Backlash," *The New York Times,* as reprinted in the *World Herald* (October 24, 1993): Sec. D, pp. 1–4.

32. Ibid.

CHAPTER 4

REGULATORY CHALLENGES

CHAPTER OUTLINE

CHAPTER OBJECTIVES

① To identify the primary principles of the federal employment discrimination laws.

② To understand the key role HR professionals play in the development and enforcement of policies that protect employees from unlawful discrimination.

③ To appreciate the need for employers to develop sexual harassment policies and complaint procedures.

④ To identify the key elements of the Americans with Disabilities Act and the Civil Rights Acts of 1964 and 1991.

⑤ To describe the purpose and advantages of employment arbitration agreements.

⑥ To identify common forms of religious discrimination in the workplace.

⑦ To appreciate the role the U.S. Supreme Court has played in defining employment discrimination laws.

⑧ To recognize the differences and similarities between affirmative action and equal employment opportunity.

⑨ To understand the application of recent U.S. Supreme Court decisions on employer sexual harassment policies and affirmative action.

⑩ To appreciate the pay gap between men and women in the United States.

During the civil rights movement of the 1960s, it became apparent that prejudice against African Americans would not disappear easily. In every area of society—education, religion, and politics—the challenge was to change the way white Americans thought and felt about black Americans. More important, there was an urgent need for white Americans to change the way they treated black Americans.

Changing hearts and minds would take generations. Changing behavior became a matter of legislating rights and responsibilities. Thus, Congress and the courts initiated reforms to ensure that all individuals have an equal chance of being selected for employment and that they will be treated equally once they are hired. Special emphasis was given to veterans and to minorities, which had experienced discrimination in past decades. The various acts of Congress that apply to recruitment and selection must be understood in detail by HR administrators and line managers.

EQUAL PAY ACT

Because of many publicized cases of female employees being paid substantially less than their male counterparts while performing identical work, the **Equal Pay Act** (EPA) was passed by Congress in 1963. The act requires organizations of all sizes to pay men and women substantially the same wages for **substantially equal work** or approximately equal "skill, effort, responsibility, and working conditions." Substantial equality is the basis on which jobs should be compared. In practice, this means that jobs do not have to be identical to command the same basic wage; nor do employers have to pay a different wage for each different job. They must pay equal wages for substantially equal work. Has the EPA achieved equal pay? See Figure 4–1.

Of particular importance are the exceptions allowed by the EPA: Differences in pay can be based on seniority, merit, quality of work, or quantity of work. Therefore, paying different wages to men and women performing the same job can be justified by these differences.

This act has caused many organizations to develop a wage-and-salary system based on formal job evaluation plans. Under such plans, employees are paid according to the jobs they are performing and not other factors such as sex or supervisory bias.

In addition to women's earnings still lagging behind men's overall, further analysis indicates that while the pay differential between men and women may have decreased over the past 30 years, a primary reason for the change is the decrease in the number of blue-collar males. Other factors include downsizing, outsourcing, and the greater use of temporary workers, none of which have generally been good for women workers.[1]

CIVIL RIGHTS ACT OF 1964

The primary federal law that regulates employment practices is the **Civil Rights Act of 1964,** an act

FIGURE 4–1 30 YEARS AFTER THE EQUAL PAY ACT, WOMEN'S WAGES STILL LAG BEHIND

The Equal Pay Act, passed in 1963, was supposed to close the gap between the wages paid to men and women. On the thirtieth anniversary of the act, however, the median annual wage paid to women was only 70 percent of that for men. At least it was an increase from the 1963 median of 60 percent. Minority women in the 1990s fare even worse: the median income for black women is only 62 percent and for Hispanic women it is 54 percent.

Critics and supporters of the Equal Pay act generally agree that it failed to achieve its goal. The modest 10 percent gain registered by women in 30 years probably would have occurred without the act due to the increased presence of working women. Employers have claimed that the gap in pay is due largely to women's lack of seniority and credentials. However, research has shown that with the same credentials and seniority, men average 18 percent higher pay than women. The gap varies substantially according to occupation, as the following graph illustrates:

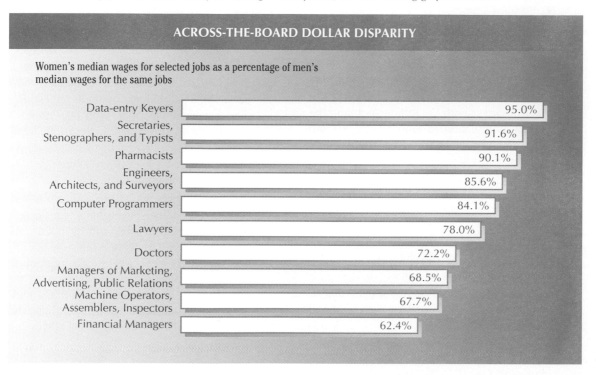

ACROSS-THE-BOARD DOLLAR DISPARITY

Women's median wages for selected jobs as a percentage of men's median wages for the same jobs

Job	Percentage
Data-entry Keyers	95.0%
Secretaries, Stenographers, and Typists	91.6%
Pharmacists	90.1%
Engineers, Architects, and Surveyors	85.6%
Computer Programmers	84.1%
Lawyers	78.0%
Doctors	72.2%
Managers of Marketing, Advertising, Public Relations	68.5%
Machine Operators, Assemblers, Inspectors	67.7%
Financial Managers	62.4%

Part of the problem, according to some experts, is that women are more hesitant to ask for a raise and are less likely to engage in self-promotion. The Equal Employment Opportunity Commission may also be part of the problem—in 1992 it filed only *two* lawsuits under the Equal Pay Act.

SOURCE: Joan E. Rigdon, "Three Decades After the Equal Pay Act, Women's Wages Remain Far from Parity," *The Wall Street Journal* (June 9, 1993): B1, 3; and the Bureau of Labor Statistics.

passed while the nation mourned the death of John F. Kennedy. Only months before his assassination, the nation had witnessed demonstrations throughout the country as minorities demanded recognition of their civil rights. **Title VII** of the act requires employment and compensation of employees without discrimination:

Title VII, Section 703 It is unlawful for an employer to discriminate against an individual with respect to his compensation, terms, conditions, or privileges of employment because of such individual's race, color, religion, sex, or national origin; or to limit, segregate, or classify his employees in any way which would deprive or tend to deprive any

individual of employment opportunities or otherwise adversely affect his status as an employee, because of such individual's race, color, religion, sex, or national origin.

Two basic forms of discrimination are addressed in Title VII. One, **disparate treatment,** is easier to understand. It refers to intentional discrimination against an individual by an employer. If, for example, a person was not hired because he or she was Hispanic, then disparate treatment occurred. In a disparate treatment case, the plaintiff (protected-class applicant or employee) must prove a prima facie case of discrimination, meaning actions taken by the employer that enable one

FIGURE 4–2   EMPLOYMENT LAW LINGO

Using the wrong word, not fulfilling the duties required by new statutes, or inadvertently taking on responsibilities that are not actually required by law can lead to a variety of harsh consequences for today's employers. Employers need to learn employment law "lingo" to best protect themselves from litigation. Below are just a few definitions to help clarify some common misunderstandings.

- **Equal Employment Opportunity.** Equal Employment Opportunity is an umbrella term that encompasses all laws and regulations prohibiting discrimination and/or requiring affirmative action. More specifically, Title VII, the Americans with Disabilities Act, and the age Discrimination in Employment Act are all federal Equal Employment Opportunity statutes. Most states also have statutes that prohibit discrimination. Some are broader than the federal laws. For example, in many states, marital status is protected. Also, in a few jurisdictions, sexual preference and orientation are protected.

- **Civil Rights Act of 1991.** For the most part, the Civil Rights Act of 1991 does not make anything illegal that was not already illegal. What the act does is increase the likelihood that employees will sue by making their discrimination cases easier to win and by making the damages they can be awarded even more substantial.

    The act makes it easier for them to win by relaxing the burdens of proof and introducing jury trials. No longer limited to lost earnings, a successful litigation now can recover damages for pain and suffering, and in some cases, punitive damages.

- **Harassment.** Sexual harassment is a form of sex discrimination that violates federal, state, and most local laws. Sexual harassment can take two forms. The first, *quid pro quo,* occurs when a supervisor conditions the granting of some economic benefit on a subordinate's

providing sexual favors or punishes the subordinate for not providing such favors.

    The second, *hostile work environment,* occurs when supervisors and/or co-workers create an atmosphere so infused with unwelcome sexually oriented or otherwise hostile conduct that an employee's reasonable comfort level or ability to perform is undermined.

- **The Americans with Disabilities Act.** The Americans with Disabilities Act prohibits discrimination against a qualified person with a disability with regard to all aspects of employment. An applicant or employee is qualified for employment if, with or without a reasonable accommodation, the applicant or employee can perform the essential functions of the job [without creating an undue hardship on the employer].

- **Quotas.** A quota is a fixed, inflexible percentage or number of positions that an employer agrees or decides can be filled only by members of a certain minority group. Quotas are a form of reverse discrimination and are strictly scrutinized by the courts for reasonableness and necessity. Quotas are almost always illegal, notwithstanding the laudatory goals of enhancing diversity.

- **Affirmative Action.** Affirmative action usually does not involve the setting of specific quotas, but rather general aspirational goals to increase the number of minorities and women in specific positions. Affirmative action is lawful if ordered by a court as a remedy for past discrimination.

    Affirmative action is also required of certain federal contractors. Compliance with such affirmative action obligations is monitored by the Office of Federal Contract Compliance Programs. Finally, voluntary affirmative action programs may be upheld where there has been past discrimination and where the plan is limited in time and scope.

SOURCE: Jack Trager-Planer, "Employment Law Lingo," *HR Magazine* (May 1992): 48. Used by permission.

to reasonably infer discrimination. The employer must provide evidence that the employment decision was not motivated by discrimination. The second form, **disparate impact,** occurs when an employment policy or practice that is racially neutral results in a dis-

proportionate number or percentage of protected-class individuals not being hired or promoted. Examples include tests, educational requirements, or physical requirements. The intent of the policy or practice may have been nondiscriminatory, but if the result of its utilization is discriminatory, then disparate impact has occurred. The two types of discrimination are not exclusive.[2] In fact, often an individual files a disparate treatment lawsuit and it becomes a disparate impact case including hundreds or even thousands of persons who may have been affected by a discriminatory policy or practice. For example, in 1993 State Farm Insurance agreed to pay $157 million to 814 women who had applied for sales positions from 1974 to 1987. During that period, State Farm hired 586 agents, all men except one. A suit filed by Muriel Kraszewski, who had become a successful Farmers Insurance Agent, resulted in the disparate impact case.[3]

The Civil Rights Act also established the **Equal Employment Opportunity Commission (EEOC).** The EEOC was given the authority to investigate employee complaints of job discrimination. Where the EEOC finds such complaints justified, it cannot directly order organizations to make personnel changes. But it can bring suit in federal courts against employers if job discrimination is suspected.

Under Title VII, the EEOC is empowered to investigate employee complaints and to act as their attorney. The employer is obligated to show personnel records and other requested material to the EEOC. In addition, all employee applications must be kept for three years in case they are needed in an EEOC complaint or other action. Typically, a discrimination complaint is processed in the following steps:

1 The employee's *inquiry* is filed with the EEOC or a state commission dealing with human rights. The employee is interviewed by a professional, who ascertains all facts of the case. The EEOC then reviews the facts and determines whether the case warrants further investigation.

2 If the EEOC finds that there may be **probable cause**—a reasonable possibility—of discrimination, the commission requests the employer's records. These records may include application blanks, interview results, or test results. The EEOC then determines if there was probable cause for the complaint.

3 The EEOC arranges a *conciliation meeting* with the employer to discuss the employee's complaint if the EEOC feels that it has probable cause. The purpose of the conciliation meeting is to arrive at a mutual agreement that will satisfy both the employer and the aggrieved employee. If this is not possible, then the EEOC

weighs the severity of the complaint and discusses alternative actions with the employee.

4 If there is no satisfactory conciliation agreement, the EEOC may issue a **right to sue** to the complainant, indicating that the commission does not feel that it should take the case to court; however, the complaining employee does have the right to sue with a private attorney. Many times this action is an indication that the EEOC does not feel that the complainant has a strong case. The alternative to giving the complainant a right to sue is for the EEOC to take the case of the complainant to court. Title VII covers attorney's fees for complainants if the EEOC does so.

In 1997 congressional testimony, attorney Richard T. Seymour presented a report of the Lawyers Committee which found the EEOC has not been effective in pursuing discrimination cases. The reason cited was the "harsh reality of inadequate resources." The EEOC at that time had 810 investigators for about 80,000 cases per year, or 99 cases per investigator, or four times the expected load. Today almost all discrimination cases, noted Seymour, must rely on circumstantial evidence, which requires much more investigation. Thus, many charges languish for years before meaningful action occurs—which is bad for victims and for respondents whose exposure increases over time. The result has been greater use of mediation of charges—a new EEOC program. Mediation is now used in a majority of cases, and is faster and easier than trials.[4]

COURT PROCEDURES

When a disparate treatment complaint is taken to court, the case usually proceeds according to the *McDonnell-Douglas* v. *Green* case that was litigated in 1972.

In a 1993 landmark case, the U.S. Supreme Court modified the 20-year old *Green* case guidelines and made it harder to prove job discrimination cases. Under the 1972 *Green* decision, where there was no "smoking gun" employees could still prove discrimination. However, under the 1993 *Hicks* case, one must prove that discrimination occurred. Under the 1972 decision, cases followed three steps:[5]

1 A prima facie case is established—a job was available, the alleged victim was a protected-class minority, and a non-protected-class person was hired.

2 The employer presents a legitimate nondiscriminatory reason for the decision.

3 The alleged victim proves the employers reason was a cover-up for discrimination—pretext.

The *Hicks* decision changed the third step, pretext. The alleged victim must not only prove pretext, but must also prove discrimination.[6]

The organization may put forward one of a number of defenses. For instance, the organization may claim that the employee did not have the requisite **bona fide occupational qualification (BFOQ).** Title VII provides that in certain instances religion, sex, or national origin is a BFOQ if such a qualification is reasonably necessary to the normal operation of the organization. BFOQ is a vague and seldom used defense for discrimination cases. An example of a BFOQ might be a firm's hiring a male to serve as a men's room attendant or a church's refusing to hire someone of a different religion to serve as a minister. The courts have ruled that it is not a BFOQ for flight attendants to be female. Title VII also states that an organization must make reasonable accommodation for employees of specific religious beliefs or employees with handicaps. Exactly how much is "reasonable accommodation" is subject to interpretation.

Another defense is that it was a **business necessity** *not* to hire the complainant. If safety or profitability requires hiring a specific person, then discrimination could be defended under Title VII. For example, if a company hired an individual to work specific hours during the week, and after being hired the individual could not work those hours due to personal circumstances, management may claim a business necessity as a defense. Another example is a dress shop that claims that it is a business necessity to hire young females as salesclerks so that they may better match the public they are serving.

Still another defense is that the person hired is better qualified for the job than the complainant. This is the most common defense for an organization charged with employment discrimination. HR records should prove that the results of the tests or interviews indicate that the person hired was better qualified. HR departments with standardized and documented records, using valid selection techniques, have a strong defense. If, however, their defense is based solely on what they remember about a case or what they believe occurred, then they have a weak defense.

The EEOC usually hears complaints from applicants who were discriminated against in the process of hiring or promotion, not in matters of unequal pay. Under Title VII, employment discrimination refers to much more than the initial hiring process; it encompasses all "terms, conditions, or privileges of employment" and includes selection, promotion, transfers, and employee training. Therefore, all organizational decisions that relate to an employee's job classification are included under the Civil Rights Act.

MIXED-MOTIVE DISCRIMINATION

Mixed-motive discrimination occurs when an employer uses discriminatory criteria, as well as other factors, in making an employment decision. If the employer can prove that it would have made the same decision in the absence of discriminatory criteria, then it cannot be punished. The U.S. Supreme Court, in *Price-Waterhouse* v. *Hopkins* (1989), found that Price-Waterhouse had the burden of proving that a woman who was denied a partnership because of "sexual stereotyping" would have still been denied the partnership in the absence of any sexual discrimination. The court ruled that Hopkins had been denied a partnership because sexual stereotyping was "a substantial factor" in decision making and not simply "a factor."[7]

EQUAL EMPLOYMENT OPPORTUNITY ACT

In 1972 the Civil Rights Act of 1964 was amended by the Equal Employment Opportunity Act. The amendment effectively changed Title VII of the 1964 act to include all private employers and labor unions with 15 or more employees or members, state and local governments, and public and private educational institutions. More important, the Equal Employment Act considerably strengthened the 1964 act by giving the EEOC power to bring suits directly to federal courts when conciliation efforts proved unsuccessful. Previously, the EEOC did not have such power and relied on employers to comply voluntarily with conciliation efforts. State and local EEOC offices were established to provide local-level counseling for complainants who felt they had suffered discrimination.

PREGNANCY DISCRIMINATION ACT

A type of sex discrimination openly practiced in the past is one based not entirely on sex but on so-called *sex plus.* A typical example of sex–plus discrimination occurred when a manager openly told all women with small children that they would not be hired because of their child-care responsibilities. The courts found the policy illegal because it was not equally imposed on men.[8] Sex-plus discrimination has also been used against pregnant women. The U.S. Supreme Court had held that such discrimination was legal. But the Pregnancy Discrimination

Act of 1978, an amendment to the 1964 Civil Rights Act, prohibited sex discrimination, including but not limited to pregnancy, childbirth, and related medical conditions. The 1978 act also required employee medical insurance to cover pregnancy as fully as it covers other long-term disabilities.[9]

SEXUAL HARASSMENT

Sexual harassment has developed into one of the most controversial, complex, and perhaps widespread HR problems in the United States.

A national study of over 13,000 workers found that 42 percent of the women and 14 percent of the men had experienced some form of sexual harassment in a three-year period. The study also found that only 5 percent of the men and women who had experienced harassment chose to report it. The primary reasons why the other 95 percent did not report their harassment include the following:[10]

- The fear of losing one's job.
- The need for a future job reference.
- The possibility of being considered a trouble-maker.
- The assumption that nothing would change if harassment was reported.
- Concern about being accused of inviting the harassment.
- A reluctance to draw public attention to private lives.
- The prospect of emotional stress for filing a lawsuit and undergoing long, costly legal procedures.

The EEOC guidelines describe harassment known as *quid pro quo:* sex in exchange for favors and/or to avoid adverse actions. The guidelines also describe a type of harassment that results in a *hostile work environment.* Regardless of which type of harassment is involved, the same criterion applies: The conduct, whether physical or verbal, must be both unwelcome and of a sexual nature.

Unwelcome Sexual Advances   It is critical to understand what *unwelcome* means in the EEO guidelines. A person may have acquiesced in some type of conduct, but the conduct can still be unwelcome. Acquiescence to the conduct may have happened because the person feared loss of the job or some other retaliation.

If the conduct was unsolicited or if the victim viewed the conduct as undesirable or offensive and did nothing to initiate it, even if it was agreed to, it could still be considered unwelcome. Questions about *welcome* and *unwelcome* sexual advances are fact based and particular to each case. Consider, for instance, a woman who went out of her way to visit her supervisor in the hospital and in his brother's home and allowed him to visit her home. Later, this woman may not be able to convince a jury that the supervisor's conduct of which she complained was unwelcomed. Nor, in another example, might a woman who claimed that a hostile work environment existed be able to prove it when she began most of the discussions about sex herself.

Sexual Nature   For harassment to be based on sex, as that term is used in the Civil Rights Act, there must be something of a sexual nature in the conduct. Usually that test is met when a person is propositioned, comments or jokes are made about the person's anatomy, or pictures of people nude and/or in sexually suggestive poses are displayed. Conduct of a sexual nature can also be found when a *but for* situation arises. In one case, male crew members harassed female crew members by pulling such pranks as locking the restroom door at the work site and disabling their trucks.[11] "But for" the harassed victim being women and unwanted by this particular male work crew, the harassment they experienced would not have happened. This, then, became a "but for their sex" situation.

QUID PRO QUO

Quid pro quo sexual harassment occurs when a threat or promise is made in exchange for a sexual favor. In order to threaten or promise, the harasser must be in a position to follow through. Usually the harasser is the immediate supervisor, but sometimes he or she is higher up on the organizational ladder.

Monetary damages must be provable. Generally in a quid pro quo situation, actual losses can be demonstrated. The victim may have been denied a promotion or raise or may have been fired for refusing the harasser.

This type of harassment need happen only once to be actionable. If the truth of the harassment can be demonstrated, there is no necessity to show a pattern of other violations. *Once is enough* in quid pro quo cases.

Employers have been held *strictly liable* for the sexual harassment by one of their supervisors under a *respondeat superior* theory, which states that the employer is responsible for his or her agents. Actual knowledge on the part of the employer about how the supervisor acts is not required.[12] The employer has placed the supervisor in a position of authority and has given the supervisor the opportunity to misuse the authority.

Employers must ensure that there is a policy prohibiting sexual harassment, that the policy is communicated to all employees, that an effective complaint procedure exists, and that all managers have been trained in the policy.

HOSTILE ENVIRONMENT

Harassing conduct that interferes with an individual's work performance can come from anyone in the workplace: supervisors, co-workers, and even outsiders such as visitors or customers. One incident of harassment cannot establish a hostile work environment. Generally, the offensive conduct is frequent, repetitive, and part of an overall pattern that cannot be explained by coincidence. A victim may not be able to prove a particular monetary loss through a demotion or any specific job action. In fact, money damages may not have occurred. Unlike quid pro quo, job or money losses are not required; hostile environmental harassment includes unwelcome sexual advances, requests for sexual favors, verbal or physical conduct of a sexual nature, and actions that alter the conditions of the victim's employment and create an abusive working environment. In general, the courts have determined that a hostile environment was created when (1) the actions were unwelcome; (2) serious actions were repeated (an isolated sexual advance that was not repeated and that resulted in no retaliation is usually not sufficient); and (3) the actions were so severe as to alter the conditions of employment.[13]

In a hostile environment case, the conduct complained of is so offensive as to be objectionable to an uninvolved third party. Courts have traditionally used what was known as the **reasonable person standard** to judge what the community as a whole considers acceptable, despite individual peculiarities. For purposes of sexual harassment, the EEOC advised investigators to view the conduct as a reasonable person would, keeping the victim's perspective in mind.

A Florida court went further and decided the case on a *reasonable woman standard* because the court felt that men viewed sexual harassment as a comparatively harmless amusement.[14] Another court, in using a reasonable woman standard, relied on research that found that two-thirds of males interviewed would be flattered

HR IN THE NEWS

LANDMARK SEXUAL HARASSMENT CASES

In 1998 the U.S. Supreme Court handed down two landmark rulings on sexual harassment. In *Faragher* v. *City of Boca Raton,* Florida, a "hostile work environment" type of sexual harassment, the employer had a harassment policy, but never distributed it to supervisors. Faragher, a lifeguard, reported "unwanted and offensive touching, comments, and gestures" to her supervisor. The supervisor was unaware of the city's policy and took no action. The Court held the city liable even though it was unaware of the complaints. In the second case, *Gebser* v. *Lago Vista Independent School District,* a teacher had frequent sexual intercourse with a student for two years. The Court, even though the school district had no written policy as required, found against the student because the district was never notified and thus given a chance to correct the situation.

The Court advised employers desiring to limit their liability to:

1 Develop and publish a sexual harassment policy.

2 Include how to report an incident of harassment.

3 Distribute the policy to all employees.

If an alleged victim who has been given the harassment policy of his or her employer fails to report alleged incidents, the employer may not be held liable.

SOURCE: David C. Slade, "Schools, the Workplace, and Sexual Harassment," *The World & I,* 13, (October 1, 1998): 92.

by a sexual approach in the workplace, while only 15 percent would be insulted. The response from women to the same question was reversed.[15]

REDUCING SEXUAL HARASSMENT

The Anita Hill testimony during well-publicized U.S. Senate confirmation hearings for Supreme Court nominee Clarence Thomas awakened many employers to the need for clear policies and guidelines in the area of sexual harassment. Employers realized that developing procedures and training supervisors in how to investigate a claim after it is filed is too late. Once a person complains, emotion rather than reason is likely to dominate, and thus an objective investigation is often impossible. It is important to establish policies and investigation procedures in cases of alleged sexual harassment that take into account the following points.[16]

- *Don't Presume Guilt* All claims should be taken seriously, but if the investigation is influenced by a presumption of guilt, the employer may be subject to a viable defamation suit. Few allegations are potentially more damaging to one's professional and home lives than a claim of sexual harassment. Individuals once charged usually fight back and, if the process appears unfair, may countersue the employer. Employers should be considerate of the rights of both the victim and the accused and conduct an impartial investigation.
- *Use the Reasonable Woman Standard* This standard is significant in court cases (see *HR in the News:* Landmark Sexual Harassment Cases). Investigations conducted only by men may reach invalid conclusions and lack credibility with a jury that must determine if the conduct would have been offensive to a reasonable woman. Thus women should play a key role in all phases of any investigation and decision making.
- *Maintain Confidentiality* To minimize potential defamation claims by alleged harassers, the allegations should only be made known to people on a need-to-know basis. In general, an HR official, not supervisors, should conduct harassment investigations to maximize confidentiality. Any personnel questioned in the process should be strongly warned to not discuss the case with others.
- *Document All Complaints* Employees often discuss a hostile environment situation informally with someone but then plead with this person to take no action. Even if no action is taken at the employee's request, the complaint should still be filed, with all

pertinent information noted. A copy given to the employee may prevent the employee from changing his or her story later or denying the request that no action be taken. In addition, the employer must consider investigating such complaints even when the employee requests otherwise because the employer has a duty to protect other employees who may be affected. The employer may be held liable for a hostile environment if the company failed to take appropriate action.

- *Establish Clear Policies* Policies should define and prohibit sexual harassment and provide an explicit code of conduct for all employees. All written and oral complaints should be investigated. Any refusal to provide a written complaint does not release the employer from the responsibility to investigate.
- *Provide Training* Training is essential, and can increase awareness among all employees and reduce the number of incidents. A growing number of companies including DuPont, Digital Equipment, Honeywell, Corning, and Pacific Gas & Electric are training most or all of their employees. Sexual harassment can be an uncomfortable and tough subject, according to Corning HR Manager Tom McCullough, who has directed awareness seminars. Videos are effective tools because they can show subtle actions better than words alone. Employees generally want to discuss the entire range of harassment behaviors (Figure 4–3), as well as the gray areas of relationships. Discussing all the examples cited in Figure 4–3 can be critical because sexual harassment does not mean the same thing to everyone. But by viewing each act as a point on a continuum, people better understand the seriousness of all acts, as well as how some minor actions may lead to more serious ones or become part of a hostile environment. The desired outcome is that some unintentional harassment may be stopped.[17] It is also important to make employees aware that a *continuing pattern* of the acts on the left of the spectrum in Figure 4–3 may constitute a hostile environment.

WWW.DUPONT.COM
WWW.HONEYWELL.COM
WWW.CORNING.COM

RELIGIOUS DISCRIMINATION

Discrimination based on religion is prohibited by Title VII of the 1964 Civil Rights Act, Executive Order 11246, the 1991 Civil Rights Act, and various state and local laws.

FIGURE 4–3   SEXUAL HARASSMENT

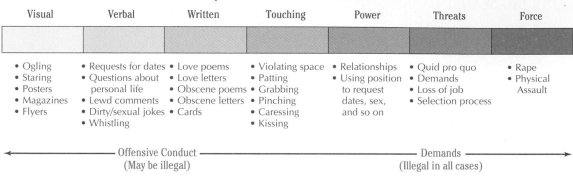

SEXUAL HARASSMENT
A Spectrum of Behavior Patterns

Visual	Verbal	Written	Touching	Power	Threats	Force

• Ogling	• Requests for dates	• Love poems	• Violating space	• Relationships	• Quid pro quo	• Rape
• Staring	• Questions about	• Love letters	• Patting	• Using position	• Demands	• Physical
• Posters	personal life	• Obscene poems	• Grabbing	to request	• Loss of job	Assault
• Magazines	• Lewd comments	• Obscene letters	• Pinching	dates, sex,	• Selection process	
• Flyers	• Dirty/sexual jokes	• Cards	• Caressing	and so on		
	• Whistling		• Kissing			

←——————— Offensive Conduct ———————   ————— Demands ————→
(May be illegal)   (Illegal in all cases)

- Individual perceptions and reactions determine harassment
- Behaviors unwanted by recipient are harassment
- Behaviors may not be intended to harass, but that is often the result
- Illegal if the result is perceived as harassment

- Behaviors are intentional; goal is to intimidate, harass or hurt another person

SOURCE: *Sexual Harassment Manual,* General Electric Corporation.

All aspects of the employment process are included in these acts. In the past, the number of cases based on **religious discrimination** was relatively few. However, with the workforce becoming more culturally diverse, it is expected that the number will increase. The federal laws define *religion* to include "all aspects of religious observance, practice, and belief." However, the legitimacy of some religions and their practices has been questioned.[18] Thus, to clarify the definition, the courts have identified three major characteristics that should be present: (1) the belief is based on a theory of "man's nature or his place in the universe," (2) which is not merely a personal preference but has an institutional quality about it, and (3) which is sincere.[19]

Religious discrimination issues have mostly focused on one of the following issues:[20]

- *Dress Policies* Many employers have grooming and dress policies designed to maintain an appropriate image or provide employee safety. The courts have generally upheld these policies if they have been fairly and uniformly enforced. Restaurants, for example, have successfully defended the policy of no facial hair and have required uniforms as a business necessity to maintain a public image of cleanliness.
- *Work Schedules* Employees requesting time off for religious observances are a problem for many employers. In general, employers are required to make reasonable accommodations if no undue hardship is placed on the business or on other employees. In one

case, for example, the U.S. Supreme Court upheld TWA's firing of an employee who refused to work on Saturday for religious reasons. In a previous TWA position, the employee had had enough seniority to avoid Saturday work. After requesting for, and receiving, another position that required Saturday hours, the employee started on a new seniority list and thus was scheduled to work Saturdays. He repeatedly failed to report on Saturday and was terminated. The Court upheld TWA's decision and cited the seniority system as a reasonable means of meeting employees' religious and secular needs.

- *Harassment* Prohibited religious discrimination also includes jokes, slurs, taunts, or tricks by coworkers and/or supervisors. If such activities occur repeatedly, the situation is viewed as a hostile environment and may violate the law.
- *BFOQ* Church-run organizations may consider religion a bona fide occupational qualification (BFOQ). Employees can then be required to be members of the church, and nonmembers can be discriminated against on the basis of religion.
- *Atheists* Discrimination against atheists is also legally prohibited because religion has been found to include belief and nonbelief. For example, an atheist bank employee refused to attend staff meetings because they opened with a prayer. She eventually felt forced to resign due to her absences. The Court found in her favor, noting that her quitting was not voluntary.

AGE DISCRIMINATION IN EMPLOYMENT ACT

The **Age Discrimination in Employment Act (ADEA)** was passed in 1967 and amended in 1978 and 1986. The act makes it illegal for employers with 20 or more employees, governmental bodies, and labor unions to discriminate against individuals over age 40. Employers cannot refuse to hire or discriminate in terms of compensation, promotion, or other conditions solely due to an individual's age. Nor can age be used as a preferential criterion in recruitment.

Section 4(f) of the ADEA allows employers to discipline or terminate an employee for a job-related reason such as incompetence, theft, or some other just cause that is "not age related." The courts have upheld employers' age policies where health and safety are of concern. In a landmark case, *Hodgson* v. *Greyhound Lines, Inc.*, a court of appeals upheld Greyhound's policy of barring applicants over the age of 35 for the job of bus driver.[21]

The 1986 amendment prohibits any mandatory retirement age for workers (previously set at age 70 [1978 amendment] and originally at age 65 [1967 act]). The 1986 amendment also requires employers to continue the same group health insurance for employees over age 70 that is offered to younger employees. The elimination of the mandatory retirement age received ardent support from senior citizens, labor leaders, and civil rights groups.[22]

The 1978 amendment to the ADEA transferred the enforcement responsibility to the EEOC and provided for jury trials. The change to jury trials greatly increased the number of cases that go to court. Jurors tend to be sympathetic to individuals who are generally the same age as themselves, and they are often prejudiced against large corporations. At the same time, companies began "retiring" many older employees due to economic pressures.

In recent years the number of age discrimination cases has increased dramatically—34 percent from 1989 to 1993 alone. The American Association of Retired Persons (AARP) believes the jump is due to the fact that 25 percent of older persons are discriminated against when applying for a job.[23] An additional reason may be a Supreme Court decision which closed a major loophole in the 1967 act. The 1996 decision determined that the age of a replacement employee in a termination case is irrelevant—even if he or she is also over age 40. Previously, if a victim over age 40 was tired and replaced by another person over age 40, he or she was barred from bringing the suit to court. The Court noted the act doesn't say anything about who a person may be replaced with in a termination case.[24]

The result of these different forces has been a large increase in age discrimination cases. The typical complainant in ADEA cases is a managerial or professional employee over age 50. Most cases involve mandatory retirement, demotion, or direct termination.[25] An analysis of over 300 cases filed showed that while the EEOC was involved in less than 25 percent of the cases, it was able to win 79 percent of the cases it chose to pursue. Employees generally had a greater likelihood of winning cases that contested mandatory retirement and pension-related employer actions. Age-conscious remarks by employers can help an employee's case (see Figure 4–4). Employers can increase their chances of winning age discrimination cases if they do the following:[26]

- Make all decisions on the basis of documented performance appraisals.
- Eliminate organizational policies that might indirectly be age discriminatory and formalize HR policies that are not.
- Train managers and other personnel to refrain from making references to age, especially in front of potential witnesses.
- Chart ages and any other employee characteristics protected against discrimination and analyze any possible discrimination by age.
- Document employee responses to early retirement programs that may be needed as evidence of their voluntary participation.

SEPARATION AGREEMENTS

An employer and an employee may both benefit from the employee's early retirement. In fact, employers often offer "retirement windows" to employees close in age and seniority to retirement. The window is a fixed period of time, usually a month, during which the employee must decide whether or not to accept and sign a **separation agreement** that provides enhanced retirement benefits such as continued healthcare coverage or a higher monthly pension. The 1986 ADEA amendment requires early retirement programs to be voluntary.

In a landmark case, *Sullivan* v. *Boron Oil Company* (1987),[27] an employee's written separation agreement was upheld as legal and binding. In this case, an

FIGURE 4–4   AGE-CONSCIOUS REMARKS THAT CAN BE USED AGAINST YOU

Employees have clearly become more aware of employer age-discrimination practices—and they know their rights under the Age Discrimination in Employment Act (ADEA). Unlike most race-discrimination cases, age-discrimination cases are decided by juries, which may be more sympathetic to the worker. Age-conscious remarks by managers can influence a jury's decision.

Examples of age-conscious communications that have been found to be discriminatory included:

● A piece of paper with the official reason for layoff that says: "Lay off—too old."

● Memo recommending a reduction in [the work] force to promote "a younger image."

● Job advertisements seeking: "college student," "recent college graduate," or "retired person."

● Direct comments by supervisors who affect employment decisions: "For men your age, there isn't going to be a future in the new [company]"; or the company was "going to get rid of the 'good old Joes' and get some younger folks in."

In lawsuits involving age discrimination the employee must prove that age . . . was a determining factor in an employment action—but age need *not* have been the sole reason for the action taken. Employers can avoid liability by eliminating age-conscious remarks in official communications and by documenting a well-organized campaign to sensitize all managers to the need to avoid age-conscious remarks and thinking.

SOURCE: John J. Coleman, III, "Age-Conscious Remarks: What You Say Can Be Used Against You," *Personnel* 62, no. 9 (September 1985): 22–29. Used by permission.

employee of the Standard Oil of Ohio (SOHIO) Company signed an agreement titled "Release of Claims," which stated that "In consideration of the benefit provided me . . . , I release the Standard Oil Company . . . from all claims." The employee claimed age discrimination because he was mentally and physically fatigued when he signed the release. The U.S. Court of Appeals applied a five-part test to determine the validity and fairness of the agreement and found that (1) the release was clear and unambiguous, (2) the plaintiff knew his rights as stated in the agreement, (3) the plaintiff understood the agreement, (4) the plaintiff had an opportunity to negotiate, and (5) the plaintiff voluntarily accepted the release for personal compensation. This decision provides employers with specific guidelines for developing voluntary early retirement plans that can be legally executed without fear of successful litigation.

OLDER WORKERS BENEFIT PROTECTION ACT

The ADEA was again amended in 1990 by the **Older Workers Benefit Protection Act (OWBPA).** Title I of the OWBPA effectively nullified the 1989 *Betts* decision by the U.S. Supreme Court. That Court decision had allowed age discrimination in the administration of benefit plans, thus allowing employers to offer benefit plans of greater value to younger workers, regardless of cost considerations. Title I of the OWBPA includes employer benefit plans under the ADEA. Therefore, an employer cannot make age-based distinctions in designing employee benefit plans unless the costs are greater for older workers than for younger ones. In addition, early retirement plans are permitted as long as they are voluntary and employees receive a financial incentive for electing to participate.

Under Title II of the OWBPA,[28] an individual may not waive any right or claim under the ADEA unless the waiver is "knowing and voluntary." In general, the most common scenario involves an employee over age 40 who is told that his or her position is no longer needed due to downsizing (or rightsizing), merger, or reorganization. The HR director offers the employee a separation agreement, reviews it with the employee, and provides time for it to be reviewed by the employee's attorney. In general, the release offers the employee more compensation than he or she would normally receive in pension benefits in exchange for a written release and covenant not to sue under the ADEA or OWBPA. The employee may later decide that he or she was discriminated against because of age and coerced to sign the agreement. The employer's attorney, however, may file a countersuit based on the employee's breach of the agreement. A court must then decide if someone was wronged. Decisions have been made in favor of both sides, but more often in favor of employees if age was a factor in their being selected for termination. Here is an example of separation agreement:[29]

> In consideration of these undertakings by the company, the employee agrees to release from, and covenants not to sue the company for any and all claims, including but not limited to those arising out of the employee's employment with the company and cessation thereof, and also including but not limited to any and all claims of discrimination on account of . . . age. . . . I [each employee] understand that by signing this release I am releasing the company from any and all claims I may have against the company to date. I certify that I do so knowingly and voluntarily in exchange for the company's agreement to perform the actions outlined above.

VOCATIONAL REHABILITATION ACT

Under the **Vocational Rehabilitation Act** of 1973, employers with government contracts of $2,500 or more must have approved affirmative action programs for the handicapped. Programs include special recruitment efforts for the handicapped, as well as procedures to promote and develop the handicapped within the organization. Employees are also required to make environmental changes, such as adding ramps, to make their business more accessible to the handicapped. The act is administered by committee members from the Civil Service Commission, the U.S. Department of Veterans' Affairs, the U.S. Department of Labor, and the U.S. Department of Health and Human Services. Handicapped individuals who feel that their rights have been violated under the act may file complaints with the U.S. Department of Labor.

Although the term *handicap* is usually associated with physical impairments, the act also covers such mental impairments as retardation and emotional disorders. In addition, the act covers certain illnesses sometimes used by employers as grounds for rejecting applicants, including diabetes, heart disease, epilepsy, and cancer. Individuals who are alcohol or drug users are included unless their illness affects their ability to perform their job.[30] In practice, the Department of Labor's guidelines for contractors require them to make a "reasonable accommodation" for the handicapped, which generally includes the following:[31]

- ● *Job Accessibility* Adding wheelchair ramps, Braille signs on elevators, air conditioning for workers with respiratory problems, and so on.
- ● *Job Design* Eliminating tasks that a handicapped person cannot perform but that are not really necessary to do the job.
- ● *Qualifications* Eliminating unnecessary job specifications, such as a physical exam that might limit the entry of handicapped applicants.
- ● *Unprejudiced Treatment* Eliminating hiring decisions based on people's fear or uneasiness about handicaps such as epilepsy or speech impairment.

VIETNAM-ERA VETERANS READJUSTMENT ACT

This act was a special effort to help Vietnam War veterans who had particular difficulty in securing jobs when they returned to the United States. The **Vietnam-Era Veterans Readjustment Act** of 1974 requires all organizations holding government contracts of $10,000 or more to hire and promote Vietnam War veterans. The act is administered by the Veterans Employment Service of the U.S. Department of Labor. Employers holding government contracts are required to list their job openings with local state employment offices in order that these offices may contact unemployed veterans as well as other individuals. One side effect of the act has been a demonstrated increase in job openings listed by state employment offices, which has increased their effectiveness in many communities.

IMMIGRATION REFORM AND CONTROL ACT

Congress in 1986, after years of debate, passed a comprehensive federal immigration-control law. In effect, the **Immigration Reform and Control Act (IRCA)** shifted much of the burden of immigration enforcement from the federal government to employers. This shift was accomplished by making it illegal for an employer to hire, recruit, refer for a fee, or continue to employ a person whom the employer knows is not eligible to work in the United States. Employers are required to verify and maintain records of each new employee's identity and work eligibility for three years of employment or for one year after termination.

A second major feature of the IRCA makes it unlawful for employers to discriminate against individuals who look or sound "foreign" but legally reside in the United States. This section of the act was passed in response to concerns of Hispanic-American groups and others who feared that the new employer requirements might lead to unintentional employment discrimination.[32] Specifically, Section 274B(a)(1) of the act provides the following:

> It is an unfair immigration-related employment practice for a person or other entity to discriminate against any individual (other than an unauthorized alien) with respect to the hiring, or recruitment or referral for a fee, of the individual for employment or the discharging of the individual for employment—(a) because of such individual's national origin, or (b) in the case of a citizen or intending citizen . . . , because of such individual's citizenship status.

The preamble to the regulations emphasizes that policies such as "English-only" rules, lengthy residence requirements, or unnecessary documents for employee verification can be challenged if adopted for discriminatory purposes.

Employers of four or more employees are covered by the act. The Department of Justice is charged with its enforcement. The Act requires employers to refuse employment to unauthorized aliens. It is unlawful to continue to employ individuals whom the employer knows are using fraudulent documents or whose temporary work authorization has expired. The Act specifically excludes union hiring halls from any documentations or certification requirements. Employers of union referrals, however, are covered by the act.

The Act includes civil penalties of $250 to $2,000 per person for the first offense of knowingly hiring undocumented workers. Subsequent offenses may bring penalties of $2,000 to $5,000. Penalties of $100 to $1000 can be imposed on employers who fail to comply with the documentation requirements.

AMERICANS WITH DISABILITIES ACT

The **Americans with Disabilities Act (ADA)** was enacted in 1990, and full coverage of all of its wide-ranging provisions (see Figure 4–5) became law in 1994. In general, the ADA prohibits discrimination against persons with disabilities in four broad areas:[33] employment (Title I); governmental programs and services (Title II); public accommodations and services, including hotels, restaurants, retail stores, service establishments, and other public facilities (Title III); and telecommunications (Title IV).

A U.S. Census Bureau report showed only 34.6 percent of working age persons with disabilities are employed, compared to 79.8 percent of those without disabilities. Furthermore, those with disabilities are primarily employed in low-status jobs. Why? Attitudinal biases and employer stereotypes are still the primary reasons. In fact, these stereotypes have been proven incorrect by research. In general, people with disabilities do not have different job-related abilities, performance levels, absenteeism, or turnover than other employees.[34]

The ADA provides assistance to the over 43 million American workers who have disabilities by acknowledging "that they have a role in the workforce," according to Alan Emery, a San Francisco-based health specialist. It will also help the nondisabled become more aware of the ability of many disabled to be productive on the job and therefore end many myths concerning the disabled. Much of the compliance required by the ADA simply involves sensitivity and common sense, as described in Figure 4-6. As nondisabled workers see and work with more disabled workers, they may at first feel uneasy or uncomfortable. However, over time, they will likely change their attitudes and appreciate the skills and motivation of disabled co-workers.[35]

The ADA's employment discrimination provisions (Title 1), administered by the EEOC, primarily include the following:

- *Disability Defined* Section 1630 defines *disability* as "a physical or mental impairment that substantially limits one or more of the major life activities." The act also includes individuals with a history of physical impairment such as cerebral palsy and muscular dystrophy or of diseases such as mental illness, cancer, epilepsy, or AIDS. In addition, it includes individuals who are regarded as having a substantial impairment—meaning that their disability is not substantially limiting but is perceived to be so by others. It does not include transvestites, homosexuals, or people with emotional disorders. Are obese workers covered? Yes, obese people have been given new protection from discrimination by the EEOC under the ADA. The ADA defines an individual with a disability differently from other discrimination laws, and since obesity was found to fall under the act's definition of limiting "one or more of the major life activities," the EEOC in 1993 determined that people who have been extremely overweight for a long period of time may qualify for

FIGURE 4–5   ADA EMPLOYER OBLIGATIONS

The following points summarize employers' legal obligations under the Americans with Disabilities Act.

1 An employer must not deny a job to a disabled individual because of a disability if the individual is qualified and able to perform the essential functions of the job, with or without reasonable accommodation.

2 If an individual who has a disability is otherwise qualified but unable to perform an essential function without an accommodation, the employer must make a reasonable accommodation unless the accommodation would result in undue hardship.

3 An employer isn't required to lower existing performance standards for a job when considering the qualifications of an individual who has a disability if the standards are job-related and uniformly applied to all employees and candidates for that job.

4 Qualification standards and selection criteria that screen out or tend to screen out an individual on the basis of a disability must be job-related and consistent with business necessity.

5 Any test or other procedure used to evaluate qualifications must reflect the skills and abilities of an individual rather than impaired sensory, manual, or speaking skills, unless those are the job-related skills that the test is designed to measure.

With respect to the recruitment and job application process, including pre-employment inquiries, employers:

1 Must provide an equal opportunity for an individual who has a disability to participate in the job application process and to be considered for a job.

2 May not make pre-employment inquiries regarding any disability, but may ask questions about the ability to perform specific job functions and, with certain limitations, may ask an individual who has a disability to describe or demonstrate how he or she could perform these functions.

3 May not require pre-employment medical examinations or medical histories, but may condition a job offer on the results of a post-offer medical examination, if all entering employees in the same job category are required to take such an examination.

4 May use tests for illegal drugs, which are not considered medical examinations under ADA.

SOURCE: Wayne E. Barlow and Edward Z. Hane, "A Practical Guide to the Americans with Disabilities Act," *Personnel Journal* (June 1992): 59. Used by permission.

protection under the ADA. This protection applies even if the individual was given a goal and time to lose weight but was unsuccessful.

- ***Discrimination*** (Section 102(a)) No covered employer shall discriminate against a qualified individual with a disability. This includes the following employment practices.[36]

Application	Compensation
Testing	Leave
Hiring	Benefits
Assignment	Layoff
Evaluation	Recall
Disciplinary actions	Termination
Training	Promotion
Medical examinations	

Qualified individuals with disabilities include those who have a disability and meet the skill, experience, education, and other job-related requirements.

Step 1. The individual possesses the prerequisites for the position, such as experience, license, skill, and education. Any requirement must be demonstrably job related.

Step 2. The individual can perform the **essential job functions** with or without reasonable accommodation. Essential job functions can be identified through job analysis and are often found in job descriptions. The descriptions should, however, distinguish between essential and marginal job functions and be current. An essential job function is one that

FIGURE 4–6   DISABILITY ETIQUETTE IN THE WORKPLACE

HOW TO TREAT DISABLED EMPLOYEES WITH RESPECT

Interviews. Interviews offer a time when courtesy and reasonable accommodation work together. The interviewer needs to know the essential functions of the job (thus job descriptions are important), questions related to essential functions, and the ability to determine the person's skill level as it relates to the job.

The initial interview is the first time many will have contact with a person who has a disability, and they may be unfamiliar with how to approach these individuals. Be aware of:

- **Greetings.** Treat the person who has a disability as you would anyone else: maintain eye contact, sit at the interviewee's eye level, maintain proximity and attention. Give that person the same orientation and assistance you would a nondisabled individual. Do you shake hands with someone who has no use or limited use of arms? What if he or she has short arms or a prosthesis or is visually impaired? The answer is yes. If you usually shake hands, that's what you would expect to do in these situations.

- **Eye contact and eye level.** It's important to maintain eye contact and eye level because it gives a person who has a disability a non-verbal message that creates the tone of the interaction and lets that person know that you're comfortable in his or her presence; that you're focused on the individual, not the disability; and that you're extending the same courtesies you would to anyone else. Maintain eye contact at all times with someone who's hearing impaired even when he or she is looking at the interpreter and when the interpreter is repeating the person's words to you. Pretend the interpreter isn't there.

- **Proximity and attention.** During a conversation or interview, sit as you do when you're interviewing other candidates. For example, some people choose to have a barrier (for example, a desk) between themselves and the interviewee; others choose to have none. Regardless of the disability of the person, maintain the same level of attentiveness.

- **Assistance.** Usually a disabled person will ask for help if it is needed; otherwise don't offer or assist without first asking if help is needed.

- **Information access.** This is one of the most important aspects of the work day. It's crucial for everyone to have access to vital information in the organization—and at the same time. With employees who have a disability, the form of communication may be one that hasn't been used before. For example, if your company uses a public address system, [use] a "buddy system" in which a hearing person can transmit the information. If there's going to be a meeting the next day that involves a 40-page report and a person who's visually impaired, give that person an audiotape.

- **Physical space.** Consider the person's disability and be aware of the environment as it affects that person. Think in terms of what the person can and can't do for him or herself, how long it will take, and the safety factors involved. For instance, if the mail slots are far from the desk of an individual who uses a wheelchair, other arrangements might be made, or co-workers might regularly check his or her slot as well as their own.

SOURCE: Patricia Morrissey, "Disability Etiquette in the Workplace," as reported in "How to Treat Disabled Employees with Respect," *Personnel Journal* (June 1992): 71.

is critical to the success of the job and that must be performed by the incumbent (see Figure 4–7). Marginal job functions may be performed by the incumbent or others and are incidental to the main purpose of the job.

- ***Reasonable Accommodation*** (Section 102(b) (5)(A) Discrimination includes not making **reasonable accommodation** to the known physical or

mental limitations of an otherwise qualified individual with a disability who is an applicant or employee, unless the employer can demonstrate that the accommodation would impose an undue hardship on the operation of the business. . . .

Under the ADA, however, the employer is not required to provide employees with personal items such as hearing aids, wheelchairs, corrective lenses,

FIGURE 4–7   ESSENTIAL JOB FUNCTIONS UNDER THE ADA

To comply with the ADA, employers must determine which job functions are essential to a position and which are marginal. The ADA regulations specify several factors which should be considered when making this determination. These factors can be evaluated by answering the following:

1 Does the position exist to perform these functions? If the performance of a particular function is the principal purpose for hiring a person, it would be an essential function.

2 Would the removal of the function fundamentally alter the position? If the purpose of the position can be fulfilled without performing the function, it isn't essential.

3 What's the degree of expertise or skill required to perform the function? The fact that an employee is hired for his or her specialized expertise to perform a particular function is evidence that the function is essential.

4 How much of the employee's time is spent performing the function? The fact that an employee spends a substantial amount of time performing a particular function is evidence that the function is essential.

5 What are the consequences of failure to perform the function? The fact that the consequences of failure are severe is evidence that the function is essential.

6 How many other employees are available among whom the function can be distributed? The smaller the number of employees available for performing a group of functions, the greater the likelihood that any one of them will have to perform a particular function.

SOURCE: Wayne E. Barlow and Edward Z. Hane, "A Practical Guide to the Americans with Disabilities Act," *Personnel Journal* (June 1992): 54. Used by permission.

or prosthetic devices that people use in their daily lives. The Job Accommodation Network at West Virginia University has estimated that of those items that must be provided under the reasonable accommodation statute, about half cost less than $50. Some, however, such as a new portable reading machine for the blind, can cost over $5,000. Common low-cost items include:[37]

- Modification of doorknobs with a lever-type handle; cost: $11.
- Telephone headsets to replace the handset for people with mobility limitations; cost $25 to $150.
- Use of a lazy-susan type of file folder system on a desk for people with impaired mobility; cost: $150.

The ADA has caused some larger employers to hire an assistive technology coordinator to help them make reasonable accommodations.

- *Selection Criteria* (Section 102(b)(6)) Discrimination includes using qualification standards, employment tests, or other selection criteria that screen out or tend to screen out an individual with a disability— or a class of individuals with disabilities—unless the standard, test, or other selection criteria is shown to

be job-related for the position in question and is consistent with business necessity.

- *Medical Examinations* (Section 102(c)) Employers shall not conduct a preemployment medical examination or make inquiries of a job applicant as to whether the applicant has a disability or as to the nature of such disability. An employer may make preemployment inquiries into the ability of an applicant to perform job-related functions. In addition, an employer may require a medical examination after an offer of employment has been made, and the employer may condition an offer on the results of an examination if all employees are subjected to such an examination.

- *Drug Testing*   Section 1630.3 states that "employers may discharge or deny employment to persons who illegally use drugs, on the basis of such use, without fear of being held liable for discrimination." Illegal drug use is defined to include both the use of unlawful drugs and the unlawful use of prescription drugs. Employers are specifically permitted wide latitude in regulating drug and alcohol use in the workplace. Employers may prohibit alcohol as well as the use of drugs. In addition, a drug test is *not* considered a medical examination (as discussed in the previous section); thus, requiring a drug test prior to an employment offer is permissible. It should be noted, however, that individuals disabled by alcoholism are included in the ADA definition of disability.[38]

The general purpose of the ADA is to prohibit job discrimination against individuals with disabilities. In the past, such discrimination typically occurred in the form of application blanks or job interviews that inquired into the *existence of a disability* rather than the *ability to perform* the functions of a job. Another common form of discrimination consisted of slotting the disabled into menial or dead-end jobs.[39]

While the ADA has received praise for its intention to prohibit employment discrimination, critics complain that it is replete with vague terms, such as *reasonable accommodation* and *undue hardship,* which will likely be interpreted by the courts. Section 10(A) simply defines undue hardship as "an action requiring significant difficulty or expense" when considered in light of four factors: (1) the nature and cost of the accommodation needed; (2) the overall financial resources of the facility, the number of persons employed, and the impact of such accommodation; (3) the overall size of the business; and (4) the type and geographic separateness of the facilities. Under the ADA, reasonable accommodation may include eliminating nonessential job duties, permitting part-time or modified work schedules, and acquisition of new equipment or devices that would enable the disabled employee to perform the job. Examples of such equipment include adaptive computer hardware, Braille devices, and hearing aids or amplifiers. The act does not provide guidelines for employers to follow in determining which job duties are nonessential to a job and therefore should be transferred to another employee as part of an employer's reasonable-accommodation requirement.

Title III of the ADA has also had significant impact on employers who serve the public, including hotels, restaurants, bars, theaters, stadiums, retail stores, banks, gas stations, professional offices, schools, daycare facilities, parks, zoos, and other public buildings. All such facilities, regardless of size, must make their premises accessible to the disabled by removing architectural and communication barriers.

Cases filed under the ADA are decided by juries. This substantial change provided by the Civil Rights Act of 1991 altered the course of history in the area of employment discrimination. Previously, for over 25 years, judges (who were typically white, male, and middle-aged or older) decided discrimination cases. The change occurred because, as one attorney noted, "Juries decide cases with their guts and hearts, not necessarily with their heads."

CIVIL RIGHTS ACT OF 1991

In response to several U.S. Supreme Court decisions on civil rights and employment discrimination, the U.S. Congress passed the **Civil Rights Act of 1991.**[40] It is the most important federal employment legislation to be enacted since the 1964 Civil Rights Act. Supporters claimed it was needed to eradicate the U.S. Supreme Court decisions (Table 4–1) they believed had turned back the clock on employment discrimination practices.[41] The signing of the act ended a bitter two-year struggle between President George Bush and Congress. The central issue was whether the bill required employers to resort to quotas as the only way of avoiding discrimination claims. The act does not contain such a requirement.[42] It does, however, include a significant number of major provisions:[43]

1 *Disparate Impact* The act requires that an employer justify an employment practice that has been shown to have disparate impact. The employer must show that the practice is a business necessity, which is defined to be job related for the position(s) in question. This provision overturns the 1989 *Wards Cove* decision by the U.S. Supreme Court and supports the 1971 *Griggs* v. *Duke Power Co.* court decision (Table 4–1). The *Wards Cove* decision had shifted the burden of proof to the employee at all times during a case. Under the 1991 Civil Rights Act, a disparate impact claim is established if[44]

> a complaining party demonstrates that a respondent uses a particular employment practice that causes a disparate impact on the basis of race, color, religion, sex, or national origin and the respondent fails to demonstrate that the challenged practice is job related for the position in question and consistent with business necessity.

2 *Race Norming* The act prohibits the adjustment of test scores on the basis of the religion, national origin, gender, or race of the test takers (race norming). Race norming is the employment practice of adjusting job-test scores according to separate racial percentiles. In practice, test results are separated into racial groups, and then whites, blacks, and Hispanics are ranked by percentile against members of their own race alone. Then the results are combined without reference to race and listed by rank. Effectively, a person whose real score on the test was high could be listed at a lower percentile than someone whose real score was lower but whose within-race percentile was higher. The justification for race norming generally was that it was needed to compensate for tests that were biased against minority groups.

TABLE 4–1   SIGNIFICANT EEO/AA U.S. SUPREME COURT DECISIONS

CASE	YEAR	DECISION/EFFECT
Griggs v. *Duke Power Co.*	1971	Provided first interpretation of the 1964 Civil Rights Act. Established that (1) the employer must prove that any job requirement is job related; (2) tests must be validated; and (3) the absence of discriminatory intentions does not absolve an employer.
Moody v. *Albermarle Paper*	1975	Required employer to prove test validation if the test had adverse impact on any minority group. Tests included performance appraisals.
Weber v. *Kaiser Aluminum*	1979	Upheld race-conscious AAPs that require certain positions to be filled by minorities, thus voiding the concept of reverse discrimination.
Stotts v. *Firefighters Local 1784*	1984	Maintained the use of a bona fide seniority system in the case of layoffs and recall actions, even when conflicting with affirmative action.
Wygant v. *Jackson Board of Education*	1986	Upheld the use of seniority systems in layoffs unless prior discrimination existed. Also endorsed underutilization as a basis for an AAP.
Sheet Metal Workers v. *EEOC*	1986	Supported court-ordered quotas to overcome a history of discrimination.
Firefighters v. *City of Cleveland*	1986	Upheld a voluntary union–employer agreement to promote minorities on a one-to-one basis.
Johnson v. *Transportation Agency*	1987	Established the use of sex-based hiring goals in affirmative action programs.
Martin v. *Wilks*	1989	Allowed the use of reverse discrimination theory by permitting white firefighters to challenge the promotion of black firefighters in a court-approved consent decree. Narrowed the *Weber* (1979) decision.
Hopkins v. *Price-Waterhouse*	1989	Ruled that even if gender was one factor in an employment decision, if the same decision would have been reached in the absence of discrimination, it can be allowed.
Antonio v. *Wards Cove Packing*	1989	Reversed *Griggs* by ruling that the ultimate burden of proof in a Title VII disparate impact case is on the plaintiff (employee).
Lorrance v. *AT&T Technologies*	1989	Required those adversely affected by a discriminatory seniority system to sue within 180 days of the time when the system takes effect.
St. Mary's Hand Center v. *Hicks*	1993	Revised 1972 *Green* decision to require victims prove discrimination occurred.
Faragher v. *City of Boca Raton* *Gebser* v. *Lago Vista Independent School District*	1998	Ruled employers should publish and distribute sexual harassment policies.

③ Mixed Motives An employer is prohibited from allowing race, sex, religion, or national origin to be a "motivating factor" in an employment decision. This provision overturns the 1989 U.S. Supreme Court decision in *Hopkins* v. *Price-Waterhouse*, which allowed an employer to avoid liability by showing that the same decision would have been reached even though gender had been a factor (Table 4–1). For example, assume that Jones, Chevy, and Rydell were all finalists for a position and Rydell was hired. Jones files a discrimination suit and the employer admits that her sex was a factor in the decision. However, the employer also proves that Rydell would have been selected even if sex had not been a factor.

④ Foreign Personnel The act applies Title VII of the 1964 Civil Rights Act and the ADA to employment practices by U.S. employers in foreign countries. Thus employees of U.S. companies are allowed to return to the United States and file suit against their employer for "foreign" discrimination. This provision overturns the *Boureslan* v. *Aramco* decision of the U.S. Supreme Court, which held that Title VII did not protect employees of U.S. companies who worked outside of the country and where the decision was wholly foreign.

⑤ Jury Trials Perhaps the most significant provision is the introduction of jury trials in cases involving Title VII or the ADA. Previously, plaintiffs had no right to a jury trial, which is generally more sympathetic to their cases. Also significant is the introduction of compensatory and punitive damages in cases involving intentional discrimination (not caused by an employment practice or test applied to all applicants or employees). These damages are not available in disparate impact cases, and are limited by caps:

$50,000	(employers with 15–100 employees)
$100,000	(employers with 101–200 employees)
$200,000	(employers with 201–500 employees)
$300,000	(employers with over 500 employees)

⑥ Seniority Systems Employees may file suits claiming discrimination in the operation of a seniority system, either on its adoption or on its impact on an employee. This provision overturns the 1989 *Lorrance* v. *AT&T Technologies* decision by the U.S. Supreme Court, which allowed challenges only within 180 days of the date that a seniority system was implemented.

⑦ Intentional Discrimination In the 1989 *Pattersen* v. *McLean Credit Union* case, the U.S. Supreme Court held that intentional discrimination was illegal under the 1866 Civil Rights Act in hiring decisions alone.

The 1991 act overrode the *Pattersen* decision by amending Section 1981 of the 1866 Civil Rights Act to apply to *all* employment decisions, including promotions, discharges, and demotions. This change was also significant because the 1866 act applies to employers of fewer than fifteen employees who are protected from racial and ethnic discrimination. The 1964 Civil Rights Act only applies to employers of fifteen or more employees.

The significant provisions of the 1991 Civil Rights Act increased the number of employment discrimination claims, largely due to the change in the burden-of-proof provision in disparate impact cases, the introduction of jury trials, and the introduction of compensatory and punitive damages. At the same time, the direction set by the U.S. Supreme Court in its 1986–1989 employment law decisions was clearly reversed.

EMPLOYMENT ARBITRATION AGREEMENTS

The number of employment discrimination cases filed each year was increasing rapidly *before* passage of the ADA of 1990 and the Civil Rights Act of 1991. With the addition of these two new laws, the estimated 100,000 employment discrimination case backlog in state and federal courts is expected to increase. An alternative to the court process is the arbitration of employment disputes, which can reduce the number of court cases following a 1991 U.S. Supreme Court decision.[45]

In *Gilmer* v. *Interstate/Johnson Lane Corp.*[46] the court required the arbitration of an age-discrimination suit. The employee, Gilmer, in a New York Stock Exchange application, had signed an agreement to arbitrate any dispute, claim, or controversy with his employer. After being terminated, he had filed a discrimination suit with the EEOC. The employer moved to compel arbitration as provided in the agreement, which a district court denied but the U.S. Supreme Court approved. Several lower courts have ordered the use of arbitration in similar cases on the basis of the *Gilmer* decision.[47]

The use of arbitration to settle disputes is usually a voluntary arrangement between two parties. For many years, labor unions and employers, for example, have voluntarily agreed to resolve most grievances with arbitration as the last of a series of steps. Section 118 of the Civil Rights Act of 1991 encourages the use of arbitration or some alternative dispute method:

> Where appropriate and to the extent authorized by the law, the use of alternative means of dispute resolution, including

settlement negotiations, conciliation, facilitation, mediation, factfinding, minitrials, and arbitration, is encouraged to resolve disputes arising under the Act or provisions of federal law amended by this title.

The use of arbitration to settle employment cases, in comparison to the court process, has several potential advantages:[48]

- Faster resolution of disputes (multiple lengthy court appeals are avoided).
- Less expensive.
- Avoidance of jury trials (sympathetic juries often side with employees).
- Improved supervision and employee morale (as supervisors act more reasonably in accordance with established policies).

Employers can be expected to expand the use of arbitration in employment disputes by (1) requiring the signing of an arbitration agreement on an employment application, (2) including the arbitration process in an employee handbook or personnel manual, or (3) including an arbitration clause in a severance agreement.[49] In any potential use of arbitration agreements, employers, to be fair to their employees and to maximize the likelihood that the process will be upheld by a court, should do the following:[50]

- Ensure that the agreement is voluntarily executed.
- Describe the arbitration process in precise, nonlegalistic terms detailing key issues such as what kinds of claims will be disputed, how the arbitra-

tor will be selected, who bears the expense, and when the hearing will occur.
- Require the employee to sign a statement that he or she has read and understood the agreement and freely accepts it.

Employment arbitration agreements may not always be upheld by the courts. However, the courts have generally required that the process be followed if it has been voluntarily agreed to by both parties, and arbitration awards may be given significant weight by a court if the case is pursued.

AFFIRMATIVE ACTION

By Executive Order 11246, President Lyndon B. Johnson created what is known today as **affirmative action.** Since 1965, this order has been amended several times by later presidents. An *executive order* is not a law and, therefore, does not have the wide impact of federal laws such as the Civil Rights Act of 1964. An executive order directly affects only governmental agencies and contractors or subcontractors of federal government programs. But organizations may be ordered by a court to develop an affirmative action plan. Unlike the previously discussed laws passed by Congress, which may be referred to as *neutrality laws* because they require only that organizations obey them, executive orders relating to affirmative action require that certain organizations take specific positive actions to improve the employment opportunities of minorities.

HR IN THE NEWS

MORE EMPLOYERS ADOPT MANDATORY EMPLOYMENT ARBITRATION AGREEMENTS

Circuit City, US West, Hooters of America, and Tenet Healthcare are among a growing number of American employers requiring job applicants to sign employment arbitration agreements. The success of the agreements, which usually require mediation before arbitration, is one factor—mediators settle 85 percent of their cases. The other factors

WWW.CIRCUITCITY.COM
WWW.HOOTERSOFAMERICA.COM

are cost, speed, and the fact that employers win more often than if they went to court. The greatest loss for the job applicant is the right to go to a court and jury trial should they encounter job discrimination.

SOURCE: *Sun-Sentinel,* "Arbitration Rules Force Debate: Employees Question Abandoning Their Right to Sue Employers," *The Dallas Morning News* (July 20-1998): 2D.

In employment, an *affirmative action plan* (AAP) is a formal, written process that includes the hiring and promoting of members of targeted groups. The AAP is based on an analysis of an organization's workforce. The analysis compares the gender and racial composition of the available qualified labor pool to that of the organization and determines if there is an imbalance. Where an imbalance (or underutilization) exists, goals and timetables for hiring additional females and minorities are established for the purpose of ending the imbalance. These hiring goals are not rigid quotas. Only courts can impose a hiring quota (a specified percentage of new hires that must be female or minority), and they have done so where employers have been found guilty of substantial past discrimination practices.

Affirmative action may be remedial or preferential. *Remedial affirmative action* refers to efforts to ensure equality of access to all employment opportunities for those denied access or overlooked in the past. Targeted recruiting or training programs may be remedial. *Preferential affirmative action* refers to preferential treatment given to someone because of his or her race, gender, disability, or veteran status. An *affirmative action employer* is one that gives preferential treatment to minorities, women, the handicapped, and Vietnam veterans. The purpose of preferential treatment is to end an imbalance of minority representation in an organization's workforce. The differences between affirmative action and equal employment opportunity (EEO) are outlined in Table 4–2. Affirmative action does not require an employer to hire or promote an unqualified or less-qualified individual. It does mean that when there are comparably qualified applicants for a position, affirmative action considerations may be the determining factor.[51]

Employers practice affirmative action because they (1) are so ordered by a court, (2) are government contractors or subcontractors, or (3) do so voluntarily. AAPs must be approved by the Office of Federal Contract Compliance Programs (OFCCP) and must include the entire organization, not only one branch office or unit. Generally, valid plans must meet four conditions:[52]

1 Have the remedial purpose of ending statistical imbalances within certain job categories.

2 Exist only temporarily to achieve a balanced workforce (not for maintenance).

3 Not totally bar hiring and/or promotion opportunities for white males.

4 Not include layoffs or other actions that would harm current employees.

PROGRAM DEVELOPMENT

Development and administration of an affirmative action program usually requires an organization to perform specific acts.

First, an organization must give a copy of the EEO policy to all employees and applicants. The policy must specify a commitment to EEO and affirmative action. The organization must reaffirm these commitments in all ads and employee notices.

TABLE 4–2 MAJOR DIFFERENCES BETWEEN EEO AND AFFIRMATIVE ACTION

ENFORCEMENT AGENCY	BASIC REQUIREMENT	FACTORS INCLUDED	EMPLOYERS COVERED
EEOC	Prohibit discrimination in employment based on any factor(s) (EEO)	Minorities Women Handicapped Veterans Aged Religion	2 or more (EPA) 25 or more (Title VII) 15 or more (ADA and governments) 20 or more (ADEA)
OFCCP	Best good-faith efforts to achieve balance between local labor force and employers (Affirmative Action)	Minorities Women Handicapped Veterans	Court ordered Government contractor/ subcontractor Voluntary

SOURCE: Adapted from John A. Gray, "Preferential Affirmative Action in Employment," *Labor Law Journal* (January 1992): 23–30.

Second, an organization must give a specific, top-ranking company official the authority and responsibility for affirmative action program implementation. This manager or coordinator should have the authority to secure necessary information and demand assistance in developing and carrying out an AAP. This person must receive complete support from top management to ensure cooperation from lower-level employees, who may not place affirmative action problems at the top of their daily agenda.

Third, an organization must complete a *workforce analysis* of the organization. The first step is to count the employees in the organization by number and percentage of minorities and women in each major job classification. The next step is to determine whether the organization has **underuse of minorities or women** in any job classification. Underuse can be defined as having fewer minorities or women in a particular job category than would be found in the relevant labor market. The next step for the organization is to compare its own employment figures with those of the Metropolitan Statistical Area (MSA); these data are available from the local U.S. Department of Labor office. The workforce analysis should also identify any concentration of minorities or females in a particular job category. A *concentration* exists when there are more members of a particular minority group in a job category than would be expected when compared to the labor market figures. The final step in the workforce analysis is to determine which job categories have an underuse or concentration of minorities or women. If either underuse or concentration occurs, then management must take affirmative actions in order to end the discriminatory activities that caused the situation.

Fourth, an organization must establish goals and timetables. Once managers have determined where an organization may have discriminated in the past, they can develop specific goals and timetables to improve performance in those job categories. Managers then determine if any discrimination barriers may have limited participation of minorities and women in certain job categories and decide how to ensure that sufficient minority group members and women will be hired in the future.

Fifth, an organization must develop recruitment plans. Such plans may include advertising at colleges and universities that traditionally have large minority and female enrollments. Current minority and female employees are also usually good sources of information about reaching interested female and minority applicants.

SUPREME COURT DECISIONS

The federal employment laws passed by Congress and the affirmative action executive orders have been interpreted through landmark decisions by the U.S. Supreme Court. Those decisions, as summarized in Table 4–1, have had a significant impact on HR practices as employers strive to follow the intent of the decisions, which is likely to be applied in the lower courts, where the great majority of cases are decided. For many years, employers generally applied the Court's decisions in the *Griggs* (1971) and *Albemarle* (1975) cases in matters of employment selection. The need to validate tests, determine possible adverse impacts of selection criteria, and utilize job analysis to develop job-related position requirements was firmly established. The 1978 EEOC Selection Guidelines provided substantial additional guidance for employers striving to comply with federal selection laws.

REVERSE DISCRIMINATION

The term **reverse discrimination** generally refers to situations in which minorities and/or females are given preference over white males beyond affirmative action requirements. The Supreme Court has directly addressed this concept only in cases involving a seniority system and the layoff and recall of employees. In the *Stotts* (1984) decision, the Court upheld the use of seniority systems even when they adversely affect an employer's affirmative action program.

In other cases involving a white male claiming illegal discrimination under Title VII, several circuit courts have generally not given claimants the same rights as minorities and females. Instead, the white male plaintiff must show either a discriminatory intent or highly unusual circumstances. The general theory applied in reverse discrimination cases has been that while members of majority groups are protected, historically they as a group have shown no need for additional protection. Thus, white males must show evidence, apart from race and sex, that an employer discriminated against them.[53]

In a series of cases from 1986 to 1987, the Supreme Court upheld and extended the general principles of affirmative action as they had evolved since the 1960s. The Court upheld voluntary and court-ordered AAPs, including numerical standards to address the underutilization of minorities and women. Such plans could require employers to hire or promote women and minorities over more-qualified white males. In cases of layoff and recall, however, seniority system plans continued to be upheld.

Then the Court, whose membership was changing, in 1989 decided four landmark cases that appeared to signal a new direction. The theory of reverse discrimination was given new life, the burden of proving discrimination in disparate impact cases was shifted from the employer to the plaintiff, and bias as one factor in an employment decision was allowed if the same decision would have been reached without any bias. Considering that these cases were all decided in one year, only a few years after the 1986–1987 cases, and that they appeared to partly overturn some earlier landmark cases, it seemed clear that the Court was changing course.

Therefore, the U.S. Supreme Court has, at least as perceived by some civil rights advocates, handed down rulings that lessen the impact of the 1964 Civil Rights Act. These cases and their new direction caused Congress to enact the 1991 Civil Rights Act, which largely overturned the 1989 cases and reaffirmed the federal government's commitment to the 1964 Civil Rights Act.

In 1998, the Supreme Court handed down a decision which substantially changed affirmative action in the workplace. In *Piscataway Township Board of Education v. Taxman* the Court decided an employer may not consider race, even as part of an affirmative action plan, for purposes other than remedying past discrimination. The decision seriously questions the legality of strictly voluntary affirmative action plans. In the case Taxman, a teacher, had been laid off and a black teacher with equal seniority was hired (both started the same day) as part of the school district's cultural diversity plan. The Clinton Administration supported the school district. The Court noted the 1964 Civil Rights Act bars employment discrimination based on race or gender, and thus a nonremedial affirmative action plan cannot supercede the 1964 Act.[54] Therefore reverse discrimination, when not part of a remedial affirmative action plan according to the *Taxman* decision, is likely to be an unlawful practice.

SUMMARY POINTS

● Federal laws and court decisions have greatly affected the selection process. Employers must ensure that their hiring practices are nondiscriminatory and that each applicant is given an equal opportunity.

● In recent years, many more discrimination suits have been filed under the ADEA and ADA. Employers have increased their efforts to guard against age discrimination by making employment decisions on the basis of documented performance data and by offering early retirement programs only on a voluntary basis. In addition, reasonable accommodations must be made for employees with a disability who can successfully perform essential job functions.

● Affirmative action programs by employers seek to determine areas of underuse of women and minority group members. Employers establish goals and timetables to increase recruitment and selection of women and minorities in underutilized job categories.

● Sexual harassment has developed into a complex but critical HR issue. Both quid pro quo and hostile environment forms of harassment are clearly prohibited by the Civil Rights Act. Employers should publish and distribute policies.

● Employment arbitration agreements can provide a faster, less expensive means to settle employer–employee disputes. The 1991 Civil Rights Act encourages the use of arbitration or other methods of dispute resolution that are effective and provide relief to the overburdened court system.

● Reverse discrimination is likely to be unlawful if not part of remedial affirmative action plan.

CASE STUDY

FIRE DEPARTMENT PROMOTION

Everett Mann is the HR director of the fire department in a metropolitan area. Today he must make a decision that will greatly affect the morale of the entire department and quite possibly lead to a major lawsuit. Mann must recommend to the mayor one of two finalists for the position of captain of the Third District. The promotion decision has become highly controversial both within the fire department and at City Hall. Mann knows that his recommendation will be accepted by the mayor and implemented, but he must be ready to defend it to critics and, if necessary, in the courts.

The two finalists are both qualified and deserving of the position. Both graduated from local high schools the same year, and both come from good middle-class backgrounds. Both are 40 years old and have worked together in the Third District. Now for the differences:

Continued next page.

CASE STUDY—cont'd

Michael Wines Twenty-two years' experience with the fire department; excellent record. Joined after graduating from high school.

James Barlow Twelve years' experience with the fire department; excellent record. Joined ten years after graduating from high school.

Michael Wines White, male.

James Barlow Black, male. (Joined the fire department the first year blacks were eligible.)

Michael Wines Ranks first in seniority in the Third District and first among those who applied for the position.

James Burlow Ranks second in seniority in the Third District and second among those who applied for the position.

Michael Wines Ranked ninth among those who took the Civil Service Promotion Examination.

James Barlow Ranked eighty-sixth among those who took the Civil Service Promotion Examination.

Michael Wines Promoted to lieutenant three years ago.

James Barlow Promoted to lieutenant four years ago.

Michael Wines On affirmative action: "The Civil Rights Act passed 25 years ago, and a whole generation has come up since then. Where's affirmative action going to end? I say end it now. My kids shouldn't have to pay for it."

James Barlow On affirmative action: "It's not totally fair, but was it fair that I couldn't be a fireman back in the 1960s? If there had been black firemen then, there wouldn't have been a consent decree in the first place."

The consent decree Barlow refers to was issued by a federal court to settle a discrimination suit against the city for not hiring blacks as firefighters. In the past, the city had a whites-only hiring policy and, after it was dropped, promoted the first black fire department supervisor only eight years ago. The consent decree, agreed to by the city, black firefighters, the U.S. Department of Justice, and the NAACP, provides that the city will give half of each year's jobs and promotions to blacks. That was eight years ago, and since then the percentage of black firefighters has increased from 10 to 24 percent and the percentage of black lieutenants and captains from 0 to 28 percent. The consent decree provides that the long-term hiring and promotion goals should be equal to the percentage of black civilians in the county— 28 percent.

Mann, then, must recommend that either Wines, the top-ranked white candidate, or Barlow, the top-ranked black candidate, receive the promotion.

QUESTIONS

1 If you were Everett Mann, whom would you recommend? Why? What would be the legal basis of your defense?

2 Are AAPs with hiring quotas, such as the one in this case, still appropriate more than thirty years after the Civil Rights Act?

3 Does the consent decree's quota system, in fact, require reverse discrimination? Is that legal?

4 Are consent decree hiring goals the same as quotas?

SOURCE: Adapted from Barry Siegel, "Battling to Climb the Ladder," *The Los Angeles Times* (February 7, 1990): A1, A14, A15.

EXPERIENTIAL EXERCISES

1. WHAT DO *YOU* THINK IS SEXUAL HARASSMENT?

PURPOSE

The concept of sexual harassment is not one which everyone can agree on when specific examples are discussed. Open, honest examination of the following questions can help all parties better understand the views of others and realize this is not a simple issue.

T/F TASK

Answer each of the following questions according to *your personal beliefs*. The instructor will then provide the answers according to experts' interpretations of the law.

1. Unwanted sexual attention will usually stop if no one pays attention to it.

2. It isn't sexual harassment if I don't mean to impose on another worker.

3. Some people won't complain about another person's behavior even though it bothers her or him just so the other person won't get in trouble.

4. Most healthy people will usually tell you that you said or did something that bothers her or him.

Continued.

EXPERIENTIAL EXERCISES — cont'd

5. To avoid sexually harassing a woman worker in a traditionally male workplace, men should not haze her.

6. A sexual harasser may be told by a court to pay part of a settlement to the employee he or she harassed.

7. My employer has a policy which says that employees who sexually harass other employees can be fired.

8. A sexually harassed man does not have the same legal rights as a harassed woman.

9. Men who offend women co-workers usually know that their comments/attention is not welcome.

10. Men are more likely than women to be flattered by sexual comments and overtures.

11. Most cases of sexual harassment involve a supervisor requesting sexual favors in exchange for preferential treatment.

12. A person who has been harassed usually could have done something to prevent the incident.

13. Men in male-dominated workplaces usually have to change their behavior when a woman begins working there.

14. An employer is not liable for the harassment of one of its employees unless it knows about the incident.

15. A policy forbidding sexual harassment protects an employer from liability for incidents of which it is unaware.

2. ACTUAL EMPLOYMENT DISCRIMINATION CASES

PURPOSE

To learn about actual situations involving employment discrimination and discuss their implications.

TASK

The instructor will give you two 3×5 cards. On the first card, describe an episode of employment discrimination (race, gender, religion, age, national origin) that involved you or that you are aware of from another person who was involved in the incident. If you are not aware of any such incidents, leave the card blank; do not create a hypothetical situation. On the back of the card, write "serious" and explain why you considered the incident to be one of serious discrimination.

On the second card, describe an actual discrimination incident that *you* would not consider serious, but only a joke, a casual comment, or innocent decision or practice. If you are not aware of an innocent situation, leave the card blank. On the back of the card, write "innocent."

The instructor will collect the cards, randomly select one, and read the description of the incident. The class will then be asked to decide whether it was serious or innocent. The instructor will then read the back of the card and *may* ask the author to explain his or her evaluation.

KEY TERMS AND CONCEPTS

Affirmative action
Age Discrimination in Employment Act (ADEA)
Americans with Disabilities Act (ADA)
Bona fide occupational qualification (BFOQ)
Business necessity
Civil Rights Act (1964 and 1991)
Discrimination
Disparate impact
Disparate treatment
Equal Employment Opportunity Commission (EEOC)
Equal Pay Act (EPA)
Essential job functions
Immigration Reform and Control Act (IRCA)
Older Workers Benefit Protection Act (OWBPA)

Probable cause
Reasonable accommodation
Reasonable person (woman) standard
Religious discrimination
Reverse discrimination
Right to sue
Separation agreement
Sexual harassment
Substantially equal work
Title VII
Underuse of minorities or women
Vietnam-Era Veterans Readjustment Act
Vocational Rehabilitation Act

REVIEW QUESTIONS

1. How can an employer minimize its legal liability in the area of sexual harassment?

2. What should employers learn from the *Taxman* decision?

3. What is the approximate median annual wage paid to working women—expressed as a percentage of that paid to men? What was the percentage in 1963 when the EPA was passed? Has progress been made?

4. Define the two major types of sexual harassment—quid pro quo and hostile environment. Which occurs more often? Which is more serious?

5. What prompted Congress to pass the 1991 Civil Rights Act? What are its major provisions?

6. Why should employment arbitration agreements be used to resolve employer–employee disputes? Should employers be allowed to require employees to sign them?

7. List common employer policies that might cause unlawful religious discrimination.

8. How should employers be prepared to meet the provisions of the ADEA?

9. What is the primary purpose of the Immigration Reform and Control Act?

10. What are the employment provisions of the ADA?

DISCUSSION QUESTIONS

1. Federal laws designed to prohibit workplace discrimination have existed for over thirty years. Have they been effective? Will they ever be unnecessary?

2. What actions should an employer take to prevent sexual harassment in the workplace and comply with the law?

3. Do you agree with the EEOC's decision to include obese workers as a disabled group under the ADA? What about employers' concerns that obese workers increase their health care costs?

4. If you believed you were discriminated against, under what circumstances would you contact the local EEOC or let the situation ride? Why?

5. Is there a group of American workers that you believe suffers employment discrimination yet is not protected by federal law? Should a new law be passed to provide such protection?

6. Should an employer be able to legally make a reverse discrimination hiring decision to increase the cultural diversity of its workforce?

7. Is the Age Discrimination Act adequate to protect the employment rights of baby boomers?

ENDNOTES

Chapter 4

1. Suzanne M. Crampton, John W. Hodge, Jitendra M. Mishra, "The Equal Pay Act: The First Thirty Years," *Public Personnel Management* (September 22, 1997): 335–45.

2. Paul S. Greenlaw, "Proving Title VII the Discrimination," *Labor Law Journal* (July 1991): 407–17.

3. Richard B. Schmitt, "State Farm's $157 Million settlement Caps Discrimination Suit by 814 Women," *The Wall Street Journal* (April 28, 1993): A3.

4. Equal Employment Opportunity Commission: Richard T. Seymour Congressional Testimony (October 21, 1997).

5. William H. Freivogel, "High Court Narrows Bias Test: St. Louis Case Changes Twenty-Year-Old Precedent," *St. Louis Post-Dispatch* (June 26, 1993): A1.

6. Ibid.

7. Michael J. Lotilo, "The Civil Rights Act of 1990: Practical Considerations for Business," *HR News* (July 1990): 10–11.

8. *Phillips* v. *Martin Marietta,* 440 U.S. 542 (1971).

9. Public Law 95-955, 92 Stat. 276–77 (1978).

10. Donald J. Peterson and Douglas P. Massengill, "Sexual Harassment Cases Five Years After *Meritor Savings Bank v. Vinson,*" *Employee Relations Law Journal* (Winter 1992–1993): 489–515.

11. *Hall* v. *Guss Construction Co.,* 46 FEP Cases 573 (8th Cir. 1988).

12. Stacey J. Garvin, "Employer Liability for Sexual Harassment," *HR Magazine* (June 1991): 101–107.

13. Petersen and Massengill, "After *Meritor Savings Band* v. *Vinson.*"

14. *Ellison* v. *Brady,* 924 R. 2d 871 (9th Circuit 1991).

15. *Robinson* v. *Jacksonville,* 86-927-CIV-J-12 (MD Fla., January 18, 1991).

16. Jonathan A. Segal, "Proceed Carefully, Objectively to Investigate Sexual Harassment Claims," *HR Magazine* (October 1993): 91–94.

17. Ann Meyer, "Getting to the Heart of Sexual Harassment," *HR Magazine* (July 1992): 82–84.

18. Teresa Brady, "The Legal Issues Surrounding Religious Discrimination in the Workplace," *Labor Law Journal* (April 1993): 246–251.

19. 398 U.S. 300 (1970).

20. Brady, "Legal Issues."

21. *Hodgson* v. *Greyhound Lines, Inc.,* 499 F. 2d 859, 7th Circuit (1974).

22. Michael R. Carrell and Frank E. Kuzmits, "Amended ADEA's Effects on HR Strategies Remain Dubious," *Personnel Journal* 66, no. 5 (May 1987): 111–120.

23. Maria Maciejczyk Clapham and Mark D. Fulford, "Age Bias in Assessment Center Ratings," 9, *Journal of Managerial Issues* (September 22, 1997): 373(15).

24. *O'Connor* v. *Consolidated Coin Caterers Co.* (1996).

25. Herbert Field and William Holley, "The Relationship of Performance Appraisal System Characteristics to Verdicts in Selected Employment Discrimination Cases," *Academy of Management Journal* 25, no. 2 (March 1982): 392–406.

26. Nicholas J. Mathys, Helen La Van, and Frederick Schwerdtner, "Learning the Lessons of Age Discrimination Cases," *Personnel Journal* 63, no. 6 (June 1984): 30–32.

27. *Sullivan* v. *Boron Oil Co. et al.,* 86-00076 (3d Cir. 1987).

28. Public Law No. 101–433, 104, Stat. 978.

29. Philip M. Halpern, "Age Discrimination in Employment: Releases

Protect Employers Too!" *Labor Lawyer* (1992): 948–950.

30. James Ledvinka, *Federal Regulation of Personnel and Human Resource Management* (Boston: Kent, 1982), 62–63.

31. Ibid.

32. Lawrence Lorber and Craig Freger, "Employment Discrimination under the IRCA of 1986," *HRM Legal Reporter* (Winter 1987): 4–7.

33. *Americans with Disabilities Act of 1990,* Congressional Report 101–596 (July 12, 1990): 3–12.

34. Dianna L. Stone, Adrienne Colella, "A Model of Factors Affecting the Treatment of Disabled Individuals in Organizations" (Special Topic Forum on Diversity within and among Organizations), *Academy of Management Review* 21 (April 1, 1996): 352(50).

35. Charlene M. Soloman, "What the ADA Means to the Nondisabled," *Personnel Journal* (June 1992): 70–76.

36. Wayne E. Barlow and Edward Z. Hane, "A Practical Guide to the Americans with Disabilities Act," *Personnel Journal* (June 1992): 53–59.

37. Neville C. Tompkins, "Tools That Help Performance on the Job," *HR Magazine* (April 1993): 87–91.

38. Samuel J. Bresler and Roger D. Sommer, "Take Care in Administering Tests under ADA," *Personnel Journal* 69, no. 8 (August 1990): 81–83.

39. J. Freedley Hunsicker, Jr., "Ready or Not: The ADA, *Personnel Journal* 69, no. 8 (August 1990): 81–83.

40. Civil Rights Act of 1991, Public Law No. 102–166, 105 Stat. 1071 (1991).

41. Thomas J. Piskorski and Michael A. Warner, "The Civil Rights Act of 1991: Overview and Analysis," *The Labor Lawyer* (1992): 9–17.

42. W. Randall Kanmeyer, "Disparate Impact Cases under the Civil Rights Act of 1991," *Labor Law Journal* (October 1992): 639–650.

43. David A. Cathcart and Mark Snyderman, "The Civil Rights Act of 1991," *The Labor Lawyer* (1992): 849–922.

44. Civil Rights Act of 1991, Section 105(a).

45. Evan J. Spelfogel, "New Trends in the Arbitration of Employment Disputes," *Arbitration Journal* (March 1993): 6–15.

46. 111 S. Ct. 1647 (1991).

47. Robert A. Shearer, "The Impact of Employment Arbitration Agreements on Sex Discrimination Claims: The Trend toward Nonjudicial Resolution," *Employee Relations Law Journal* 18, no. 3 (Winter 1992–1993): 479–489.

48. Spelfogel, "New Trends," 6-15.

49. Todd H. Thomas, "Using Arbitration to Avoid Litigation," *Labor Law Journal* (January 1993): 3–13.

50. Ibid.

51. John A. Gray, "Preferential Affirmative Action in Employment," *Labor Law Journal* (January 1992): 23–30.

52. Ibid.

53. Sue Ann Unger, "Should Men Benefit from the Same Presumption of Unlawful Sex Discrimination That Helps Women Claimants under the Equal Pay Act?" *Labor Law Journal* (March 1993): 186–91.

54. *Piscataway Township Board of Education* v. *Taxman* (1998).

PART

II

ATTRACTING HUMAN RESOURCES

CHAPTER 5

JOB ANALYSIS

CHAPTER OUTLINE

CHAPTER OBJECTIVES

① To understand the basic elements of a job analysis program.

② To describe the end products of an analysis.

③ To identify the major methods of job analysis.

④ To discuss the future use and updating of analysis information.

⑤ To recognize the major elements of job descriptions.

⑥ To cite techniques useful in writing job descriptions.

⑦ To understand the uses of job descriptions.

⑧ To be aware of the pros and cons of generic job descriptions.

ARE JOB DESCRIPTIONS UNIQUELY NORTH AMERICAN?

According to David Hickson and Derek Pugh, North Americans put more weight on analyzing work, breaking it down, and identifying the essential and nonessential components, before repackaging it into something called a job description. This propensity for formalized documentation (their term) differs from most other cultures. If it is true, where might this tendency have originated?

It probably began during the era of scientific management. Industrial engineers emphasized packaging work that needed doing into jobs, including written instructions, manuals of procedures, work schedules, and legal contracts. The more precise they were, the better everyone liked them—particularly unions. Of course, British, French, and German companies also analyze and prepare written job responsibilities; however, Americans generate more. Latins and Asians, for all practical purposes, pay little attention to the procedure and product.

One explanation for the U.S. "love affair" with the detailed job description, Hickson and Pugh claim, is because older cultures have unifying customs where the United States doesn't, resulting in American workers needing more explicit guidance and control at work. Perhaps a century ago, when workers were not expected to think for themselves but left that job to their bosses, that assertion had a ring of truth. Today, more likely, companies are reluctant to risk a discrimination lawsuit for wage inequity or wrongful termination. A meaningful job description can be a useful tool in assessing the value and components of a given position and the credibility (or intent) of management.

Regardless of the reason, Houston Industries Incorporated, the parent to Houston Lighting & Power Company, has no expectation of its foreign subsidiaries creating detailed written job analysis procedures anytime soon. According to Jason Schweizer, a senior HR consultant at HII: "The home office leaves the definition of specific jobs to local customs and prevailing management practices."

Indeed, Latins and Asians do not use utilize them at all. "Our South American subsidiaries don't pay much attention to job descriptions for different reasons, but the most common are an absence of tradition and a genuine lack of positive outcome awareness," according to Schweizer. "We need to make a better case for job analysis."

In Japan, job duties are generally broader and more ambiguous than those found in the United States. It is assumed that those who are good enough to be hired can develop the necessary skills and versatility to perform a variety of positions, much like players on a volleyball team. There are no clearcut job specifications and duties.

SOURCE: Adapted from *Management Worldwide* by David J. Hickson and Derek S. Pugh (London: Penguin Books, 1995), 59–68. Interview: Jason Schweizer, Ph.D., Houston Industries, Houston, TX. James Bowman, "The Rising Sun in America," *Personnel Administrator* 31, no. 9 (September, 1986): 67.

No, everyone doesn't use job descriptions and no law anywhere requires them. However, courts in the United States and Canada have repeatedly ruled that human resource systems must be supported by job analysis, and any company without a systematic, adequately detailed job analysis is at legal risk.

What exactly is a **job analysis**? It is a *systematic investigation and identification of the tasks, duties, and responsibilities necessary in the performance of work*. What is identified are actual task requirements, including the level of decision making exercised, skills performed, essential mental effort, direct reports, key interactions with other people, and expected outcomes. Machines and equipment operated, reports completed, and specific financial or other responsibilities must be included in an analysis of a job. Also examined are the working conditions—the context—such as the levels of temperature, light, offensive fumes, and noise.

The process will produce an adequately detailed and demonstrably job-related job description or worker-trait specification. The end result matches job requirements and people, resulting in a good person–job fit, low turnover, and a high-performance organization.

While job analysis is prevalent in the United States and Canada, job analysis is not uniquely North American either. Many countries, especially in northern Europe, follow established procedures for analyzing a job and preparing descriptions and specifications. The increased importance of job analysis in North America reflects more than the notion of a love affair with formalized documentation.[1]

IMPORTANCE OF JOB ANALYSIS

Political, economic, and social forces in the North American environment, combined to stimulate the creation of legislation and regulations few employers can afford to ignore. In fact, there are so many laws that influence the employer–employee relationship most firms voluntarily employ job analysis as a means for complying with those regulations.

The federal government, in particular the judicial system, has encouraged the use of job analysis and job descriptions so that organizations have specific, objective methods of determining HR decisions. Fuzzy, vague, or obsolete job descriptions make it hard to document and defend a company's HR policies.[2]

The Uniform Guidelines on Employment Selection Procedures (1978) requires a systematic job analysis program to provide information necessary in the recruitment and selection process.[3] Although the term **job description** is not found in the guidelines, the courts clearly look hard at what is articulated in the job duties and qualifications. For example, a particular job description contains a requirement that a driver's license is necessary. However, the job doesn't really depend on the applicant needing to drive. The courts would interpret this requirement as discriminating against a person who is physically unable to drive and a violation of the Americans with Disabilities Act.

Additionally, some states have enacted discrimination laws that are more stringent than the federal laws, extending coverage to the smallest of companies. Laws prohibiting discrimination because of sexual orientation are spreading across states as well.

From a legal perspective, the job analysis process helps support why one applicant is qualified and another is not, why one employee is paid more than another, or why an employee is terminated for poor performance. In a litigious climate, not having a process in place that validates these types of decisions is a risk most organizations refuse to take.

The justification for job analysis is obvious on legal arguments alone, but there are other reasons, just as compelling, for investing the time and effort. A job analysis is not the end product; instead, it provides the input to obtain end products systematically. A job analysis determines both the minimum and the most desirable qualifications necessary to perform a job. Such information is crucial when creating a recruitment strategy.

From the perspective of both the HR manager and line managers, job analysis is essential in the effective performance of all the activities depicted in Figure 5–1. For example, depending on the information collected, the job analysis can directly affect workflow processes and lead to more efficient methods for improving the product or serving the customer.

In the selection process, line managers are as critical as the HR manager. It is the line manager who really understands the work environment. That knowledge, combined with a systematic job analysis, will paint the most accurate picture of what it takes to accomplish the task plus the qualifications necessary to excel. By using that information during an interview, either manager can evaluate the candidate's fit.

Once hired, the new employee will need to be introduced and oriented to the new job. While it may not say much about the company as a whole, the job analysis can paint an accurate picture of the job. It describes the key tasks that need to be performed, as well as answer the universal questions new employees ask: what, why, where, when, and how. It may also stimulate the new employee to seek out answers. Taking it another step, a thorough job analysis will reveal important skills and knowledge which can be used as a basis for future training and development programs needed within the existing workforce.

Performance appraisal—determining how well employees have performed their jobs in the past—as well as promotion decisions are easier and more valid when based on a system that has produced an adequately detailed, demonstrably job-related job description. In addition to satisfying many legal issues, it makes the difficult assignment of evaluating people much easier when it is based on job-related criteria.

The process also helps determine worth or value of jobs. Establishing job worth is a delicate process. Economic and psychic forces are at work. There are the wage market forces outside the company, and there are the forces pushing for internal pay equity. If either one of these systems is grossly out of line, inevitably it negatively impacts on morale and retention. Job analysis is the foundation for an equitable compensation system that balances internal and external wage determination.

FIGURE 5–1   JOB ANALYSIS

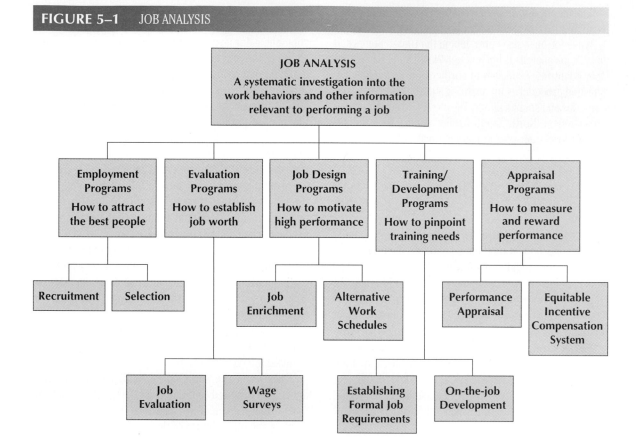

In today's accelerating competitive environment, there is intense pressure to leverage competitive advantage from an organization's human assets. Having a job analysis system with a proactive focus may be more important in fast and fluid industries than concentrating solely on the way things have been done, a reactive focus. A popular strategy under these conditions involves the identification of behavioral competencies needed to define and drive high performance.

A competency goes beyond baseline skills (for example, typing 60 words per minute). **Competencies** are the exhibited behaviors that distinguish superior from average performance. They are the observable behaviors, skills, and personal traits that contribute to enhanced organizational success.[4] The job analysis is the preferred method among HR professionals for identifying competencies.[5]

Job analyses affect most areas of employment and therefore indirectly affect employee performance and productivity. In an era of unprecedented change, where new industries and new work expectations are explod-

ing, opportunities abound, but only to those companies who can charge forward with the right skill sets. The next section reviews programs and procedures needed to discover the right skill sets.

PROGRAM IMPLEMENTATION

Larger firms typically have specially trained HR staff, called *job analysts,* whose primary function is to collect and process job information. Job analysts may conduct the review on their own or in consultation with job incumbents (that is, employees who perform the work) and their supervisors.

The creation and implementation of a job analysis program varies from firm to firm. Nonetheless, most organizations follow a standard format in conducting a job analysis that generally includes committee review, information collection, choosing a job analysis method, product completion, and updating.

COMMITTEE REVIEW

Experience indicates that the best way to initiate an effective program is through a representative committee. The committee must make critical decisions in choosing the appropriate job analysis technique and the important job elements to be evaluated.[6] Working with the HR department and the job analyst, the committee reviews information about each job within the organization and then makes difficult decisions in comparing job factors such as relative responsibility or working conditions.

Committee membership should represent all the major departments to be studied in the job analysis system. That is, if jobs to be analyzed are from six departments, then each department should have representatives on the committee who understand the department's jobs and procedures. The committee should include HR staff members who collect and evaluate job analysis information on a firsthand basis. All the people assigned to this committee should understand the standard operating procedures within the organization and be able to work well together.

The quality of the job analysis will depend on the accuracy of the information gathered by the job analyst, the consistency and objectivity of the job analyst's evaluation of the information, and the ability of the committee members to make critical decisions when necessary. In this first step, the committee should decide the end products of the job analysis: Will the information be used to write job descriptions? Will the analysis be the basis for a system of job evaluation? Will it be used to determine minimum specifications for jobs in the organization? There may be more than one end product of job analysis.

The committee needs the cooperation of both employees and supervisors during information gathering. One reason for having each department represented is to allow committee members to report back to their departments about how the job analysis will proceed and to reassure fellow employees that the program is accurate and fair.

INFORMATION COLLECTION

As noted previously, job analysis is a systematic investigation into the tasks, duties, and responsibilities of one or more jobs. Information involving job content is collected, analyzed, and interpreted. There is a variety of ways to collect this information, but the most common ones include the *Dictionary of Occupational Titles (DOT)*, site observation, interviews, and questionnaires.

Background research must always be among the first steps in a job analysis. Learning something about job analysis techniques employed by other organizations, the problems they encountered, and their results could save the analyst an enormous amount of time, not to mention money. One of the best sources of job-relevant documents is the *DOT.*

U.S. Department of Labor   The U.S. Department of Labor (DOL) has developed a standardized method for job analysis that uses four major categories.[7]

1 **Worker Function** What the worker does in relation to people, data, and things.

2 **Work Fields** The methods by which the worker carries out the technological, sociological, or scientific requirements of the job.

3 **Equipment Utilization** The tools, machines, and equipment that the worker must utilize.

4 **Products and Services** The materials worked on, products produced, knowledge assembled, or services rendered.

One advantage of the Department of Labor method is that it utilizes the U.S. Employment Service's ***Dictionary of Occupational Titles (DOT).*** The *DOT* classifies jobs by field of work, tasks performed, and the relationship of the job to data, people, and things. Each job title in the *DOT* system is given a six-digit code. The first digit indicates the general occupation, as shown in Table 5–1. The second and third digits provide a finer

TABLE 5–1	GENERAL OCCUPATION CODE OF THE *DOT*

DOT FIRST DIGIT	OCCUPATION
0,1	Professional, technical, managerial
2	Clerical, sales
3	Service
4	Farming, fishery, forestry
5	Processing
6	Machine trades
7	Bench work
8	Structural work
9	Miscellaneous

SOURCE: U.S. Department of Labor, *Dictionary of Occupational Titles,* 4th ed. (Washington, D.C.: U.S. Government Printing Office, 1977).

breakdown with respect to industry and function. The last three digits of the code are derived from the work-function code, as illustrated in Table 5–2. A tax accounting job, for example, is given the code 160.162; where 1 indicates professional; 60 indicates the accounting field; 1 indicates data coordinating; 6 indicates speaking or signaling (people contact); and 2 indicates operating or controlling.

Internal Methods   In addition to external research, job analysts have to use a variety of internal sources to obtain job information, including documents such as technical manuals, training materials, organization charts, and previous job analyses.

Job incumbents represent the most common internal source because they probably know best how to perform a job. Of course, what incumbents report may reflect how a task is done rather than the best way. Other subject matter experts (SMEs), such as supervisors, can provide additional perspectives. Whether one source or several sources are used, there are several methods of collecting this type of information.

Site Observations   Observing people at work permits the analyst to pinpoint precise details about the timing, frequency, and complexity of various tasks and duties; gather information about workflow, production efficiencies, work conditions, materials, and equipment used on the job; and assess the actual physical tasks that make up the job. When several employees perform the same job, the analyst would observe only the one or two who perform the job most effectively. Site observations minimize the likelihood of job incumbents' biasing the data by misleading, embellishing, or overlooking important aspects of the job. It can be accomplished by having a job analyst review film or tape of a job being performed, as well as by site observations.

One problem with site observation is that it can be used only on jobs that are easily discernible or measurable. An analyst would not learn much from observing an accountant who manipulates figures all day or a systems analyst who creates an accounts receivable program. Another problem is that some employees may resent being observed or may be uncomfortable, and thus may not perform in their normal manner. Such changes caused by observation are examples of the Hawthorne effect, first discovered in the early Hawthorne studies of human motivation.[8]

Work Sampling   One variation of site observation is work sampling, in which a job analyst randomly samples the content of a job instead of observing all of an employee's behavior. Work sampling is particularly useful for highly repetitive, mostly mental jobs, as are often found in clerical and service concerns. The job analyst must take care to ensure that what is observed is representative of the entire domain of tasks involved and not simply isolated or one-of-a-kind job behaviors.[9]

Interviews   A common alternative to observation is to interview either job incumbents or the job supervisor. Usually the analyst will ask similar questions regarding a particular job, thus giving the interview some structure. One-on-one sessions, meetings with a sample group of incumbents or supervisors, or discussions with SMEs are a few of the interview options available. This method of collecting job information is particularly valuable when the primary purpose of the job analysis is for designing performance appraisal

---

TABLE 5–2   WORK FUNCTION CODE OF THE *DOT*

DATA (FOURTH DIGIT)	PEOPLE (FIFTH DIGIT)	THINGS (SIXTH DIGIT)
0 Synthesizing	0 Mentoring	0 Setting up
1 Coordinating	1 Negotiating	1 Precision working
2 Analyzing	2 Instructing	2 Operating-controlling
3 Compiling	3 Supervising	3 Driving-operating
4 Computing	4 Diverting	4 Manipulating
5 Copying	5 Persuading	5 Tending
6 Comparing	6 Speaking-signaling	6 Feeding-offbearing
	7 Serving	7 Handling
	8 Taking Instructions—helping	

SOURCE: U.S. Department of Labor, *Dictionary of Occupational Titles,* 4th ed. (Washington, D.C.: U.S. Government Printing Office, 1977).

standards, identifying training needs, and determining job worth. Interviews, unlike observation, offer the opportunity to probe and clarify areas of confusion about complex portions of the job.

The primary disadvantage of the interview method is that the analyst must spend a great deal of time with each employee. Some employees may not respond to questions carefully because they feel on the spot during an interview. Also, comparison of information gathered from different interviews is difficult. Even structured interviews result in a lack of standardized information, particularly if more than one analyst is conducting interviews. Caution must be exercised to ensure that the final summary of interview findings adequately reflects day-to-day job duties. Nevertheless, the interview can capture the complexity and uniqueness of some jobs better than standardized methods when basic guidelines such as those in Figure 5–2 are followed.

Questionnaires Perhaps the most efficient method of gathering job information is to use a questionnaire. Use of the questionnaire is faster and easier than an interview, and it almost always results in standardized, specific information about the jobs in an organization. Figure 5–3 is a sample of a job analysis questionnaire that has been used by both service and manufacturing organizations.

Whenever information gathered through a questionnaire is insufficient, follow-up interviews can be scheduled with certain employees. Thus, the advantage of the interview—exploring specific topics the analyst is unclear about or gaining information not in the standardized questions—can often be achieved with a questionnaire.

Keep in mind that rigorous legal requirements apply when the purpose of the questionnaire is to gather data for selection decisions such as staffing or promotion. Figure 5–4 provides guidelines for compiling the job analysis questionnaire.

JOB ANALYSIS METHODS

After the initial review, the committee or analyst must decide whether information should be collected by a method developed specifically for use in that organization or by a standardized method of job analysis. Standardized methods have the advantage of being previously tested and utilized, which increases their general validity. But one significant drawback of standardized methods is that they are not designed for use by a specific organization. Each method, whether standardized or not, has various strengths and weaknesses. Thus, a combination of methods may be used in an attempt to realize the strength of each.[10]

FIGURE 5–2   JOB ANALYSIS INTERVIEW GUIDELINES.

1. *Consult the supervisor* of the job before deciding which persons to interview. If six or eight employees perform the same job, ask the supervisor which two perform the job best and thus would respond accurately.

2. *Make sure the interviewee understands the purpose* of the job analysis. Many times employees fear that the interview will be used against them, for example, to increase a job's expected output. Develop rapport with the employee as soon as possible, and express the stated goals of the job-analysis program before the interview begins. Often it will be necessary to emphasize that there will be no increase in workload or reduction in pay as a result of the job analysis.

3. *Structure the interview* as much as possible; decide what questions will be asked of all employees before any interviews begin. A structure assures standardization of format and comparability of information gathered. It also helps keep the interviews from deteriorating into bull sessions or complaint sessions.

4. *Complete a rough draft* of the interview and then go back to the employee to verify that your interpretation of the employee's statements is correct. After verification, contact the supervisor to check the accuracy of the information.

5. *And above all, prepare beforehand* by studying the job in order to ask the right questions.

FIGURE 5–3   A JOB ANALYSIS QUESTIONNAIRE

1. EMPLOYEE'S NAME: _____   Date Completed: _____

   Position Title: _____   Department: _____

   Title of Immediate Supervisor: _____

2. List the names and job titles of persons that you supervise and the percentage of time spent in supervision.

Name	Title	Hrs. Per Day/ Week Supervising
_____	_____	_____
_____	_____	_____

3. What is the lowest grade of grammar school, high school, or college that should have been completed by a person starting in your position?

   _____

4. What special type of training, skill, or experience should a person possess before starting in your position?

   _____

5. What training or experience have you received in your position, and how long would it take the average person to perform this work satisfactorily without close supervision?

   _____

   _____

6. What machines or equipment do you operate in your work and for what percentage of your time per day, week, or month?

Machine	%	Period
_____	_____	_____
_____	_____	_____

7. What do you consider to be the most important decisions that you alone make in the course of your work, and what percentage of your time is devoted to making such decisions?

   _____

   _____

8. What responsibility do you have for handling money, securities, inventory, or other valuables, and what is your estimate of their worth?

Responsibility	$ Worth per Week
_____	_____
_____	_____

FIGURE 5–3   A JOB ANALYSIS QUESTIONNAIRE—cont'd

9. What responsibility do you have in dealing with customers or other persons outside the company?

Person Contacted	Position	Nature of Contact	Frequency of Contact
_____	_____	_____	_____
_____	_____	_____	_____
_____	_____	_____	_____

10. What unusual aspects about your work and your work surroundings (working conditions, hours, out-of-town travel, physical requirements, etc.) should be included in a description of your job?

_____

_____

_____

11. What activities do you perform only at stated periods (weekly or monthly) or at irregular intervals?

Activity	Purpose	Interval
_____	_____	_____
_____	_____	_____
_____	_____	_____

12. List the specific duties you perform in the usual course of your daily work and approximately what percentage of your workday is spent in each activity. (Please try to use active verbs such as type, file, interview, etc. On the following page you will find a sample list of duties that may be helpful in preparing your answer to this question.)

_____

_____

_____

13. Discuss any considerations not covered in this questionnaire that you consider important in writing a description of your job.

_____

_____

_____

THANK YOU FOR FILLING OUT THE QUESTIONNAIRE

FIGURE 5–4   JOB ANALYSIS QUESTIONNAIRE GUIDELINES

1. *Review questionnaires used by organizations, professional groups, or university researchers.* Many items on other questionnaires may not have occurred to you. You can learn from other analysts' experiences.

2. *Keep the questionnaire short.* Most people do not like completing questionnaires. Thus, the longer the questionnaire, the less attention will be paid to the items during its completion.

3. *Have each questionnaire completed at work.* Questionnaires completed at home often are not done earnestly. Because job analysis is important to the organization, it should be done on company time so that employees have adequate time to provide the information and do not look upon completion as an extra burden they must bear.

4. *Categorize answers.* Structure questions so that responses can be categorized as much as possible. Whenever possible, design closed-end questions; have employees check one of several responses or indicate numbers or percentages for responses. Such a design avoids gathering information that is hard to compare or cannot be used by the analyst.

5. *Test the questionnaire with several trusted employees.* Many times the analyst will find that questions may be vague and misleading, or that important aspects of the jobs have been omitted.

6. *Include one open-ended question.* Always include at least one question that allows the employee to give any additional information that has not been elicited in the rest of the written questionnaire. In that way, the analyst may discover important information about particular qualities of some jobs.

The DOL   Although designed more for information collection than as a method of job analysis, the DOL method is used by smaller firms, where personnel specialists can quickly classify each job and use the *DOT* job descriptions; over 12,000 job titles are included. In other firms, specialists use the *DOT* as a starting point, modifying the standardized descriptions to fit their jobs.

The *DOT*'s greatest asset is its acceptance by federal employment agencies. According to the *Uniform Guidelines on Employee Selection Procedures*, "It is desirable to provide the user's job title(s) for the job(s) in question and the corresponding job title(s) and code(s) from the U.S. Employment Service's *Dictionary of Occupational Titles*."[11] It is also considered a fundamental mechanism by which different occupational job families are related to each other.[12]

Position Analysis Questionnaire (PAQ) Ernest J. McCormick's Position Analysis Questionnaire is another standardized method of job analysis that describes jobs in terms of worker activities. The PAQ contains job elements that fall into 27 job dimensions,

FIGURE 5–5   POSITION ANALYSIS QUESTIONNAIRE JOB CATEGORIES

Information input: How information to do the job is received.

Mental processes: The extent and type of decision making, planning, and organizing.

Work output: Tools, machines, and physical activity associated with the job.

Relationships: Associations with co-workers, supervisors, customers, and so on.

Work situation and job context: Working conditions, including hours and physical surrounding.

Other job characteristics: Work schedules, method of pay, responsibility, job demands, and the like.

SOURCE: Adapted from E. J. McCormick, P. R. Jeanneret, and R. C. Mecham, "A Study of Job Characteristics and Job Dimensions as Based on the Position Analysis Questionnaire (PA/Q)," *Journal of Applied Psychology* 56 (1972): 349.

which in turn fall into six major job categories (shown in Figure 5–5).[13]

The 27 dimensions are the job families most common to organizations. Examples of the job families include use of decision making, tools, interpersonal associations, and working conditions (see Figure 5–5). Use of the PAQ requires that job incumbents and job su-pervisors be familiar enough with the job being analyzed to check the questionnaire items that apply to the job in question. Figure 5–6 shows one page from the PAQ concerning information input.

The PAQ has the obvious advantage of being quantitative. Having a quantitative system is helpful because the job analyst can easily differentiate between jobs by

---

FIGURE 5–6   A PAGE FROM THE PAQ

1 INFORMATION INPUT

1.1 Sources of Job Information

Rate each of the following items in terms of the extent to which it is used by the worker as a source of information in performing the job.

NA	Does not apply
1	Nominal/very infrequent
2	Occasional
3	Moderate
4	Considerable
5	Very substantial

1.1.1 Visual Sources of Job Information

1. __4__ Written materials (books, reports, office notes, articles, job instructions, signs, etc.)

2. __4__ Quantitative materials (such as graphs, accounts, specifications, tables of numbers, etc.)

3. __1__ Pictorial materials (picturelike materials used as sources of information, for example, drawings, blueprints, diagrams, maps, tracings, photographic films, X-ray film, TV pictures, etc.)

4. __NA__ Patterns/related devices (templates, stencils, patterns, etc., used as sources of information when observed during use; do not include here materials described in item 3 above)

5. __1__ Visual displays (dials, gauges, signal lights, radarscopes, speedometers, clocks, etc.)

6. __1__ Measuring devices (rulers, calipers, tire pressure gauges, scales, thickness gauges, pipettes, thermometers, protractors, etc., used to obtain visual information about physical measurements; do not include here devices described in item 5 above)

7. __NA__ Mechanical devices (tools, equipment, machinery, and other mechanical devices which are sources of information when observed during use or operation)

8. __NA__ Materials in process (parts, materials, objects, etc., which are sources of information when being modified, worked on, or otherwise processed, such as bread dough being mixed, workpiece being turned in a lathe, fabric being cut, shoe being resoled, etc.)

9. __NA__ Materials not in process (parts, materials, objects, etc., not in the process of being changed or modified, which are sources of information when being inspected, handled, packaged, distributed, or selected, etc., such as items or materials in inventory, storage, or distribution channels, items being inspected, etc.)

10. __NA__ Features of nature (landscapes, fields, geological samples, vegetation, cloud formations, and other features of nature which are observed or inspected to provide information)

11. __NA__ Features of environment created by people (structures, buildings, dams, highways, bridges, docks, railroads, and other altered aspects of the indoor or outdoor environment which are observed or inspected to provide job information; do not consider equipment, etc., that an individual uses during work, which are covered by item 7).

SOURCE: Adapted from the *Position Analysis Questionnaire: Visual Sources of Job Information* (Logan, UT: PAQ Services, Inc.), Used with permission.

comparing the point totals of one job to those of another and, therefore, can assign jobs to different pay grades. The PAQ also has the advantage of being standardized: Each job is looked at with the same criteria in mind. The PAQ has demonstrated a high degree of reliability even when the level of cooperation of employees is quite low or when attempts are made to manipulate the information provided. Furthermore, the PAQ is supported by a considerable number of human resources information system (HRIS) software programs already on the market.[14]

The PAQ, in many respects, was clearly developed with the goal of making the job analysis process faster, cheaper, and for some functions, better. They are not suited for every personnel function, but it is well-suited for most, including the creation of job descriptions and worker specifications.[15] The PAQ is perhaps the most widely used standardized job analysis method available that produces accurate and valid results for certain types of jobs.[16]

Functional Job Analysis
A modification of the DOL method was developed by Sidney A. Fine, at one time a member of the employment services division of DOL. Fine named his standardized system **Functional Job Analysis (FJA).**[17] In FJA, the job analyst gathers background research, interviews job incumbents and supervisors, makes site observations, and then prepares detailed task statements with a standard questionnaire that specifies what a worker *does* and what gets *done* on a job. These statements are reviewed and verified by subject-matter experts. Once approved, the job analyst uses the FJA questionnaire to rate each job.

In addition to tasks statements, worker functions are identified. Like the *DOT*, the function level describes differing levels of complexity in three areas of task performance: data, people, and things. For each task within a job, a measure of complexity of data, people, and things is taken. For example, a scale for measuring worker instructions is depicted in Figure 5–7.

INFORMATION REVIEW

Regardless of the method selected to collect information, the next step is to assemble and review that information with the employees and the job analysis committee. After writing a first draft of the standardized information collected, the analyst needs to make sure that the data are factually correct and complete and that a clear picture of the job is being presented. After checking with the employees and supervisors involved in gathering information, the analyst must take these first drafts to the job analysis committee, which reviews each analysis to make sure that it is both objective and easily comparable with analyses of other jobs. The establishment of standardized categories of information about the jobs—such as work environment, decision making required, and supervision—makes comparisons among jobs easier. The more effort put into these first drafts, the easier it will be to determine the desired end products.

PRODUCT COMPLETION

The fourth step involves the completion of whatever end products are desired by management. For example, job analysis data may be used to write job descriptions or job specifications, to conduct a job evaluation for wage and salary purposes, to determine training and development needs, and to create tests for employee selection.

FUTURE USE AND UPDATING

The last step in the job analysis procedure will be to determine how the information will be stored for future use. The HR department should have access to this information in case additional end products are desired. Also, the job analysis committee will need to determine how to update the information periodically because information gathered in the job analysis process has a tendency to become obsolete over time. Changes will occur as supervisors train employees to accept more responsibility, as additional tasks are developed, or as organizational changes are made. Updating the information in the job analysis program maintains its accuracy and guarantees its usefulness in the future.

JOB ANALYSIS PROBLEMS

Any job analysis will run into certain problems, regardless of the size of the organization, the status of employee relations, or the abilities of those performing the analysis. Particularly in an era of continuous delayering and downsizing, one of the most common problems is employee fear. Often employees see a job analysis as a threat to their current jobs or pay levels or both. In the past, job analysis was used as a means of expanding jobs while reducing the total number of employees. Job analysis has also been used to increase production rates and, therefore, decrease employees' pay. Organizations must overcome employees' fears so that employees and their supervisors will give accurate information.

One of the most successful methods of reducing employee fear is to involve employees or their

FIGURE 5–7   THE WORKER INSTRUCTIONS SCALE OF THE FJA

Worker Instructions Scales: Levels of Responsibility

The worker instructions scale defines *responsibility* in terms of the mix of specifications (that which is prescribed) and judgment (that which is specifically left to discretion) assigned to the worker. A worker's responsibilities may encompass several levels, depending on the activity(ies) involved.

Level 1

Inputs, outputs, tools, equipment, and procedures are all specified. Almost everything the worker needs to know is contained in the assignment. The worker is to produce a specified amount of work or a standard number of units per day.

Level 2

Inputs, outputs, tools, and equipment are all specified, but the worker has some leeway in the procedures and methods used to get the job done. Almost all the information needed is provided in the daily assignment. Production is measured on a daily or weekly basis.

Level 3

Inputs and outputs are specified, but the worker has considerable freedom in procedures and timing, including the use of tools and equipment. The worker may have to refer to several standard sources for information (handbooks, catalogs, wall charts). Time to complete a particular product or service is specified, but this varies up to several hours.

Level 4

Output (product or service) is specified in the assignment, which may be in the form of a memorandum or of a schematic (sketch or blueprint). The worker must work out ways of getting the job done, including selection and use of tools and equipment, sequence of operations (tasks), and acquisition of important information (handbooks, etc.). The worker may

either do work or set up standard and procedures for others.

Level 5

Same as Level 4, but in addition the worker is expected to know and employ theory—the whys and wherefores of the various options available for dealing with a problem—and can independently select from among them. Reading in the professional and/or trade literature may be required to gain this understanding.

Level 6

Various possible outputs are described that can meet stated technical or administrative needs. The worker must investigate the various possible outputs and evaluate them in regard to performance characteristics and input demands. This usually requires creative use of theory well beyond referring to standard sources. There is no specification of inputs, methods, sequences, sources, or the like.

Level 7

There is some question about what the need or problem really is or what directions should be pursued in dealing with it. In order to define it, to control and explore the behavior of the variables, and to formulate possible outputs and their performance characteristics, the worker must consult largely unspecified sources of information and device investigations, surveys, or data-analysis studies.

Level 8

Information or direction comes to the worker in terms of needs (tactical, organizational, strategic, financial). The worker must call for staff reports and recommendations concerning methods of dealing with them. The worker coordinates organizational and technical data in order to make decisions and determinations regarding courses of action (outputs) for major sections (divisions, groups) of the organization.

SOURCE: Adapted from the scale developed by Sidney A. Fine, Ph.D., Advanced Research Resources Organization, Washington, D.C. Used by permission.

representatives in as many aspects of the job analysis procedure as possible. Before the procedure begins, employees should be told why it has to be instituted, who will initiate it, how the employees will be affected, and why their input is critical. Management may want to make a written commitment that the organization will not terminate any employee, lower the pay of any employee, or decrease the total number of jobs because of the results of the job analysis. Such measures may enable the job analysts to obtain complete information from employees. It is unfortunate for job analysts that in past years job analysis was sometimes used improperly.

A second problem of job analysis is the need to update the information gathered. While any job analysis is being completed, jobs will be changing as the organization changes. As jobs expand, as work is reassigned within a department, and as supervisors develop, the description of their jobs will necessarily have to change. The problem, then, becomes how to keep the information current. One method is the annual review of the job analysis information, in which the HR department sends the information to supervisors, asking them to note any changes that have occurred during the past year. A second method is to have managers submit proposed changes in jobs or reclassifications. This method is especially important when the reclassification may result in a change in pay.

Both methods have their problems. The annual review is quite time consuming because every job must be reanalyzed each year. Also, when jobs are reviewed annually, employees sometimes expect that their jobs will always be reclassified—with accompanying pay increases. Another problem with an annual review is that whenever the content of a job is substantially increased only a week or two after the initial job analysis, employees in that job may be underpaid for the next 40 or 50 weeks. Finally, the annual review looks at all jobs, even those that have not changed. Possibly 90 percent of the jobs do not need to be reexamined; only the 10 percent that have changed during the year need to be reviewed.

Constant updating by managers implies that only those jobs that need to be changed will be looked at. Also, this method produces more current data and ensures that employees will not have to wait for months to have their jobs reclassified, with a possible change in salary or other benefits. A primary disadvantage of this method is that management may forget to keep up with changes. Thus, employees become frustrated, feel underpaid, or do not realize what must be done to have their jobs reclassified.

The two methods may be combined in some form, such as having biennial performance reviews with constant updates by managers who want to reclassify jobs. Yet combining the two methods contains the advantages as well as the disadvantages of the two methods separately, and therefore combinations are less common than using one method or the other.

Another problem with job analysis occurs when a job is held by only one or two employees. In such a case, the analysis is often of the person's performance and not of the job itself. The analyst must look at what the job should entail and not at how well or how poorly one employee is performing the job.

A problem commonly occurs when job analyses form the basis for job descriptions handed out to new employees. Employees often feel that the description is a contract describing what they should and should not do on the job. When asked occasionally to do extra work or an unusual task, employees may respond, "It's not in my description"—and by that reasoning resist performing the task. Management can change job descriptions by assigning added tasks to employees, but if a task is done rarely or is never to be repeated, changing the job description for a single situation is unnecessary. Many organizations use **elastic clauses** in job descriptions, such as "performs other duties as assigned." An elastic clause allows supervisors to assign employees duties different from those normally performed without changing the job descriptions.

JOB DESCRIPTIONS

The most common end product of a job analysis is a written **job description.** One of the oldest HR tools, job descriptions have attracted renewed interest in recent years, primarily because of governmental regulatory guidelines. Job descriptions have no exact format and are often used for many different purposes.

USES OF JOB DESCRIPTIONS

Over 100 major uses of job descriptions in the HR function have been identified. Most employers, however, typically use them for five or six functions.[18] Job descriptions serve a variety of purposes for HR professionals. Several employment and compensation activities depend on job information normally included in the organization's job descriptions. In addition, the basic job information needed for such legal requirements as equal employment opportunity, affirmative action, overtime qualifications, and employee safety can be included in job descriptions. Collective bargaining agreements may also specify which duties are to be performed by each union employee covered by the agreement.

Recruitment   Job descriptions may be used to develop recruitment advertisements and to provide applicants with additional information about the job openings.

Interviewing
Job descriptions are often used when they include job specifications as a means of providing the interviewer with concise, accurate information about the job. The interviewer can then better match the applicant to the job opening and make sure that the minimum qualifications of the job are met by the applicant.

Orientation
New employees may be given job descriptions to spell out job requirements and areas to be evaluated.

Training
Organizations use job descriptions to specify both the training an employee requires for effective performance and the type of training current employees may need to become promotable.

Job Evaluation
Job descriptions often specify comparable factors in the process of **job evaluation** so that a job evaluator can compare various jobs and make pay decisions. HR practices and federal laws require that such comparisons be based on job-required skill, effort, responsibility, and working conditions. The required documentation of such information is usually found in job descriptions. Thus, there is an inevitable link between pay and job descriptions. That link sometimes tempts managers to use fancy language and elaborate generalities to describe job duties in order to justify higher pay levels. HR professionals are then forced to act as police officers to guard against such problems. The growth of computerized personnel systems has greatly assisted the personnel manager in maintaining descriptions and evaluations that accurately match the job content within an organization.[19]

Wage Compensation Survey
Job descriptions give the HR administrator the opportunity to estimate whether the wages being paid for a job are equitable in comparison with wages for similar jobs in other organizations in the community or throughout the country. Thus, job descriptions provide information for both internal comparisons (through job evaluation) and external comparisons (through survey analysis).

Performance Appraisal
Job descriptions may specify the basis on which an employee will be judged during performance appraisal. If employees are told which areas and duties they are responsible for performing, they are forewarned about what will eventually be evaluated.

Outplacement
Job descriptions may also play an important role in the career-change process. Organizations that lay off workers temporarily or downsize permanently often want to assist affected employees. The HR staff can use an employee's job description to help prepare a resume that gives detailed information. The HR staff may also refer to the description when providing reference information to prospective employers.[20]

ELEMENTS OF JOB DESCRIPTIONS

Although there is no universal format for job descriptions, most have certain common elements. A list of job duties is one element found in all job descriptions. Most will contain some identification and a brief job summary. They often contain job specifications, though it is also common practice to list specifications on separate forms.

Job Identification
The first part of a job description, the identification section, usually includes the title of the job, the location of the job (for example, plant, department, or division), the title of the immediate supervisor, the job status (exempt or nonexempt), and the pay grade or pay range. This information is needed for general administrative and record-keeping functions. Job titles can be used to identify a particular job within an organization, but generally they cannot legally be used to compare jobs for pay purposes. The content of the job is described in the duties and responsibilities section. The content must be evaluated for pay considerations because job titles can be misleading; an administrative assistant in one organization may be quite different from one in another organization. A statement of location is required by the 1978 *Uniform Guidelines* when the job description is used to provide evidence of legality in an organization's selection procedures.[21]

Other useful elements sometimes included in the identification section are the name of the job analyst who approved the description, the name of the employee who provided the basic information, the date the description was approved, and, if applicable, the standard code number published in the *DOT,* the equal employment and affirmative action (EEO-1/AAP) reporting category, and the point total in a point system of job evaluation.

Figure 5–8 is a sample job description. That description of a chief quality control engineer contains a particularly good example of job identification. The identification includes not only the usual information—such as job title, department, and title of the immediate supervisor—but also the job code or the *DOT* job number. The exempt status of the job indicates a salaried position that does not pay overtime wages. The inclusion of a date on which the description was approved and the name of the person who approved it eliminates future questions or conflicts

FIGURE 5–8   A SAMPLE JOB DESCRIPTION

Chief Quality Control Engineer		*156.132*	
Job Title		Job Code	

Manager of Quality Control		*Quality Control*	
Title of Immediate Supervisor		Department	

7	*Louisville*	*Exempt*	*August 12, 1990*
Bldg.	Plant	Status	Date

Robert Myers	*Kathy Johnson*	*16*	*751*	*1/2*
Approved by	written by	Grade	Points	EEO/AAP

SUMMARY

Supervises six salaried quality control personnel; plans, organizes, coordinates, and administers manufacturing activities.

JOB DUTIES

1. Establishes and maintains supplier contacts to assist in solving quality problems by evaluating contacts' quality capabilities, facilities, and quality systems. (10%)

2. Establishes and reviews goals, budgets, and work plans in the area of quality, cost schedule attainment, and operator/equipment utilization. (10%)

3. Reviews product and process designs, identifying problems which might result in customer dissatisfaction or failure to meet established goals or allocated costs. (20%)

4. Specifies quality control methods and processes to support quality planning. Provides cost estimates and procures necessary tools and equipment to support overall project schedule. (10%)

5. Supplies input to manufacturing engineers on producibility and other quality matters. (20%)

6. Provides feedback on quality levels and costs during test runs and during production to measure system effectiveness. (10%)

7. Supervises six to eight salaried personnel assigned to the quality control engineering area. Trains new personnel in proper procedures and policy. Completes performance appraisals of subordinates. (20%)

---

concerning accuracy or completeness. A pay grade is given so that employees or applicants can estimate the pay range for a job and its level within the organization. The 751 points refers to evaluation points; if the point total is close to the next highest pay grade, future reclassifications may move it up to the next highest pay grade.

Job Summary

A job summary is a one- to three-line description of the essence of the job. Job summaries usually start with a verb, such as *supervises, coordinates,* or *directs.* Job summaries should emphasize either the most common function, the primary output, or the objective of the job.

Job Duties and Responsibilities

Job duties and responsibilities are the heart of the job description.

There are two common formats for the duties section. One is a paragraph describing the job. The problem with this format is that a reader may find it difficult to recognize immediately which functions are important. A more popular format is grouping the tasks of a job and listing them separately, as for example in Figure 5–8. The tasks might be grouped by functional categories, such as "supervision given," "organization of work," "physical demands," and "financial accountability." As with job summaries, each duty or responsibility should begin with a verb, such as *supervises* or *performs.* The intention of the duties section is to give the reader a complete and concise account of what is being performed on the job—though it is not intended to be a training instrument to teach a novice how to perform the job. The estimated time spent on each duty often appears in parentheses after each duty is explained.

Job Specifications **Job specifications,** or minimum qualifications, state the qualifications job applicants must possess to be considered for the job. These qualifications are often grouped into three categories: **skills, knowledge,** and **ability (SKAs).** *Skills* include observable capabilities performed on the job. *Knowledge* constitutes the body of information in a particular subject area that is required by a new employee to perform the job satisfactorily. *Ability* refers to any mental or physical activities required of a new employee. For example, a section supervisor might be required to know the safety regulations that affect the plant, to have the skill to operate a quality-control laser machine, and to have the ability to write daily work assignments. SKAs are most useful in personnel decision-making situations, such as selection, training, and performance evaluation.[22]

Job specifications may also include required education, experience, and training, as well as any specific certification required for the job. As a job specification, *effort* might encompass specific physical tasks the jobholder must be able to perform or some necessary experience in a supervisory position. *Responsibility* might encompass reporting responsibility, supervisory responsibility for inventory maintenance, or financial responsibility such as making up shortages in a cash drawer. Job specifications might also include working conditions such as the hours the employee must be available, as well as other unusual conditions such as high levels of noise or fumes.

Figure 5–9, a description of a word processing secretary's job, contains job specifications that would allow an interviewer to decide easily and objectively if an applicant meets the qualifications. Although a specification may not always be quantitative in nature, it should be whenever possible. The first three specifications for the job are examples of measurable or **verifiable qualifications;** the interviewer can verify that a person has a high school degree or college experience and can measure an applicant's typing and filing ability with

---

FIGURE 5–9   A SAMPLE JOB DESCRIPTION

Job Title: *Word Processing Secretary*
Department: *Branch Administration*
Position of Immediate Supervisor: *Branch Administrative Manager*

I. GENERAL SUMMARY OF RESPONSIBILITIES:
   Types, edits, and distributes various correspondence to clients and internal staff. Transmits and proofs various essential status reports for day-to-day operations.

II. SPECIFIC JOB RESPONSIBILITIES:
   Types daily correspondence and sales orders from nine representatives from machine dictation and hard copy. (40%)

   Proofreads and prepares final copies for distribution. (10%)

   Receives handwritten copies and maintains priority file of reports and correspondence. (5%)

   Types special projects such as proposals, quotations, systems, analyses, and office surveys for marketing department. (20%)

   Transmits computer programs via magnetic card typewriter and other telecommunication equipment. (10%)

   Logs and maintains records of completed staff and client work. (4%)

   Receives and assigns priority to special client and staff requests and special projects. (5%)

   Serves as backup for receptionist. (5%)

   Performs other duties as assigned. (1%)

III. JOB SPECIFICATION:
   High school diploma required, with one or two years of college preferred.

   Training or one year's experience on magnetic card typewriter. Type 50 wpm.

   Able to file 10 documents per minute without error.

   Must be able to consistently produce accurate, professional-quality documents.

   Ability to work well with people in developing proposals is essential.

standardized tests. The fourth and fifth specifications are important but are more vague and subjective—and thus subject to interviewer bias. Notice that the sample job description shown in Figure 5–8 does not contain a section on job specifications.

GENERIC JOB DESCRIPTIONS

Not interested in conducting a detailed job analysis? There are several software and hardware products currently on the market which provide generic descriptions to assist companies in creating job descriptions. Of course, the idea is not new, but merely a more elaborate

version of the *Dictionary of Occupational Titles* mentioned previously. The canned descriptions usually require generalizing the title and descriptions to a specific situation.

There are merits to this service, as the accompanying *HR in the News* suggests, but the best argument in its favor seems to be as a starting point for conducting a detailed job analysis. Perhaps the generic version might serve as a vehicle for communicating employee expectations, roles, and accountabilities. However, if the service were used to produce the *end* product rather than serve as a starting point, there would probably be legitimate concerns regarding validity.

HR IN THE NEWS

POINT–COUNTERPOINT: GENERIC OR NONGENERIC JOB DESCRIPTIONS

Along with practically everything else available on the Internet is an online service where a person can go, search a job bank for potential templates of job descriptions (JD), and go through a customization process; it will then send you an ADA-compliant JD. To quote from one Web page:

> Just choose from one of the thousands of built-in job descriptions, answer some relevant questions, and let One Stop Job Descriptions (not their real name) write sections on supervisory responsibilities, qualifications, physical demands, and work environment. You'll get results in about five minutes.

Charlie Jones, an adjunct professor at Boston University says:

> I believe the generic approach provides a better management tool than the specific approach, because it's more flexible and easy to maintain. The descriptions usually require some tailoring to fit the individual organization, but such commercial products are a starting point and a viable, cost-effective alternative.

> With a generic JD, one gains flexibility because the description addresses expectations and accountabilities and doesn't get into the details of how a task should be performed. As more and more companies try to improve their products, generic descriptions keep employees focused on results rather than tasks. They are also easier to maintain because they don't have to be modified for minor changes in tasks.

Glenn Nosworthy, an industrial psychologist with the Royal Canadian Mounted Police says:

> A job description not based on a systematic job analysis cannot provide all the necessary information on the context and specifics of the job. On many occasions, we have gathered groups of job incumbents with identical job titles and descriptions only to find the nature of their work varied substantially. When this occurs, job descriptions often don't reflect the actual job requirements.

> There also are important legal considerations. Courts in North America have repeatedly ruled that job analysis is expected and that it must be valid. Consequently, using generic JD in lieu of job analysis may place an organization in peril with the courts.

> You cannot get something for nothing. There are no quick fixes in HR management. Taking a job description from a website, cutting and pasting it onto your organization, is highly unlikely to produce a legally defensible human resource system.

SOURCE: Adapted from Brenda Sunoo, "Answerline," *Personnel Journal,* 76, no. 2 (February, 1996): 102.

Summary Points

● A sound job analysis program produces many benefits for an organization. Information critical to employment and compensation is collected on a systematic basis. Job descriptions, job specifications, and job evaluations can easily be produced from the job analysis data. Thus, critical HR practices such as hiring, wage determination, and administrative record keeping are assisted by job analysis.

● Information collection should always begin by conducting background research. One excellent source is the Department of Labor (DOL), especially the *Dictionary of Occupational Titles (DOT)*. Internal sources can be either standardized or unstructured and include previous job analyses, interviews with job incumbents and job supervisors, site observations by the analyst, and questionnaires.

● There is a variety of standardized job analysis methods, with each having certain advantages depending on the purpose, cost, and time. For smaller companies, the *DOT* is often the basis for constructing job descriptions. The most popular method is the PAQ.

● The methods of information collection are two: standardized and internal. Internal written questionnaires are often faster and easier and can be tailored to the needs of the organization. Interviews with employees and supervisors can also be used to ensure complete and accurate information.

● Job analysis is necessary to comply with the primary employment provisions of the ADA. It requires all selection criteria that tend to screen out the disabled to be job related and consistent with business necessity. The process itself helps to determine essential functions and whether an individual can carry out the essential functions with or without reasonable accommodation.

● The federal government and the courts have increased the pressure on HR managers to utilize job analysis as a means of producing job-related job descriptions, hiring criteria, and compensation systems.

● Job descriptions generally should contain a complete identification of the job and its location within the organization. The section on duties and responsibilities should group all tasks into major functional categories, and each entry should begin with verbs. Job specifications should include all SKAs needed to perform the job, as well as other minimum qualifications.

Case Study

Good Intentions Aren't Enough

Melanie's company downsized four times in three years, and each time management made an effort to find a job for her. She had always been a dependable and productive employee, and her bosses did not want to lose her. In their efforts to keep Melanie, she was assigned three different jobs in two different workgroups over the three-year span. Ted, Melanie's current boss, thought Melanie was particularly resourceful and smart. She was the kind of employee the company had to retain once the difficult times were over.

Ted and the other managers also thought Melanie knew how lucky she was that she still had her job. Ted and his colleagues were wrong. As far as Melanie was concerned, the last three years had been a nightmare.

Every time she began to catch on to a new job, the company announced more restructuring, and she ended up with another assignment. She desperately wanted to do a good job, but she did not completely understand what she was supposed to do until weeks into each new assignment. There were occasional pats on the back encouraging her to hang in there, but there was also the increasing pressure to do more.

Each day, Melanie reported to a work space designed for ten people and now home to just three. Abandoned files and photos of bygone office parties haunted her. Making matters worse, her own workload soared, partly as a result of the workgroup's shrinking to three from sixteen.

Melanie could not help but feel at least a pang of "survivor's guilt" whenever she moved into a new job once held by a dismissed co-worker. Despite her success in still holding on to a job, she felt distrustful toward management, overworked, and more insecure than ever. In addition, she sensed resentment from other survivors and co-workers who wanted to know what skills and knowledge she was expected to bring to the job. A question kept popping up in her mind: "Why was I any better than the person I replaced?"

Melanie was afraid to tell Ted how she felt. She could not handle the stress of constantly figuring out what was expected of her. Admitting her faults to Ted could only jeopardize her already precarious future. Talking to Ted about the confusing nature of her work, she reasoned, would be the straw that would break the camel's back and result in her own organizational demise. It would be better to hide these frustrations until things improved. So she plodded to work each day, did what she could, and asked no questions.

Melanie attempted to vent her frustrations by combing through the help-wanted ads in the local paper. And while the number of possibilities was smaller than in years past, eventually

CASE STUDY—cont'd

Melanie's search paid off. She interviewed for another job and was made an offer at less pay, which she quickly accepted.

Melanie's boss was flabbergasted. Ted had no idea she was any more unhappy about her job than any of the other survivors. And for her to leave abruptly after he had bent over backward to make sure she wasn't laid off was simply ingratitude. Ted thought that what he and the other managers had done to protect Melanie from a layoff was a marvelous act of allegiance to employees.

QUESTIONS

1. Did Ted and the other managers do Melanie any favors by protecting her from a layoff?

2. What did Melanie suffer from? What should Ted and the other managers have done to encourage Melanie to communicate her frustrations?

3. How might job analysis have prevented Melanie's defection?

4. In terms of job analysis, what steps should Ted have taken to rescue the survivors, such as Melanie, following the restructuring?

EXPERIENTIAL EXERCISES

1. WRITING JOB DESCRIPTIONS

PURPOSE

To conduct a brief job analysis and to create a job description.

PROCEDURE

Break the class into small groups of four or five each. Have the group select a member's job, preferably a student who is currently employed or has recently been employed.

TASK

Using the information in this chapter, group members will perform a perfunctory job analysis with the student concerning his or her job. Once the job analysis has been performed, write a job description for that job. Be sure that your job description conforms to the characteristics of good job descriptions discussed in this chapter. Once this has been completed, visit the Website *http://www.jobdescription.com* Locate a description of the job in question. How does it compare with the group's description? Which of the two descriptions is more accurate? Be prepared to share with the class the pros and cons of using "canned" job descriptions.

2. JOB ANALYSIS FOR RECRUITING

The job analysis is the foundation for a number of important activities. One of the most important is recruiting. Information gathered about a job can provide a solid foundation regarding specific openings. When designed with recruiting in mind, the job description can serve as a road map detailing who the candidate is and where you can look for the best people. This exercise is designed to give students a chance to search for the unique, detailed information necessary for attracting the best people in today's recruitment marketplace.

Form teams of four or more. Contact an HR representative in a nearby company and request an interview with any person whose position is being advertised. It is important to talk with a person who is most familiar with the open position—not necessarily the hiring HR officer, or even the manager, because they may be too far removed from the position to have an accurate idea of what this person will be doing from day to day.

The first question addresses the position title, duties, and description of an average workweek. This information is useful but, for recruitment purposes, hardly enough to sell an applicant. Request information on the salary range, including all bonuses, perks, and company benefits. Be prepared for refusals because compensation is a sensitive issue (but there is no harm in asking).

Second, request recruiting information, including the background of the ideal candidate, what level of education is necessary, how much experience is needed, what kind of person best fits the job, and where the best applicant might be found (industries, companies, departments within those companies, big or small businesses, and so on).

Third, what are the long-term opportunities for the applicant? Why would someone who is happily and securely employed leave his or her job and come to work here? Are there any negative aspects of the job? What happened to the previous people holding this position? Depending on the answers, this may be the most important recruiting information for persuading an applicant to work here.

EXPERIENTIAL EXERCISES—cont'd

Finally, ask the person what types of questions (with answers that require knowledge, skill, or experience regarding the open position) may be asked of the applicant fairly early in the selection process. In technical fields, this is a critical stage because it will help the HR staff decrease the interview-to-hire ratio and the time spent with unqualified applicants.

After gathering all of this information, the team will present its findings to the class. The team should be prepared for questions from the instructor and other students.

KEY TERMS AND CONCEPTS

Competencies
Critical incident technique (CIT)
Dictionary of Occupational Titles (DOT)
Elastic clauses
Functional job analysis (FJA)
Job analysis

Job description
Job evaluation
Job specifications
Position Analysis Questionnaire (PAQ)
Skills, knowledge, ability (SKAs)
Verifiable qualifications

REVIEW QUESTIONS

1 Define the practical relationship among job analysis, job descriptions, and job specifications.

2 What information is necessary to develop job descriptions? What are some of the qualities of a well-constructed job description?

3 How can a firm benefit from having a complete and accurate system of job descriptions and job specifications?

4 Outline the advantages and disadvantages of the various methods of job analysis.

5 How do governmental influences affect the process of job analysis?

6 If an organization has no formal system of job analysis, how might the objectives of job analysis be obtained?

DISCUSSION QUESTIONS

1 If you were an HR specialist in a company that was introducing job analysis, how would you reassure employees who felt threatened?

2 When faced with the problem of updating job analysis information, would you favor an annual review or reclassification? Explain why.

3 Describe the methods you would use to gather job information in a bank, a small manufacturing firm, or a newspaper.

4 Discuss how job analysis could or could not resolve the following problems: (a) an employee who produces less than others doing the same job; (b) an employee who complains about a dirty work environment; (c) an employee who feels passed over when promotions are announced.

5 As an HR manager, you must describe job analysis to employees. Which ideas would you stress for blue-collar workers? For white-collar workers?

6 Assume that you are the director of a medium-sized HR department and happen to be attending a staff meeting with all the department heads and the CEO. During the meeting, suppose that a manager from the manufacturing division suddenly and forcefully starts criticizing the need for job descriptions of managers. He says that they reflect a set of static, predetermined duties created by management and evaluated by the HR department, which also assigns salary levels to them based on the number of people he supervised. He goes on to say that these job descriptions tend to be snapshots of what is needed at a particular point in time. He points out a few that he says have been frozen in place, even as technological advances and competitive challenges occur. You have heard his criticisms and note that the CEO is now looking to you to respond to his comments. Are job descriptions unnecessary? If so, what would take their place?

Endnotes

Chapter 5

1. David J. Hickson and Derek S. Pugh, *Management Worldwide* (London: Penguin Business, 1995), 58–68.

2. Robert J. Sahl, "Pressing New Reasons for Accurate Job Descriptions," *The Human Resources Professional* (Fall 1992): 18.

3. "Uniform Guidelines on Employee Selection Procedures," *Federal Register* (August 25, 1978): 38302, 38306.

4. Colleen P. O'Neill, "Competency—A Powerful Tool for Driving Business Results," *Human Resource Professional* (Nov.–Dec. 1996): 22–24.

5. Bruce Meger, "A Critical Review of Competency-Based Systems," *Human Resource Professional* (Jan.–Feb. 1996): 22–25.

6. Edward C. Brett and Charles M. Canning, "Job Evaluation and Your Organization: An Ideal Relationship?" *Personnel Administrator* 29, no. 4 (April 1984): 115–24.

7. U.S. Department of Labor, Manpower Administration, *Handbook for Analyzing Jobs* (Washington, D.C.: U.S. Government Printing Office, 1972), 340–51.

8. Alex Carey, "The Hawthorne Studies: A Radical Criticism," *American Sociological Review* 32, no. 3 (1967): 403–16.

9. W. H. Weiss, "How to Work-Sample Your People," *Administrative Management* (June 14, 1982): 37–38, 49–50.

10. E. L. Levine et al., "Evaluation of Job Analysis Methods by Experienced Job Analysts," *Academy of Management Journal* 26 (1983): 339–48.

11. "Uniform Guidelines," 38304, 38306.

12. P. Geyer, J. Hice, K. Hawk, R. Boese, and Y. Brannon, "Reliabilities of Ratings Available from the Dictionary of Occupational Titles," *Personnel Psychology* 42 (1989): 547–60.

13. Ernest J. McCormick, Paul J. Jeanneret, and Robert C. Mecham, "A Study of Job Characteristics and Job Dimensions as Based on the Position Analysis Questionnaire (PAQ)," *Journal of Applied Psychology* (August 1972): 347–68.

14. Ed McCormick and R. Jeannerette, "The Position Analysis Questionnaire," in *The Job Analysis Handbook for Business, Industry, and Government*, ed. S. Gael (New York: John Wiley & Sons, 1988), 880–901.

15. Robert J. Harvey, "Job Analysis," in *Handbook of Industrial and Organizational Psychology*, 2d ed., eds. M. Dunnette and L. Hough (Palo Alto, CA: Consulting Psychologists Press, 1991), 30–43.

16. R. D. Arvey et al., "Narrative Job Descriptions As Potential Sources of Job Analysis Ratings," *Personnel Psychology* 35 (1982): 618–29.

17. Sidney A. Fine and Wretha Wiley, "An Introduction to Functional Job Analysis: A Scaling of Selected Tasks from the Social Welfare Field," *Methods for Manpower Analysis* no. 4 (Kalamazoo, MI: Upjohn Institute for Employment Research, 1979), 3–20.

18. Philip Grant, "What Use Is a Job Description?" *Personnel Journal* 67, no. 2 (February 1988): 45–53.

19. E. James Brennan, "Job Descriptions and Pay: The Inevitable Link," *Personnel Journal* 63, no. 7 (July 1984).

20. Grant, "What Use Is a Job Description?" 48–49.

21. Mark A. Jones, "Job Descriptions Made Easy," *Personnel Journal* 63, no. 5 (May 1984): 31–34.

22. Ibid.

CHAPTER
6

DESIGNING WORK

CHAPTER OUTLINE

CHAPTER OBJECTIVES

1 To be aware of the dramatic changes occurring in global corporations and their effect on the design of work throughout the world.

2 To recognize that old industrial models of job design continue at a very high human price.

3 To understand how the design of work affects employee motivation and performance.

4 To become familiar with the variety of ways work can be structured, depending on organization, industry, and people.

HR IN THE NEWS

"JOB MISFITS"

Their eyes sparkled with enthusiasm—ten young, fresh-faced graduates—all smiling broadly on the cover of *Fortune* magazine. They worked for ASSI, "a company," the magazine cover declared, "where the employees take charge of their future."

And how! Within a year, all but two of them had walked out, embittered and divided against the very company that gave them control. "It was a revolt," says owner Vic Williams. What went wrong?

The ASSI business provides computer-aided design services to architects. When they landed the big contract, Home Depot, the owner truly believed the "best" people needed to be hired. The company began hiring hotshot young designers from well-to-do backgrounds who attended the best schools.

WWW.HOMEDEPOT.COM

The new hires were given new jobs using the latest HR job-design concepts including teams, empowerment, profit sharing, and no hierarchies. It was this plan, policies, and new staff that put the company on the cover of *Fortune.* Later the company was featured in a management textbook as a case study in modern management.

But while the experts were fawning, the staff was fuming. These new young designers were expected to schedule their own jobs, but they were offended if Vic pointed out they were behind schedule. They were asked to deal directly with customers, but they chafed when customers made big demands.

When the owners leased an extra-large suite so everyone could sit by a window, employees complained about the glare on their computer screens. When some of them were offered an opportunity to attend professional development classes, they took it as a slight. The message to management: "Get out of my face."

The reality, in retrospect, wasn't terribly complicated. The owner had given the young staff plenty of authority but too little accountability. There were no formal performance reviews. No one was ever fired. They had created not a sense of fulfillment, but of entitlement. In short, Vic had hired a group of misfits—people who simply were not cut out for these jobs.

In early 1995, "the walkout" began. In the space of a few weeks, the entire design staff jumped to clients and competitors.

What lessons had Vic learned? One lesson: Recruit people who understand teamwork, not a bunch of "cowboys." He also started recruiting at community trade schools instead of four-year colleges. He wanted people who were eager to learn, too. Just as important, he began hiring from a wider, multicultural pool.

"The key difference," according to Vic, "the new staff is also held more accountable." Formal reviews, dismissals, and more controls have been instituted. "Maybe it was too naïve to think those guys could handle their own work design without more direction from me."

Are things any better? "The better mix of employees take direction and provide leadership," says Vic, "rather than a lot of people the same age rebelling and feeding off each other."

SOURCE: Adapted from Thomas Petzinger, "A More Diverse Staff Finds Strength in Its Differences," *The Wall Street Journal* (April 11, 1997): B–1.

A SEA CHANGE

Claiming people as their "greatest resource" has long been a business cliché. In the past decade, however, the phrase is weighted not only with more sincerity but with increasing anxiety. The opening story confirms this last point. Businesses must commit unprecedented resources of time, money, and ingenuity to fill their payrolls and keep their workforce competitive.

The reason? New models of working together are emerging thanks to technology, fast-moving economies, and global-minded management. The events taking place represent a **sea change**—a paradigm shift—that is rewriting the rules of work design, organizational structure, and management styles.[1] These forces contribute significantly to the need for more educated, more flexible workers. Folded into this mix are demographic patterns not to be underestimated in their effects on the American workforce and the nature of American business.

The workers available today are more diverse in race, cultural background, gender, age, and ability—and they are in a position to make demands, such as the young designers did in the opening story. Slow population and labor force growth are helping to create a seller's market for workers. Businesses are less able to fill their customary slots with generically suitable workers; instead, they must adjust jobs, training programs, and benefits to fit the people available.

Compounding the difficulties is the so-called "skills gap." In the next 20 years, America's jobs will require higher levels of skills than today's jobs, but its educational system lags behind in its ability to prepare people for the work available. Well-educated workers will be especially hard to come by, and businesses will have to compete hard for them.

CHANGING NATURE OF WORK AND WORKPLACES

A major component of changing work expectations is the changing nature of the workforce itself. For example, there are more women than ever working in today's offices. There are younger people in management positions, and the new generation of management is rapidly crafting new ways of relating to their work associates. Clearly, the demographics alone are changing work expectations. In addition, the emergence of knowledge work and knowledge workers has created an expectation for greater control and personalization in the workplace. Companies that want to attract and retain the best and brightest workforce need to pay close attention to these emerging expectations.

It's clear that the workplace of today and tomorrow will be home to a group of people with a whole new set of expectations. That means the workplace itself will need to adapt. A new set of work expectations has some direct implications for the workplace, how it's designed, the tools it provides, the flexibility it accommodates, and the processes that determine how it is used. Just the demographic shifts in today's workforce create a new set of expectations and subsequent workplace needs. A younger, more highly educated workforce that is more accustomed to high stimulation needs a different workplace from the population profile that used to inhabit office spaces.

The shifts in values and the overall vision of the place of work in one's life also make an impact on the design of the workplace. For example, a higher expectation for personal control creates a need for a workplace that accommodates more individual adaptability than group uniformity. It might involve allowing groups to participate in the design of their own worksettings, enabling them to inject very personal needs into the process. It might even involve the inclusion in the workplace of elements that were previously considered "inappropriate" such as personal art, individual or group music systems, personal effects, or even more residential-style furniture. The sacrifice of the appearance of the former "corporate office" may well be proportionate to the gain in peoples' satisfaction level with their workplace.

Organizations are rapidly being transformed from a structure built out of jobs into a field of work needing to be done. Hierarchy is being dramatically reduced. Look for jobs, the packaged 8-hour day variety, to become as rare as guarantees of job security. Anticipate a workforce that is largely self-employed and who, as a result, need to keep learning.[2]

Individuals will need different skills and different concepts of what constitutes a successful career. "Adding value" is the mantra.[3] An employee who is able to handle more sophisticated tasks adds value. Or, an employee who can manage herself adds value. Members of teams who can coordinate their work with other teams add value to the company. Finally, suggesting ideas about better ways to design work, new products, or improving customer service are value-added activities.

If the creative juices of a workforce are to be unleashed, organizations will need to transform themselves. Effective companies such as Wal-Mart, Southwest Airlines, Nucor, and many others have already begun the process.[4] They are moving from the old management emphasis on hierarchical, top-down control to structures that encourage employee involvement, lateral interaction, and customer focus.

All the experts agree, tomorrow's worker will be far more technologically literate, independent, and self-directed than today's. Videoconferencing via desktop computers, for example, will significantly increase the number of face-to-face interactions in daily work even when the individuals "meeting" are thousands of miles apart.[5] Juggling multiple tasks, working on teams, and the continuous learning of new skills are just a few of the changes for the 21st century workforce.

Work design will be governed by the demands of the task, customer focus, and technological factors—not by efficiency studies. Established systems of mass production, which once could be counted on to last for decades, now last only a few years. Clearly, the era of scientific management is declining. Nevertheless there remain numerous companies and a few industries that continue to practice it.

OLD PARADIGMS

In the old industrial model—laid out by Adam Smith, Frederick Taylor, and Henry Ford—profitability was based on efficiency and economies of scale, not quality, flexibility, and/or customer service.[6] Companies were organized by function, for example sales, manufacturing, finance, and the like. Complex work was broken down into simple, repetitive tasks performed in sequence by specialists. The primary job of supervisors was to control the quantity, quality, and cost of the work performed. Creativity and flexibility were only secondary goals.

Traditional industrial methods for managing labor took deep root in North America's manufacturing sectors. For example, the U.S. automotive industry prior to the 1980s concentrated on designing low-skilled, assembly-line, "idiot proof" jobs that required a minimum of training and individual decision making. Managers made the important decisions.

It is obvious now, but efficiency and control clearly come at a human cost. Employee job dissatisfaction, absenteeism, and turnover—factors that make a great difference in a competitive, labor-intensive industry—tend to be high. Perhaps a greater cost is the apathy and lack of involvement that is created. When people are involved in the business, their energy and creativity are directed to improving the system, instead of beating the system.

Yet the principles of scientific management are found throughout North America and in many developing countries. A few experts caution against premature dismissal of scientific management.[7] United Parcel Service has been an advocate for years. In labor-intensive industries, worker specialization has withstood the test of time. Unfortunately, the emergence of a boundary-less economy opened U.S. doors to foreign competitors.

And did they come! First the Japanese came, using flexible manufacturing methods. The Germans with their advanced manufacturing processes followed them. Others soon entered the fray, and everyone began building markets for high-quality, low-cost products.

Finally, with the emergence of new nations and new markets, labor-intensive industries began chasing low wages to developing countries, thus the departure of thousands of jobs from the United States. Of course, most of those jobs involved minimal skills and lots of repetition.

In a quest for global competitiveness, U.S. companies began to reinvent themselves, turning to restructuring, business process reengineering, delayering, downsizing, de-jobbing, and outsourcing. The result has been many changes in the design of work. Not only are companies moving toward quality and customer satisfaction, they are *empowering* their employees to make important decisions by giving them the skills and authority previously reserved for their bosses.

Many American companies have succumbed to a bad case of program-of-the-month syndrome. The *HR in the News* article "Forget Empowerment, This Job Requires Brainpower" mentions Monarch Marking Systems as one such example. However, Monarch solved the problem by replacing petty concepts of **"empowerment"** with a system that forces ideas into action. At Monarch, employees did not leave their minds out in the parking lot, but were required to use them.

At the risk of sounding trite, the only sustained source for competitive advantage comes from learning faster than competitors. Learning and putting to use critical knowledge depends entirely on workforce ability, opportunity to learn, and the willingness to try. Assuming that an organization has recruited competent people—and learning opportunities are provided—the only remaining variable is willingness.

No job, regardless of its design, can overcome an employee's lack of interest or motivation. If the employee doesn't care about his job, it seems highly unlikely he will make an effort to adapt, create, or add value to his job. The design of work must include opportunities for people to motivate themselves, or at least make it clear to management what motivational buttons to push.

HR IN THE NEWS

FORGET EMPOWERMENT, THIS JOB REQUIRES BRAINPOWER

In her 20 years at Monarch Marking Systems, Effie Winters lost count of the front-office weenies who tried to "empower" her, only to waste her time and theirs. So when new management rolled out yet another employee-involvement program, she flat-out refused to participate. "I thought it was a big joke," says Ms. Winters, who assembles a high-tech bar-code reader. "I wanted no part of it."

This time, however, participation wasn't optional. Kicking and screaming, Ms. Winters was ordered into a team studying the assembly process for Monarch's hottest product. The outcome? A 100 percent increase in productivity—and a new Effie Winters. "We're not just pieces of equipment anymore," she says. "My input means something."

WWW.PAXAR.COM

What makes the Monarch system different? Teams were charged with executing their own solution to the point of working out any necessary changes with other departments and making arrangements with vendors. Combining ideas with implementation would motivate people to think hard for the most practical solution. Also, no team would last beyond 30 days.

Results were almost instantaneous, but it wasn't as easy as it sounds. In fact, Ms. Winters and several of her teammates rebelled at one point when asked to come up with a more efficient assembly process for a hand-held bar-code reader. The manager, Steve Schneider, literally called the team to a conference room and told them in no uncertain way: "You *will* do this."

Finding themselves alone with a problem and a deadline, the thinking came with startling ease. They knew it was ridiculous to build a two-pound product on a mechanical conveyor belt. By eliminating it, they could face each other around a large workstation and simply pass around the product by hand. Anyone could easily talk to anyone, and anyone who got ahead could help anyone who fell behind. By the time it was over, they had doubled productivity.

SOURCE: Thomas Petzinger Jr., "The Front Lines," *The Wall Street Journal* (October 17, 1997): B1.

MOTIVATION

Lower productivity, lost opportunities, sloppy output, stifled creativity, and employees who are simply indifferent to their jobs are just a few of the symptoms of unmotivated people. How to turn apathetic people around, put quality in everyone's mind, and encourage innovative thinking are daily challenges to line managers, HR professionals, and conscientious employees.

The manager, in particular, is often in a "no-win situation." She is nearly always expected to be *The* person who should increase or maintain motivation of her staff by both the staff themselves and the manager's superiors alike. In order to be seen to build-up and achieve success and show results, a manager is very often tempted to "hang her hat" on one or more available motivational theories and hope that some of these work.

What is motivation? **Motivation** is the force that *energizes* behavior, gives *direction* to behavior, and underlies the tendency to *persist*, even in the face of one or more obstacles. Motivators are, to a large extent, specific to the individual.

A manager should attempt to meet the employee's important *needs*, or basic requirements for working productively. As the workforce becomes more diverse, recognizing the individuality of needs becomes quite a challenge. Undoubtedly a great deal of time talking with employees and observing their behavior is required. What will work for one employee may not work for another. There are hundreds of learned needs and dozens of different motivational theories, but only the popular ones will be reviewed. Each will focus on why people might do what they do—and how managers might motivate them to do what the organization might want them to do.

HIERARCHY OF NEEDS

Abraham **Maslow's Hierarchy of Needs** is probably the best known and the most intuitively appealing theory for managers today. Maslow suggested there are categories of needs: *physical, security, social, esteem,* and *self-actualization.* Figure 6–1 depicts each category.

All people have these categories of needs to some degree. People, Maslow found, strive to fulfill progressively higher levels of need, from nourishment to fulfilling one's potential.[8] However, only a single category can operate at any point in time. Once the need is satisfied, the next level takes over.

The most basic, or prepotent, needs dominate all others. In a work environment, besides compensation and benefits, maintaining a safe and hazard-free job is essential. For a single mother, benefits and programs that meet such needs as childcare would prove quite effective. Many organizations now using work teams are discovering how well they meet the social needs of their members.

Esteem needs include an individual's drive for mastery, competence, and recognized status. Being recognized as an "expert" is a powerful motivator. This category of need also includes **self-efficacy,** or the way a person feels about herself and her ability to perform. Self-actualization needs reflect the person's desire to grow and develop on the job, to be creative and independent.

Once employees' needs have been identified, there are an array of ways to meet them as suggested in Figure 6–1. While people often share similar need levels, the choice of behavior that leads to the satisfaction of the need may vary. Two employees, both with high recognition need, may choose very different paths: For example, one person might seek approval from his boss, whereas the other person might rather have the approval of his co-workers.

Maslow coined the phrase *"enlightened management"* to describe the work conditions leading to self-actualization. Teams, he found, made better workers, and better workers made better teams. "Generosity can increase wealth rather than decrease it. The more influence and power you give to someone else in the team situation, the more you have yourself."[9]

ACHIEVEMENT MOTIVATION

Almost as popular as the hierarchy of needs, **achievement motivation** was created by David McClelland. Only three needs are emphasized: achievement, affiliation, and power.[10] The *need to achieve* (N ach) is defined as a preoccupation to focus on goals, improving performance, and tangible results. Also it is associated with

self-discipline, schedule-keeping, accepting responsibility, and becoming success oriented. Unfortunately, the need to achieve is often associated with a lack of group orientation.

The *need for affiliation* (N aff) motivates people to make friends, to become members of groups, and to associate with others. The focus is on human companionship, interpersonal relations, and concern for others.

The *need for power* (N pow) refers to the desire to obtain and exercise control over others, resources, and the environment. McClelland found that when affiliation and power were both strong, the individual either demonstrated a propensity for either totalitarian methods of control or more democratic methods.[11] A combination of achievement and power lead to different types of assertive behaviors and management styles.

The need for achievement was the greatest concern for McClelland. He emphasizes this need as critical to the success of most organizations—since most organizations want their employees to achieve. He also looked at job design and its role in creating challenge in work.

GOAL SETTING

Edwin Locke has shown that job performance can be increased through **goal setting**—when individuals are given specific, challenging goals—rather than vague directions such as "do your best." The goal setting process is remarkably flexible. The important thing is the goal itself, not necessarily who sets it or how it was determined.[12]

Participation in the process does lead to setting more difficult, challenging goals. The more complex and sophisticated the goal, the more important participation becomes in the process.

One element often overlooked is the quality, quantity, and timeliness of critical *feedback* available to the participants. It must be constructive, not destructive. The availability of accurate measures can make a huge difference in giving credibility to the pro0cess. Feedback that is too little or too late ultimately undermines the effectiveness of mid-course corrective actions. Feedback is also a powerful motivator when it is linked to personal accomplishment.

MOTIVATION ACROSS CULTURES

The need and goal theories described are all based on the work of American scholars. A major issue centers on whether these theories are culture bound. Although the concept of needs holds across cultures, people with different cultural backgrounds can express and satisfy those needs differently. Each theory described has

FIGURE 6–1   HR PRACTICES THAT SATISFY VARIOUS LEVELS
OF HUMAN NEEDS IN MASLOW'S HIERARCHY

Physical Needs

1. Furnish pleasant and comfortable environment.
2. Provide for ample leisure.
3. Provide for "comfortable" salary.
4. Programs that provide childcare or elder-care service.

Security Needs

1. Adhere to protective rules and regulations, hazard-free work.
2. Minimize risk-taking requirements.
3. Provide strong directive leadership and follow chain-of-command policy.
4. Provide well-defined job descriptions.
5. Minimize negative stroking and threatening behavior.
6. Provide information about firm's financial status and projections.
7. Provide "just" compensation and supportive fringe benefits.
8. Union contracts that include employment guarantees.

Social Needs

1. Encourage the team concept.
2. Systematically use organization-wide feedback survey.
3. Use task groups to execute projects.
4. Provide for firm and/or office business and social meetings.
5. Provide close personal leadership.
6. Encourage professional-group participation.
7. Encourage community-group participation.
8. Compensate on basis of total team performance.

Self-Esteem Needs

1. Include employees in goal-setting and decision-making processes.
2. Provide opportunity to display skills and talents.
3. Provide recognition of advancement—for example, publicize promotions.
4. Provide recognition symbols—for example, name on stationery.
5. Assign associates and support staff for coaching and development.
6. Provide personal secretary to associates.
7. Use positive-reinforcement program.
8. Pay attention to office size, office location, parking spaces, and so forth.
9. Institute mentor system.
10. Compensate as recognition of growth.

Self-Actualization Needs

1. Provide for participation in goal-setting and decision-making processes.
2. Provide opportunity and support for career-development plan.
3. Provide staff job rotation to broaden experience and exposure.
4. Offer optimum innovative and risk-taking opportunities.
5. Encourage direct-access communication to clients, customers, suppliers, vendors, and so on.
6. Provide challenging internal and external professional development opportunities.
7. Provide supportive leadership that encourages a high degree of self-control.
8. Compensate as reward for exceptional performance.

different application from culture to culture. The French, for example, do not respond nearly as well to goal-setting strategies as the Americans.

McClelland's need for achievement theory is more controversial. Some say it is very robust. Others see a distinct U.S. cultural base in the desire for action and accomplishment. Hofstede saw clear differences among countries for the need to achieve.[13] He felt the concept was applicable only for the Anglo-American countries, India, South Africa, the Philippines, and Hong Kong.

Maslow's theory, for example, may not generalize to workers in other countries. It must be modified as different needs appear as a driving force in different countries.[14] People in the United States have a high need for achievement. The Japanese worker may value security over self-fulfillment. Security and affiliation needs in Latin America are high. Cooperative affiliation orientations are high in New Zealand. Workers in Scandinavian countries, which emphasize the quality of life, are reacting to strong social needs. In France and Germany, people highly value security.

It appears that motivation theories are limited in application in developing countries. With the employee focusing on satisfying basic needs, higher level needs are not even considered. Of course, this is an aggregate observation, and motivational strategies work best when customized to no more than small groups of people.

The common sense approach of treating staff well, communicating, training, and providing appropriate rewards are cornerstones to all the theories. But as people are different, there cannot be one universal theory that could be sufficient to work in all circumstances and for all situations. Therefore, it is natural for managers to keep searching for new ideas or develop old ones as they manage.

MOTIVATOR–HYGIENE THEORY

This theory, created by Frederick Herzberg, is widely known by practicing managers. **Herzberg's two-factor theory** is based on identifying characteristics of jobs that will operate as motivators and the characteristics that will act as dissatisfiers—or hygiene factors.[15]

Generally, *hygiene factors* deal with the work environment, or *context,* and will never create real satisfaction with a job—they will only decrease job dissatisfaction. *Motivators* are tied to the work itself—job *content*— and may increase or decrease satisfaction with the task itself. Money, for example is not seen as a motivator. If a person hates his job—he shovels horse dung—he will still hate it if he is paid a million bucks a year to do it. Figure 6–2 identifies the different context and content factors that affect job satisfaction.

The Motivator–Hygiene theory has received praise and criticism. Legitimate questions have been raised regarding methodology and about the confusing relationship between satisfaction and motivation. Nevertheless, managers should pause and consider: Are attempts to use monetary incentives, as Herzberg says, only good for the short term? Even Herzberg is reputed to have his doubts (see *HR in the News:* "Well . . . on the Other Hand . . .").

FIGURE 6–2   HERZBERG'S THEORY: FACTORS AFFECTING JOB SATISFACTION

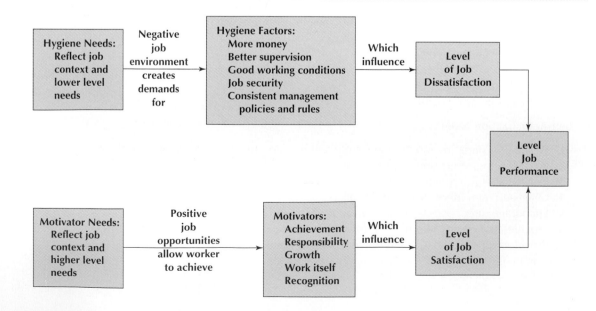

"WELL . . . ON THE OTHER HAND . . ."

An interesting story, if true, is that Herzberg, while negotiating a fee for a lecture on why pay motivation doesn't work, suddenly had the tables turned. A perceptive business agent, who had obviously done his homework and was familiar with Herzberg's point of view, politely pointed out that the lower offer ought to stand because "after all, money doesn't motivate, so why haggle over it?"

"Money, in fact, doesn't motivate me," Herzberg said without embarrassment, "but it sure as hell helps me sort out my priorities."

DESIGNING JOBS

Two of the most important concerns of HR managers are employee productivity and job satisfaction. A critical factor affecting these areas is the type of work performed by the employee. Job design greatly affects how an employee feels about a job, how much authority an employee has over the work, how much decision making the employee performs on the job, and how many tasks the employee should complete. Managers realize that job design determines both their working relationship with their employees and the relationship among the employees themselves.

Job design is the manipulation of the content, functions, and relationships of jobs in a way that both accomplishes organizational purposes and satisfies the personal needs of individual job holders.[16] The content of a job encompasses the variety of tasks performed, the autonomy of the job holder, the routineness of tasks performed, the difficulty of the tasks performed, and the identity of the job holder, or the extent to which the whole job is performed by the person.[17] The functions of a job encompass the work methods utilized, as well as the coordination of the work, responsibility, information flow, and authority of the job. The relationships of a job encompass the work activities shared by the job holder and other individuals in the organization.[18]

Figure 6–3 shows the framework of design to both the worker and the organization. At stake is a worker's satisfaction with the job situation—that is, the work itself. A worker's favorable reaction to job design means greater accomplishment, less absenteeism, fewer grievances, and less turnover.

How should jobs be designed? This topic has been discussed widely since the Industrial Revolution. Traditional approaches to job design have been seriously questioned in recent years. Some job design problems in the last 25 years have been the result of workers' increasing dissatisfaction with jobs designed for robots or mindless machines. Henry Ford's assembly line is an excellent example of the job design method known as *job specialization*.

SPECIALIZATION-INTENSIVE JOBS

Job specialization is characterized by jobs with very few tasks, tasks that are repeated often during the workday and require few skills. These are called **specialization-intensive jobs.** Job specialization was the primary component of scientific management.[19]

1 The manager determines the one best way of performing the job.

2 The manager hires individuals according to their abilities, which must match the needs of the job design. For example, a strong person is hired to carry heavy loads and a diligent person is hired to file records.

3 Management trains workers in the one best way the job should be performed. All planning, organizing, and control are done by the manager.

At United Parcel Service (UPS), the principles of scientific management are clearly evident—even at the close of the 20th century. Most of the work is routine, repetitive, and easy to learn. Everything is measured, from timing drivers and stoplights to measuring sorting-hub efficiency and package mishaps.[20]

The Problem of Overspecialization Job specialization evolved from a preoccupation with command-and-control systems. Jobs are narrowly designed

FIGURE 6–3   A FRAMEWORK FOR JOB DESIGN

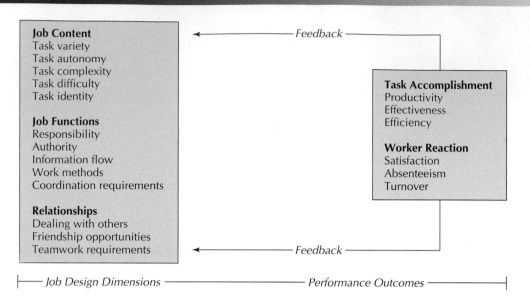

SOURCE: Andrew D. Szilagyi and Marc J. Wallace, *Organizational Behavior and Performance,* 2d ed. (p.1 49). Copyright © 1980 by Goodyear Publishing Company. Reprinted by permission.

to achieve standardization, simplification, and division of labor. Maximum efficiency is the goal. There is no doubt that specialization offers economic benefits, especially when there is an abundant supply of unskilled labor.[21] Why, then, are many organizations dropping specialization and redesigning work around human needs?

The answer is found in overspecialization. It is a frequently cited reason for workers feeling alienated from work and their bosses. **Overspecialization** has several symptoms.[22]

Repetition   Employees performing only a few tasks, which must be repeated many times during a work shift, will quickly become bored. Most people need to be stimulated and challenged.

Mechanical Pacing   Employees who are restricted by an assembly line and required to maintain a certain pace of work will soon divert their attention to anything other than the task at hand. Identifying the optimum pace is not easy, however. What is just right for one may be too fast for another.

No End Product   Overspecialization makes it difficult for employees to identify the end product. Employees need to have **line-of-sight** between their performance and the ultimate outcome. Consequently, they will have little pride in and enthusiasm for their work.

Little Social Interaction   Employees will complain that because the assembly line requires constant atten-

tion, there is little chance to interact on a casual basis with co-workers. This makes it difficult for employees to develop significant social bonding at work.

No Input   Employees tend to complain that they have little chance to determine how they perform their jobs, the tools they use, or their work procedures. The lack of personal control creates a lack of interest in the job because there is nothing they can improve or change.

Job Dimensions   The degree to which a job is highly specialized can be determined by measuring scope and depth. Job **scope** is how long it takes a worker to complete a piece of work. For example, an assembly line worker in an early Ford plant might have taken five minutes to add a wiring harness to an automobile as it moved down the assembly line. Thus, the scope of the job, or the job cycle, was five minutes.

The second dimension is job depth. This dimension is more difficult to determine. It cannot be measured in easily identifiable terms. **Depth** refers to how much planning, decision making, and controlling the worker does in the total job. For example, to what extent can a worker vary the methods used on the job? How many decisions can the worker make without supervisory approval? If various techniques and tools are determined solely by management, the job is said to have very little depth. At the other end of the continuum, a job in which a worker performs independently has great depth or a great deal of autonomy.

MOTIVATION-INTENSIVE JOBS

Modern management has found that the increased cost of employee absenteeism and turnover, as well as decreased productivity and quality, may outweigh the advantages of highly specialized jobs. The challenge is to balance the employees' human needs and the employer's economic goals. Table 6–1 shows the advantages of each of the two approaches to job design.

Motivation-intensive job approaches include: job rotation, enlargement, enrichment, and work teams.

JOB ROTATION

Job rotation is the periodic assignment of employees to alternating jobs or tasks. For example, an employee may spend two weeks attaching bumpers to vehicles and the following two weeks making final checks of the chassis. During the next month, the same employee may be assigned to two different jobs. The advantage of job rotation is that employees do not have the same routine job day after day.

Does job rotation solve the problem of boringly repetitious jobs? No. Job rotation addresses only the problem of assigning employees to jobs of limited scope; the depth of the job does not change. Some employees dislike job rotation. Rather than being assigned to one boring job, they are assigned to several. Workers quickly realize that job rotation does not increase their interest in their work.

Why, then, is job rotation still a common practice? One reason is it does give managers a means of coping with frequent absenteeism and high turnover. When absenteeism or turnover occurs, managers can quickly fill the vacated position because each employee can perform several jobs.

Job rotation is often effectively used as a training technique for new, inexperienced employees. At higher organizational levels, rotation also helps develop managerial generalists because it exposes them to several different operations.

JOB ENLARGEMENT

Another means of increasing employees' satisfaction with routine jobs is **job enlargement,** or increasing the scope of tasks performed. Job enlargement, like job rotation, tries to eliminate short job cycles that create boredom. Unlike job rotation, job enlargement actually increases the job cycle. When a job is enlarged, either the tasks being performed are enlarged or several short tasks are given to one worker. It does not increase the depth of a job.

The focus of designing work for job enlargement is the exact opposite of that for job specialization. Instead of designing jobs to be divided up into the fewest number of tasks per employee, a job is designed to have many tasks for the employee to perform. Worker satisfaction should increase because boredom is reduced as the job scope is expanded. However, job enlargement programs are successful only if workers are more satisfied with jobs that have increased scope.

The Maytag Company undertook fifteen job enlargement projects during a three-year period. At the conclusion, Maytag managers observed the following.[23]

- Quality and efficiency were improved.
- Production costs were lower.
- Employees reported higher job satisfaction. They especially preferred the slower work pace that resulted from an enlarged job that did not have a repetitious cycle and that required a greater variety of skills.

Although job enlargement is still considered a valid means of addressing specialization problems, it has been augmented by a more sophisticated technique known as job enrichment.

JOB ENRICHMENT

Organizations with employees who have high levels of knowledge and skills should consider job enrichment

TABLE 6–1	ADVANTAGES OF THE MAJOR APPROACHES TO DESIGN

SPECIALIZATION-INTENSIVE JOBS	MOTIVATION-INTENSIVE JOBS
High productivity of unskilled workers	High productivity of challenged workers
Less training time required	Less absenteeism
Easy to replace workers	Less turnover
Few mental work errors	Higher product quality
Greater manager control of operations	More employee ideas, suggestions
	Greater employee job satisfaction

programs. With **job enrichment,** jobs are redesigned in both scope and depth. Typically, the worker decides how the job is performed, planned, and controlled. The overall purpose is to make a job more exciting and challenging.

Job enrichment goes further than job enlargement by grouping a set of tasks of sufficient complexity to require choices about how to bring together the varied operations and get the job done. For example, instead of simply feeding material into a machine, the worker with an enriched job might perform machine setup, feed the machinery, inspect the output, accept or reject the output, and, if necessary, adjust or perhaps even repair the machine. Not only are more tasks added, thus increasing *variety,* but the worker can see the process through from start to finish, what is called *task identity.* Prior to the change, the worker probably had a hard time believing that quality of the work really mattered. Now the worker can take *responsibility for a significant portion* of the overall product, and by inspecting the completed product, the worker receives timely *feedback* on whether it was made properly or not.[24]

Clearly, this type of program requires a great deal of commitment and planning by top-level management, retraining of employees, and substantial changes in leadership styles from supervisors and managers. The last change is particularly difficult for managers accustomed to tight controls. Convincing leaders to change their styles is perhaps the most critical step when implementing job enrichment programs.

Labor leaders are becoming less skeptical of job enrichment programs. Restructuring and downsizing are constantly occurring so taking on additional duties is not the problem it was in the past.

WORKING IN TEAMS

A large portion of the work in most organizations occurs within groups. Most jobs do not exist in isolation but instead involve formal workgroups (departments, sections, and so on), as well as informal groups of employees whose strong friendships affect their working relationships. The effectiveness of these employee groups or teams can be critical to the success of the entire organization.

In many union and nonunion organizations, formal groups of employees responsible for an identifiable work process, a specific project, or the solution of a problem are called *employee teams.* These groups have been called the productivity breakthrough of the 1990s, even though the first ones, like those at General Foods in Topeka, Kansas, have been in existence for over 30 years.[25] A *Chicago Tribune* survey of the 500 largest companies in the United States found that about 80 percent utilize some form of committees, employee involvement groups, or employee teams.[26]

Formal employee teams can generally be divided into three categories: special project teams, problem-solving teams, and self-managed teams (see Figure 6–4). **Self-managed teams** are characterized as permanent groups of employees who perform all tasks required of one general activity, as well as the supervisory duties related to their work. Special project teams are usually formed by combining labor and management people from different functional areas to design, develop, and produce new products or services. **Problem-solving teams** usually meet on a regular basis to analyze, recommend, and implement solutions to selected problems. In the 1980s, a handful of U.S. companies began using a new approach to new product development—the project team. **Project teams** most often consist of 10 to 15 people from different functional areas such as research and development, engineering, manufacturing, and marketing brought together to design and develop a new product quickly and successfully. The project team is viewed as an autonomous group operating independently within the organization.

The factors that have caused a growing number of employers to turn to project teams include the following: (1) Rising global competition has greatly increased the need to reduce the time required to put a new product on the market; (2) employees today expect and are able to provide more meaningful input into the development of new products; (3) the past successes of project teams, as well as of other employee teams, have convinced more managers to relinquish their authority to project teams; and (4) the synergy factor discussed earlier is believed to be a significant force that drives team members to be more creative, work harder, and achieve greater productivity than they would if they were given only a limited view of the project.

Problem-solving teams have increased in popularity but are generally used to a lesser extent. They can, however, be highly successful groups. Many problem-solving teams have their roots in quality circles and may be characterized as mature, fully empowered quality circles. The creation of permanent problem-solving teams should not be surprising. An American Society for Training and Development survey of organizations with employee teams found that the most common objective of the teams is problem solving (72 percent of those responding listed this as an objective), team building was second (61 percent), and improving quality was third (58 percent).[27] Thus, many organizations with positive

FIGURE 6–4   WHAT'S A TEAM?

There are several types of teams. Here are three of the most common:

Problem Solving	Special Project	Self-Managed
Usually 5 to 12 members of labor and management who meet a few hours a week to discuss ways of improving quality, efficiency, and work environment.	Usually 10 to 15 people from different functional areas. May design and introduce work reforms or new technology or may meet with suppliers and customers. In union shops, labor and management collaborate at all levels.	From 5 to 15 nonmanagement workers who learn all production tasks and rotate from job to job. Teams do managerial duties such as schedule work and order materials.

SOURCE: Aaron Bernstein, "Putting a Damper on That Old Team Spirit," *Business Week* (May 4, 1992): 60.

experiences with quality circles and problem solving as an ongoing concern allowed the evolution of quality circles or similar groups into permanent problem-solving teams.

Self-managed employee teams (also called *employee groups* or *employee involvement groups, autonomous work groups,* or *self-directed teams*) are becoming more common in many American organizations. Special-project teams and self-managed teams are perhaps the best-publicized types of employee teams. They have even been called "the new American industrial weapon" in cover stories in *Business Week, Fortune,* and other business publications.[28]

Exactly what are self-managed employee teams?

A *self-managed team* is a small group of employees responsible for an entire work process or segment. Team members work together to improve their operation or product, plan their work, resolve day-to-day problems, and manage themselves.[29]

They are not groups formed to design and develop special projects or new products or to analyze and solve problems. Instead, these teams are permanent nonmanagement employees within the organization that get the work out on a daily basis. The key difference is that their work is assigned to a team, rather than to a department with a supervisor or head who then assigns portions of the work to individuals within the department.

Common characteristics include:[30]

- They plan, control, and make decisions about their work (they self-manage!).
- Within limits, they set their own productivity goals and inspect their own work.

- They set their own work schedules.
- Members select, appraise, and discipline each other.
- Members receive a portion of their compensation on the basis of team performance.

Organizations that have chosen to organize work to be performed by self-managed teams may be quite different from traditional organizations with highly specialized jobs (see Figure 6–5). They often have far fewer levels of management. For example, the Nucor Corporation (a highly successful steel manufacturer which extensively uses teams) has only 4 levels of management compared to an average of 10 in the steel industry. The teams may perform many of the functions normally performed by the additional layers of management—assign work, check to see that it is done properly, discipline people when necessary, hire employees, appraise performance, and so on. Thus, savings occurs from the elimination of many supervisors and managers due to the use of self-managed teams.[31] Another difference is that members are often cross trained and can perform a variety of team tasks.

When most organizations install teams, they simply don't make the many changes that are needed in order to create effective teams, whether they be problem solving, special project, or self-managed. Lucent Technologies employed teams and achieved success (see *HR in the News:* "No Skeptics at Lucent Technologies"). Their secret consisted of designing human resource management systems and information systems that provided the right kinds of selection, training, feedback, and recognition for teams and individuals.

WWW.LUCENT.COM

FIGURE 6–5   KEY DIFFERENCES BETWEEN TRADITIONAL ORGANIZATIONS AND SELF-DIRECTED TEAM ORGANIZATIONS

Element	Traditional Organizations	Self-Directed Teams
Organizational structure	Layered/individual	Flat/team
Job design	Narrow, single-task	Whole process/multiple-task
Management role	Direct/control	Coach/facilitate
Leadership	Top-down	Shared with team
Information flow	Controlled/limit	Open/shared
Rewards	Individual/seniority	Team-based/skills-based
Job process	Managers plan, control, improve	Teams plan, control, improve

SOURCE: Richard S. Wellins, William C. Byham, and Jeanne M. Wilson, *Empowered Teams* (San Francisco: Jossey-Bass, 1991), 6. Used by permission.

HR IN THE NEWS

NO SKEPTICS AT LUCENT TECHNOLOGIES

The skeptics persist in doubting the potential for self-direction in the workplace. They think workers lack initiative and that bosses will never give up control. If you're among the naysayers, please meet Phillip Dailey of Lucent Technologies in Mount Olive, New Jersey.

Dailey works on an assembly line, stringing digital cables for cellular phone systems. While studying a bottleneck along the line, he realized that output could increase by 33 percent if there were only 25 percent more staff. At his initiative, he recruited temporary workers from other teams and set out to prove his theory. His idea worked. Only then did he clue in the bosses.

How does Lucent's self-directed workforce of 480 stack up? Total labor costs have decreased to just 3 percent of product cost. And, there hasn't been a missed delivery in two years.

Lucent teams, when asked how they do it, shared a few simple principles.

1 Hire attitude over aptitude. Applicants are put through tests intended to weed out loners and curmudgeons. People come in as contractors and are "anointed" as employees only after proving they're self-starters and team players.

2 Let teams monitor quality, training, scheduling, and communication with other teams. At Lucent, team members are often overheard in the locker rooms gently chiding one another for failing to uphold a standard.

3 No vague mission statement, but a one-page list of "working principles." Teams do not get stuck on mission but have a very clear picture of where they need to be. They have enough authority to alter the manufacturing process and even the product design itself.

4 Nurture communication and feedback among all stakeholders. Operating statistics, performance charts, schedules, and other measures are posted everywhere. Teams take responsibility for each other and their customers.

5 Measure and reward teamwork, but don't ignore individual achievements. The yearly bonus is 15 percent and is based equally on individual and team performance.

SOURCE: Adapted from Thomas Petzinger Jr., "The Front Lines," *The Wall Street Journal* (March 7, 1997): B1.

THE OFFICE ENVIRONMENT

Many people think of office environments simply as physical settings—something quite separate from the people, their work activities, and organizational structures. However, a holistic view of the office domain—considering people, production structures and processes, and place together—provides a better approach for understanding and responding effectively to dynamic problems in the workplace.

In the industrial era, many organizing concepts from the factory were adopted as the model for office work, including a linear flow of work and a high differentiation of tasks. Consequently, clerical and technical jobs, for example, have often consisted of repetitive tasks that encompass only a small part of the product or service being produced. Under this scheme of work, people have had little sense of how their part of the work contributed to the final result.

Organizations have varying attitudes toward space and facilities. Some companies think of buildings and furniture primarily in economic terms, as costs to be contained, expending little effort to make full use of the physical environment to support the social, cultural, and productive processes. Progressive companies, on the other hand, use buildings and furniture to enhance productivity and express the corporate culture. Changing the physical environment is an effective way to signal and support changes in culture.

At Union Carbide, for example, the board chairman wanted to improve company performance, in part by changing the culture—flattening the hierarchy, increasing participation, and decentralizing decision making. He also reinforced the emerging culture through facility changes. In the new headquarters building, managers and professionals regardless of job level got the same size and type of office. In this way, Union Carbide effectively aligned its facilities and space policies with the new egalitarian corporate culture.[32]

WWW.UNIONCARBIDE.COM

While the physical environment of the office tends to be rated lower in importance than many other factors,[33] research indicates that people often unconsciously adapt to their surroundings in ways that are not always good for them, for example, by adjusting to inferior seating, ineffective keyboard support, or poor lighting.[34] Regardless of the importance attributed to facilities by individuals, in actuality the quality of the physical environment does make a significant difference in work performance as well as in satisfaction.[35]

In today's office environment, dealing with change is a major challenge. Because the core elements (people, production, and place) have an impact on key outcomes such as productivity, satisfaction, safety, and long-term effectiveness, a holistic understanding of the office environment can support positive changes and enhance an organization's chance of success.

WORKPLACE FLEXIBILITY

Earlier the comment was made that life is not as predictable as it once was. Many Americans do not work a 40-hour week anymore, and they probably do not waltz out the company door at 5 P.M. They have the unpredictable demands of childcare, elder care, and their own personal well-being. Trying to mesh their personal life with their work life has become a challenge, one that many people solve by using flexible work agreements. It is becoming so important that organizations include it in their strategic plans. The workplace-flexibility challenge is to construct the best scheduling mix between employees' needs and the organization's staffing requirements in ways that are consistent with the company's culture and mission.

Workplace flexibility includes programs such as flextime, job sharing, telecommuting, and compressed workweeks. It has been hailed as a relatively inexpensive way to help employees balance their lives and their livelihoods. Yet, telecommuting, job sharing and compressed workweeks are not used as often as they are needed in the workplace mostly because organizations and managers are slow in giving the green light to arrangements they simply do not know how to cope with. When a manager ignores a flexible workplace request, key employees simply search for employers who are willing to work with them on flex arrangements.

Getting started in providing flex arrangements does take some planning.[36] Start small, with only a few employees or a pilot project. Let employees know these arrangements will be reviewed regularly to see if the needs have changed and if it is working out. Most important, make sure other employees do not feel they are getting the short end of the stick. Keep everyone informed on who is working when and how long it can be expected to last. Also, make sure employees know that the company is willing to listen to anyone who needs flexible hours. Once started, consider the guidelines outlined in Table 6–2.

HR IN THE NEWS

FLEXTIME INITIATIVES CAN PROVE PROFITABLE

When Xerox Corporation employees tried flextime at their Dallas customer-service center, the results seemed almost too good to be true. Work got finished quicker, absenteeism dropped 30 percent, customers were better served, and a key project came in under budget, the company said.

How employees scheduled their working hours was left up to them. Flexibility is the one component workers consistently identified as critical to creating balance between work and family.

The change at the Dallas center is one of a number of such initiatives adopted by Xerox, Tandem Computers, and Corning. Employees at each company also tried telecommuting, compressed workweeks, part-time work, and simply hanging "Quiet Time" signs on office doors.

SOURCE: "Flextime Initiatives Can Prove Profitable," *Reuters* (New York: May 28, 1997).

TABLE 6–2   FLEXIBLE WORKPLACE GUIDELINES

1. It's a partnership. Flexibility is a context, not a policy or program. The cooperation of several people is needed: manager, employees, co-workers, and the company.

2. Focus on results. Just because you don't see an employee all the time does not mean the work is being forgotten. Keep in mind that allowing workers to take more responsibility for when and how they do their work is consistent with more modern business practices. Set up goals and timetables and manage those results.

3. Always communicate. Keeping everyone informed of changes that affect the workplace or an individual is critical to making sure that any glitches are caught early. At the same time, shared successes encourage others to experiment, too.

4. Continually observe and make adjustments.

SOURCE: Barney Olmsted and Suzanne Smith, *Managing in a Flexible Workplace* (New York: AMACOM 1997), 83-106.

TELECOMMUTING

New technological opportunities such as electronic mail (e-mail) and groupware networking have created a new alternative in work scheduling called **telecommuting.** Workers can complete some or all their assigned duties at home.

There are all sorts of opportunities for people to work at home, and the numbers are growing. The proportion of company employees working at home at least part time rose 15 percent in 1993 to 7.6 million, according to Link Resources, a New York research concern.[37] More would like to join the trend; 20 percent to 40 percent of employees say that they see telecommuting as a desirable option.[38]

But as the number of telecommuters increases, some who work at home find that it does not work for them. It can foster a sense of isolation, stagnation, family problems, and even compulsive overwork.[39] While some of the skills required to succeed as telecommuters, are obvious, others are harder to measure. An ability to solve problems alone and nurture client and co-worker relations from home, for example, may be obvious requirements.

Less obvious, many telecommuters fear that losing visibility at work can lead to derailing a career. No doubt, the old adage "Out of sight, out of mind" is in the minds of many ambitious telecommuters. Suggestions for minimizing this problem include, first, making sure that the "home work" delivers significant benefits to the boss and the business; second, staying flexible; third, cultivating the boss's active support for the home arrangement; and fourth, keeping in touch and interested.[40]

Telecommuters should be prepared to use the telephone and e-mail frequently.

TEMPORARY HELP AND CONTRACT WORKERS

In the past, temporary workers played an insignificant role, but that situation has changed. Global competition, as well as an ongoing campaign to control labor costs and make businesses more flexible, are the reasons. Firms are beginning to manage their workforces in a just-in-time manner, much like the practice of keeping their inventories lean and ordering as needed. Some employers hire temporary workers to adjust to sharp peaks and valleys of demand. Many of the workers want more time off to take care of their families or for other personal needs or interests.

The Wyatt Company, a Washington, D.C. consulting firm, reports that approximately 27 percent of U.S. companies hired temporary employees in 1993. This was a 3 percent increase. They also reported many more companies are contracting with outside vendors to handle operations formerly performed by the company.[41]

Although temporary workers are a tiny percentage of the overall workforce, their share of total employment has risen over the past decade. The National Association of Temporary Services estimates that temporary-help jobs represented 1.2 percent of total nonfarm employment in 1992, up from 0.9 percent in 1988 and 0.4 percent in 1982.[42]

From top management's perspective, the flexibility to turn a company around "on a dime" has great appeal. Being able to change products or work locations quickly is a strategic core competence that can be attained only with a flexible workforce. With the diminishing power of organized labor, employers are allowed more leeway in using temporary and contract labor to fill in when there are sudden surges in demand beyond the capabilities of the core workforce.

But there is a down side. One problem is that more employers are hiring part-timers to become "lean and mean" in a competitive world regardless of the harm it does to workers and company efficiency as a whole. In fact, involuntary part-time employees—workers who would prefer full-time jobs—account for most of the growth in the part-time sector.[43] Most of these new jobs pay less than regular jobs, and few come with good benefits. The standard U.S. job, with a 40-hour workweek, medical benefits, and a pension at age 65 is on the wane, many labor experts are saying, because of the availability of temporary or contract workers.

Managing temporary and contract workers can be challenging, especially when they are mixed with permanent employees. One difference between the two groups may result from the insecurity involuntary part-time temporaries often show because they are not on the company's regular payroll but want to be. While some may have quietly resigned themselves to this fact, others may be surreptitiously job hunting, looking for a better deal while giving the company only a minimum of effort or results.

Another difference between these two groups is their agenda. Permanent employees are interested in events that most temporaries will never experience, for example, promotions, new or revised company benefits, news on who is doing what and when, and local gossip. Temporary employees are more interested in issues that directly affect their status and pay because politically "they're not on the food chain."[44] Involuntary temporaries also see themselves as having the worst schedules, the least interesting jobs, and poor long-term expectations. Maintaining a balanced blend of permanent and temporary employees is becoming a constant challenge for managers. Figure 6–6 offers a few suggestions on how it might be done and what to avoid.

PERMANENT PART-TIME WORKERS

Part-time employment makes up a growing share of jobs in the United States. About half of the jobs people find are part-time. These employees represent almost one-fifth of the U.S. work force.[45]

Most part-timers work in clerical, sales, and service occupations. These occupations are predominantly low-paid and low-skilled. Perhaps as much as one-third of all **permanent part-time work** is available for the highly skilled.[46] Retail organizations, for example, rely extensively on a permanent part-time workforce while maintaining only a small core of full-time employees.

Organizations create good part-time jobs to attract and retain valued employees whose personal circumstances prevent them from working full time. Many of these positions are highly skilled. Unlike temporary or contract employment, permanent part-time employees may receive high compensation for high productivity and low turnover, rates are not uncommon. Employers often accommodate the worker's schedule rather than ask the worker to accommodate the needs of the job.

JOB SHARING

In recent years, job sharing has evolved as an opportunity for career part-time employment. **Job sharing**

FIGURE 6–6   GUIDELINES FOR MANAGING A MIX OF PERMANENT AND TEMPORARY WORKERS

1. Refer to temporaries as *associates* or *consultants;* avoid the term *temporary* or even *contingent.*

2. Be as consistent in giving out rewards with temps as with permanent employees—particularly praise and interesting work.

3. Communicate to combat slacking off and cynicism—make an extra effort to keep temps in the loop without implying that they're permanent.

4. Include them socially—if the company sponsors a softball team and temps want to play, let them; it can only build esprit de corps.

5. Be careful when discussing the company's future plans and make no sympathy-fueled promises of permanent positions.

Source: Adapted from Marilyn Kennedy, "A Nightmare Scenario," *Across the Board* (July-August 1993): 12.

HR IN THE NEWS

JOB-SHARING TRAILBLAZERS

With companies stretching fewer workers further, job sharing, it seems, has gone the way of the leisure suit. There's been hardly any growth in policies allowing two part-timers to share one job, and few employees use the policies that do exist. Many managers groan at the mere mention of job sharing, loath to add another ingredient—compatibility with a partner—to the long list of qualities required of a good employee.

But though their ranks are thin, job sharers are anything but a dying breed. Janice Decker and Wendy Riley are two people who have solved the problem of achieving a balance between work and life. Wendy had been a 12-year veteran of HR management who wanted more time to be with her daughter and still make a professional salary. Janice, HR consultant and published author, had decided to restructure her life to live as a fiction writer. They conformed their resumés and sent out a joint cover letter promising "enhanced flexibility in coverage, with no job burnout."

Anticipating every objection, the two put together a strategy. Unlike most job sharers, who typically each get all or most of a full benefits package, they agreed to split one benefits package if necessary. Money was divided up 60/40. Work hours reflected the split and whatever best suited the job and the employer. Similarly, they decided how to split up the benefit package: health insurance for Janice, flexible-spending plan for Wendy; Social Security for both (no way out of that one); pension plans 50–50 as allowed by the plan. What didn't fit inside the box, they found a way to split up out of the box. The biggest hurdle was to convince the employer that they could provide client service with continuity and coherence.

What happened? A few interviewers were overwhelmed by the concept; other interviewers got lost in the details, concluding the risk was too great; and a few interviewers, however reluctant, admitted that their companies put more emphasis on "face time"—how many hours employees were visible at the worksite—above other, perhaps more meaningful measures of productivity.

The two trailblazers persevered, however, eventually landing a job at Aetna Life & Casualty. Michelle Carpenter, their Aetna manager, was impressed with the "entrepreneurial initiative" as "the kind of thinking we're trying to get employees to do."

WWW.AETNA.COM

Source: Adapted from Janice Decker and Wendy Riley, "They Don't Get It," *Across the Board* (October 1996): 44–45.

generally refers to dividing full-time jobs into two or more part-time positions, often without particular regard for how the full-time job is divided. In personnel work, the term generally means that two employees hold a position together, whether as a team jointly responsible for the position or as individuals responsible for only half of the position. *Leisure sharing* refers to a couple sharing a single position because they prefer the increased leisure time that two household members gain by sharing a job. In this way, both of them can pursue careers.[47]

Job sharing as an alternative scheduling technique provides the organization with several possible advantages: increased productivity, a greater pool of qualified applicants, and reduced costs. The most common result is an influx of new energy and enthusiasm brought to the job by a second person (see *HR in the News:* "Job-Sharing Trailblazers"). The company often gets more than twice the talent from having two workers perform the same job. When job sharing was studied in the mass assembly department of a southeastern manufacturing firm, the scrap ratio was 12 percent lower and output was 7 percent higher for the shared-job positions. Workers found four hours to be far less tiring than eight and so worked at a faster pace. Also, fatigue-caused errors were greatly reduced.[48]

The supervisor of a Wisconsin state telecommunications department stated that the primary advantage of job sharing is that employees working a few days a week or four hours a day are happier about their jobs than full-time workers. Many times the expenses of training, hiring temporary workers, and overtime are reduced. Training costs are often reduced because one job-sharing employee can give on-the-job training to the other. Turnover costs are often reduced, because job sharers with hours specifically tailored to their personal needs are less likely to leave the job.

Job sharing has disadvantages. Communication problems may increase between job-sharing partners and between them and other members of the workforce. Job sharing may make it difficult to assign responsibility to a particular individual. Benefit costs to the organization may increase, particularly if the Social Security (FICA) tax or state taxes for unemployment insurance cannot be prorated. Companies employing job sharers whose incomes exceed the FICA ceiling may pay additional FICA taxes. However, benefit costs usually decrease because the two part-time employees do not receive all the benefits of full-time employees. Perhaps the greatest obstacle to job sharing is the fact that surveys show job sharing is not positively viewed by managers. Generally, they feel that job sharers lack the commitment to a job that a full-time employee would have.

In Grand Rapids, Michigan, Steelcase, one of the nation's largest manufacturers of office furniture, first offered job sharing in 1983. After several years, Steelcase has concluded that job sharing lowers absenteeism and turnover by retaining employees who want part-time work.[49]

COMPRESSED WORKWEEKS

Compressed workweeks are schedules with fewer than the traditional five workdays a week for 40 hours, or 5/40. The hours worked per day are increased so that the hours worked per week still total 40. The most common compressed workweek is the four-day workweek.

4/40 Workweek
The usual **four-day workweek** consists of four 10 hour days, or 4/40. Sixty percent of all compressed workweeks fall into the 4/40 category. In practice, some of the 40-hour workweeks have actually become four 9-hour work periods as employees trade coffee breaks and clean-up time for extra hours off. With this scheme, managers believe that they are getting as much work accomplished in four 9-hour days as they might in a 5/40 workweek because they save start-up time as well as maintenance, which is often scheduled for the fifth day of work.[50]

4/48 and 3/36 Workweeks
An alternative to the 4/40 compressed workweek is a week that rotates four-day and three-day shifts. In this arrangement, employees who work four 12-hour days are off for three days. Then they work three 12-hour days, followed by four days off. Thus, employees work 48 hours one week and 36 hours the next, or 4/48 and 3/36. For 48-hour weeks they automatically receive eight hours of overtime pay. This system requires two crews of employees for each shift. One crew works from 9 P.M. to 9 A.M. as the night shift, while the other crew works from 9 A.M. to 9 P.M. as the day shift. In total then, four shifts of employees work 12-hour days, with three-day workweeks alternating with four-day workweeks throughout the year.[51]

DISCRETIONARY WORKWEEKS/FLEXTIME

A second type of alternative work schedule is the **discretionary workweek,** which offers employees greater freedom in regulating their own lives. Retail stores, service agencies, and some manufacturers have met the demands of business with more satisfied, more productive employees working varied schedules.

Flextime   A system of **flextime** provides a true alternative work schedule for employees, who may follow different schedules of work each day of the workweek. Flextime has been particularly beneficial to service organizations such as retail outlets, banks, savings-and-loan associations, and insurance companies.

Almost every survey shows companies reporting more advantages than disadvantages to flexible work schedules, regardless of type. Savings in employee turnover, absenteeism, and tardiness are reported so often and over such long periods of time that these advantages must be considered valid attributes of flexible schedules.

In a typical flextime system, the employer establishes a *core* time when all employees must work. For service organizations, core time is a time during which most customers arrive; for example, from 10:30 A.M. to 1:00 P.M. for a retail outlet where most customers come in during their lunch breaks or 5:00-to-9:00 for suburban shopping locations. As Figure 6–7 shows, the employer also establishes the total hours of operation during which the employee must work. Normally, the employee must work the core hours within the total eight hours worked. If the core time is not worked, the employee does not get credit for the workday; usually an employee does not arrive at work at all if the core time cannot be worked. The employee may choose a different starting and stopping time each day of the week, as long as the core time is worked and the total hours worked are

within the hours the organization is open. The organization may alternate core times for different days of the week if this is necessary to meet customers' demands.

Most employees in the United States and elsewhere favor flextime operations. Employees particularly like the control flextime gives them over their personal lives. They can better schedule leisure activities and family responsibilities, and take care of personal business during normal work hours.

Other flextime advantages for employees include reduced commuting time and faster shopping during slack times. Parents enjoy the advantages flextime gives them because they are often responsible for school-age children.

Organizations that have experimented with flextime report many advantages to the system: improved employee morale, increased productivity, and decreased absenteeism and turnover. Tardiness is practically eliminated since employees can start their total workday later and still work the same hours. Flextime also reduces timekeeping by supervisors. Employers report that employees usually arrive ready to begin working since personal needs can be taken care of before work. Another advantage is the reduction of overtime costs. By setting core hours during the busiest periods of the day, managers avoid scheduling overtime or hiring part-time employees for busy periods. Often retail and service organizations must overstaff to be sure that an adequate number of employees is available during a rush period. Overstaffing is less necessary with flextime.[52]

Flextime may be a key factor for employers who successfully attract and retain employees with diverse ethnic backgrounds. Arnold Manseth, director of employee

---

FIGURE 6–7   FLEXIBLE WORK SCHEDULES

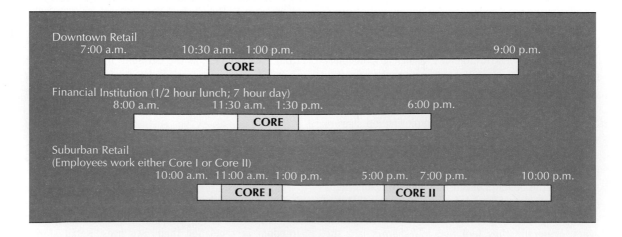

relations at the Pacific Northwest Bell Telephone Company, believes that trust between employer and employees is all that is required to implement flexible work hours. Manseth claims, "Today's employees are no longer content to follow their fathers' footsteps and put the job above everything else. Instead, they have learned to balance the job with other aspects of life, and are asking the employer to understand. For those [employers] who do, they'll find the quality of work will not drop. A happy employee is a productive one."[53]

Creating a flexible workforce will also enable employers to retain older employees. In the 1990s, the United States has the oldest workforce in its history. Flextime allows older workers the opportunity to ease their work demands while remaining productive.

Gus Tyler, assistant president of the International Ladies Garment Workers Union, believes that flexible work hours will enhance U.S. competition in the international marketplace. If American companies were more willing to "loosen the boardroom grip" and encourage rather than disdain greater flexibility among their employees, they might find that they do not need to relocate to other countries. Instead, claims Tyler, we could regain paradise in America if companies were more flexible instead of cutting benefits and complaining about government overregulation.[54]

DISADVANTAGES OF WORKPLACE FLEXIBILITY

The alternatives just discussed are only the beginning of a trend toward new and varied work schedules. Managers, realizing that they cannot redesign all jobs to make them more challenging or interesting, use various scheduling techniques to give employees increased freedom to plan work or leisure time. The major alternatives—compressed workweek, job sharing, flextime, telecommuting, and part-time work—have been successful for the most part. The advantage of workplace flexibility is a substantial gain in employees' satisfaction with their jobs and work environment. However, there are also disadvantages associated with alternative work schedules. These will now be discussed.

Employee Resistance   Employees often resist change of any type. Uncertain of what the new system will bring and at least partially satisfied with the current system, many employees resist possible changes in their basic routine. When asked for their input about a possible change in work schedule, employees are con-

cerned about the new schedule's effect on (1) their personal life, including their family; (2) organizational effectiveness, particularly work coordination; and (3) customer service. Their attitudes toward new work schedules tend to focus not only on personal and family effects, as might be expected, but also on the effects on the employer's cooperation and relations with customers. If such perceived problems materialize, managers will need to take action to alleviate the cause of the concern.[55]

Communication Problems   Possibly the most common disadvantage encountered by any company using alternative work schedules is communication problems. Inconsistent work hours change common communication patterns; at times, some employees may be inaccessible for group meetings or casual discussions. This problem can be minimized by proper management planning and correct implementation of the work schedule alternative that has been adopted.

Fatigue   A major complaint of some employees about compressed workweek schedules is fatigue. Obviously, many compressed workweek schemes that involve longer days and mental and physical fatigue may become a real hardship. While many employees may not complain of fatigue directly, the later hours of the workday must be carefully monitored to make sure that fatigue is not becoming a major cause of increased injuries or decreased productivity during a compressed workweek schedule.

Interdependence of Jobs   Real problems for flextime or part-time alternative work schedules are created by the interdependence of jobs. In fact, highly interdependent jobs such as assembly-line operations probably make these scheduling procedures impractical. Flextime and other discretionary workweek programs have been utilized primarily by service or small manufacturing organizations that do not have highly interdependent jobs.

WORK DESIGN GUIDELINES

In modern management, the problem of designing work that is appealing to employees yet results in high productivity is a common one. When implementing a program designed to increase both the motivation and productivity of employees, management should consider the following issues:

- Is the problem one that can be addressed by enlarging the scope of most employee's jobs? Jobs traditionally designed to be routine and dull can often be improved by giving employees more and varied tasks to perform. Job rotation and job enlargement usually require minimal management, planning, and cost. More complete programs increase not only the scope of the job but, more important, its depth in order to increase motivation. These programs are usually more expensive to develop and implement. Although job enrichment, work teams, and work simplification may involve greater cost and time, they often reap greater returns.

- Any job design program should have two objectives: (1) to increase the general morale of employees in order to bring greater productivity and lower costs to the organization, and (2) to increase employee job satisfaction through more interesting and challenging work. The objectives of both management and employees must be given equal weight because each must cooperate completely if such a program is to succeed.

- Different employees satisfy different needs in doing their jobs. Any job designer must consider that not all employees want either increased responsibility and authority or increased scope. A certain proportion of the workforce prefers specialized jobs so that they can easily learn their work, become proficient, and not worry about their job security. These employees often find personal achievement and growth outside the organization and do not seek high levels of autonomy and achievement through their jobs.

- Before considering a job-design program, an organization should carefully investigate the exact causes of employee problems. The design of the work may not be at the heart of those problems; rather, they may be caused by poor supervision, lack of advancement, poor working conditions, or low pay.

- Finally, when embarking on a job design program, management should tap its greatest source of ideas and knowledge: its employees.

Job enrichment, work teams, or any of the flexible work schedules may breathe new life and competitive fire into organizations. There seems to be unabashed optimism in the HR profession for all of them. But while these approaches may promise more highly motivated employees, improved quality, and better productivity, the results may be less than expected. HR professionals must be prepared to tinker with—or perhaps abandon—these programs.

While the risk of failed job design is real, the benefits far outweigh the detriments for most organizations. Implementing a bad program can lead to mistakes, but doing nothing can lead to extinction. Without a doubt, traditional job designs, particularly those emphasizing overspecialization, will continue giving way to motivation-intensive programs.

SUMMARY POINTS

- Organizations are being designed in terms of processes rather than by functions. The changes are the result of global competitive forces.

- Older industrial engineering models, such as scientific management, concentrated on attaining efficiency and control to achieve economies of scale. Certain industrial sectors, especially manufacturing, depended on specialization using work simplification, standardization, and training to keep costs down. Human concerns were secondary.

- Understanding how people are motivated, that is, their needs and goals, is critical to modern work design. Important motivational theories include Maslow's hierarchy of needs, goal setting, and Herzberg's two-factor theory.

- One controversial issue is whether money ought to be linked closely to job performance. Does money motivation detract from the intrinsic satisfaction that can come from doing a good job? The evidence is mixed.

- The tasks employees perform on the job and the variety, difficulty level, and autonomy of the job greatly affect job satisfaction and productivity.

- Employees, individually or in work teams, are being asked to take on greater responsibility for the design and control of their jobs. Simple, repetitious tasks are being eliminated whenever possible, generally resulting in jobs that are more motivating and challenging. At the same time, some degree of job specialization is necessary so that new employees can learn their jobs quickly and make fewer errors.

- Programs such as job enrichment and self-managed workgroups, have resulted in redesigned jobs that were previously highly specialized and boring. There is also a trend toward multiskilling, whereby team members learn multiple tasks. Organizations are adopting work teams and giving them more freedom and responsibilities.

- Technology plays an important role in modern job design. The office environment can improve employee creativity, productivity, and quality.

- In addition to job design, organizations may choose to implement programs that increase workplace flexibility. These programs tend to adopt a scheduling mix between

SUMMARY POINTS—cont'd

employees' needs and the organization's staffing requirements in ways that are consistent with the company's culture. Compressed workweeks, flextime programs, telecommuting, temporary and contract work, and permanent part-time work are the more common approaches.

Employees who desire greater control over work hours, who would like easier commuting, or who want a different lifestyle will be attracted to organizations that offer these types of programs.

CASE STUDY

AND YOU THOUGHT YOUR JOB WAS BAD . . .

Judy Adkins is having a miserable night. The 58-year-old telemarketer is on her 21st phone call on the evening shift, but so far, she has sold just one bank credit card application. She is becoming impatient as she waits for her computer to dial the next prospect. Finally, she hears the beep in her headset and the prospect's name appears on her computer.

"About time," she mutters. There is confusion all around her, but it is rather tame tonight. Everyone except Judy is close to meeting their goals. For some unexplainable reason, tonight is not going well for her.

A young supervisor—not yet 30, Adkins guesses—has now moved into position just behind her. Adkins knows she is in for some tough comments.

"You're not holding up your end of the wagon tonight, Judy." The supervisor is gone before the words are out of her mouth.

"I don't need to hear that now!" she says.

But Ms. Adkins knows that the pressure goes with the job. She is a seasoned veteran, having over six years experience in a variety of telemarketing industries. Adkins is one of the most senior people in her current job, having just finished her second year. For her and other experienced callers, the daily goal is 100 calls for an eight-hour shift. The expected "conversion rate" is 15 percent of those who listen long enough to count as a presentation.

Adkins's current supervisor is intense, demanding, and quick to criticize. Frankly, all of them have been that way. "Their job is just as tense as mine," she says. "If they don't fill their sales targets, they're history, just like us."

Because most supervisors occasionally eavesdrop on calls with cordless phones, they are quick to give feedback. Some are positive, such as "Judy is a goal buster—way to go, Judy!"

More often, however, what employees hear are "suggestions" for improving their sales pitch, such as "Slow the presentation down" or "Don't ad-lib on the script!" While Adkins wants recognition as much as anyone, she has become somewhat jaded from the insincerity. She would rather have more pay or benefits, but neither is in the cards.

Most telemarketers are paid an hourly wage plus commissions. For Adkins that amounts to $7.50 per hour plus approximately $5 for commissions—around $12 per hour on a good day. There are no health benefits, and if you believe telemarketing executives, no prospects for any in the future.

Adding to the tension are the customers. Telemarketing is tough, stressful work. Besides the fact that the boss may well be listening in, some hostile customers will verbally heap abuse on the telemarketer. Profanity is common, and there is nothing to do but continue to be polite and take it.

The constant stress takes a toll on everyone. The turnover rate is one of the highest in the country. The average time worked as a telemarketer is only 11 weeks (not months or years). Those who want to make it a career hope to break into management, where pay and benefits are much better. But that usually requires more education and youth. The last opening for a supervisor's position drew over 50 applications from telemarketers.

QUESTIONS

1. Assume you are a management consultant called in to analyze the turnover problem. You are told that pay and benefits are fixed and cannot be substantially altered. It is clear that whatever you recommend must not bring productivity down. What would you recommend to management?

2. How might the telemarketer's job be redesigned so that employees are more satisfied and challenged by their work? Is telemarketing a job that can be enriched and remain highly productive or is it more like an assembly line?

3. How might the supervisors be contributing to the problem? What recommendations would you make about changing their styles?

4. How might recruitment be part of the solution?

5. Consider such strategies as team competition and alternative work schedules. What do you think would happen if they were implemented?

EXPERIENTIAL EXERCISES

1. CAN THIS JOB BE ENRICHED?

PURPOSE

To explore the concept of job enrichment by determining whether a routine job has the potential for enrichment.

The basic steps to implement job enrichment include the following:

1. Select the job or jobs to be enriched. Criteria for selection include:
   a. Can changes be made without costly engineering modifications?
   b. Are job attitudes poor?
   c. Will motivation improve some area or areas of performance?
2. Thoroughly analyze the job and develop a list of ways in which it may be enriched.
3. Screen out ideas that are considered "hygienic"; for example, working conditions, pay, benefits, peer and supervisory relationships, and so on. Include only motivators, such as job factors that enable employees to make more decisions and have greater responsibility for their work, as well as increased recognition.

TASK

For the following scenario, answer the following questions:

1. *Can* the job be enriched?
2. *Should* the job be enriched?
3. If you decide to enrich the job, *how* would you do so?
4. If you decide to enrich the job, what performance criteria would you use to determine whether your job enrichment strategy was a success?

BERT GARNER: ASSEMBLY LINE WORKER

Bert Garner works for General Electronics, Inc., a large manufacturer of home appliances. Garner is employed in a large plant that builds refrigerators. The refrigerators are built on an assembly line that snakes several hundred yards through the plant. Garner is responsible for attaching the freezer door to the refrigerator. As the refrigerator reaches his station, he picks up a door, several screws, and a screwdriver and screws the door to the refrigerator. He does this more than 200 times a day.

Stacks of freezer doors are delivered to Garner's workstation by another employee. Down the line, an inspector checks his work in addition to the work of other operators. Any item that needs to be reworked is removed from the refrigerator and set aside. The speed of the line—thus the productivity rate—determined by plant management. Any job changes are generally initiated by the industrial engineering staff.

When asked about his work, Garner responded, "It's a job. I'm not crazy about it, but it puts food on the table. Hell, who likes their job anyway? With the economy the way it is, I feel lucky just to have a job."

General Electronics' refrigerator assembly plant is about 35 years old. Capital improvements in the plant are seriously being considered by management to improve plant efficiency. Plans are to install more robot-type machines, particularly for jobs in which quality problems often exist. The labor–management climate is satisfactory, but the union's concern over management's plans for installing advanced technology has strained relations quite a bit.

2. MY IDEAL JOB

PURPOSE

To help you better understand how the different elements comprising any job affect job satisfaction and motivation and to understand that people are motivated by a variety of job elements.

TIME

30 to 45 minutes.

TASK

1. The instructor will break the class into small groups. Each group will review and discuss the common job factors from the list to be presented. Each group will be expected to reach a consensus on the two factors that are most important to the group. The group is not limited to the factors identified on the list.
2. The group will present its list to the class and present a rationale for its selection.
3. Following brief group presentations, the instructor will lead the class through a discussion of the most important job factors.

JOB FACTORS

Job satisfaction is the goal of most workers. What would it take for you to be a satisfied employee? Consider each of the job factors identified here. All of them are commonly found, but it is possible that some other factor not listed is more important to you. If that is the situation, list it as well. Place a weight from 1 (least important) to 10 (most important) for each factor.

EXPERIENTIAL EXERCISES — cont'd

1. Job security
2. Good pay
3. A friendly boss
4. Pleasant office environment or work conditions
5. A job with prestige and status
6. Challenging, stimulating, and interesting work
7. A job you can master and control
8. Increased responsibility and authority
9. A satisfying, high-quality personal life
10. Recognition and appreciation for your work
11. Sensible company policies, procedures, and rules
12. A desire to continue to learn new skills, gain more knowledge, and so on

KEY TERMS AND CONCEPTS

Achievement motivation
Compressed workweeks
Depth
Discretionary workweek
Empowerment
Flextime
Four-day workweek
Goal setting
Herzberg's two-factor theory
Job design
Job enlargement
Job enrichment
Job rotation
Job sharing
Line-of-sight
Managing by walking around

Maslow's Hierarchy of Needs
Motivation
Motivation-intensive job
Overspecialization
Permanent part-time work
Problem-solving teams
Productivity
Project teams
Scope
Sea change
Self-managed teams
Self-efficacy
Specialization-intensive jobs
Telecommuting
Workplace flexibility

REVIEW QUESTIONS

1. Describe some of the forces at work leading to the dramatic changes taking place in the workforce and in the workplace.

2. Clearly efficiency and control of workers can produce a competitive advantage, but it can also create long-term problems. What is the downside of work that is designed solely in terms of increased efficiencies?

3. What is the only true source of building a sustained competitive advantage? Why?

4. Describe different ways that office work can satisfy an office worker's needs using (a) Maslow's hierarchy of needs; (b) McClelland's model; and, (c) goal-setting strategies.

5. Herzberg's two-factor theory has been widely criticized, yet still seems to be popular with business practitioners. Explain the discrepancy.

6. Describe the differences between job rotation, enlargement, and enrichment.

7. Working in teams appears to be something in which most people should become accustomed; nevertheless, for some people, it is not something they are good at or want to be good at. What are the qualities of people who make good team members?

8. Explain why the actual physical layout of an office can make a significant difference in the satisfaction and productivity of the group.

9. Workplace flexibility is becoming one of the most important considerations in managing a contemporary workforce. What are the different strategies available for managing a diverse workforce?

DISCUSSION QUESTIONS

1. Employers are always looking for workers who will be motivated. How important is "being motivated" if the job is (a) sales clerk, (b) assembly-line worker, (c) programmer, (d) telecommuter?

2. Part-time and contract workers give an employer flexibility, but are managers likely to question their work commitment? What issues will occur should the employer rely more on a contingent workforce than on a full-time, permanent workforce?

3. Assume you are an expatriate employee for Ford Motor USA, and have been assigned to work in their new factory in China. You are interested in motivating the factory employees, and you happen to believe in the Maslow hierarchy of needs model. What kind of success would you anticipate by using that model for motivating Chinese factory workers?

4. The numbers of telecommuters are increasing quickly. What are the critical issues in deciding whether a (a) particular job can be done away from the regular work environment via telecommuting, and (b) the human qualities needed to handle telecommuting responsibilities?

5. Balancing the demands of work and home is becoming an important consideration for many workers. What strategies should HR professionals consider for balancing work–family responsibilities?

ENDNOTES

Chapter 6

1. William Bridges, "The End of the Job," *Fortune* (September 19, 1994): 62–64.

2. Edward E. Lawler III, *From the Ground Up: Six Principles for Building the New Logic Corporation* (San Francisco: Jossey-Bass, 1996), 5.

3. Ibid., 33.

4. Ibid., 161.

5. John A. Byrne, "Paradigms for Postmodern Managers," *Business Week/Reinventing American* (1992): 62.

6. Christopher Farrell, "A Wellspring of Innovation," *Business Week/Enterprise* (1993):61.

7. John Schermerhorn, Jr., James Hunt, and Richard Osborn, *Managing Organizational Behavior,* 5th ed. (New York: Wiley, 1994), 703–706.

8. Abraham Maslow, "A Theory of Human Motivation," *Psychological Review* 50 (1943): 370–396.

9. Abraham Maslow, *Eupsychian Management, A Journal,* 1963 portions of text are available at this Website: http://www.scarlet-fire.com/maslow.

10. David McClelland, *The Achieving Society* (Princeton, NJ: D. Van Nostrand, 1961), 15.

11. David McClelland and D. Burnham, "Power Drive Managers: Good Guys Make Bum Bosses," *Psychology Today* 7 (1985): 69–71.

12. Edwin Locke, "Toward a Theory of Task Motivation and Incentives," *Organizational Behavior and Human Performance* 3 (1968): 157–180.

13. Lisa Hoecklin, *Managing Cultural Differences: Strategies for Competitive Advantage,* (Reading, MA: Addison-Wesley Publishing, 1995), 23–39.

14. Ibid., 5–7.

15. Frederick Herzberg, *The Motivation to Work* (New York: Wiley, 1959), 59–83.

16. John Ivancevich, Andrew Szilagyi, and Marc Wallace, Jr., *Organizational Behavior and Performance* (Santa Monica, CA: Goodyear, 1977), 141–42.

17. Ibid., 141.

18. Ibid., 142.

19. Frederick W. Taylor, *The Principles of Scientific Management* (New York: Harper & Row, 1947), 23–53.

20. Robert Frank, "Efficient UPS Tries to Increase Efficiency," *The Wall Street Journal* (May 24, 1995): B1.

21. Bernard J. Reilly and Joseph A. DiAngelo, Jr., "A Look at Job Redesign," *Personnel,* 65, no. 2 (February 1988): 61.

22. Although dated, the comprehensive study of the automobile industry by Walker and Guest continues to reflect an accurate assessment of life on the assembly line. See C.R. Walker and R.H. Guest, *The Man on the Assembly Line* (Cambridge, MA: Harvard University Press, 1952).

23. M. D. Kilbridge, "Reduced Costs Through Enlargement: A Case," *Journal of Business* (October 1989): 357–362.

24. J. R. Hackman and G. R. Oldham, *Work Design* (Reading, MA: Addison-Wesley, 1980). See also "You See the Package from Beginning to End," *Business Week* (May 16, 1983): 103; and R. H. Waterman, *The Renewal Factor* (New York: Bantam Books, 1987), 4.

25. S. Dillingham, "Topeka Revisited," *Human Resource Executive* 4, no. 5 (May 1990): 55–58.

26. Steve Jordan, "Union Defies U.P. Quality Concept," *The Omaha World Herald* (April 6, 1993): M1.

27. Richard Wellins and Jill George, "The Key to Self-Directed Teams," *Training and Development Journal* 45 (April 1991): 26–29.

28. Frank Shipper and Charles C. Manz, "Employee Self-Management Without Formally Designed Teams: An Alternative Road to Empowerment," *Organizational Dynamics* 20 (Winter 1992): 48–61.

29. Wellins and George, "Self-Directed Teams," 27.

30. Richard S. Wellins, William C. Byham, and Jeanne M. Wilson, *Empowered Teams* (San Francisco: Jossey-Bass, 1991), 3–5.

31. Lawler, *From the Ground Up*, 158–161. See also D. Keith Denton, "Multi-skilled Teams Replace Old Work Systems," *HRMagazine* (September 1992): 48–56.

32. Charles Handy, *The Age of Unreason* (Boston: Harvard Business School Press, 1989).

33. David Jamieson and Julie O'Mara, *Managing Workforce 2000* (San Francisco: Jossey-Bess, 1991). See also Eric Sundstrom, *Work Places* (New York: Cambridge University Press, 1986), Jean D. Wineman (ed.), *Behavior Issues in Office Design* (New York: Van Nostrand Reinhold, 1987).

34. Robert Sommer, *Personal Space: The Behavioral Basis of Design* (Englewood Cliffs, NJ: Prentice Hall, 1969); and Jacqueline C. Vischer, *Environmental Quality in Offices:* (New York: Van Nostrand Reinhold, 1989).

35. Michael Brill (ed.), *Using Office Design to Increase Productivity* (Buffalo, NY: Workplace Design and Productivity, Inc., 1984, 1985). See also Vischer, *Environmental Quality* and Barney Olmsted, "Workplace Flexibility: From Employee Accommodation to Business Strategy," *The Human Resources Professional* (Fall 1992): 27.

36. Olmstead, "Workplace Flexibility."

37. Sue Shellenbarger, "Some Thrive, But Many Wilt Working at Home," *The Wall Street Journal* (December 14, 1993): B1.

38. Ibid.

39. Ibid.

40. Sue Shellenbarger, "I'm Still Here! Home Workers Worry They're Invisible," *The Wall Street Journal* (December 16, 1993): B1.

41. "Shift to Temporary Help Appears Permanent," *Sunday World-Herald*, Omaha, Nebraska (September 5, 1993): G-1.

42. Ibid.

43. Marilyn Kennedy, "A Nightmare Scenario," *Across the Board* (July–August 1993): 11.

44. Ibid., 44.

45. Chris Tilly, "Reasons for the Continuing Growth of Part-time Employment," *Monthly Labor Review* (March 1991): 10–18.

46. Ibid., 12.

47. Michael Frease and Robert A. Zawacki, "Job-Sharing: An Answer to Productivity Problems?" *The Personnel Administrator* (October 1979): 35–37.

48. Grett S. Meier, *Job Sharing* (Kalamazoo, MI: Upjohn Insitute, 1978), 1–3.

49. Kirkland Ropp, "The Solution: Steelcase Inc.," *Personnel Administrator* 32, no. 8 (August 1987): 79.

50. "Flexible Work Schedules," *Small Business Report* (October 1978): 24–25.

51. Ibid., 24–25.

52. Keith Bernard, "Flextime's Potential for Management," *The Personnel Administrator* (October 1979): 51–54.

53. James Fraze, "Preparing for a Different Future," *Resource* 7, no. 1 (January 1988): 1, 10.

54. Ibid.

55. Randall B. Dunham and Jon L. Pierce, "Attitudes Toward Work Schedules: Construct Definition, Instrument Development, and Validation," *Academy of Management Journal* 29, no. 1 (March 1986): 170–82.

CHAPTER

7

EMPLOYEE RECRUITMENT

CHAPTER OBJECTIVES

1 To explain how the labor market operates.

2 To understand the need for human resources planning.

3 To recognize the advantages of filling vacancies with internal job applicants.

4 To cite the keys to a successful job-posting program.

5 To identify the advantages of filling vacancies with external job applicants.

6 To describe methods of recruiting qualified and available job applicants.

7 To evaluate alternatives to recruiting permanent new employees.

HR IN THE NEWS

COLLEGE RECRUITMENT BECOMES LAVISH!

WWW.DELL.COM

"It has happened overnight", says Pamela Hamilton of Dell Computer Corporation, "All of a sudden you need the same intensity to hire undergrads as you do MBAs, and that has never been the case." The market for undergraduates "is as intense as anybody's ever seen it," says IBMs Dave Ferrell. The 1.2 million 1998 college seniors were part of the strongest U.S. job market in decades. One senior, Courtney Meltzer, a business major at the University of Colorado was flown to New York by Smith Barney for its "Super Saturday" recruitment fair and offered a $6,000 signing bonus, $40,000 salary, and first-year bonus of $17,000– $27,000—she signed.

NOW, *THIS* IS A JOB MARKET

- National unemployment rate (April, 1998): **4.3%**
- Last time unemployment was lower: **Feb. 1970 (4.2%)**
- Lowest unemployment rate in the nation: **Columbia, SC (1.3%)**
- Highest unemployment rate: **Merced, CA (19.0%)**
- Companies saying job candidate has "upper hand" in negotiating salary and benefits: **63%**
- Companies saying the employer has upper hand: **13%**
- Average number of job offers for male college undergraduates this year: **2.65**
- Average number of job offers for female college undergrads: **2.53**
- Companies saying there is a shortage of qualified job candidates: **88%**
- Workers who say they would change jobs for "slightly higher pay": **40%**
- Average bonus given to employees at Cambridge Technology Partners Inc. who refer new hires: **$2,500**
- Total bonuses paid out under the program this year: **$570,000**
- Employees hired as a result of program this year: **230**

SOURCES: Carl Quintanilla, "College Recruiting Becomes Lavish," *The Wall Street Journal* (June 4, 1998): B1, 7; Bureau of Labor Statistics, Marra Peters & Partners, Hanigan Consulting Group, William M. Mercer Inc., Robert Hall International Inc., Cambridge Technology Partners Inc.

RECRUITMENT STRATEGIES IN A DIVERSE WORKFORCE

What's the toughest, most important challenge in business today? Recruiting and hiring qualified people quickly enough to keep a business prospering. Many employers are chronically short of the best talent. HR professionals, owners, and managers find they must constantly focus on attracting and retaining talented workers. The old time tested recruiting methods will fill some jobs, but employers need to create their own unique techniques for fast powerstaffing. How? A company with a good reputation as a workplace has an advantage. In general the most successful companies are as serious about recruiting, hiring, and retaining good people as they are about their products and services.

Traditional methods, discussed later in this chapter, such as classified ads, employment agencies, referrals, walk-ins, and so on still work in many cases. However, new recruiting tools are challenging the traditional methods in usage, cost-effectiveness, and success. One method (see Figure 7–1) is Internet recruiting which includes a large number of online job banks, career fairs, internships, and minority training programs. Cisco Systems in San Jose, for example, hires 1,200 people per month from its multiple Web sites.[1]

Every organization, regardless of its size, product, or service, must recruit applicants to fill positions. **Recruitment** is the process of acquiring applicants who are available and qualified to fill positions in the organization. Most often, HR administrators will actively recruit only as positions become vacant. Through direct applications by individuals and by walk-in applicants, an organization can

FIGURE 7–1   RECRUITMENT METHODS

TRADITIONAL

- Classified ads
- Employee referrals
- Employment Agencies
- Walk-in Applicants
- State Agencies
- Internal Promotions
- Colleges/Universities

NONTRADITIONAL

- The Internet
- Career Fairs
- Minority Programs
- Hiring Bonuses/Finder's Fees
- Internships/Mentoring Programs

WEBSITES: LOOKING FOR A NEW JOB?

- **CareerBuilder**
http://www.careerbuilder.com
Jobs: 3,000–5,000. **Employers:** 200, including Sallie Mae, Southwestern Bell, Taco Bell.

- **CareerMart**
http://www.careermart.com
Jobs: 5,000. **Employers:** 500, including IBM, Philips, Burger King.

- **CareerSite**
http://www.careersite.com
Jobs: 5,000–7,000. **Employers:** 400, including AT&T, Booz Allen Hamilton, CIGNA Insurance, Ford.

- **Career Path**
http://www.careerpath.com
- **E.Span**
http://www.joboptions.com
Jobs: 15,000. **Employers:** 1,000, including Caterpillar, Compaq, IBM, Lotus, MCI, Microsoft, Texas Instruments, Westinghouse.

- **The Monster Board**
http://www.monsterboard.com
Jobs: 25,000. **Employers:** 4,000, including CVS, Compaq, IBM, Intel, McDonald's, Price Waterhouse.

- **4Work.com**
http://www.4work.com
Jobs: 6,000. **Employers:** 1,735, including Blockbuster, Norell, United Way.

- **The Wall Street Journal**
http://careers.wsj.com
An online discussion about the job market for college graduates.

- **America's Job Bank**
http://www.ajb.dni.US
The U.S. Department of Labor lists jobs in all fifty states.

SOURCE: Adapted from Margaret Mannix, "Putting the Net to Work," *U.S. News and World Report* (October 27, 1997): p. 94.

maintain a large pool of available and qualified applicants without much additional recruitment effort. But because of federal guidelines and the increasing competition for the best applicants, HR administrators find it necessary to recruit even when they have a large number of available and qualified applicants. Sometimes the process provides unexpected, humorous events, as presented in Figure 7–2.

Recruiting workers in other countries differs substantially from the American process. Japanese and German employers, for example, develop long-term employee relationships and primarily recruit from the best and brightest high school students. Students in those countries are aware that their final examinations taken at the end of high school determine their job potential, which in turn makes the exams very competitive. Honda and Toyota, for example, select their future workers directly from high school based on their final examination scores. In Germany, half of each high school graduating class goes directly into employers' apprenticeship programs.[2]

Significant demographic shifts in the available labor supply are having a profound impact on recruitment strategies utilized by employers.

Recruiting good applicants has always been challenging; however, demographic and economic factors in today's society require employers to utilize more flexible and innovative recruitment methods. The reality, which

FIGURE 7–2   RESUMANIA

Robert Half, a New York employment specialist who recruits financial executives, accountants, and data processors, has for many years been c ollecting inappropriate, unintentional, humorous, and self-defeating material that job candidates have included in their resumés. He calls it "resumania."

For example, a Salt Lake City bookkeeper wrote, "I am very conscientius and accurite." A Boston accountant stated, "My consideration will be given to relocation anywhere in the English-speaking world and/or Washington, D.C." A Cleveland computer programmer stipulated, "Will relocate anywhere—except Russia, Red China, Vietnam, or New York City."

Here's what some job hunters had to say when asked why they left their last job: "The sales manager was a dummy." "Responsibility makes me nervous." "The company made me a scapegoat—just like my three previous employers." "They insisted that all employees get to work by 8:45 every morning. Couldn't work under those conditions."

Under the heading of "I don't think they meant to say that," Half includes: "I am also a notary republic." "The firm currently employs 20 odd people."

Prospective employers are still trying to figure out the resumé of a San Jose, Calif., man who wrote, "Please call me after 5:30 P.M. because I am self-employed and my employer does not know I am looking for another job."

Resumania may be avoided, Half advised, by using logic and common sense and by making sure the completed resumé is written in a factual, business-like, readable, and tactful manner. Examples of what not to do include the resumé of a Pittsburgh job seeker who described her ideal employer: "Perfect would be an organization beset with a variety of problems while simultaneously beginning to stir with the fever of acquisitions and diversification. As the nature of the job declines in the hierarchy of preferences, so obviously would come into play the decisiveness of compensating subordinating factors."

A New York credit manager (who should have pursued a career in law) wrote: "While I am open to the initial nature of an assignment, I am decidedly disposed that it be so oriented as to at least partially incorporate the experience enjoyed heretofore, and that it be configured so as to ultimately lead to the application of more rarefied facets of financial management as the major sphere of responsibility."

Finally, we are left to ponder the fate of an Omaha bank officer whose resumé read, "I can type, pitch hay, and shear sheep. I am also skilled at groundhog hunting and ballroom dancing." And what do you suppose ever happened to the Philadelphia computer operator who bragged, "I was proud to win the Gregg Typting Award"?

SOURCE: Byron Crawford, "Resumania," *The Louisville Courier-Journal* (February 25, 1985): B-1. Reprinted by permission of *The Louisville Courier-Journal*, copyright 1985. All rights reserved.

was projected by the Bureau of Labor Statistics, is an aging workforce that has fewer young people entering the job market to replace retirees; in addition, of those new entrants, 83 percent are women, members of minority groups, or immigrants.[3] This changing workforce enables employers to achieve diversity, as discussed in Chapter 6.

To attract and keep good people today requires flexibility. Workers today place a high value on interesting work, open communication, and a positive family/work atmosphere. At IBM, the HR department regularly surveys all employees. "There's a message that comes in

loud and clear," according to IBM spokesman Mike Shore, "and that's flexibility." The growing labor shortage caused by the aging workforce requires employers to be more flexible. However, according to a National Association of Colleges and Employers, new college graduates still place traditional benefits—medical insurance, retirement plans, salary increases, and vacations—above more exotic perks such as fitness programs, onsite drycleaning, casual dress, and so on.[4]

Employers are responding to the labor shortage with a number of nontraditional recruitment strategies, including the following:

- **Minority training programs** At a time when 50 percent of all jobs require a high school diploma and 30 percent require a college degree, many minority applicants have difficulty meeting these basic requirements. To assist minority applicants and achieve a more diverse workforce, Aetna Life & Casualty, for example, offers training programs covering basic writing and mathematics skills, as well as job-specific instruction.

- **Internships and mentoring programs** Employers are introducing students to the opportunities available through education by means of internships and mentoring programs. Inroads, Inc., in St. Louis, matches minority students seeking internships in the sciences with employers. The program has four steps: (1) *prescreening*, sending employers only three to four students for every position; (2) *training*, Saturday classes on personal and professional development topics to get students "corporate ready"; (3) *coaching*, monthly meetings with Inroads counselors to help bridge the gap from school to work; (4) *internship*, practical on-the-job experiences over two to three summers. The Inroads program has a record of about two-thirds of all students being hired full-time by the internship sponsor.[5]

- **Career fairs** Employers are increasingly trying to attract retirees back into the workforce. Days Inn of America sponsors national career fairs in locations that are likely to attract retirees. At the fairs, they emphasize special incentives designed to attract older applicants, such as tuition reimbursements for grandchildren. The hotel chain has been able to recruit over one-quarter of its reservation clerks through the program and has experienced a 39 percent reduction in turnover in those positions.

WWW.DAYSINN.COM

- **Finder's fees** A traditional effective source of new applicants—current employees—is being given a new twist by employers offering bonuses or finder's fees to employees who recruit new hirees. Chicago's Continental Bank offers a $300 finder's fee to employees.

- **The Internet** Thousands of employers have developed a national job market by posting positions with online job banks (see Figure 7–1). Some only post positions on the Internet. At first, only computer-related jobs were listed; today everything—from grill-cook jobs at Wendy's to laser-physicist positions at Lockheed Martin Corporation are listed. The advantages to employers are speed and cost according to Robert Worley, Director of Employment Resources at First Union Corporation in Charlotte,

North Carolina. Compared to a two-week process for newspaper ads, "you can post a job today and start getting resumés overnight," and the cost of job searches on the Internet is less.[6] Some job banks offer "personal search agents" which are interactive and let applicants search for job openings by key criteria such as by position, industry, and location. Career experts warn, however, that search agents can miss many desirable possibilities.[7]

- **Telerecruiting** Technology has created other new avenues for recruitment. Cable television has enabled employers to buy time on "employment channels" to air thirty-second want ads on stations such as Chicago's WGBO-TV/Channel 55 (the Television Employment Network) and Channel 21 in Washington, D.C. (the Employment Channel). Interested persons typically call the advertising employer, and the initial interview is conducted over the telephone (that is, telerecruiting). The resumé information is entered on a computer data bank, which is then accessed when openings occur.

LABOR MARKET INFORMATION

An organization's recruitment efforts must compare favorably with its competitors'. A firm's HR department is competing with other organizations in the local and regional area for the same good job applicants. In most instances, a wage survey is used to maintain labor market information for the local area. Most professional organizations will conduct surveys not only for the local area but for regional and national areas as well. Professional positions require a greater regional and national emphasis because individuals seeking professional jobs are often more willing to relocate to take challenging jobs.

One widely used survey statistic is the **unemployment rate.** Observing changes in the unemployment rate over a period of time can help a firm determine the labor market conditions of a local area. But the **labor force participation rate** for an area is also an important statistic that should be understood and utilized in the recruitment process. Many persons are part of the **labor reserve,** such as housewives, students, and retired individuals who take jobs in hard times to supplement family incomes. The result is that more individuals are employed at the same time that the number of unemployed in an area increases due to layoffs and economic conditions. Consequently, the unemployment rate increases even though more individuals are working in a labor market area.

LABOR MARKET SOURCES

The people most available for recruitment are the **unemployed,** who can be contacted through direct application, employment agencies, or advertisements. Other sources often need to be considered when recruiting top candidates.

Part-time employees are good examples of recruitment sources. In past years, some managers believed that part-time employees were not loyal to the organization and did not produce at the level of full-time employees. However, organizations today realize that part-time employees are very productive and that there are qualified applicants who wish to work on a part-time basis. Due to a decrease in benefit costs and lower wages, part-time employees are often less expensive to the organization; if part-time employees can produce at the same level as full-time employees, they then become an attractive alternative. Owners and managers have also found that part-time employees may have greater enthusiasm for jobs that are traditionally boring and routine because they do not face constant repetition, day after day, for long periods of time.

Underemployed individuals are another group of applicants who can be successfully recruited. Some full-time employees feel they are underemployed because their jobs are unrelated to their interests and training. Many of these people are not actively looking for jobs, but they can be recruited by another organization because they would prefer jobs more in line with their training and skills.

Pirating takes place when search firms actively recruit employees from other organizations. Administrators may become aware of an able employee at a competitive firm or at a firm in a related industry. They pirate an individual away from another employer by offering a more attractive salary, better working conditions, or other benefits. In some industries and for some large firms, pirating is preferred to hiring recent college graduates because trained, experienced persons can more quickly become productive and successful.

Redeploying occurs when an employer does not want to lose the investment it has made in workers whose jobs are eliminated. Instead, the affected employees are offered other permanent jobs in the organization or temporary short-term jobs until they find a permanent position. This "temporary pool" of workers provides a transition phase as an alternative to layoffs or termination. At Public Service Electric and Gas in Newark, New Jersey, for example, when 445 employees were downsized, 77 percent were redeployed into other jobs, 22 percent retired, and only a total of 30 employees were terminated.[8]

A rapidly growing labor market source is the **older worker.** Employers are increasingly turning to the recruitment of workers in the expanding 40 to 70 age group as the number of workers in the 16 to 24 age group continues to decrease. Several industries including fast-food, retailing, insurance, and temporary office help are actively recruiting the older worker.[9] Besides the change in demographics, Jim von Greup, director of public affairs for Wal-Mart Department Stores, believes that there are other valid reasons to recruit older workers: "The older workers have good ethics and work habits. Generally, they have very good skills in dealing with the public, and in many cases they are good teachers for younger workers." Philip Johnson, HR director of the Winn-Dixie supermarket chain, adds, "They have the self-discipline to stick with a job and see it through."[10]

Kathryn Rocha, vice-president of human resources at Salomon Brothers in Tampa, Florida feared the record low unemployment rate of 3 percent would make it impossible to fill over 100 openings. Salomon's job fairs and campus recruiting had lured young college graduates in past years, but no longer were attracting enough applicants. Then, Rocha held an "open house" which included breakfast, a tour of facilities, talks by company officials, and a basic skills test. An "amazing thing" happened, said Rocha. The people who came were not the expected college students or unemployed, but recent retirees—she filled the 100 positions and had a backlog of 40 more! This and similar experiences by other employers using nontraditional recruitment methods has convinced some labor economists that the unemployment rate is misleading. In most regions, there may be far more qualified people who will take jobs they find appealing. Many are retirees, at-home mothers, or temporary workers. This change represents a fundamental change in the world of work—and how HR managers can successfully recruit qualified people even in a tight market.[11]

Another whole new breed of applicants are the *downsized* workers: those who were forced into retirement or, more likely, into positions with less income and challenge. These ex-middle managers may not be actively seeking positions, but may respond to career fairs or open houses like that of Salomon Brothers.[12] Most have skills and expertise greater than required by their current positions.

When many corporations cut payrolls in the 1980s, these newly downsized employees often were glad to escape the corporate "rat race" and chose to play golf or start their own business. After working long hours as owners/managers, watching their small businesses struggle, or tire of leisure time, by 1997 95 percent of downsized workers preferred to work for another corporation, up from only 75 percent 10 years earlier.[13]

FIGURE 7–3   WHAT RECRUITERS ARE LOOKING FOR

SOUTHERN CALIFORNIA GAS COMPANY
Los Angeles–based natural gas supplier
Joyce Ridley, employment manager

> In new employees we look for an ability to take initiative in whatever situation is presented. Our employees should also have a positive attitude and a flexibility in their attitudes and approaches. We also want people with a strong work ethic and a commitment to doing a good job. . . . We are also looking for females to perform jobs that have traditionally been filled by males.

HUGHES AIRCRAFT COMPANY
Westchester County, New York–based defense contractor
Robert Williams, director of employees research, education, and development

> The skills we're looking for when we promote someone depends on the level of management we're recruiting for. If it's a fairly low level of management then we're emphasizing technical skills because this person will be supervising workers in a fairly hands-on way. In middle management, we are looking for strong interpersonal skills because these people are supervising the hands-on managers and communicating the results upward in the management chain. At the highest level of management, we look for people who have strong conceptual skills and who are adept at long-range planning and goal setting.

AST RESEARCH INC.
Irvine-based computer maker
Howard Derman, director of human resources

> We like to see people with personal accomplishments and achievements. We want people with creativity and flexibility in their style and approach to the job. It's nice to have people who are book smart, but it's better to have people who have flexibility and creativity to apply their knowledge in a common sense kind of way. Unfortunately, a lot of people don't have this. We also look for the personal chemistry between the corporation and the employee. We have to know if the style and aspirations of the applicant match the culture of the company because if they don't the employee won't be happy.

Continued.

1994 was a historic year for older workers in America. That year the median age for all working Americans, which has been steadily climbing, reached 40. Thus, half of the U.S. labor force was included in the "older" category, as defined by the ADEA. Discrimination against older workers continues, largely due to prejudiced thinking and myths, according to Sally Dunaway, attorney for the American Association of Retired Persons. Such unfair stereotypes include the following: "older workers can't learn computer skills," "they get sick more often," "they are closed-minded and won't take direction from younger supervisors," and "they have too many accidents." These myths often lead to discriminatory treatment and over 30,000 age discrimination suits each year. More employers, however, are actively recruiting older workers. Days Inn President John Russell began a campaign to hire older workers because "they are good for business." After eight years, the program produced significant results including lower turnover, better customer relations, and reduced stress.

In addition, according to Russell, "if you need someone to stay, the seniors are the first to volunteer."[14]

The Travelers Insurance Company was one of the first to establish a *retiree job bank*. Bringing back its own retirees to work part-time has become common at Travelers. Small-business owners have also utilized the expertise of retirees. The Travelers' Retiree Job Bank is a pool of retirees that serves as an in-house temporary agency to fill positions during peak periods, vacations, and illnesses. Travelers has found that 90 percent of its retirees are interested in working part-time and provide an excellent pool of trained, low-cost (few benefits) labor. Similar retiree programs have been successful at Bank of America, Polaroid Corporation, Kentucky Fried Chicken, Lockheed, and Motorola.[15]

WWW.TRAVELERS.COM

What attributes in candidates do recruiters look for most often? According to the recruiters in Figure 7–3, the top criteria include initiative, technical skills,

FIGURE 7–3   *(continued)*

WALT DISNEY COMPANY
Burbank-based entertainment company
Curtis Kishl, manager of employment and professional staffing

> We want people who can take an innovative approach to traditional business situations and problems, and we try to find these people by asking a variety of hypothetical questions in our interviews. We're also looking for analytical skills and the ability to present clear solutions to various business situations. Our employees should also be familiar with children's products, possess a feel for the social significance of Mickey, and understand that the Disney company stands for family entertainment.

FLOUR CORPORATION
Irvine, California-based engineering and construction firm
Karen Vari, manager of human resources

> Beyond the appropriate skills and background for the particular job, we are looking for strong communication skills, a willingness to do the work required by the job, an ability to be a team player and take an innovative and creative approach to the job. We like to hire what we call "committed champions," a term that means internally motivated people who are willing to take some risks. We also look for people who are flexible and can perform many tasks. Because we are a worldwide organization and globalization is an increasingly important part of business, we also look for our employees to be fairly mobile and comfortable with change.

FIRST INTERSTATE BANK
Los Angeles–based bank
Shirley Perkins, senior vice president

> Aside from the purely technical skills which vary from job to job, we look for people with good interpersonal skills. We want people who are sales oriented, people who are comfortable selling themselves, selling the corporation, and selling the products of the corporation. This means we need people who are self-confident, have the ability to communicate, and are able to convey their enthusiasm for their job and the products they are selling.

SOURCE: Adapted from "What Employers Are Looking For," *The Los Angeles Times* (September 17, 1989): 2, 5. Copyright 1989, *Los Angeles Times.* Reprinted by Permission.

communication skills, analytical skills, and internal motivation.

HUMAN RESOURCES PLANNING

How many people will we need? What specific skills will be needed by employees three years from now that they do not currently possess? These are two of the most difficult questions faced by HR managers. Overstaffing causes excessive costs, but understaffing causes quality to suffer and opportunities to be missed. Thus, **human resources planning,** also called *manpower planning,* can be important in holding down costs while providing a productive workforce.[16]

FORECASTS

Determining the future supply and demand for human resources is a first step in developing a manpower plan. The *supply forecast* is the result of direct interviews with employees and the use of standard HR data such as work histories, skills acquired, job progression, and demographics. Modern computerized HR systems have simplified the process of generating supply reports such as the one shown in Figure 7–4.

The estimate of the total number of employees needed as well as the skills required is known as the *demand forecast.* Planners find it difficult to develop precise demand forecasts for various reasons, such as changes in sales patterns, technological innovations, and company reorganizations. Precise demand forecasts are not as important when

FIGURE 7–4 A SUPPLY REPORT

JOB TITLE, NAME	SOCIAL SECURITY	DATE ASSIGNED	EEO	STATUS	STATUS DATE	PROMOTABLE TO
Plant Superintendent						
Jackson, Ralph	123-45-6789	05-87		R	10-98	
Plant Engr. Mgr.						
Robinson, Larry	234-56-7891	08-89		P	10-98	Plant Super.
Plant Controller						
Brown, Sarah	345-67-8912	01-88	1F			
Supv. Process 1						
Miles, Jack	456-78-9123	10-77	5M	Q		
Fleming, Mark	567-89-1234	02-79		R	12-96	
Pressler, Roy	678-91-2345	09-87		P	10-98	Plant Engr. Mgr.
Supv. Process 2						
Johnson, Tom	789-12-3456	04-84		R	09-97	
Plant Pers. Mgr.						
Powers, John	891-23-4567	11-88		P	09-97	Supv. Process 2
Indust. Engr. Mgr.						
Rodriguez, Tom	912-34-5678	06-90	3M	P	06-99	Supv. Process 1
Safety Mgr.						
White, Judy	134-56-7891	02-89	2F	P	09-97	Plant Pers. Mgr.
Qual. Cont. Tech.						
Ling, Sam	245-67-8791	11-91	4M	S		

Status Codes
S = Satisfactory but not moving
P = Place/promote, hence moving
R = Replace/retire, hence moving
Q = Questionable: employee is on probation and is not moving
EEO Codes
F = Female
M = Male
1 = White
2 = Black
3 = Hispanic
4 = Asian
5 = American Indian

SOURCE: Charles F. Russ, Jr., "Manpower Planning Systems: Part I," *Personnel Journal* (February 1982). Reprinted with the permission of *Personnel Journal*, Costa Mesa, California; all rights reserved.

there is great flexibility in an organization's workforce, when employees are mobile and multiskilled, and (most important) when workers are easily found and hired. Why, then, bother with forecasting? Because people are geographically less mobile (less willing to relocate) today than in the past, employees are retiring earlier, and jobs have often become too specialized to be learned quickly.[17]

Demand forecasts are developed from two main sources: standard statistical data and knowledgeable personnel. Statistical techniques such as correlation analysis can be used to detect significant relationships between staffing levels and such variables as the economic climate, the unemployment rate, the competition, and sales levels. But all statistical approaches contain a bias: They predict the future based solely on the past. Thus, critical factors may be omitted. Such factors might include a plan for a new product line, the introduction of new machinery, the loss of an important contract, or a change in government regulations.

Once the demand-and-supply forecasts have been made, HR administrators can plan on how to address projected shortages or surpluses. Specialized training, early-retirement incentives, and increased outside recruitment are a few of the techniques available to address an organization's needs. Keep in mind that the forecasts are not airtight: Not all mismatches are cause for action. It may be preferable to wait for further information or to see if projected changes take place.

Management succession planning (MSP) is commonly used to deal with changes in mid- and top-level personnel. The process involves identifying projected vacancies and choosing replacement candidates for each position, estimating the promotability of each candidate, and, most important, identifying development and training needs to ensure the availability of qualified personnel for future openings.[18]

WWW.EEOC.GOV

MSP is a method for career planning designed in part to satisfy Equal Employment Opportunity Commission and affirmative action (EEOC/AA) requirements. The MSP system generates three reports. The first is the supply report, which classifies each individual listed as satisfactory but not ready for promotion or placement on another job; promotable; replaceable or retiring; or questionable because of probation or some other status. The second is the demand report, which shows new positions due to expansion, turnover, or promotion. The third is the HR report, which shows the supply–demand equation, including the name, job, and location of all those suitable for promotion. The purpose of the HR report is to develop a zero balance between the projected career changes and the expected demand changes.[19]

An excellent example of how human resource planning can be tied to a firm's strategic business planning is provided by Robbins and Meyers, a multiproduct manufacturer with over 2,500 employees. The company instituted an annual planning cycle starting in September, as shown in Figure 7–5. Managers were provided background material, and planning dates were set. The planning process comprised the following steps:[20]

1 *Identify Strategic Issues* Managers identified issues that would constrain or enhance a business plan.

2 *Conduct Organizational Analysis* Managers developed a one- to two-year organizational plan to deal with structural changes.

3 *Forecast Staffing Requirements* Managers identified open positions caused by turnover or growth.

4 *Develop Succession Plans* Managers developed individual succession plans for important positions.

5 *Identify Training Requirements* Training managers developed programs based on individual and organizational needs.

6 *Identify Development Plans for Selected Employees* Those singled out in the succession plans were given individual development plans.

7 *Conduct Organizational Review* The HR plan of each division was reviewed by the president and manager of corporate planning.

8 *Develop Budgets* Approved plans were given budgets for implementation.

Management at Robbins and Meyers developed their human resources planning as a logical outgrowth of their strategic business planning. Their human resources planning constituted a continuous process—developing from the corporate business plan and helping that plan succeed.[21]

ENTRY-LEVEL PLANNING

Human resources planning for mid- and top-level positions focuses on specific individuals—their replacement on retirement or their training, development, and promotion. Human resources planning is also used for entry-level positions, where the focus is not on career planning but on the forecasting of the number of entry-level applicants that will be needed at various times.

The HR manager anticipates the company's needs, the training time that may be required, and employee turnover. As Figure 7–6 indicates, the recruiter with a simple formula can estimate the number of applicants needed in order to fill various entry-level positions. The process can be used for each different entry-level position; thus, four or five different estimates may be made. If a firm typically hires a large number of entry-level clerical workers or sales representatives during the year, such estimates can minimize the time such positions are left open because of a lack of qualified trainees.

Human resources planning balances the long-run demand for employees with the long-run supply of internal and external applicants. Adjustments in training, the transfer of employees, and external recruitment can

FIGURE 7–5 ROBBINS AND MEYERS, INC., OF DAYTON, OHIO, INSTITUTED HUMAN RESOURCES PLANNING THAT WAS CLOSELY TIED TO THE COMPANY'S STRATEGIC BUSINESS PLANNING. AS THIS FLOWCHART SHOWS, THEIR ANNUAL PLANNING CYCLE BEGINS IN SEPTEMBER AND PROCEEDS THROUGH A NUMBER OF SPECIFIC STEPS.

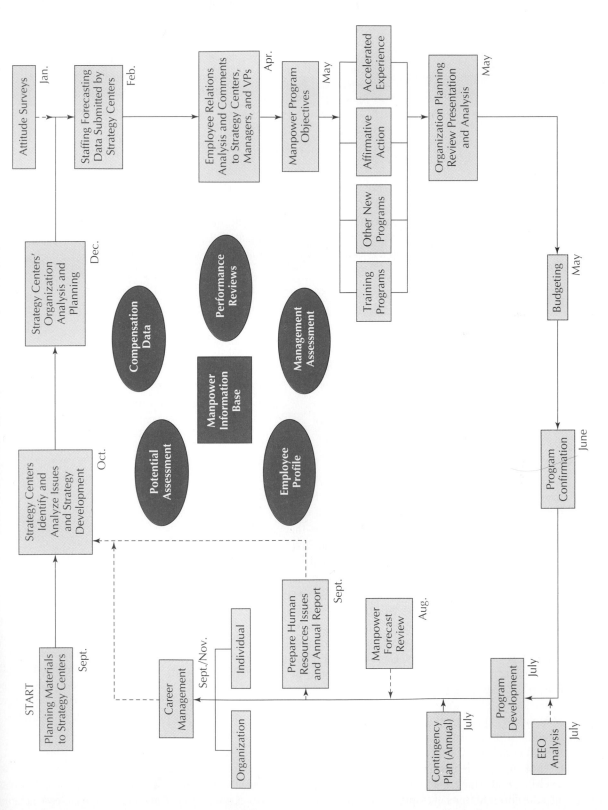

SOURCE: David R. Leigh, "Business Planning Is People Planning," *Personnel Journal* 63, no. 5 (May 1984): 44–50. Used by permission.

FIGURE 7–6   DETERMINING THE NEED FOR ENTRY-LEVEL APPLICANTS

Formula

$$\begin{array}{c}\text{Applicants Needed}\\\text{Annually}\end{array} = \begin{array}{c}\text{Current and Future}\\\text{Entry-level Positions}\\\text{Needed}\end{array} \times \begin{array}{c}\text{Turnover}\\\text{Rate}\end{array} \times \begin{array}{c}\text{Ratio of}\\\text{Applicants}\\\text{Needed to Every}\\\text{Applicant Hired}\end{array}$$

Example

$$\begin{array}{c}\text{Applicants Needed}\\\text{Annually}\end{array} = 40 \text{ (clerical positions)} \times 0.5 \text{ (rate)} \times \frac{3}{1} \text{ (ratio)}$$

$$\begin{array}{c}\text{Applicants Needed}\\\text{Annually}\end{array} = 60$$

If training programs begin on the first of each month, then

$$\frac{60 \text{ Applicants}}{12 \text{ Months}} = \begin{array}{l}\text{5 applicants needed to start}\\\text{each training program each month}\end{array}$$

TABLE 7–1   ADVANTAGES OF RECRUITING INTERNALLY AND EXTERNALLY

INTERNAL RECRUITMENT	EXTERNAL RECRUITMENT
Increases morale of all employees	Applicant pool is greater
Knowledge of personnel records	New ideas, contacts
Chain effect of promotion	Reduces internal infighting
Need to hire only at entry level	Minimizes Peter Principle
Usually faster, less expensive	

then minimize severe personnel shortages in future years.

There are a number of steps in determining the number of positions a company will need to fill. First, future customer demands are estimated by examining the market for products and services, the competition, and long-term growth potential. Once customer demands are estimated, decisions must be made regarding financial resource availability. Those resources determine the two critical inputs in the organization process: capital and materials. Once financial determinations are made, the level of operation must be decided. Management estimates the required level of operation in future months and years so that it can economically purchase materials and equipment. Sometimes overlooked is an estimate of the level of operation and its effect on HR needs. Estimating the level of operation is critical to HR planning because it involves not only the number of employees needed but also the different types of employees required for current and future positions.

RECRUITMENT SOURCES

Once management has determined an organization's staffing requirements, the recruitment process begins. The first decision made is whether a particular job opening should be filled by someone already employed or by an applicant from outside. Normally, firms recruit both internally and externally. In each case, the advantages of recruiting outside the organization must be weighed against the advantages of recruiting inside the organization.[22] Table 7–1 shows a few advantages of each type of recruitment. As Figure 7–7 illustrates, however, the use of sources by employers varies by industry.

INTERNAL APPLICANTS

Of the several advantages to recruiting within the organization, probably most important is the increase in morale for employees who believe that the organization will

FIGURE 7–7   MOST PREVALENT RECRUITING SOURCE BY JOB CATEGORY

PERCENTAGE OF COMPANIES

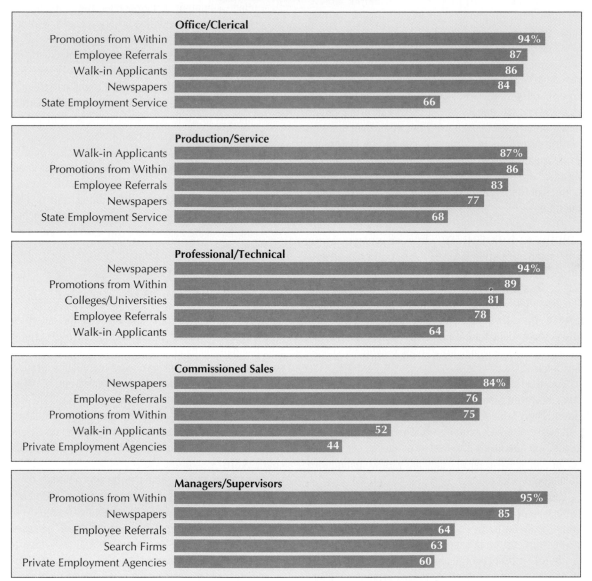

Office/Clerical

Promotions from Within	94%
Employee Referrals	87
Walk-in Applicants	86
Newspapers	84
State Employment Service	66

Production/Service

Walk-in Applicants	87%
Promotions from Within	86
Employee Referrals	83
Newspapers	77
State Employment Service	68

Professional/Technical

Newspapers	94%
Promotions from Within	89
Colleges/Universities	81
Employee Referrals	78
Walk-in Applicants	64

Commissioned Sales

Newspapers	84%
Employee Referrals	76
Promotions from Within	75
Walk-in Applicants	52
Private Employment Agencies	44

Managers/Supervisors

Promotions from Within	95%
Newspapers	85
Employee Referrals	64
Search Firms	63
Private Employment Agencies	60

SOURCE: Compiled from information provided by the Bureau of National Affairs, Inc.'s *Personnel Management, BNA Policy and Practice Series,* as published in K. Michele Kacman, "Look at Who's Talking," *HR Magazine* (February 1993): 57.

reward successful performance and that they will be promoted to higher positions. The lack of possible promotion and advancement opportunities within an organization can be a major cause of turnover and dissatisfaction.

Managers recruiting within the organization also have the advantage of using HR data maintained by the company. Interviews with supervisors and analysis of employee performance records can be added to the ap-

plicant's file during the recruitment process. At best, the organization can only guess at the completeness and objectivity of information received from other organizations. Only after years of interaction with the other organizations can an HR officer begin to measure the accuracy of external applicants' HR files.

A promotion within the organization often leads to a vacant position, which can then be filled from within the organization. This chain effect on promotion means that two or more positions will often be filled at one time when internal recruitment is used. Thus internal promotions have a positive effect on employee morale because each promotion positively affects several employees.

When organizations promote from within, often only entry-level vacancies are filled from the outside. The advantage of this approach is that it is not necessary to experiment with unknown people at high levels in the organization; individuals have a chance to prove themselves in lower-level positions first. Rewarding employees for successful performance also can be faster and less expensive than external recruitment. Therefore, because an organization uses its own records and sources of testing, internal recruitment can save money and time.

Employee Relocation

Internal promotion with large companies often involves the relocation of an employee from one city to another. The workforce of today may be less mobile than that of 20 years ago. The lure of a new home, better job, and higher salary has waned; instead, the prospect of locating in a new city often brings the anticipation of higher house payments, real estate hassles, and unhappy spouses who must find new jobs.

Transferring an employee from one location to another, however, remains one means of filling a vacant position. The obvious advantage is that the employer is well aware of the employee's abilities and work record. In addition, the newly transferred employee can quickly become productive on the new job with a minimum of training and orientation.

Employee relocations do have disadvantages. The average cost of relocating an employee within the United States is between $20,000 and $50,000. The costs include direct moving expenses, realtor's fees, temporary housing, travel allowances, and assistance in finding employment for spouses. Another disadvantage often involved is disruption of the spouse's career. In dual-career marriages, women are especially concerned about limiting their own careers to accommodate the transfer of a spouse. Most single parents also dislike relocating because of the disruption in the lives of their children or problems with ex-spouses. Overall, employees are increasingly concerned with their quality of life and therefore less willing to relocate, even if it means passing up a promotion.[23]

Therefore, employee resistance to relocating has increased in recent years. HR managers must provide even greater assistance in relocation to persuade reluc-

tant employees to move. Complete relocation programs, such as the one at US Sprint, may include the following:[24]

Complete Reimbursement of Costs Costs include shipment of belongings, travel for house-hunting trips, temporary living expenses, realtor's fees, closing costs, and storage costs.

Counseling Stress or psychological counseling for employees and family members may be needed. Why? Relocating is one of the ten most stressful lifetime occurrences. Assistance with matters such as locating school districts, good neighborhoods, and so forth is essential.

Spousal Assistance This may include job-hunting trips, income protection if the job search is not successful, and search firm expenses.

Marketing Assistance Expediting the selling of the old home and buying the new one, including financing assistance, can save the employer money.

EXTERNAL APPLICANTS

One of the advantages of recruiting from the outside is that a greater number of applicants can be recruited than could normally be recruited internally. Outside applicants may bring new ideas, work techniques, production methods, or training to the organization, resulting in increased employee productivity.

External applicants also may have contacts that internal employees do not have. In sales, research and technology, and purchasing, for example, good external contacts are critical, and the recruitment of outside applicants with these contacts may be very helpful.

Recruitment of outside applicants for mid-level and higher positions may eliminate infighting by employees jockeying for promotion. Wherever infighting is severe, organizations begin to do more external recruiting to decrease internal dissension.

In recent years, organizations have sought applicants from the outside to minimize promoting employees to levels where they are unable to perform successfully. The concept that every employee will be promoted beyond his or her level of competence is called the **Peter Principle.** This theory has validity; managers often have promoted employees who cannot perform as expected in their new jobs.[25] The theory may be a self-fulfilling prophecy for policymakers who blame the Peter Principle for their own lack of good internal recruitment methods. However, any firm that promotes exclusively from within will experience the effects of the Peter Principle to some extent.

One common method of avoiding the effects of the Peter Principle—and the resulting dissatisfied employee—is the use of temporary titles. For example, an employee is promoted to "acting department head" for an unspecified period of time. If the employee is not capable of performing the job, a permanent department head can be recruited. Thus, the employee does not suffer the embarrassment of failing to handle the position; nor is a demotion or termination made part of the employee's permanent record. Whenever an acting department head proves capable, that employee can be made the permanent department head.

Whether employees are recruited from inside or outside should be determined by the availability of qualified employees in the organization, the size of the organization, and the desire to keep up with contemporary ideas and methods. Employees should realize that external recruitment does not mean that no one is qualified to fill the position internally. Rather, it indicates the need for fresh ideas and new approaches to old problems.

METHODS OF RECRUITMENT

The two most common methods of internal recruiting are bidding and job posting. Bidding is common with unionized organizations; when an opening exists, qualified employees are notified that they may bid on the position if they wish to be considered for it. The employee with the most seniority receives the promotion. This structured process is usually specified in the union contract; promotions are based on seniority and ability. There are a number of methods of external recruiting, including direct applications, employee referrals, campus recruiting, employment agencies, and temporary help.

JOB POSTING

One of the most popular methods of filling positions within organizations is **job posting.** A survey of over 6,000 companies indicated that job posting is the most common means of filling open positions.

Job posting methods include at least three proven, effective processes: (1) traditional bulletin boards, (2) computer electronic mail-based systems, and (3) telephone voice mail-based systems. All three methods can be effective, but the last two offer benefits over traditional bulletin boards that include the following:[26]

- Easy access by all employees.
- 24-hour availability.

- Minimum paperwork.
- Immediate notification to all employees.

More organizations are developing computer- and telephone-based systems (see Figure 7–8, "Telephone Job Posting Systems at AMP") due to these advantages, as well as positive employee responses.

Although job posting is an effective, useful management tool, it can create severe employee morale problems if not handled properly. Managers should consider several aspects of the job-posting process.

First, the job-posting procedure should be clearly explained to the employees and should be followed to the letter each time a position is open. If the procedure varies according to the job or the particular employee applying for a position, employees may suspect that employer subjectivity is unfairly entering into the process.

Second, job specifications should be clear and should include the years of experience, skills, or training employees must have to apply for the posted position. This will make the decision process easier for management, assuming that strict seniority will not be used as the only criterion and that other factors such as an employee's HR record and the results of interviews will be considered. When only a few job specifications are included in the posted position, the HR specialist will have a larger number of applicants to review during the selection process.

Third, job-posting procedures should specify the exact period during which posted positions will remain open. For example, a position may remain open for fourteen working days after it is first posted, and applications will be taken until 4:30 P.M. on the fourteenth day. Also, the procedure should specify that employees on vacation or laid off will be notified by mail or employee publication of posted positions. The exact media to be used in the job-posting process—that is, bulletin boards, e-mail, the employee newspaper—should not only be specified but also consistently used unless employees are notified about a change.

Fourth, the application procedure should be clear. For example, an employee may apply for a posted position through the HR department or a supervisor. If the employee applies directly to the HR department, supervisors feel that the chain of command has not been used. On the other hand, employees going through their supervisors sometimes feel that their supervisors may not wish them to receive the positions. A common compromise is to have employees submit written applications for a posted position to the HR department, with a copy to the supervisor. Finally, and perhaps most important, the HR department should ensure that applicants

FIGURE 7–8   TELEPHONE JOB POSTING SYSTEMS AT AMP

WWW.AMP.COM

AMP Incorporated Inc., a Harrisburg, Pennsylvania firm, is the world's largest manufacturer of electrical and electronic interconnection products. After over 50 years of utilizing a traditional "bulletin board" job posting system for its 15,000 employees, AMP decided it needed a better system. Problems with the old weekly posting system included:

- Employees weren't made aware of openings.
- Supervisors didn't have to inform employees that they were considering them for open positions.
- No feedback process existed.
- The form limited employees to only three career choices.
- Some supervisors and managers believed that employees who participated did so because they were unhappy with their current position.
- Some business units refused to allow their employees to be considered for jobs in other units.
- The process created a tremendous amount of paperwork.

After reviewing traditional systems, computer-based systems, and telephone-based systems at other organizations, AMP chose a voice-mail telephone system. The new *Career Opportunities Program* involves five steps:

1. New openings are input into the system by an HR employee and thus are immediately posted for seven days.

2. Any employee can access the system, which lists all openings by job title and job code 24 hours a day. using voice response, the system guides employees through a series of prompts.

3. To apply for a position, an employee leaves their name, employee number, the name of their supervisor, and job number. Additional steps or permission is not required.

4. After seven days, all employee responses are listed with the employees' work history and given to the hiring supervisor.

5. After the position is filled, the system generates a letter to each applicant which includes positive and negative feedback information.

After a trial period, the new posting method produced several impressive results:

- 61 percent of the new vacancies were filled internally compared to 44 percent under the previous system.
- Recruitment costs decreased from $311,000 to $87,000 for the year despite more than twice the number of positions being filled.
- Positions stayed open 16 percent fewer days.
- Employees and managers preferred the new system. Employees liked its flexibility, the control they have over their career decisions, and the fairness of the new system.

SOURCE: William C. DeLone, "Telephone Job Posting Cuts Costs," *Personnel Journal* (April 1993): 115–18.

receive adequate *feedback* once a selection is made. For example, when nine applicants apply for a posted position and one is accepted, the other eight employees may feel rejected. Although no amount of communication will entirely eliminate this feeling, it is imperative that the rejected employees receive feedback on the selection process. Otherwise, the morale of one employee may increase while the motivation of eight other good employees may significantly decrease.

The rejected employees should be given a counseling interview by the HR department or the hiring supervisor. The interview, which can help cushion the person's disappointment, should include the following:[27]

- Reasons for nonacceptance, but with emphasis on the person's qualifications and strengths that made him or her a strong candidate.

- Suggested remedial measures such as training and education to improve performance in the person's current job, possible new duties, and so on. Such counseling should be aimed at strengthening any weaknesses of the candidate.

- Information concerning possible openings the candidate might apply for in the future.

- Assistance in the posting process, such as how to bid for a new job and how to conduct a job interview.

If properly used, job posting helps employees feel that they have some control over their future in the organization. Job posting often uncovers employee talent that supervisors would not voluntarily reveal.

DIRECT APPLICATIONS

For most organizations, direct applications by mail or by individuals applying in person are the largest source of applicants. In the case of blue-collar jobs, walk-ins are often called **gate hires.** Direct applications can provide to the organization an inexpensive source of good job applicants—especially for entry-level, clerical, and blue-collar jobs. In recent years, direct applications from new college graduates have been used to fill other entry-level positions.

The usefulness of direct applications will often depend on the image the organization has in the community and, therefore, the quality of applicants who will apply directly to the organization. The size of an organization and its reputation determine whether applicants will seek out the organization rather than respond to other recruitment methods. Only the largest, best-known organizations in the labor market will receive a large number of direct applications. Organizations that receive many direct applications must develop an efficient means of screening those applications and keeping a current file of qualified candidates. While the cost of recruitment is low if large numbers of applications are received, the cost of screening and maintaining a file of applicants can be quite high. Medium-sized and smaller firms do not receive a large enough volume of direct applications to fill all their positions with available and qualified candidates without using further recruitment methods.

Some newspapers have increased the advantages of newspaper advertising by utilizing a telephone voice-response system to speed up the process, reduce the number of applicants who provide incomplete information, and provide the employer a computerized database of applicants for easier screening and sorting. An example of a local newspaper ad that offers voice resumé systems to employers appears in Figure 7–9.

FIGURE 7–9   "APPLY-BY-PHONE" NEWSPAPER ADVERTISING

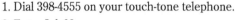

How to respond to Apply-By-Phone Voice Resumes

1. Dial 398-4555 on your touch-tone telephone.
2. Enter Job No.
3. Be prepared to answer the following questions:
   1. "Please tell us your name, address and home phone number."
   2. "Please tell us about your educational background."
   3. "Please tell us about the company where you last worked, time frame of employment, and a brief description of your job responsibilities."
   4. "Please tell us your current salary or desired salary."
   5. "Please tell us briefly why you believe you are the best person for the position."
   6. Advertiser's custom question.

Invalid or expired box #? Please check to make sure your touch-tone phone is set on tone rather than pulse. If you have additional questions call 342-6633.

Omaha World-Herald

SOURCE: The *Omaha World-Herald* (July 18, 1993): 15–16.

EMPLOYEE REFERRAL PROGRAMS

In recruiting, **employee referrals** are one of the best means of securing applicants. Employees can be encouraged to help their employers locate and hire qualified applicants by rewards, either monetary or otherwise, or by recognition for those who assist the recruitment process.

Employees who recommend applicants place their own reputations on the line; therefore, they are usually careful to recommend only qualified applicants. When recommended applicants are hired, employees take an active interest in helping new employees become successful in their jobs.

HR research has indicated that people hired through employee referral programs have higher degrees of job satisfaction and longer tenure with the organization. Yet only 10 to 15 percent of positions nationally are filled by referrals. Why not more? The three most common obstacles to employees making referrals are: (1) they don't see recruitment as their problem or as a high organizational priority; (2) they can't easily match the skills of friends-associates with those required by job openings; (3) they make faulty assumptions about the interest level of friends or don't realize they are looking for a better job. The Vanguard Resource Group reviewed the practices of organizations with highly successful referral programs and found most contained elements similar to those listed in Figure 7–10.[28] Thus, by implementing an innovative employee referral program, most employers could enhance the recruitment of good applicants.

In past years, the **old boy network** filled positions in some organizations with friends and relatives. This hiring of former college friends or neighborhood associates leads to a distorted mix of employees and usually an underrepresentation of minority groups in various job categories. Today, **networking** has replaced the old boy network, both in name and in practice. The informal interpersonal network of professional contacts and resources that each employee establishes is an invaluable recruitment source.

CAMPUS RECRUITING

A new level of sophistication in campus recruiting began in recent years. Employers' prescreening of students has, in many cases, replaced the old method of selection from the placement office's resumé book. Prescreening programs are designed to identify top students, often as juniors, and to begin to introduce them to employers. Professors may play a critical role in identifying such students. Citibank in New York, for example, hires professors to teach specific programs and involve their students where possible. Texas Instruments encourages company executives to teach at the university level, thereby identifying top students on the basis of first-hand experience.

Students who have difficulty finding their first postgraduation job should use the ten leads discussed in Figure 7–11.

Recruitment videos, which can be used on campuses or for other recruitment efforts, have been effectively used by employers who want to emphasize the quality of their work environment or community.

Career days on campuses have increased in recent years due to tight job markets. More employers are making campus visits in combination with other methods.

NCR College Recruiting
In many ways NCR Corporation, a 52,000-employee worldwide computer manufacturer headquartered in Dayton, Ohio, is similar to many other corporate recruiters. Almost all of the college graduates hired were once NCR interns or scholarship winners. NCR believes in identifying high-performance students early in their college careers and then grooming them for success in the corporation. The company spends about $350,000 annually on college scholarships and offers several hundred summer internships which provide meaningful work assignments and give both parties a chance to evaluate each other. What is unique about NCR is that it hires about 75 percent of its new employees from colleges.

WWW.NCR.COM

This high percentage is due to an evaluation conducted by NCR that resulted in the conclusion that recent college graduates were more adaptable and stayed longer than other hires. Thus, NCR, after reviewing the success of all of its employees, decided to focus its recruitment on college graduates instead of experienced workers. Then NCR targeted 75 to 80 colleges according to several criteria, including the following:[29]

- Faculty quality, measured partly by the number of full-time Ph.D.s on staff.

- Student quality, determined by the schools' entrance requirements.

- The percentage of women and minority enrollments (to support the company's efforts to achieve diversity).

- Supportive services, such as the number of computers in the laboratories compared with the total number of students, research facilities, and so on.

FIGURE 7–10   SIX WAYS TO IMPROVE EMPLOYEE REFERRAL PROGRAMS

Organizations with highly successful programs (30 percent or more of all vacancies are filled by referrals) credit the following practices:

1 *Public recognition of successful referrals.* Harris Bank in Chicago hires 300 to 400 people each year through employee referrals. Enthusiasm for the employee referral program (ERP) is linked to acknowledgment of successful referrals in company meetings. When possible, managers who benefit from the new hire are present to show gratitude and present bonus checks or other nonmonetary awards (coffee mugs with corporate logo, desk nameplates).

2 *Prompt bonus rewards.* When bonus payouts occur months after the initial referral, the reward has less impact. Understanding the concept, Acuson, a manufacturer of ultrasound devices in Mountain View, California, changed its payout policies a few years ago. Referral bonuses are paid immediately after the new hire reports to work. Acuson's philosophy is that employees create value when the referred person reports to work. Because the company evaluates and selects the new employee, the organization accepts the risk of retention. Therefore, bonuses are paid immediately after the new hire reports to work.

3 *Regular promotional incentives.* Quarterly (or semi-annual) promotional drawings can reinforce enthusiasm for a program. When a new hire reports to work, the referring employee's name goes into the drawing box. If an employee provides three new hires in the quarter, three chances to win are entered. The top prize might be a three- or four-day trip for two people to an exotic location like St. Thomas in the Virgin Islands.

4 *Converting the program from a passive to a proactive tool.* Many problems with employee referral programs are traced to their passive design. The HR department posts vacancy announcements, then waits and hopes for referrals. Passive designs also perpetuate imbalances in minority representation in the workforce. Naturally, people tend to nominate those in their demographic peer group.

A proactive employee referral program begins when the vacancy notice triggers a discussion with the hiring manager about job requirements:

- Identify competitors and worksites where suitable candidates are likely to work. This information helps HR representatives prescreen incoming resumés and applications. It also help HR target employees who formerly worked at the organization.

- Search the database for current employees who were formerly employed at target employers.

- Contact those most likely to know the right people. Find related technical skills. For example, if the vacancy is for a systems analyst, a cost accountant would be more likely to interact with the systems group than an outside sales representative or a mechanic.

- With employee assistance, develop a list of people who seem to meet the job requirements. Sometimes, this takes a little coaxing.

- Coach co-workers about making calls. Some role plays may be necessary to guide employees unfamiliar with the recruiting process.

5 *Creative devices to enhance employee participation.* Atlantic Richfield, for example, gives business cards to employees who don't normally have them. The cards have both the employee's information and the contact information for the HR department. The employee can then simply give the card to someone and say, "I enjoy working here. If you are interested in a job, call the HR department."

6 *Good communications feedback about referrals.* Employees get frustrated and discouraged when they don't receive feedback about the disposition of referrals. If a referral is given, but no feedback returns, employees lose enthusiasm. The HR department is viewed as unresponsive and disorganized, and the likelihood of future referrals dwindles.

SOURCE: Andy Bargerstock and Hank Engel, "Six Ways to Boost Employee Referral Programs," *HR Magazine* 39, no. 12 (December 1994): 72–78.

FIGURE 7–11   JOB LEADS FOR COLLEGE STUDENTS

College students often have difficulty landing their first real job. A poor economy can make the challenge even greater. Ten proven sources for good leads include the following:

1 *Internships.* Many firms are increasingly hiring only students who have proven themselves through an internship with the employer. It is best to find an internship related to your major; however, if that is not possible, find one with a highly desirable employer in a related type of work.

2 *Referrals.* Former employers, professors, neighbors, and relatives can provide valuable leads. Give them a resumé and tell them of your job interests.

3 *Placement Offices.* Don't overlook the obvious! Employers often depend on the college placement office for initial contacts.

4 *Nationalize.* Don't count on opportunities in your local area. Other cities and regions may have stronger economies and more job opportunities. You can always move closer to home after you have gained work experience.

5 *Job Fairs.* Check local and out-of-town newspapers for job fairs; attend as many as possible. An employer may not have open a position of interest, but you might sell yourself to a recruiter who has a new opening in your field within a few weeks.

6 *Volunteer.* If you have a strong desire to work for a particular organization or person, offer to volunteer your services for a few weeks to secure the opportunity to sell yourself.

7 *Part-Time Jobs.* It may not meet your career or financial needs immediately, but a part-time position can give you the opportunity to transfer to a full-time position once you have a good work record.

8 *Nonprofit and Government Employers.* Don't ignore the large percentage of jobs that exist in these important and growing segments of the economy.

9 *Self-Employment.* This may be the best time in your life to start your own business. Consider taking a partner if you need help and encouragement. The U.S. Small Business Administration can provide useful assistance.

10 *Small Towns.* Explore the small towns that offer a reasonable commute from your home. Small-town employers are having increasing difficulty hiring qualified workers and therefore may provide that important first job opportunity.

PRIVATE EMPLOYMENT AGENCIES

HR departments have increased their use of private employment agencies, and their use of some public agencies such as Goodwill Industries which, in some states, provides a training program that prepares women for jobs in the construction industry (see *HR in the News:* "Goodwill Trains Women in Construction"). With private agencies, sometimes the expense involved is prohibitive. The employer may pay a percentage of the applicant's first-year salary as a fee to the agency. However, in some cases, a good employment agency can save the personnel office valuable time by screening out unqualified applicants and locating qualified ones. Effective agencies may actually save the organization money by reducing recruitment and selection costs. Use of private employment agencies does not relieve HR departments of any requirements under federal employment laws.

Only two or three competent agencies should be used by one organization; one specific agency should be used for a position when that agency typically has a good number of qualified applicants for that type of position. A **source trust** should be developed with a particular agency counselor so that unqualified applicants are not sent. A counselor will work harder to retain repeat business than to fill just one immediate opening.

HR managers should limit the number of applicants they allow an agency to send to four or five; this will keep them from being flooded with marginal applicants who probably could have been located without the agency. When limited to only four or five applicants, the agency counselor will do a better job of screening and will send only the people who have the best opportunity to be hired.

The relationship between an employer and an agency may result from one of several situations: (1) a

HR IN THE NEWS

GOODWILL: TRAINING WOMEN IN THE CONSTRUCTION INDUSTRY

Goodwill Industries is far more than a clothing store operation, it also provides some employers a recruitment source. It also offers NEW (Nontraditional Employment for Women) Choices for Women, a preapprenticeship training program that prepares women to enter careers in carpentry, plumbing, electrical work, painting, highway construction, and other construction-related and building-industry fields. Graduates are qualified to take entry-level jobs with companies such as apartment management corporations, independent contractors, hospitals, and hotels; government agencies such as the Department of Transportation or public housing authorities; or begin apprenticeship programs through local unions or independent contractors, during which they are required to work. The goal is to enable women to pursue careers that can meet the basic needs of their families and give them the economic incentive needed to avoid public assistance.

WWW.GOODWILL.ORG

NEW Choices combines classroom instruction and hands-on training for the acquisition of skills and exposure to industry. Students construct a partial house on-site for exposure to all aspects of construction, to enable them to decide which trade interests them most. Each student works as a partner with a case manager to ensure that personal needs are met and plans are in place for self-sufficiency after training. Field trips to job sites occur throughout the training period, and the students work all day, once a week, on a Habitat for Humanity house. In addition, guest instructors from industry demonstrate skills throughout the program. New Choices was developed through a partnership of construction-industry professionals, social-service providers, and training-and-employment experts. This Leadership Team (EAC/CAC), initiated by Goodwill Industries, includes representatives from local joint apprenticeship-and-training committees as well as merit shops in the region.

For over a year, the Leadership Team and Goodwill staff researched the best practices of established and highly successful nontraditional programs for women across the country including Nontraditional Employment for Women in New York City, Hard Hatted Women in Cleveland, Milwaukee Nontraditional Employment Training, and Chicago Women in the Trades. These programs have placed thousands of women in construction-related jobs and apprenticeship programs over the past 20 years. Goodwill's Leadership Team then designed a curriculum for NEW Choices that was customized to meet local needs.

SOURCE: Cindy Henning and Susan Carrell, Goodwill Industries of Kentucky (1998).

written agreement between the two parties, which specifies the fee and the basis of its obligation—usually when the agency produces an applicant who is hired; (2) an oral agreement such as an HR official asking a recruiter over lunch to "send me some resumés"; (3) an implied agreement, which may occur if two parties continue to operate as they had when a written agreement existed. For example, a recruiter learns of an opening in a firm with which she has conducted business in the past. The recruiter sends several resumés, with a cover letter explaining why they were sent, and one of the applicants is hired; (4) an applicant's resumé includes information about an agency relationship—"property of recruiter Jones, fee expected from employer."[30]

ADVERTISING

In a growing number of fields, including engineering, computer science, aircraft operation and maintenance, and health care, employers are having a difficult time attracting qualified applicants. These employers are increasingly relying on recruitment advertising and have begun using more-creative advertisements. A new generation of recruitment ads, such as the one in Figure 7–12, while very different and distinctive, generally have in common the following:[31]

- Images that sell the company first and specific jobs second.
- Recognition of high-tech professionals as people, not just as techno-buffs.
- Strong visuals as attention getters that are "flipper proof"—meaning that the most casual observer cannot flip the page without reading them.
- Humor as well as graphics to attract attention.

Employers who have won *Personnel Journal's* Vantage Award for recruitment advertising excellence include Relational Technology, a software manufacturer; Hewlett-Packard/Colorado; Bell Aerospace Textron, a Buffalo, New York–based defense systems company; GTE Laboratories, the Massachusetts engineering firm; Lockheed, the Los Angeles defense industry company (see Figure 7–12); and Mercury Computer. In the case of Relational Technology, the company was largely unknown to potential applicants even though its database management software, Ingres, was among the best-known products in its field. The relational ad "Modern Art" shows a photo of art gallery onlookers pondering a framed canvas with the word *Ingres* in bold letters. The ad (which appeared in *Computerworld*) produced the highest response rate in the history of the company and led to the hiring of 110 new employees.[32]

Recruiters can develop successful recruitment advertising for local newspapers, as well as for trade and professional publications, by incorporating the elements of consumer advertising. Often an organization using advertising is not really trying to recruit the unemployed person, who will diligently follow up on most ads, but rather the underemployed person, who if given the right opportunity would welcome a change of jobs. To recruit this type of employee, the ad must be attractive enough to stimulate the employee to respond.

A successful recruitment advertisement is based on the answers to four questions, according to Bernard Hodes, president of a Chicago advertising firm. The four questions are:[33]

1 *What do you want to accomplish?* Decide who you want to hire, how many people you want, and in what time frame. Develop accurate, current job descriptions and summarize critical job functions to be included in an ad.

2 *Who do you want to reach?* Estimate the demographics and motivations of those you want to respond. This helps to select and shape the best media. Develop a psychographic profile of the target audience. The profile can be used to select benefits of the job or organization that would motivate a reader to respond.

3 *What should be advertising message convey?* Identify the facts that must be included, such as job duties and minimum qualifications. Also, decide what image of the organization the ad should convey. Often the general advertising copy, logo, product lines, and the like can be incorporated into the ad so that the reader sees a connection between the common image of the company and the recruitment ad.

4 *How and where should you advertise?* Decide which of the nine major types of advertising media should be used. One or more possibilities may be used after considering the strengths and weaknesses of each. After one is chosen, a specific agent must be selected. For example, if a trade magazine is the medium, should *Engineering News-Record, Civil Engineering, Building Digest,* or some other agent be used?

Direct Mail   A relatively new tool for recruitment advertising is the direct-mail campaign. This technique is generally used to lure professionals who are employed but willing to consider a job with greater opportunities. For mid- and top-level management jobs, the best candidates may not respond to newspaper or trade-journal ads, because these candidates are not actively seeking jobs.

Direct-mail recruitment enables a recruiter to get the attention of desirable candidates and gives the employer an advantage over other employers looking for some prospects.[34] A highly successful direct-mail recruitment program was developed by the Martin Marietta Corporation. The company, which needed to staff a new program, had little success attracting experienced professionals with over two years of experience. Martin Marietta was looking for professionals who were successful in their current jobs, who were not actively looking in the market and thus not responding to conventional ads, and who would be motivated by a new and greater challenge. The company's direct-mail program comprised primarily three steps:[35]

Obtain a Mailing List   From various list directories or other firms, a target mailing list was obtained.[36] Martin Marietta used a 10,000-person list that concentrated on targeted disciplines within a 200-mile radius of Baltimore. For discretion, only home addresses were used.

Develop a Mail Package   Martin Marietta used a three-part mail package. First, the outer envelope was designed to capture attention. Second, the package contained an attractive company brochure carefully designed to cover Martin Marietta's growth and technological successes, job descriptions for open positions, the

FIGURE 7–12   AWARD-WINNING RECRUITMENT ADVERTISEMENT

HIGH PAY, FREE HOUSING, NO TAXES. WHAT'S THE CATCH?

The catch is you'll be living in Saudi Arabia. And while the life-style for Westerners there is very comfortable, it is nevertheless a country where customs are very different from America's. As the tour would also be unaccompanied, you might imagine that the compensation would be generous.

You'd be right.

The benefits for C-130 specialists are extraordinary. We have abundant opportunities in our Mideast Operation for people with the following backgrounds:

C-130 Aircrew (Instructor Qualified)
C-130 Classroom Instructors
C-130 Maintenance Techs

Besides the excellent pay and allowances, the free housing, and tax exemption, you'll also enjoy liberal vacations, travel opportunities, wonderful benefits and a free trip back to the States every year.

For a C-130 experienced professional just leaving the service, this opportunity is a unique and exciting bonanza. Call us toll free, 1-800-472-2203. Or write Lockheed Aircraft Services Company, P.O. Box 33, Dept. 1-782-064, Ontario, California 91761-0033. Lockheed is an equal opportunity, affirmative action employer.

INNOVATION: giving shape to imagination

SOURCE: R. M. Dombrowski, Lockheed Aircraft Service Company, Ontario, California.

company's location, and employee benefits. Third, the package contained a response card, a mini-resumé requesting an applicant's name, address, present position, and college degree.

Follow Up Quickly   The response card was critical because it facilitated immediate response from individuals who were unlikely to have current resumés. A Martin Marietta representative telephoned each respondent quickly to keep interest high.

The results of Martin Marietta's program were typical of successful direct-mail programs: a high response rate of 4 to 5 percent compared to a 2 percent industry standard; a low cost per hire for executive positions; and the filling of all open positions with highly qualified applicants.[37]

TABLE 7–2	COMPARISON OF ALTERNATIVE METHODS OF ADDING LABOR				
CRITERIA	RECRUIT NEW PERMANENT EMPLOYEES	ASSIGN OVERTIME TO PERMANENT EMPLOYEES	OUTSIDE TEMPORARY AGENCY	IN-HOUSE TEMPORARY SERVICE	LEASING
Additional HR administrative activities required	Yes	No	No	Yes	No
Government regulations (OSHA, EEO, etc.)	Yes	Yes	No	Yes	No
Wages and benefits costs	Normal payroll	1 1/2 time wages	Varies, usually higher	Usually lower benefits	5–10% above normal payroll
Additional training required	Yes (initially)	No	Yes (varies)	No	Yes (initially)
Fast, easy to hire and fire	No	No	Yes	Yes	Yes
Fatigue possibility	No	Yes	No	No	No
Loyalty (potential problem)	No	No	Yes	No	Yes

HIRING ALTERNATIVES

In recent years, employers have increasingly sought alternatives to the recruitment and selection of permanent new employees. They are willing to pay a premium to escape the legal responsibilities, paperwork, and commitment required in the traditional hiring of additional employees. The alternatives of assigning overtime to permanent employees, using temporary employees (outside or in-house), or leasing employees, must be carefully reviewed and the criteria included in Table 7–2, considered before one or more are chosen. In recent years, however, an increasing number of employers have chosen alternative methods of adding labor to the workplace, decreasing their dependence on hiring new permanent employees.

The three most immediate sources of additional labor are (1) current employees who work overtime, (2) temporary employees, and (3) leased employees.

ASSIGNING OVERTIME

Assigning overtime to employees is an attractive alternative because it is a temporary situation rather than a permanent staff increase. Choosing overtime means using experienced, knowledgeable employees who do not require any additional training or orientation. But overtime also means additional fatigue for employees who have already worked their full shift and usually the expense of time-and-a-half or double-time pay.

TEMPORARY HELP

Temporary help may be less costly than hiring new permanent employees, particularly for companies with great seasonal demands or for an unforecasted temporary absence of important personnel. In office administration, accounting, and engineering, temporary help can quickly be trained to be productive on the job with relatively low start-up costs.

The temporary-services industry in the United States is booming. An estimated nine out of ten American companies use temporary services. Over 1 million orders are filled *daily*. Why the demand from employers?

Even during a strong economy, many employers are very careful in hiring permanent employers due to the cost and potential liability of a bad hire. Thus, increasingly they choose from their pool of experienced temps, until it is the third most common recruitment source (see Figure 7–13). The recruiting specialist at Herman Miller, Lee Sullivan, even advises college graduates to first get some experience—through Manpower Temporary Services.[38] Manpower today is the world's largest employer and places people in all types of jobs worldwide.

Employers who use temporary services most often no longer view them as just a source of replacement secretaries. Certainly that is still a large portion of the business, but the downsizing of corporate America has provided temporary services with a large supply of highly trained individuals and many corporate clients, needing temporary manpower, that are wary of adding full-time personnel.

Employers considering using temporary services should review the following suggestions on how best to use the temporary service.[39]

WWW.MANPOWER.COM

1 Develop a partner relationship with one service rather than a vendor relationship. Working primarily with one service allows them to learn your specific needs.

2 Invite service representatives into your working environment to assess your needs before submitting orders.

3 Before placing an order, compile as much information as possible about your needs—work experience, equipment, software, communication skills, and so on.

4 Treat the temporary worker with the same courtesy as you would a permanent employee.

In-House Temporaries   Instead of calling an outside agency to fill a temporary position, larger employers may operate an in-house temporary service. The employer recruits a pool of part-time and full-time workers who are kept available to departments that need to fill a position temporarily due to a regular employee's vacation, illness, or other reasons, or to departments experiencing a seasonal or other sudden increase in workload.

FIGURE 7–13   RECRUITMENT SOURCES USED BY HR EXECUTIVES

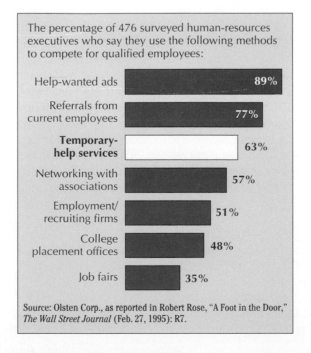

The percentage of 476 surveyed human-resources executives who say they use the following methods to compete for qualified employees:

Help-wanted ads — 89%
Referrals from current employees — 77%
Temporary-help services — 63%
Networking with associations — 57%
Employment/recruiting firms — 51%
College placement offices — 48%
Job fairs — 35%

Source: Olsten Corp., as reported in Robert Rose, "A Foot in the Door," *The Wall Street Journal* (Feb. 27, 1995): R7.

Crestar Bank, headquartered in Richmond, Virginia, operates a large and successful in-house temporary service called Tempo. Out of 1,100 positions at Crestar's headquarters, 60 to 100 each week are filled with temporary employees. Tempo, a unit within the bank's HR department, recruits and trains employees to work in all departments. The unit was created to replace Crestar's use of more-expensive outside temporary-agency employees. Ellen Barnard, HR vice president at Crestar, sees the greatest advantage of an in-house service as the quality of work. Since the temporaries are employees of Crestar, Barnard believes that they are more committed to their work. Successful in-house temporary services are also in operation at Aetna Life & Casualty Company in Hartford, Connecticut; Eastern Milk Producers Corporation in Syracuse, New York; Sharp Health-Care in San Diego, California; and Agway, a farm cooperative in Syracuse. Aetna's program, Aetna Temporary Services, may be the largest in the country, with over 1,500 positions filled each year. All the programs report similar advantages: lower costs and higher-quality workers than those of outside agencies. In addition, they report that many of the temporary-unit workers are hired by the departments they serve as permanent positions become available. This process works well for both sides: The temporary employees know in advance if they like the nature of the work and the people they will be working with, and the department is already familiar with their work. Another advantage reported by these companies is the ease of recruiting in today's changing workforce. In particular, former employees who retired or left to raise a family can be more easily recruited for part-time or limited temporary jobs, and they are often already trained in the work. The major problem associated with in-house programs is maintaining the pool of workers. It can take as many as six people to fill each job order due to availability, skill requirements, and specific job needs. In comparison to using outside agencies or leasing, the in-house service also has the disadvantage of being responsible for all required normal HR activities such as hiring, payroll, and benefits. Also, even the largest in-house program must utilize outside agencies when unique skills are needed.[40]

LEASING EMPLOYEES

A new alternative to the traditional method of recruiting new employees is the practice of **leasing employees.** While the concept of employee leasing is not entirely new, there is a new breed of companies, such as Contract Staffing of America, headquartered in Tustin, California. CSA hires workers and then contracts them out to employers that request employees with certain skills and abilities. Why the new interest in employee leasing? James Borgelt, general manager of Omnistaff, a Dallas leasing firm, believes his customers lease employees for several reasons. For example, small businesses cannot afford a pension program or other benefits that compete with those of large corporations. Thus they lose many good employees to large firms. However, Borgelt contends that his firm offers a competitive salary and benefits to its employees because it can take advantage of group rates. Omnistaff then leases the employees to small employers. Small employers also like not having the EEO/AA administration duties such as payroll, W-2 forms, benefit claims, and so on, which are handled by Omnistaff.[41]

To be considered the common-law employer by the Internal Revenue Service, the leasing company must perform the hiring and firing. The leasing company, as the legal employer, is responsible for all HR functions, including employee records, payroll, complying with government regulations, workers' compensation insurance, and employee benefits. The client employer, however, retains approval of who works in its facility. If a client becomes dissatisfied with an employee or terminates the position, the leasing firm removes the employee and may fire, lay off, or transfer the employee to another client.

The primary advantage to the client employer remains freedom from the administrative burden. This time-saving advantage alone can save the employer 5 to 10 percent of payroll costs generally charged by the leasing company. Another advantage to the client is that management can spend more time running the business and less time on HR functions. The client can also save money by not providing benefits that are provided by the leasing company.

There are also areas of potential advantage to the employees. Leasing companies that provide workers to many clients enjoy the economies of scale that enable them to offer employees benefits that many small employers cannot afford. Employees may also realize greater job security if they work for a successful leasing company. They can be transferred to another client rather than be fired if their relationship with the current client becomes unsatisfactory for either the client or the employee. Thus, employees who simply do not get along with the supervisor have more options than if they were hired directly by the client.[42]

INTERNATIONAL HR: STAFFING

One of the more challenging issues facing multinational firms is staffing. Should a firm relocate home-country staff to its foreign operations or hire host-country personnel?[43] The multinational firm can choose to relocate experienced personnel from the home country or employ and train nationals (that is, citizens of the host country). The choice is often determined on the basis of trade-offs between technical expertise that may be available only from the home country and the firm's need to adapt to local customs.

If the type of employee needed to staff the overseas operation is technically or professionally unique (for example, a computer engineer), chances are high that the person will be transferred from the United States. However, this strategy is very expensive.

The cost of sending personnel overseas from the United States is expensive—two to eight times salary, depending on the country of assignment.[44] Of course, this cost will vary in terms of hardship to the employee, distance from the United States, and family obligations. Big-ticket expenditures for relocating personnel may include bonuses for hardship, education of children, visits back to the United States, and additional expenses to maintain an American standard of living. The high cost of expatriates is a major reason fewer and fewer companies continue this personnel practice.

By and large, international firms are depending more on local labor sources to meet their staffing needs.[45] Recruiting local workers is less expensive and, with the exception of a few countries, there is usually an adequate and available labor pool from which to recruit. An added advantage is that it creates career opportunities, goodwill, and loyalty to the company. It may also be politically astute, because governments have been known to impose constraints on the number of foreign managers and specialists brought into their countries. An American mining company in Africa, for example, was required to hire all lower-level workers locally and to phase out all American workers within 10 years.

McDonald's, one of the most recognized names around the world, has focused its international recruiting on finding people who have similar values and expectations to those of McDonald's in the United States (see HR in the News).

WWW.MCDONALDS.COM

INTERNATIONAL HR IN THE NEWS

MCDONALD'S GLOBAL RECRUITING: CORE VALUES

Most U.S. employers have adopted an international recruiting strategy of adapting to specific cultural differences in each foreign country. But McDonald's—which has been an international player for 30 years and is currently doing business in 101 countries—takes a different approach. "A lot of times, people who don't have international experience focus on the cultural differences," says Bob Wilner, home office director, international human resources in Oakbrook, Illinois. *"We look at how they're the same.* There's a lot more common ground than people think in all the countries in Asia. There are people who share our values everywhere, and part of our selection process is to try to find them. We look for people who are seeking advancement, like training, and think they'll be rewarded for hard work."

Sticking to core values is important to McDonald's, no matter where it operates. But the company is sensitive to cultural norms in each country and remains flexible in implementing its policies, Wilner says. "We take our overall philosophy and work to integrate it into each culture and market," he says. "When we opened in Korea, the concept of performance-based merit increases was pretty much unheard of. People got the same raises without regard to performance. McDonald's is committed to rewarding by merit, so we tried to devise a system that would fit into the culture and still allow us to do that." The result: "We went with a merit-based system, with a differential that didn't make a huge difference in overall compensation," says Wilner. "It was a first step, allowing us to introduce the concept."

He also notes that the company has "extremely low turnover and very high retention." What's McDonald's secret for success? On top of good salaries, benefits, and training—which other firms also offer—the company creates a sense of family and offers opportunities for career advancement, says Wilner "We want our company to be part of our workers' families and lives. When we open a restaurant, we invite the families of our workers to eat there first—even before the local dignitaries. People really get a sense of pride, and it pays off," he notes.

SOURCE: "McDonald's Focuses on Similarities," 42, no. 7, *HR Magazine* (July 1997): 107–109.

Coca-Cola's International Recruiting   The Atlanta, Georgia–based Coca-Cola Company operates in 160 countries and employs about 400,000 people. Thus, its HR department must recruit professional and managerial staff that can successfully operate internationally. Mike Semran, director of international resources for Coca-Cola, believes that "As you look to the future, the people who are running companies are going to be people who have operated in more than one culture." Therefore, he has concluded that Coke's management needs to be multilingual and multicultural. While the global language of business is English, according to Semran, applicants who have additional language skills are more valuable to the company. Coca-Cola's managerial recruitment program focuses on candidates at the college level in U.S. schools with strong international programs. A large percentage of its new hires are from the company's formal internship program. According to an International Orientation Resources study, Coca-Cola's international recruitment practices are similar to those of other U.S. companies. In general, the qualities international firms require in recent college graduates include technical expertise, management ability, previous overseas experience, and a second language.

SUMMARY POINTS

- Recruitment requires the HR specialist to acquire a pool of available and qualified applicants. The recruiters can tap a variety of sources including current employees, retirees, part-time workers, the unemployed, and employees of other organizations who feel they are underemployed.

- Human resource planning is a key method by which the HR department can hold down recruitment costs and minimize the time positions remain vacant. By developing demand-and-supply forecasts, the HR specialist can develop training programs, retirement incentives, management succession planning, and other techniques to aid future recruitment efforts.

- Job-posting programs are widely utilized to recruit applicants for positions. New voice-mail and electronic-mail systems offer several advantages to traditional bulletin boards.

- Effective recruitment advertising has increased due to the use of common marketing research tools. The need for advertising has increased because of two-career couples and a general unwillingness to relocate on the part of professional and technical employees.

- Current employees are the most common source of applicants for higher-level positions. They offer the organization several advantages over external applicants and give all employees the incentive of knowing that they may be promoted as a reward for hard work.

- Overtime, temporary help, and leasing are alternative sources of additional labor. Depending on the number of hours and skills needed, these recruitment sources may be more desirable than hiring permanent employees.

- College campus recruitment has become more competitive and employers more sophisticated in their methods. A poor economy should signal to students the need to use innovative job leads.

CASE STUDY

AN EMPLOYEE REFERRAL PROGRAM

Annabelle Adams is the HR director for Missouri Telemarketing in St. Louis. The company employs about 2,500 people, of whom 90 percent are part-time telemarketing sales personnel. Most of these employees are college students, housewives, or retired people who work part-time for $7 to 10 per hour, depending on their seniority and shift. Annual job satisfaction surveys indicate that the employees like their supervisors, wages and benefits, and the workplace facility. Turnover, however, is currently averaging 25 percent due to the hours (evening and weekend shifts must be worked by all employees for at least half of their total hours) and stress due to the constant pressure of meeting sales targets. Employees also complain of the lack of social interaction at work due to their isolation (each employee sits in a small cubicle with a computer that performs the dialing and recordkeeping functions).

The company is growing rapidly, and thus must constantly recruit and train new sales personnel. The president, Mary Anne Ryan, has decided that the company should try an employee prize referral program as a means of recruiting. She has just returned from a conference in Morro Bay, California, where she heard several other CEOs describe how they successfully utilized referral programs. Ryan has directed Adams to develop an employee referral program that will recruit at least 300 new workers in the next three months. She has provided a budget of $150,000 to cover all prizes and expenses directly related to the program (routine HR staff time is not included).

CASE STUDY—cont'd

QUESTIONS

1. What prizes should Adams recommend the program offer to employees? Why?

2. How should the program be communicated to the employees?

3. How should the success of the program be determined?

4. Whom should Adams consult for advice in designing the program?

EXPERIENTIAL EXERCISES

1. THE TEMPORARY HELP ALTERNATIVE

PURPOSE

To gain an understanding of the temporary help alternative as a method of increasing personnel.

TASK

Contact five temporary help agencies and ask each to provide the following information for each of the positions listed: (1) their charge for one week (40 hours); (2) the number of people with at least one year's experience they have available; and (3) how quickly an employee could be provided. If additional information is needed, improvise.

POSITION	COST/WEEK	NO. AVAILABLE	WHEN AVAILABLE
1. Secretary (experience: word processing, spreadsheet, database)			
2. Cashier (must be bonded)			
3. Salesperson (experienced in retail clothing)			
4. Accountant (BS/BA degree)			
5. Driver (current driver's license, experience with delivery trucks)			

2. EFFECTIVE HELP-WANTED ADS

PURPOSE

To understand the criteria for evaluating help-wanted recruiting advertisements and the effectiveness of several actual help-wanted ads.

INTRODUCTION

What are the characteristics of effective help-wanted ads? Consider the following questions and dos and don'ts.

WHO DO YOU WANT?

Important information that you will need *before* you write your ad:

- Is this person likely to be working? If so, where?
- How many people do you need?
- What skills and abilities are required?
- What publications is this person likely to read regularly?

- Which job rewards—compensation, benefits, career opportunities, and so on—is this person likely to be looking for?
- How competitive is the market for this person?
- What is the likely level of job satisfaction the person has with his or her present job?

Once you have answered these basic questions, you will need to create a strategy for effectively communicating the challenges and opportunities of the available job.

SOME DO'S AND DON'TS

- *Headlines are important.* Use a distinctive headline to *sell* the job to the candidate. Don't just list the job title.
- *Use graphics carefully.* Ad graphics vary widely, ranging from the simple to the complex. Graphics that are

confusing or misleading are worse than no graphics at all, so make sure that graphics make sense. A basic question to ask is: Do the graphics convey a message that you want to communicate?

● *Don't misrepresent the job.* Don't make promises you cannot keep. Be honest about opportunities for advancement, challenge, responsibility, and so on. Honesty is the best policy.

● *Don't be vague.* Be specific about the job title, salary range, and closing date.

● *"Sell" the employee.* Without tooting your own company horn too loudly, make sure the ad contains the benefits of working for your firm.

● *Avoid stereotypes.* Beware of sexism, racism, and other stereotypes. Make sure that the ad will not be seen as offensive to anyone.

● *Help prospective candidates identify themselves.* To avoid sifting through countless resumés, define the qualifications you are looking for. You will cut down considerably on unqualified applicants if you specify the three to five key requirements and be specific—for example, "Experience as the manager of ten or more industrial salespeople for at least three years."

● *Use advertising space economically.* Space cost is not cheap. Don't use a full-page ad when a half-page ad will do the job just as effectively. Don't use too many graphics and too little prose; conversely, don't use a space so small that the applicant will get eyestrain from reading. The size of the ad should be in proportion to the size of the firm, importance of the position, number of candidates sought, and so on.

● *Select recruitment media carefully.* Study the reading habits of potential candidates to determine what they read. Also, study the readership demographics of the various media you are considering. A great-looking ad is no good if the right people are not reading it.

TASK

Illustrated are several help-wanted advertisements. All were taken from the same newspaper on the same Sunday morning. Using the criteria listed, evaluate each ad, using the grid provided. Your instructor will lead you in a discussion of the results of your analysis.

SOURCE: Adapted from Margaret Magnus, "Recruitment Ads at Work," *Personnel Journal* (August, 1985). Reprinted with the permission of *Personnel Journal*, Costa Mesa, California; all rights reserved.

CRITERION*

ADVERTISEMENT

	1	2	3	4	5	6	7
Distinctive headlines							
Effective graphics							
Clever and creative							
Avoids sounding too glamorous							
Specifies nature of job and qualifications							
"Sells" the employee							
Avoids stereotyping							
Helps candidate identify self							
Uses space economically							
Effective typeface							
Proper recruitment media							
TOTALS:							

Ranking (most effective to least effective)

1.
2.
3.
4.
5.
6.
7.

*Rank each ad for each criterion using the following scale:
5 = Excellent; 4 = Very Good; 3 = Satisfactory; 2 = Below Average; 1 = Very Poor

REVIEW QUESTIONS

1 How can an employer recruit a diverse workforce?

2 Discuss hourly and professional applicants' knowledge of labor markets.

3 What are the advantages of recruiting applicants internally? Externally?

4 List the three major methods of job posting. Why should an employer consider a voice-mail system?

5 Has advertising increased as a recruitment technique in recent years? Why?

6 Why might hiring temporary help be preferable to assigning overtime or hiring new employees?

7 How can U.S. firms successfully recruit local residents in foreign nations?

DISCUSSION QUESTIONS

1 If you were an underemployed MBA, what steps would you take to find a more satisfactory position?

2 From an inexperienced job applicant's point of view, which recruitment method is more attractive? From the point of view of an applicant with 20 years' experience?

3 How should applicants prepare for job interviews? What questions should they expect to answer?

4 How should the HR director compare alternative recruitment sources?

5 Compared to their grandparents, what factors are important to today's workers as far as the workplace and employer are concerned?

6 How can an employer recruit more older workers if past efforts have not been successful?

KEY TERMS AND CONCEPTS

Employee relocation
Employee referrals
Gate hires
Human resources planning
Job posting
Labor force participation rate
Labor reserve
Leasing employees
Management succession planning
Networking
Old boy network

Older worker
Part-time employees
Peter Principle
Pirating
Recruitment
Redeploying
Source trust
Temporary help
Underemployed
Unemployed
Unemployed rate

ENDNOTES

Chapter 7

1. Mary Cook, "Choosing the Right Recruitment Tool," *HR Focus* 74, no. 10 (October 1997): 57–58.

2. John Bishop, "High School Performance and Employee Recruitment," *Journal of Labor Research* (Winter 1992): 41–44.

3. Elizabeth Blacharczyk, "Recruiters Challenged by Economy, Shortages," *HR News* (February 1990): B1, 4.

4. Hal Lancaster, "Will Hiring . . ." *The Wall Street Journal* (April 28, 1998): B1.

5. Michelle Neely Martinez, "Looking for Young Talent? Inroads Helps Diversity Efforts," *HR Magazine* 41, no. 3 (March 1996): 73.

6. Alex Markels, "Job Hunting Takes Off in Cyberspace," *The Wall Street Journal* (September 9, 1996): B1, 5.

7. Margaret Mannix, "Putting the Net to Work," *U.S. News and World Report* (October 27, 1997): 94.

8. Jennifer Laabs, "Create Job Orders, Not Pink Slips," *Personnel Journal* (June 1996): 97–99.

9. "Older Workers Rapidly Becoming a New Force in the Labor Market," *Resource* (August 1987): 2.

10. Pat O'Connor, "As the U.S. Grows Up, More Firms Turn to Older Workers," *The Courier-Journal* (July 13, 1987): B12, 7.

11. Greg Jaffe, "Many Employers Find That Hiring Is Easier Than Data Suggest," *The Wall Street Journal* (July 31, 1997): A1, 8.

12. Michael Peterson, "A Recruiter's Crystal Ball," *Recruit!* 2, no. 1 (June–July 1996): 8.

13. "Corporations Lure Back Job Seekers," *Workforce* (August 1997): 23.

14. Barry Stavro, "Job-Hunting After 40: Abridged Resumés and Touched-Up Hairs," *The Los Angeles Times* (May 17, 1993): 12.

15. David V. Lewis, "Make Way for the Older Worker," *HR Magazine* 35, no. 5 (May 1990): 75–77.

16. Richard Frantzreb, "Human Resource Planning: Forecasting Manpower Needs," *Personnel Journal* 60, no. 11 (November 1981): 850–51.

17. Ibid., 850–54.

18. Kendrith M. Rowland and Scott L. Summers, "Human Resource Planning: A Second Look," *Personnel Administrator* 26, no. 12 (December 1981): 73–80.

19. Charles F. Russ, Jr., "Manpower Planning Systems: Part I," *Personnel Journal* 61, no. 1 (January 1982): 44–45. For a complete discussion of commitment manpower planning see Charles F. Russ, "Manpower Planning Systems: Part II," *Personnel Journal* 61, no. 2 (January 1982): 119–123.

20. David R. Leigh, "Business Planning Is People Planning," *Personnel Journal* 63, no. 5 (May 1984): 44–45.

21. Ibid.

22. *Employee Promotion and Transfer Policies,* PPF survey no. 120 (Washington, D.C.: Bureau of National Affairs, Inc., 1978), 2–4.

23. Linda T. Thornburg, "Relocation Costs Up, Transferees Less Happy," *HR News* (June 1990): 10.

24. Kathryn Scovel, "The Relocation Riddle," *Human Resource Executive,* (June 1990): 46–51.

25. Lawrence J. Peters and R. Hull, *The Peter Principle* (New York: Bantam Books, 1969), 55–57.

26. William C. De Lone, "Telephone Job Posting Cuts Costs," *Personnel Journal* (April 1993): 115–18.

27. Lawrence S. Kleiman, "An Effective Job Posting System," *Personnel Journal* 63, no. 2 (February 1984): 20-25, 81–84.

28. Andy Bargerstock and Hank Engel, "Six Ways to Boost Employee Referral Programs," *HR Magazine* 39, no. 12 (December 1994): 72–78.

29. Dawn Gunsch, "Comprehensive College Strategy Strengthens NCR's Recruitment," *Personnel Journal* (September 1993): 58–62.

30. J. Jonathan Schraub, "Avoiding Unexpected Fee Liability," *HR Magazine* (October 1993): S2–S3.

31. Beyond Nuts and Bolts," *Personnel Journal* 69, no. 2 (February 1990): 70–77.

32. Ibid.

33. Bernard S. Hodes, "Planning for Recruitment Advertising: Part II," *Personnel Journal* 62, no. 6 (June 1983): 492–99.

34. Richard Siedlecki, "Creating a Direct Mail Recruitment Program," *Personnel Journal* 62, no. 4 (April 1983): 304–307.

35. Rick Stoops, "Direct Mail: Luring the Isolated Professionals," *Personnel Journal* 63, no. 6 (June 1984): 34–36.

36. Siedlecki, "Creating a Direct Mail Program," 307. Consult the *Direct Mail List Rates and Data,* published by Standard Rate and Data Service, Inc., 5201 Old Orchard Road, Skokie,

IL 60077, or contact Direct Mail/Marketing Association (DM/MA), 6 East 43 Street, New York, NY 10017.

37. Stoops, "Direct Mail," 34–36.

38. Robert Rose, "A Foot in the Door," *The Wall Street Journal* (February 27, 1995): R7.

39. Steve Bergsman, "Setting Up a Temporary Shop," *HR Magazine* 35, no. 2 (February 1990): 46–48.

40. Ibid.

41. "Leasing Employees," *Changing Times* (May 1985): 50–54.

42. Paul N. Keaton and Janine Anderson, "Leasing Offers Benefits to Both Sides," *HR Magazine* 35, no. 7 (July 1990): 53–58.

43. D.McFarlin and P. Sweeney, *International Management* (Cincinnati, OH: South-Western College Publishing, 1998), 223–254.

44. For more information on the costs of expatriates, see P.J. Dowling, R.S. Schuler, *International Dimensions of Human Resource Management, 2nd ed.,* (Belmont, CA: Wadsworth Publishing Co., 1994), 70–171.

45. For some staffing issues associated with expatriate managers, see J.B. Cullen, *Multinational Management: A Strategic Approach* (Cincinnati, OH: South-Western College Publishing, 1999), 408–478.

46. Jennifer J. Lambs, "The Global Talent Search," *Personnel Journal* (August 1991): 38–44.

CHAPTER 8

EMPLOYEE SELECTION

CHAPTER OUTLINE

CHAPTER OBJECTIVES

1 To explain the Uniform Guidelines on Employee Selection.

2 To develop a selection decision process.

3 To cite useful application blank information.

4 To develop a structured employment interview.

5 To distinguish among different types of preemployment tests.

6 To understand the need for complete background checks.

7 To identify significant issues related to staffing in foreign countries and major hiring alternatives.

8 To understand the use of preemployment medical exams and drug tests.

9 To describe negligent hiring and understand its complexity and impact on the selection process.

10 To explain how the final selection decision is made.

The selection process begins when there are more qualified and available job applicants than there are open positions. It may be necessary to fill one particular position or several positions as they become open or to fill positions continuously through training programs so that people are ready to take jobs as they become vacant. In large organizations, which may continuously recruit and select job applicants for future job openings, the time that positions remain vacant is minimized.

SELECTION DECISIONS

Human resource selection is the process of choosing qualified individuals who are available to fill positions in an organization. In the ideal personnel situation, selection involves choosing the best applicant to fill a position. After the position opens, the HR manager reviews the available, qualified applicants and fills the position from that pool. The ideal situation, however, seldom occurs. The selection process involves making a judgment—not about the applicant, but about the fit between *this* person and *this* job. Almost half of the employees who voluntarily quit their jobs within the first year cited a wrong fit as the reason.[1]

There is no fail-safe method of determining the best person to fill any position. Many subjective factors are involved in the selection process because there is no perfect test or gauge of applicants. But there are objective techniques that increase the validity of the process. The selection process is perhaps the heart of an organization's HR program. If the selection process is well ad-

ministered, the employee will be able to achieve personal career goals and the organization will benefit from a productive, satisfied employee.

In the new era of globalization, the key to success is the human factor—people. Unlike products, land, equipment, and money, people experience unique problems when moved across national borders. Thus, even greater care must be taken to select, orient, and assist people who must work in different countries and cultures. Most people are raised, educated, and indoctrinated in only one culture. Yet the magic of successful international business lies in people who have developed knowledge of and respect for more than one culture and thus can interface successfully between two or more cultures. An American Management Association survey of Forbes 500 CEOs found that of the 60 most common problems of international business operations, 12 were related to selecting, training, and developing people (see Figure 8–1).[2] The process also works in reverse—that is, with foreign companies selecting American workers for their U.S. operations. For example, Toyota, the Japanese car manufacturer, developed an extensive, highly successful selection process for its first U.S. assembly plant in Georgetown, Kentucky.

AN HR RESPONSIBILITY

The selection process is usually centered in the HR department, though it involves many individuals from other departments. Particularly in larger organizations, centralizing the recruitment and selection process in the HR department is both efficient and effective. Both current employees and job applicants have one place to

HR IN THE NEWS

GENETIC TESTING: IT'S NO JOKE

The U.S. Government's Human Genome Project (HGP) will completely map the entire human genetic system by the year 2005. It will provide detailed knowledge of the human genetic structure, a great medical advance allowing for early diagnosis and treatment of many conditions and diseases.

The HGP will also enable potential employers to identify people who have a "high risk" to develop conditions and diseases. Employers have a strong incentive to require genetic testing by job applicants—their enormous healthcare costs. The costs of genetic tests, once prohibitively high, are dropping ($2,000 in 1991, $800 in 1998). Genetic testing raises significant medical opportunities and, in the workplace, significant ethical, legal and social issues.

SOURCE: "ACLU's Genetic Testing Report," *Workforce Tools* (July 1997): 1, 2.

FIGURE 8–1   MOST COMMON HR PROBLEMS IN INTERNATIONAL BUSINESS

An American Management Association survey of CEOs of Forbes 500 companies found 12 of their top 60 most common problems of conducting international business to be HR issues:

1. Selecting and training local managers.

2. Generating companywide loyalty and motivation.

3. Speaking the local language and respecting the culture.

4. Appraising overseas managers' performance.

5. Planning systematic manager development.

6. Hiring indigenous sales personnel.

7. Compensating foreign managers.

8. Hiring and training foreign technical employees.

9. Selecting and training U.S. managers for overseas operations.

10. Dealing with unions and labor laws abroad.

11. Promoting and transferring foreign managers.

12. Compensating U.S. nationals abroad.

SOURCE: S. Hayden, "Our Foreign Legions Are Faltering," *Personnel* (August 1990): 40–44.

apply for jobs, transfers, or promotions, as well as to inquire about related HR matters. In most situations, the cost of recruiting and selecting employees is minimized with centralization because HR specialists can perform these functions more effectively than managers in different departments. The trained HR specialist can also save money by ensuring that an organization's HR selection practices comply with federal laws and restrictions. In addition, the HR manager can ensure that the selection process is objective. Centralizing the selection function minimizes the bias of department managers or others who may wish to promote employees or hire applicants who are not the best qualified.

While the HR department is usually responsible for selection, individual managers are often involved in the interviewing process. Frequently, the applicant's second or third interview is with the department manager, who has valuable insights about work methods and departmental goals and can evaluate the applicant's qualifications. The selection process also relies on managers to assist in developing job specifications and writing job descriptions, which are critical in determining the needs for a particular position and identifying the best-qualified applicants.

The centralization of the hiring process within the personnel department and the sharing of decision making with line managers have evolved over many years. As outlined in Table 8–1, hiring procedures have been greatly altered by outside influences such as World War II, federal legislation, and new technology. Many common techniques—such as testing, employee training, and test validation—are the direct result of social movements and government statutes. Yet despite the increased role of the HR department, final selection decisions are often made by line managers.

THE SELECTION PROCESS

As Figure 8–2 indicates, the selection process pulls together organizational goals, job designs, and performance appraisals, as well as recruitment and selection. The first element in the selection process is the *setting of organizational goals,* which must include the general hiring policy of the organization. Management can either employ the best people in the marketplace for particular jobs—often involving high salaries and benefits—or pay relatively low wages and salaries, unconcerned with employee turnover or dissatisfaction about wages, benefits, and working conditions. Policymakers must

TABLE 8–1   A CHRONOLOGY OF HIRING PRACTICES AND INFLUENCES IN THE U.S.

EVENT OR INNOVATION	DATE	EXPLANATION OR SIGNIFICANCE
First personnel department	1890s	John H. Patterson, president of the National Cash Register Company, Dayton, Ohio, establishes the first personnel department.
Scientific management	1912	Frederick Taylor testifies before a special U.S. House committee on the principles and virtues of scientific management. This approach would reduce waste by hiring the right people and simplifying their jobs. Extremely popular for many years, it was no longer in favor by the end of the 1920s.
Testing	1918	The first group intelligence test, *Army Alpha,* is developed by personnel managers and psychologists to "match each enlisted man to a job." Shortly after World War I, industry and the Civil Service Commission adopt testing as a breakthrough in hiring practices, believing that each job can be scientifically filled with the right person.
	1920s	The first professional journal in personnel, *The Journal of Personnel Research* (forerunner of *Personnel Journal*), describes in issue after issue the profession's infatuation with testing as the means of making hiring decisions with objective and scientific information.
Staff designation	1923	Line managers believe personnel should stay out of day-to-day decisions (including hiring), but personnel offices continue to take over the employment function to make it more scientific. In 1923 the National Personnel Association, in support of line management's views, changed its name to the American Management Association.
Great Depression	1930s	Massive unemployment stops almost all hiring and cruelly shows America that work is not appreciated until it is gone.
Wagner Act	1935	The once unified field of industrial relations is split into two—personnel and labor relations—in the years following enactment of the Wagner Act and the growth of union membership.
World War II	1940s	Organizations rapidly grow in size, and supervisors' preoccupation with production demands often forces them to relinquish all hiring and government-regulations concerns to personnel departments.
		The War Manpower Commission assumes control of most industrial hiring and introduces widespread use of manpower planning and training programs, which remain long after the war. Universities are encouraged to develop "industrial education" personnel programs.
		Nondiscriminatory hiring orders are first issued by President Roosevelt. By 1945, women account for 36 percent of the workforce due to the shortage of men. Both managers and women themselves are confronted with the fact that women are successful in jobs previously closed to them.
The age of Sputnik	1950s	The combination of the GI Bill and the national "space race" with the USSR ignites a trend for organizations to hire college graduates in unprecedented numbers, particularly scientists, engineers, and businessmen.
Federal laws	1960s	The movement toward "fair and open" hiring practices begun during World War II crystallizes into federal legislation: the Equal Pay Act of 1963, the 1964 Civil Rights Act, affirmative action (1965 executive order 11246), and the Age Discrimination in Employment Act (ADEA) of 1967.
		The new hiring legislation forces personnel managers to consider the validity and reliability of selection methods; the use of written tests and the old boy network decline as structured interviews, nondiscriminatory application blanks, assessment centers, and weighted application blanks grow in use.
The new employee	1970s	"Matching the needs of the person with those of the organization" becomes the common hiring practice. A new wave of better-educated, less loyal employees armed with employment laws demand flexible working hours, quality circles, increased leisure time, compressed workweeks, quality of working life, and so on.
		Employers, because of court decisions, become more concerned that their hiring practices must be defensible to their employees and government.
Reagan administration	1980s	Employers perceive a swing of the government-regulation pendulum in their direction. The Supreme Court and federal agencies, inspired by the 1978 EEO hiring guidelines, order less stringent government regulation of hiring practices, except in cases involving age discrimination, due to new "teeth" in the 1978 amendment to the 1967 ADEA. Unions suffer several setbacks from the National Labor Relations Board and the courts.
New global economy	1990s	Congress reaffirms nondiscriminatory hiring practices with the 1990 Americans with Disabilities Act (ADA) and the 1991 Civil Rights Act. The U.S. Supreme Court reaffirms its strong position on sexual harassment.
		Downsizing of corporate America, followed by unprecedented economic growth and tight labor market. The diversity of the U.S. workforce become a major issue.

SOURCE: Adapted from A. S. T. Blackburn, Sam Ervin, Jonathan Glassman, Martha Harris, and John Thelin, "Sixty Years of Hiring Practices," *Personnel Journal* 59, no. 6 (June 1980): 462–82.

FIGURE 8–2   BASIC ELEMENTS IN THE SELECTION PROCESS

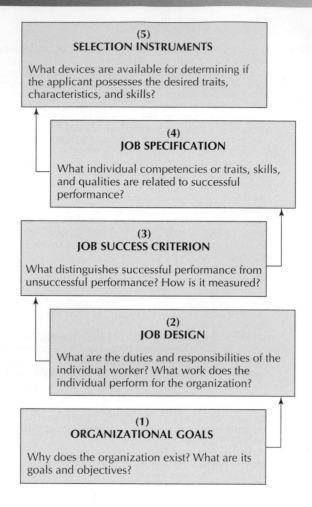

SOURCE: Mitchell S. Novit, *Essentials of Personnel Management* (Englewood Cliffs, NJ: Prentice-Hall, 1979), 70. Reprinted by permission of Prentice-Hall, Inc.

determine how the employees fit into the overall framework of the organization and must establish the relationship among the employees in the organization.

The second element, *job design,* involves determining what duties and responsibilities each job will entail. How motivating or repetitive each job becomes greatly affects the performance of employees on that job. The performance of employees will be affected by their ability and motivation. The job design will greatly affect both of these factors.

The third element involves the *measurement of job success.* The discovery of which employees are successful will determine what kinds of employees to recruit and select in the future.

The fourth element, *job specifications,* comes from the job analysis, which specifies what traits, skills, and

background an individual must have to qualify for the job. In the 1990s **competency-based hiring** replaced traditional job skills in many organizations. Ideally, competencies are accurately identified (see Figure 8–3) that link individual competencies to organizational objectives to improve overall performance because employee behaviors are better-aligned with organizational values.[3]

Finally, policymakers must determine which combination of interviews, tests, or other selection devices to use in the selection process. There is no magical combination of selection instruments that will minimize the cost of selection and facilitate choosing the best candidates available. Although there are few new selection techniques in HR management, there have been improvements in particular areas. The steps in the typical

FIGURE 8–3   EXAMPLES OF COMPETENCIES

MANAGEMENT COMPETENCIES:

Delegating responsibility

Motivating employees

Solving problems

Project management

Presentation skills

INDIVIDUAL COMPETENCIES:

Job/product knowledge

Technical knowledge

Computer skills

Time management

Managing interpersonal conflict

SOURCE: Ann Vineda, "Performance Management Through a Work/Life Lens," *HR Focus* (February 1998): 9–10.

selection process are outlined in Figure 8–4. They may change from one organization to another, but all the steps are normally completed at one time or another. The sequence may vary within organizations according to the types of jobs being filled and the size of the organization. The process usually begins by reviewing current applications gathered through the organization's recruitment effort.

Applicants who appear to be qualified for the position are then screened. Initial screening looks for the minimum requirements still available in the job market, as determined by the job specifications. The third step is to have the applicants complete an application blank, which standardizes information about all of the applicants to be considered. Any tests relevant to the job and validated by the organization are then administered to applicants. The next step is usually to interview applicants within the HR department. The background of desirable applicants is checked next, especially their references and employment history. Finally, the few applicants remaining are interviewed by the departmental supervisor or department head. During this in-depth interview, job requirements are discussed so that the applicant, as well as the supervisor, will be able to judge each other's interest in the job. At this point, a job offer can be made to the applicant best qualified for the job. If that applicant rejects the offer, management can either contact other qualified applicants or begin the recruitment process again if there are no other qualified applicants available. When the applicant accepts the offer, the process of placing the applicant in the organization begins.

EVALUATING ABILITY AND MOTIVATION

Maximizing employees' future performance is the objective of the selection process. An employee's performance on the job depends on the employee's **ability**

and motivation to perform the job as is illustrated in Figure 8–5. The entire selection process hinges on determining which applicants have the necessary ability and the greatest motivation to be successful employees.

Often, failure on the job is due not to a lack of skill or ability to perform the job adequately but to a lack of motivation. Skills and abilities can be developed in employees through training inside and outside the organization, but motivation cannot be developed to the same extent. For example, 85 percent of the persons who failed to be successful sales representatives in one company lacked motivation rather than ability. The single most important indicator of how a job applicant will perform appears to be past performance on the same job. Therefore, during the selection process, obtaining an accurate and verifiable record of the applicant's past job performance is critical, though often very difficult.[4]

The key to accurately assessing a person's motivation may be the measurement of his or her values. If the applicant shares the same values as the employer, they are much more likely to be committed to achieving the same goals. At the Toyota automobile manufacturing plant in Kentucky, for example, over 200,000 applicants have gone through an exhaustive 20 hours of selection, testing, and interviewing to determine if their basic values match those of the company. Toyota believes that **Kaizen,** a philosophy of continuous improvement, requires employees who are strongly motivated and who place a high value on quality. The Toyota selection process focuses not on skills, which will be given to new employees through training, but on certain traits and values, specifically the following:[5]

- **Problem solving** People who think for themselves and are self-motivated to address problems.
- **Teamwork** Interpersonal skills, diplomacy, and willingness to communicate.
- **Flexibility** Ability to adjust to changing needs.

FIGURE 8–4   THE STEPS IN THE TYPICAL SELECTION PROCESS

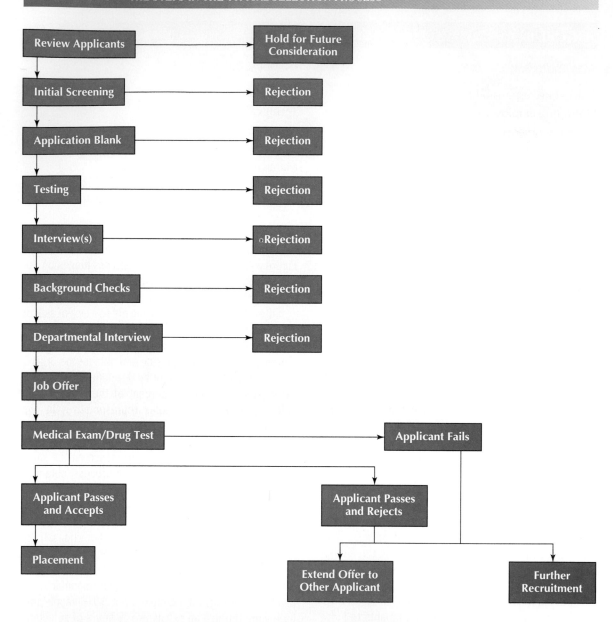

FIGURE 8–5   JOB PERFORMANCE IS PRIMARILY A FUNCTION OF TWO FACTORS

● *Continual learning* Desire to constantly explore new processes and implement new work methods.

STEPS IN THE SELECTION PROCESS

INITIAL SCREENING

Initial screening minimizes the time the HR department must spend during the selection process by removing obviously unqualified or undesirable applicants. For most jobs, many applicants do not deserve the serious attention and time of the HR specialist, particularly if many applications are blind resumés or walk-ins. To maintain a favorable corporate image, every applicant must be given courteous treatment. Primarily, the initial screening determines if the applicant possesses the critical job specifications and expedites the departure of the unqualified applicants to minimize the total cost of the selection process.

In reviewing resumés or letters from applicants, the HR officer must determine which applicants have the minimum qualifications indicated in the job description.

Once the cornerstone of the job search process, the resumé today must be carefully scrutinized. While resumés can provide effective descriptions of individuals' work histories, the validity of their content should be questioned since about 36 percent contain misleading or false information. Most distortions (see Figure 8–6) involve: (1) education—degrees claimed, but not earned; (2) dates of employment—stretching to cover gaps due to unemployment; (3) inflation—of past job titles or salaries; (4) embellishment—of past duties or achievements; and (5) omission—of criminal convictions, firings.[6]

Qualified applicants are then queried about their interest in the position. If the initial screening can be done by direct contact with the applicant, then the interviewer may pursue a number of strategies. The interviewer can ask so-called *knockout questions.* Such questions may cause an applicant to withdraw from further consideration. Knockout questions include: What are your salary requirements? Can you work weekends and nights? Can you work shift hours? Can you work out of town three nights per week?

Applicants who are rejected at this point in the selection process or at any other point must be included in an **applicant flow record.** The Equal Employment Opportunity Commission (EEOC) requires that companies with federal contracts record for each job applicant the name, race, national origin, sex, reference source, date of application, and position applied for. The applicant flow record should also indicate whether a job offer was made to the applicant and the reason why an offer was not made or was rejected.

Resumé Tracking Systems   An increasing number of employers are utilizing computer resumé scanning and tracking systems to provide initial screening of resumés. Companies like MCI, Disney, and Nike, have found that these software systems reduce the administrative and storage costs associated with paper resumés. While such systems vary, in general they involve HR clerks inputting all resumés received into a computer database. The resumé is then edited and stored according to key words, and a response letter is sent to the applicant. A recruiter can then scan the database for all applicants who meet certain criteria for positions. If the program produces a list that is too long or too short, the criteria can be changed. HR professionals have found that resumé scanning provides several advantages compared to filing, copying, and sorting through paper resumés:[7]

● Reduced utilization of recruitment agencies due to the speed and capacity of the system.

● Ease and speed of storage, which enables all resumés (even thousands of unsolicited ones) to be stored and retrieved.

● Faster recruitment of applicants due to computerized screening of resumés.

● Improved service to applicants.

● A paperless system that eliminates filing, copying, and sorting of resumés.

APPLICATION BLANK

An **application blank** is a formal record of an individual's application for employment. This record is later used by the HR department and may be reviewed by government agencies. The application blank, which provides pertinent information about the individual, is used in the job interview and in reference checks to determine the applicant's suitability for employment. An example of an application blank appears in Figure 8–7. The agreement section at the end should be read carefully. It contains five critical aspects of a good application blank:

❶ The applicant certifies, with his or her signature and the date, that all information provided is correct. Falsification of such information is generally legal grounds for termination.

❷ The applicant agrees to submit to a medical examination, with passage being a condition of employment.

FIGURE 8–6   WHAT'S REALLY IN A RESUMÉ

Why you need to check it out

What you read on a resumé might not be the whole truth. Here are some examples for a fictitious resumé.

	On the resumé	The truth
Objective	Senior financial position with a major company	Get a nice title with big salary at a company that doesn't check backgrounds
Experience **1995–present:** Vice president and chief financial officer, Fish Industries	Worked closely with CEO to restructure the company's businesses and improve profitability	The company is in bankruptcy
1993–1995: Controller, Fish Industries	Installed computer bookkeeping system and expanded internal auditing functions	Company updated bookkeeping/auditing systems to stop embezzlement, but they couldn't catch me.
1989–93: Assistant controller, Fish Industries	Revamped annual report and improved financial reporting to shareholders	Imaginative bookkeeping beats kickbacks any day
1985–87: Purchasing director, Bilco Inc.	Restructured company's employee benefits program.	Got kickbacks; set up phony vendors to rip off Bilco.
1982–85: Staff assistant, purchasing department, Bilco Inc.	Wrote employee benefits handbook.	Used embellished resume to get hired for clerical job.
Education	MBA, Harvard University, 1989 BS, Finance, University of Kentucky, 1982.	Studied business and accounting at Kentucky State Prison while serving two years for embezzlement, 1987–89; Attended, University of Kentucky, 1980–82.
Affiliations and memberships	Member and former president, Jaycees, 1983-present; member and former president, Society for Purchasing Management, 1985-present; Big Creek Baptist Church, finance committee chairperson, 1990.	
Volunteer activities	Girl Scouts of America, Habitat for Humanity, God's Pantry and Meals on Wheels.	Are you kidding? But no one checks anyway.
References	Mike Smith, president, Fish Industries	Good reference guaranteed; he wants to get rid of me.
	Karen Smart, vice president, Fish Industries	Afraid to say anything negative about anyone.
	B.J. Bland, human resources manager, Bilco Inc.	Died a month ago.

SOURCE: Jim Jordan, "Truth or Consequences," *The Lexington Herald-Leader* (May 4, 1998): 10. Adapted from Edward C. Andler, *The Complete Reference Checking Handbook* (New York: AMACOM Books, 1997).

FIGURE 8–7 AN EXCELLENT EXAMPLE OF A COMPLETE APPLICATION BLANK FROM THE KENTUCKY FRIED CHICKEN CORPORATION.

KFC Management Company — KFC Corporation
Employment Application
Zantigo MEXICAN RESTAURANT

MO	DAY	YR

All Applicants Will Receive Consideration Without Regard To Age, Race, Color, Religion, Sex, National Origin, Handicap, Or Military Status

PLEASE COMPLETE ALL SECTIONS—FRONT AND BACK

PERSONAL

Last Name	First Name	Middle Name	Social Security#

Present Street Address	City	State	Zip	No. Yrs.	Home Phone (Including Area Code)

Last Address	City	State	Zip	No. Yrs.	If Under 19 Years Of Age, Date Of Birth:

Are You Legally Eligible To Work In The United States? ☐ YES ☐ NO | Have You Ever Been Convicted Of A Felony? ☐ YES ☐ NO | If Yes, Please Explain:

Notify In Emergency: State Name, Complete Address And Phone (Including Area Code):

Minors Indicate Parent or Guardian

JOB INTEREST

Position (Type of Work) Desired: | Starting Monthly Salary Expected: $ | Have You Ever Previously Applied To Our Firm? ☐ YES ☐ NO

Date You Can Start Work: | List Any Relatives Or Acquaintances Working For Our Company:

Type Of Employment Desired:
☐ Full Time ☐ Permanent Part Time ☐ Temporary Full Time ☐ Temporary Part Time ☐ Summer

Are There Any Times When You Are Unavailable For Work? If So, Please Specify: | Are You Known To Schools/References By Another Name? If Yes, By What Name:

Special Interests Or Qualifications That May Help Us In Considering Your Application:

EDUCATION

Circle Highest Grade Completed In Each School Category:

	Grade School	High School	College	Graduate School
	1 2 3 4 5 6	7 8 9 10 11 12	1 2 3 4	1 2 3 4

Schools	Name And Address	Dates Attended From / To	Diploma Or Degree	Grade Average	Areas Of Specialization
High School					
College					
Graduate School					
Other					

HEALTH

Are you able to perform, with or without accommodation, the essential job tasks?	☐ YES ☐ NO
If hired, could you perform all the tasks in the job description?	☐ Standing ☐ Lifting

If No to the Above, Explain.

VETERANS AND DISABILITY INFORMATION

Answering the questions in this section is completely voluntary and will not affect your chances for employment with the company. They are being asked because the federal government requires the company to maintain records of Vietnam era veterans, disabled veterans, and handicapped individuals seeking employment. The answers to these questions will help fulfill our responsibility in this area, and the company would appreciate your help.

Did you serve in active military duty 180 days or more between August 5, 1964 and May 7, 1975? ☐ YES ☐ NO

Were you released from active military duty between August 5, 1964 and May 7, 1975 because of a service connected disability? ☐ YES ☐ NO

PLEASE CONTINUE ON REVERSE SIDE

FIGURE 8–7   AN EXCELLENT EXAMPLE OF A COMPLETE APPLICATION BLANK FROM THE KENTUCKY FRIED CHICKEN CORPORATION.—cont'd

EMPLOYMENT   RECORD: List Each Job Held Starting With Your Present Or Last Job. Include Military Service, Summer Employment and Volunteer Activities. If You Need Additional Space, Please Continue On A Separate Piece Of Paper.

Name Of Company	Type Of Business	From (MO & YR)	To (MO & YR)
Address (Including City And State)		Starting Salary	Last Salary
Name And Title Of Supervisor	Telephone	Titles And Duties:	
Reason For Leaving:			

Name Of Company	Type Of Business	From (MO & YR)	To (MO & YR)
Address (Including City And State)		Starting Salary	Last Salary
Name And Title Of Supervisor	Telephone	Titles And Duties:	
Reason For Leaving:			

Name Of Company	Type Of Business	From (MO & YR)	To (MO & YR)
Address (Including City And State)		Starting Salary	Last Salary
Name And Title Of Supervisor	Telephone	Titles And Duties:	
Reason For Leaving:			

Name Of Company	Type Of Business	From (MO & YR)	To (MO & YR)
Address (Including City And State)		Starting Salary	Last Salary
Name And Title Of Supervisor	Telephone	Titles And Duties:	
Reason For Leaving:			

Name Of Company	Type Of Business	From (MO & YR)	To (MO & YR)
Address (Including City And State)		Starting Salary	Last Salary
Name And Title Of Supervisor	Telephone	Titles And Duties:	
Reason For Leaving:			

REFERENCES

List Names And Addresses Of People Who Have Known You Over 3 Years. (DO NOT LIST RELATIVES.)

Name	Address	Occupation	Phone

AGREEMENT

I certify that all statements given on this application are correct, and understand that falsification or misrepresentation in this or any other personnel record can result in my dismissal if I am employed by the company. If requested to do so, I agree to submit to a physical examination which I must successfully pass as a condition of being accepted for employment. I agree to provide proof of age upon notification of hire. I authorize my former employers and other individuals to give the company information concerning me, whether or not it is part of their written record, and I release them and their companies from any liability whatsoever on account of such information furnished to KFC. I understand that the above noted examination and reference inquiries will be kept confidential and will not be released to anyone by KFC without my written consent. Also, I agree that if I am offered employment by KFC and accept, my employment will be employment at will, that my employment and compensation can be terminated, with or without cause, and with or without notice, at any time, at the option of either KFC or myself. I am hereby informed and I understand that no representative of KFC, other than the Chief Executive Officer, has any authority to enter into any agreement for employment for any specified period of time or to make any agreement contrary to the foregoing and that any such agreement must be in writing and must be signed by the Chief Executive Officer of KFC.

Public Law 91-508 requires that we advise you that a routine inquiry may be made during our initial or subsequent processing which will provide application information concerning character, general reputation and credit, personal characteristics and mode of living. Upon written request, additional information as to the nature and scope of the inquiry, if one is made, will be provided.

Signature:_____ Date: _____

WE APPRECIATE YOUR INTEREST AND THE TIME YOU HAVE TAKEN TO PREPARE THIS APPLICATION.

SOURCE: KFC Corporation. Used by permission.

3 The applicant authorizes former employers and references to provide background information.

4 The applicant understands and accepts that his or her employment is "employment at will" and thus can be terminated at any time, with or without cause.

5 Only a written employment agreement, signed by the CEO, is a valid offer of employment; thus, any promises or suggestions that may have been casually made by others during the hiring process are not valid.

Although future court decisions may alter the items that should not appear on application blanks, those questions that can appear on the application blanks concern the following:

- Applicant's name.
- Applicant's home address and telephone number.
- Whether the applicant is of minimum working age.
- Whether the applicant can speak or read and write one or more foreign languages (if job related).
- Applicant's educational background (if job related).
- Applicant's work history, including dates of employment, salary progression, job responsibility and duties, and reasons for leaving.

- Whether the applicant can meet special job requirements such as working in the evening or on weekends.
- Applicant's military experience.
- Applicant's criminal conviction record (if job related).
- Applicant's willingness to travel.
- Applicant's special skills or training.
- How the applicant heard about the position.
- Membership in professional organizations.
- Names of relatives who are employed by the company.
- Other current employment, either full-time or part-time.

Uses of the Application Blank   The application blank is a permanent record of the applicant's qualifications for a job. In addition to providing information required for the selection process, the application supplies input for the EEO/AA report. Human resource specialists use the application to develop background checks and interview questions. An important part of the selection process is verification of the applicant's past work history and references. Applicants and their previous employers sometimes disagree about the duties, responsibilities, and importance of previous jobs,

HR IN THE NEWS

U.S. MANUFACTURERS SEEKING EDUCATED WORKERS

Thomas Williams quit his high school teaching job to work on the Ford Motor Company assembly line in Avon Lake, Ohio. Why? Williams says, "I've changed my focus, from molding lives to molding products"—to more than double his teaching salary to over $50,000 a year.

Yes, the U.S. automobile industry began hiring again in the '90s, up to 75,000 workers at Ford and Chrysler alone. However, they hired a different kind of worker than those hired in the '50s and '60s. The car makers today want employees who are quick to learn their job, require limited supervision, and are flexible and productive. Ford and Chrysler have adopted employee selection techniques similar to those used by Toyota when they select new employees. Applicants are tested in areas such as mathematics and manual dexterity as well as problem-solving skills and teamwork. Chrysler stopped giving preference to relatives of current employees because of criticism from the United Auto Workers union. The new selection techniques have resulted in a more educated workforce at Ford Motor Company.

Manufacturers in other industries have also adopted selection methods that hire an educated and skilled workforce. Workers are viewed as "a major capital investment."

Continued.

HR IN THE NEWS—cont'd

The new breed of manufacturing employee views assembly line jobs, which were once disdained, as "plums."

For example in Chrysler's sprawling minivan plant in Windsor, Ontario, you will see Jeffrey Pancheshan, who has a master's degree in business administration from the University of Windsor, tightening catalytic-converter shields to the bottom of each passing minivan. "The reason I got an education was so I could get a good job," declares Mr. Pancheshan, who worked at the plant part time while going to college. "I feel like I have a good job right now."

Twenty-six percent of the new workers at the Windsor plant have college degrees. Only a few years ago many had trouble reading and writing.

The new hires are not quitting after only a few days on the assembly line as they commonly did in previous decades. Arthur Johnson, supervisor of training at Ford Motor Company, credits the lower turnover partly to the tight job market, but mostly to Ford's doing a better job of selecting employees.

Ford gives applicants a $3\frac{1}{2}$-hour test in arithmetic, reading, and technical material as well as dexterity tests such as quickly attaching washers in the right order to a pole. Ford also tests applicants on their ability to work together in teams, the same exercise the Japanese car makers utilize. Ford then selects applicants who score roughly in the top half and who have solid work histories, which demonstrate their motivation level. Candidates are also interviewed by at least two assembly-line employees. They must also pass a drug test and a medical exam.

A major reason for the desire to hire more skilled and educated workers is the new corporate structure, which has fewer supervisors and thus demands more decision making from its workers. Chrysler, for example, had 1 salaried worker for every 25 hourly workers in 1991, 1 per 48 in 1994, and expects 1 per 100 in 1999.

"Before you change the caliber of workforce you bring in, you have to change the environment they work in," preaches Mr. Pawley at Chrysler Corporation. "You have to say to yourself, 'I'm going to pull my people out and turn that assembly line over to an empowered workforce.'"

SOURCE: Neal Templson, "Auto Plants, Hiring Again, Are Demanding Higher-Skilled Labor," *Wall Street Journal* (March 11, 1994): A1, A4. Reprinted by permission of *The Wall Street Journal.* Dow Jones & Company, Inc. All rights reserved worldwide.

length of employment, salary levels, and especially the reason for leaving employment. In an effort to obtain accurate, complete information from the applicant, the HR specialist starts with the application and follows through with background checks and an interview. During the interview, some applicants will give different accounts of prior experience as well as skills from what they provided on their application blanks.

Application blanks can also be used as screening devices to generate **global assessments,** wherein the HR specialist reviews the total applications and determines the general desirability of each applicant. A very subjective technique, global assessment is often used when many applicants are being considered and those lacking an appropriate background or skills can be quickly screened out.

A more objective screening technique using application blanks is to have the HR specialist rate each applicant on particular job-related areas, such as the level of specific skills or experience in particular work areas or in supervisory positions. Such a rating would change from job opening to job opening as different skills and background requirements become more relevant. Generally, if one particularly relevant job specification does not appear on completed application blanks, then these applicants can be screened out.

The former HR director of PepsiCo and Texas Instruments, Brooks Mitchell, recommends a selection strategy which combines two widely used techniques: (1) a biographical test based on application blank information including education, past work experience and hobbies, and (2) a structured interview. His employee selection focus is on the hiring of entry-level people, rather than executives or managers because the entry-level jobs produce the products, work with customers, and so on. This application blank–based strategy followed by a structured interview is still the core of many selection strategies.[8]

UNIFORM GUIDELINES ON EMPLOYEE SELECTION PROCEDURES

In 1978, the Uniform Guidelines on Employee Selection Procedures were adopted by four federal agencies: the EEOC, the Civil Service Commission, the U.S. Department of Labor, and the U.S. Department of Justice. In order to comply with suggested practices and avoid potentially costly litigation, both managers and HR practitioners must be familiar with the guidelines' basic principles. The more significant sections are printed here and then interpreted in light of practical experience.

Section 2. B. Employment Decisions These guidelines apply to tests and other selection procedures which are used as a basis for any employment decision. Employment decisions include—but are not limited to—hiring, promotion, demotion, membership (for example, in a labor organization), referral, retention, and licensing and certification to the extent that licensing and certification may be covered by federal equal employment opportunity law. Other selection decisions, such as selection for training or transfer, may also be considered employment decisions if they lead to any of the decisions listed above.

Remember that guidelines apply to tests of the paper-and-pencil variety and "other selection procedures." Thus, the guidelines apply to any reference check, interview, application blank, or other selection instrument utilized by an organization.

Section 3. Discrimination Defined Relationship between use of selection procedures and discrimination. Procedures having adverse impact constitute discrimination unless justified. The use of any selection procedure which has an adverse impact on the hiring, promotion, or other employment or membership opportunities of members of any race, sex, or ethnic group will be considered to be discriminatory and inconsistent with these guidelines, unless the procedure has been validated in accordance with these guidelines, or the provisions of Section 6 . . . are satisfied.

In Section 3, the guidelines link discrimination directly to adverse impact. **Illegal discrimination** occurs when an individual who has an equal probability of being successful on a job does not have an equal probability of getting the job.

An **adverse impact** (or disparate impact) on an employment practice causes members of any race, color, sex, religion, or national origin to receive unequal consideration for employment. If an employer's selection procedure, such as an interview, results in an applicant's not having an equal chance to be hired or promoted, then that procedure caused the organization to discriminate against that applicant. A selection procedure or policy that has adverse impacts on the employment opportunities of any race, sex, or ethnic group is normally illegal under Title VII unless the employer can offer a legal defense.

Section 3 states that using a properly validated selection procedure is not wrongful. **Validity** in testing means that a test actually measures what it is intended to measure. If a test is valid, then the employer knows that it is directly measuring the applicant's ability to perform the job and not something else. A valid test is not influenced by personal bias. For example, a person measuring a sapling with a yardstick and finding it to be 38 inches high thinks that is a valid measurement. The yardstick could not measure a friend's ability to estimate the height of the same tree correctly. The friend's point of view—size and proximity to the tree—influences the "guesstimate." The same type of influence occurs when individuals' points of view consciously or unconsciously influence decisions concerning job applicants. Since there once were no standard means available to measure the validity of employment tests, the guidelines offer standards for test validity.

Section 5. General Standards for Validity Studies A. Acceptable types of validity studies. For the purposes of satisfying these guidelines, users may rely upon criterion-related validity studies, content validity studies, or construct validity studies in accordance with the standards set forth in the technical standards of these guidelines. B. Criterion-related content and construct validity. Evidence of the validity of a test or other selection procedure by a criterion-related validity study should consist of empirical data demonstrating that the selection procedure is predictive of or significantly correlated with important elements of job performance. Evidence of the validity of a test or other selection procedure by a content validity study should consist of data showing that the content of the selection procedure is representative of important aspects of performance on the job for which the candidates are to be evaluated. Evidence of the validity of a test or other selection procedure through a construct validity study should consist of data showing that the procedure measures the degree to which candidates have identifiable characteristics which have been determined to be important in successful performance in the job for which the candidates are to be evaluated.

Criterion-related validity can be established by collecting data from job applicants and employees. This form of validation correlates test scores with employee success on the job. There are many measures of employee productivity that may be used, such as absenteeism, sales levels, supervisory evaluations, or quantity of production. Two primary methods of establishing criterion-related validity are predictive validation and concurrent validation.

Predictive validity, preferred by the EEOC, is usually the most difficult to determine. Establishing predictive validity requires testing the entire pool of job applicants, hiring them, and then correlating their test scores with their criterion (performance) scores.

For example, to determine the predictive validity of a test given to applicants for sales representative positions, all applicants during the previous month are tested. All applicants are then hired, given equal training, and assigned to sales routes. After one year, the total commission sales of the new employees (the criterion of job success) are correlated with their test scores. The resulting figure, called a *correlation coefficient,* can vary from −1 to +1. For example, if the correlation coefficient *(r)* is .67, then the test *is* valid for sales representatives because individuals' test scores have been shown to be related to job performance.

If the comparison of the applicants' test scores with their criterion scores produces a high correlation coefficient, then the organization may use the test for future applicants because it has evidence that the test is a valid predictor of employee performance.

Concurrent validity is similar to predictive validity in that test scores are compared to job performance measures. But to establish concurrent validity, both test scores and performance measures are collected at the same time.

This is accomplished by testing current employees, for whom the organization already has performance scores, such as supervisory ratings. The major difference between predictive validity and concurrent validity is that the former concerns applicants and the latter concerns present employees. This difference is very important because, in establishing predictive validity, the firm gets test scores from the total range of individuals who might apply for the job. By contrast, in establishing concurrent validity, the firm tests only those individuals who have been kept as employees. For practical reasons, establishing concurrent validity is preferable. One impor-

tant reason is that administrators do not like to hire all applicants, some of whom very likely will fail as employees. Another reason is time. Concurrent validity can be established within a few weeks; predictive validity requires at least six months to a year to be established.

Content validity is a nonempirical (nonstatistical) approach to validation. To establish content validity, the organization shows—often through job analysis—that the content of the test is actually a *sample* of the work performed on the job. For example, a typing test could be given to applicants for clerical positions that require typing. Another example would be testing bank teller applicants' speed and accuracy with figures.

Construct validity is another nonempirical approach to validation. This type of validation is based on the theoretical relationship between a test and a construct, a characteristic in which an employee should have to be successful. Giving store manager applicants a general IQ test because management believes they need a certain level of intelligence to be successful is an example of construct validity. Giving sales clerks "personality" tests to determine if they will work well with customers could be considered construct validation.

In general, the EEOC gives the greatest preference to predictive validity and the least to construct validity. Both criterion-related validations, predictive and concurrent, are strong because they involve empirical data collection and statistics, which generally are not discriminatory. Content validity is at least a direct test of individuals' ability to perform some—usually not all—of the tasks required on the job. Construct validity is often management's last choice and may be hard to defend in court.

Section 4.D. Adverse Impact and the Four-fifths Rule   A selection rate for any race, sex, or ethnic group which is less than four-fifths (4/5) (or 80 percent) of the rate for the group with the highest rate will generally be regarded by the federal enforcement agencies as evidence of adverse impact, while a greater than four-fifths rate will generally not be regarded by federal enforcement agencies as evidence of adverse impact.

The **four-fifths rule** or *80 percent rule* in the guidelines raised serious questions by private industry. The rule provides a quantitative definition of adverse impact, not a legal definition. For example, if 8 out of 50 white male applicants (16 percent) and 3 out of 20 black male applicants (15 percent) were hired, the four-fifths rule has been met because four-fifths of 16 percent (12.8 percent) is less than the 15 percent hiring rate for blacks. No evidence of adverse impact is present.

Section 1.B. Purpose of Guidelines   These guidelines do not require a user to conduct validity studies of selection procedures where no adverse impact results. However, all users are encouraged to use selection procedures which are valid, especially users operating under merit principles.

These sections of the guidelines permit one component of the selection process to have an adverse impact if the total selection procedure does not produce an adverse impact. If an employer's total selection process meets the four-fifths rule but the interview—one of several components—violates it, the federal government usually will not take action or require validation of the interview process as part of the entire selection procedure.

Section 4.A. Information Required Records concerning impact. Each user should maintain and have available for inspection records or other information which will disclose the impact which its tests and other selection procedures have upon employment opportunities of persons by identifiable race, sex, or ethnic group . . . in order to determine compliance with these guidelines. Where there are large numbers of applicants and procedures are administered frequently, such information may be retained on a sample basis, provided that the sample is appropriate in terms of the applicant population and adequate in size.

PREEMPLOYMENT TESTING

The use of testing in the selection process has had periods of growth and periods of decline. Once the cornerstone of the selection process, selection tests, particularly paper-and-pencil ones, came under attack by the EEOC and the courts. Some tests were not reliable, and others were found not to predict employee job performance accurately. The primary problem in the past was the use of very general tests for many different jobs without serious thought about their validity. Today most employers are more careful in the selection and use of tests, although use of tests is increasing.

From a 1988 case, *Daniel Construction Company* v. *International Brotherhood of Electrical Workers,* three critical criteria a selection test should meet to withstand legal challenge can be outlined:[9]

❶ The test is a valid predictor of employee performance.

❷ The test is developed, administered, and evaluated by professionals.

❸ Those who fail a test can appeal the results or have an opportunity to increase their chances through other selection criteria.

Employee testing is generally far more objective than other selection procedures; testing has often proved to be the most valid selection procedure. In fact, one of the most rigorous and complete studies of employment testing concluded that, in general, standardized tests do not discriminate against blacks; blacks and whites with similar test scores do equally well in job performance. Although blacks, Hispanics, and Native Americans as groups do not score as well as white applicants, those differences may be due to less education and other social factors, not to the standardized tests themselves. Most important, no better alternative to a standardized test has been developed. Thus, at least some of the cynicism about testing in recent years has been unfair.[10] Many employers are increasingly using tests to select a skilled workforce. The U.S. manufacturing industry, for example, is generally seeking a more skilled workforce and using tests to select applicants (see *HR in the News:* "U.S. Manufacturers Seeking Educated Workers").

Franciscan Health System of Dayton

An example that illustrates how preemployment testing can be effective in the selection process is the Franciscan Health System of Dayton (FHSD). A problem common in the health-care field is employee turnover; yet, employees are critical to the service delivery system in nursing-care facilities like FHSD. Headquartered in Dayton, Ohio, FHSD operates three care facilities with 2,700 employees. A few years ago, the organization experienced extremely high turnover (146 percent) and poor employee performance. It was concluded that better employees who would make a long-term commitment to health-care delivery and could excel at difficult and stressful jobs were needed. It was also decided that the selection process, which was based solely on interviews and reference checks, was not effective. At the same time, FHSD implemented a total-quality improvement process and HR Director Delores Shuermann concluded that "getting the right people in the first place is crucial." Thus, a new preemployment series of tests— *Nursing Assistant Test Battery*—was developed, validated, and given a trial period. The battery consists of three separate tests:[11]

❶ *Employment Inventory* Measures the motivation level of applicants.

❷ *Personality Test* Identifies applicants who are cheerful, tolerant, and don't worry much, all needed qualities in the nursing-care industry.

❸ *Job Preference Inventory* Estimates the match between the working conditions of the job and the applicant's preference for certain working conditions. For example, a person who prefers a predictable, stable workday would not be a good match for a nursing assistant position.

The ten-month trial period produced solid results: Turnover decreased from 146 percent to 27 percent employee productivity increased, and supervisors reported that the newly hired employees were "showing more compassion, displaying competence, and collaborating with their co-workers." The test battery was placed in permanent use, and similar batteries were developed for other employee groups. The nursing battery successfully predicted the probability of applicants becoming above-average employees. Applicants' scores on the tests placed them in one of three categories: hire, don't hire, and proceed with caution (see Figure 8–8). While FHSD would prefer to extend offers only to applicants who fall in the "hire" category, the lack of good candidates or the urgent need to fill positions sometimes forces it to consider applicants in the middle category—hire with caution.[12]

General Intelligence Tests

Decades ago, general **intelligence tests** were developed to predict the success of young children in school. Some think that testing the success of young school children in their academic careers is still what general intelligence tests are best suited for. However, intelligence has been found to be positively correlated with performance in many occupations.

Aptitude Tests

Natural ability in a particular discipline or the ability to learn quickly or to understand a particular area reveals an aptitude for that area or discipline. **Aptitude tests** indicate the ability of an individual to learn certain skills.[13]

As the official U.S. Employment Services aptitude test, the General Aptitude Test Battery (GATB) is recognized as the basic denominator in estimating aptitude requirements. It is the aptitude test by which jobs are categorized in the *Dictionary of Occupational Titles (DOT)*. Also, many state and local employment agencies use the GATB, which tests the following:

- General intelligence
- Verbal ability
- Numerical ability
- Spatial perception
- Form perception
- Clerical perception
- Motor coordination
- Finger dexterity
- Manual dexterity

FIGURE 8–8   USING TESTS IN THE SELECTION PROCESS

The FHSD utilizes a preemployment test battery. Applicants' scores have been divided into thirds, and successfully predict their performance and turnover.

Outcome	Decision	Predicted Performance
Red-light candidate (scored in bottom third)	Do not hire	• Shows a less than 50% chance of above-average performance • Estimated annual productivity contribution: − $2204/hire
Yellow-light candidate (scored in middle third)	Hire with caution	• Shows between a 50% and a 63% chance of above-average performance • Estimated annual productivity contribution: + $727/hire
Green-light candidate (scored in top third)	Hire immediately	• Shows a better than 63% chance of above-average performance • Estimated annual productivity contribution: + $1989/hire

SOURCE: Franciscan Health System of Dayton.

The GATB consists of twelve timed tests (parts)—eight paper-and-pencil tests and four apparatus tests. Each part requires performance of familiar tasks such as name comparisons, arithmetic computations, reasoning, pegboard manipulations, and so on. Employer use of the GATB in employee selection is related to its use by the U.S. Employment Service. The Employment Service conducted validity studies of the GATB over a 45-year period and found three general abilities (cognitive, perceptual, and psychomotor) to be valid predictors of job proficiency. The Employment Service then began implementing the testing in local Job Service (unemployment) offices. Employers may use the GATB when validated as predictors of employee success.[14]

Personality and Interest Tests

Both personality and interest tests seek to measure an individual's motivation in particular fields. Personality tests, such as the Bernreuter Personality Inventory, measure neurotic tendency, self-sufficiency, introversion and extraversion, sociability, and self-confidence. The Thematic Apperception Test (TAT) is a common projective personality test in which the subject is asked to interpret certain situations. The TAT assesses the individual's need for achievement and has been successful in predicting individual motivation. Other personality tests, such as the California Psychological Inventory (CPI) and the Thurstone Temperament Survey (TTS), have been developed to assess specific personality aspects. The Guilford-Zimmerman Temperament Survey is a broad personality measure that assesses the individual's ability to positively interact with others.

There are three primary problems with personality tests. First, they are generally not reliable or valid predictors of job performance. Second, to be useful, such tests assume that job applicants have sufficient insight to describe themselves accurately—often an unjustified assumption. Third, in a desire to perform well, candidates may give false responses to produce what they believe to be the desired "test score," despite there being no right or wrong answers on personality tests.

Interest tests generally are designed to measure individuals' activity preferences. For example, individuals are asked if they would rather watch a baseball game on television, read a novel, or attend a local Little League game on a Saturday afternoon. Interest tests such as the Strong Vocational Interest Blank (SVIB) have been found to predict the occupations people will enter with reasonable accuracy. By matching the interests of individuals successful in different occupations, the SVIB indicates to applicants which fields most closely match their inter-

ests. The SVIB has shown that, within professions, people's interests have been fairly stable over time.

Interest tests like the Job Preference Inventory estimate the match between the working conditions of a job or organization and the extent to which a person likes or prefers to be in a certain type of environment. A match between the actual conditions and those desired by an individual can mean an easier adjustment to a new job and possibly a longer tenure.

Achievement Tests

Aptitude tests assess a person's capacity to learn, whereas **achievement tests** assess the degree to which a person has learned. Because achievement tests measure current behavior, they may be an excellent predictor of future employee behavior. Therefore, HR departments may use achievement tests to determine whether a person can do the job and aptitude tests to measure whether or not someone can be trained to do the job. Through a job analysis for a specific occupation, a list of questions can be developed that will test an applicant's occupational experience. The U.S. Employment Service has developed a series of trade tests that measure an individual's knowledge of the behavior, tools, and equipment of a particular job. Because achievement tests can be validated, they are useful predictors of job performance where specific knowledge or experience is necessary to perform in a skilled occupation.

Work Samples

One step beyond the achievement test, which measures knowledge of a particular job or occupation, is the use of **work samples,** in which the applicant performs part of the job as a test. Examples of work samples are typing tests for secretaries, assembly tests for production-line workers, and trial-balances computation tests for accountants. Work samples are generally valid predictors of job performance since they measure those behaviors required for successful job performance. But work samples have limited use due to their specific nature; that is, they can only test an individual's ability on certain duties within the job setting. Other criteria are measured by other selection devices. Work samples are usually limited to jobs that are physical rather than mental in nature. In the future, more work samples for conceptual jobs may be developed.

Polygraph Tests

The **polygraph** is a device that measures the emotions of an individual by directly measuring galvanic skin response, blood pressure, and breathing rate. A 1988 federal law restricted the use of a polygraph in employment decisions. Before the law was passed, polygraph use in corporations fell into three common areas: (1) verification of employment application information; (2) periodic surveys to determine employee honesty and loyalty; and (3) investigation of a specific instance of theft within the company.

In 1988, Congress passed the *Employee Polygraph Protection Act,* which prohibits the use of polygraphs to screen job applicants or investigate employees' backgrounds. The act also outlaws voice-stress analyzers, psychological-stress evaluators, and deceptographs as applicant screening devices. Exempted employers include security-service firms and pharmaceutical manufacturers and distributors. The act does permit polygraph testing of employees as part of workplace investigations into theft or vandalism, but only under strict regulations.

The passage of the act came after years of congressional debate. Supporters of polygraph testing argued that when operated by a trained professional, the device can be a valuable tool in screening job applicants. Problems occurred, they contended, because no national licensing program existed to ensure professional testing. Opponents (and supporters) of the act maintained that stress detected by the equipment is not proof of untruthfulness and that the test results can be unreliable.[15]

Honesty Tests

Preemployment **honesty tests,** as defined by the U.S. Government, are written tests designed to identify job applicants who have relatively high propensities to steal money or property on the job or who are likely to engage in behavior of a "counterproductive" nature, including tardiness, sick leave abuse, and absenteeism.[16] While these paper-and-pencil tests have been used in employee selection for over forty years, their widespread use by employers began only after the *Employee Polygraph Protection Act* limited the polygraph's use in selection. *Integrity* (honesty) tests were then viewed as logical substitutes. Their use is limited in some states, including Massachusetts, Rhode Island, and Minnesota. The primary concern over their use in employee selection is the lack of sufficient evidence of their validity. The U.S. Office of Technology Assessment (OTA) has not yet been convinced of their validity even though it has conducted extensive research and worked with the publishers of the tests.[17] One credible 1989 review of a large number of validity studies published by test publishers did, however, support their validity.[18] A comprehensive review of a taskforce of the American Psychological Association concluded that "for those few tests for which validity information is available the preponderance of the evidence is supportive of their predictive validity." The report also noted that many test publishers have not come close to meeting validation standards for their honesty or integrity tests.[19]

One major problem with honesty tests reported by the OTA is the high percentage of honest people who fail the test. This result may be caused by the broad range of behaviors covered by the tests, including theft, absenteeism, and falsification of expense records, which make it difficult to define accurately the concept of *honesty* and to predict who is dishonest. A second problem is the disagreement over whether honesty is an individual trait or is something that is situationally determined. If it is situationally determined, then the problem could be addressed by management practices that support honest behavior. The third, and perhaps the most significant, problem with honesty tests is that they fail to predict accurately which persons are likely to engage in theft, generally considered the most critical dimension of employee honesty. Thus, they are not ideally useful as preemployment tests for applicants. At least three major types of honesty or integrity tests are currently in use.[20]

1 *Overt* These tests contain items that deal directly with the applicant's attitudes toward theft and dishonesty and admission of past dishonesty.

2 *Personality* These tests strive to predict a variety of counterproductive work behaviors such as low motivation, resistance to following directions, lack of personal pride in work, and unnecessary absences.

3 *Multidimensional* Several scales are measured including integrity, drug use, property damage, waste, and causes of personnel turnover.

Medical Exam/Drug Tests

As indicated in Figure 8–9, a job offer is usually made contingent on the applicant's passing a **medical exam** and a **drug test.** Under the ADA, the medical examination must focus on the applicant's ability to perform the essential job functions. The ADA specifically allows preemployment drug testing (which is not considered a medical examination). To provide maximum validity, most employers do not perform in-house drug tests but instead utilize an external laboratory certified by the **National Institute on Drug Abuse (NIDA).** NIDA standards must be met by federal drug-testing programs and are the recognized industry standards. When testing applicants, NIDA recommends that the drug-testing requirement be included in the position announcement. In addition, the job offer should be made contingent on the applicant's having a negative test result. Applicants who refuse to take the test or who test positive can be

FIGURE 8–9   U.S. PREEMPLOYMENT DRUG SCREENING BY INDUSTRY

Industry	Percentage
Transportation	88.5%
Manufacturer	87.4
Public Administration	76.2
Wholesale/Retail	72.5
Healthcare Provider	69.9
Miscellaneous Services	69.0
Business/Professional Services	54.3
Financial Services	34.1

Legend: Required to Test · Test Without Requirement

SOURCE: American Management Association, *HR Focus* (June 1992): 7.

rejected. Not all employers require that applicants pass a drug test, and no federal law requires private sector employers to utilize a medical examination or drug test. In addition, 17 states have passed laws limiting the use of drug testing in the workplace.[21]

A national survey of the American Management Association indicates that 75 percent of major U.S. employers engage in drug testing. Also, about 33 percent of all job applicants offered positions will be tested. The use of preemployment testing varies greatly according to the industry involved (see Figure 8–9). The industries with the highest rates of testing include transportation and manufacturing.[22]

Employer drug-testing programs have contributed to the overall decline in casual drug use, according to experts. About 90 percent of all testing involves job applicants, and employer programs have made drug use more difficult and less socially acceptable. Virtually every employer that has instituted a drug-testing program has witnessed a steep drop in positive test results. Mobil Corporation and Hoffman-LaRoche (a pharmaceutical company), for example, found that about 7 percent of their job applicants failed their tests in the mid-1980s but that 10 years later less than 1 percent failed. Tropicana Products found 25 percent of its job applicants us-

ing drugs when its drug-testing program started. After six years of testing, the rate dropped to 5 percent, accidents dropped by 50 percent, and turnover dropped by 20 percent.[23]

HIV-Positive Employees   Under the ADA, employers are prohibited from discriminating against a qualified person with a disability. A 1998 U.S. Supreme Court decision (see *HR in the News* "AIDS Landmark Case") stated that individuals who have AIDS or AIDs-related complex or who are HIV positive are considered disabled and protected from discrimination. Furthermore, the ADA prohibits discrimination against an applicant or employee because he or she has a family member or associate who has a disability. An employer can take action when an HIV-related condition becomes job related. A job-related condition, however, does not result from unfounded fears or prejudices of co-workers, clients, or customers. Generally, an HIV-related condition may become job related and thus allow an employer to take appropriate action under the following conditions:[24]

➊ The condition renders the employee incapable of performing the essential job functions.

HR IN THE NEWS

AIDS LANDMARK CASE

In 1998, the U.S. Supreme Court decided a landmark AIDS case, the first Court ruling dealing with the legal rights of people with an HIV infection. In the case, a dentist refused to fill a cavity at his office (instead of a hospital) because the patient was HIV positive.

"HIV infection, even in the so-called asymptomatic phase, is an impairment which substantially limits the major life activity of reproduction" and therefore qualifies for coverage under the law, Justice Anthony Kennedy wrote for the Court.

The decision means that even people with no visible signs of AIDS are protected under the 1990 Americans with Disabilities Act against discrimination in employment selection, housing, and public accommodations.

SOURCE: Laurie Assco, Associated Press, "Those with AIDS Virus Covered by 1990 Law," *The Courier-Journal* (June 26, 1998):A4.

2 The condition poses a significant risk to others with whom the employee must come in contact in the context of performing his or her job.

INTERVIEWS

The job **interview** is the most commonly utilized selection method. Yet interviews are often not good predictors of future job performance due to low validity, low reliability, and untrained interviewers. Often, the final hiring decision rests on the interview, and to conduct successful interviews the manager or HR professional should: (1) Let the candidate do the talking!—about 80 percent of the time; (2) use a panel of three or more people—to increase reliability; (3) use a structured approach—to increase consistency of information gained and double the validity; and perhaps most important, (4) avoid old vague questions such as, "Tell me about yourself," "Why did you major in accounting?" Instead, ask behavioral questions which require the candidate to give specific job-related samples of their experience or knowledge (see Figure 8–10). Such questioning is based on the concept discussed earlier in the chapter, that the best predictor of a person's future behavior is their past behavior on the same job.[25]

The interview process should seek answers from candidates in three general areas: First, does the person have the *ability* to do the job; second, is he or she sufficiently *motivated* to do the job for some time; and third, will he or she *fit* into the department and organization—can they work well with other employees or team members?

For many reasons, there is low validity or consistency in the interview process. First, interviewers must constantly work to reduce personal biases. Even when interviewers recognize their personal biases, an interviewee's sex, race, religion, school, or hobbies may influence the final decision. Biases can be positive as well as negative. The sex of the interviewer or the interviewee affects the total evaluation of the interview situation. This problem occurs even with trained, experienced interviewers.[26]

Second, all interviews are different, as are all interviewees. The content of interviews changes because no two interviewees have the same background and experience; different aspects of the individuals, their skills, and their work histories must be discussed with each individual.

Third, the setting of the interview may affect the outcome. If one interview takes place early in the morning when the interviewer is fresh and the next interview is conducted late in the afternoon when the interviewer is in a hurry to leave, the second interviewee may receive less support when the interviewees are compared. For another example, an applicant interviewed right after an extremely impressive applicant the interviewer has seen is more likely to get a less positive interview evaluation than normal, but an applicant following a poor applicant the interviewer has seen may get a higher evaluation than normal.

Fourth, if the company has established a maximum number of people to interview and a deadline for filling the position, additional pressure is placed on the interviewer. The last applicant to be interviewed may be offered the position if the interviewer is in a hurry to fill it.

FIGURE 8–10   BEHAVIORAL INTERVIEW QUESTIONS AND DESIRABLE RESPONSES

A. Ability to Solve Problems

Sample Questions—"Tell me about a difficult situation you encountered with another person and how you handled it." "What has been your greatest challenge, and how did you overcome it?"

Positive Indicator—The applicant gives a scenario that focuses on how he or she resolved the situation to a win–win conclusion.

B. Ability to Make Decisions

Sample Questions—"What was the process you used when you bought your last automobile or other major purchase?" "Which factors were important to you in that process?"

Positive Indicator—Desirable applicants will display a thorough approach to decision making by gathering information, evaluating choices, and acting on the option that is most feasible. Applicants' responses to these questions can also provide insight into their value system.

C. Ability to Assume Responsibility

Sample Question—"Tell me about a mistake you made and what you learned from it."

Positive Indicator—Desirable applicants will not have to think too long to come up with a mistake where they've learned valuable lessons. Be wary of applicants who tell you they cannot think of any mistakes. Everyone makes mistakes: The best employees learn from them.

D. Interpersonal Skills

Sample Question—"What types of people do you have the most problems dealing with and why?"

Positive Indicator—Applicants who have a long list of people with whom they have had problems obviously needs to improve their interpersonal

skills. On the opposite end of the spectrum, interviewers should not accept a blanket statement from applicants who say they have never had a problem dealing with people. Everyone has experienced situations with other people where there was friction.

E. Flexibility

Sample Questions—"When was the last time you were asked to work on a weekend when you had already made plans?" "How did you feel about it?"

Positive Indicator—While no one wants to give up their weekend plans for work, the interviewer should look for applicants who are able to adjust quickly to the change with minimum stress. Applicants who indicate they were very upset about last-minute change will more than likely have problems dealing with other types of change inherent in the workplace.

F. Ability to Communicate

Sample Question—In many ways, it is easy to discern communication skills from responses presented in an interview. To delve deeper, the interviewer should ask for specific examples of presentations and written documents such as business correspondence, reports, and memorandums. If the position requires a lot of writing, be sure to ask for writing samples.

Positive Indicator—Look for clarity of thought in responses and pay attention to grammar and vocabulary. Applicants who use poor grammar in their verbal responses will also use poor grammar in their written communications. But beware of the applicant who has the gift of gab that may not translate well in written communication.

SOURCE: Carol Zyles and Alisa Mosley, "Hiring the Best," *Business and Economic Review* 44, no. 1 (October–December 1997): 19–22.

Thus, the applicant may fill a position that otherwise would not have been offered.

A Structured, Objective Process
The problems with the traditional interview process are well known. They usually result in the interviewer's hiring whomever he or she felt most comfortable with, often a "junior me." Today companies like Johnson Wax, Mobil, and Marriott have developed structured, objective interview processes with the goal of achieving "controlled

subjectivity." A critical change in this process is the shift from broad, vague questions such as "How would you discipline an employee?"—for which applicants can give canned responses—to specific behavioral questions such as "Describe a recent example in which you disciplined an employee with absenteeism or tardiness problems."[27]

Conducting objective interviews is primarily a two phase process. The first phase is to create a good interview setting before the applicant actually arrives and to prepare for the interview. The second phase is to establish a useful questioning period during the interview. These eight steps encompass the following characteristics of interviewing:

① ***Setting*** Prepare a setting that will put the applicant at ease and provide consistent surroundings for each interview. Allow 30 to 60 minutes for an adequate interview.

② ***Documentation*** Prepare a system of written records and formalized procedures for the interview. Determine how the interview will be documented at its conclusion to provide a formal record of the outcome.

③ ***Standardization*** Standardize the interview format. Determine a line of questioning that includes the applicant's prior work history, special abilities, skills, and educational background. This will provide a framework for consistency in the information-gathering process.

④ ***Scoring*** Determine how the interview will be scored. That is, on what criteria will the applicant ultimately be evaluated as a result of the interview process? An applicant may be scored in each area relevant to the job description, as well as on the basis of the applicant's response to questioning. If several people interview the same applicant, they should compare scores afterward and challenge each other to support their scores.

⑤ ***Reviewing Job Specifications*** Review the description and specifications for the particular job before each interview. Since the interviewer may see applicants for different jobs, the important aspects of each job must be fresh in the interviewer's mind.

⑥ ***Reviewing the Application Blank*** Review the application before the interview, looking for possible problem areas that require additional information and areas of possible strengths and weaknesses that should be discussed in more detail during the interview.

⑦ ***Training the Interviewer*** Train the interviewer to recognize personal biases and other possible detriments to interview reliability.

⑧ ***Job-Related Questions*** Prepare a line of questioning that keeps the interview job related and does not waste time by straying from the subject or delving into personal areas which could be seen as discriminatory. Questions should require candidates to relate specific examples of their past behavior rather than describe "what I think I would do in that situation."

The end of the job interview is a critical time. At the end, the applicant should be able to ask questions concerning the job, pay, or working conditions. The interviewer should ask when the applicant will be available to work and tell the applicant when the job will be filled. If more people will be interviewed or if there will be a waiting period for a final decision to be made, the applicant should be given an estimate—such as ten days or two weeks—of when a decision should be reached. The applicant should also be told whether to call to find out the results of the job decision or to wait for notification. Interviewers should be positive toward all applicants, even those who may have to be ruled out, because applicants may be available and suited for other positions at a later date.

A board or panel interview can replace the traditional one-on-one interview technique. The *panel interview* minimizes individual bias since all panel members score the applicant. The final evaluation for each applicant is an average of several individuals' evaluations and, therefore, balances out one individual's bias. The panel technique also forces interviews to become more structured and to the point. The only disadvantage of the panel interview is the increased cost to the organization of having more than one interviewer.

The Structured Interview   A structured or patterned interview requires the interviewer to ask a series of predetermined job-related questions. The answers are often scored on a set scale such as 1 for poor, 2 for marginal, 3 for acceptable, 4 for above average, and 5 for outstanding. The interviewer, shortly after the interview is completed, completes an evaluation form, and includes a brief rationale for the evaluations. Validity studies indicate that structured interviews have an *r* or validity coefficient of .28 compared to .14 for unstructured interviews.

REFERENCE CHECKING

The thorough checking of a candidate's background is an important step in the selection, especially since more people are providing misleading or false information on their resumé or application blank. Thus, the primary reasons for conducting **reference checks** are (1) to verify information about the candidate and (2) to uncover information not provided—such as poor attendance, inability to work with team members, criminal record, suspended driver's license, and so on.

In past years, employers were caught in the middle of two countervailing forces when seeking background information. Federal and state laws prohibiting unfair discrimination and defamation led many former employers to only release basic information such as job title, salary, and dates of employment. On the other hand, future employers needed much more job-performance information to avoid *negligent hiring* litigation and make good hiring decisions. By 1995, most employers felt compelled to only release basic data on their former employees, yet wanted much more information from other employers on job candidates. Then the Society for Human Resource Management (SHRM) developed a model reference-checking law and lobbied in statehouses for its passage. Today over 30 states have enacted the law which provides protection to employers who release truthful information and require job applicants to sign a release form. The result has been that many employers, like Winning Ways, in Lenexa, Kansas, have changed their policies and will release valid negative information on former employees.[28] Today, reference checking is a frequent practice for many jobs (see Figure 8–11), and a variety of useful information can be obtained, including reason for leaving, personality traits, violent or bizarre behavior, and human relations skills.

There are several methods of checking references. The HR specialist can personally visit previous employers or friends of the applicant. This method should be reserved for candidates being considered for high-ranking positions because of the extra time and expense incurred. A second method is to check references by mail. This method has two disadvantages: Several days to weeks are required, and it lacks the depth of information that a personal phone call can provide. In addition, most employers are increasingly wary of putting their perceptions about former employees in writing (see Figure 8–12). The third method, the telephone call, is a time-efficient, accurate means of getting complete information on applicants. Previous supervisors and employers are more likely to give complete information regarding a candidate's background over the phone. The HR specialist can go into detail or ask particular questions concerning the applicant. A final method for checking references involves the use of outside services which, for a fee, will investigate the background of applicants. Such services conduct interviews with former employers and check criminal records, credit files, and educational credentials.

Therefore, experienced HR specialists have learned that checking references by telephone provides several advantages:[29]

- *Immediate clarification* of significant issues can be gained.
- *More information* can generally be obtained than through mailed forms.
- *Relatively little expense* is involved, especially when compared to using outside agencies or direct contact.
- *Additional areas* of needed inquiry can be uncovered during the conversation.
- *A structured form* can be utilized, which makes a fast, efficient conversation possible and provides the necessary documentation of the findings.

A major problem with telephone checks is the resistance that may be encountered from some individuals, particularly if the applicant had previous work-related problems. Experience indicates that any such resistance may be minimized if the caller emphasizes that the information is necessary for the applicant to be considered for the position and that the lack of information would probably remove the candidate from further consideration. The caller should begin with "I would like to verify some information given to us by _____ who is a candidate for a job opening." This may put the person at ease because the caller already has information on the applicant and the purpose of the call is to verify that information.[30]

In making reference calls, HR specialists often encounter resistance, regardless of their efforts. After the very first question the response comes, "I am sorry but we only give dates of employment, job title, and wage or salary levels." Why? Employers increasingly refuse to disclose reference information on former employees for fear of incurring liability. Former employees may sue for defamation of character or invasion of privacy, *however, few actually do* (see the Preface for more information). Unfortunately, if employers refuse to provide information about former employees, other employers increase their exposure to negligent-hiring lawsuits (when the employer fails to investigate an employee's background), an interesting legal paradox.[31] One irate company president recalled:

We hired her and after only three months terminated her for frequent absences and tardiness. . . . I talked with her former employer one day who told me they let her go for the same problem! I asked Personnel why they didn't check her references. They said the previous employer would only verify dates of employment, salary, and job title. Then I really got mad until, that is, my HR director pointed out that we only give out dates of employment, salary, and job title!

FIGURE 8–11 REFERENCE CHECKING SURVEY OF HR PROFESSIONALS

A. Conducting Reference Checks

1. Does your organization have a written policy that addresses conducting reference checks on job applicants?
   ☐ Yes   ☐ No   ☐ Don't know

2. How frequently does your organization conduct reference checks on each of the following job candidates? (Check ONE box per row)

	Regularly	Sometimes	Rarely	Never	Don't know
Executive	☐	☐	☐	☐	☐
Professional	☐	☐	☐	☐	☐
Administrative	☐	☐	☐	☐	☐
Technical	☐	☐	☐	☐	☐
Skilled labor	☐	☐	☐	☐	☐
Temporary	☐	☐	☐	☐	☐
Part-time	☐	☐	☐	☐	☐
Seasonal	☐	☐	☐	☐	☐

3. Are job candidates required to sign a waiver allowing you to contact references and/or former employers?
   ☐ Yes   ☐ No   ☐ Don't know

   If yes, is the waiver part of the application or a separate document?
   ☐ Part of the application
   ☐ A separate document
   ☐ Don't know

4. How frequently does your organization, or an agency hired by your organization, check any of the following references for its job candidates? (Check ONE box per row)

	Regularly	Sometimes	Rarely	Never	Don't know
Verification of schools attended	☐	☐	☐	☐	☐
Verification of degrees conferred	☐	☐	☐	☐	☐
Driving records	☐	☐	☐	☐	☐
Credit checks	☐	☐	☐	☐	☐
Criminal records	☐	☐	☐	☐	☐
Verification of Social Security number	☐	☐	☐	☐	☐
Verification of former employers	☐	☐	☐	☐	☐
Verification of lengths of employment	☐	☐	☐	☐	☐
Verification of past salaries	☐	☐	☐	☐	☐
Verification of former titles	☐	☐	☐	☐	☐
Other _____	☐	☐	☐	☐	☐

5. How frequently are the following methods used to check references? (Check ONE box per row)

	Regularly	Sometimes	Rarely	Never	Don't know
Telephone	☐	☐	☐	☐	☐
E-mail	☐	☐	☐	☐	☐
Mail	☐	☐	☐	☐	☐
Internet	☐	☐	☐	☐	☐

   ☐ We don't check references

6. Has the passage of the 1997 Fair Credit Reporting Act changed your practice of checking credit reports?
   ☐ Yes it has changed; we no longer check credit reports
   ☐ No, it has not changed; we still check credit reports
   ☐ Yes it has changed; we now do check credit reports
   ☐ We never did check credit reports
   ☐ Don't know

7. Of the references your organization checks, how often do you find job candidates have falsified the following pieces of information? (Check ONE box per row)

	Regularly	Sometimes	Rarely	Never	Don't check this info.
Verification of schools attended	☐	☐	☐	☐	☐
Verification of degrees conferred	☐	☐	☐	☐	☐
Driving records	☐	☐	☐	☐	☐
Credit checks	☐	☐	☐	☐	☐
Criminal records	☐	☐	☐	☐	☐
Verification of Social Security number	☐	☐	☐	☐	☐
Verification of former employers	☐	☐	☐	☐	☐
Verification of lengths of employment	☐	☐	☐	☐	☐
Verification of past salaries	☐	☐	☐	☐	☐
Verification of former titles	☐	☐	☐	☐	☐
Other _____	☐	☐	☐	☐	☐

8. Does the job application used by your organization contain a statement warning candidates that any falsehoods discovered during the hiring process are grounds for dismissal from consideration for the position?
   ☐ Yes
   ☐ No
   ☐ We don't check references
   ☐ Don't know

9. Who at your organization is PRIMARILY responsible for conducting reference checks of job candidates? (Check ONE box)
   ☐ HR staff
   ☐ Legal staff
   ☐ Outside agency
   ☐ Person for whom the candidate would work
   ☐ Other _____
   ☐ We don't check references
   ☐ Don't know

10. On average, how many references does your organization check for each job candidate? # _____

11. When a job candidate's reference is contacted by your organization, is he or she asked to provide additional names of others who could speak about the job candidate?
    ☐ Yes
    ☐ No
    ☐ We don't check references
    ☐ Don't know

12. When checking the references of job candidates, how often do the people you speak with provide adequate information in the following areas that will help you make a hiring decision? (Check ONE box per row)

	Regularly	Sometimes	Rarely	Never	Don't check this info.
Dates of employment	☐	☐	☐	☐	☐
Salary history	☐	☐	☐	☐	☐
Reason candidate left previous employer	☐	☐	☐	☐	☐
Work habits (absence, tardiness, etc.)	☐	☐	☐	☐	☐

FIGURE 8–11   REFERENCE CHECKING SURVEY OF HR PROFESSIONALS—cont'd

12. (Cont'd)

Personality traits	☐	☐	☐	☐	☐
Violent/bizarre behavior	☐	☐	☐	☐	☐
Human relations skills	☐	☐	☐	☐	☐
Qualification for a particular job	☐	☐	☐	☐	☐
Overall impression of employability	☐	☐	☐	☐	☐
Eligibility for re-hire	☐	☐	☐	☐	☐

13. Has the amount of time spent on checking references increased, stayed about the same or decreased at your organization in the past 3 years?
    ☐ Increased   ☐ Stayed about the same
    ☐ Decreased   ☐ Don't know

B. Providing References

1. Does your organization have a written policy that addresses you, as a representative of the organization, or any other staff members providing references about former employees?
   ☐ Yes   ☐ No   ☐ Don't know

2. Does your organization provide references when asked?
   ☐ Yes   ☐ No   ☐ Don't know

   If no, why not? _____
   _____

3. Who at your organization is PRIMARILY responsible for providing references about former employees? (Check ONE box)
   ☐ HR staff
   ☐ Legal staff
   ☐ Ex-employee's supervisor
   ☐ Other_____
   ☐ We don't provide references
   ☐ Don't know

4. How frequently does your organization provide the following pieces of information when a reference is requested? (Check ONE box per row)

	Regularly	Sometimes	Rarely	Never	Don't provide this info.
Dates of employment	☐	☐	☐	☐	☐
Salary history	☐	☐	☐	☐	☐
Reason candidate left previous employer	☐	☐	☐	☐	☐
Work habits (absence, tardiness, etc.)	☐	☐	☐	☐	☐

Personality traits	☐	☐	☐	☐	☐
Violent/bizarre behavior	☐	☐	☐	☐	☐
Human relations skills	☐	☐	☐	☐	☐
Qualification for a particular job	☐	☐	☐	☐	☐
Overall impression of employability	☐	☐	☐	☐	☐
Eligibility for re-hire	☐	☐	☐	☐	☐
Other _____	☐	☐	☐	☐	☐

5. In the past 3 years, has your organization had a defamation claim brought against it as a result of a reference given about a former employee?
   ☐ Yes   ☐ No   ☐ Don't know

6. In the past 3 years, has your organization been sued for negligent hiring for hiring an individual who later harmed another employee or committed another crime while an employee?
   ☐ Yes   ☐ No   ☐ Don't know

7. Have you personally, as an HR professional, ever given a positive reference about a former employee known to engage in violent or harassing conduct?
   ☐ Yes   ☐ No   ☐ Don't know

8. Have you personally, as an HR professional, ever given a positive reference about an employee with poor performance just to help get them out of your organization?
   ☐ Yes   ☐ No   ☐ Don't know

9. Has anyone in your organization ever refused to provide information about a former employee for fear of being sued?
   ☐ Yes   ☐ No   ☐ Don't know

10. Are you aware if your state has enacted reference checking legislation protecting employers from civil liability when providing references in good faith?
    ☐ Yes   ☐ No

11. Has your organization changed its policy on providing references as a result of increased state laws that protect employers from civil liability when they give references in good faith?
    ☐ Yes, as a result of the laws we now provide references
    ☐ No, there has been no policy change
    ☐ Yes, as a result of the laws we no longer provide references
    ☐ We don't have a policy on providing references
    ☐ Don't know

Do you have any unique reference checking experiences you would like to share with us?

SOURCE: *Reference Checking Survey,* Society for Human Resource Management, 1998, pp. 12–15.

FIGURE 8–12   THE UNFAVORABLE BUT POSITIVE RECOMMENDATION

For the person who desires to send a letter of recommendation that sounds positive yet contains unfavorable information, Robert J. Thornton of Lehigh University developed the Lexicon of Inconspicuously Ambiguous Recommendations (LIAR):

- To describe a candidate who is woefully inept: "I most enthusiastically recommend this candidate with no qualifications whatsoever."

- To describe a candidate who is not particularly industrious: "In my opinion you will be very fortunate to get this person to work for you."

- To describe a candidate who is not worth further consideration: "I would urge you to waste no time in making this candidate an offer of employment."

- To describe a candidate with lackluster credentials: "All in all, I cannot say enough good things about this candidate or recommend him too highly."

- To describe an ex-employee who had difficulty getting along with fellow workers: "I am pleased to say that this candidate is a former colleague of mine."

- To describe a candidate who is so unproductive that the position would be better left unfilled: "I can assure you that no person would be better for this job."

Any of the above may be used to offer a negative opinion of the personal qualities, work habits, or motivation of the candidate while allowing the candidate to believe that it is high praise. In any case, whether perceived correctly or not by the candidate, the phrases are virtually litigation-proof.

SOURCE: Robert J. Thornton, "I Can't Recommend the Candidate Too Highly: An Ambiguous Lexicon for Job Recommendations," *The Chronicle for Higher Education* 33 (February 25, 1987): 42. Copyright 1984, The Chronicle of Higher Education. Reprinted with permission.

Defamation of character may occur when one person makes a statement, either oral or written, to another person that is false, harms a third person's reputation, and lowers his or her status in the community. Employers who release information about previous employees do have considerable legal protection under the "qualified privilege doctrine," which protects them when the person receiving the information had a need to know. The doctrine states that exchange of information about employees is in the best interest of employers, who have a common interest in hiring desirable applicants, and in the best interest of the public.[32] Employers, however, are protected under the doctrine only under the following conditions:[33]

- The information is given in good faith. Only factual, documented information should be given. If an employee stole inventory, that should be stated. If a supervisor *"thinks* he is a crook," that should not be stated.

- The information should be limited to the inquiry. If asked about the employee's absenteeism, do not mention that he or she had poor peer reviews.

- The information must be related to job performance. Do not discuss the employee's personal life.

- The information is valid. The truth is generally an absolute defense to a charge of defamation.

School Records

An increasing number of employers are requiring school records—high school or college transcripts. School records contain valuable information on attendance, exams, and specific courses and skills needed for certain jobs (see *HR in the News:* "School Records").

Consumer Credit Reports

Many employers utilize consumer-credit reporting agencies to provide background information on applicants. They must comply with the Fair Credit Reporting Act (FCRA) if such information is used to evaluate job applicants. The FCRA allows employers to use a consumer report as a preemployment measure, but only if the report contains information on the applicant alone—not on a spouse or any other individual. In general, there are two types of reports that an employer may access: (1) *consumer*

HR IN THE NEWS

SCHOOL RECORDS—HIRING PROCESS REQUIREMENT

A nationwide campaign called *Making Academics Count* began in 1998. It's goal was to "send a very powerful message that we in business do care about what goes on in schools." According to Anne Miller, director of corporate education at Eastman Kodak. At Kodak and over 10,000 other businesses, an HR policy is to ask for transcripts for entry-level jobs as well as middle-level and higher positions. The hiring process of these companies require applicants to demonstrate academic achievement through school-based records, portfolios, academic transcripts, certificates, and other evidence. The campaign was initiated by the National Alliance of Business, a coalition of 13 national business organizations (*www.nab.com*).

SOURCE: "Employers Agreed Work Is on the Record," *Work America* 15, no 3 (March 1998): 1–3.

---

reports, which contain information on creditworthiness, and (2) *investigative consumer reports,* which contain information on general reputation and character gained through personal interviews with neighbors, friends, or associates. If an applicant is denied employment based solely or in part on report information, the employer under the FCRA must tell the applicant that the report was secured and that the information at least in part caused him or her to be denied employment. In addition, the employer must supply the applicant with the name and address of the agency making the report. Possible penalties for failing to comply with this FCRA disclosure requirement are substantial since they can include damages for humiliation and mental distress, injury to reputation, and injury to creditworthiness.[34]

NEGLIGENT HIRING

An employer's liability for the **negligent hiring** and retention of employees who engage in criminal or other illegal acts is a question of significant importance. In negligent hiring cases, the courts have generally found the employer's liability to depend on the soundness of the employer's investigation into the employee's background. If the employee was hired for a job that might include a risk of injury or harm to customers or co-workers, the employer's liability is particularly great. Negligent liability cases are generally decided by a jury, which determines whether the employer should bear all or part of the cost associated with injury or harm to a third party.[35]

In one case, the parents of a young boy received an out-of-court settlement of $440,000 from the employer of the boy's murderer. The employer knew of the employee's extensive criminal background, including a second-degree murder conviction. The employee was hired to provide security in a construction-skills training program, where he met the young boy.[36] In another case, a homeowner was assaulted in her home by an employee of a pest-control company. An appellate court ruled that the homeowner had the right to sue for damages on the basis of negligent hiring and retention.[37] Pinkerton's Security Company lost a $300,000 suit for the negligent hiring of a security guard who was convicted of theft. Pinkerton's was found liable because it failed to check adequately the employee's references and previous employers.[38]

How can employers avoid negligent hiring liability? Unfortunately, there are no certain answers. However, following the reasoning of the courts in such cases, employers should do the following:[39]

- Ask about conviction records on the application and during the interview. It is alright to ask an applicant about a crime if he or she was convicted. However, unless the conviction is for a crime directly related to the current job opening (that is, embezzlement and a financial control position), the conviction cannot be the sole reason to refuse to hire an applicant. Refusing to hire an applicant solely because of a conviction unrelated to the job is a violation of EEOC guidelines.
- Ask about gaps in time in the employment, educational, and military section of the application.
- Clarify unclear statements during the interview.
- Have applicants sign a release granting you permission to obtain background information.
- Check as many personal and employment references as possible.

- Document in writing all reference-check inquiries.
- Ensure the investigation inquiries are job related for the position being sought.

Of course there is no way to totally prevent hiring a problem employee, but being proactive in hiring practices can always reduce the risk.

Personal References   Many employers continue to request that applicants list the names, occupations, and addresses of three or more individuals who are not previous employers or relatives but who can attest to the applicants' suitability. In reality, almost all applicants list individuals who will say something very positive about them and give good recommendations. Realizing this, the HR specialist does not use a good recommendation to determine the applicant's suitability for the position. A realistic use of personal references includes the following:

- Verifying the data received on the application blank or during the interview. Often personal recommendations can verify information on the application blank. For example, individuals did attend certain schools, do have certain work experiences, or lived at listed addresses for certain periods of time.
- Evaluating the quality of the personal recommendation. Applicants who give professional people or business executives as references have a definite advantage over applicants who use their next-door neighbors or former high-school classmates as references.
- Determining how well the person knows the applicant. An HR specialist may call a personal reference and find that the person has little or no knowledge of the applicant other than that the applicant lives down the street or went to the same high school. In some cases, the references do not even give applicants good recommendations, simply saying that they really do not know much about the person. A lukewarm recommendation by a personal reference may be an indication of the applicant's lack of suitability for a position.

THE SELECTION DECISION

Deciding which applicant should be offered the position may be accomplished by one of two processes: compensatory selection or multiple hurdles selection. The **multiple hurdles selection process** requires the applicant to pass each hurdle: initial screening, application blank, testing, interview, background checks, and departmental interview. See Figure 8–4 for an example.

In the *compensatory selection process* all applicants who pass the initial screening complete the application blank and are tested; *each* applicant is interviewed before the final choice is made. The applicants are then compared on the basis of all the selection information. In compensatory selection, an applicant may score low in one area, but the score might be offset by a very high mark in another area. This is particularly beneficial to candidates who receive low interview scores because they are very nervous and lack self-confidence during interviews but perform very well on aptitude and background checks. Diversity may be considered one element of a compensatory process. The disadvantage of compensatory selection is its cost: A larger number of candidates must be processed through the complete selection procedure before a final decision is made. Primarily due to the cost factor, the multiple hurdles selection technique, in which a candidate can be rejected at each stage of the process, is more common.

INTERNATIONAL HUMAN RESOURCE MANAGEMENT

EXPATRIATE RIGHTS

When Ali Boureslan, a naturalized American citizen, was fired by his Saudi Arabia–based American employer, he sued for discrimination. What Boureslan began as a relatively straightforward case involving one man, one company, and one incident has evolved into an important test case in international employment law. Boureslan's complaint was no longer the central issue. Whether he was discriminated against was no longer the relevant question. Boureslan, a Lebanese native and a Muslim, was hired by ARAMCO in the United States. After he was transferred to ARAMCO's Saudi Arabian operation, he reported that a British co-worker was harassing him because of his religious obligations. The co-worker was eventually fired. Boureslan, however, was later laid off, along with other ARAMCO employees in Saudi Arabia. His suit claims that his termination was really part of the harassment that began with his co-worker.

The issue then concerned the administration of HR policies by American companies with overseas operations. Do Title VII of the Civil Rights Act of 1964 and other employment laws apply to expatriate Americans who are working for U.S. companies?

"The internationalization of the world's economy does not require or even suggest that the domestic social practice of this country or any country be made the standard of practice around the world," said attorney Lawrence Z. Lorber, who argued the Boureslan case.

Boureslan's attorney, James Tyson, agreed that there might be inequality in the treatment of workers of different nationalities, but that is not a sufficient argument, he said, to deny American workers their rights under Title VII. One argument has been used by both sides to support their cases: the chilling effect on Americans' careers if they are guaranteed or denied civil rights protection overseas. Without Title VII protection, said Tyson, few American workers would be willing to accept overseas assignments and expose themselves to the capriciousness of foreign supervisors and foreign cultures.

On the other hand, Lorber said that with the protection—and almost certain resulting cultural conflict—of combined American law and local law, American companies operating abroad would hesitate to hire American workers. This would place an unfair limitation on qualified American employees for whom an overseas assignment would benefit their careers. Lorber added that the combined legal burden would undermine the competitiveness of foreign-based American companies and create unfair conditions that would favor American workers on the job site.

The case was decided in a landmark 1991 decision. In **_Boureslan_ v. _ARAMCO, Arabian-American Oil Co.,_** the U.S. Supreme Court ruled that the EEOC had no jurisdiction outside the United States and its territories and that Congress did not intend to impose Title VII on American companies employing American citizens outside of the United States.[40] However, the 1991 Civil Rights Act overturned the Supreme Court decision. Thus, employees now do have the right to sue an American employer for "foreign" discrimination.

STAFFING THE NEW EUROPE

The economic unification of Europe and the fall of communism, as well as the growth of China, has caused HR managers in the United States to learn the intricacies of staffing their organizations in countries previously closed to Western businesses. These new operations primarily employ three types of employees:[41]

1 **Local (Host Country) nationals** Citizens of the country where the facility is located, working in their home country.

2 **Third country nationals** Non-U.S. citizens who are on the payroll in their home country but working in a third.

3 **Expatriates** (American foreign-service employees) U.S. citizens who are on the payroll in the United States but working overseas.

The cost differences among the three types of overseas employees can be substantial and must be carefully weighed in planning the workforce requirements of foreign operations. Generally, according to Neil B. Krupp, vice-president of the international division of Runzheimer International, a foreign-service employee costs an employer at least three times as much as a local national. It is, of course, more costly to conduct business in some countries, such as Belgium and Germany.

The major factors responsible for cost differences among countries and types of employees are the allowance packages required by foreign-service employees (incentives, housing differentials, goods and services differentials, educational expenses) and taxes. Most employers assume responsibility for all the employee's foreign tax obligation. A Chicago resident earning an annual salary of $45,000 in the United States would incur $38,000 of foreign tax liabilities if relocated to Germany, compared to only about $10,000 in Illinois. Thus, the U.S. employer must pay the $28,000 difference.

Employers can potentially reduce their foreign staffing costs by:

1 Employing local nationals when possible.

2 Locating American expatriates in low-allowance and low-tax countries.

3 Minimizing relocation costs by moving foreign-service employees as infrequently as possible.

4 Considering hiring single employees first, without violating federal or state discrimination laws.[42]

Staffing is the single key issue to U.S. businesses expanding in Asia. Staffing is why it is critical for U.S. firms to find a joint-venture partner in China. The enormous influx of foreign companies to China has put severe pressure on the small number of educated Chinese workers. These local nationals who have received Western training and experience are in short-supply. The success of a joint venture in China often hinges on the building of contacts and positive relationships or _guanxi_ (see Figure 8–13), many on-site visits, and the hiring of expatriate and local staff. A model program for setting up business in China is the McDonald's Corporation. Bob Wilner, the McDonald's director of international human resources, went to China at least

FIGURE 8–13   KEYS TO SUCCESSFUL HIRING IN CHINA

1. COMMUNICATION, CONTACTS, AND BUSINESS BEHAVIOR—Build good contacts and relationships or *guanxi*. It's of the utmost importance. Face-to-face communication works better than written contracts.

2. HR INVOLVEMENT—HR people should visit the operation sites and research the on-site conditions for expatriates well in advance.

3. EXPATRIATE STAFF SELECTION AND PLANNING—Expatriate staff members should be carefully selected and assessed on their adaptability, flexibility and cultural sensitivity in addition to their technical skills. The general manager needs to be a good leader, receptive to cultural differences and accommodating to the way business is done in China. Don't underestimate family issues in expatriate selection.

4. CULTURAL BRIEFING AND PREPARATION—It's extremely important to prepare employees and families thoroughly in the area of cultural issues and differences. This includes a knowledge of Chinese culture and history, awareness of the isolation factor, and using performance measures of business success appropriate in China.

5. LANGUAGE—Although language training is provided by most companies, it's far more important to have cultural sensitivity than fluency in Mandarin, Taiwanese, Cantonese, or other Chinese language.

6. LOCAL STAFF—Recruit local staff members, but be careful with interregional expatriates. Developing the skills and careers of local staff is essential and a priority. It's advisable to hire a good legal person who knows about local benefits and compensation policies.

Source: ECA International, London as published in Charlene M. Soloman, "The Big Question," *Global Workforce* 2, no. 3 (July 1997): 10–16.

once a month for the first ten years as the firm started looking at the China market. China is a society which highly values—and expects—a demonstration of long-term commitment as displayed by Wilner. McDonald's, says Wilner, takes a global approach to HR, not a U.S.-based approach. "Unlike the way we cook our hamburgers exactly the same in all 101 countries, the way we manage, motivate, reward, and discipline is more sensitive to the culture." McDonald's has been highly successful in China by stressing HR basics: communication, performance feedback, clear policies, and an open mind. The McDonald's selection system in China and other countries focuses on initial interviews followed by candidates spending three days working in a restaurant, during which time the restaurant manager evaluates them on specific skills. Wilner emphasizes that candidates, and employees, are encouraged to openly discuss what they like and don't like, and suggest how things can be improved. Employees are rewarded based on performance in two areas: team effort and individual performance. The career development program—most store managers and upper-level managers are promoted from within—has been credited as the key to McDonald's success in China, because it rewards loyalty and commitment, which are highly valued in the Chinese culture.[43]

- The selection process generally centers on the HR office. It is one of the most critical functions in HR because an organization's effectiveness depends on its employees. The selection process is not, however, one of scientific precision. Instead of finding the one best person, managers strive to select an applicant who has the ability and motivation to perform the job for many years.

- Selection screening devices, such as the interview and the application blank, each have advantages and disadvantages. Employers must carefully consider the cost and validity of each method.

- The interview tends to be the most commonly used and decisive selection technique. Subject to reliability problems, the structuring of the interview questions, training, and the scoring of answers can greatly improve reliability and usefulness of the interview as a decision tool.

- Preemployment tests can be effective tools in the selection process. If carefully selected, validated, and monitored, they can help select applicants who will match the position's requirements.

- Reference checking has increased in use but has been subjected to legal challenges. Employers can legally provide factual and accurate information, but they should be able to verify any job-related information they release.

- U.S. employers hiring employees in foreign nations should carefully consider the substantial cost variations related to different staffing alternatives. Most employees were raised, educated, and indoctrinated in only one culture and thus must develop respect for and learn to value another culture to interface successfully between the two cultures. The McDonald's model of global HR practices should be considered by companies starting business abroad.

- Negligent hiring liability has become a major concern for employers. While no practices can guarantee an employer protection, reasonable-effort background checks, requesting police and credit records, and investigating complaints are good precautions.

CASE STUDY

BLUE GRASS STATE UNIVERSITY

Blue Grass State University President Glenn Wood had decided that the traditional method of selecting faculty had not been successful. In the past twenty years, when a department had an open position, the chair would attend the regional conference of the appropriate discipline and place a position announcement with the placement service. Interested candidates at the conference would contact the chair and request an initial interview. These professional meetings provided a placement process as a service to faculty and schools. The chair would then return to the campus with vitae and interview notes on several candidates. The department faculty would review this applicant pool and select three to five candidates to be invited to the campus for a formal interview. After all the interviews, an offer was made to the top-rated (by the faculty) candidate. If it was turned down, the offer was extended to the second choice, and so on. Candidates were rated by each faculty member on three factors, with the following weights: (1) teaching interests (specific graduate and undergraduate courses), 40 percent; (2) research interests and publication record, 40 percent; (3) quality of Ph.D. training and fit with departmental needs, 20 percent. The weighted rating determined each candidate's aggregate score.

President Wood has several problems with the traditional process, and as a former president of a local bank, he was inclined to question it. His specific concerns are the following:

1. The process had produced several faculty members who were not outstanding teachers. Some had poor communication skills; many were satisfactory, but few were outstanding. Wood considered teaching to be the highest priority of the university and research and community service the other two important priorities.

2. The cost per hire had averaged $5,000 per position due largely to the expenses related to bringing several candidates to the campus.

3. Many faculty members hired under this process were unable to work effectively in the community in either the private or the nonprofit sector. Since Blue Grass was an urban community, Wood considered active community involvement to be an important role of everyone employed at the university.

4. The process has produced a faculty that contains only 20 percent women and 4 percent minorities. Wood has set university diversity goals of 40 percent women and 20 percent minorities for each job classification, including faculty.

President Wood has assembled a task force to consider the recruitment and selection process. The task force consists of four students, four faculty members, and two administrators. Wood has given the task force responsibility for developing a new faculty selection process that will address all of his concerns and hire top-quality faculty.

QUESTIONS

① How should the task force proceed to address the change?

② Do you agree with President Wood that the problems he listed are probably caused by the faculty selection process?

③ Design a recommended selection process that would meet President Wood's concerns. Consider using each of the selection methods discussed in the chapter. Be specific about what stakeholders (faculty, students, community representatives, alumni, and so on) should be included in using each method.

④ How should President Wood determine whether the new process proposed (question 3) has been effective after a five-year trial period?

EXPERIENTIAL EXERCISES

1. IS THIS APPLICATION BLANK LAWFUL?

PURPOSE

To recognize the legal issues surrounding the use of application blanks and to analyze an actual application blank for potentially unlawful items.

TASK

Illustrated on the following page is an actual application blank used by a retail clothing chain. How many potentially illegal items on the application blank can you identify? Following your analysis, your instructor will lead you in a discussion concerning this exercise.

2. INTERVIEWER PERSPECTIVES

PURPOSE

To recognize the difficulty of conducting effective job interviews and to learn how several interviewers can reach different conclusions on the same applicants.

TASK

The class should be divided into groups of three to five students. An even number of groups is required. Each group will assume the roles of HR professionals or job applicants.

Step 1: Members of each HR group will write a brief job description based on a job with which they have some familiarity.

Step 2: The job description developed by the HR group will be given to members of the applicant group, who will then study it and prepare themselves for a job interview. The in-

structor may wish to allow one or two days to pass before step 3 for the applicants to prepare themselves.

Step 3: Members of the HR group will prepare a list of interview questions to ask the applicants and a list of criteria that they will use to score the interview.

Step 4: The HR group will interview each applicant (other applicants should be out of the room) and individually score the applicant after the interview is completed.

Step 5: All members of each pair of HR and applicant groups will review the interview scores together. Each HR member should be required to explain or defend his or her scoring.

Step 6: If the class contains multiple pairs of groups, one representative of each pair will lead a discussion of the activities of their session.

KEY TERMS AND CONCEPTS

Ability and motivation
Achievement tests
Adverse impact
Applicant flow record
Application blank
Aptitude tests
Boureslan v. *ARAMCO*

Competency-based hiring
Criterion-related validity
Defamation
Drug test
Expatriates
Four-fifths rule
Global assessments

APPLICATION FOR EMPLOYMENT

We are an equal opportunity employer, dedicated to a policy of non-discrimination in employment on any basis including race, creed, color, age, sex, religion or national origin.

PERSONAL INFORMATION

DATE

NAME

SOCIAL SECURITY
NUMBER

LAST	FIRST	MIDDLE

PRESENT ADDRESS

STREET	CITY	STATE

PERMANENT ADDRESS

STREET	CITY	STATE

PHONE NO.

REFERRED
BY

DATE OF BIRTH   HEIGHT   WEIGHT   COLOR OF HAIR   COLOR OF EYES

MARRIED   SINGLE   WIDOWED   DIVORCED   SEPARATED

NUMBER OF CHILDREN   DEPENDENTS OTHER THAN WIFE OR CHILDREN   CITIZEN OF U.S.A.   YES ☐   NO ☐

RACE

REFERRED
BY

EMPLOYMENT DESIRED

POSITION   DATE YOU CAN START   SALARY DESIRED

ARE YOU EMPLOYED NOW?   IF SO MAY WE INQUIRE OF YOUR PRESENT EMPLOYER?

EVER APPLIED TO THIS COMPANY BEFORE?   WHERE?   WHEN?

EDUCATION	NAME AND LOCATION OF SCHOOL	YEARS ATTENDED *	DATE GRADUATED *	SUBJECTS STUDIED
GRAMMAR SCHOOL				
HIGH SCHOOL				
COLLEGE				
TRADE, BUSINESS OR CORRESPONDENCE SCHOOL				

* The Age Discrimination in Employment Act of 1967 prohibits discrimination on the basis of age with respect to individuals who are at least 40 but less than 65 years of age.

GENERAL

SUBJECTS OF SPECIAL STUDY OR RESEARCH WORK

DO YOU HAVE ANY PHYSICAL DISABILITIES? IF YES, EXPLAIN:

WHAT FOREIGN LANGUAGES DO YOU SPEAK FLUENTLY?   READ   WRITE

U.S. MILITARY OR NAVAL SERVICE   RANK   PRESENT MEMBERSHIP IN NATIONAL GUARD OR RESERVES

[CONTINUED ON OTHER SIDE]

HAVE YOU EVER BEEN ARRESTED? IF YES, FOR WHAT REASON:

LAST   FIRST   MIDDLE

KEY TERMS AND CONCEPTS—cont'd

Honesty tests
Illegal discrimination
Intelligence tests
Interest tests
Interview
Kaizen
Local (host country) nationals
Medical exam

Multiple hurdles selection process
National Institute on Drug Abuse (NIDA)
Negligent hiring
Polygraph
Reference checks
Third country nationals
Validity (*predictive, concurrent, content,* and *construct*)
Work samples

REVIEW QUESTIONS

1. Why is the selection process usually centralized in the HR department?

2. Should the HR office ask an applicant for his or her date of birth, marital status, or a photograph?

3. How does the HR specialist use the application blank?

4. What are the real purposes of background checks?

5. How can preemployment tests be utilized in employee selection?

6. What questions may an interviewer legally ask under the ADA to determine if and under what circumstances an applicant could perform a job?

7. Why have employers increased the use of honesty or integrity tests in recent years? What are their limitations?

8. How can a battery of tests be utilized to select applicants for jobs?

9. When U.S. companies staff new overseas operations, where can they secure the needed personnel? What steps should they follow in hiring staff?

10. Why is validity an important characteristic of a selection test?

DISCUSSION QUESTIONS

1. What inappropriate personality traits would overshadow an employee's skills and abilities enough to cause the dismissal of the following persons: a food-store checkout clerk, a research assistant, an elementary school teacher?

2. If you inherited a shoe factory that had a history of high turnover and low wages, would you attempt to attract only the best workers by raising salaries or continue a minimum-wage policy and disregard employees' dissatisfaction? What factors would influence your decision?

3. While interviewing two well-qualified applicants for an accounting manager's position, you notice that one applicant has had one job for seven years and the other has had five jobs in ten years, each change involving a salary increase. Would this information affect your decision?

4. Due to costs and other reasons, some employers require medical exams or drug tests only on applicants for

selected jobs. For what types of jobs do you think all employers should be required to test their applicants?

5. You work in a department store's personnel department. The owner requests that all of the store's employees take honesty tests periodically to minimize employee theft. Employees find this approach insulting and demand that you do something. What would you do?

6. How has the U.S. Supreme Court affected the concept of affirmative action in recent decisions? Do you agree with the Court's general direction?

7. Do you agree with the U.S. Supreme Court's decision in the *Boureslan* v. *ARAMCO* case? Explain your position.

8. Some HR professionals believe that Congress should pass a law (as many states have done) requiring employers to provide complete, accurate information on their former employees to prospective employers conducting background checks. Do you agree? Why?

ENDNOTES

Chapter 8

1. T. L. Brink, "A Discouraging Word Improves Your Interviews," *HRMagazine* (December 1992): 49–52.

2. S. M. Jameel Hasan, "HRM in a New Era of Globalization," *Business Forum* (Winter 1992): 56–59.

3. Ann Vincola, "Performance Management Through a Work Life Lens," *HR Focus,* 75, no. 2 (February 1998): 9–10.

4. Arthur Within, "Commonly Overlooked Dimensions of Employee Selection," *Personnel Journal* 59, no. 7 (July 1980): 573–75.

5. Gary Dessler, "Value-based Hiring Builds Commitment," *Personnel Journal* (November 1993): 98–102.

6. Jim Jordan, "Truth or Consequences," *The Lexington Herald-Leader* (May 4, 1998): 10.

7. Larry Stevens, "Resumé Scanning Simplifies Tracking," *Personnel Journal* (April 1993): 77–79.

8. Brooks Mitchell, *Bet on Cowboys, Not Horses: A Technological Breakthrough for Employee Selection* (Shaker Heights, OH: York, 1993).

9. Gerard P. Panaro, "Psychological Testing: Three Key Strategies," *Personnel Practice Ideas* 5, no. 8 (April 1990): 6.

10. Dale Yoder and Paul D. Standohar, "Testing and EEO: Getting Down to Cases," *Personnel Administrator* 29, no. 2 (February 1984): 67–74.

11. Mark Thomas and Harry Brull, "Tests Improve Hiring Decisions at Franciscan," *Personnel Journal* (November 1993): 89–92.

12. Ibid.

13. *Webster's Unabridged Dictionary* (Springfield, MA: Merriam, 1986), 108.

14. Robert M. Madigan, K. Dow Scott, Diana L. Deadrick, and Jil A. Stodard, "Employment Testing: The U.S. Job Service Is Spearheading a Revolution," *Personnel Administrator* 31, no. 9 (September 1986): 102–112.

15. "How to Comply with the Polygraph Law," *Nation's Business 77,* no. 12 (December 1989): 36–37.

16. U.S. Congress, Office of Technology Assessment, "The Use of Integrity Tests for Pre-Employment Screening," OTA-SET-0442 (Washington, D.C.: U.S. Government Printing Office, September 1990), 1.

17. Carolyn Wiley and Doria L. Rudley, "Managerial Issues and Responsibilities in the Use of Integrity Tests," *Labor Law Journal* (March 1991): 152–59.

18. Paul R. Sackett, Laura R. Burris, and Christine Callahan, "Integrity Testing for Personnel Selection: An Update," *Personnel Psychology,* 42 (1989): October 491–528.

19. Lewis R. Goldberg et al., *Questionnaires Used in the Prediction of Trustworthiness in Pre-employment Selection Decisions: An A.P.A. Task Force Report* (Washington, D.C.: American Psychological Association, 1991), 26.

20. Wiley and Rudley, "Managerial Issues," 152–53.

21. Rob Brookler, "Industry Standards in Workplace Drug Testing," *Personnel Journal* (April 1992): 128–132.

22. Eric Rolfe Greenburg, "Test-Positive Rate Drop as More Companies Screen Employees," *HR Focus* (June 1992): 7.

23. Joseph B. Treaster, "As More Companies Test Employees for Drugs, Usage Drops," *The New York Times* (November 21, 1993): D1.

24. Jonathan A. Segal, "HIV: How High the Risk?" *HRMagazine* (February 1993): 93–100.

25. Carol Douglas Lyles and Alisa G. Mosley, "Hiring the Best," *Business and Economic Review* 44, no. 1 (October–December, 1997): 19–22.

26. Gerald Rose, "Sex Effects on Managerial Hiring Decisions," *Academy of Management Journal* 21 (1978): 104–112.

27. Julie Soloman, "The New Job Interview: Show Thyself," *The Wall Street Journal* (December 4, 1989): A1.

28. Frances A. McMorris, "Ex-Bosses Face Less Peril Giving Honest Job References," *The Wall Street Journal* (July 8, 1996): B1.

29. Erwin S. Stanton, "Fast-and-Easy Reference Checking by Telephone," *Personnel Journal 67,* no. 11 (November 1988): 123–130.

30. Ibid.

31. Kenneth L. Sovereigns, "Pitfalls of Withholding Reference Information," *Personnel Journal 69,* no. 3 (March 1990): 116–122.

32. *Circus Hotels* v. *Witherspoon,* 667 P.2d 101 (November 1983).

33. Sovereigns, "Pitfalls of Withholding Reference Information," 116–122.

34. David Israel and Anita Lechner, "Use of Credit Reports Requires Disclosure," *HRMagazine* (April 1992): 93–96.

35. Ronald M. Green and Richard J. Reibstein, "It's 10 P.M. Do You Have to Know Where Your Employees Are?" *Personnel Administrator* 32, no. 4 (April 1987): 71–76.

36. *Henley* v. *Prince George's County,* 305 Md. 320, 503, A. 2d 1333 (1986).

37. *Abbot* v. *Payne,* 457 So. 2d 1156, Fla. Dist. Ct. App. (1984).

38. *Welsh Manufacturing* v. *Pinkerton's, Inc.,* 474 A. 2d 436 R.I. (1984).

39. Saundra Jackson and Andríenne Loftin "Proactive Practices Avoid Negligent Hiring Claims," *HR News* (September 1995): 9.

40. *Bareslan* v. *ARAMCO, Arabian-American Oil Co.,* no. 87–2206 (5th Cir. 1990).

41. Neil B. Krupp, "Overseas Staffing for the New Europe," *Personnel 67,* no. 7 (July 1990): 20–25.

42. Ibid.

43. Charlene M. Soloman, "The Big Question," *Global Workforce* 2, no. 3 (July 1997): 10–16.

P A R T III

ASSESSMENT AND DEVELOPMENT

CHAPTER

9

PERFORMANCE APPRAISAL AND PERFORMANCE MANAGEMENT

CHAPTER OUTLINE

CHAPTER OBJECTIVES

1 To explain the evaluative and developmental objectives of performance appraisal.

2 To describe the major performance appraisal methods.

3 To recognize common appraisal problems.

4 To develop an effective appraisal interview.

5 To design and evaluate a program of performance appraisal.

6 To evaluate who should perform the appraisal.

HR IN THE NEWS

WANT TOP FINANCIAL PERFORMANCE? STUDY SAYS USE *PERFORMANCE MANAGEMENT*

Although companies have had a love–hate relationship with performance management programs (PMPs) there is recent evidence that may change that. PMPs have been documented to be positively associated with firms' *financial* performance.

Hewitt Associates, an Illinois HR consulting firm, analyzed the financial performance of 437 publicly held U.S. companies for five years during the 1990s. They divided these into firms which had been using a PMP for at least two years and those in the same industry who had not. Hewitt found those firms using formal performance management systems to be superior to their competitors based on three important financial indicators:

- **Stock return to market index**   This measure generates a true picture of wealth creation by management by removing all common market influences. PMP firms have an average stock-return-to-market index of 1.435 compared to 1.023 for non-PMP firms—over a 40 percent difference.

- **Price to book total capital** (ratio of current market value of a company to total book value of its invested capital)   A ratio over 1.0 indicates investors are optimistic about the company's future growth; under 1.0 indicates pessimism. PMP firms average 1.64 (high) compared to 1.34 for non-PMP firms—over a 22% difference.

- **Real value to cost**   This measure also looks at the returns senior managers generate from the capital that is available to invest, but specifically estimates how much confidence investors have in the ability of management to use shareholders' money wisely. PMP firms average 1.67 compared with 1.31 for non-PMP firms—over a 27 percent difference.

This study was performed by Abbie Smith, professor of accounting at the University of Chicago Graduate School of Business along with Hewitt Associates; cited in Helen Rheem, "Performance Management Programs," *Harvard Business Review* 74 (September–October 1996): 8.

PERFORMANCE APPRAISAL AND PERFORMANCE MANAGEMENT

Are employers interested in managing the performance of their employees? Of course. In fact, employers use many tactics and approaches to assess the level of performance of all factors at work—human and technolog-ical. **Performance management** refers to the entire box of tools which management uses to control, guide, and improve the performance of employees. Tools such as reward systems, job design, leadership approaches, training efforts, and the performance appraisal can all be seen as part of an effective human performance management system and a big part of most managers' jobs.

Other chapters discuss various tools employers use to manage employee performance; in this chapter, we want to deal primarily with one, a tool that has been recently called one of the "most important human resource systems" and "most widely researched" tool.[1] The **performance appraisal (PA)** is the ongoing process of evaluating and managing both the behavior and human outcomes in the workplace. We want to cut through the jungle of studies, advice, and lingo to examine the core objectives for PA, the typical process, the methods and instruments used, and 360-degree feedback systems, as well as to discuss how managers handle PA interviews.

The jungle starts with all the different terms used to name the PA process. Your employer may call PA the *performance review, annual appraisal, performance evaluation,* or some other term. Care must be used to avoid confusing different HR processes. For instance, *job analysis* (see Chapter 5) is very different from the PA because it examines issues such as which tasks and responsibilities are included in the design of a particular job. *Job evaluation* (see Chapter 12) focuses upon how much a job is worth and helps to set pay ranges for jobs.

For example, at Federal Express the position of labor relations manager would first have undergone job analysis in which the duties of conducting FedEx's labor negotiations, guiding employee involvement programs, and training managers in employee relations were identified. Next, the job evaluation process was used to determine the relative value of this job compared with others at FedEx. This ended in specifying a pay range. Finally, whoever happens to be the labor relations manager now has her or his performance assessed regularly using the PA process.

WWW.FEDERALEXPRESS.COM

PERFORMANCE APPRAISAL OBJECTIVES

Performance Appraisals are actually a relatively recent development as a formal tool for managing performance, with some observers citing the 1940s as the genesis of the PA.[2] However, there is nothing unusual or new about judging and guiding the work performance of a subordinate. Indeed, these two concepts—judging and guiding—form the two core objectives of the PA: the **evaluative objective** and the **developmental objective** (see Figure 9–1). If a PA program can fulfill its objective of evaluating performance fairly and helpfully and can also fulfill its purpose of guiding and improving the employee's performance, then the PA program is effective. Effective PAs are essential for use in making decisions about pay, promotion, and retention. Effective appraisals can significantly contribute to the satisfaction and motivation of employees—if they are used correctly.[3]

EVALUATIVE OBJECTIVES

One of the primary purposes of PAs is to look at past performance. The most common decisions based on evaluative objectives concern compensation, which includes merit increases, employee bonuses, and other increases in pay. Thus, the term *merit review* may be found in organizations using the PA to determine pay increases.

A PA normally has a two-part effect on future pay. In the short run, it may determine merit increases for the following year; in the long run, it may determine which employees are promoted into higher-paying jobs.

FIGURE 9–1   EVALUATIVE AND DEVELOPMENTAL OBJECTIVES IN PA

OBJECTIVES OF PERFORMANCE APPRAISAL

Evaluative
- Compensation Decisions
- Staffing Decisions
- Evaluate Selection System

Developmental
- Performance Feedback
- Direction for Future Performance
- Identify Training and Development Needs

Staffing decisions are also affected by the PA because managers must make decisions concerning promotions, demotions, transfers, and layoffs. Past PAs which reflect performance help determine which employee is most deserving of a promotion or other job change.

Performance appraisals can also be used to evaluate the recruitment, selection, and placement system. The effectiveness of these functions can be partially measured by comparing employees' PAs with their test scores as job applicants. For example, management may find that applicants who scored about the same on selection tests show a significant difference in performance after one year on the job; thus, the tests may not accurately predict behavior.

DEVELOPMENTAL OBJECTIVES

The second type of objective PAs—developmental objectives—encompasses developing employee skills and motivation for *future* performance.

Performance feedback is a primary developmental need because almost all employees want to know how their supervisors feel about their performances. Motivation to improve performance increases when employees receive feedback that suggests goals, which in turn enhances future career moves.[4]

Developmental performance appraisal is mainly focused on giving employees direction for future performance. Such feedback recognizes strengths and weaknesses in past performances and determines what direction employees should take to improve. Employees want to know specifically how they can improve.

The results of appraisal influence decisions about the training and development (T&D) of employees. Below-average evaluations may signal areas of employee behavior that may be strengthened through on- and away-from-the-job training. Of course, not all performance deficiencies may be overcome through T&D. Supervisors must distinguish performance problems resulting from lack of a critical skill or ability from those caused by low motivation or a poor work ethic.

THE APPRAISAL PROCESS

A variety of appraisal techniques are available to measure employee performance. In creating and implementing an appraisal system, administrators must first determine for what purposes the PAs will be used and then decide which technique will work best. These decisions are just as important as how the appraisal is conducted or the actual content of the appraisal. If employees believe the appraisal was undertaken lightly or haphazardly, they may take the process less seriously than they should. Possible legal ramifications exist whenever management is not consistent in its PA procedures. A loss of morale or employee productivity may also result from poorly administered PAs.

STEPS FOR CREATING AN EFFECTIVE PA

The specific steps followed when creating or changing a PA system can vary. According to *HR Magazine*, the official publication for the Society for Human Resource Management (SHRM), the following 10 steps can help organizations construct an effective PA system.[5]

1 Obtain the active support of top management. Any HR system must be integrated into the firm's overall strategy. Top management must support PA development and implementation and must utilize the PA results in management decisions.

2 Appoint an implementation team. This is a taskforce used to develop and lead in the use of the PA. Using a crossfunctional team—rather than the HR manager—to guide PA development creates the opportunity for involvement that a successful PA will need.

3 Determine all of the purposes the system will be expected to serve. If the main use is to allocate pay raises, then the system will operate differently than if pay-raise allocation is secondary. We believe that the PA should always play a role in pay increases if the pay system is based upon performance. However, if pay increases are based upon seniority, then obviously there is no pay-relevant function to the PA.

4 Design the form. If early versions of the form are made available to employees, the team will receive input in response. There are many sources for developing forms (instruments). Many PA instruments require the team to identify the most important performance dimensions. Often different forms are used for different groups (for example, executive, managerial, nonmanagerial). Ensure that both evaluative and development objectives are addressed.

5 Make sure all administrative issues and executive biases are addressed. If management is committed to an annual appraisal, the team must address this. Is 360-degree feedback important? Do individual appraisals make sense if we are organized into workteams?

6 **Ensure ongoing communication during development.** Allow a generous amount of development time and operate openly so that employees can be aware of the details of the developing PA system.

7 **Train all appraisers.** Raters need a great deal of discrimination, insight, and observational skills. Annual training is often essential to develop these skills.

8 **Orient all employees being appraised.** It is uncomfortable to be evaluated and not know how you will be assessed. All forms have ambiguities and issues associated with them. This is complicated further with 360-feedback or other nonsupervisory involvement in ratings.

9 **Use the results.** Everyone will know the PA system is a joke if it is not important in promotion, pay, training, and discipline decisions. The PA should be the employers' primary tool which relates performance with important HR decisions.

10 **Monitor and revise the plan.** Research the completed forms to look for errors and biases. Hold meetings to discuss the PA after it has been used and seek continuous improvement.

LEGAL CONSIDERATIONS

The possibility of judicial and agency review of PAs continues to expand in the United States. The expansion of discrimination laws, erosion of the employment-at-will doctrine, and an unending appetite for suing in our society all create a climate where PAs have become a critical legal concern. Policymakers and practitioners must be mindful of the possibility of legal review of terminations, promotions, pay decisions, and other HR decisions.

For instance, a black female manager was discharged as part of a general workforce reduction. The employer stated that the reason she was part of the cutback was that she had a tendency to criticize others, which prevented her from achieving management's goals of building morale and encouraging a team spirit. The discharged manager sued, believing that she was a victim of race discrimination. The court held that the employer's stated reason was merely a *pretext* for racial discrimination. Why? The discharged manager had received consistently good performance ratings and two merit raises. Her only negative ratings were part of a set of appraisals that she had never seen. Further, the supervisor of the discharged manager had been pressured by upper management to lower her ratings on the unseen appraisal after they had decided to fire her.[6] Chapter 4

discusses the huge amounts that such a case can cost employers under the Civil Right Act of 1991.

The judgments in EEOC complaints and wrongful-discharge cases often go against the employer because the plaintiff-employee frequently does the following:

- Produce records of consistently favorable PAs and no warning of trouble.
- Show that no formal PAs criticizing performance were received.
- Prove that the employer's PA system is inherently biased against members of a protected class.[7]

Where EEOC's Uniform Guidelines regulate employment (and other) tests, they regulate PAs as well, since PAs are also measurements affecting employment. In general, such measurements must be valid and administered fairly (refer to Chapter 8). According to other agency regulations and court decisions, the validity and fairness requirements have been interpreted to mean that the instrument measuring performance must be linked to specified job requirements, that a good score means good performance, that the rating reliably predicts future performance, and that the appraisal is a valid measure of motivation and intelligence.[8]

Legal Checklist

- **Written appraisals should be conducted regularly for all employees, not limited to lower-level employees.** These written appraisals should never be backdated or altered later. The Americans with Disabilities Act (ADA) requires any request for *reasonable accommodation* to be recorded and a request might surface during a PA interview.

- **Supervisors and other appraisers should be trained thoroughly in proper appraisal procedures.** Emphasize that PAs should be truthful, candid but constructive, and not malicious.

- **Appraisers should apply consistent, explicit, and objective job-related standards when preparing PAs.** Performance, not the individual, should be judged. The ADA requires that appraisals of an employee or applicant be related to the *essential functions* of the job.

- **An audit system should be established to guard against leniency and other rater errors to ensure that the appraisals are unbiased.** For instance, before the PA interview is held with the employee, the PA could be reviewed by another manager. The HR department can review ratings to help identify rater errors such as central tendency, harshness, and leniency.

- **Problem areas should be detailed and documented.** If problems are not specifically identified, the employee will have a hard time knowing exactly what behavior to improve. Documentation of particular problems is crucial.

- **When problems have been identified in assessing substandard performance, specific goals and timetables should be established for improvement.** PAs are most effective when they contain a compliance timetable and secure the employee's commitment to comply.

- **Employees should be given a clear opportunity to respond to negative appraisals.** If the employee with substandard performance gives her or his version of the facts, this may "smoke-out" future legal claims and will help gain the employee's involvement in the PA process. An opportunity to appeal ratings within the organization may also help ensure a perception of justice and provide a real opportunity to respond.

- **The employer should be able to prove that the employee received the PA.** Employees who disagree with their ratings may be reluctant to sign the PA form, assuming that their signature indicates agreement. Allowing them to sign and indicate that they were "present" will still supply the proof of receipt. Receipt can also simply be witnessed by another supervisor.

- **Circulation of appraisals should be restricted to those in management with a need to know.** Unrestricted access to a PA, including negative ratings, may expose the employer to a defamation suit (see *HR in the News: "PAs That Make the Case"*).

- **Check past PAs.** If termination for unsatisfactory performance is being considered, past PAs should be scrutinized to see if the employee was adequately informed of his or her performance deficiencies and if the PAs are consistent with the stated reasons for the employee's dismissal.[9]

APPRAISAL METHODS AND INSTRUMENTS

The methods chosen, and the instruments (or forms) used to implement these methods, are critical in

HR IN THE NEWS

PAs THAT MAKE THE CASE

The following three cases indicate how important following good PA procedure can be in avoiding complaints and lawsuits.

- After working 23 years for Bissell, an employee was fired for uncooperativeness, poor attitude, and lack of leadership. Bissell's policy stated that an employee must be given notice of work deficiencies and a chance to improve before termination. The PA just before discharge did not indicate any problems, though the supervisor admitted to considering termination even at that time. The Michigan court held that Bissell can be sued for "negligent evaluation" in this case.[10]

   WWW.BISSELL.COM

- Dominic complained to his supervisor about age discrimination. Later, the supervisor fired Dominic for unsatisfactory performance. The employer believed his supervisor had given Dominic a negative PA but discovered at trial that the supervisor had lowered Dominic's ratings without Dominic's knowledge after the discrimination complaint. Dominic won a $450,000 verdict.[11]

- Bals was fired by Inland Steel after several unfavorable PAs. Bals filed a defamation suit against Inland, arguing that related information damaged his reputation inside the corporate community and that this was as bad as if it been leaked to people outside Inland. The Indiana Supreme Court held that there was "publication"—necessary for defamation—but Indiana law also allows employers to retain a "qualified privilege" if negative HR information is communicated "in good faith" to people with a "legitimate need" to know.[12]

determining whether the organization manages its performance successfully. The dimensions listed on a PA form often determine which behaviors employees attempt and raters seek and which behaviors are neglected. PA methods and instruments should signal the operational goals and objectives to individuals, groups, and the organization at large.

Traditionally, PA methods were broken down into two categories based on the standards for success chosen. **Comparative methods,** such as ranking or forced distribution, rate the overall performance of one employee directly against that of other employees. **Absolute standards methods,** such as rating scales or management by objectives (MBO), rate the employee against some objective or imaginary goal(s).

Work standards are used primarily to measure the performance of clerical and manufacturing employees whose jobs are production or output oriented. Work standards establish the normal or average production output for employees on the job. Standards are set according to the production per hour or the time spent per unit produced or served. Today, production standards are used as *part* of an appraisal process, especially if the firm pays on a piece-rate basis. Whether rating an individual or a team, quantity of production is only *one* aspect of performance; other aspects (quality, safety, planning, training, maintenance activities, and so on) must be included. Other more modern methods of PA have become more common (see Figure 9–2).

RATING SCALES

Graphic Rating Scale
The **graphic rating scale** rates the employee-ratee on some standard or attribute of work. Traditionally, the focus was on personal traits (for example, friendliness and coopera-

tion), but recently, it has been on work behaviors and outcomes (for example, "does job right the first time" and "greets every customer who enters store"). The rating is often done on some 1–5 Likert-type scale, with 1 representing "very unsatisfactory" and 5 representing "excellent." The rating scale is one of the oldest and most common methods, and has survived the many recent innovations in instruments.

As shown in Figure 9–3, graphic rating scales itemize factors such as attendance and safety (which are factors 2 and 3 under "Behavioral Factors"). The Marley Cooling Tower Company in Mission, Kansas, has the employee (E) and the supervisor (S) both rate the employee using a 1–5 scale on various factors, including factor 3, "Exhibits safe practices in work performance." Marley's PA form also uses the modern approach of self-rating along with supervisor rating on a traditional graphic rating scale form.

Nongraphic Rating Scale
Shown in Figure 9–4 is the **nongraphic rating scale.** A nongraphic scale may be more valid than a graphic scale, because the former contains a brief description of each point on a scale rather than simply low and high points of a scale. The rater can give a more accurate description of the employee's behavior on a particular attribute because a description clarifies each level of the rating scale. On the graphic scale, raters arbitrarily decide what various numbers on the scale represent about an attribute; for example, what is "2 below-average" cooperation?

In general, both graphic and nongraphic rating scales are quick, easy, and less difficult for supervisors to use than many other methods of PA. Also, decision makers find rating scales to be satisfactory for most evaluative purposes because they provide a mathematical evaluation of performance, which computes a useable number and can be used to justify compensation or job changes

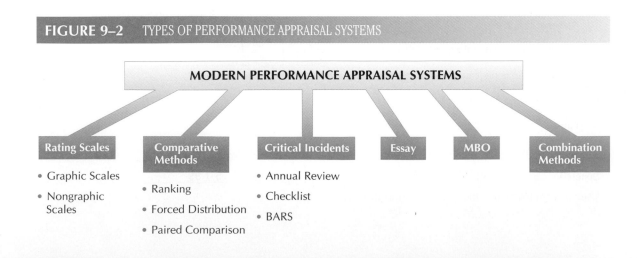

FIGURE 9–2   TYPES OF PERFORMANCE APPRAISAL SYSTEMS

MODERN PERFORMANCE APPRAISAL SYSTEMS

Rating Scales
- Graphic Scales
- Nongraphic Scales

Comparative Methods
- Ranking
- Forced Distribution
- Paired Comparison

Critical Incidents
- Annual Review
- Checklist
- BARS

Essay

MBO

Combination Methods

Job and Behavioral Summary
Factors Important to MARLEY® Mission and Personal Development

Both [E] employee and [S] supervisor shall answer separately, and record together answers on supervisor's form. Openly discuss variation.

Name: _Pat Dugan_   Date: _5-7-99_

Current Job: _Training Specialist II_   Dept.: _HR_

Job Factors

Mark X at level of current belief   1 2 3 4 5 (high)

Factor	E/S	Rating	Comment
1. Aim of process is clearly understood	E	4	
	S	4	
2. Role in process is clearly understood	E	4	
	S	4	
3. Information input to job is good	E	3	
	S	3	
4. Training for job is sufficient	E	2	*Pat has just entered T & D program*
	S	4	
5. Equipment, materials, etc. provided are sufficient	E	1	*Budget limits purchases / need supplies*
	S	2	
6. Management support is sufficient to accomplish goal(s)	E	4	
	S	4	
7. Expectations of position are realistic	E	3	
	S	4	
8. Team participation is encouraged	E	3	
	S	3	
9. Recognition/reward is a positive factor	E	5	
	S	5	
10. Impact of job on overall system is clear	E	5	
	S	5	

Behavioral Factors

Performance level   1 2 3 4 5 (high)

Factor	E/S	Rating	Comment
1. Education/experience	E	5	*Pat's MBA helps*
	S	5	
2. Attendance & punctuality	E	3	*We have discussed goals & timetables*
	S	3	
3. Exhibits safe practices in work performance	E	5	
	S	5	
4. Personal effort and enthusiasm	E	5	*very enthusiastic!*
	S	5	
5. Attitude toward mission/vision	E	4	
	S	5	
6. Interest in understanding and delighting customer	E	5	
	S	5	
7. Promotes teamwork in word & action	E	4	
	S	4	
8. Does job right the first time	E	4	
	S	4	
9. Communication skills	E	5	
	S	5	
10. Personal initiative	E	4	
	S	4	
11. Demonstrates tact and diplomacy	E	4	
	S	5	

Include a copy of this page in my personnel file ☑ yes   ☐ no

I have discussed job factors and behavior with my supervisor:

☑ I agree   ☐ I disagree   ☑ Comments are attached

Employee signature: _Pat Dugan_   Date: _5-7-99_

Supervisor signature: **Mel Fitzpatrick**   Date: **5-7-99**

Used by permission from the Marley Cooling Tower Co.

FIGURE 9–4   AN EXAMPLE OF THE NONGRAPHIC FORM OF RATING SCALES

Name: _____ For period ending: _____

Department: _____ Job title: _____

Instructions: Listed below are a number of traits, abilities, and characteristics that are important for success. Place an "X" mark on each rating scale, over the descriptive phrase which most nearly describes the person being rated.

ACCURACY is the correctness of work duties performed.

Usually accurate; makes only average number of mistakes	Makes frequent errors	Requires absolute minimum of supervision; is almost always accurate	Requires little supervision; is exact and precise most of the time	Careless; makes recurrent errors

ALERTNESS is the ability to grasp instruction, to meet changing conditions, and to solve novel or problem situations.

Requires more than average instructions and explanations	Slow to catch on	Exceptionally keen and alert	Grasps instructions with average ability	Usually quick to understand and learn

CREATIVITY is talent for having new ideas, for finding new and better ways of doing things, and for being imaginative.

Continually seeks new and better ways of doing things; is extremely imaginative	Has average imagination; has reasonable number of new ideas	Frequently suggests new ways of doing things; is very imaginative	Rarely has a new idea; is unimaginative	Occasionally comes up with a new idea

PERSONAL APPEARANCE is the personal impression an individual makes on others. (Consider cleanliness, grooming, neatness, and appropriateness of dress on the job.)

Very untidy; poor taste in dress	Generally neat and clean; satisfactory personal appearance	Unusually well groomed; very neat; excellent taste in dress	Sometimes untidy and careless about personal appearance	Careful about personal appearance; good taste in dress

JOB KNOWLEDGE is the information concerning work duties which an individual should know for a satisfactory job performance.

Lacks knowledge of some phases of work	Has complete mastery of all phases of job	Understands all phases of work	Poorly informed about work duties	Moderately informed; can answer most common questions

QUANTITY OF WORK is the amount of work an individual does in a work day.

Volume of work is satisfactory	Very industrious; does more than is required	Does just enough to get by	Superior work production recorded	Does not meet minimum requirements

STABILITY is the ability to withstand pressure and to remain calm in crisis situations.

Thrives under pressure; really enjoys solving crises	Goes "to pieces" under pressure; is "jumpy" and nervous	Tolerates most pressure; likes crises more than the average person	Has average tolerance for crises; usually remains calm	Occasionally "blows up" under pressure; is easily irritated

OVERALL EVALUATION in comparison with other employees with the same length of service on this job:

Definitely Unsatisfactory	Substandard but making progress	Doing an average job	Definitely above average	Outstanding

Signature of Supervisor	Date	Signature of Employee	Date
Signature of Reviewing Officer	Date	Signature of Personnel Officer	Date

Remarks:

SOURCE: Kentucky Department of Education, Frankfurt, Kentucky. Used by permission.

and to validate selection instruments. For example, if the rating scale contains 20 attributes with a 5-point scale for each attribute, employees can receive 100 points.

Rating scales have several disadvantages. Using the scale, raters can easily make halo or central-tendency errors. Since everyone can quickly be rated very high or average on most items, raters who want to use central tendency or leniency in their appraisals can easily do so. Most rating scales also have the disadvantage of not being related to a specific job.

COMPARATIVE METHODS

Regardless of the effort spent in developing a PA system, appraiser's tend to assign uniform ratings to employees regardless of performance. One study of over 7,000 managerial and professional employees found that 95 percent of the employees were crowded into only two of up to six rating categories.[13] Supervisors often do not (and are not forced to) differentiate between employees despite real differences in performance. Comparative methods can be used to tease out differences between employees by providing direct comparisons.

Ranking   **Ranking** employees from most effective to least effective is a common appraisal method. Ranking is comparative because raters judge employees' performances in relation to each other instead of against an absolute standard, as is the case with rating scales.

Supervisors rank their employees from most effective to least effective in total job performance. This results in as many different rankings as there are departments or areas within the organization, as shown in Figure 9–5.

Some managers merge departmental rankings into a ranking for the total organization. When a total organizational ranking is used, employees receiving the highest rankings may receive the highest merit increases or avoid being "downsized."

The advantage of ranking is that it is fast and easy to complete. A numerical evaluation given to the employees can be directly related to compensation changes or staffing considerations.

There are, however, serious disadvantages. Ranking is seldom developmental because employees do not receive feedback about performance strengths and weaknesses or any future direction. Also, ranking assumes that each department has employees who can be distributed fairly over a range from best to worst. Finally, when ranking is used, there is no common standard of performance by which to compare employees from various departments. Many employers rank employees and use other PA methods so that they can gain the advantages while avoiding the pitfalls of this method.

Forced Distribution   Another comparative method of performance appraisal is called **forced distribution.** Similar to ranking, forced distribution requires that supervisors spread their employee evaluations in a predescribed distribution. As illustrated in Figure 9–6, the supervisor places employees in classifications ranging from poor to excellent. Forced distribution has the same disadvantages as ranking. Often, administrators will use forced distribution to compare employees from different departments. However, this is valid only if each department has an equal number of excellent employees, above-average employees, and so on.

Paired Comparison   Perhaps an improvement on the ranking method, **paired comparison** requires that a chart be made of all possible pairs of employees. One overall chart can be used, or a copy of the chart can be used for different dimensions. In Figure 9–7, we see that the rater is comparing a staff of four employees on two dimensions.

FIGURE 9–5   AN EXAMPLE OF RANKING EMPLOYEES BY DEPARTMENT

SALES	OFFICE	WAREHOUSE	DELIVERY
1. Dugan	1. Godfrey	1. Lionel	1. Cooper
1. Hansbrough	2. Weber	2. Ellis	2. Grover
3. Douglas	3. Hui	3. Aschbacher	3. Crooker
4. Krug	4. Kelley	4. Ferre	4. Baldwin
5. McCalman	5. Delahanty	5. Futtrell	
	6. Fitzpatrick	6. Wagner	
	7. Hadley		

FIGURE 9–6   AN EXAMPLE OF FORCED DISTRIBUTION

POOR 10%	BELOW AVERAGE 20%	AVERAGE 40%	ABOVE AVERAGE 20%	EXCELLENT 10%
Fitzpatrick	Futtrell	Grover	Dugan	Godfrey
Hadley	Crooker	Hansbrough	Lionel	Cooper
	Wagner	Hui	Weber	
	Baldwin	Douglas	Ellis	
		Aschbacher		
		Krug		
		Kelley		
		Ferre		
		Delahanty		
		McCalman		

FIGURE 9–7   AN EXAMPLE OF USING THE PAIRED COMPARISON METHOD

JOB KNOWLEDGE

COMPARED TO	ABBY	BOB	CARLOS	DONNA
Abby		Abby	Carlos	Abby
Bob			Carlos	Donna
Carlos				Carlos
Donna				

Carlos is rated highest on "Job Knowledge" winning in 3 comparisons.

HELPING THE CUSTOMER

COMPARED TO	ABBY	BOB	CARLOS	DONNA
Abby		Abby	Abby	Abby
Bob			Carlos	Donna
Carlos				Carlos
Donna				

Abby is rated highest on "Helping the Customer" winning in 3 comparisons.

Like ranking and forced distribution, paired comparison is quick and fairly easy to use if few employees are being rated. In fact, raters may prefer paired comparison to ranking or forced distribution because they compare only two employees at a time rather than all employees to one another.

The number of comparisons required equals $N(N - 1)/2$. Therefore, for 20 employees, 190 comparisons would be necessary $[(20 \times 19)/2 = 190]$. Thus, this technique is time-consuming with large numbers of employees.

Another disadvantage of paired comparison is that employees are often compared to each other only on overall performance rather than on specific job criteria. The advantage of not forcing the employee evaluations into set distributions makes paired comparison attractive.

CRITICAL INCIDENTS

Several modern PA methods employ the use of **critical incidents** to make the appraisal process more job related. The critical-incident methods of PA use specific examples of job behavior that have been collected from supervisors or employees or both. Normally, several employees and supervisors compile a list of actual job experiences involving extraordinarily good or bad employee performances. Neither normal procedures nor average work performance is included. Outstandingly good or bad job performances separate employees into excellent, average, and poor performers. Thus, the emphasis is on specific actions as critical examples of excellent or poor behavior.

Annual Review File or Calendar

One form of the method is for the supervisor or appraiser to keep an ongoing record of his or her employees' critical incidents contemporaneously during the period of appraisal. If the review period is one year, the supervisor can keep a file or calendar in which the extraordinary examples of subordinates' performance are entered. The supervisor would then make an annual review of this file or calendar before preparing for the PA. Employees who have little or no record during the year are doing their jobs satisfactorily, not performing much above or below job expectations. The advantage of the **annual review file** is that it is usually very job specific. With specific dates and incidents included in the PA, the supervisor is less affected by bias.

The main disadvantage of using an annual review file is the difficulty of keeping an accurate record. With other interests having a much higher priority, maintaining records for employees is often not given adequate time. Another disadvantage of the annual review is that it is very difficult to compare the performances of different employees using only records of critical incidents.

Checklist of Critical Incidents

Critical incidents may also be used in PA by developing a checklist of critical *behaviors* related to employee performance. Such an appraisal form may have 20 or 30 critical items for one specific job. The rater simply checks whether the employee has performed in a superior manner in any one of the incidents. Outstanding employees would receive many checks, indicating that they performed very well during the appraisal period. Average employees would receive few checks because only in a few cases did they perform outstandingly.

The **checklist of critical incidents** often involves giving different weights to different items in the checklist to indicate that some are more important than others. The checklist method of critical incidents is fairly fast and easy to use, and it can produce a mathematical total for employees. It is also evaluative as well as developmental. But the checklist is expensive to develop because checklists for each job must be produced.

Behaviorally Anchored Rating Scales (BARS)

The most common use of critical-incident performance appraisals is in combination with rating scales. Instead of using broad employee attributes, the points on the rating scale are critical incidents. The **behaviorally anchored rating scale (BARS)** is quick and easy to complete. Such scales are evaluative because mathematical totals can be easily related to merit increases and promotion probability. They are also job related and more developmental than typical rating scales because the items being evaluated are specific and are critical to good performance.

The Ohio State Highway Patrol developed a BARS appraisal system in four stages. Stage one involved detailed job analysis. Critical tasks were determined from interviews with troopers and supervisors. Stage two entailed assigning weight to each task according to how critical the task was and how frequently it was required. Descriptions of "excellent," "average," and "poor" performance levels of each task were developed in stage three. The fourth stage included a statistical validation of the appraisal instrument. As an example, the critical task "secure accident scenes" was given the following three levels of evaluation:[14]

1 Uses available equipment and solicits any available assistance to secure scene of accident quickly and efficiently. (Excellent)

2 Generally secures scene adequately before beginning accident investigation. (Average)

3 May fail to secure the scene adequately before beginning accident investigation. (Poor)

BARS systems have been favored by federal agencies and personnel researchers because they are job related. As with the other critical-incident systems, the primary disadvantage of a BARS system is the time and effort involved in adapting critical incidents to a rating-scale format. A BARS system requires a separate rating scale for each job. An older but interesting example of a BARS for the job dimension "organizational skills" for a college professor is shown in Figure 9–8. Try rating one of your professors.

FIGURE 9–8   A BARS FOR COLLEGE PROFESSORS

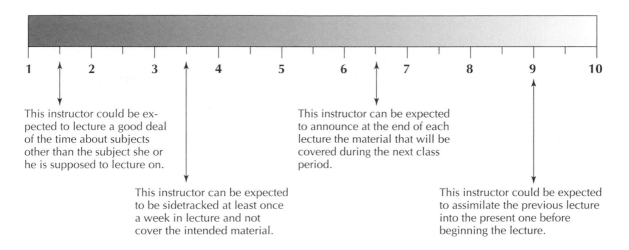

Organizational skills: A good constructional order of material slides smoothly from one topic to another; design of course optimizes interest; students can easily follow organizational strategy; course outline followed.

Makes no use of a course syllabus; lectures on topics randomly with no logical order.	Prepares a course syllabus but only follows it occasionally; presents lectures in no particular order, although does tie them together.	Follows a course syllabus; presents lectures in a logical order; ties each lecture into the previous one.

1   2   3   4   5   6   7   8   9   10

This instructor could be expected to lecture a good deal of the time about subjects other than the subject she or he is supposed to lecture on.

This instructor can be expected to announce at the end of each lecture the material that will be covered during the next class period.

This instructor can be expected to be sidetracked at least once a week in lecture and not cover the intended material.

This instructor could be expected to assimilate the previous lecture into the present one before beginning the lecture.

SOURCE: Reprinted with permission from H. J. Bernardin, "Behavioral Expectation Scales versus Summated Scales: A Fairer Comparison", *Journal of Applied Psychology,* 62 (1977): 422–427.

ESSAY METHOD

The written essay method requires the supervisor or appraiser to write an essay, in narrative style, describing the employee's performance, specifying examples of strengths and weaknesses. Because the **essay method** forces the rater to discuss specific examples of performance, it can also minimize supervisory bias and rater error. It can also be easily added to any form.

The essay method often has a distinct disadvantage: The time the supervisors must spend writing separate essays about each employee can be formidable. Also, essays are not very useful for evaluative purposes; 200 essays describing different employees' performances cannot easily be linked to merit increases and promotion because there is no common standard.

MANAGEMENT BY OBJECTIVES

One of the more widely used appraisal methods is **management by objectives (MBO).** Although individual

approaches may vary somewhat, most MBO programs contain the same essential elements.

Goal Setting   Goal setting lies at the heart of the MBO process. With MBO, the goal-setting process begins at the top with the formulation of long-range objectives and "cascades" through organizational objectives, departmental goals, and finally down to individual goals.

At the individual goal-setting level, goals are mutually set by the employee and his or her manager. The aspect of participation in goal setting is one of MBO's major strengths. There is general agreement that participation in decision making strengthens employee motivation and commitment.

MBO concentrates on setting *measurable* goals as opposed to vague or subjective goals. Characteristics of good MBO goals include (1) a description of specifically what is to be accomplished and how the accomplishment of a goal will be measured, (2) target dates for goal accomplishment, and (3) the amount of resources (for example, time, money) to be used in accomplishing the goals.

For example, an HR manager's goal might be to "create a new employee orientation program by December 31 with an expenditure of no more than 100 staff hours and at a cost in materials and supplies of no more than $5,000." In this case, the manager knows specifically what his or her expectations are. Compare that goal to being told by the boss to "put together a new employee-orientation program ASAP and spend as little money as possible."

Action Planning

Goals specify *what* is to be achieved; action plans specify *how* goals are to be achieved. Action plans provide direction as well as a mechanism (often called *milestones*) for measuring accomplishment toward goals.

Self-Control

A primary assumption of MBO is that employees will accomplish their goals if given management and organizational support. Inherent in this assumption is that those who are being appraised with MBO have a fairly high level of motivation, commitment, and achievement drive.

Periodic Review

Most MBO systems include a mechanism for periodically measuring progress toward goals. A review process is particularly important to discuss problems that an employee may be experiencing. Typical MBO review periods are quarterly or monthly.

The advantages of the MBO method are many. Both the supervisor and the employee participate in the appraisal process. The focus of the appraisal process is on specific goals and not on broad personality traits such as "dependability" or "cooperation." What is unique about the MBO procedure is that goals and objectives are determined before the appraisal period begins.[15] Since the MBO process gives employees direction before the appraisal period begins, it is developmental. A disadvantage of the MBO procedure is that much time and effort must be spent by both the supervisor and the subordinate in the MBO process.

COMBINATION METHODS

It has become a common practice to combine two or even three PA methods into an employer's overall PA program. For example, on the form used at Marley (Figure 9–3), there is room to write essay-style comments (they also supply an additional page, not shown in the figure) along with the graphic rating scales. The essay and MBO approaches can be added to a rating-scales ap-

proach for a fuller, perhaps more effective, PA system. Team and individual ratings also can be combined to provide a more in-depth appraisal.

APPRAISAL SCHEDULE

How often to formally appraise employee performance is an important and difficult question. Probably the most common answer fixes a specific interval such as one year or six months between formal appraisals. The schedule provides consistency in the evaluation process because all employees are evaluated for the same period of time. A variable-interval process can be used when a goal-setting approach establishes specific time periods to achieve certain goals. Thus, at the end of each time period, an appraisal determines the achievement level for a particular goal. When goal achievement does not have to be tied to a specific time period, it may be linked with the company's standard appraisal period in order to maintain appraisal consistency.

PROBLEMS WITH PA METHODS AND INSTRUMENTS

COMMON RATER ERRORS

One set of problems with PAs is the errors raters make when filling out PA forms. Appraisers should not only become aware of the most common **rater errors,** but should also learn how to avoid committing them. Training and information can minimize many errors. Raters should not only note the following rater errors, but should be aware that employees use *political tactics* to create such errors as the halo effect.

Supervisory Bias

The most common error that exists in any appraisal method is conscious or unconscious **supervisory bias.** Such biases are not related to job performance and may stem from personal characteristics such as age, sex, disability, or race or from organization-related characteristics such as seniority, membership on an organization's athletic team, or friendship with top administrators. For example, a supervisor may give an undeserved high rating to a subordinate with whom she or he plays golf.

Halo Effect

When a rater lets one particular and accurately rated aspect of an employee's performance influence the evaluation of other aspects of performance, a **halo effect** has occurred. For example, the manager who knows that a particular employee always arrives at work early and may let the halo caused by that employee's punctuality influence the appraisal of other areas such as quality of work or job knowledge. Thus, even though the employee may be only mediocre in terms of quality of performance, the employee receives all high ratings because he or she is punctual.

A negative halo, or "devil's horns" effect, is part of this same effect. If an accountant performs poorly only when working directly with plant managers on annual budget projects, the supervisor may allow this one accurately rated negative behavior to cloud the objectivity on ratings given on the accountant's other behaviors.

The halo problem can be minimized with training. Supervisors should be trained to recognize that all jobs—even routine, low-level jobs—require the application of many different skills and behaviors. Training should also focus on the fact that it is not unusual for employees to perform well in some areas and less effectively in others.

Central Tendency
When raters evaluate everyone as average, the result is **central tendency.** They may find it difficult and unpleasant to evaluate some employees higher or lower than others, even though performances may reflect a real difference. The problem of central tendency also occurs when supervisors cannot evaluate employee performance objectively because of a lack of familiarity with the work, lack of supervisory ability, or fear that they will be reprimanded if they evaluate individuals too highly or too strictly.

Leniency
Inexperienced or poor supervisors may decide that the easiest way to appraise performance is simply to give everyone a high evaluation, sometimes called the "Lake Wobegone" ("Where everyone is above average"—Garrison Keillor) effect. **Leniency** assumes that employees will not complain if they all receive high appraisals. However, the best performers in the department will complain about such ratings because those who are working hard receive no more credit than fellow employees who are not.

Salary considerations may also often lead managers to inflate appraisals to justify pay raises for their employees. Lack of accurate appraisal can lead to turnover among the best employees, who go to organizations that can appraise their performance accurately and give them the recognition and pay they deserve.

Strictness
Sometimes, supervisors consistently give low ratings even though some employees may have achieved an average or above-average performance level. **Strictness** or harshness is the opposite of leniency.

Some supervisors are guilty of strictness in ratings because they feel that none of the subordinates is living up to standards of excellence. Research also indicates that people believe that they will appear smarter to their bosses if they are more critical.[16] Unreasonable performance expectations that employees find impossible to achieve, and a negativity bias, can be demoralizing.

Recency
When organizations use annual or semi-annual PAs, there may be a tendency for supervisors to remember more about what their employees have done just before the appraisal than in prior months. It is human nature to remember recent events more clearly than events in the distant past.

To avoid the **recency** error, raters could conduct frequent appraisals—for instance, monthly or quarterly—and/or keep a log of critical incidents or extraordinary examples of the employee's behaviors and outcomes. These notes could be kept in a special file or simply on a calendar.

Overall Ratings
Many appraisal forms require the supervisor to provide an **overall rating** of an employee's performance in addition to evaluations of specific performance areas. Often compensation decisions are determined by the employee's overall rating. The supervisor may be required to rate the employee overall as "outstanding," "above average," "average," "substandard but making progress," or "unsatisfactory." It is difficult for a rater to combine all the separate performance dimensions into one accurate overall rating. Behavioral research indicates that raters are not consistent in this process. Some raters may also weigh all areas as equal, whereas others may only consider two to three items important in determining an overall rating.

PROBLEMS WITH PA FORMS

We have been discussing errors that raters make when filling out PA forms. There are also three problems—validity, reliability, and practicality—that are best illustrated by thinking about the forms themselves. Since PAs are increasingly likely to be used as evidence in an employee complaint (see *HR in the News:* "The Law, PAs, and E-mail Discussion Groups"), and since organizations can't afford to administer useless PAs, we must examine our forms carefully.

Validity asks the question, "Does the PA form do what it claims?" Does it accurately measure the employee's performance? When a form includes items that are not important aspects of performance, or don't apply at all, the form has a validity problem

HR IN THE NEWS

THE LAW, PAs, AND E-MAIL DISCUSSION GROUPS

HR professionals, academics, and consultants exchange opinions, problems, and updates at a furious pace on the HRNet, a Cornell University listserv, associated with the Academy of Management. On January 12, 1999, the following discussion was part of a 45 e-mail-discussion on various topics.

Subject: Subpoenas for PA Documents

It is about five years since I was involved in industrial tribunals in the UK. These deal with claims of unfair dismissal as well as other matters. When someone is dismissed and feels it was unfair, the tribunals are interested in how employers make decisions to dismiss. What systems are in place to assess performance, what records are kept, what discussions take place, what remedial action is taken to try to improve performance before dismissal is considered. So whether there is a formal system or not the tribunal will expect evidence to support the case. Often tribunals will comment on the lack of objective written assessments, therefore wise employers will ensure that some kind of documentation is available.

Some would say this is only fair.

—Alistair McEwen, Training for Profit,
Edinburgh, Scotland

I am involved in two types of cases where PA documentation is requested.

In our representation of companies in front of the NLRB, PAs are routinely asked for. Usually there is an unfair labor practice charge that has been filed against the company for a disciplinary action that has been taken. The NLRB will usually ask to see the last two years [of] PAs for this employee. Worse yet, they will ask to see the PAs of the rest of the employees.

In most cases, you have to provide the information—although it is not automatic. The fact that PAs are often not written properly gives the NLRB ammunition. However, it's only one piece of the argument. If there is other strong documentation that shows that the employee who was disciplined was afforded internal due process (warnings), and that other employees have been treated similarly, then the PA can be overcome.

The other type of case involves human rights and Employment Security Commissions. These are discriminatory cases where the complainant alleges discrimination on some illegal basis. PAs are routinely made part of the proceeding. These Commissions have the right to this information so it is usually not a good idea to make them issue a subpoena.

—Fred B. Grubb, SPHR, managing director
TWG Consulting Group

If a company doesn't have a PA system, the data can't be requested by the NLRB or HRC/EEC. Is the company in a stronger position to defend itself if there is no data to request? Of if there is data, and it supports the company's position?

—Jack Zigon, president,
Zigon Performance Group, Wallingford, PA

. . . . it is OK from a legal perspective not to have any formal documented PAs. You do, however, have to document negative personnel actions that are taken and provide employees with some measure of due process. If absolutely no decisions are documented then all the employee has to do is make the prima facie case and you're sunk.

Good question. I would have to say that there is always "data." The question is the form it is in.

Aside: Wrongful termination and discrimination cases are very difficult to prove. The vast majority of these cases are won by the employer. We hear about the high-profile cases on TV. Those are really quite rare. I see many firms settling when they don't have to, usually because of poor advice.

—Fred B. Grubb, SPHR managing director
TWG Consulting Group

—Edited for reasons of space. Permission granted by Alistair McEwen, Fred Grubb, and Jack Zigon.

called **contamination.** Rating the president of the United States on "Personal Safety" would probably contaminate the validity of the PA used for presidents. Conversely, omitting an important aspect of performance from a PA is a validity problem called **deficiency.** If a rating form for the U.S. president did not include the variable "Skill in International Affairs," most would consider it deficient and lacking in validity. The costs of using a PA system which lacks validity can be great.

Reliability refers to the consistency of the ratings. The worse the PA form is, the more likely it is that two different raters would rate the employee differently (interrater reliability). Further, consistency over time is important. Rating one construction worker in the summer—the busy season—and another in winter when there is little work would likely yield inconsistent ratings (test–retest reliability).

Practicality involves the usability of the form. There are PA forms which contain more than twenty pages and therefore simply don't get used. We can conquer problems of validity and reliability; but if the form becomes impractical, too time consuming, or too controversial, then it is of little value to an organization. Forms need to be free of major validity problems, reliable as possible, and yet practical.

WHO SHOULD DO THE RATING?

Performance management systems are in a state of change. An estimated 90 percent of Fortune 1000 firms use some form of multisource assessment rather than the traditional "manager as only rater" approach.[17] The popular term **360-degree feedback** refers to the fact that the employee (often a manager) may be rated by a complete circle of five "S observers"—supervisors, same job peers, served (customers and clients), self, and subordinates. (see *HR in the News:* "360-feedback—The Second Wave"). We begin by discussing each of these five S's and end by examining team appraisal raters.

SUPERVISORS

The person in the best position to observe the employee's behavior and determine whether the employee has reached specified goals and objectives is the most appropriate rater. Indeed, EEOC has preferred the appraiser to directly observe the employee being rated.

Traditionally, this has been the supervisor, and in many cases this continues to be the best choice.

The performance appraisal process is a major *management* tool. The performance rating is the basis upon which numerous career decisions are made. Like an airplane pilot, the supervisor is the individual who "flies" the traditional PA process. Supervisor error in the PA process, like pilot error, can have disastrous consequences. Employees, therefore, judge supervisors on their "flying" or rating skills.[18]

SAME JOB PEERS

In some situations, if an employee is working very closely with other employees in a functional workgroup environment, employees in the same job may be in the best position to evaluate a co-worker's performance. Peers can, in some situations, provide information that the organization could not get from the employee's supervisor due to a lack of direct contact between the supervisor and employee. These subordinates, however, may not give objective, honest appraisals because of possible retaliation. Further, some research has indicated that factors such as race may have more of a biasing effect when co-workers rate a employee than when a supervisor does the rating.[19]

The technique of allowing a panel of peers to review the behavior of employees, or to review the appraisal itself, may have started at General Electric in the 1980s. GE's **peer review** procedure gives employees the right to have a grievance heard by a panel of three fellow workers and two managers. The panel's decision is final and binding, all proceedings are confidential, and panelists must be trained and be selected randomly from a group of volunteers.[20] This pushing of decision making further down the organizational ladder also may help keep employers out of court by giving employees a *voice* in the workplace. Companies like Public Service Company of New Mexico not only allow the outcomes of PAs (like terminations and demotions) to be challenged, but the PAs themselves can be appealed to peer panels.[21]

THE SERVED

An increasing number of jobs are now considered service jobs, so evaluations by customers and clients are becoming more valuable as part of the multiple-rater PA process. We are all familiar with customer comment cards located everywhere from banks to restaurants to electronics stores. Specialized customer questionnaires, telephone follow-up surveys, and other techniques are used in addition to comment cards to try to get the customer's evaluation of the employee's performance. However, it would be difficult or impossible for customers and clients to give a total PA because they generally view only part of the employee's performance.

The reactions of customers is being emphasized even in nonservice jobs, such as those in manufacturing. TQM and similar programs, make quality the responsibility of all employees, not just of quality inspectors. The end user of each department's output can be thought of as an internal customer. When PQ Corporation, a Pennsylvania chemical manufacturer, was converting to a performance-based pay system to fit with its new TQM program, it also adjusted its PA system. Evaluations from each employee's internal customers were added to those from supervisors.[22]

SELF

A growing number of employers are including **self-ratings** in the PA process—ratings that employees give to themselves. The appraisal instrument used by Marley (Figure 9–3) formally records the employee's self-ratings (E) as well as the ratings given by the supervisor (S) on each factor. According to Marley's PA packet, the rating scales shown are *not to rate or judge the person but to encourage employee development, build genuine teamwork, and to connect job performance with company goals.*[23]

Research suggests that supervisors may "cave in" to employee self-ratings. Supervisors who learned that certain employees' self-ratings were higher than their own changed their initial ratings. Supervisors generally changed the ratings in a positive direction, gave these employees larger raises, and were less willing to sit down and discuss the appraisal with these high self-raters.[24]

A recent meta-analysis has found that employee PA participation is strongly related to satisfaction. Further, "value-expressive" participation (simply having one's "voice" heard) was even more important than "instrumental" participation (trying to influence the end result).[25]

SUBORDINATES

While traditional appraisals have the supervisor rate the employees, in **reverse appraisals,** or upward evaluations, the employees rate the supervisor. As a college student you have probably rated your instructors, and they have graded you.

Many employers have made reverse appraisals part of their appraisal process. A manager at Seventh Generation, a Vermont retailer of consumer products, likes the subordinate appraisal process. She said, "One of

the things for me is, people tell me that they feel I'm too busy to approach, so it's helped me to take a look at my style. . . . It also tells you to spend more time asking people 'how's it going?'"[26]

Use of reverse rating must be approached with care. "If all you're getting is 'This guy's a schmuck,' that's not going to do anything," explained Frank Sadowski, HR and management consultant in Vermont.[27] He states that evaluations must identify particular strengths and weaknesses, rather than consist of vague comments, to be helpful. He also believes that anonymity is necessary unless there is a high level of trust at the workplace. Finally, fear of retaliation must be eliminated for this employee voice mechanism to be effective.

TEAM PORTFOLIO APPRAISALS

Closely related to peer review is the multiple-rater approach of having a team appraise the performance of individual team members. U.S. employers are not completely following through with the team concept. In a survey of 500 organizations, with some 4,500 teams operating, only a small percent consider team issues in their PAs.[28]

At Digital Equipment Corporation, in Colorado, using work groups has led to a more participatory PA. Here is a slight modification of their system:

1 The employee to be rated is contacted about thirty days before the PA is due. At this time, the ratee chooses a PA chair, usually an advocate of her or his work.

2 The PA chair selects the members of the PA committee, which is composed of the PA chair, the employee-ratee, the management consultant, and two other coworkers in the group chosen at random.

3 The ratee sends mail to the team members outlining his or her accomplishments and training during the past year.–Goes into the portfolio.

4 Team members provide input to the PA chair within the next two weeks, a copy of which is forwarded to the ratee.—Goes into the portfolio.

5 The ratee writes her or his own PA portfolio from the input received from the team and from the self-rating. This portfolio is sent to the committee for review.

6 The committee reviews the portfolio for one week and then meets with the ratee. If the PA needs further

360-DEGREE FEEDBACK—
THE SECOND WAVE

While enthusiasm for the multiple-rater approach continues, firms who were early adopters of the 360-degree approach are learning and fine-tuning their systems. Two of the central concerns are (a) *who gets access to the input* from peers, subordinates, customers, and so on and (b) *for what purposes can the feedback be used?*

The first step at most early 360-degree companies was to only allow the ratees (for instance, managers) to see comments from others. Now, a number of companies, such as NORTEL and Texaco have decided to allow ratee managers to share with their supervisors issues which were suggested in the feedback from others.[29] Universities routinely force faculty to present feedback from others (like students and peers) to their supervisors. Therefore, some variations have evolved on who gets access.

However, UPS began by sharing feedback from others with the ratee's supervisor but now sees that as a mistake. Managers realized that individuals completing evaluations were influenced by the feedback results, and thus the process was not clearly developmental. There seems to be a clearer trend on this second "purpose" issue.

There are strong opinions that if you do not limit the use of multiple-rater feedback to the developmental purposes raters will change (usually raise) ratings if they think pay is involved, game playing may be increased so that political goals of a manager may become more important than organizational goals, and some groups of employees may consider peer or reverse ratings taboo and boycott participating. However, NORTEL allows managers the chance to use the ratings of others to provide evidence of development in the employee's weaker areas—serving an evaluation purpose.[30]

revision, another meeting is scheduled. If not, a final appraisal is determined based upon the portfolio, and the committee jointly sets the goals for the next year.

7 Finally, the PA chair writes a summary of the meeting and attaches the rating and any promotion. A completion document is printed and signed by the entire PA committee. This is forwarded to the personnel department.[31]

While all team appraisal approaches do not have to be as elaborate as this one, team reviews should be considered as a possible improvement at many workplaces.

MONITORING EMPLOYEES ON THE JOB

Look in on Sue's computer screen . . . in fact, Sue doesn't even know you're there! Hot key again and off you go on your rounds of the company. Viewing one screen after another, helping some, watching others. All from the comfort of your chair.

The above excerpt from an ad by a computer networking software company exemplifies one way today's information technology can be used to monitor employees. With the advent of this and similar technological advances, many people have raised concerns about balancing perceived employee privacy rights with the rights of employers to manage their organizations.[32]

Sixty-three percent of employers record employee voice mail, electronically monitor phone calls, review computer files, or videotape workers according to an American Management Association survey in 1997. Further, up to 23 percent of those employers fail to tell their employees about the monitoring. The most common forms of monitoring are: tallying the phone numbers called and duration of calls (37 percent); videotaping of employees' work (16 percent); reviewing e-mail (15 percent); and reviewing and storing files (14 percent). Bankers and brokers are the professions which are most highly monitored.[33]

Electronic monitoring, the collection and analysis of individual or group behavior at work using electronic devices, differs from earlier monitoring in two ways: (1) Electronic monitoring allows the employer to monitor in detail many employees simultaneously; and (2) while employees usually knew when the boss was there, electronic monitoring is "there" all the time[34]— and sometimes in very unexpected places.

Many employees object to the increased use of the performance management technology of monitoring. A few years ago, nurses at Silver Springs Holy Cross Hospital were "channel surfing" at lunch when they found their dressing room "live" on Channel 16. The hospital explained that the camera was there because of suspicious activity, but soon removed it.[35]

We also know where you are. Employers are using an "active badge" developed by Olivetti, the Italian computer company. Employees who wear the credit card–sized badge can be located by infrared technology wherever they happen to be in the building.

The general rule is that the *government* needs a warrant to search your house and desk at home, but in the case of "searching" at the workplace (1) your employer is *not* the government (in the private sector), and (2) it is not your desk (or locker, file, computer, telephone, and so on)—it is the employer's.

Further, there are solid business-related reasons to monitor. Employers are attracted to monitoring since technology makes such performance measurement possible and inexpensive. Elan Financial Services, a division of First Wisconsin National Bank, Milwaukee, uses keystroke monitoring as part of its PA system.[36] Objective measures and other proofs gathered through monitoring may supply evidence for the employer to use in defending against the increasing number of wrongful discharge suits.

Legislation to limit employee surveillance has been repeatedly introduced, and clearly this topic will be debated in the future. Meanwhile, video, computer, and telephone surveillance are likely to spread because such monitoring is currently legal, technology is improving, costs are dropping, and demand for such objective performance measurement is growing.

EFFECTIVE PA SYSTEMS

Organizations prefer quantitative PA approaches, and the consistency of using the same rating scales over time for all employees offers a sense of equity and predictability. However, the TQM-type programs have started a shift in philosophy regarding who should be evaluated. TQM programs may allow *individual assessment* of employees, but they are much more interested in a *systems* (or organizational) *assessment.* Effectively meshing this refocus into the PA systems of the future

will be a challenge. HR professionals want PA systems to be designed to (1) help determine merit pay increases and bonuses, (2) comply with the various employment laws, and (3) be easy to administer.[37]

DESIGN INPUT

HR Department Input
In creating or modifying a PA system, employment involvement has now become the standard approach. The old approach required the personnel department to write the PA instrument or to use an appropriate one from an HR book or periodical. Employees who would be rated had little or no input into its selection or implementation. HR departments continue to be involved in the PA system, but they no longer dominate the entire process.

Team Approaches
Technical Services Company, a midwestern professional services firm with 5,000 employees worldwide, approached a performance management system redesign by using employee involvement. TSC significantly improved the management and outcomes of employee performance, resulting in an improvement in the performance of the organization.[38] TSC started with an in-depth assessment followed by a redesign of the performance management system, with employee teams working on each step.

One of the many changes at TSC was a change from rating (or guessing) the employee's traits to assessing work outcomes. For example, instead of rating a manager on a 1–5 scale on a trait like "leadership," the rater(s) would now respond to an outcome-based statement like this:[39]

> *Directing:* Provides clear and timely instructions on specific assignments and responsibilities; is accessible to staff and allows ample time to answer questions; provides necessary guidance on other resources; reviews work on a timely basis; provides regular performance feedback to the project team.
>
> Evaluation: _____
>
> _____

The following are suggested steps to involve employees in a PA design or redesign project.[40]

Step 1. Group Formation
A cross-functional team should be assembled. The group size might range from 12 to 25 employees. The charge to this team from management should be clear. For instance, what are the required outputs and deadlines during implementation?

Step 2. Objectives and Concerns

Team members should discuss their own goals and the problems they would like the new PA system to overcome. Employee surveys, customer inputs, and inputs from other sources should be considered at this step. The team should develop general sections of the PA form that conform to the objectives members have identified. These sections will likely address employee feedback, employee development, work goals, and others.

Step 3. Dimensions of Performance

The team should identify the dimensions of performance that need to be evaluated. Brainstorm, then trim the list by requiring that each dimension of performance be directly observable, behavioral, and job related. Working in subgroups, members should then write definitions of each of the final dimensions of performance. These dimensions and definitions will appear on the final PA instrument.

Step 4. Policies and Procedures

Finally, the team should prepare guidelines for implementing the new PA system that support the objectives established in Step 2. The team must decide such issues as PA schedule, access, formalization and justice (appeals). Meetings and training sessions must be discussed. Review and evaluation of the new PA system should also be addressed.

TQM or Systems Approach

W. Edwards Deming, the "father" of TQM, listed PAs as one of the "seven deadly diseases" of U.S. management practices. Deming argued that PAs should be completely abandoned. TQM advocates contend that the PA is actually a harmful device because it misdirects managerial attention.[41] Their argument is that PA systems are attempts by management to place blame for poor organizational performance on lower-level employees.

TQM is founded on the philosophy that quality products are a function of the *system* in which they are produced. System variables can include anything that influences the final product or service. Availability of raw materials and supplies, the leadership style of supervisors, and the efficiency of the manufacturing line are all system variables. TQM should promote a **systems assessment** and should minimize the individual differences between employees that are the focus of traditional PAs.[42]

Many modern organizations are trying to straddle the TQM versus traditional PA argument. While companies have shifted to the continuous improvement and total quality responsibility tenets of TQM, they have sabotaged the success of their TQM programs by continuing their anti-TQM appraisal programs, according to TQM purists.

One HR vice president described this situation. "We didn't figure this one out until it was time to do the reviews [PAs]. Julie walked out and put a stack of [PAs] on my desk—and I had no supervisors to give them to."[43] After committing to a TQM-team concept, the employer had neglected to reexamine the appraisal system, which apparently had a life of its own. This company, like many modern firms, was faced with the question of who or what to rate. Should employers appraise the entire system or each team within the system? Should they continue to appraise individuals or should they use some combination?

We suggest that since TQM and 360-degree programs are both part of the Human Relations (or humanist) philosophy movement discussed in Chapter 1, they should work smoothly together. This means that:

1. Raters should be trained in person *and* system performance factors.

2. Ratings should be collected from multiple raters.

3. PA interviews should focus on potential performance barriers (system *and* person).

4. Differentiation between employees should be minimized.

5. PA measures should be tailored to the specific organization.[44]

TRAINING APPRAISERS

Modern Approaches There is disagreement about whether the most effective rating flows from the rater's trained skill or from natural ability.[45] However, there is general agreement that training will improve the appraiser's ratings. Every rater needs information about the PA system, forms, legal issues, ethics, and common errors. Practice exercises, videotapes, cases, and role playing are common PA training methods. We believe that the common rater errors can be drastically reduced through the analysis of the completed forms followed by acknowledgment of such errors as central tendency among the raters.

Impression Management A topic often overlooked in PA training sessions is the strategy used by employee-ratees to get favorable ratings. How often does a boss hold a PA meeting in which she details major performance problems she has observed and then the subordinate says, "You are right, I AM tardy, sloppy, petty, and unmotivated, and I intend to continue this way . . ."? While such a response may be honest, we as individuals want to disguise our shortcomings and dramatize our strengths—and get a PA rating higher than our actual performance warrants.

When employees are managing and disguising the impressions they make, they are engaged in **impression management.** If raters will identify the shrewd political tools employees use to bias PA in their favor, raters can protect themselves from making invalid ratings. The two general strategies employees use are demotion-preventative and promotion-enhancing strategies.[46]

Demotion-preventative strategies seek to minimize responsibility for some negative event. They include (1) giving accounts or excuses ("I couldn't finish, I was sick"), (2) apologies, and (3) dissociation ("I was the only person on the team who saw the problem coming."). **Promotion-enhancing strategies** seek to gain credit or enhance the employee's viability. They include (1) entitlements ("Perhaps you remember my last suggestion? It's already saved us money!"), (2) enhancements ("Not only is my suggestion saving money, but morale has improved as well."), (3) obstacle disclosure ("I had to overcome reluctant co-workers and red tape to succeed."), and (4) association ("When I was talking with the marketing vice president about this . . .").[47]

FORMAL AND INFORMAL METHODS

Many supervisors think about the appraisal process only annually—whenever the HR department notifies them that an employee's anniversary date is approaching and the PA must be completed. Feeling greatly relieved on completing the mandatory appraisal, some supervisors do not tackle the often painful subject of performance until it is time to complete another PA form. This mechanical approach to appraisal may help with pay-increase decisions, but it neglects the fact that performance feedback for developmental purposes is a continuous responsibility. Regular informal appraisal sessions let employees know how they are doing and how they can improve their performances. Good work should not go unnoticed, and frequent supervisory recognition is an important technique for sustaining high levels of employee motivation.

APPRAISAL SYSTEM EVALUATION

An organization's PA program is generally created and implemented to meet both evaluative and developmental objectives. Many organizations fail to assess periodically whether those objectives are being achieved. Often, appraisal programs are set in motion and left to function—sometimes dismally for years—without a thorough examination of their effectiveness. Ill-conceived and poorly implemented appraisal programs may contribute to negative feelings between employees and management, perceptions of unfairness, hindered career development, and discriminatory (and illegal) employment practices. The periodic evaluation of the organization's PA program is an indicator of effective management.

How can an appraisal system be evaluated? One company with approximately 20,000 employees followed these procedures:

- ● *Interviews.* Managers from various departments were interviewed. Discussions focused on strengths and weaknesses of the present system and on recommendations for improving the system.

- ● *Analysis of employees' records.* A random sample of almost 200 PA forms was selected to uncover possible discrimination. The forms were also examined to spot rater errors such as central tendency, leniency, and the halo effect.

- ● *Analysis of the relationship between the employees and their ratings.* Employee ratings were correlated with certain personal and work factors (such as age, tenure, and race). Employees were also asked whether appraisal results were discussed with them.

- ● *Analysis of PA systems in comparable settings.* The organization's appraisal was compared to the systems used by 39 similar organizations.[48]

THE APPRAISAL INTERVIEW

One of the final—and most important—steps of the PA process is discussing the appraisal with the employee. Performance-related feedback has been described as one of the most important methods for enhancing employee development and improving individual performance.[49] Most PA systems require that these interviews take place to provide performance feedback for employees. Thus, employees learn where they stand in the eyes of the organization and are counseled about how performance may be improved.

Both parties generally perceive the appraisal interview as a stressful event. Even well-constructed, job-related appraisal forms can only reduce what is inherently a stressful process. Important to the success of the interview—that it affect the employee's future behavior—is the supervisor's behavior during the interview.

There are three types of information that supervisor-raters generally try to relay in PA interviews: (1) performance improvement feedback, (2) corporate goal feedback, and (3) salary information. Practitioners and researchers argue about whether the "split roles" approach (separating discussions of performance feedback and salary) is helpful or harmful. Some recent research indicates that including salary discussions *helps* the PA interview since it strengthens the motivational utility of performance and enhances employee satisfaction with the interview.[50]

PQ Corporation refers to these interviews as *performance improvement discussions (PIDs)*. These PIDs become central to their TQM approach. Breaking with tradition, during the PID the supervisor acts as a coach and counselor, not as a judge or evaluator.[51]

PROBLEMS WITH THE APPRAISAL INTERVIEW

The appraisal interview is a troublesome and difficult obligation for many managers. Some managers devise ways to avoid or minimize the interview even though it may be required.

A recent study found that supervisors avoid performing formal PAs for a complex set of reasons. The study identified five *situational* variables that contributed to supervisors' failure to rate subordinates: if the subordinate had worked for the current supervisor for only a short time; if the subordinate had little job experience; if there was little trust between the supervisor and the subordinate; if the supervisor does not initiate a lot of structure for the subordinate; and/or if the subordinate had little confidence in the appraisal system or the supervisor.[52] There are at least four *psychological* variables that are also important to address.

Playing God
In a classic article, behavioral scientist Douglas McGregor pointed out that many managers who view the appraisal as playing God are uncomfortable in simultaneously playing helper and judge. According to McGregor:[53]

> The modern emphasis upon the manager as a leader who strives to help his subordinates achieve both their own and the company's objectives is hardly consistent with the judicial role demanded by most appraisal plans. If the

manager must put on his judicial hat occasionally, he does it reluctantly and with understandable qualms.

The solution to this fear may be found in the following suggestion: "Make the manager and employee equals in the appraisal meeting, to eliminate the parent/child relationship. If we don't want employees to act like children, we shouldn't act like parents."[54]

Inability to Give Criticism
Many supervisors have difficulty giving criticism constructively, and many employees have difficulty accepting criticism even though it may be given with sensitivity and diplomacy. One important study showed that defensiveness and poor performance can result from criticism given during the appraisal interview. Further, about half of all employees become defensive when criticized, and a majority of employees feel they performed more favorably than their supervisors' assessments indicate.[55]

Personality Biases
Some supervisors assume the role of amateur psychologist and attempt to bring about personality changes in the ratee that may improve job performance. But such an approach is unwise, according to McGregor. In citing the advantages of the objective-oriented appraisal process, whereby the supervisor and subordinate set performance targets, McGregor states:[56]

> Consider a subordinate who is hostile, short-tempered, uncooperative, insecure. Rather than facing the troublesome prospect of forcing his own psychological diagnosis on the subordinate, the superior can, for example, help the individual plan ways of getting "feedback" concerning the impact on his/her associates and subordinates as a basis for self-appraisal and self-improvement.

Inability to Give Effective Feedback
For the interview to be a truly developmental process, the employee must receive some specific feedback on areas in need of improvement. Too often, supervisors cloak criticism in vague, subjective terms such as:

- "Your absenteeism rate is too high."
- "You need to dress a little more conservatively."
- "You need to change your attitude."

Comments such as these provide little basis for positive behavior change. Supervisors are responsible for making their expectations clear to employees. For example, do not say, "Your absenteeism rate is too high." It is more constructive to state, "You have accumulated six unexcused absences in the past three months and we expect no more than one unexcused absence per month. Can you suggest ways you may be able to achieve this standard in the future?"

INTERVIEW FORMAT

The various problems associated with interviews may be minimized by following a planned, standardized approach. These five steps should be generally covered:

1 *Prepare for the interview.* Preparation is important in a successful appraisal interview. During preparation, the supervisor should gather and review all relevant performance records. The supervisor will want to make note of the specific items to discuss. Finally, preparation includes setting a date for the appraisal interview that gives the employee lead time to prepare for the interview and develop a list of items to discuss.

2 *State the purpose of the interview.* The employee should be told if the interview will cover compensation and staffing decisions (merit increase, promotion, transfer, and so on), employee development, or both. Some managers avoid mixing compensation and staffing decisions with employee development issues in the same appraisal interview.

3 *Indicate specific areas of good performance and areas that need improvement.* How do you break the bad news or criticism to the employee? Mitchell Marks, senior director of Delta Consulting Group suggests the "sandwich" approach. You begin the discussion with the positive parts, then say, "Now, here's the bad news . . ." You finally end your part in the positive. It is important that the bad news in this sandwich be "meaty" and full of specific performance related facts. "You can't get wimpy about it."[57]

4 *Invite participation.* In a survey of companies, only 38 percent of employees said that their managers do a good job of seeking their opinions and suggestions. Only 29 percent said that they do a good job of acting upon their suggestions. Worse, both of these percentages have declined since the same study was done earlier. Perhaps the most serious comment was that only 18 percent of employees felt that their suggestions were *not* being ignored.[58]

Throughout the appraisal interview, employee should be invited to comment. This enables the employee to "let off steam" and perhaps explain why certain problems exist. It is also an opportune time to clear up any misunderstandings that may still exist about job expectations. According to Dick Grote, author of *The Complete Guide to Performance Appraisals,* "Managers

have an unrealistic expectation about what should come out of the performance review. What you should look for is gaining not agreement but understanding."[59]

5 *Focus on development.* The next step involves setting up the employee's development program. Employees are much more likely to be committed to developmental programs if they agree with the supervisor that the program is necessary to improve job skills and abilities. Employees who feel that no performance problems exist or that a program of development is unnecessary to promote career goals will be uncommitted to development. Employees may react more positively to a "problem solving" rather than a "tell and sell" supervisory approach.

VIOLENCE RELATED TO THE APPRAISAL

Have you ever feared that a PA could stir up a violent reaction?

According to the National Institute for Occupational Safety and Health (NIOSH), 750 people die every year as a result of occupational homicides.

Many observers believe that mergers and downsizings place stress on employees that may lead to violence. In one case, John, a poor performer, had been receiving average ratings for years because his supervisor did not want to deal with his unsatisfactory performance. After a merger, the company culture changed. John received an accurate PA that threw him into a panic. The appraisal was so sensitive that the supervisor and the HR manager both attended to lend some objectivity to the event. "He was very controlled but totally devastated by the criticism," said the HR manager. "He was told the people he had to work with found him intimidating."

"Perhaps they know I've been trained to kill," John said. Then he began to attack the supervisor verbally. The HR manager says, "We told him to take the review . . . think about it, and that we would get him on an improvement program. We didn't specify any date by which his performance needed to improve, and we didn't make any threats."

"On Monday, he called . . . sobbing and hysterical . . . [by] Wednesday, I got a call from the local hospital claims department. He was in the psychiatric unit," the manager said. Though later released by his psychiatrist, he twice failed to show up at work. John later called and said, "I can't come to work because I wouldn't be able to back down from those people; I'd have to hurt somebody."[60]

What can management expect to do to handle violence that can be set off during or after a PA interview?

- *Think about change and how to survive it.* "You need to let employees verbalize their concerns and listen—really listen," says Jon Christensen, associate director of the Center for Employee Assistance in Racine, Wisconsin. Christensen recommends that the CEO meet with workers and tell them what is really going on during turbulent organizational times. He believes that an outside employee assistance program (EAP) can also be helpful.
- *Prevent the stress syndrome.* Jim Martin, an EAP professional with the Detroit Fire Department, does "critical incident debriefing." About 46 hours after a violent event, he gathers together those who witnessed the incident to talk about their reactions. For those directly involved in the incident, Martin uses a seven-phase process.
- *Develop policies and procedures.* "Every employer should have policies and procedures to address the possibility of employee violence," says Joseph Kinney, executive director of the National Safe Workplace Institute in Chicago. Kinney suggests a "threat assessment team" to manage existing threats and to review policies and programs.[61] Proper handling of PAs can be key.

INTERNATIONAL APPLICATIONS

Multinational firms have problems when appraising the performance of expatriate employees. As international activities of firms increase and more employees are sent on foreign assignments to implement either global or regional strategies, accurate expatriate PAs will become more critical. Suggested practices include (1) using standardized forms customized for local assignment contexts, (2) conducting PAs annually or semiannually, (3) include raters located geographically with the expatriate (host-country supervisor), and (4) balance the location of raters between inside and outside the host country.[62]

However, research indicates that many firms do not follow these practices because they require extra effort. For expatriates, the employer's failure to pay attention to important international criteria may lead to career derailment during or after the overseas assignment. For the firm, it may fail to respond to local competitive conditions and exert more corporate headquarters control over foreign operations than is strategically advisable.[63] Such negative outcomes should lead firms to more carefully weigh the importance of effectively appraising their employees on international assignments.

SUMMARY POINTS

- Employees and supervisors find the PA process stressful. Employees tend to be satisfied with the process if the appraisal interview is constructive, if the chosen method is job related and provides specific direction for future performance, and the employees' input is heard.

- The PA process generally has two goals: (1) the evaluation of employees' past performance for salary and selection decisions and (2) the improvement of future performance as a part of career development. The evaluative objective tends to dominate specific organizational uses of appraisal information.

- To pass scrutiny by the EEOC and the courts, the appraisal process should contain certain features. A standardized process should evaluate all employees in a consistent manner. Job analysis should be used in the content development to ensure job relatedness. Supervisors should be trained in the process and should provide employees with direct written feedback from the process.

- Certain rater errors such as supervisor bias, halo effect, or recency can only be minimized; others, such as leniency

or central tendency, can be stopped, but forms that eliminate these problems generally contain their own problems. Each PA method has unique advantages and disadvantages, but rating scales continue to be used most often by HR managers.

- The appraisal interview is the most important element in the PA process. Supervisors who dislike "playing God" find it hard to act simultaneously as judge and coach. Supervisors need to be trained for, and give adequate attention to, the appraisal interview. Employee preparation can also help them to provide useful input into the discussion, as well as to be psychologically prepared for any possible negative feedback.

- Organizations can benefit by periodically evaluating their appraisal program. The HR department can provide feedback to supervisors about the quality of their appraisals and check for rater problems. Multiple raters—such as peers, subordinate customers, and team ratings—may be used as information added to supervisors' ratings.

CASE STUDY

BORDON ELECTRIC

Helen Horn joined the Bordon Electric Company eight months ago as director of human resources. Bordon Electric is a small regional public utility serving 50,000 customers in three communities and the surrounding rural area. Electricity is generated at a central plant, but each community has a substation and its own work crew. The total labor force at the central plant and three substations, exclusive of administrative and clerical personnel, numbers 280 people.

Horn designed and introduced a Performance Evaluation and Review System (PERS) shortly after joining Bordon. This system was based on a similar system she had developed and administered in her prior position with a small company. She thought that the system had worked well and that it could be easily adapted for use at Bordon.

The purpose of PERS, as conceived by Horn, is to provide a positive feedback system for appraising employees that would be uniform for each class of employees. Thus, the system would indicate to employees how they were performing on the job and help them correct any shortcomings. The plant supervisors and field supervisors are responsible for administering the system for the plant workers and the substation crew workers, respectively. The general supervisors are responsible for the plant/field supervisors. Employees get personal PERS reports monthly informing them of their current status, and there is a review and an appraisal every six months.

PERS is based on a point system in an attempt to make it uniform for all workers. There are eight categories for evaluation, with a maximum number of points for each category and a total of 100 points for the system. The eight categories for the plant and crew workers, and the maximum number of points in each category, are as follows:

Categories	*Points*
1. Quality of work	15

Points are deducted if the job must be redone within 48 hours of completion.

| **2. Productivity** | 15 |

Points are deducted if the work was not completed within the time specified.

| **3. Safety on the job** | 15 |

Points are deducted if the employee does not use safe work habits on the job.

| **4. Neatness of work area or repair truck** | 15 |

Points are deducted if the work area or truck is not clean and neat.

| **5. Cooperation with fellow workers** | 10 |

Points are deducted if an employee does not work well with others.

| **6. Courtesy on the job and with the public** | 10 |

Points are deducted if an employee is rude and unpleasant with the public.

| **7. Appearance** | 10 |

Points are deducted if an employee does not wear standard work clothing or if the clothing is sloppy and dirty at the shift's beginning.

| **8. Tardiness/excess absenteeism** | 10 |

Points are deducted if an employee arrives late or is absent for causes other than illness or death in the immediate family.

| **Total Points** | $\overline{100}$ |

The list of categories used to evaluate the plant/field supervisors is slightly different.

Each employee begins the year with 100 points. If an infraction in any of the categories is observed, 1 to 5 penalty points can be assessed for each infraction. Notification is given to the employee indicating the infraction and the points to be deducted. A worker who is assessed 25 points in any one month or loses all the points in any category in one month is subject to immediate review. Similarly, anytime an employee drops below 40 points, a review is scheduled. The general supervisor meets with the employee and the employee's plant/field supervisor at this review.

If an employee has no infractions during the month, up to 12 points can be restored to the employee's point total—2 points each for categories 1 to 4 and 1 point each for categories 5 to 8. However, at no time can a worker have more than the maximum allowed in each category or more than 100 points in total.

When Horn first introduced PERS to the general supervisors, they were not sure that they liked the system. Horn told them how well it had worked where she had used it before. Horn's enthusiasm for the system and her likable personality convinced the general supervisors that the system had merit.

There were a few isolated problems with the system in the first two months. However, Larry Cox, a crew worker, is very unhappy with the new system, as evidenced by his conversation with Bob Cambron, a fellow crew worker.

Cox: "Look at this notice of infraction—I have lost 22 points! Can you believe that?"

Cambron: "How did your supervisor get you for that many points in such a short time?"

Cox: "It's all related to that bad storm we had two weeks ago. He disagreed with me on the work at Del Park and Madeline Court. It was dangerous, and I probably did fly off the handle. It was late at night after I had been working 15 to 16 hours straight. Look what he got me for: 5 points for lack of cooperation, 5 points for a dirty uniform, 5 points for a messy truck, including lunch bags and coffee cups in the cab, 4 points for slow work, and 3 points for being 10 minutes late the next morning. Can you imagine that—

CASE STUDY—cont'd

being docked for 10 minutes when I worked a double shift the day before? I didn't get home until 1:00 A.M. I even cleaned the truck up after he left that night—on my own time, no less!"

Cambron: "At least you won't get reviewed."

Cox: "Sure, but I bet he planned it to come out less than 25 points."

Cambron: "Boy, we worked ourselves to a frazzle that night and the next two days. You know, one of the guys over in substation 3 told me that his supervisor adds back points to their PERS reports over and above the normal monthly allowances."

Cox: "Well, don't that tell you what a screwy deal this whole PERS system is?"

DISCUSSION QUESTIONS

1. Without regard to Larry Cox's recent experience with the system, evaluate the PERS in terms of its:
   a. Design for a performance management and appraisal system.
   b. Value as a motivational device.

2. What problems might occur in the administration of the PERS system, and how might these administrative problems affect employee motivation? Explain your answer.

3. Could a similar PA system be set up to evaluate work crews on a team basis? How?

EXPERIENTIAL EXERCISES

1. INDIVIDUAL: IT'S GREAT TO BE "LOYAL"—BUT WHAT DOES IT *MEAN?*

PURPOSE

To recognize the difficulty of performing a valid PA using a trait-oriented form that includes vague and subjective personal traits.

TASK

Listed here are a number of traits taken from PA forms used in a variety of organizations.

A. Write a one-sentence definition for each trait that is related to performing a job. As an example, the first item, "initiative," has been completed. Your instructor may lead a discussion concerning your definitions in class.

1. Initiative: Seeks better ways to do the job without being asked.

2. Cooperation:

3. Judgment:

4. Sensitivity:

5. Effort:

6. Dependability:

7. Honesty:

8. Leadership:

9. Character:

10. Loyalty:

B. Reword three of these traits in behavioral terms that may be used for a more objective appraisal.

2. GROUP: REVIEWING THE U.S. PRESIDENT

PURPOSE

To recognize how multiple raters may rate the same person differently, to experience the difficulty of rating someone whose performance you do not often observe directly, to practice team appraisal using a rating form, and to identify instances of deficiency and contamination.

TASK

Return to Figure 9–3, the job and behavioral summary rating form.

1. Use the 10 items listed under "Behavioral Factors," starting with "Education/experience," and rate the president of the United States. Remember, the president is a public servant and, therefore, theoretically, works for us.

EXPERIENTIAL EXERCISES—cont'd

2 Next, form into small groups in class and attempt to reach a consensus on each of the 10 rating items. Your goal is to come up with a *team rating* on which all team members can agree.

3 Each team should report its group rating, and your instructor should list each of the teams' ratings so that a comparison can be made. Discuss whether the teams rated the president similarly and why.

4 Discuss which of the 10 items was most difficult to rate. Why did you have difficulty? Was it due to deficiency or contamination problems on the rating form?

5 Discuss whether the rating form covered all of the important aspects of the president's job.

KEY TERMS AND CONCEPTS

Absolute standards methods
Annual review file
Behaviorally anchored rating scale (BARS)
Central tendency
Checklist of critical incidents
Comparative methods
Contamination
Critical incidents
Demotion-preventive strategies
Developmental objective
Electronic monitoring
Essay method
Evaluative objective
Forced distribution
Graphic rating scale
Halo effect
Impression management
Leniency

Management by objectives (MBO)
Nongraphic rating scale
Overall ratings
Paired comparison
Peer review
Performance appraisal (PA)
Performance management
Promotion-enhancing strategies
Ranking
Rater errors
Recency
Reverse appraisals
Self-ratings
Strictness
Supervisory bias
Systems assessment
360-degree feedback
Work standards

REVIEW QUESTIONS

1 What are the major purposes and general objectives of PA?

2 How are PA and performance management different?

3 What are the common steps in the appraisal process?

4 Describe the major methods used in PA systems.

5 What are the major problems associated with many PA systems?

6 What can raters do to ensure that PA interviews are productive and helpful to both the employee and the organization?

7 Should employers monitor the performance of their employees secretly?

8 What is the best way to perform a PA on a workteam or an autonomous workgroup?

9 What is the system appraisal that many TQM advocates prefer, and how is it different from standard PA programs?

DISCUSSION QUESTIONS

1. Think of two instructors you have had—one very good and one very poor. What specific behaviors distinguish the two instructors? If you were the dean who had to conduct performance appraisals for the instructors, what method would you use to gather performance data?

2. Write five MBO objectives for an individual selling computers at a computer "superstore." How would you weigh each objective in terms of the overall performance of the salesperson?

3. A number of organizations have subordinates rate the performance of their supervisor. What advantages do you see in doing this? What problems may occur?

4. Supervisors may ask employees to furnish a self-rating at the appraisal interview for discussion. What are the benefits and drawbacks of this procedure?

5. What methods would you use to appraise the performance of the following kinds of employees: keypunch operator, first-line supervisor in a manufacturing plant, professor of management, airline pilot, office clerk in large government office, exotic dancer, and police officer?

6. When the process of evaluating employees is viewed as purely perfunctory, supervisors show little or no interest in completing the forms and conducting the interview. In some cases, the appraisal interview is not conducted. Why do these problems exist? What can be done to reduce them?

7. As an HR administrator who is developing a PA system for department store sales personnel, you have decided to implement the BARS method. Write three behavioral statements that illustrate good performance and three that describe poor or mediocre performance.

8. Should the government pass a law limiting the employer's right to monitor employees? If so, what specifically should such a law prohibit?

9. If a manufacturing employer decided to use multiple raters for PA instead of having only the supervisor perform all of the appraisal, what other raters might be most helpful? What if the employer was a retail store or the state government?

ENDNOTES

Chapter 9

1. Brian D. Cawley, Lisa Keeping, and Paul Levy, "Participation in the Performance Appraisal Process and Employee Reactions: A Meta-Analytic Review of Field Investigations," *Journal of Applied Psychology* 83 (1998): 615.

2. Archer North & Associates, "Performance Appraisal: The Complete On-line Guide" at *http://www.performance-appraisal.com/intro.htm.*

3. Roy W. Regel and Robert W. Hollmann, "Gauging Performance Objectively," *Personnel Administrator* 32, no. 6 (June 1987): 74–78.

4. Beverly L. Kaye, "Performance Appraisal and Career Development: A Shotgun Marriage," *Personnel* 61, no. 2 (March–April 1984): 57–66.

5. "Creating a Terrific Appraisal System," *HRMagazine* 43 (October 1998): 56.

6. "Making a Case for Accurate Appraisals," *Personnel Journal* 71 (November 1992): 116.

7. David I. Rosen, "Appraisals Can Make—or Break—Your Court Case," *Personnel Journal* 71 (November 1992): 113.

8. Ibid., 113.

9. Adapted from Rosen, 113–118.

10. "Making a Case for Accurate Appraisals," 116.

11. Ibid.

12. Harry N. Turk, "Questions—and Answers," *Employment Relations Today* 20 (Spring 1993): 133—134.

13. Kevin J. Murphy, "Performance Measurement and Appraisal: Merck Tries to Motivate Managers to Do It Right," *Employment Relations Today* 20 (Spring 1993): 47.

14. G. Rosinger, L. B. Myers, G. W. Levy, M. Loar, S. A. Mohrman, and J. R. Stock, "Development of a Behaviorally Based Performance Appraisal System," *Personnel Psychology* 35, no. 1 (Spring 1982): 75–88.

15. Dallas de Fee, "Management by Objectives: When and How Does It Work?" *Personnel Journal* 56 (January 1977): 37–39.

16. Teresa M. Amabile, "How to Kill Creativity: Keep Doing What You're Doing . . ." *Harvard Business Review* 76, (September–October 1998): 83.

17. Leanne Atwater and David Waldman, "Accountability in 360-Degree Feedback," *HRMagazine* 43 (May 1998): 96.

18. Dennis M. Daley, "Putting the Super in Supervisor: Determinants of Federal Employee Evaluation of Supervisors," *Public Personnel Management* 26 (September 1997): 301.

19. Scott H. Oppler, John P. Campbell, Elaine D. Pulakos, and Walter C. Borman, "Three Approaches to the Investigation of Subgroup Bias in Performance Measurement: Review, Results and Conclusions," *Journal of Applied Psychology* 77 (1992): 201–217.

20. Dick Grote and Jim Wimberly, "Peer Review," *Training* 30 (March 1993): 51–52.

21. Ibid., p. 52.

22. Jeanne C. Poole, William F. Rathgeber III, and Stanley W. Silverman, "Paying for Performance in a TQM Environment," *HRMagazine* 38 (October 1993): 70.

23. Performance appraisal training packet written by Jim Way, vice president of administration, Marley Cooling Tower Co., Mission, KS, January 8, 1993. The appraisal instrument itself was developed by an employee task group.

24. Gerald L. Blakely, "The Effects of Performance Rating Discrepancies on Supervisors and Subordinates," *Organizational Behavior and Human Decision Processes* 54 (1993): 57–80.

25. Brian D. Cawley, Lisa M. Keeping, and Paul E. Levy, "Participation in the Performance Appraisal Process and Employee Reactions: A Meta-Analytic Review of Field Investigations," *Journal of Applied Psychology* 83 (1998): 615.

26. Joyce E. Santora, "How Chrysler Developed and Implemented Its Reverse–Appraisal Program," *Personnel Journal* 71 (May 1992): 42.

27. Alex Rothenberg, "Vermont Firms Let Workers Review Bosses" (Barre-Montpeller, VT) *Times-Argus* (May 24, 1992): C7.

28. "Work Teams Have Their Work Cut Out for Them," *HR Focus* 70 (January 1993): 10.

29. Atwater and Waldman, "Accountability in 360-Degree Feedback," 98.

30. Ibid., 99.

31. Carol A. Norman and Robert A. Zawacki, "Team Appraisals—Team Approach," *Personnel Journal* 70 (September 1991): 101.

32. Paul S. Greenlaw and Cornelia Prundeanu, "The Impact of Federal Legislation to Limit Electronic Monitoring," *Public Personnel Management* 26 (Summer 1997): 227.

33. The Associated Press, "Don't Look Now, But Your Boss Might Be Surveying: Most Employers Spy on Workers," *Newsday* (May 23, 1997): A60.

34. Greenlaw and Prundeanu, "The Impact of Federal Legislation to Limit Electronic Monitoring," 228.

35. Kim Clark, "Who's Watching You?" *Baltimore Sun* (March 21, 1993): B5.

36. Erik Gunn, "The Boss Has New Ways to Watch," *Milwaukee Journal* (September 23, 1990): G8.

37. Douglas B. Gehrman, "Beyond Today's Compensation and Performance Appraisal System," *Personnel Administrator* 29, no. 3 (March 1984): 21–33.

38. Sandra O'Neal and Madonna Palladino, "Revamp Ineffective Performance Management," *Personnel Journal* 71 (February 1992): 93. "Technical Services Co." is a disguised name for a company that wished to remain anonymous.

39. Ibid., 98.

40. Steps 2, 3, and 4 are adapted from James G. Goodale, "Improving Performance Appraisal," *Business Quarterly* 57(Autumn 1992): 65-66.

41. Kenneth P. Carson, Robert L. Cardy, and Gregory H. Dobbins, "Upgrade the Employee Evaluation Process," *HRMagazine* 37 (November 1992): 88.

42. Ibid.

43. John Case, "What the Experts Forgot to Mention," *Inc.* (September 1993): 76.

44. Carson et al., "Upgrade," 89–92.

45. Many studies, unfortunately, have found little or no improvement in selection or PA "skills" as a result of training. This suggests that selection and rating are not based solely on skills that can be improved through traditional training. For a recent example where modern training had little or no effect see Danny L. Balfour, "Impact of Agency Investment in the Implementation of Performance Appraisal," *Public Personnel Management* 21 (Spring 1992): 1–15.

46. Robert A. Giacalone, "Image Control: The Strategies of Impression Management," *Personnel* 67 (May 1989): 52–55.

47. Ibid.

48. Brian L. Davis and Michael K. Mount, "Design and Use of a Performance Appraisal Feedback System," *Personnel Administrator* 29, no. 3 (March 1983): 47–51.

49. Jane R. Goodson, Gail W. McGee, and Anson Seers, "Giving Appropriate Performance Feedback to Managers: An Empirical Test of Content and Outcomes," *The Journal of Business Communication* 29 (1992): 329.

50. Ibid., 331.

51. Poole et al., "Paying for Performance," 72.

52. Yitzhak Fried, Robert B. Tiegs, and Alphonso R. Bellamy, "Personal and Interpersonal Predictors of Supervisors' Avoidance of Evaluating Subordinates," *Journal of Applied Psychology* 77 (1992): 462–468.

53. Douglas M. McGregor, "An Uneasy Look at Performance Appraisal," *Harvard Business Review* 35 (May–June 1957): 89–94.

54. Catherine Petrini, "In Practice," *Training and Development* 47 (July 1993): 13 (quoting Dave Lynn of Blessing/While, Inc.).

55. H. H. Meyer et al., "Split Roles in Performance Appraisal," *Harvard Business Review* 43 (January–February 1965): 127.

56. McGregor, "An Uneasy Look at Performance Appraisal," 91–94.

57. Kathleen Driscoll, "Question: I Have an Employee Who's Going Through a Difficult Problem . . ." *Gannet News Service* (September 14, 1995).

58. Citing The Wyatt Company and The Hay Group in Ludeman, "Upward Feedback," 87.

59. Shelly Donald Coolidge, "Yearly Event Can Be a Work-in-Progress," *The Christian Science Monitor* (December 7, 1998).

60. The preceding account was adapted from Linda Thornburg, "When Violence Hits Business," *HRMagazine* (July 1993): 40–45.

61. Ibid.

62. Hal B. Gregersen, Julie M. Hite, and J. Stewart Black, "Expatriate Performance Appraisal in U.S. Multinational Firms," *Journal of International Business Studies* 27 (Fourth Quarter, 1996): 711.

63. Ibid., 711.

EMPLOYEE TRAINING AND MANAGEMENT DEVELOPMENT

CHAPTER OUTLINE

CHAPTER OBJECTIVES

1. To identify the major purposes of training and development (T&D).

2. To recognize the differences and similarities between employee training and management development.

3. To identify key internal and external influences upon T&D.

4. To identify the many on-the-job and away-from-the-job T&D techniques.

5. To learn the four steps of training and recognize the importance of each.

6. To identify the different needs for T&D within the modern organization.

7. To understand the principles of learning and learning styles that apply to T&D programs at the workplace.

U.S. companies spend a total of $61 billion on formal training, offering training programs totaling 2 billion hours of instruction to up to 55 million employees. Just over half of that $61 billion flows toward programs for managers and professionals, with those in the sales profession most likely to receive formal training. The fastest growing slice of the budget is the outsourcing of training. Today, almost one-third of all training is delivered by outside contractors. While an increasing proportion of training (19 percent) involves the computer in some way, live, face-to-face instruction (70 percent) is still by far the most common training approach.[1]

The real spending and energy directed toward training and development activities is actually much higher than the figures given above. The statistics only include companies of 100 or more employees and do not include the largest single expenditure in training, the salaries still paid to employees even though they are participating in training.

As the *HR in the News* about Advanced Microelectronics indicates, training has become part of any effective HR program and is strategically related to key company objectives such as productivity and employee recruitment and retention.

TRAINING AND DEVELOPMENT (T & D)

There are several different terms used when discussing the training and developing of employees. Labor economists divide programs into general and specific training. *General training* refers to training so basic that any worker would profit from it, like learning to read. Employers increasingly offer "employee education"

HR IN THE NEWS

ADVANCED MICROELECTRONICS DISCOVERS THAT TRAINING AFFECTS TURNOVER AND PRODUCTIVITY

Two years ago, Advanced Microelectronics, a fast-growing computer services company, let its employee training programs lapse. Within months, productivity sagged and turnover soared at the Vincennes, Indiana, firm. CEO Steve Burkhart recalls departing workers repeating refrains such as "I'm out of date" and "I'm not keeping up."

Those complaints surprised Burkhart, one of the firms founders. Just a decade ago, he had instituted internal training programs in partnership with nearby Vincennes Community College to teach his workers added skills, but he had not anticipated the degree of his staff's zeal for learning. "I'm over 50," he says, "and I always thought: When I'm out of school, I'm out of school." What he found, however, was that he had "60 people each wanting $10,000 worth" of continuing education.

Burkhart responded by reinstating the training programs with "even more focus." The result, he says, was higher morale and lower turnover. Training is "just a 7-day-a-week process around here now," Burkhart says. It seems to be almost a demanded benefit, or people don't feel like they have a valuable job."

Now, the revitalized training program not only targets his computer repair and network service technicians, but also bookkeepers and other administrative staffers. At first he feared a low turnout, so he offered free pizza. But workers, who signed up in big numbers said no enticement was necessary. Training is "a big deal for companies—no matter what size they are," says this enlightened CEO.

Burkhart is just one of countless American employers who have discovered that finding and keeping good workers is one of the greatest challenges facing them today. An expanding U.S. economy and low unemployment rates have created a powerful demand for intelligent, well-trained workers. A 1998 survey of small but growing companies found that two-thirds of such firms said that a lack of skilled workers will limit their revenue growth this year—up from 27 percent in 1993.

SOURCE: Adapted from Steve Bates, "Building Better Workers," *Nation's Business* 86 (1998). Reprinted with permission. All rights reserved.

programs to teach fundamental math and English skills. *Specific training* refers to training which is unique to a specific workplace, like learning Wal-Mart's specific approach to inventory control.

Traditionally, employee training and management development have referred to different approaches. In this chapter, we examine T&D activities in a more unified way. The flattening of organizational structures and the accompanying emphasis upon empowerment and teams has blurred the boundaries between management skills and employee skills. Historically, **employee training** had as its goal the acquisition of narrow, short-term, technically oriented skills by nonmanagerial employees. **Management development** had as its goal the sharpening of broad, long-term skills associated with planning, organizing, directing, and controlling. Learning how to operate a scanner at a grocery checkout lane was employee training, while learning multiple approaches to motivating subordinates was management development.

The term **Human Resource Development (HRD)** spans the boundaries of the training vs. development argument. HRD refers to any planned actions by a firm to improve the knowledge, skills, and abilities of employees. Many employers have adopted the HRD designation, while most use some combination of the other T&D terms.

TRADITIONAL MANAGERIAL SKILLS

The reorganization of, and redesign of jobs within, cutting-edge organizations means that some of the skills traditionally thought of as managerial are now needed among all employees. Many other workplaces remain somewhat traditional, clearly dividing duties between management and nonmanagerial employees. In either context, it is important to examine "managerial skills." Figure 10–1 illustrates how the mix of these three skills varies according to the level of the traditional management job, per Katz's classic model.

Technical skills, or front-line skills, include knowledge of equipment and work methods and are the focus of traditional first-line supervisory and nonmanagerial training. **Conceptual skills,** or vision skills, include the ability to view the organization as a whole and to coordinate and integrate complex functions and goals. **Human relations skills,** or people skills, are needed equally at all levels of management. Human relations skills verify the popular definition of manager—"Someone who accomplishes work through the efforts of others."

PURPOSES OF T&D

What are the general purposes of T&D programs for managerial and front-line employees? There are at least seven major purposes:

- Improve performance.
- Update employees' skills.
- Avoid managerial obsolescence.
- Solve organizational problems.
- Orient and socialize new employees.
- Prepare for promotion and managerial succession.
- Satisfy personal growth needs of employees.

However, these and other general purposes for training activities depend on influences which come from both internal and external sources. In other words, the internal and external environments shape the needs that an employer has which can then be satisfied by T&D.

INTERNAL INFLUENCES ON T&D

Business Strategy   To play an important role within an organization, T&D must help it achieve its business strategy. Business strategy refers to the plan and posture a firm adopts which flows from the firm's mission and integrates its goals and actions. In complex

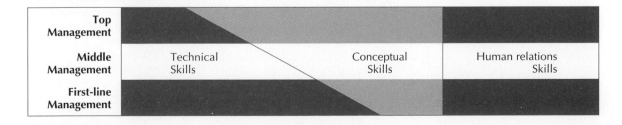

FIGURE 10–1   A DIFFERENT MIX OF SKILLS TRADITIONALLY HAS BEEN REQUIRED AT EACH LEVEL OF MANAGEMENT

Top Management		
Middle Management	Technical Skills	Conceptual Skills	Human relations Skills
First-line Management		

organizations, each line of business adopts a business strategy which then drives the organizational plans.

Research indicates that there is a relationship between business strategy and training.[2] Figure 10–2 shows four distinct strategies: concentration, internal growth, external growth, and disinvestment. The figure shows the different implications for training that each strategy creates.

Competitive Position   Although companies in the United States are spending more on training than ever before, the gap between the leading-edge compa-nies and the average company is widening—and companies that don't bridge the gap may face bottom-line repercussions, according to the American Society for Training and Development (ASTD). These more successful employers, classified as "leading edge" within their industries, are each spending almost $5 million on training annually, while the industry average is $2.1 million. Leading-edge employers also train a higher percentage of their employees than do the average employers—86 percent versus 74 percent.[3]

Employers who spend more on T&D have:

FIGURE 10–2   IMPLICATIONS OF BUSINESS STRATEGY FOR TRAINING

STRATEGY	EMPHASIS	HOW ACHIEVED	KEY ISSUES	TRAINING IMPLICATIONS
Concentration	• Increase market share • Reduce operating costs • Create or maintain market niche	• Improve product quality • Improve productivity or innovate technical processes • Customize products or services	• Skill currency • Development of existing workforce	• Team building • Cross-training • Specialized programs • Interpersonal skill training • On-the-job training
Internal growth	• Market development • Product development • Innovation • Joint ventures	• Market existing products/add distribution channels • Expand global market • Modify existing products • Create new or different products • Expand through joint ownership	• Create new jobs and tasks • Innovation	• Support or promote high-quality communication of product value • Cultural training • Help in development of organizational culture that values creative thinking and analysis • Technical competence in jobs • Manager training in feedback and communication • Conflict negotiation skills
External growth (acquisition)	• Horizontal integration • Vertical integration • Concentric diversification	• Acquire firms operating at same stage in product market chain (new market access) • Acquire business that can supply or buy products • Acquire firms that have nothing in common with acquiring firm	• Integration • Redundancy • Restructuring	• Determining capabilities of employees in acquired firms • Integrating training systems • Methods and procedures of combined firms • Team building
Disinvestment	• Retrenchment • Turnaround • Divestiture • Liquidation	• Reduce costs • Reduce assets • Generate revenue • Redefine goals • Sell off all assets	• Efficiency	• Motivation, goal setting, time management, stress management, cross-training • Leadership training • Interpersonal communications • Outplacement assistance • Job-search skills training

SOURCE: Raymond A. Noe, *Employee Training & Development* (Boston: Irwin/McGraw-Hill, 1999), 35. Reprinted by permission.

- higher net sales per employee,
- higher gross profits per employee, and
- higher ratio in market-to-book values.[4]

Ability to invest in T&D varies with the competitive position of the organization. The average workplace spends 0.9 percent of its payroll budget on training. However, firms in more favorable competitive positions invest about 3.0 percent. T&D advocates recommend a 3–6 percent investment in training for those companies seeking to be a true "learning organization."[5] Of course, money is no insurance that effective T&D will take place. However, it is clear that companies lacking the ability to pay are at an important competitive disadvantage.

Workforce and Workplace Characteristics

The needs of the employees are an important influence on training requirements. If the workforce is only semi-literate, too often a problem, then general training requirements will be enormous if the work requires reading and writing. Specific training will be a constant demand for companies such as those in the fast-food industry because of high turnover rates.

EXTERNAL INFLUENCES ON T&D

Many *standards* influence T&D. International Standards Organization (ISO) 9000 and QS-9000 both dictate specific and heavy requirements for T&D within qualified organizations. Comprehensive training requirements are part of the criteria for The Malcolm Baldridge National Quality Award and are also benchmarked among certain industries, like the National Association of Manufacturers (NAM). However, the U.S. workplace lags behind that of workplaces of some of its international competitors in the amount of training given to employees.[6]

Spending varies across *industries.* Some industries are really scrambling to fill needed jobs. For instance, the worldwide market for informational technology training was up to $19 billion in 1998.[7] With the continuing growth of service jobs, there are calls for big increases in T&D for that industry. Fast-food, retail, and other industries with high turnover rates need constant technical and orientation training.

The characteristics of the relevant *labor pool*—level of education, training, and experience—also drives training needs. During the late 1990s relatively low unemployment often created a comparatively small selection pool for job openings. Expanding employers find it difficult to find educated, trained, or experienced employees.

SYSTEMS APPROACH TO T&D

The thought of training often brings to mind a trainer, participants, and traditional training techniques: a film being shown, workbooks being completed, or a chalkboard-assisted lecture. But the actual process of training people is only a small part of the training process. Successful T&D involves considerable effort both before and after the trainer and trainees are brought together. In other words, training is best thought of as a complex *system* that involves a number of distinct but highly interrelated phases.

A **training systems model** is shown in Figure 10–3. The five major steps of training are assessing needs, identifying objectives, selecting training approach, conducting training, and outcome evaluation.

FIGURE 10–3   FIVE-STEP TRAINING SYSTEMS MODEL

1. Assess training needs.
   ↓
2. Identify outcome objectives.
   ↓
3. Select training approach.
   ↓
4. Conduct training.
   ↓
5. Evaluate training outcomes.

STEP 1: ASSESSING TRAINING NEEDS

The first step in the training model, **needs assessment,** may be conducted at three levels: organizational analysis, operations analysis, and person analysis.[8]

Organizational Analysis

Organizational analysis involves analyzing organizationwide performance criteria (for example, accidents and injuries, absenteeism, turnover, productivity, labor costs, sexual harassment charges, EEO complaints, and so on). The purpose of this analysis is to uncover major problem areas that may indicate a need for training.

Operations Analysis

The purpose of operations analysis, also called *task analysis,* is to determine *how* a job should be performed—specifying the desired level of performance. Through operations analysis, data is collected that enables training personnel to create programs that focus on the right way to perform a job.

Person Analysis

The two purposes of person analysis are to determine (1) who currently needs T&D and (2) what skills, knowledge, abilities, or attitudes need to be acquired or strengthened. Person analysis is important to ensure that employees who need training are the ones who actually receive it and that programs are designed to fill the gap between actual and desired performance, called the **performance gap.**

There are numerous ways to collect person analysis data. The more common techniques include requests from management, employee interviews, and the following:[9]

- *Advisory Committees* Advisory committees generally comprise various levels of management, and some organizations create multiple crossfunctional committees to represent the workforce. Committees often determine whether a particular problem is a T&D problem and establish training objectives.
- *Assessment Centers* Used mostly for management selection and development, the assessment center has participants undergo a series of exercises to determine their strengths and weaknesses in performing managerial tasks.
- *Attitude Surveys* Attitude surveys are most effective in measuring the general level of job satisfaction, and the data may show T&D needs.
- *Group Discussions* This method generally involves meeting with employees who represent a specific work area. A primary benefit of group dis-

cussions is that the employees are more committed to the training as a result of active participation in the assessment process.

- *Questionnaires* Some organizations use questionnaires to identify T&D needs. The employees themselves are generally the respondents. The questionnaire usually specifies vital skill areas, the importance of the skill, and the employee's perception of training need for each area.
- *Skills Test* A test of necessary skills, such as word processing, computer programming, or driving, may also be used to measure training needs.
- *Observations of Behavior* Trainers or supervisors may directly observe employees' behavior to identify training needs. This method is generally limited to the assessment of technical skills and behaviors.
- *Performance Appraisals* A valid, job-related appraisal system will point out strengths and weaknesses in employee performance and should indicate T&D needs.
- *Performance Documents* Most organizations regularly gather data on employee performance such as productivity, absenteeism, accidents, and turnover. Such information may be used to point out training needs.
- *Exit Interviews* A high turnover rate may spell organizational problems and a need for training. The validity of exit interviews greatly depends on an unbiased and skilled interviewer and on honest answers from the employee who is leaving.

Finally, you should be aware that many employers perform no formal needs assessment. See *HR in The News:* Needs Assessment—A "Taboo" Training Term. Employers and some HR departments simply buy into a current fad in training and guess that that fad will be of use to their particular workplace. Training modules in personality (like Myers-Briggs), diversity, TQM, managerial grid, and other concepts have surely helped some organizations. However, many other organizations will purchase or mimic such popular programs without having first identified a need that requires a training intervention. After a need has been identified, training objectives should be specified; only then should a particular program be developed. Otherwise, the firm may buy a T&D program that people enjoy but provides little objective benefit.

The Special Case of Needs Assessment for Managers

Long-range T&D needs of managers

HR IN THE NEWS

NEEDS ASSESSMENT—A "TABOO" TRAINING TERM?

HERE'S AN ASSESSMENT QUICKIE According to consultants, there are certain terms that a trainer should never use in front of managers. Use training jargon in your own office, "but never in the presence of the client," says Bob Mager, president of Mager Associates in Carefree, Arizona. Here are some training terms likely to frustrate managers: "needs assessment," "needs analysis," "subject matter expert," "just-in-time training," and "instructional technology." Patti Shank, an "educational designer" with InSight Ed in Sykesville, Maryland, says never say "I'm here to diagnose your *performance gaps.*" If you do, you're asking for a dope-slap.[10]

One reason the term "needs assessment" gives managers the willies is that traditionally it means a time-consuming, academic research project. That's hard to sell to impatient, penny-pinching line managers. Harried trainers think, "Don't drag your feet with that assessment stuff! We've gotta show 'em we're team players with a 'bias for action.' Ready, shoot, aim!"[11]

Jack Asgar, chairman of Practical Management Inc., of Las Vegas, suggests a list of questions to replace traditional needs assessment. These questions often end in training other than that first indicated, or no training at all.

1. What are the operating problems? *(Never ask, "What is the training need?")*

2. Are the operating problems caused or contributed to by human behavior? If yes, describe the present behavior and the desired performance.

3. Could the employees perform correctly if they had to? Have they performed the task correctly lately? *(A "yes" suggests that training is not the solution.)*

4. Is the desired performance now being demanded by the employees' manager? If yes, explain how. If no, what assurance do you have that the new behavior will be reinforced on the job after training has been completed?

5. What evidence shows that present performance is a problem? What would be some observable signs that the problem has been solved?

6. What other issues might be contributing to this operating problem?

7. Based on this analysis, is training needed? If yes, what skills should be learned?

8. If training is needed, will managers commit themselves to active involvement in the training process before, during, and after the training?

SOURCE: The eight questions are from Rebecca Ganzel, Jack Gordon, Michele Picard, David Stamps, and Ron Zemke, "Speedy Needs Assessment," *Training* 35 (July 1998): 13. Reprinted by permission of *Training*, Minneapolis, MN.

---

are linked to the HR and strategic planning of the organization. Assessing long-range development needs begins with a forecast of the demand for managers. If the organization promotes from within, the promotion potential of current managers, as well as candidates, must be determined. Strengths and weaknesses are closely examined to predict how managers will perform if promoted. During this assessment, managers with many skills and broad experience may be considered promotable without formal development. A certain percentage of managers may have "peaked" in their present jobs. Others may be judged promotable but only after further preparation. For the last group of managers, an analysis must be made of the specific skills and abilities they will need in order to be successful after being promoted.

To assist in making that analysis, some organizations prepare an HR planning tool called a management (or *executive*) succession chart. Succession charts indicate successors for each position in the management hierarchy and often combine current performance data with a judgment of promotion potential. Figure 10–4 illustrates the information normally contained in a management succession chart.

The assessment of development needs should result in a program of T&D approaches somewhat individualized for each manager. No two management jobs are exactly alike, nor is the performance of any two managers identical. An assessment of one plant supervisor may find weaknesses in counseling employees and conducting performance appraisals. Another supervisor may be strong at counseling employees but weak in dealing with PAs, and motivation. The T&D effort should attempt to meet employees where they currently stand and address their individual needs.

STEP 2: SETTING OBJECTIVES

Following an assessment of training needs, **training objectives** should be written to reflect what the participant should be able to do on completion of training—skills, knowledge, abilities, and attitudes the participant should possess after training. Well-written objectives have three major benefits:

1. They help determine which methods are appropriate by focusing on the areas of performance that need to change.

2. They clarify what is to be expected of both the trainer and the participants.

3. They provide a basis for post-training evaluation.

A well-written T&D objective will have three parts: (1) a statement of outcome behavior—what the employee will be able to do after training; (2) a description of the conditions under which the outcome behavior is expected to occur; (3) a statement of the minimum

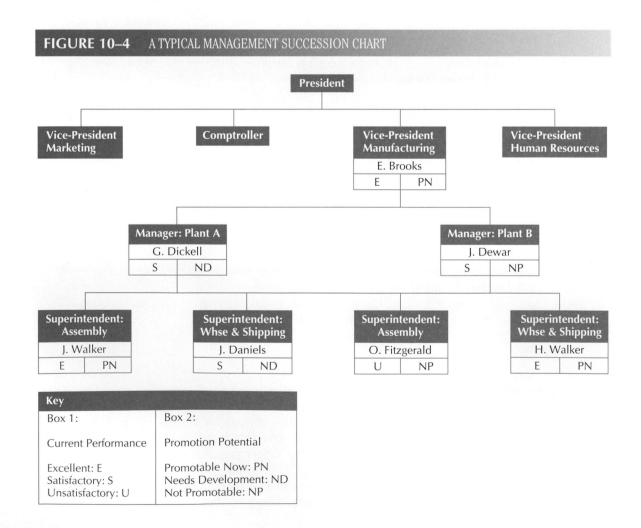

FIGURE 10–4 A TYPICAL MANAGEMENT SUCCESSION CHART

Key

Box 1:

Current Performance

Excellent: E
Satisfactory: S
Unsatisfactory: U

Box 2:

Promotion Potential

Promotable Now: PN
Needs Development: ND
Not Promotable: NP

FIGURE 10–5 THREE SAMPLE T&D OBJECTIVES

TERMINAL BEHAVIOR	CONDITION	MINIMAL ACHIEVEMENT
To word process	Given a standard word processing operator's examination	60 words per minute, with an error rate no higher than 2 percent
To perform maintenance	Given a standard set of tools	Preventive maintenance on a lathe within 30 minutes, according to company standard
To locate and correct errors	Given a business letter containing grammatical errors	Locate 95 percent of all errors after studying the letter for no more than 5 minutes

level of achievement that will be accepted as evidence that the employee has accomplished what was required. Figure 10–5 shows a few examples of what should be included in written T&D objectives.

STEP 3: SELECTING THE TRAINING APPROACH

After a needs assessment has identified a performance gap (the difference between desired and actual performance) or another specific set of developmental needs, and after particular objectives have been set that a T&D approach should accomplish, the organization is ready to seek or design a T&D program. The organization should be careful to select or design a T&D program that will yield verifiable results; otherwise, the large financial investment in training will not pay off. Employers should avoid choosing a popular or entertaining T&D program without having performed an assessment study, and a reasonable search for a program. Employers should use the same business standards for need substantiation and purchasing that they would demand for other business investments.

T&D techniques may be used while employees are either on the job or away from the job.

On-the-Job Techniques

On-the-job training, commonly referred to as OJT, typically involves job instruction given by an employee's supervisor or an experienced co-worker. Many studies indicate that 70 percent of all T&D is performed on the job. OJT may involve learning how to run a machine, conduct an interview, or sell a service or product. While employees may say that they learned their jobs "OJT" with a chuckle, learning by doing is a solid educational technique.

OJT is not limited to nonmanagerial or front-line employees. Managers essentially learn by doing. OJT techniques enable managers to practice management skills, make mistakes, and learn from their mistakes under the guidance of an experienced, competent manager. OJT methods include job rotation and lateral promotion, enlarged and enriched job responsibilities, job instruction training, apprentice training, coaching, mentoring, and committee assignments. (See Figure 10–6 for the assets and liabilities of OJT.)

Job Rotation Also referred to as *crosstraining,* job rotation involves placing an employee on different jobs for periods of time ranging from hours to weeks. At lower job levels, job rotation normally consumes a short period of time, such as a few hours or one or two days. At higher job levels, job rotation may consume much longer periods. For example, OJT for a bank lending officer may consist of one or two months in each department, including loan operations and collections, bookkeeping, trust operations, data processing, and commercial lending.

For middle- and upper-level management, job rotation serves a slightly different function. At these levels, job rotation assignments normally involve **lateral promotions,** which may last for one or more years. In contrast to a vertical promotion, in which an employee takes over a supervisor's job, a lateral promotion involves a move to a different work environment so that the manager may develop competence in general management decision-making skills. Much like the short-term job rotation assignment, a lateral promotion allows the manager to be exposed to many organizational operations and management styles.

Enlarged and Enriched Job Responsibilities By giving an employee added job duties, and increasing

FIGURE 10–6   OJT TRAINING TECHNIQUES: THE BALANCE SHEET

The widespread use of OJT training is, no doubt, due to the many benefits it offers. Among the potential assets of this type of training are the following:

- The employee is doing the actual work, not hypothetical or simulated tasks.
- The employee receives instructions from an experienced employee or supervisor who has performed the task successfully.
- The T&D is performed in the actual work environment under normal working conditions and requires no special training facilities.
- The T&D is informal, relatively inexpensive, and easy to schedule.
- The T&D may build cooperative relationships between the employee and the trainer.

Among the potential liabilities of OJT training are the following:

- The trainer may not be motivated to train or to accept the responsibility for T&D; thus, training may be haphazard.
- The trainer may perform the job well but lack the ability to teach others how to do so.
- The trainer may not have the time to train and may omit important elements of the T&D process. While the employee is learning OJT, resources will be inefficiently used, performance (at least initially) will be low, and costly errors may be made.

the autonomy and responsibilities associated with the job, the firm allows an employee to learn a lot about the job, department, and organization. Redesigning the job can be seen as a T&D approach because the employee can be stretched and tested in new ways.

Job Instruction Training (JIT)   Faced with massive training needs during World War II, the federal government developed job instruction training to enable supervisors to train their employees quickly and effectively. Because of its simplicity, JIT remains a popular tool for many modern trainers. The simple steps in the "monkey-see, monkey-do" JIT system are preparation, presentation, performance tryout, and follow-up.[12]

Apprentice Training   A combination of on- and away-from-the-job training, apprentice training is widely used in the skilled trades, such as carpentry, printing, welding, and plumbing. Apprentice training involves cooperation among employees, the government, educational institutions (usually vocational or technical schools), and labor unions. The U.S. Department of Labor regulates apprentice training programs and determines the length of apprenticeships and the minimum requirements for classroom instruction.

Coaching   As in athletics, the organizational coach assumes the role of helper and teacher. The coach—often the new manager's or exceptional employee's boss—achieves developmental objectives by setting

goals, by providing assistance in reaching goals, and by giving timely and constructive performance feedback. Coaching is not problem-free. Coaching may fail unless a rapport conducive to learning is created between the manager and the employee. The coach must be willing to give sufficient time to the development process and allow the subordinate to assume some risks and make mistakes.[13]

Mentoring   The term mentor comes from Greek mythology. Mentor was the wise teacher asked to watch over Odysseus' son during Odysseus' participation in the Trojan War. Mentor gave support and guidance. Thus we have come to know mentors as those who guide and nurture the career growth of their younger "protégés."[14]

Mentoring starts in two ways—formally and informally. Because a mentor can "show the ropes" to the protégé, many organizations have set up formal mentor programs, often as part of their affirmative action or orientation efforts. Informal mentoring relationships seem to have always existed, generally based on a judgment by the mentor that the employee has promise and that the mentor's advice and counsel will not be wasted. The effectiveness of formal, somewhat artificial, mentoring programs has not been established to be the same as in the traditional informal relationships, where the mentor and protégé are perhaps more genuinely committed to each other.

Recent research indicates that there is now little difference in the mentoring relationships between the genders if males and females have the same education. While there are still relatively few women in top-level management positions, and while cross-gender mentorships can be sensitive, top-performing women are now as likely to be mentored as their male counterparts. Females and males both report receiving more promotions, having higher incomes, and being more satisfied with their pay and benefits than those who experience little or no mentoring.[15]

Committee Assignments   A great deal of a manager's time is spent as part of committees. Serving on a committee and participating in decision making enables a manager to strengthen a variety of skills.

While working on a committee assignment, a supervisor may gain a greater understanding of complex issues and meet and discuss problems with personnel from other departments. Junior managers or particular front-line employees can be placed on such committees as regular members or may be sent as substitutes by the regular members.

Away-from-the-Job Techniques   **Away-from-the-job training** includes any form of training performed away from the employee's immediate work area. Two approaches are used:

1 In-house programs that are conducted within the organization's own training facility, either by training specialists from the HR department or by external consultants (often a combination of both).

2 Off-site programs held elsewhere and sponsored by an educational institution, a professional association, a government agency, or an independent T&D firm.

According to a recent study by the Center for Workforce Development, up to 70 percent of what employees know about their jobs they learn informally from the people they work with. Formal training programs account for 30 percent or less.[16] Still, there are a wide range of training methods employed to train and develop employees away from their jobs. Some methods are used more often for managerial employees, while others more often for nonmanagerial employees. However, the differences in responsibilities between these two levels of employees are dissolving in many organizations as reorganization and empowerment initiatives are implemented.

Videotapes   Videotapes bought off the shelf or produced internally are used by 90 percent of organizations,

according to a recent survey. New concepts and ideas can be introduced in this convenient format and videotapes can supplement several of the other techniques to be discussed. See *HR in the News;* "Kodak Develops Humor—Increases Performance" for an unusual use of videotape and other technologies.

Lecture   The lecture is the second most popular away-from-the-job T&D technique, with some 85 percent of organizations using this controversial method. Its strength lies in delivering uniform information to a large group of people in a timely manner.[17] Almost all T&D methods contain at least some lecture. Two complaints are made about this method: Behavioral skills seem to be learned more effectively through more interactive methods, such as role playing or case studies; and "adult learning" advocates say trainees get bored and listen poorly. As a student, you probably understand the shortcomings of lectures all too well. However, research indicates that lecture is as effective as more-interactive forms of teaching at creating learning in trainees.[18]

Conference/Discussion   Many training programs focus on organizational problems and innovative ideas. Discussing problems and critical issues in a conference/discussion format permits a dialogue between the trainer and trainee, as well as among the trainees. This two-way communication provides trainees with immediate feedback on their questions and ideas and heightens motivation for the learner.

Vestibule or Simulation   In a training area created to resemble the employee's actual work area, vestibule or simulation training is performed with the aid of an instructor who demonstrates tasks on the same kinds of machines and/or the same processes the trainee will use on the job. Vestibule training has been successfully used for a variety of skilled positions including retail sales personnel, bank tellers, machine operators, and aircraft pilots.

Case Study   A case study is a written description of an organizational problem. The case method was developed at the Harvard Business School in the 1920s to develop problem-solving skills and remains a popular teaching technique, primarily at the graduate level of study. Case studies require participants to identify and analyze specific problems, develop alternative courses of action, and recommend the best alternative.

Role Playing   During role playing (or *reality practice*), participants play the roles of those involved in an organizational problem. Usually there are no scripts, and participants have limited data on which to base their

HR IN THE NEWS

KODAK DEVELOPS HUMOR—INCREASES PERFORMANCE

Surveys of executives show that 96 percent think that people with a sense of humor do better at their jobs than those who seem to lack a funnybone. Kodak decided on an unusual development technique and created a "humor room" to help increase creativity in its manufacturing, research, marketing, and other departments.[19] The humor development room contains a resource library stocked with humorous books, videotapes, and comfortable chairs; group meeting areas with photos of Charlie Chaplin and Groucho Marx on the wall, where groups can brainstorm; a "toy store" where punching bags, "boss dolls" (with pull-off arms and legs), and other silly items are free to employees; and an area where computers, or "humor processors," are loaded with software to help employees be more creative in problem solving and generating new ideas.

Tax consultants—stereotyped as serious—at Price-Waterhouse in New York, attended a humor program where they wrote with pens shaped like vegetables, wore red clown noses, and gave each other standing ovations for achievements on the job.

Case studies indicate that improved performance results from humor training. At Digital Equipment Corporation, managers who participated in a humor workshop increased their productivity 15 percent and cut their sick days in half in the nine months after the training. Employees who viewed funny training films and went to humor workshops at Colorado Health Sciences Center in Denver had a 25 percent decrease in downtime and a 60 percent increase in job satisfaction.

roles. For example, assume that managers are receiving instruction in the use of employee counseling. One member of a group may play the role of an employee who has been tardy and absent several times. Another member plays the role of the employee's supervisor. With as much realism as possible, the two players act out their roles. Discussion normally follows role playing, which itself lasts for only a few minutes.

Management Games Management games (or *simulation exercises*) are designed to replicate conditions faced by real organizations and usually involve competing teams that both make decisions concerning planning, production, finance, and control of a hypothetical organization.[20] The winner is typically the team that achieves the highest net profit at the completion of the game. Teams may receive a printout detailing the specific impacts of their decisions on the effectiveness of the enterprise. Such simulations are used in the strategy courses in modern business schools.

In-basket Exercise An exercise called the in-basket exercise, is designed to develop the analytical and problem-solving skills of lower-level managers. The technique centers on a series of hypothetical problems that a supervisor may find in a typical in-basket. See the

experiential exercise "Supervision—A Basket Case?" at the end of this chapter for an example.

The in-basket exercise forces the trainee to make decisions and to prioritize. For this reason, this exercise is often part of an assessment-center program.

Assessment Center The assessment center is a technique that requires managers to participate in activities designed to identify their job-related strengths and weaknesses. It is used primarily as a manager-selection device, but it has been increasing use as a manager-development tool.

During an assessment center, which normally lasts for two to three days, a small group (six or seven participants, each from a different department or company) is observed and evaluated by trained assessors. The participants are evaluated on qualities considered important for effective management at *that* firm. Exercises include interviews, leaderless group discussions, role playing, and in-basket exercises. Following the exercises, participants normally receive detailed feedback about their performance and their developmental and growth needs.

Wilderness Training Many managers have swapped business attire for hiking boots hoping to become more-motivated and more-skilled managers. Wilderness training is a generic term used to describe a variety of management and executive development programs that take place in outdoor settings and include mountaineering, backpacking, ocean sailing, white-water rafting, canoeing, cross-country skiing, and cycling. The purpose of wilderness training is not to develop technical skills, but to develop and hone interpersonal skills such as confidence, self-esteem, teamwork, goal setting, and trust. Some are one-day excursions in the woods involving team exercises such as scaling a 14-foot wall or using group methods to cross a simulated river. Also popular are short "ropes courses" where participants, both individually and with the aid of team members, complete a series of exercises high above the ground.

Also popular are *Outward Bound* courses, which generally last for about a week and involve a group of managers who, for example, climb mountains, backpack, or canoe with one or two facilitators who not only serve to assist in the physical aspects of the experience but also lead discussions about leadership, teamwork, trust, and other human qualities important for success in the business world.

One of the key ingredients, challenge, is also an aspect which provokes some new criticism. The Institute of Personnel and Development (IPD), an international HR organization, has recently released a guide on outdoor training. The IPD warns that employers not only check out the physical threats, but the psychological threats as well. IPD suggests that participants may be asked to do things which might make them feel *uncomfortable.*[21]

Membership in Professional Organizations   One way to keep abreast of new theories, principles, methods, and techniques in a field is through membership in a professional organization. Hundreds of such associations exist, with memberships varying from a handful to several thousand.

Many professional organizations publish journals for their membership. Examples include the American Society for Training and Development's (ASTD) monthly, *Training and Development,* Society for Human Resource Management's *HRMagazine,* and the American Management Association's *Management Review, Supervisory Management,* and *Personnel.*

Behavior Modeling   A classroom-oriented technique generally used to teach problem-solving skills to first-level supervisors is called behavior modeling. The technique focuses on individual "skill modules" that address a common problem most supervisors face, such as absenteeism, tardiness, or employee orientation. Each module contains the following elements:[22]

- Trainers introduce the topic.
- A model of effective supervisory behavior is illustrated by videotape or acting. A discussion of key learning points follows.
- The group discusses the model of effective behavior.
- Trainees practice desired behaviors, using role playing, as other trainees observe (each participant acts out the desired behaviors).
- Trainees receive feedback on the effectiveness of their behavior from their fellow observers.

Sensitivity Training   Through sensitivity training (also called *T-group—T* for training), individuals hopefully become more aware of their feelings and learn how one person's behavior affects the feelings, attitudes, and behaviors of others. In the purest form of sensitivity training, an open and honest "no holds barred, tell it like it is" discussion takes place among participants. Perhaps for the first time, many participants learn how their behavior is perceived by others. For some participants, the experience is a tremendous emotional high; others may leave the training session depressed, demoralized, and contemplating a lawsuit.

Does sensitivity training result in greater managerial effectiveness? Research has proven inconclusive.[23] According to studies, sensitivity training can produce such behavioral changes as greater openness, trust, and respect for the feelings of others. It has not, however, been demonstrated that behavioral change has led to more effective job performance.

The popularity of T-groups waned until the technique became a favored tactic in **diversity training programs.** No recent T&D topic has been more controversial. Some employers hiring a "diversity specialist" during the *first wave* of diversity training programs were shocked when they discovered that their entire programs were dedicated narrowly to an aggressive anti-white or anti-male political agenda. (See *HR in the News:* "FAA Training Coerces *Groping* to End Sexual Harassment?") During the *second wave* of diversity T&D programs, employers focused beyond differences based only upon the legal protected-class status categories (for example race, gender, religion). These broader programs realize that diversity of personality, style, region, education, and work history generally reveal even greater differences among employees. Of course, the success of Japanese industry, one of the least diverse yet most successful, challenges some of the premises upon which simplistic diversity training programs are based. While the push for new diversity T&D has slackened, the following guidelines are offered:

HR IN THE NEWS

FAA TRAINING COERCES *GROPING* TO END SEXUAL HARASSMENT?

How would you like to be the manager at the Federal Aviation Administration (FAA) responsible for approving the following sexual harassment and sensitivity training?

Douglas Hartman, an air traffic controller, and other men were forced to run a gauntlet of female employees who were encouraged to grab the crotch and bodies of the men passing through.[24] Hartman, who sued, said the female co-workers grabbed his body and commented derisively on his attributes. He was offended, saying "You can't use abusive behavior to correct abusive behavior."[25] However, Louise Eberhardt, president of the training firm who designed the program, told CNN, "It was . . . what women in male-dominated organizations experience often, daily. . . ."[26] Really?

Also as part of a sexual harassment training program, the FAA paid at least one female air traffic controller $75,000 in damages for a nervous breakdown she claimed was brought on when she disclosed her sexual history during the training. Notice it is the *employer,* not the trainer, being held responsible and liable for outrageous training.

How about yet another FAA training program where black employees at "sensitivity training" sessions have been encouraged to go off by themselves, discuss their problems in a "white, male-dominated society," and then return to the main room and verbally assail some individual white male employees? Nobody really knows how many federal agencies are more likely poisoning, rather than improving, workplace relations.[27]

- Avoid trainers who have a single political agenda.
- Integrate any T&D program into the firm's overall approach to diversity.
- Avoid beginning such training too soon after an EEO complaint.
- Differentiate among the concepts of valuing diversity, pluralism, EEO, affirmative action, and managing across cultures.
- Avoid basing diversity on the "political correctness" movement.
- Don't pressure only one group to change.
- All viewpoints should be allowed expression, even concepts such as *reverse discrimination.*[28]

Technology Based Training   There are two main types of **computer-based training**—CD-ROM approaches and web-based training. In the years prior to the ubiquity of computers, employers often used programmed instruction training. **Programmed instruction** allows trainees to learn the information or skill in small segments and at the learner's own pace. We have shifted from the old booklet-based applications to computers using this same idea. Anyone who has been through a tutorial for programs such as Quicken,

Windows, or PrintShop realizes how well computers can apply the programmed instruction approach.

Off-the-shelf training CDs are available, but often the employer wants or needs to modify or totally invent the materials. One study found that it can take 300 hours for a T&D department to create one hour of training "burned" onto a CD.[29]

No educational or training approach has ever exploded onto the scene faster and with as much promise as **web-based training (WBT).** The Internet offers training opportunities not bound by either time or place. Universities and employers are busy testing the promise that the web has for instruction. For instance, high-tech firms like Automated Concepts and Noblestar Systems employ companies like DigitalThink, a leading WBT company, to provide information technology (IT) training for their professionals. Initially more than 55 courses on Java, Microsoft Windows NT, C++ programming, web programming, and other topics were offered. "WBT is the solution to the conflict between keeping Noblestar employees trained in keeping with obligations to our clients." says Wayne Jackson, director, emerging technologies group at Noblestar. "Before [WBT] the best and busiest people at Noblestar were often unavailable for instruction in new technologies. Now we get tutor-supported training to those people and keep their skill 'state of the art'."[30] An integrated training management system lets managers see which employees have enrolled in courses and tracks student progress.

Satellite linkages, compressed video, and other videoconferencing techniques are technology-based approaches that are popular for organizational communications and training. These techniques can make technology-based programs cost efficient if used on a large scale since the set costs of the technology can be spread over a greater number of trainees for a lower per-trainee cost. Further, linking together multiple sites to receive a single electronic transmission can capture the advantages of immediacy and standardization of training across locations.

Packages of T&D Programs   Away-from-the-job T&D programs can come as an integrated package or program of courses. Many such "total" T&D programs are offered as formal courses and seminars conducted by either in-house or off-site by a university, consulting group, or nonprofit association such as the American Management Association, American Society for Training and Development, or Society for Human Resource Management.

The length and breadth of these courses vary considerably. A one- or two-day seminar normally focuses on a specific management technique or problem such as time management or executive speaking. One- or two-week courses may focus on a variety of managerial methods and processes. For example, the American Management Association's popular five-day course "Developing Supervisory Leadership Skills" covers leadership, communication, discipline, employee development, job satisfaction, and morale.

Some universities sponsor advanced management programs that closely resemble a highly concentrated master's degree program in business administration. One of the most popular courses of this nature is the Harvard Business School's Advanced Management Program. For more information about T&D packages examine Figure 10–7.

OJT or Away-from-the-Job T&D?   A contingency approach is required when deciding which general approach to T&D should be used. In some situations, OJT will be a very effective approach while in others the best T&D program will be available at an external site. See Figure 10–8 for the pros and cons for using away-from-the-job training.

FIGURE 10–7   CHECKLIST FOR SELECTING A TRAINING PACKAGE

How do you pick a good training package off the shelf?

Many employers are interested in purchasing a package which might include videotape and/or computer-based instruction. The following is a guide to selecting such a package.

1 Do you have a specific training need which the package addresses?

2 Will it meet your very specific training objectives?

3 Is the package well-organized, and does it allow flexibility in using its modules?

4 Will the copyright holder permit modification of the package?

5 What limitations will you have to duplicate or "site-license" the package?

6 Are the media portions of high technical quality, current (year?), and believable?

7 Does the package employ multiple and sound principles of learning?

8 Are there opportunities for trainees to practice new skills and knowledge?

9 Are useful trainer/facilitator aids part of the package?

10 Are there workbooks and other trainee aids?

11 Are there available statistics demonstrating validity and effectiveness?

12 Does the supplier have a good reputation and customer service?

13 Is the package a good value (total costs/number of trainees)?[31]

FIGURE 10–8   AWAY-FROM-THE-JOB TRAINING: THE BALANCE SHEET

Among the potential assets of away-from-the-job training are the following:

- Training is cost efficient because groups rather than individuals are usually trained.
- Trainers, usually full-time instructors or training personnel, are likely to be more competent trainers than ad hoc on-the-job trainers.
- More planning and organization often go into away-from-the-job training than into OJT.
- Away-from-the-job training enables the trainee to learn in an environment free from the normal pressures and interruptions of the workplace.
- Off-site courses and seminars enable small companies with limited resources to train employees without the formidable expenses of a large training staff and training facilities.

Among the potential liabilities of away-from-the-job training are the following:

- Employees attending away-from-the-job training are not performing their jobs. This is an added expense of training, though training benefits should exceed costs in the long run.
- Away-from-the-job training often has problems of **transfer of learning.** Sometimes this training is of limited practical value to the trainee—particularly when the training is conducted away from the organization. Because it is impossible for the trainer to customize a course for each participant, away-from-the-job programs normally contain limited applications for a trainee's specific problems and situations.

The learning climate of the workplace needs to be taken into account as well. It is impossible to escape job duties when on the property of some employers, while other employers, like Aetna with its own T&D "campus," provide an excellent transfer climate. An effective **transfer climate** is one in which the environment—including leadership and rewards and punishments—assists rather than hinders, T&D efforts.[32]

The goals and objectives of the T&D effort need to be identified early. Wexley and Latham have developed a 3×3 **training goals matrix** to suggest what type of training might be indicated, depending on the goals sought and strategies favored (see Figure 10–9). Using their figure, if the organization wishes to increase motivation, then an appropriate strategy that is behavior based would involve coaching and behavior modeling (column "Motivation" and row "Behavioral"). Similarly, if the employer wished to increase job skills using a cognitive (or intellectual) approach, then lectures, audiovisual aids, case study, and computer-based training would all be reasonable approaches.[33]

Other considerations relating to training selection are resources and money. Smaller employers, employers who lack human resource development (HRD) professionals, and employers who have no appropriate equipment will generally have to opt for off-site T&D methods. When budgets shrink, two things happen: Employees generally have to perform at higher levels, and staff budgets such as T&D budgets are often cut. For the small, financially strapped organization, OJT and low-cost away-from-the-job programs (such as university and government-sponsored courses) are often the only economically feasible training alternatives.

STEP 4: CONDUCTING TRAINING

There are responsibilities which go with this step. Often HRD or T&D departments use checksheets to ensure that all rooms, supplies, and technologies are available on time. The logistics required are complex at Xerox's new "Document University," where print shop and other customers learn to build their own businesses through TQM.

In away-from-the-job situations, HRD employees need only follow through with pre- and post-training planning.

STEP 5: EVALUATION

One very important question remains: Was the training *effective?* Did the trainees actually gain the needed

FIGURE 10–9   TRAINING GOALS MATRIX OF WEXLEY AND LATHAM

GOALS

STRATEGIES		SELF-AWARENESS	JOB SKILLS	MOTIVATION

COGNITIVE		Career development
		Management role theory
		Need for achievement
		Double-loop learning
		Sensitivity training
		Self-directed manage-
		  ment development
		Transactional analysis
			Orientation training and
			  socialization of new
			  employees
			Lecture
			Audiovisual
			Vroom-Yetton model
			Case study
			The incident process
			Job aids
			Computer-based training
			Teleconferencing
			Corporate classrooms/
			  colleges
			Seminars and workshops
				Role motivation theory
				Need for achievement
				Training
				Survey feedback

BEHAVIORAL		Interactive skills training	On-the-job training Apprenticeship Programmed instruction Equipment simulators Computer-assisted instruction Rational manager training Conference discussion Assessment centers Role playing Management games Grid seminars Leader-member exchange Juniors boards Understudy assignments Mentoring	Coaching Behavior modeling
ENVIRONMENTAL		Leader match		Job rotation Behavior modification

skills, knowledge, or behaviors? Over $100 billion a year is spent nationwide on T&D activities, and the cost of T&D to large organizations can run into the millions of dollars. With such costs, any prudent manager should ask: Are we getting our money's worth?

There are several strategies that may be used to evaluate training. *Cost-benefit analysis* measures T&D costs against the monetary benefits of T&D. While T&D costs (materials, supplies, lost work time, travel expenses, consultant fees, and so on) are relatively easy

to measure, T&D benefits are difficult to translate into economic terms. For example, how does an improvement in communication skills affect the bottom line? While cost-benefit analysis is theoretically appealing, it sees little actual use in practice.

Another strategy for evaluating T&D is to assess the extent to which the objectives were met. As we discussed earlier, T&D objectives define the performance gap between actual and desired performance and may be used to measure training success.

Levels of T&D Evaluation   One popular evaluation strategy includes four different levels of T&D evaluation. In fact, it comprises four separate evaluation strategies. The designer of this system, D. L. Kirkpatrick, advocates applying each level of evaluation to a program. He suggests measuring the participants' *reaction,* participants' *learning,* change in participants' *behavior,* and impact of the program on *organizational effectiveness.*[34]

Level 1: How Did Participants React?   Throughout training, each trainee formulates opinions and attitudes about the overall effectiveness of the program. Perhaps the trainee is favorably inclined toward the content of the program but thinks that the trainer is too cold or too impersonal. At this level of evaluation, the trainee normally completes a questionnaire about the adequacy of T&D facilities, the skill of the trainer, the quality of the program content, and the relevancy of T&D techniques. After the questionnaires are tabulated and reviewed, the program's quality is judged on the basis of the overall responses.

This first level of evaluation is highly subjective, and training administrators should ensure that the participants are not responding favorably simply because they enjoyed the program or instruction. Figure 10–10 is a questionnaire used for evaluating T&D programs offered through Indiana state government.

Level 2: What Did Participants Learn?   Learning is often assessed by testing a trainee both before and after a program. For example, if a program is designed to teach a word processing program, the trainee would be expected to score significantly higher on a test after training than before. This second level of evaluation is easily conducted if tests are readily available to measure learning, but trainers are often reluctant to test trainees—it is often viewed as not conforming to "adult learning" theories. Because managers are also reluctant to spend the time to create learning tests, learning often regrettably goes unevaluated. In addition, it is difficult to create a test to measure many behavioral skills such as communication skills, interpersonal relations, and leadership skills.

Level 3: How Did Participants' Behavior Change?   Participants in T&D are expected to learn a skill or body of knowledge that results in a positive change in job behavior. Learning time management techniques, for example, is purely an academic—and costly—ability unless behavior is changed on the job. Learning needs to be *applied.* The important questions to ask concerning this level of evaluation is whether learning was transferred from training to the job and how can this be objectively evaluated?

Level 4: What Organizational Goals Were Affected?   Ultimately, T&D is expected to result in a more effective organization. The fourth level of evaluation examines the impact of T&D on organizational goals of productivity, quality, and job satisfaction, as well as decreased turnover, accidents, and grievances. Although this level of evaluation is appealing in both theoretical and practical terms, it is difficult. How can the effects of T&D be separated from the effects of other organizational changes (for example, reorganization or job redesign)? Where it is difficult to connect acquired skills directly to organizational goals, the administrator may implement a less sophisticated evaluation strategy.

Applying Evaluation Strategies   T&D effectiveness can be evaluated by the simple, uncomplicated—and perhaps useless—process of measuring participants' reactions or by sophisticated strategies that compare T&D costs and benefits and measure organizational results. Flexibility should be the key to evaluating T&D programs; T&D personnel should apply the most sophisticated strategy that is both relevant and economically feasible. Combining the four levels of T&D evaluation with a cost-benefit strategy would certainly enable management to ascertain whether a program was contributing to the effectiveness of the organization. At the very least, measurable objectives should be written during the assessment phase and evaluated after T&D has been completed.

Costs of T&D Programs and Departments

At the beginning of the 21st Century, American employers are easily investing over $100 billion annually on T&D activities—$61 billion in formal programs among only the larger employers. Still, the amount of formal T&D given to U.S. workers compares unfavorably to employers in many other countries. New production workers in Japan receive 380 hours of T&D, and new workers in Japanese-owned plants in the United States receive 370 hours. U.S. employers offer only 47 hours of T&D to their new employees.[35]

Employers should be shrewd shoppers for T&D approaches. For budgeting a T&D project the following equation has been offered: *Development cost equals the number of developer hours per hour of T&D, multiplied by the development cost per hour multiplied by the number of hours of T&D.* Of course, if a T&D program cost $10,000 (using the equation) but resulted in $50,000 in

FIGURE 10–10   EVALUATION OF TRAINING

EVALUATION OF TRAINING
Indiana State Government
State Form 45910 (4-93)

NOTE: Our agency is committed to providing quality training. To assist us in this effort, please complete this evaluation form for both the course content and the course instructor. Doing so will assist us in monitoring our services and enable us to better meet your needs and the needs of other employees.

Your name (optional):	Date: 4-1-99
Course title: MOTIVATION	Instructor: D. McCALMAN

REGARDING COURSE CONTENT . . .

Did this course meet your expectations?	Yes ☑	No ☐
Was the content of the course logically organized?	Yes ☑	No ☐
Was adequate time allowed for the material covered?	Yes ☑	No ☐

If you responded "No" to any of the above, please explain: _____
_____

What additional information, if any, would you incorporate into the course? _____
_____

What information would you remove from the course content? Please explain. _____
_____

Were the following helpful:

Audio visuals	Yes ☐	No ☐	Some ☑	N/A ☐
Overhead transparencies	Yes ☐	No ☐	Some ☑	N/A ☐
Role plays	Yes ☑	No ☐	Some ☐	N/A ☐
Demonstrations	Yes ☑	No ☐	Some ☐	N/A ☐
Handouts	Yes ☐	No ☐	Some ☑	N/A ☐
Reading assignments	Yes ☐	No ☐	Some ☐	N/A ☑
Discussion	Yes ☑	No ☐	Some ☐	N/A ☐
Lecture	Yes ☑	No ☐	Some ☐	N/A ☐

Did you have ample time to practice <u>newly acquired</u> skills?   Yes ☑   No ☐

Additional comments: _____ we could have used additional time-- _____

_____ enthusiastic Instructor/speaker _____

REGARDING THE INSTRUCTOR . . .

Was the instructor:

Well-informed on the subject	Yes ☒	No ☐
Well prepared/organized	Yes ☒	No ☐
Enthusiastic	Yes ☒	No ☐

Did the instructor:

Encourage participation	Yes ☒	No ☐
Adequately answer questions	Yes ☒	No ☐
Present a professional appearance	Yes ☒	No ☐

Continued.

FIGURE 10–10   *(continued)*

Please summarize your <u>overall</u> rating of the instructor:

Knew the material very well

SUMMARY INFORMATION . . .

How will you apply what you have learned in this course to your job?

– gained several ideas on how to

motivate my employees

– will re-think my job descriptions for

2 employees.

ADDITIONAL COMMENTS:

Thank you!

SOURCE: Indiana State Government (1999). Used by permission.

savings, what did the T&D really cost? Figure 10–11 gives some of the comparative costs of several popular methods of T&D.

PRINCIPLES AND STYLES OF LEARNING

Training is a form of life-long learning. In *Future Shock,* futurist Alvin Toffler projected that "The illiterate of the year 2000 will not be the individual who cannot read and write, but the one who cannot learn, unlearn, and re- learn."[36] Research in education has gone in many direc- tions trying to identify prescriptions for effective learn- ing. Traditionally, trainers have relied upon basic learning principles. Modern research has also examined learning styles and adult learning.

LEARNING PRINCIPLES

Most lists of **learning principles** include motivation, participation, feedback, organization, repetition, and ap- plication. *Motivation* is required to have the trainees apply themselves. Showing the trainees how the training

FIGURE 10-11 COMPARATIVE FORMAL TRAINING COSTS

METHOD	TRAINEE TIME-OFF COSTS	OTHER COSTS	PROS	CONS
Lecture and Discussion	High if away from work, low otherwise	Lecturer costs vary $200–$500/hour	Familiar; effective learning; can be interactive	Boring; scheduling problems
Videotape— off the shelf	Low	Equipment expense; tapes range $100–$500	Familiar, effective learning, holds attention	Non-interactive, can be dated or irrelevant
Computer-based— CD and Web-based	Low	Equipment expense if dedicated to training; packages range widely $100+	High interactivity among good products; flexible on time/place	May intimidate; may not match needs
Video conference	Low	Equipment expensive; expense of transmission time	Effectiveness similar to face-to-face; allows access to great trainers	Scheduling problems for trainees and technology needs

will improve their own performance and letting trainees choose or plan the training are two motivational approaches.[37] *Participation* is assured when the training is interactive or involves the trainees in another direct manner. *Feedback* to the trainees about how they are doing each step of the way helps maximize learning. *Organization* of material, through outlining or other natural progression, can break down even complicated material into reasonable "bites." *Repetition* is exemplified by the standard advice, "tell them what you are going to tell them; tell them; then tell them what you told them." Allowing trainees to practice what they are learning improves learning. Finally, *application* focuses upon the transfer of learning issue. Can the trainee actually apply the learning back to the workplace in a useful manner? Training should focus on such applications.

Away-from-the-job techniques frequently have transfer-of-learning problems. There are some specific tactics a trainer can take to improve the "transfer climate":

- Maximize the similarity between the training and the job.
- Provide as much experience as possible with the task being taught.
- Provide a variety of examples.
- Identify important features of the employee's task.
- Make sure that general principles are understood.
- Make sure that the training is rewarded on the job.
- Design the training so that the applicability is obvious.
- Use questions to guide trainees' attention.

There are several approaches to studying learning styles, including learning styles, wholebrain, and experiential learning theories.

Learning styles or neurolinguistic programming (NLP), suggests that people have a preferred way of learning and communicating that is tied to the senses. When you want to remember certain information, you try to access a certain "file" in your brain where you have stored the data—either in visual (pictures), auditory (sounds), or kinesthetic (physical feelings) form.[38] Training needs to take the different learning styles into account. This is sometimes called "accelerated learning." Visual learners want to see; auditory learners focus in on the sound; and kinesthetic learners want to move, feel, and do.

Whole-brain learning theories emphasize the preference for either the right or left hemisphere of the brain. The right side is considered to hold the seat of creativity and emotion while the left is considered to hold the seat of logic and reason.[39] Some whole-brain theories are complex, but the simplest implications are that a *logical* approach to training will work for some, while an appeal to *creativity* may be more successful for others. Men have less integration across the hemispheres (due to testosterone), resulting in their being influenced exclusively by one side at a time.

Finally, there has been some controversy over the validity of **adult learning theory.** Writer Malcolm Knowles suggested "andragogy," the study of adult learning, was vastly different from pedagogy. He identified four assumptions of adult learners which distinguish them from nonadults: self direction, experience, readiness to learn, and orientation to learning. Many would suggest that all learners share the needs which Knowles attributes exclusively to adults. From either perspective, the following assumptions are important.

Knowles says that: (1) Adults have a deep psychological need to be self-directing (visit my three-year-old!). This means adults (or all learners) resist training situations which do not allow self-direction; (2) adults have a reservoir of experience that serves as a resource for learning and should be used as a way to relate to learning (the only noncontroversial point); (3) adults (or all learners) are most ready to learn when they need to know the information; and finally, (4) adults tend to have a problem-centered orientation to learning. Knowles argues that children are subject-centered[40] (perhaps Knowles is confusing a teacher's lesson plans with a child's interest pattern). All of these, save the experience, are fundamental concepts for all learners. If it makes adults feel better about learning by suggesting that they are different, so be it.

LEGAL ISSUES

As explained in Chapter 4, civil rights laws forbid discrimination in terms or conditions of employment because of race, color, religion, sex, national origin, age, or disability. The act covers T&D activities, just as it does any other personnel activity.[41]

1 T&D required to obtain a job or a promotion must be job related.

2 Selecting employees for a T&D program must not be done in an illegally, discriminatory manner.

3 The training itself must not be illegally discriminatory. For example, to comply with federal legislation, AT&T redesigned pole climbing so that women could successfully complete the pole-climbing training course.[42]

4 If career decisions are made on the basis of success during training, it should be shown that training success is a valid "test". For example, if preferred job assignments are given to employees who performed effectively during training, a correlation between training success and subsequent job success should be shown.

5 Preferential treatment for training minorities *is* legal if an affirmative action program exists. Such treatment was supported in the Supreme Court case *United Steelworkers* v. *Weber* in 1978. The Court ruled that affirmative action programs involving training *are* legal where prior evidence of racial discrimination exists.

TOP MANAGEMENT SUPPORT

An organization's T&D activities must receive a strong endorsement from top management. Without this support, T&D programs may be viewed as a form of entertainment or a second-rate, marginally effective activity. Support also means a sufficient budget to carry out a full T&D program.

Support of top management must be earned by demonstrating how programs are contributing to the strategic and operational goals of the organization. Because of the importance of the bottom line, demonstrating the cost effectiveness of investing in training may be the most productive way to gain support. Unfortunately, that form of evaluation is the most difficult to demonstrate.

What specific skills should HRD professionals possess? One model suggests that HRD professionals acquire four sets of skills: power skills, relationship skills, technical skills, and entrepreneurial skills.[43] For instance, HRD staff who perceive themselves as entrepreneurs rather than administrators view HRD as a profit center and recognize the strategic link between training and the organization's long-term corporate goals.

CLIMATES FOR CHANGE

Problems of transfer of learning become significant when managers attempt to apply new ideas in rigid, uncompromising climates. Therefore, the transfer climate in the organization plays an important role in T&D success for managers.

One classic problem of transfer of learning involved a widely used human-relations training program for supervisors. Testing before and after the program revealed that supervisors did undergo an attitude change about people-oriented leadership. However, supervisors' on-the-job behavior changed only when their new attitude was supported by their bosses.[44]

In the end, the organizational climate and culture has a significant effect on performance. Management development cannot be effective if it conflicts with existing organizational culture.

INTERNATIONAL HR: INTERCULTURAL PREPARATION

In their book *Going International,* Lennie Copeland and Lewis Griggs tell how Motorola lost out in France to the Japanese when France's Thomson Group chose the Oki Electric Industry Company to expand the French company's semiconductor business. After working with Motorola for six years, a Thomson Group executive said: "We may just have more in common with the Japanese than we do with the Americans." He explained, "We both attach great importance to form and style."[45]

How can a gap as large as the one between Motorola and Thomson be bridged? And what caused the gap in the first place? The reasons for the gap can be summed up in two words: *cultural ignorance.* Generally speaking, the American manager is hurried, abrupt, direct, and objective. Managers in many other countries have opposite traits.

The best solution for closing the gap lies with **intercultural preparation.** The objective is not to make U.S. managers behave like people from other cultures; rather, the objective is to help managers (and other expatriates) cope with unexpected events in a new culture.

A large number of T&D techniques are available for preparing expatriates for overseas assignments, and they can be categorized into five categories[46]:

1 Area studies that expose people to a new culture through materials on the country's sociopolitical history, geography, etc.

2 Cultural assimilator, a programmed instruction method that exposes trainees to specific incidents critical to successful interaction with a target culture.

3 Language preparation.

4 Sensitivity training, in which people's self-awareness is increased.

5 Field experiences, or exposing trainees to minicultures within their own country during short field exercises.

A survey found that of 288 North American companies with international operations, only 30 percent provide formal cultural orientation to employees being sent overseas.[47]

SHARED RESPONSIBILITY

Like many staff functions, responsibility for T&D is shared by line management and staff administrators. Effective T&D requires that line and staff work closely together on all phases of the T&D process and that both parties understand and recognize their shared authority. Although the responsibility for various functions of T&D will differ from organization to organization, certain responsibilities are usually reserved for either line managers or staff personnel. For instance, it is often the role of HRD to procure the training package once the objectives are agreed to by line and staff.

SUMMARY POINTS—cont'd

● The training process includes five distinct but related steps: needs assessment, setting objectives, selection of training, the training itself, and evaluation.

● Effective T&D includes a balance of both on-the-job and away-from-the-job activities. Individual programs should be created, particularly for managers, and should be built on current strengths and weaknesses, career potential, and personal needs.

● Only through a sound evaluation will trainers obtain support from top management and show how T&D improves organizational effectiveness. Major T&D efforts should include the following levels of evaluation: reaction, learning, behavior change, and results.

● Both line and staff trainers must be aware of the legal environment surrounding the T&D function. Race, religion, sex, color, national origin, or age generally should not be a factor in determining who receives training or who is selected to be developed for promotional opportunities. The only exception to this rule is where an organization has an approved affirmative action program.

● T&D must reflect certain principles of learning, learning styles, and theories to be successful.

● T&D involves close cooperation between line and staff personnel, and each must recognize their shared authority. T&D efforts also require the support of top management and a positive transfer-of-learning climate.

CASE STUDY

THE WALKAROUND MALL

Yolanda Gonzales is the mall manager for the Walkaround Mall, located in Charleston, West Virginia. Walkaround is owned by an investment group, RDH, which owns 11 other malls and two dozen strip shopping centers. Gonzales manages Walkaround on behalf of RDH Investments and was recently transferred to this mall after achieving notable success at a similar mall in central Indiana. Walkaround features over one hundred stores and businesses, each of which has either a short- or a long-term lease managed by Gonzales. All leases are computed on the basis of a minimum plus a percentage of store (or business) sales dollars.

Two other malls operate in the area, one larger and one smaller. Wal-Mart and Sam's stores moved into the area, in new strip shopping centers, for the first time in 1998. The population of Charleston is stable. Large employers are located in the area, but the unemployment rate is a little higher than the national average.

Part of Gonzales's role as mall manager is to help develop the overall business of the mall. She was able to show 12 percent total mall sales increases annually during her three years in Indiana. Typically, mall strategy is to focus on three conditions in order to increase mall sales:

1 Increase the occupancy rate.

2 Make the mall more attractive.

3 Ensure that the workforce within the mall is skilled and motivated.

Gonzales was concerned when Walkaround had only a 4 percent increase in total sales in 1997, so when she moved to Charleston at the beginning of 1998, she focused on the three crucial conditions. During 1998, she lost six shops, but replaced

each with a similar store. All four of the "anchors," or large department stores (Sears, Lazarus, Penneys, and Kaufmans), remained on long-term leases. RDH Investments approved a general facilities "facelift," but there was no new construction, and none was likely during the next two to three years.

Gonzales decided that she needed to move on condition 3 and focus on the managers and sales employees. All employees work for their own stores, not for the mall, but Gonzales met with some of the store managers and developed a T&D plan to help the stores train their employees. The manager of Shoes-Are-You told Gonzales, "If you can help train our employees to be better salespersons, I know we could increase our sales."

By May 1998, Gonzales had scheduled a one-hour training program titled "Increase Your Sales and Smile!" The program would be repeated at various times over a two-month period so that every employee would have a chance to attend. A business professor from a local college presented the program using a videotape, a brief lecture, and a short role-playing exercise to emphasize the basics of effective selling. Almost 50 percent of mall employees attended the sessions, and many of the trainees said that they really enjoyed the program and that it was helpful. Gonzales made hopeful predictions when talking with RDH managers at their offices that summer.

However, in mid-January 1999, Gonzales was distraught as she sat in her office and read the numbers. Overall sales had increased—but only by 4.5 percent. Had the training program, which she had designed with the professor, had only a 0.5 percent effect? She now wonders what she can do to influence the employees working in the mall to help boost sales since her hands are tied on conditions 1 and 2.

She has a meeting scheduled for Monday to discuss the mall performance figures with RDH in Dallas.

CASE STUDY—cont'd

QUESTIONS

1. What were the flaws in her training approach?

2. Should she design another training approach to help increase 1999 sales?

3. Did she follow the five steps of an effective T&D plan?

4. What objectives for training would be appropriate for her situation?

5. Is examining the total sales of all mall stores the best, or only, evaluation method available?

6. Can the sluggish sales at Walkaround be solved by an effective T&D program?

EXPERIENTIAL EXERCISES

1. INDIVIDUAL: SUPERVISION—A BASKET CASE?

PURPOSE

To understand how the in-basket technique for developing managers works by participating in an in-basket exercise.

INTRODUCTION

The in-basket is a simulation consisting of notes, letters, memos, and other information that is typical of the kind of printed material that daily crosses a manager's desk. The term *in-basket* is derived from the fact that supervisors and managers face a constant barrage of written requests, questions, concerns, and problems that must be attended to—the kinds of things that often end up in a manager's in-basket. This management T&D technique forces the manager to make decisions: more specifically, decisions about how to act on (if at all) the things that land in the in-basket. The exercise itself teaches the training participant how to act on a variety of problems that confront managers.

TASK

Assume that you supervise 25 blue-collar employees in a mid-sized manufacturing company (1,200 employees) and that you are participating in a management T&D program that uses the in-basket technique. Listed below are brief descriptions of items sitting in your in-basket. For each item, answer the following two questions:

1. How important is this item? (Assign one of the following numbers: 1: not important at all; 2: somewhat important; 3: important; 4: very important; and 5: extremely important.) Be prepared to defend your answer.

2. What specifically should be done with this item? Some options to consider (you may develop others) are: 1: **Act** on the item immediately; 2: **Postpone** acting on it until a later date (specify how much later); 3: **Delegate** the item to someone else to act on (assume you have a secretary or an assistant and that the organization you work for has a normal line/staff orga-

nizational structure with staff assistance from the human resource department, and others; if you chose this option, specify *who* should act on the item; 4: **Seek more information** about the item (specify what information you would seek); and 5: **Do nothing.** Be prepared to defend your answer.

IN-BASKET ITEMS

1. A request from a company to provide a work reference on a former employee you supervised. The employee was a machine operator. He worked for you for about a year and, overall, did satisfactory work, but nothing exceptional.

2. A telephone message to call your spouse immediately.

3. An anonymous letter, signed "concerned female employee," who complains of sexual harassment in your work group. A male employee who is one of your subordinates is named as the harasser.

4. A letter from an excellent employee who wishes to set up an appointment to discuss her future with the company. She states that she is "burned out" in her job and wants a promotion to a more responsible job. She insinuates that she will look for other employment if she is not promoted soon. There are no job opportunities in your work unit and only a handful in other areas of the company.

5. A letter from the HR manager, who expresses concern about the plant's becoming unionized. He wants to meet with you to discuss specifically what you can do to stop "all this talk about a union."

6. A letter from an EEOC representative who wants to talk to you about a complaint filed against your company by a former employee. She (a black female) alleges that you fired her not because of poor performance (as you stated to her) but because she was black.

EXPERIENTIAL EXERCISES — cont'd

7 An anonymous letter stating that alcohol and illegal drugs are being consumed in cars and vans in the company parking lot during lunch hour.

8 A note from your boss that a supervisory position will be open in a few months. He wants to know who, if anyone, among your current nonsupervisory employees might be a good candidate for the job.

2. GROUP: TEACHING THE TEACHERS

PURPOSE

To experience the work that is required when assessing actual training needs and trying to develop an evaluation method that will provide the information employers really want. Group discussion may expose the student to needs and outcomes that she or he did not think were important.

TASK

Perhaps every semester you perform student evaluations on some or all of your instructors. Unless you are guilty of the rater error of leniency, or unless you are taught by an exceptional instructor, you give negative ratings to one or more items describing your instructor.

1 Write down three specific weaknesses of one of your ineffective or mediocre instructors. Do not write down the instructor's name since it is his or her teaching in which we are interested.

2 Form into a small groups, four to six to a group, and discuss your lists. Next, your group should rank-order these identified weaknesses into a group list of at least five weaknesses. Discard any weaknesses that cannot be improved through training.

3 Write training objectives that you would like to see met through some type of T&D program. However, the group should not yet choose what type of training should be conducted.

4 Briefly specify which T&D methods could be used to achieve these objectives.

5 Describe a different evaluation technique for each objective your group specified. Will your evaluation techniques really prove that the weaknesses you originally identified (in step 1) will be corrected after the training?

6 How might you go through these same steps if you were the academic department chair, the academic vice president, a parent, or a state legislator?

KEY TERMS AND CONCEPTS

Adult learning theory
Away-from-the-job training
Computer-based training
Conceptual skills
Diversity training programs
Employee training
Human relations skills
Human Resource Development (HRD)
Intercultural preparation
Job rotation
Lateral promotions
Learning principles
Learning styles

Management development
Management (executive) succession chart
On-the-job training (OJT)
Performance gap
Programmed instruction
Technical skills
Training goals matrix
Training systems model
Transfer climate
Transfer of learning
Web-based training (WBT)
Whole-brain learning theories

REVIEW QUESTIONS

1. What are the major internal and external influences on T&D programs?

2. What are the three levels at which a T&D needs assessment can be made? Describe some of the methods available at the different levels.

3. Name and distinguish the various OJT and away-from-the-job training techniques.

4. When, and in what circumstances, will OJT be more effective than away-from-the-job training techniques? Which approach is more expensive to the organization?

5. How do the training needs of managerial employees differ from the needs of professional nonmanagerial employees, or from those of front-line employees in service or production industries?

6. What are the important principles of learning and learning styles discussed in this chapter? How should knowing these improve the design of a T&D program?

7. How have technology advances changed the T&D methods available to employers? Are high-tech training programs superior to lecture and discussion approaches?

8. Discuss the legal issues that may be involved in T&D. What should an HRD professional do to guard against a complaint or lawsuit involving training?

9. What are the major mistakes employers make in choosing the methods and topics for training programs? Which of the five steps of T&D is most neglected in the workplace?

10. How can an employer enhance the transfer climate of the workplace? What can an organization do at work to help employees learn and remember the training they receive away from the job?

DISCUSSION QUESTIONS

1. Listed are six T&D methods and five situations. From the six T&D selections, select the best answer to the needs in the five situations.

   1. Lecture
   2. Vestibule
   3. OJT instruction
   4. College-sponsored seminar
   5. Apprentice training
   6. Programmed instruction

   _____ A. Train 30 new employees to run a large printing press.

   _____ B. Small employer needs to familiarize two HR employees with new guidelines on the Americans with Disabilities Act.

   _____ C. Office needs to teach one new clerical employee how to run various office machines.

   _____ D. Organization of 500 needs training to prepare raters to handle upcoming performance appraisals more effectively.

   _____ E. Airline needs to train 50 new pilots.

2. If you were a newly hired T&D director for a medium-sized manufacturing company of 750 employees, how would you communicate the importance of T&D to top management? Could you prove the value of T&D programs in objective terms if necessary?

3. How did operating "lean and mean" after downsizing influence T&D programs in the United States? While it is easy to say that we all need more training, do we really? What proportion of the payroll should be spent on formal T&D programs?

4. Should employers invest in basic skills general training? Who has (or shares) the responsibility for teaching and learning basic reading, writing, and math skills? Will there be a greater need for such basic skills training in the workplace during the next 20 years?

5. Is T&D more important in some industries than in others? Which industries need what kind of T&D programs?

6. What are the problems of people and organizations that cannot be solved with training? List five problems that exist in your workplace (or one you know) that cannot be substantially improved through T&D.

7. It is often very hard to assess the value of a T&D program. What are the problems in evaluating the effects of training?

8. If mentoring can be very helpful to the careers of protégés, what can an employee do to be mentored? Can an employer force a manager to mentor an employee? Do the genders of the mentor and the protégé matter?

9. If you were a top manager and wanted your HRD staff to help your managerial employees become better managers, what five courses would you suggest as part of a managerial T&D program? What topics would be most helpful to managers at various stages of their careers?

E N D N O T E S

Chapter 10

1. "Industry Report 1998," *Training* 35 (October 1998): 43.

2. S. Raghuram and R. D. Arvey, "Business Strategy Links with Staffing and Training Practices," *Human Resource Planning* 17 (1994): 55–73.

3. "ASTD Releases 1999 State of the Industry," *Business Wire* (January 12, 1999).

4. Ibid.

5. Gillian Flynn, "Training Budgets 101," *Workforce* 77 (November 1998): 91.

6. Nancy Chase, "Raise Your Training ROI," *Quality* 36 (September 1997): 28.

7. Barb Cole-Gomolski, "Training Benefits Scrutinized, Link to Profitability Hard to Prove," *Computerworld* 32 (July 15, 1998): 24.

8. William McGehee and Paul Thayer, *Training in Business and Industry* (New York: Wiley, 1961), 124–125.

9. J. W. Newstrom and J. M. Lilyquist, "Selecting Needs Analysis Methods," *Training and Development Journal* 33 (1979): 178–82. *See also* K. N. Wexley and G. P. Latham, *Developing and Training Human Resources* (Glenview, IL: Scott, Foresman, 1981), Chapter 3; F. L. Ulschak, *Human Resource Development: The Theory and Practice of Need Assessment* (Reston, VA: Reston, 1983).

10. Bob Filipczak, "Taboo Training Terms," *Training* 34 (July 1997): 36.

11. Ron Zemke, "How to Do a Needs Assessment When You Think You Don't Have Time," *Training* 35 (March 1998): 38.

12. Methods for JIT are discussed in Fred Wickert, "The Famous JIT Card: A Basic Way to Improve It," *Training and Development Journal* 28 (February 1974): 6–9.

13. Harry Levinson, "A Psychologist Looks at Executive Development," *Harvard Business Review* (November–December 1962): 69–75.

14. Diane C. Andrica, "Mentoring: Executive Responsibility?" *Nursing Economics* 14 (March 13, 1996): 128.

15. George F. Dreher and Ronald A. Ash, "A Comparative Study of Mentoring among Men and Women in Managerial, Professional, and Technical Positions," *Journal of Applied Psychology* 75 (1990): 539–546.

16. Jack Stack, "The Training Myth," *Inc.* 20 (August 1998): 41.

17. Carolyn Wiley, "Training for the '90s: How Leading Companies Focus on Quality Improvement, Technological Change, and Customer Service," *Employment Relations Today* 20 (Spring 1993): 84; see also "ASTD Effort Pushes for Better Training of America's Workforce," *Training and Development* 45 (March 1991): 7.

18. Robert D. Bretz and Robert E. Thompsett, "Comparing Traditional and Integrative Learning Methods in Organizational Training Programs," *Journal of Applied Psychology* 77 (1992): 941–951.

19. Adapted from Shari Caudron, "Humor Is Healthy in the Workplace," *Personnel Journal* 71 (June 1992): 63–68; and "How Kodak Made Room for Humor," *Personnel Journal* 71 (June 1992): 66.

20. C. Craft, "Management Games," in R. Craig, *Training and Development Handbook* (New York: McGraw-Hill, 1976).

21. "IPD: Identify the Psychological Risks of Outdoor Training Advises New IPD Guide," *PressWIRE* (March 31, 1998): M2.

22. Wexley and Latham, *Developing and Training Human Resources* (1981), 178.

23. John P. Campbell and Marvin D. Dunnette, "Effectiveness of T-Group Experiences in Managerial Training and Development," *Psychological Bulletin* 64 (August 1968): 73–104; and Robert J. House, "T-Group Education and Leadership Effectiveness: A Review of the Empiric Literature and a Critical Evaluation,"

Personnel Psychology 20 (Spring 1967): 1–32.

24. Linda Chavez, "Diversity's the Name, Spending's the Game," *USA Today* (September 28, 1994): 13.

25. Maria Puente, " 'Reverse Tailhook:' Male Controller Sues FAA," *USA Today* (September 22, 1994): 4.

26. Daniel Seligman, "Thinking about the Gauntlet," *Fortune* 130 (October 17, 1994): 214.

27. Ibid.

28. Ideas adapted from Michael Mobley and Tamara Payne, "Backlash! The Challenge to Diversity Training," *Training and Development* 46 (December 1992): 45–52.

29. Kenneth N. Wexley and Gary P. Latham, *Developing and Training Human Resources in Organizations*, 2nd ed. (New York: HarperCollins, 1991), 6.

30. "Systems Integrators Choose DigitalThink to Provide Web-Based Training; Automated Concepts, Inc. and Noblestar Systems Corporation among Latest Clients of Web-Based Training Leader," *Business Wire* (June 21, 1998).

31. Includes points freely adapted from William R. Tracey, "Customizing Off-the-Shelf Training Programs," *HRMagazine* (January 1993).

32. For a discussion of the concept of transfer climate, see J. Z. Rouillier and I. L. Goldstein, "Determinants of the Climate for Transfer of Training," presented at the meeting of Society of Industrial/Organizational Psychology (1991), as cited in Scott I. Tannenbaum and Gary Yukl, "Training and Development in Work Organizations," *Annual Review of Psychology* 43 (1992): 399–441.

33. Wexley and Latham, *Developing and Training Human Resources* (1991), 6.

34. D. L. Kirkpatrick, "Four Steps to Measuring Training Effectiveness," *Personnel Administrator* 28 (November 1983): 19–26. *See also* K. Bunker and S. Cohen, "The Rigors of

Training Evaluation, A Discussion and Field Demonstration," *Personnel Psychology* 30 (1977): 525–541.

35. Ray A. Faidley, "Build a Lean, Clean, Training Machine," *Training and Development* 47 (October 1993): 69.

36. From Alvin Toffler, *Future Shock,* as quoted in Ron Zemke, "In Search of Self-Directed Learners," *Training* 35 (May 1998): 68.

37. Wexley and Latham, *Developing and Training Human Resources* (1991) 75–77.

38. "Learning-Style Theories," *Personnel Journal* 71 (September 1992): 91.

39. Ibid.

40. Chris Lee, "The Adult Learner: Neglected No More," *Training* 35 (March 1998): 50.

41. Wexley and Latham, *Developing and Training Human Resources* (1991), 22–27.

42. E. I. Smith, *Small Climber Development* (Basking Ridge, NJ: AT&T, 1978).

43. Lyle Sussman and Frank Kuzmits, "The HRD Professional as In-House Consultant," *Personnel* 64 (June 1987): 18–22.

44. Edwin A. Fleishman, "Leadership Climate, Human Relations Training, and Supervisory Behavior," in Edwin A. Fleishman, ed., *Studies in Personnel and Industrial Psychology* (Homewood, IL: Dorsey Press, 1967), 250–263.

45. Lennie Copeland and Lewis Griggs, *Going International* (New York: Random House, 1985), xvii.

46. P. Christopher Earley, "Intercultural Training for Managers: A Comparison of Documentary and Interpersonal Methods," *Academy of Management Journal* 30, no. 4 (December 1987): 686.

47. "Preparing Expatriates," *Training and Development* 47 (September 1993): 10.

CHAPTER 11

INTERNAL STAFFING AND CAREER MANAGEMENT

CHAPTER OUTLINE

CHAPTER OBJECTIVES

1 To recognize the various kinds of internal-staffing decisions that have an impact on the HR function and to describe how these decisions may be effectively made.

CHAPTER OBJECTIVES—cont'd

2 To discuss the importance of making sound promotion decisions and to describe both effective and ineffective criteria for making these decisions.

3 To understand the inherent dangers in making promotion decisions solely on the basis of past performance.

4 To identify the HR department's role in assisting the laid-off employee to gain employment as quickly as possible.

5 To understand the legal issues that surround the internal staffing process.

6 To explore a career management model and to illustrate the elements necessary for a successful career management function.

7 To examine the problems that typically confront employees when seeking to advance their careers.

8 To identify the problems that women and minorities have when trying to move up the organizational ladder.

HR IN THE NEWS

TWO LINES AT THE TELLER WINDOW? THE DILEMMA OF HAVING TWO CAREER PATHS IN BANKING

Employees reach a certain level of their career or age and they look around and wonder: Is this it?

The challenges confronting the banking industry are magnified because of the hierarchical structure of the industry in general. In banking, the two worlds—the *branch* side (retail) and the *corporate* side (administrative)—seem diametrically opposed. Here's the career track: Employees start out as tellers or management trainees. Good, motivated employees will move through the ranks, from teller to platform duties to assistant manager to manager and then hit the corporate wall. To move up, they must go corporate.

This is bad for the industry. The unique skills which made them good branch managers may not be fully utilized at corporate. According to Roger Raber, America's Community Bankers member services director, many branch mangers love their job and have key skills, like great sensitivity to customer needs, abilities to handle crises, and abilities to manage people. Raber says that sometimes branch managers leave their bank for a larger bank or another retail environment. "There isn't a clear career track where you could become a vice president and stay in the branch."

A few banks, like Hudson City Savings Bank of Paramus, NJ, take the career track to a new level. They offer ongoing training and vice president–level jobs in the branch. Hudson has 75 branches and 1000 employees, 700 of which are in branches. Michael Lee, vice president of retail operations, says "If you try to move that number of people to corporate, it's not a very easy task. Therefore, we are in a way forced to keep people at the branch level."

To retain and motivate these managers, Hudson has established three approaches:

1 *Job enrichment programs* with the goal of keeping branch managers in mind of overall bank operations and goals, not just what's going on at their branch.

2 *A senior branch manager program* for each region. "It gets them involved in the functions of the region and gives them . . . more challenge and helps them focus on the needs of the (entire 17-branch) region," Lee says. "We also rotate that position to let senior people get their hands wet and do some more administrative work."

3 *Task forces for special projects,* such as the Y2K problem, revising manuals, and testing transaction procedures. "We try to bring the managers in on these projects and let them be creative," Lee says.

SOURCE: Caroline Wilson, "The Problem with Good Branch Personnel: Do You Transfer Them to Corporate?" *America's Community Banker* (January 1999) 8: 28–31. Edited and reprinted by permission of America's Community Banker.

The 1990s were turbulent times for many organizations and for their employees. Mergers and acquisitions, massive reorganizations, shifts toward service-sector jobs, social pressures, demographic changes, and stable economic growth have all lead to workplace changes.

The typical organizational chart, with neatly drawn and labeled boxes connected by horizontal and vertical lines, often fails to convey the great amount of movement by personnel that takes place in modern enterprises. People are shifted up, down, across, and out in organizations of all kinds and sizes. These decisions about **internal staffing,** involving promotions, demotions, transfers, and layoffs, represent an important area of HR policy and management. Effective internal staffing plans, policies, and procedures will promote the achievement of both organizational and personal goals. However, mismanagement of internal staffing may result in a great deal of job dissatisfaction and reduced organizational effectiveness.

In this chapter, we will discuss internal staffing decisions and the issues connected with them. In Chapters 7 and 8, the primary concern was with external hiring. The focus here will be on the staffing decisions that affect the firm's internal human resources (see *HR in the News:* "Two Lines at the Teller Window," for an example of such issues).

The second part of this chapter concentrates on career management and individual career planning.

The last part of the chapter deals with the special problems that women, minorities, and older workers face in their careers. While progress has been made in removing obstacles to advancement for these groups in many organizations, a "glass ceiling" still exists in others.

FACTORS INFLUENCING INTERNAL STAFFING DECISIONS

Figure 11–1 illustrates the important factors that influence internal staffing decisions. These include the following:

- **Organization Growth** Expansion generally results in filling new positions by promoting existing employees. Increases in the number of new positions are particularly common for companies in growth industries. See Figure 11–2 for information on where organizational and job growth will be through 2006.
- **Reorganization** A major restructuring of an organization will result in various types of personnel actions. During the 1980s and 1990s, mergers and reorganizations became popular. Also, a management philosophy of operating with a flatter organizational structure has had a wide range of effects on staffing considerations.

FIGURE 11–1   FACTORS INFLUENCING INTERNAL STAFFING DECISIONS

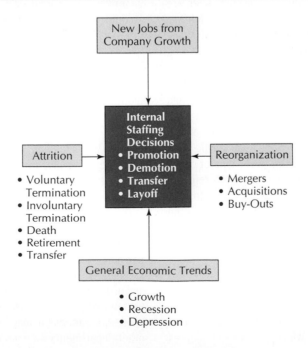

FIGURE 11–2   WHERE WILL JOB GROWTH OCCUR IN THE 2000s?

Fast Growth Occupations 1996–2006.

According to the Bureau of Labor Statistics (BLS), total employment is projected to increase by about 19 million jobs during the 1996–2006 period to a total of 151 million workers. This 14 percent growth is considerably less than the 19 percent growth enjoyed during the previous 10-year period. Expect occupational growth rates to change. These occupations are projected to have the fastest 10-year growth by the following percentages:[1]

1	Computer engineer	+156%	6	Childcare worker (private)	+93%
2	Systems analyst	+152%	7	Physical and corrective therapy assistant	+91%
3	Electronic pagination system worker	+137%	8	Occupational therapist	+91%
4	Physical therapist	+101%	9	Technical writer	+86%
5	Medical assistant	+98%	10	Home health aide	+85%

Fast Growth Industries (percentages). Computer and Data Processing Services—including database administrators, computer support specialists, desktop publishing specialists, and DP equipment repairers.

Health Services—including personal and home care aids, home health aides (tops in growth 1986–1996), medical records technicians, medical assistants, dental hygienists, physicians' assistants, human services workers, and respiratory therapists.

Specialties—including paralegals, special-education teachers, residential counselors, adjustment clerks, and bill collectors.

Largest Growth Industries (number of jobs)—retail trade, business services, health services, and educational services.

Biggest Decline Occupations (number of jobs)—*industry employment changes hurt:* sewing-machine operators, farmers, various textile machine operators, electrical and electronic equipment assemblers, cleaners and servants; *occupational structure changes hurt:* typists and word processors; payroll and timekeepers; bookkeeping, accounting, and auditing clerks; duplicating, mail, and other machine operators; secretaries (except legal and medical); general office clerks; statistical clerks; mainframe computer operators; and *combination changes hurt:* farm workers, along with various telephone, printing, and machine-shop industry jobs.[2]

- **General Economic Trends** Economic cycles are clearly an important variable in changes in internal staffing. The United States has experienced stable growth over the past several years. This has allowed firms to plan HR movements. However, relatively low unemployment rates, along with other demographic factors in the workforce, has led to various hiring and staffing problems. Recessions in the Pacific Rim nations have led to layoffs and other reorganizations.
- **Attrition** Employee reductions that result from termination, resignation, retirement, transfer out of the business unit, and death are collectively referred to as *attrition.* Early-retirement programs to deal with attrition, have become an HR option since the downsizing moves in the early 1990s.

PROMOTION

A **promotion** involves the reassignment of an employee to a higher-level job. When promoted, employees generally face increasing demands in terms of skills, abilities, and responsibilities. In turn, employees generally receive increased pay and (sometimes) benefits, as well as greater authority and status.

Promotions serve many purposes and provide benefits to both organizations and employees. First, promotions enable organizations to use their employees' abilities to the greatest extent possible. Second, promotions can motivate performance. Third, there is a significant correlation between opportunities for advancement and high levels of job satisfaction.[3]

RECRUITING FOR PROMOTION

Two main approaches are used to recruit employees for promotion. The more common approach is the **closed promotion system,** which places the responsibility for identifying promotable employees with the supervisor of the job to be filled. In addition to reviewing the past performance and assessing the potential of subordinates, a supervisor may inquire about employees in other departments who may be qualified for the job.

A drawback to the closed promotion system is that many employees who may be qualified and interested in promotion may be overlooked.

An approach that may lead to recruiting more qualified persons is the **open promotion system** or *job posting*. Job vacancies are publicized on bulletin boards and internal communication systems so that all interested employees may apply. Job posting enhances participation and equal opportunity efforts, but increases administrative expenses and takes time. A survey by the Bureau of National Affairs showed that open promotion is used mostly at the clerical and blue-collar levels in government and unionized companies. Open and closed systems are used about equally for professional and technical employees. Closed systems are used almost exclusively for managerial personnel.[4]

PROMOTION CRITERIA

For many, a promotion is a highly sought prize. Climbing the organizational ladder has long been a part of the American dream. Status, satisfaction, and financial rewards accrue to those who are able to rise in an organization. But frustration, stress, and even severe depression may occur when personal goals of upward mobility are unmet by an organization—particularly when an employee feels passed over for a deserved promotion. Because organizational effectiveness and job satisfaction are influenced by the way in which promotions are made, it is important for organizations to gather reliable data for making decisions about promotions. There are a number of criteria that organizations examine in deciding which candidates to promote.

Seniority   Many organizations place significant weight on an employee's seniority or tenure when making a promotion decision. **Seniority** refers to an employee's length of service and has long been an important factor. Salaries and benefits such as vacation time and sick leave are also often tied to seniority.

Students of management may think that seniority should be given little or no weight in promotion decisions. There are, however, sound arguments for using seniority as a criterion. First, seniority avoids the problems of biased managers, who may promote favorite employees. Second, seniority is a quick and easy method. Third, seniority and performance are correlated up to a point. Employees usually become more competent at their jobs as they gain experience. Fourth, seniority rewards loyalty and so helps in retention efforts.

Seniority provisions are not required by federal laws except in the public sector, nor is seniority an "inherent

right" of employees. However, formal seniority systems are common in virtually all unionized organizations and rare among nonunion employers.

There are a variety of seniority approaches. The most common is *plantwide seniority*, where an employee receives credit that becomes applicable whenever that employee competes with any other employee from another department for the same position. Other common seniority approaches include departmental, trade, classification, and companywide. For example, in a *departmental seniority* system, employees accrue seniority according to the amount of time they worked within a particular department, and that seniority credit is valid only within that department.

In situations involving layoffs, seniority systems often use **bumping;** that is, employees with greater seniority whose jobs have been phased out have the right to displace, or bump, employees with less seniority. Such bumping rights may be limited to departmental or job classification seniority instead of plantwide seniority. In a *combined seniority system*, plantwide seniority is frequently used only to determine bumping rights.

Management often disagrees with the use of seniority as the sole determinant of promotion decisions. The Bureau of National Affairs estimates that seniority is a determining factor in promotional policies, as provided by collective bargaining agreements, in 67 percent of labor contracts. However, only 9 percent of labor contracts require promotion decisions to be based solely on seniority. Another 33 percent provide that the most senior individual will receive promotion if he or she is qualified for the job.[5] In most promotional policies, seniority is treated as a "tie-breaker" or as just one determining factor.

Past and Current Performance   Because of the potential drawbacks in using seniority as the sole promotion criterion, most nonunion organizations generally focus upon current performance when promoting employees to jobs of increased responsibility. Seniority is often given little weight. Instead, a candidate's performance, training and development, education, awards, and other performance data are often used to predict the employee's chances for success in a higher-level job. Using this approach, the chances that the organization will make an effective promotion decision are relatively good when both the candidate's present job and the higher job require similar skills and abilities (for example, receptionist to secretary or first-line supervisor to superintendent).

In these situations, past work performance is a fairly good predictor of future success. But past performance is not always a valid indicator of future performance, particularly when the employee is promoted to a job that requires different skills and abilities. A common situation involves the promotion of a nonmanagerial employee to manager, such as advancement from assembly-line worker to first-line supervisor. The skills required for effective supervision are almost totally different from those required for successful assembly-line work.

Assessment Centers

To improve the chances of making successful promotional decisions—particularly from nonmanagement to management—many organizations are using assessment centers. Job candidates are brought to **assessment centers** for evaluation of their promotability and to participate in a series of exercises. These exercises focus on the kinds of skills and abilities required to effectively perform the higher-level managerial jobs that the candidates seek.[6]

WWW.ATT.COM

American Telephone and Telegraph's (AT&T) assessment-center program is one of the oldest and largest. AT&T sets up over 50 assessment centers across the United States. Each assessment center is located in a conference room or seminar area away from the worksite.

An AT&T employee may ask to attend an assessment center, or a supervisor may feel that an employee is supervisory material and suggest that the employee attend. In either case, the final decision to participate is the employee's.

About a dozen participants undergo exercises designed to determine their potential as successful managers. Employers who do not have a corporate center may send a single employee who will participate with others from various employers. Common exercises during AT&T's two-and-one-half-day assessment include: mental ability, reasoning ability, and current affairs knowledge tests; in-basket exercises and management games; role playing; and in-depth interviews concerning career goals.[7]

Throughout the session, six assessors and a director observe and evaluate each participant. They are experienced, successful line managers who volunteered to be trained as assessors. The assessors pool their evaluations and place each participant into one of the following categories: more than acceptable, acceptable, less than acceptable, and unacceptable. These ratings become important criteria for selecting managers in the future, though they are not the sole criterion used.

The results of AT&T's studies, and of the studies of many other researchers, show that the assessment center is a more effective selection method than such traditional practices like performance appraisals, interviews, and supervisory recommendations.[8] In comparing the method to traditional methods, one researcher stated that "the average validity of the assessment center is about as high as the maximum validity attained by use of . . . traditional methods."[9]

"UNOFFICIAL" PROMOTION CRITERIA

A common retort to a discussion of criteria used for promotions is this: "Where I work, promotions depend on who you know, not what you do." All too often, a gulf exists between the theory and practice of promotions. Criteria such as seniority, performance, and assessment-center ratings may be cast aside for political reasons. **Unofficial promotion criteria** may influence or even dominate a decision. Such criteria include personal characteristics, nepotism, social connections, and friendships.

Personal Characteristics

The Civil Rights Act, the Age Discrimination Act, and the Americans with Disabilities Act prohibit discrimination in all terms and conditions of employment on the basis of age, race, color, religion, sex, national origin, or disability. Internal staffing decisions fall under the domain of these acts, just as external recruiting, selection, and placement practices do. Although organizations profess to abide by EEOC guidelines, not all organizations practice what they preach. Being of the "wrong" sex, race, age, or religion may create a real, though unspoken, obstacle to advancement. Prejudice causes a sizable pool of valuable human talent to be overlooked.

Nepotism

Being of a certain bloodline sometimes helps one's progression to a higher-level job. **Nepotism,** from the Italian *nepotismo* ("favoring of nephews"), is the showing of favoritism or patronage to relatives. Nepotism is often criticized because family members get desirable jobs by virtue of their lineage.[10] At the highest ranks of the pyramid, nepotism is still practiced at many well-known firms, such as Ford and Toyota motor companies, DuPont, and Playboy Enterprises.

Employers have policies that either encourage or discourage nepotism. Courts will generally uphold either approach as long as the policy is clear and consistently applied. Employers may restrict nepotism with a written policy prohibiting the hiring of applicants who are related to current employees. However, the possibility of two employees marrying must also be considered. Because such a situation may involve two current, valued employees, it becomes a difficult policy question. A common policy is that if two employees within the same department marry, the junior employee must accept a transfer.

Social Connections   Membership in a certain club, even graduation from the "right" university, and participation in the "right" sport (traditionally golf) are important in getting promoted in some organizations, particularly at the upper management and staff levels. One classic account of the importance of these factors in decisions of promotion was published by sociologist Melville Dalton. Dalton asked, "What are the things that enable men to rise in the plant here?" This response came from a 53-year-old first-line supervisor:[11]

> You know as well as I do that getting in and running around with certain crowds is the way to get up. Nearly all the big boys are in the yacht club, and damn near all of 'em are Masons. Hell, these guys all play poker together. Their wives run around together, and they all have their families out to the yacht club hobnobbing together. Everybody knows it. It's the friendships and connections you make running around in these crowds that makes or breaks you in the plant.

Friendships   In organizations of all forms and sizes, strong informal bonds are created between employees who share common interests, values, and attitudes. In turn, such informal bonds between decision makers and candidates for promotion may play a significant role in, deciding who gets promoted. People naturally prefer to work with people whose thoughts and perceptions mirror their own.

OTHER INTERNAL MOVES

Promotions are not the only way an employee may move in an organization. In fact, until about 2010, when baby-boomers retire, promotions for junior employees may be fewer than for any recent cohort.[12] For many reasons, employees may have to be moved over, down, or even out. Thus, HR professionals must be prepared to deal with demotions, transfers, layoffs, and some less traditional approaches.

DEMOTION

A **demotion** is the reassignment of an employee to a lower job with less pay, often involving fewer responsibilities. Demotions may take place for reasons within or beyond the control of the employee. Typically, there have been five reasons for using the exceptional tool of demotion:

1 A failed promotion

2 Inability to perform assigned duties

3 Incapacitation

4 Downsizing, or the results of a reduction in force

5 Voluntary request by the employee for personal reasons[13]

Surveys indicate that HR directors in manufacturing do not think that demotion is a useful personnel tool (56 percent) and that the incidence of demotion for managers and professionals is extremely low and seldom used.[14]

Some observers say that getting fired may be final, but the worst thing that can happen to you is to be demoted. Mark McCormack, author of *What They Don't Teach You at Harvard Business School,* says that demotion is paralyzing and "leaves you twisting in the wind." Some employees, which McCormack calls "*demotionally* impared" have trouble understanding that they have even been demoted. "The shock is so painful they automatically go into denial . . . tell(ing) themselves that they still have a job . . . dignity and friends at work."[15]

Though demotions are reportedly unpopular tools, employers can get sued both for demoting or for not demoting. In the first of two publicized cases, a former supervisor for the Texas Child Protection Agency sued because she was demoted after she removed a foster child that had been placed with a lesbian couple and placed the child with relatives.[16] On the other hand, Denise Brunetti sued her employer, the Internal Revenue Service, because it took two years for the IRS to demote or discipline her boss for sexual harassment. Brunetti claimed that her female boss, the branch chief, followed Brunetti around like a bodyguard, escorted her to the restroom and breaks, started each day by summoning Brunetti to a private office to talk on a sofa complete with burning scented candles, insisted on adjoining hotel suites with the doors between rooms left open when traveling, bumped against Brunetti's body, stroked her hair, followed her home, and courted her with gifts, and so on. Based upon similar testimony verifying Brunetti's complaints and establishing similar unwelcome sexual advances involving other female employees, the IRS demoted the chief to a $75,000 a year nonmanagerial position two years after the complaint.[17]

In a small number of situations involving unsatisfactory performance, employees may be the recipients of the *promotion-demotion*. Here employees are "kicked upstairs" to higher-paying jobs that typically involve less responsibility.

TRANSFER

A **transfer** is the reassignment of an employee to a job with similar pay, status, duties, and responsibilities. Whereas a promotion involves upward movement, a transfer involves horizontal movement from one job to another.

Transfers take place for several reasons. First, because personnel placement practices are not perfect, an employee–job mismatch may have resulted. A transfer moves the employee to a more suitable job. Second, an employee may become dissatisfied with the job for one or a variety of reasons: serious conflicts with co-workers or a supervisor that appear unresolvable or a dead-end job from which a transfer would advance career goals. Third, organizational needs may require that employees be transferred. Voluntary or involuntary turnover, promotions, demotions, and terminations may result in job vacancies that may be filled most effectively through transfers.

Fourth, as organizations flatten their structures, there is a growing emphasis on lateral transfers for employee development. Having employees hold different jobs within the organization at a given level for a significant period results in a more flexible workforce with broader skills, not only for front-line employees on the shop floor, but for managers as well. Employees should become more willing to accept lateral promotions. One observer says that new ground rules are developing, including the following:

❶ The employee can no longer expect to rely on promotions as their primary measure of job success and satisfaction.

❷ The old notion that employees who make several lateral moves are dead wood is out.

❸ Learning new skills or getting an MBA will no longer guarantee a promotion.[18]

LAYOFF

A **layoff,** sometimes called a *reduction in force (RIF),* occurs when an employer cuts jobs from the payroll. If the need for employees increases after a layoff, some or all of the employees who have been laid off may be *recalled.* If the demand for the organization's products or services does not increase, then the layoff becomes

permanent, and employees are formally separated from the firm. Layoffs have become a way of life due to the fluctuations inherent in a market economy (see *HR in the News:* "Layoffs Are No Longer Taboo"). Seniority often plays a major role in determining the order of layoffs for union employees. For example, a contract between Joseph E. Seagram & Sons, and the Distillery, Rectifying, Wine, and Allied Workers' International Union of America included the following layoff, recall, and job bidding provisions:

> Article XII, section 1
> The employee's length of service for the purpose of determining seniority rights shall be deemed to have commenced on the first day of employment with the employer. In all cases of promotion or recall, seniority rights of employees shall govern. The principle of seniority shall govern in all cases, including the filling of vacancies occurring in shifts or new positions created. If vacancies occur in a higher rated position, seniority including the ability to perform the work shall be the controlling factor in the selection of employees to fill such vacancies.

Production and other front-line employees are usually among the first to be laid off. But managers, staff administrators, and other skilled employees are not immune to layoffs. Employee performance usually plays a major role in deciding which nonunion employees to lay off. Some major corporations have found that the "last hired, first fired" policy may be damaging to minorities and women in their workforces. However, when AT&T cut 58,000 jobs, its proportion of minority supervisors rose from 3 percent to 9 percent and its proportion of women supervisors rose from 2.5 percent to 9 percent due to their process. DuPont, Honeywell, and Nynex corporations each had large layoffs in the 1990s, and their percentages of minorities and women in supervision were basically unchanged.[19] While seniority and performance measures remain as typical guidelines for layoff, some employers are also considering race and gender.

Legal Issues on Layoffs in Union Settings

In the 1970s, a great deal of controversy arose concerning the role of seniority in laying off minority employees under a labor contract. Blacks and women were beginning to make significant gains in many jobs that were highly unionized. As a consequence, most had less seniority than white males. Layoffs of union employees have generally had an adverse impact on minorities. But the federal courts have long upheld the validity of the **bona fide seniority system (BFSS),** holding that it is not illegal to make layoffs

INTERNATIONAL HR IN THE NEWS

LAYOFFS ARE NO LONGER TABOO: JAPAN'S ONCE-PAMPERED *SALARYMEN* ARE STRUGGLING TO ADJUST

Noriaki Kohama, a 38-year-old salesman now faces the kind of midlife crisis a "salary-man" has never considered. Kohama has worked for 15 years for Yamaichi Securities. Unfortunately, this brokerage, Japan's fourth largest, announced in November of 1997 that it is closing and laying off 7,500 employees.

By December, unless Kohama quickly finds another job, he will be out of work, out of his company-subsidized apartment, and left to support his wife and two children on Japan's meager unemployment insurance. A graduate of Tokyo's prestigious Rikkyo University, Kohama is not confident that he will land a good job. "I am angry," says Kohama, "this is the worst possible time to look for a job."

Of course it is the deep financial crisis across all of Asia which has led to Kohama's layoff. Japan's vaunted "lifetime employment" system is wrecked. Seven years of economic stagnation have brought on recession. Japan's unemployment rate is about 3.5 percent; the highest since the end of World War II. Up to 10 percent of the nation's 65 million workers might be unemployed by the year 2000.

"Salarymen" (white-collar workers) make up 30 percent of Japan's workforce. Men often join a company after college graduation and never leave. Instead of firing poorly performing managers, companies push them off to subsidiaries or promote them "up." Forget efficiency, productivity in Japan is still 38 percent lower than in the United States. "Blue-collar workers are multiskilled and can shift from one factory to another," says economist Naohiro Yashiro, "(but) white-collar workers only know how to do the work of the company that hired and trained them."

Some firms still avoid giving workers the *kata tataki*—the tap on the shoulder which means "you are laid off," (the word "layoff" is never used). Some firms offer early retirement and incentives to trim headcounts. Workers who resist may find themselves discarded into the ranks of the "window-side gang," left to sit at their desk with little to do but look out the window.

SOURCE: Adapted from Frank Gibney, Jr., in Tokyo with reporting by Irene M. Kunji, Sachiko Sakamaki, and Hiroko Tashiro in Tokyo, "Asia's Financial Crisis: Death of a Salaryman," *Time International* (February 16, 1998): 18+. Used by permission.

using a seniority system unless the seniority system was intentionally designed to discriminate. For example, in 1969 the Crown Zellerbach Company was ordered to revise its system of promotion and to adopt a plantwide seniority system instead of using what amounted to one seniority system for whites and another for blacks.

Several court decisions in the early 1980s led to an erosion of the BFSS concept, particularly in government jobs involving police officers, firefighters, and teachers. A federal judge in 1981 barred the city of Boston from reducing the fire department's 14.7 percent level of minority firefighters achieved through the city's affirmative action plan. The result was that 83 white males with greater seniority were laid off in place of minority workers. Similar court rulings took place in Memphis, Cincinnati, Toledo, and Jackson, Michigan.[20]

The seniority system was upheld under a 1984 Supreme Court decision, *Firefighters Local 1784* v. *Stotts.*

The city agreed to a consent decree to settle charges of race discrimination in the fire department and set a goal of hiring black firefighters so that the percentage of minority firefighters reflected the percentage of minorities in the relevant labor market. When the city later responded to a budget crunch by preparing to lay off firefighters based on their seniority, the district court stopped any layoffs that would decrease the percentage of blacks in the department.

However, the Supreme Court disagreed. Interference with a collectively bargained seniority system cannot be justified as an effort to enforce the affirmative action decree, the Court said, because the decree, to which the union was not a party, mentioned neither layoffs nor an intent to depart from the lawful seniority system. Nor could the district court grant "super-seniority" to black employees as a "modification" of its decree, the Court explained, because there was no finding that any of the blacks protected from layoff had themselves been victims of discrimination.[21]

OTHER APPROACHES

Telecommuting

About 25 years ago, the story goes, a man named Jack Nilles was stuck in a L.A. traffic jam when a brainstorm hit. Then and there he coined the word **telecommuting**, apparently conceiving the benefits of computer-linked worksites. Today, telecommuting, working at home with the support of computers and telecommunication, is an approach that is growing at 10 percent to 15 percent per year.[22] Accurate headcounts have been hard to derive, but conservative studies estimated the number of telecommuters for the following years as indicated: 1990, 4 million; 1997, 11 million; 2000, 14 million (projected).[23]

Georgia Power has 150 telecommuters, representing 13 percent of the Atlanta headquarters' workforce. GP's telecommuters range from hourly customer-service workers to health and safety professionals. To date, telecommuting has reduced GP's commuting by almost one billion miles and pollution emissions by close to 35,000 pounds. GP also saved $100,000 per year in office expenses. IBM's telecommuting program has allowed IBM to save about $75 million by selling buildings and reducing office leases.[24] However, some costs increase. Computer budget costs are 63 percent to 157 percent higher and telecommunications bills also soar.[25]

Guidelines for managing these "invisible employees" include the following:

- Focus on productivity, not presence. Telecommuting often forces managers to set objectives more carefully.

- Develop policy guidelines. Companies range from informal arrangements between a manager and a telecommuter to using a very specific policy manual. It is wise to clarify who is responsible for expenses.

- Ensure regular time in the office. "Out of sight, out of mind" can destroy the career of a telecommuter, so it helps if the employee works in the office on a regular basis.

- Avoid "place-based discrimination." There have been a few notable cases in which employees were stripped of their benefit packages when they took telecommuting assignments. The Internal Revenue Service (IRS) rigorously enforces the employee-contractor distinction, so employers cannot generally discriminate in benefits to argue that "employees" have become "independent contractors" merely because the location of the worksite has changed. The IRS estimates that it is losing $2 billion per year due to incorrect classifications.[26]

- Employers should use the 1099 form only for people who truly work out of the office. Providing a phone and an office can convert them to employees. Former employees or retirees rehired on contracts are also likely to be viewed as employees. Hiring through an outside agency is a good way to help insulate the employer from misclassifying employees.[27]

- Telecommute for appropriate reasons—when beneficial to both the worker and the organization—not because it is a fad.

- Write down the specifics of the arrangement and conditions of employment.

Alternatives to Layoffs

One approach is to hire **contingent workers** when the workload increases. See *HR in the News:* "Contingent Workers . . ." for a discussion of this term. Another cost-cutting HR tool is the offer of early retirement. **Early-retirement programs** give experienced, older employees additional incentives for retiring early. Many employers, including GM, IBM, and Polaroid, have offered early retirement as a way to avoid the less desirable options of layoff, termination, and demotion. There is a wide range of approaches to program design, but most do the following:

1. Strictly define who is eligible for the option, usually with a calculation of years of service and age.

2. Contain a substantially "sweetened" pay or bonus and benefit element.

3. Move forward the date at which the employee can draw the full employer pension benefit.

4. Define a precise "window" of time during which the option can be exercised by the eligible employee (usually brief).

5. Make clear that the choice is voluntary. There can be no coercion or threat because an early retirement program could be a pretext for age discrimination if older employees are told only to "take this option or be terminated."

While early-retirement programs, or *buy-outs*, were viewed initially as completely positive, some critical problems have emerged. A survey of 1,100 HR officials found that 67 percent of companies that offered early-retirement programs saw people leave whom they had hoped to retain. One-half of these companies had to hire replacements for some of these employees within two years.[31] Employers cannot meet cost-cutting goals

CONTINGENT WORKERS— INCREASING OR NOT?

Some experts estimate that one-fourth of all workers are now part of the "new" contingency, or temporary, workforce. A few analysts predicted that the U.S. workplace would continue to change so rapidly that by the year 2000 half of us will be no longer be considered full-time employees.

Others predicted that this is sheer nonsense.[28] Here are the two sides of the argument.

- *There's a big trend that will result in half of all workers being temporary.* Polls of CEOs found that 44 percent increased the use of contingent workers between 1988 and 1993. During the next five years, 44 percent said they increased their use of these temporary workers. Never have so many employees in the United States (6.4 million) said that they are working part-time but really want a full-time job. The 7,000 U.S. temporary employment agencies now employ over 1.6 million workers, up from just under half a million 10 years ago.[29]

- *The size of the contingency workforce has not gone up, and the discussion is just a faddish obsession with an old situation.* The alarmists lump together part-timers and the self-employed. Self-employed workers account for about 8.5 percent of the workforce, just as they did in 1980. Many of the self-employed are well-paid professionals like doctors and lawyers. Further, when you lump together the part-timers and self-employed in the early 1980s, 27 percent in the United States would qualify. In the 1990s the proportion was 26 percent, *down* 1 percent. Ken Nardone, who computes employment figures at the Bureau of Labor Statistics, says, "We hear a lot of anecdotal data about the growth of the contingent workforce, but we can't pinpoint the numbers."[30]

when they must recruit and train new employees who generally bring less experience to the job. The bill for replacement on a technical or specialized job can be 150 percent of the retiring employee's original salary.[32] Further, if coercion is found later on in the early-retirement offer, there may be a violation of the Age Discrimination in Employment Act. Finally, the employer plays a guessing game about whether the package is "sweet" enough to achieve the correct number of retirements but not too sweet.

INTERNAL STAFFING POLICIES

Sound internal staffing policies and practices will resolve many HR problems for the organization. When employees think they are being treated unfairly or discriminated against in promotion, transfer, or layoff decisions, dissatisfaction may result and lead to absenteeism and turnover. An employee who thinks he or she was discriminated against may file a complaint with the EEOC. Therefore, HR professionals must create and im-

plement internal staffing practices that are fair and that make the greatest use of employees' abilities. A discussion of important internal staffing policies follows.

PROMOTION FROM WITHIN

The most prudent approach to filling job vacancies is to follow a policy of promotion from within but to maintain enough flexibility to tap the external labor market when employees within the organization are not qualified. Many firms also desire some percentage of their managers to be from the external market, so new ideas will infuse the organization.

ASSISTANCE FOR LAID-OFF EMPLOYEES

Economic misfortunes may cause a firm to lay off great numbers of workers. Layoffs can be managed to reduce the strains that laid-off workers and the community face when jobs are permanently eliminated. Providing assistance to employees during layoffs reflects genuine concern and is an act of social responsibility. Laid-off employees can be helped through notification of plant closings, severance pay, supplemental unemployment benefits, and outplacement assistance.

The Worker Adjustment and Retraining Notification Act (WARN)

Commonly known as the *Plant Closing Act*, this law covers employers who have 100 or more full-time employees. WARN, which went into effect in 1989, requires these employers to give affected employees 60 days' written notice of anticipated plant closings or large layoffs (generally of 50 or more employees).[33] Employers who violate the law may be required to give back-pay to workers laid off without receiving the proper notification and to pay a fine. There are exceptions to WARN. A "faltering company" is exempt if it was seeking money during that time that would have avoided the layoff/closing. "Unforseeable business circumstances" may also provide an exemption to an employer's notification responsibilities. Several state laws place even more responsibilities on an employer who is closing or laying off employees.[34]

The biggest advantage of notification of an imminent layoff is that workers and communities are given time to prepare for the impending economic hardships or to contemplate "bailout" measures (like tax breaks), as well as giving workers a chance to find new jobs. But managers see problems; they claim that advance notice of a plant closing hurts credit ratings and reduces new customer orders. They also worry about employee morale, motivation, and absenteeism.

Supplemental Unemployment Benefits

In the 1950s, steel and automobile industry union leaders began negotiating **supplemental unemployment benefits (SUB)** plans. These plans provide additional income to supplement state unemployment benefits to employees who are laid off. SUB plans are designed to be directly supplemental; employees receive a certain percentage (for example, 90 percent) of their gross pay for a maximum number of weeks when unemployed.

Relatively high unemployment rates in prior decades led to negotiation of a few *guaranteed income stream (GIS)* plans in the auto industry. GIS plans furnish benefits to eligible workers until they retire and thus have been called a guaranteed lifetime wage; and benefits provided by a GIS plan are only partially offset by outside earnings until a breakeven point is reached. There was little expansion of GIS outside of the auto industry in the 1990s.

Severance Pay

Sometimes called *dismissal pay,* **severance pay** is pay that many employers voluntarily provide to employees who have been permanently ter-

minated. Studies indicate that among employers who pay severance, most pay when it is a discharge for economic reasons (94 percent) or if the position is eliminated (88 percent); some pay for termination for poor job performance (42 percent); but few use severance pay for disabilities, resignations, or retirements. The most common amount is one week's pay per year of service (47 percent) although some make a flat payment or leave it to the discretion of management.[35]

OUTPLACEMENT ASSISTANCE

Many firms now provide a number of services to laid-off employees that involve job-placement assistance and training for new job skills called **outplacement assistance.**

The Illinois AFL-CIO model program has been used by employers to guide their efforts in developing programs for the soon-to-be unemployed. The program includes the following:[36]

- *Advance notice* of one-half to a full year helps in all outplacement efforts
- *Labor–management outplacement committees* allow both parties to set outplacement goals and identify effective helps
- *Job search training* is very helpful to those who have not been in the job market for years
- *Job clubs* bring job seekers together, provide a place for job search training, and reduce the isolation that generally accompanies job hunting activities
- *Aggressive job development* includes contacting suppliers, customers, and the business community to locate possible jobs
- *Skills training* may enhance opportunities although only 20 percent of those laid off might use it
- *Personnel assistance* to assist the unemployed with references, training, and counseling is needed for some time after a plant closes
- *Third parties* or external consultants with expertise in outplacement activities are widely available
- *Industrial development* by many local and federal redevelopment agencies have assisted a new employer in acquiring the site of a closed plant

CAREER MANAGEMENT

Work, food, and sex are the most commonly shared behavioral traits of adult life. While the last two are subject to aesthetic taste and availability—and therefore somewhat discretionary—for 95 percent of us, *work* is entirely nondiscretionary—we have to work. "Even those of us who desperately don't want to work," poet Ogden Nash wrote "must work in order to earn enough money so that they won't have to work anymore".[37]

According to current Department of Labor statistics, today's new college graduates will average eight to ten jobs and as many as three careers in their lifetimes.[38] The *Occupational Outlook Handbook,* published every two years by the Bureau of Labor Statistics, provides information on the nature of work, work conditions, training, salaries, and job outlook for about 250 occupations. Unfortunately, there is no scientific formula for selecting a career; it's all about balancing costs and benefits.[39]

There may be two kinds of people. First, there are those who view their job as a necessary evil. Voltaire pointed out that work will at least keep you from the jaws of the three great evils of boredom, poverty, and vice. Second, there are those who revel in their work and find meaning in it for themselves and others. Novelist and film director Elia Kazan has said that the one absolute lesson he has learned in life is "that our careers and our identities are inextricably bound up." Samuel Butler said, "Every man's work, whether it be literature or architecture or anything, is always a portrait of himself."[40] Most come to believe those people who feel successful in their careers are those who enjoy their work.

HR professionals, are playing an increasingly active role in designing and implementing programs that help employees not only focus on career choices and objectives but also achieve the objectives they formulate. Such help originated with a concern for the quality of working life and a need to use the organization's human resources effectively. Programs have been created that draw on both traditional personnel tools and contemporary methods designed specifically for the development of career paths. In general, all these programs fall under the general heading of **career management.** Important terms and concepts in career management are the following:

Career   A sequence of jobs held during a person's working life.

Career Management   The process of designing and implementing goals, plans, and strategies that enable HR professionals and managers to satisfy workforce needs and allow individuals to achieve their career objectives.

Individual Career Planning   The process whereby each employee personally plans career goals.

Organizational Career Planning   The process whereby management plans career goals for employees.

BENEFITS TO THE ORGANIZATION

Well-planned and executed career programs will benefit both the organization and employees in a number of ways, including:

Staffing Inventories   Effective career management will help ensure a continuous supply of professional, technical, and managerial talent.

Staffing from Within   Because of the many potential advantages of promotion from within, most organizations like to promote employees when possible, but this requires a strong career management program to guarantee that employees can perform effectively in their new jobs. Promoting employees before they are ready to assume their new jobs will result in unsatisfactory performance, as predicted by the Peter Principle.[41]

Solving Staffing Problems   Certain staffing problems may be remedied through employees knowing that their employer has an effective career management plan.

Satisfying Employee Needs   Higher levels of education have raised career expectations. Many workers hold their employers responsible for providing opportunities so that those expectations may be realized.

Enhanced Motivation   Because progression along the career path should be directly related to job performance, an employee is likely to be motivated to perform so that career goals may be accomplished.

Equal Employment Opportunity   EEO guidelines demand fair and equitable recruiting, selection, and placement policies and the elimination of illegally discriminatory practices concerning promotions and career mobility. Many affirmative action programs contain formal provisions to enhance the career mobility of women and minorities, including the development of career paths and the design of formal T&D activities.

Successful Career Management

Four factors determine the success of an organization's career management efforts. First, career management must be planned; haphazard or ill-conceived attempts to manage careers will fail. Second, top management must support career management and provide a positive climate. Third, administrators must not neglect any of career management's many programs and processes. These include organizational career planning, individual career planning, integrating organizational and individual plans, implementation, and evaluation. A fourth factor, **career match,** has been found to be the most critical factor in career management programs. The program must seek to find a career match between the employer's plans for the employee and the employee's personal aspirations. Programs that simply explain the organization's career plans to the employees, but do not assist them in clarifying their own goals and developing a match between theirs and the organization's, are likely to fail.

Organizational Career Planning   An important part of the HR planning process involves the forecast of both long- and short-term HR needs. During this process, the major changes the organization is likely to face are predicted (growth, decline, reorganization, new technologies) as is their impact on the organization's labor force. Emphasis is placed on predicting changes in the numbers and kinds of employees that will be needed. But HR plans must be flexible enough to adjust to changes.

Some organizations develop individual career plans for managers and for professional personnel. An executive succession chart is sometimes used as an aid in career planning.

Many employers have developed two career ladders—one, the traditional managerial ladder and the other, a professional ladder. The professional ladder allows employees who have never taken a formal managerial assignment to move up the corporate ladder. For example, to become the department head in customer service, the *managerial ladder* included three steps up in technical jobs (service representative I, II, and III), then three steps in management (supervisor, manager I and II). The *professional ladder* may now allow three steps of additional technical or professional jobs (service analyst, service consultant I and II) to substitute for the steps in management. This dual ladder helps:

- Retain the best professional/technical people.
- Create a career path for those not interested in a career in management.
- Increase the morale of the technical staff.
- Create a more equitable nonmanagement compensation structure.

INDIVIDUAL CAREER PLANNING

Today individuals should be plotting their own career goals and creating strategies to achieve them. Many books have been published to assist in the planning and integrating of personal, social, family, and work goals.

Many progressive organizations offer counseling on career opportunities as a part of their career management system. Whether employees conduct career planning through a course or seminar or through formal career counseling, the first step is the assessment of personal interests, aims, skills, and abilities. It is important that employees find out as much as possible about themselves—their ambitions, needs, values, strengths, and limitations.

The second step is the collection of information about existing and future opportunities in an organization. Career counselors or HR professionals should be valuable sources. Many managers have also testified to the value of informal sources (such as mentors) in providing career insight.

The final step in the individual planning process is the development of a strategy to achieve career goals. Decisions about such a strategy are often informal, rarely put in writing, and subject to considerable adjustment as an employee progresses through a career. The realities of organizational life demand flexible planning because uncertainty and risk underscore any form of long-range planning. Formal long-term education strategies may include earning an advanced degree such as an MBA. Short-term educational strategies may include participation in short courses or seminars.

INTEGRATING PLANS

To be effective, career management efforts must strike a workable balance between the organization's HR needs and employees' career goals. In reality, this balance is difficult to achieve. The dynamic nature of organizational life sometimes makes it extremely difficult for each person to carry out career plans, especially within specific time constraints.

To a considerable extent, management can minimize employee frustration and turnover caused by career stagnation through honest and up-to-date *career counseling.* In some cases, overly optimistic personal career goals may have to be trimmed back. In others, counseling may suggest opportunities and, perhaps, alternative career paths to accelerate an employee's career aims.

IMPLEMENTING PROGRAMS

Career development is a long-term process, spanning an employee's entire working career. The primary elements in implementing a career management program include the publication of job vacancies, the implementation of employee performance appraisals, the establishment of T&D activities, and the evaluation of career progression.

Job Vacancies Publicizing job vacancies (job posting) is an excellent way to widely and fairly disseminate career information and notify employees who may be qualified for a vacant job.

Appraisal Data Supervisors have the important responsibility of honestly telling employees whether their performance is satisfactory in light of their career goals. Further, HR professionals play an important role by implementing valid PA systems.

T&D Experiences Perhaps the most meaningful aspect of career development is the accumulation of work experiences and away-from-the-job training activities that broaden employees' skills and abilities. Developmental activities (for example, job rotation, coaching, and committee assignments) are core components of career management for many firms.

Career Evaluation The final phase of the career development process is evaluation of an employee's progress toward career goals. Evaluation usually takes place annually or biannually, possibly during a formal appraisal review. During evaluation, employees may review the progress of their careers with supervisors. Particular emphasis is placed on whether career goals and timetables have been reached. If progress has been less than expected, the reasons should be explored and discussed.

Career Stages Managers should recognize that employees generally progress through four **career stages.** Each stage represents a unique set of opportunities, problems, and circumstances, and the career needs of employees change as they pass from one stage to the next.[42]

1 *Establishment* Beginning a career, the employee faces uncertainty over his or her performance potential and competency. During establishment, a supportive and caring superior is particularly important for assisting the employee.

2 *Advancement* The employee demonstrates competence and a knowledge of the politics of organizational life. Less guidance and supervision are needed than during the establishment stage. However, coaching, counseling, role models, and friendships remain important at this stage.

3 *Maintenance* People generally achieve their highest advancement during the maintenance stage, and devote a considerable amount of their energies to developing and guiding others with less experience. This stage brings a great deal of satisfaction to some—those who have achieved their career goals. But others find disappointment and frustration—those who have failed to reach career objectives.

4 *Withdrawal* Withdrawal begins as one retires or moves on to a new career. During this stage, the individual devotes greater time to leisure and to the family. Frustration, stress, and boredom may also characterize this stage because the retiree starts to lose his or her job identity and the social contacts enjoyed at work.

EVALUATION OF CAREER PROGRAMS

Even though a great deal of time and expense are expended on career development programs, few organizations evaluate their efforts formally. One research study involving 40 corporations found only 15 with formal evaluation systems, eight with informal methods, and 17 with no evaluation whatsoever.[43]

Another problem is the frustration employees feel when advancement opportunities are limited. Frustration can be minimized through candid career counseling and by telling employees that promotions are not the automatic outcomes of career programs on training.

The supervisor is the employee's most important career counselor.[44] But an American Management Association study showed that in a sample of 225 companies the majority of supervisors surveyed thought that (1) career planning was a burden, (2) career planning for subordinates was not part of their job, and (3) they were not equipped to assist employees in career planning and counseling.[45] It is critical that supervisors receive training in the skills required for career management and that they are rewarded for helping guide the careers of their subordinates.

THE PLATEAUED EMPLOYEE

Until baby-boomers begin to retire in 2010 there will likely be too large of a supply of managers. Since World War II, a career of abnormally swift promotions became the expectation in the U.S. However, in the United States there are now more people in the managerial pool than ever before but opportunities are limited. Sooner or later, for almost every employee, the process of upward movement ends. When this happens, he or she becomes known as a **plateaued employee.**

Managers are not the only ones experiencing the stress of plateauing. Professionals and employees who find themselves in jobs that offer limited mobility and few opportunities for the expansion of experience feel the same frustration and the stigma of failure.

The HR department is often expected to take the lead in addressing and resolving the plateaued employee's frustrations. This may mean encouraging employees at all levels to accept the reality that promotions do not go on forever. It certainly means more lateral assignments within the organization.

DUAL-CAREER COUPLES

Since the 1950s, the influx of women into the labor force—*the* largest single change in workplace diversity—changed both home and work. By 1997, only 17 percent of households have an employed dad, a stay-at-home mom, and one or more children (the 1950s high was in the 40 percent range). About two-thirds of married-couple households now have two employed spouses. **Dual-career couples** (DCCs), where couples are both employed, represent 45 percent of the *total* workforce. Since 85 percent of these couples cite the need for income as their chief reason for two jobs, many economists blame escalating tax rates in the United States for forcing many spouses into the work force.[46]

One study found that huge majorities of women (75 percent) and men (66 percent) want to customize their career path to make allowances for family priorities. Companies shouldn't ignore this and other needs of the DCCs since they comprise almost one half the work force. The following are workplace *programs* which DCCs report as currently helpful:

Tools (like laptops and cellphones)
Corporate climate and managerial support
Emphasis on results (rather than a time card)
Informal flexibility based on the nature of work
Having managers with kids or who are also DCCs

Here are some of the *needs* of DCCs identified in a recent study:

Flexible hours
Formal flexible work programs
Family leave time
Company-supported childcare
Help relocating the **trailing spouse**[47]

Increasingly, women's jobs are dictating where couples locate. While only 5 percent of relocating employees were women in 1980, by 1999 17 percent were women, and three-quarters of these were married and had "trailing husbands."[48] Promotions and other personnel moves are further complicated when the promotion is interna-

tional. Latest figures indicate that 45 percent of expatriate assignments include a spouse who was employed prior to relocation. Over 80 percent of companies say that family considerations are a primary reason candidates reject overseas assignments—and half cite spouse career considerations. Indeed, almost one in ten married expatriates relocate without their spouse.[49]

THE SPECIAL CASES OF WOMEN, RACIAL MINORITIES, AND OLDER WORKERS IN MANAGEMENT

During the past decade, women's share in the total U.S. workforce rose 2 percent to a total of 46 percent. Just over half of all women work full-time outside the home. Their representation in specific occupations has grown in varying rates. Women increased their share of some occupations they already dominated. Women now represent 80 percent of medicine and health managers; 65 percent of personnel, training, and labor specialists; 75 percent of recreation workers; and 84 percent of statistical clerks. Women have become a majority of workers, especially in managerial and professional jobs: financial managers, accountant and auditors, technical writers, economists, PR specialists, authors, production coordinators, dispatchers, optical-goods workers, and bartenders.[50]

However, only about 10 percent of corporate offices in the nation's 500 largest companies are held by women, and that number drops to just 3 percent for top titles like chief executive, president, chair, vice chair, COO, and executive vice president.[51] The percentages for racial minorities in such jobs are even less representative, even considering the far smaller proportion of the overall labor force which racial minorities comprise. Contrary to some diversity exaggerations, the race and gender total percentages are experiencing only small, incremental changes. Projections for 2005 expect the following workplace proportions: Hispanics 11 percent, blacks 12 percent, white females 39 percent, and white males 44 percent.

OBSTACLES TO UPWARD MOBILITY

The statistics above lead people to wonder how women could be 46 percent of the workforce, increase their representation at many managerial levels, but remain only 10 percent of the corporate leaders. There is some controversy over what these statistics mean. In 1991, the

Department of Labor (DOL) issued it's interpretation in "A Report on the Glass Ceiling Initiative." The report defines the **glass ceiling** "as those artificial barriers based on attitudinal or organizational bias that prevent qualified individuals from advancing upward in their organizations into management-level positions."[52]

DOL is conducting reviews known as Corporate Management Reviews. Focusing on federal contractors, these reviews examine whether organizational practices and corporate cultures impede the advancement of women and minorities.[53]

Employers are advised to conduct a *glass ceiling self-audit* to prepare for a Corporate Management Review and to remove any glass ceiling at their workplace. A self-audit process should follow four steps:

1 Statistical information should be collected on woman and minorities.

2 Both senior management and the corporate culture need to be analyzed as they relate to the opportunities of women and minorities.

3 Barriers to promotion opportunities should be identified.

4 A qualitative analysis of the workplace as it relates to opportunities for women and minorities within the organization should be performed.[54]

There is some controversy over the interpretation of the job statistics. Simon Howard, a senior recruitment specialist, dismisses the notion of a glass ceiling. Speaking at the European Union's Institute of Personnel and Development Howard said, "I would argue that it is not so much a glass ceiling as a 'glass escalator'." He argued that with high college graduation rates and larger numbers of women entering the workplace, employers tend to recruit women over men. "There are far more women on the first steps of that escalator. As a result, more women are going to reach the heights. There is evidence that this is already happening."[55] Indeed, encouraging research indicates that more women than men are moving into top management and at a faster rate. This is true when both women and men hold MBA degrees.[56]

Catherine Hakim has also produced controversial research which shows that the glass ceiling is essentially a myth. Her research discovered that men and women have different priorities. Men define themselves mostly in terms of work, but women (especially those with kids) see themselves in a more complicated way. She finds that women are unwilling or unable to compartmentalize their lives in the way that most men do, and

therefore many women see part-time and nonmanagerial work as an ideal way of combining roles.[57] It is important to realize that there is more than one viewpoint.

Persons with disabilities also face major obstacles on the career path. For a brief discussion of their problems and information on the recent Americans with Disabilities Act, read *HR in the News:* "Unintentional Discrimination Against the Disabled."

STEREOTYPES ABOUT WOMEN MANAGERS

One set of obstacles is the stereotypes of women that workers frequently encountered at work. Negative stereotypes of working women include the following:[58]

- All women work merely to supplement the family income; they do not need equal pay or benefits because *men* support families.

- All women avoid being managers because the extra workload would interfere with family obligations.

- All women are unable to meet certain work demands for emotional toughness and stability because of their psychological makeup. They tend to take things personally, to respond to anger and frustration by crying, and to be insufficiently hard nosed in making difficult decisions.

There are strategies for dealing with the negative stereotypes that many female managers must confront. The best is a vocal and assertive stance by top management that recognizes the workplace rights of female employees.

THE OLD BOY NETWORK

Another obstacle to the development of women and minority managers is the **old boy network,** the informal network of advice and assistance that facilitates upward mobility. The fast track on which many male managers have swiftly traveled has often been greased by membership in an old boy network. For example, at a Rotary Club luncheon, one member may ask another if he is interested in a job opening. By belonging to this club, the aspiring manager becomes privy to inside information: who to know, important positions coming up, job assignments that count, and other valued information that increases both visibility and credibility.

Having club memberships open to women and minorities helps combat the old boy exclusions. Also, many

HR IN THE NEWS

UNINTENTIONAL DISCRIMINATION AGAINST THE DISABLED?

According to the findings of Congress, some 43 million Americans have some disability that affects one or more of their life functions. The Americans with Disabilities Act (ADA) protects persons with disabilities from discrimination at the workplace. This was popular legislation, but did you know that someone sympathetic to the person with a disability may be the first to discriminate against him or her at work?

According to a couple of recent studies, people making HR decisions often favor a disabled person over a nondisabled person—if the job is "right for them." In the case where a job had duties that kept the worker away from the public (an accounting job with no public duties), the person with disabilities was discriminated *in favor of.* If the same job (accountant) required the person to have the same skills, but to meet the public as part of his or her duties, then the person with disabilities was discriminated *against.*

Further research reveals that the more "social distance" created by the disability itself, the more pronounced the discrimination. For instance, someone with a hidden disability (heart disease, deafness, and so on) is treated more like a person without disabilities, while a person with an obvious disability (in a wheelchair, blind, and so on) is more likely to be discriminated against.

Well-meaning HR professionals and managers should be very careful if they believe they "have just the job" for a person with disabilities.

SOURCE: Adapted from Robert D. Hatfield and Chun Hui, "Avoiding Discrimination Suits Under the ADA: An Analysis of When Discrimination Is Most Likely," *Proceedings,* Council on Employee Responsibilities and Rights (June 1992); and Chun Hui and Robert D. Hatfield, "Discrimination Against the Physically Disabled: When Concern for Selection Matters," *Proceedings,* Midwest Division Academy of Management (1992). Used with permission.

women and minorities are forming their own career-related information systems through **networking.** Networking provides a means to disseminate and collect valued information on jobs available, jobs becoming available, and other information helpful to the career-oriented.

ISSUES OF AN AGING WORKFORCE

One of the growing concerns of today's labor force deals with the career-related problems of an **aging workforce.** The 43 million baby boomers born between 1945 and 1955 are now "graying" to the extent that the first boomers turn 55 in 2000. People over 50 will represent 30 percent of the population in 2005. Further, workers 55 and older are the fastest-growing sector of the labor force.[59]

The graying of the workforce is forcing management to examine closely the myths and stereotypes that have long surrounded the older worker. For example, many youthful managers assume that health, productivity, attitudes, and overall usefulness to the organization decline rapidly after age 50. According to scientific research, however, the truth about the older worker is quite different from commonly held stereotypes:[60]

Physiological Changes   While physiological changes take place as one ages, they vary markedly in degree among persons of the same age. Motivated, relatively unaffected older workers are now called "the *young-old.*" In the absence of time pressures, the performance of older workers is as good as that of younger employees—and sometimes better.

Work Attitude   Research shows that age and job satisfaction are positively related in all sectors of the workforce.

Job Performance   According to research, older managers are less willing to take risks, take longer to reach decisions, and are less confident in their decisions. However, older managers are better able to appraise new information and seek to minimize risk by collecting more reliable information. In sales, clerical, and manual-labor jobs, age seems to have little effect. Absenteeism rates do not appear to be significantly affected by age.

Managing Older Workers   While differences between older workers and young workers may not be as pronounced as many believe, management should still be attuned to the unique needs and concerns of

older workers. Six areas have been suggested for in preparing for the graying of a company's workforce:[61]

① Job performance requirements Organizations should define job requirements precisely and ensure that recruiting and selection procedures are based on critical performance criteria. If selection decisions are based strictly on requisite job skills and abilities, age will not enter into the selection decision.

② Performance appraisal HR managers must closely examine their PA systems to remove any intentional or unintentional biases against the older worker.

③ Work force surveys Workforce surveys will enable management to get a clear idea of employee needs. Special HR programs can then be created to deal with the needs of various employee groups, including older workers.

④ Education and counseling Firms are beginning to counsel older workers on retirement and second-career options following retirement. Special training might also be provided for the older employee who chooses to remain on the job.

⑤ Job structure The older worker raises issues concerning how jobs are structured. Flexibility is important in regard to the work pace, the length of the work day, leaves of absence, and part-time work.

DEVELOPMENT FOR WOMEN AND MINORITIES

Each member of an organization must recognize the responsibility to eliminate inequities that may exist for female, minority, and older employees. EEO is not solely the HR department's job; it is the responsibility of every worker, regardless of position or level.

Some of the ways managers and HR professionals can facilitate the movement of women and minorities into management ranks include the following:

- Ensure that PA data used for development decisions are free of bias against women and minorities.
- Implement special programs and training that deal solely with discrimination and EEO. Examples are "Positive Approaches to EEO and Affirmative Action," "What First-Line Supervisors Must Know About EEO," "Developing Minority, Older, and Female Employees," and "Managing Diversity."
- Create programs especially for aspiring women and other minority managers. Studies of the problems of these managers suggest that women and minorities would greatly benefit from T&D activities that focus on their particular problems and needs.

SUMMARY POINTS

- Several factors result in a need for significant internal personnel changes: organizational growth, major reorganizations, changes in general business conditions, resignations, terminations, and retirements. HR administrators should closely monitor these changes to ensure that internal staffing decisions are as planned and orderly as possible and should strive to integrate both short- and long-range staffing needs.

- Decision makers should look closely at their mechanisms and practices for promotion. Open promotion systems often permit greater use of employee skills and abilities than closed systems.

- Criteria for making promotion decisions should be applied in a manner consistent with the nature of the workforce and organizational goals. Seniority and qualifications are prime factors in making promotions among unionized employees; performance and promotability are important in promoting nonunionized employees. Assessment centers are valuable tools for identifying potential managers among nonmanagerial personnel.

- It is important that decision makers write sound HR policies for making internal staffing decisions. An important issue is when to promote from within or hire from the outside.

- Appraisal data for making promotional decisions must be objective and must accurately reflect an employee's performance and promotability. Assistance should be available for laid-off employees. Internal staffing should be consistent with equal opportunity for all employee groups. Long- and short-range planning decisions should be integrated as fully as possible.

- Career management involves integration of organizational staffing needs with the career goals and aspirations of individuals. To be effective, career management should be formal and planned, should receive support from top management, and should be recognized as a process that involves coordination of a number of separate yet interrelated HR tools and techniques.

- Once organizational HR staffing needs and personal career goals have been defined and integrated, a number of

SUMMARY POINTS—cont'd

personnel practices can start a career in motion. These include job posting, PA, and T&D activities.

● Dual-career couples should be prepared to deal with problems that include potential conflicts over career paths and the division of family responsibilities. Organizations may have special policies for dual-career couples.

● Historically, women and other minorities have faced formidable obstacles in their advancement into managerial ranks.

Management development can play a dual role in removing these obstacles by (1) developing special courses dealing with discrimination in the advancement of women and other minorities and (2) creating management development programs to meet the particular needs of these workers.

● The aging workforce requires the HR department to consider policies that meet the unique needs of this growing labor group.

CASE STUDY

ASSESSMENT CENTER AT PIEDMONT INSURANCE

The Piedmont Insurance Company's personnel committee entered the executive conference room, took their seats, drank coffee from Styrofoam cups, and chatted amiably among themselves. Each of the organization's six major departments was represented, typically by the department head. They included Kathy Morris, claims manager; Allen Mazula, manager of personal lines, and Lynn Snead, manager of group insurance. They were waiting for Jerry Smyth, head of Piedmont's HR department and chairman of the personnel committee. The committee members had only a vague notion of what the meeting was about; the memo calling the session spoke sparingly of "problems with promotion decisions" and a need to develop "a system for making more effective promotion decisions."

The Piedmont Insurance Company is a medium-sized, rapidly growing insurance company based in Durham, North Carolina. Piedmont Insurance is one of 18 insurance companies owned by Tidewater, Inc., a large insurance holding company. Offering a variety of personal, home, and life insurance coverage, Piedmont has recently captured a sizable niche in the group insurance market. Piedmont's labor force totals about 4,500 employees, including about 600 line managers and staff administrators.

Smyth, about five minutes late, hurriedly took his chair at the end of the conference table. After uttering a brief apology for his tardiness, he got to the point:

Smyth: This afternoon we need to discuss a serious personnel problem that we've had in this organization for some time. As I'm sure you are all aware, we have recurring performance problems at the first level of management. Deadlines are frequently missed, and quality control is almost nonexistent. Turnover among the clerical staff and sales personnel is about twice what it should be. And our annual employee attitude surveys show that our supervisors are in dire need of both work-oriented and people-oriented skills. We have much job dissatisfaction at the clerical and salesperson levels, and all fingers point to supervision. Besides, the productivity audit

conducted last year by our management consultants, Cheek and Associates, confirmed that our first level of supervision was one of the organization's weakest links. To make a long story short, we need to consider alternative ways to strengthen our first-line supervision."

Morris: But Jerry, each new manager is required to attend a 40-hour supervisory training program offered by your department. Isn't the program having any impact?

Smyth: "Well, we haven't been satisfied with the results of our evaluation studies. Currently we're looking at ways to improve our management training.

Mazula: Jerry, you don't turn someone into a supervisor in one week. What else are we doing to develop the skills of our new managers?

Smyth: Several things. First, we generally pay for an employee to attend a seminar as long as it's related to the job. Second, we reimburse employees for expenses they receive in getting a college degree. And as you know, we also encourage all middle managers to work closely with their supervisors to develop skills through on-the-job coaching.

Snead: Besides taking a closer look at our T&D programs, what else can we do to improve our supervision?

Smyth: I think we need to make some significant changes in the way we make promotion decisions, particularly when promoting a nonmanagement employee into the first level of management. We're currently promoting about 75 employees a year into supervision. Historically, we've promoted someone because of a high degree of technical skills. But technical skills play only a minor role in supervision. I'm afraid we've tried to make supervisors out of a good number of people who simply don't have the aptitudes to be successful managers. And we're probably overlooking a lot of employees who have the basic qualities that it takes for successful supervision.

CASE STUDY—cont'd

Snead: And how do we deal with these problems?

Smyth: A couple of months ago, I sent each of you a memo and several current journal articles that described the assessment-center concept. I think this is the real key to long-run improvements at our lower management levels. I've been toying with the idea of going ahead with the project for some time and decided to make a formal request to top management. I'm going to propose that we begin an assessment center for selecting first-level managers, and I want to discuss with you several different strategies for getting the program into action.

One approach is to put our own assessment staff together under my direction. We could study other programs, select our own tests and exercises, train our own assessors, and periodically conduct our own assessment, say every three months or so. Another alternative is to hire an outside consulting firm to come in and do the assessments. And a third approach is to persuade the corporate personnel office at Tidewater to put together a program that could be used by each company. The economies of scale of this approach would be tremendous; with the great number of promotions that are made annually in the Tidewater system, a full-time professional staff would easily keep busy the year around.

Snead: "Hold on, Jerry. We all realize that a lot of successes have been recorded for the assessment-center concept, but it's not a perfect system. It won't guarantee success. Besides, it's pretty costly. How will we know we're getting our money's worth? To improve the quality of our supervision, maybe we should consider some other alternatives to the assessment center. We could beef up our supervisory training. Or we could make our promotion decisions much more carefully than we do now, perhaps by a formal committee. And to get more candidates, we could use job posting for the first level of supervision. That way all interested personnel would be welcome to apply.

But if we do finally decide to go with the assessment center, let me strongly encourage that we start slowly at first with a pilot program in one department. That way we can iron out the bugs in the system before we go any further with it."

QUESTIONS

1. Evaluate the following alternatives for improving Piedmont's first level of supervision: (a) more supervisory training for new supervisors, (b) promotion decisions made by a promotion committee, and (c) implementation of an assessment center.

2. If you recommend an assessment center for Piedmont, who should conduct it—Piedmont's HR department, Tidewater's corporate HR office, or an outside consulting group? Should the program begin on a pilot study basis?

3. Are the training and assessment-center approaches mutually exclusive strategies for improving the quality of supervision? Discuss.

EXPERIENTIAL EXERCISES

1. WHAT ARE YOU GOING TO DO WITH YOUR LIFE?

PURPOSE

To get you to start thinking about career goals, personal strengths and weaknesses, and strategies for achieving career goals.

TASK

Listed here are several areas that are normally the focus of career planning workshops for employees and students. After you complete all questions, your instructor will lead a discussion concerning career planning.

GOAL SETTING

I. *Career Goals*

Let's begin by outlining a few career goals. How much thought have you given to what you want to be? How much money you want to make? The kind of organization you would like to work for? The industry? Geographical location? Think about these questions and complete the following section.

A. Job
What *specifically* would you like to be doing in five years?

B. Salary
How much money would you like to be making? (Of course, your salary goals should be tied directly to your job goal.) Be realistic!
$ _____ per year

C. What size company would you like to work for?
1. Small (fewer than 300 employees) _____
2. Medium (300 to 1,000 employees) _____
3. Large (1,000 employees or more) _____

D. Which industry would you prefer to work in?
1. Government
Local _____
State _____
Federal _____
2. Construction _____
3. Mining _____
4. Manufacturing _____ (Which kind?—automobile? computer?) _____
5. Agriculture _____
6. Transportation _____
7. Wholesale/retail trade _____
8. Services _____ (Which kind?—banking? health care?) _____
9. Health care _____
10. Information Technology _____
11. Sales _____

E. Where would you like to live?
1. Northeast _____
2. Southeast _____
3. Midwest _____
4. Central Plains _____
5. Southwest _____
6. Northwest _____
7. Doesn't matter _____

II. *Strengths and Weaknesses*
Right now, you have several strengths—knowledge, skills, and abilities—that will be assets in achieving your job goal. You will probably also need to acquire *new* skills to realize your job goal. In addition, you may have some weaknesses that you need to overcome before achieving your goals. In relation to your job goal, think about your strengths and weaknesses and complete the following section.

A. Strengths
List your strengths—including all knowledge, skills, and abilities, work experience, technical skills such as your college major, and human skills (for example, communication, leadership, motivation).

B. Skills to develop
Think about the job you would like to have, the skills you currently possess, and the skills you think you'll need to obtain to be competent in the job you want. Needed skills may include decision making, technical, and human relations skills. List these skills.

C. Obstacles
Now think of all the obstacles that you must overcome to realize your job goal. Obstacles relate less to skill deficiencies (listed before) than to external considerations such as a reluctance to relocate if it is a condition for a promotion or perhaps the difficulties (time and money) you would face in getting an MBA at night.

EXPERIENTIAL EXERCISES—cont'd

D. Soul search

Consider all your thoughts thus far: job and salary goals, strengths, areas that need to be developed, and obstacles. In light of your shortcomings and obstacles that need to be overcome, how *realistic* are your job and salary goals? How likely is it that your goals can be achieved? Write a statement about the likelihood of meeting your job goal in five years. Be honest!

2. DESIGNING A DIVERSITY TRAINING PROGRAM

PURPOSE

To use role playing and role reversal to become aware of the range of views about the meaning of diversity at the workplace. Students should also gain a clearer understanding of how a diversity of ideas can help an organization become more competitive. Students must approach this exercise with a certain level of maturity but should also be creative.

TASK

This is a role-reversal exercise that requires students to group by race and/or gender. ***All students should show respect for all roles***. Depending on the size of the class and the composition of the class in terms of race and gender, the instructor may decide to group students in one of the following ways:

1 By gender, with females role-playing males and males role-playing females.

2 By race, with white students role-playing minority students and minority students role-playing white students.

3 By race and gender, with white males role-playing minority females, minority males role-playing white females, and so on.

4 By other categories, which may include age, disability status, and so on.

Step 1: Your group (role reversed) should meet and list the elements that you believe should be covered in a diversity training program at a hypothetical large firm in your locale. Emphasize the interests of the gender or racial group you are role-playing.

Step 2: Your class should now return, and the groups should list on the blackboard the ideas generated for the ideal diversity training program. After the lists are written, class members should be encouraged to ask any group to explain why it included certain elements.

Step 3: Your class should draw circles or lines on the board, linking elements that were common, regardless of the group. This should identify the core elements. Discuss the common, and perhaps the uncommon, elements.

Step 4: What steps, if any, need to be taken at the workplace to remove glass ceilings. Decide whether these core elements (identified in Step 3) of your diversity program will actually help remove these barriers.

Step 5: What did role playing add to the discussions? Discuss how accurate role-players portrayals were.

KEY TERMS AND CONCEPTS

Aging workforce
Assessment centers
Bona fide seniority system (BFSS)
Bumping
Career management
Career match
Career stages
Closed promotion system
Contingent workers
Demotion
Dual-career couples
Early-retirement programs
Glass ceiling
Internal staffing
Layoff

Nepotism
Networking
Old boy network
Open promotion system
Outplacement assistance
Plateaued employee
Promotion
Seniority
Severance pay
Supplemental unemployment benefits (SUB)
Telecommuting
Trailing spouse
Transfer
Unofficial promotion criteria

REVIEW QUESTIONS

1. What are the benefits of an effective system for making promotion decisions? What are the various criteria that may be used for making promotion decisions?

2. What are the major causes of employee demotions, transfers, and layoffs?

3. What are some alternatives to layoffs? How effective do you think they can be when an employer is reorganizing?

4. What are some important HR policies and practices that have an impact on internal staffing decisions?

5. What are the benefits that may be gained from a career management program?

6. What are the problems of two-career couples and how may they be overcome?

7. What are the special problems that minorities, women, and older employees face when trying to move up the corporate ladder?

DISCUSSION QUESTIONS

1. Seniority is a common criterion for deciding who to lay off among the blue-collar workforce. Should seniority be the major factor in deciding on white-collar layoffs? Defend your reasoning.

2. Most organizations used closed promotion systems when selecting candidates for promotion to managerial jobs, though it is generally recognized that this minimizes the pool of candidates from which an employee may be selected. Why do organizations continue to use the closed promotion system?

3. An advantage of using seniority as a criterion for making promotions is that it eliminates supervisory bias. *Is* there still the possibility of supervisory bias when using performance-related criteria in making promotion decisions?

4. The personnel literature generally holds the assessment center in high regard. Can you think of reasons why

an organization would not adopt the assessment center in gathering promotion data?

5. If an employee receives a promotion and fails, whose fault is it—the organization's or the employee's?

6. Do you agree with the requirements of the Plant Closings Act? Why or why not? Would you favor increasing the notification period from 60 days to 120 days?

7. What kind of lateral promotion would you be willing to take?

8. Are women, minorities, and older employees really discriminated against at the workplace? How and why?

9. Assuming that you were employed full-time, what would you perceive as some of your immediate supervisor's responsibilities in your career management process?

10. How would you evaluate your college's or university's efforts to prepare you for a career in the world of work? Cite your school's strong and weak areas.

ENDNOTES

Chapter 11

1. Vikki R. Conwell, "Money & More: Getting a Job Is a Job Itself: Enhancing Skills Important for Remaining Employable, Experts Say," *The Atlanta Journal and Constitution* (January 1, 1999): F03.

2. George T. Silvestri, "Occupational Employment Projections to 2006" (Employment Outlook: 1996–2006); *Monthly Labor Review* 120 (November 1, 1997): 58.

3. See Frederick Herzberg et al., *The Motivation to Work* (New York: Wiley, 1959).

4. Bureau of National Affairs, *Employee Promotion and Transfer Policies,*

Personnel Policies Forum survey no. 120 (Washington, D.C.: Bureau of National Affairs, 1995).

5. Bureau of National Affairs (BNA) Editorial Staff, *Grievance Guide* (Washington, DC: Bureau of National Affairs, 1978), 173–174.

6. As indicated in a previous chapter, the assessment center may also be used to assess management development needs and strengthen managerial skills. See L. C. Nichols and J. Hudson, "Dual Role Assessment Center," *Personnel Journal* 82 (May 1981): 380–387; and F. Enzs, "Total Development:

Selection, Assessment, Growth," *Personnel Administrator* 25 (February 1980).

7. Walter S. Wikstrom, "Assessing Managerial Talent," *The Conference Board Record* (March 1967). Assessment center procedures and exercises are also outlined in C. Jaffee and J. Sefcik, Jr., "What Is an Assessment Center?" *Personnel Administrator* 25 (February 1980): 35–39.

8. Wikstrom, "Assessing Managerial Talent."

9. S. D. Norton, "The Empirical and Content Validity of Assessment Centers vs. Traditional Methods for

Predicting Managerial Success," *Academy of Management Review* 2 (1977): 442–453.

10. This point may be debated. It can be argued, and often is, that the family member is the most qualified person for the job.

11. Dalton Melville, *Men Who Manage* (New York: Wiley, 1959), 154.

12. Alison Kindelan, "Older Workers Can Alleviate Labor Shortages," *HR Magazine* 43 (September 1998): 200.

13. John P. Kohl and David B. Stephens, "Is Demotion a Four-Letter Word?" *Business Horizons* 33 (March–April 1990): 74.

14. Ibid.

15. Mark H. McCormack, "Boss Sends You a Message with Demotion," *The Arizona Republic* (October 1, 1998): 4.

16. "State Worker Sues over Demotion," *United Press International* (September 1, 1998).

17. John Accola, "Secretary's Suit Says IRS Acted Late on Harassment: Manager Disciplined Two Years after Complaint," *Denver Rocky Mountain News* (October 3, 1997).

18. Adapted from John E. Hayes, Jr., "Few Fast Tracks for Tomorrow's Brightest," *HR Magazine* 38 (January 1993): 94.

19. Julie Amparano Lopez, "Companies Alter Layoff Policies to Keep Recently Hired Women and Minorities," *The Wall Street Journal* (September 18, 1992): B1, B16.

20. S. Wermiel, "Court Orders That Shield Minorities from Layoffs Generate Bitterness," *The Wall Street Journal* 32 (March 23, 1983): 33.

21. "Blacks Hired Under Consent Decree Subject to Seniority-Based Layoffs," *U.S. Law Week* 52, no. 49 (June 19, 1984): 1193.

22. Diane Stafford, "At Home with Work: With Nearly 15 percent Growth Rate, Telecommuting Trend Catching On," *The Dallas Morning News* (January 18, 1999): 2D.

23. Jenny C. McMune, "Telecommuting Revisited," *Management Review* 87 (February 1, 1998): 21.

24. Ibid.

25. Stafford, "At Home with Work,"

26. Ani Hadjian, "Hiring Temps Full-Time May Get the IRS on Your Tail," *Fortune* (January 24, 1994): 34.

27. Ibid.

28. Jaclyn Fierman, "The Contingency Work Force," *Fortune* (January 24, 1994): 30–31.

29. Ibid., 32.

30. Ibid., 31.

31. "Early-Retirement Offers Lead to Renewed Hiring," *The Wall Street Journal* (January 26, 1993): B7.

32. Ibid.

33. Paul D. Staudohar, "New Plant Closing Law Aids Workers in Transition," *Personnel Journal* 68 (January 1989): 87.

34. Ibid.

35. David Stier, "Most Pay Severance, Even If Fired," *HR News* (August 1990): 2.

36. W. L. Batt Jr., "Canada's Good Example with Displaced Workers," *Harvard Business Review* 61 (July–August 1983): 100.

37. Al Gini, "Work, Identity and Self: How We Are Formed by the Work We Do," *Journal of Business Ethics* 17 (May 1998): 707.

38. William J. Morin, "You Are Absolutely, Positively on Your Own, Outplacement Is Dead, and the Truth about Your Future Is Hard to Come By at Many Companies. No Longer Any Doubt About It," *Fortune* (December 9, 1996): 222.

39. Erik A. Savisaar, "Matching Yourself with the World of Work, 1998," *Occupational Outlook Quarterly* 42 (Fall 1998): 2.

40. Gini, "Work, Identity and Self," 709.

41. See L. Peter and R. Hull, *The Peter Principle* (New York: William Morrow, 1969).

42. L. Baird and K. Kram, "Career Dynamics: Managing the Superior/Subordinate Relationship," *Organizational Dynamics* 12 (Spring 1983): 46–64.

43. T. Gutteridge and F. Otte, "Organizational Career Development: State of the Practice," unpublished monograph (October 1982), 23.

44. J. Walker and T. Gutteridge, "Career Planning Practices: An AMA Report" (New York: AMA-COM, 1979).

45. Ibid., p. 13.

46. Nancy T. Kate, "Two Careers, One Marriage," *American Demographics* 20, no. 1 (April 1, 1998): 28.

47. "Dual-Career Couples Speak Out," *HR Focus* 75 (August 1998): S6.

48. Becky Ebnekamp, "And Now, a Word from Dad," *Brandweek* 40 (January 18, 1999): 19.

49. Reyer A. Swaak, "Today's Expatriate Family: Dual Careers and Other Obstacles," *Compensation & Benefits Review* 27 (May 15, 1995): 21.

50. Diane Crispell, "Women's Work," *American Demographics* 19 (November 1997): 37.

51. Martha Groves, "Work & Careers; Corporate Currents; Some Firms Look through Glass Ceiling to See Ways of Tapping Women's Talent," *Los Angeles Times* (July 12, 1998): B5.

52. Patrick Kelly, "Conduct a Glass Ceiling Self-Audit Now," *HRMagazine* 38 (October 1993): 66–70.

53. Ibid.

54. Adapted from Ibid., 77–79.

55. Sally Pook, "Women's Glass Ceiling Is Really 'Glass Escalator,'" *The Daily Telegraph* (October 29, 1998): 1.

56. "The 'Glass Ceiling' That Keeps Women from the Top Ranks of the Corporate World May Have a Few Cracks in It," in footnotes, *Chronicle of Higher Education* 26 (November 24, 1993): A6.

57. David Aaronovitch, "Modern Women May Decide Their Place Is at Home with the Children," *Independent* (August 11, 1998): 3.

58. Rosalind Loring and Theodora Wells, *Breakthrough: Women into Management* (New York: Van Nostrand Reinhold, 1972), 25–28. *See also* E. Mirides and A. Cote, "Women in Management: The Obstacles and Opportunities They Face," *Personnel Administrator* 25 (April 1980).

59. Michele Galen, "Myths About Older Workers Cost Business Plenty," *Business Week* (December 20, 1993): 83.

60. Jeffrey A. Sonnenfeld, "Dealing with the Aging Workforce," *Harvard Business Review* 56 (November–December, 1978): 54–71.

61. Ibid.

P A R T

IV

RETAINING HUMAN RESOURCES

C H A P T E R

12

COMPENSATION SYSTEMS

CHAPTER OUTLINE

CHAPTER OBJECTIVES

1 To understand the relationship between business strategy and compensation systems.

2 To demonstrate the various compensation strategies for attracting, retaining, and motivating employee performance.

3 To establish a systematic job evaluation process that will comply with legal considerations.

4 To understand the strengths and weaknesses across traditional, person-based, and incentive-based compensation systems.

5 To be able to create individual, team, and organization-wide incentive systems.

INTERNATIONAL **HR** IN THE NEWS

GLOBAL DILEMMA: HOW TO REWARD TRANSNATIONAL TEAMS?

David Goodall is corporate director of compensation at Motorola. The company pioneered cellular telephones and pagers, turning them into must-have products for millions of people.

WWW.MOT.COM

In order to generate the creativity to stay on the cutting edge of technology, Motorola uses transnational teams. Each team is made up of a half-dozen people representing different businesses from different regions.

While Motorola is convinced that teams can generate gains in productivity and quality, always lurking in the background are those tough questions about whether—and how—to share the financial gains with workers.

Which raises another nasty question: How important a role does national culture play in determining team rewards?

One Motorola transnational team successfully completed their project. Their reward—each individual was given a $1,000 after-tax bonus.

Three of the six members felt the money was unnecessary. "We've already had the satisfaction of being on the team, having the recognition of being able to report back to the senior staff."

They said another key had been the opportunity to travel to different regions of the world as they were doing their work.

These people were further disturbed by the fact that, irrespective of the level they were in the organization, each received the same dollar amount. "We want to be rewarded for the effort we put in as individuals," they said.

Motorola has learned that treating members as a block of interchangeable parts is not good. "We've got to focus on the individual and how the individual is performing within that team," says Goodall. "People don't want to be rewarded for team results; they know some pull more weight than others."

"What would motivate you if you were part of a team?" Motorola asked individuals at all levels as it went around the world, interviewing teams. "They all came up with the same answer," says Goodall. "The reward . . . is a sense of recognition and satisfaction."

As for the cross-cultural challenge, Asians are more comfortable with everyone receiving similar rewards. Americans, on the other hand, *want it all.* They would prefer rewarding individuals for what they contribute to the team *and a team reward, too.*

SOURCE: Adapted from Perry Pascarella, "Company Experience with Global Teams," *Across the Board* (February 1997): 16–22; and Joann Lubin, "My Colleague, My Boss," *The Wall Street Journal* (April 12, 1995): R4.

STRATEGIC COMPENSATION MANAGEMENT

Just as organizations have different business strategies, companies need compensation systems that move in step with mission and strategy. Human resource support systems—particularly compensation—need to be aligned to business competitive strategies.[1]

Usually the pay philosophy will match three different types of objectives: (1) labor cost control, (2) employee attraction and retention, and (3) employee motivation. An organization's business strategy will determine the relative importance of these objectives.[2]

A company's decision to be a low-cost leader in its industry, such as Wal-Mart, requires that labor costs be monitored closely and overhead minimized. The strategy they choose is to offer a *low hourly wage.* They expect to hold turnover down through employee empowerment, recognition, and profit sharing.

Motorola's business strategy is to develop new markets for its high-tech products. Motorola's compensation strategy is designed to attract highly-skilled people who can orchestrate and deliver high-tech products. The Motorola strategy is to *pay whatever it takes* for talented people.

Employee compensation has a substantial impact on the long-term financial position of most firms. It is a huge percentage of total operating costs, ranging anywhere from 60 percent for manufacturing companies to 75 percent for service organizations.[3]

From the employees' perspective, using Maslow's hierarchy of needs, compensation addresses the most basic of human needs—physical and security needs. It also influences perceptions of fairness by the company, and compensation experts, such as Edward E. Lawler III, have found that effectively designed pay systems motivate high performance.[4]

Wage rates are generally determined by a number of factors including the nature of the work performed, the wage rates paid by other companies in the same area for similar work, and the employer's own finances. However, there are also federal and state laws that must be considered.

The **pay mix** consists of base compensation, benefits, and incentives. The **base compensation** is fixed and is the agreed upon hourly wage or annual salary that most employees are paid for performing a set of designated duties. *Employee benefits* such as insurance, vacation pay, and a retirement plan are a substantial part of the total compensation package and will be discussed later (see Chapter 13). Monetary **incentives,** or pay-for-performance, are designed to reward improved performance. Incentive plans are a variable in the total compensation picture and disbursed only in the event of meeting defined goals. The term *incentives* also includes nonfinancial rewards, for example, special recognition awards.

COMPENSATION OBJECTIVES

The compensation challenge is daunting. It begins with the perpetual mandate from top management to keep labor costs under control. Because pay levels must reflect market realities and affect both the cost of doing business and performance, consideration must be paid to the dollar amounts as well as how they are distributed. Paying higher wages than competitors can lead to ruin. Paying wages less than competitors might make the firm's bottom line appear attractive, but it may hamper employee recruitment and retention.[5]

The method of choice for determining the competitive labor costs in a particular industry or locality is the **wage survey.** It has become an arduous process, and most firms have turned to purchasing this information from specialists such as William M. Mercer, Inc., and the Hay Group. Wage surveys provide labor-market information such as demand for specific jobs, what competitors are paying for these jobs, historical wage patterns, union influence, and more.

WWW.HAYGROUP.COM

The wage survey output would then be used to establish *external wage equity* between employees of one organization and similarly jobbed employees elsewhere in the local labor market. Achieving external equity means employees would be less likely to exit one company for a similar job with a different company simply due to wages. Balancing external wage market realities with how wages are distributed internally is an immense challenge, posing all sorts of questions.

What is a job really worth to the organization and to its competitors? Should employees be paid more as they acquire time on the job or should "results" carry the most weight? Should "effort" play a larger role as the Motorola transnational team suggested? Which compensation systems are better at motivating improved performance? In the case of Motorola and others who are using teams, rewards should be based on team performance or individual contributions? The ideal system can be summed up as follows:

FIGURE 12–1 OBJECTIVES OF A COMPENSATION SYSTEM

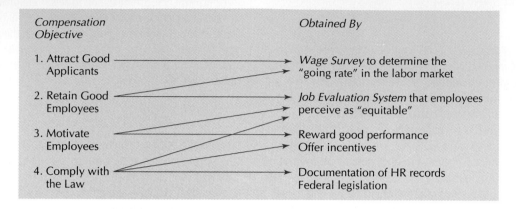

- It should *attract* qualified people to join.
- It should support *retention* once the qualified people come on-board.
- It should *motivate* employees to high levels of performance.

As simple as these objectives appear (see Figure 12–1), it is their implementation that raises many questions. If employees perceive unfair treatment due to compensation, it creates job dissatisfaction, which leads to lower commitment to the organization, and frequently an increase in absenteeism and turnover.[6] Should employees perceive more equitable treatment by another organization, their probability of leaving jumps dramatically. It is perception that drives the decision, not necessarily reality.

JOB EVALUATION

Determining what a job is worth is tricky. **Job evaluation** is the systematic process for assessing the relative value of jobs that results in establishing *internal pay equity* within the organization.

Jobs are compared on the traditional basis of skills required to complete the job, effort required to perform the job, responsibility of the job holder, and working conditions on the job. The process strives to obtain internal consistency among jobs, while wage surveys help the organization to maintain external consistency with other organizations in the local labor market.[7]

Paying for the market value of the job continues to be the predominant compensation philosophy.[8] Bureaucratic organizations, government, public-sector utilities, and some manufacturing sectors continue to depend on a traditional compensation approach invented for postwar mass-production-type systems. These companies are extremely conservative when it comes to pay, but given the tight labor markets now occurring (see *HR in the News:* "Tight Labor Markets Squeezing Bottom Lines"), many are forced to react and change their pay systems to reflect the added difficulties of retaining skilled workers.

MOTIVATION

American workers expect that their performances will correlate with the rewards received from the organization. Generally, that perceived relationship takes the form exhibited in Figure 12–2. Employees set expectations about rewards and compensation to be received if certain levels of performance are achieved. These expectations determine goals or levels of performance for the future. Employees achieving the desired level of performance expect a certain level of compensation. At some point, management evaluates and rewards the employee's performance. Examples of such rewards include merit increases, promotions, and intangible rewards such as goal accomplishment and increased self-esteem. Employees consider the relationship between their performance and the rewards related to that performance—then the fairness of that relationship. The final step in the process involves employees setting new goals and expectations based on prior experiences within the organization.

If employees see that hard work and superior performance are recognized and rewarded by the organization, they will expect such relationships to continue in the future. Therefore, they will set higher levels of performance, expecting higher levels of compensation. Of course, if employees see little relationship between performance and rewards, then they may set minimum goals in order to retain their jobs but will not see the need to excel in their positions.

HR IN THE NEWS

TIGHT LABOR MARKETS SQUEEZING BOTTOM LINES

The city of Plano, Texas, adopted a market-based compensation plan which, hopefully, will enable them to compete with the private sector for attracting and retaining skilled workers. The new plan established new salary ranges, changed some job titles, and put more people in the same pay categories. Instead of 37 pay grades, there are now 20. Each pay grade has three divisions. The lower third is for new employees or those who have only a few years of experience; the middle third applies to workers with several years of experience who are considered competent; and the upper third is for top-performing experienced workers.

In some grades, the ceiling for salaries rose, but in others, it dropped. For example, under the previous plan, the average salary for lower-level jobs such as data entry clerks, mail clerks, and warehouse workers ranged from $18,369 to $25,144. Under the new plan, the salary range dipped to between $16,791 and $23,675.

To help resolve the discrepancies, workers whose salaries are in the lower third are now eligible for higher performance pay increases than those in the middle and high end of the spectrum.

"I think it attempts to resolve some of the concerns the past plan had of having too many ranges and too narrowly defined job descriptions," City Manager Tom Muehlenbeck said of the new structure. The goal is to have most salaries in the midpoint, which is the market average.

SOURCE: J. Packer, "City's Pay Structure Changing: Study Consolidates Salary-Range Groups." *The Dallas Morning News* (October 15, 1998): 1F.

FIGURE 12–2   MOTIVATION AND PERFORMANCE MODEL

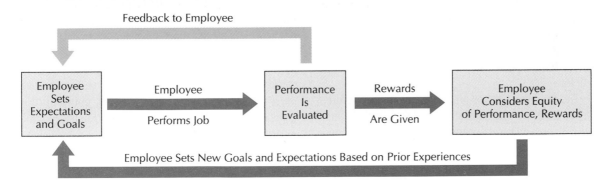

To safeguard this relationship of performance and motivation, which benefits the organization and the employee, the organization must provide the following:

- ***Accurate Evaluation.*** Management must develop a system of accurate performance appraisal in order to identify those employees who are outstanding, average, and poor performers. Although developing an accurate performance appraisal system is not easy, it is a critical link between employee performance and motivation.

- ***Performance Rewards.*** Management should identify which rewards relate to performance levels and tell employees that pay, increased benefits, change in hours or working conditions, or recognition will be directly related to high performance.

- ***Supervisors' Feedback.*** Supervisors must give complete and accurate feedback to employees when appraising their performances. Employees must be told what they are doing well and which performance areas need improvement.

LEGAL CONSIDERATIONS

A fourth major objective of the compensation system is to comply with federal legislation. Government has affected compensation by legislating pay levels and nondiscriminatory pay practices. As an employer in competition with private employers, the government also affects pay systems. At any time, government can increase its control over compensation by freezing wages; this occurred during the Korean War and from 1971 to 1974. A governmental *wage freeze* requires that federal regulatory bodies review wage increases. *Wage guidelines,* on the other hand, are not strict wage controls but simply requests to employers to comply voluntarily with wage-increase maximums.

Fair Labor Standards Act
The major compensation legislation regulating employers is the **Fair Labor Standards Act (FLSA)** of 1938. This act has been amended by Congress several times to provide higher minimum-wage levels. The provisions of this law include the following:

Minimum Wages   Under the FLSA, employers must pay an employee at least a minimum wage per hour. As shown in Table 12–1, the minimum wage per hour was $.25 in 1938 and was raised to $5.15 in 1997.

Child Labor   The FLSA prohibits hiring individuals between the ages of 16 and 18 for hazardous jobs or employing individuals under 16 in interstate commerce except in nonhazardous work for a parent or guardian. The act also requires individuals under 18 to obtain temporary work permits to be given to their employers.

The declining number of teenagers in the labor force has contributed to a substantial increase in child labor law violations in recent years. The vast majority (78 percent) were in the retail trade industry, which includes fast-food restaurants. Many teachers and parents are concerned that too many students fall asleep in class and do not complete their homework because they are working at part-time jobs. The tragic irony is that corporate America is demanding, and often contributing to, improvements in American schools—but in some respects may contribute to some teens' poor learning.[9]

Overtime Compensation   The FLSA stipulates that certain employees must receive overtime pay of one and one-half times the normal rate when they work over 40 hours per week. Certain kinds of employees are *exempt* from the overtime provision of the act.

Under the law, **exempt** most frequently means that a particular individual is exempt from the overtime provision and need not be paid overtime. In and of itself, a job title is not a sufficient basis for exemption. Rather, the actual work performed and the primary duties of the employee are what count. A person with an executive title who does not primarily manage a department or a function may not meet all conditions for exemption.

All positions are **nonexempt** (covered) unless proven exempt by the employer. Typically, exemption is determined by referring to a series of salary tests and other requirements that must be met. These are specified for four basic groups of employees: executive, administrative, professional, and outside salespersons. The test for executive, administrative, and professional employees includes a minimum salary and, most important, a primary duty condition that requires that more than 50 percent of the employee's time used is to "customarily and regularly exercise discretion and independent judgment." In addition, less than 20 percent of their time can be spent on routine, manual, or clerical work.[10]

Some organizations have tried to lower their overtime costs by classifying more employees as exempt and thus not paying them for hours worked exceeding 40 per week. The restaurant, tourist, and medical industries are exempt from the overtime provision, as are agricultural workers. When calculating overtime, a workweek is 168 consecutive hours or seven consecutive days, not necessarily a calendar week. Special provisions allow hospitals to use a 14-day period instead of a 7-day period.

The U.S. Department of Labor estimates that there are 73,000 compliance investigations annually. About half of them involve the overtime pay provision. In many cases, while the employer and many affected employees are happy with their compensation system, it is found to be in technical violation of the FLSA.

Many of the technical violations of the FLSA result from newer compensation plans that include pay

TABLE 12–1	U.S. MINIMUM WAGE CHANGES UNDER THE FLSA (WAGES PER HOUR)												
1938	1945	1950	1956	1962	1967	1974	1978	1979	1980	1985	1990	1991	1997
$.25	$.40	$.75	$1.00	$1.15	$1.40	$2.00	$2.65	$2.90	$3.10	$3.35	$3.80	$4.25	$5.15

HR IN THE NEWS

WORKERS DESIRE TIME OFF— NOT OVERTIME DOLLARS

The federal law requiring cash payment for overtime work was enacted over 60 years ago. Under the prevailing patterns of the time, the male breadwinner would focus on the added income, while his home-based wife dealt with family concerns. That pattern of family life, of course, is somewhat outdated. Working wives and single parents make up a substantial part of the workforce.

Today's workers, male and female, are repeatedly challenged to find enough time to deal with their children's school, sports, and other activities as well as with the care of aging parents, with volunteer work, and with matters of personal concern generally. The key to finding that time is increased flexibility in their working hours.

Despite the changing social environment, the Fair Labor Standards Act of 1938 remains unchanged in these closing years of the 20th century. The statute, which generally applies to workers paid by the hour, mandates that employees who work more than 40 hours in the same week be paid for the overtime hours at 150 percent of their usual hourly rate.

An hourly worker might be willing to put in two extra hours on Thursday night in exchange for leaving three hours early to attend a school conference or a baseball game the following Tuesday afternoon, but current law does not allow employers and employees to make such arrangements. Under the law as it now stands, the worker can use vacation time or, if none is available, take the time off without pay.

Because of those limited options, the idea of allowing hourly workers to take time off as compensation—so called *comp time*—for overtime worked has strong public support. A poll commissioned by the Employment Policy Foundation shows that 75 percent of Americans favor allowing workers to choose between comp time and cash payments; 57 percent of those who work overtime indicated they would sometimes choose time over cash, and 33 percent said they would choose time more often than cash. A study by the U.S. Department of Labor in 1995 showed that the top concern of working women was flexible job scheduling.

Legislation that would help workers in their effort to juggle job and personal considerations has been introduced in the U.S. Senate as the Family Friendly Workplace Act (S. 4) and in the House of Representatives as the Working Families Flexibility Act (H.R. 1).

The basic provision of each bill would allow employers and hourly workers to agree on provision of comp time at the same rate of cash reimbursement—an hour and a half for every hour worked beyond 40 hours in the same week.

In the absence of such an agreement, the employer would have to pay cash overtime. The bill contains many other worker protections, including provisions for cashing out comp time, a worker's right to withdraw from an agreement at any time, and penalties for employers who attempt to coerce employees into signing such agreements.

The legislation would extend to the private-sector workforce the same option that federal and some other government employees have had for many years.

Giving workers a comp-time alternative would ease the antiquated view of the Fair Labor Standards Act toward family priorities and end the current discrimination against the private sector on this critical issue.

SOURCE: Steven Blakely, "Flexibility on Overtime Rules Is Overdue," *Nation's Business* 85, no. 1 (April 1, 1997): 84.

incentives such as attendance bonuses, productivity bonuses, and commissions. Employers are often unaware that such bonuses and commissions must be included in the regular rate of pay when computing the overtime rate of pay. As a general rule, the act requires that all compensation be included in the employee's regular rate of pay, with seven specific exceptions:[11]

1. Gifts

2. Christmas bonuses

3. Special occasion bonuses

4. Profit-sharing payments

5. Thrift plan payments

6. Savings plan payments

7. Irrevocable contributions made to a bona fide trust

The most common mistake made by employers is to treat bonuses and commissions as discretionary income and not part of an employee's regular rate of pay, which is used to determine the overtime rate. The Department of Labor's regulations provide that if a bonus or commission is promised to employees by a specific policy or agreement, it is not discretionary income and must be included in the employee's weekly earnings. For example, if employees received a bonus of $100 for a week during which they worked 50 hours, the additional overtime due would be calculated as follows: $100/50 = $2/hour increase in hourly rate; thus, the employees are also due $1 in overtime for each of ten hours, or $10. Employers may choose to base a bonus or commission on a percentage of total earnings if the percentage is increased to one and one-half for all overtime hours.[12]

In today's labor markets, with its low unemployment rate, firms must offer more creative work arrangements in an effort to retain skilled employees. A number of polls support the notion that workers, particularly women, would like the option of receiving time off, or **compensatory time** *(comp time),* in lieu of overtime pay (see *HR in the News:* "Workers Desire Time Off . . ."). While Congress is considering comp time legislation, the main opposition comes from labor unions. Employees, unions say, are not well-protected against employer pressure to force them to "choose" comp time over paid overtime.

The Davis-Bacon Act
The Davis-Bacon Act of 1931 regulates employers who hold federal government contracts of $2,000 or more for federal construction projects. It provides that employees working on these projects must be paid the **prevailing wage** rate. In most urban areas, the union wage is the prevailing wage for that particular geographic area. If the local union wage for plumbers is $16 per hour, then any plumbers hired to work on federal construction projects in the area must

be paid at least $16 per hour. The reasoning behind the Davis-Bacon Act is that often governments will award contracts to the firm submitting the lowest bid for certain construction specifications. By requiring all employers in construction projects to pay the prevailing wage, the Davis-Bacon Act puts bidders on an equal basis and ensures that craft workers will not be underpaid.

BUILDING TRADITIONAL COMPENSATION SYSTEMS

There are a number of popular pay strategies, tactics, tools, and processes in use in organizations. The oldest and still the most common strategy is paying people on the basis of their jobs.[13] Traditional organizations pay people primarily through base salaries. The specific amounts were determined by three factors: the specific job, the need to maintain internal equity, and the need to be competitive in the local labor market. It is a job evaluation process.

Job Evaluation Committee
The process is expensive and not entirely objective. A committee is usually formed, composed of people who are familiar with the jobs under examination and who have been trained in the basic concept of job evaluation. Usually an HR functional specialist will participate and provide resources when necessary. Large organizations, like the federal government, often maintain a permanent job evaluation committee. All organizations should plan on periodically reviewing established job classifications as they tend to become outdated rather quickly in the current economic climate.

Outside Assistance
One of the first decisions for the committee is whether the organization should produce a job evaluation system or hire outside consultants. The Hay Group, for example, has developed a *point-based* measurement system which ranks jobs based on three primary criteria: know-how, problem solving, and accountability. Pay is based on the specific, individual skills a person brings to a specific job.[14]

Most job-based systems use a schedule of pay grades and steps such as the one in Table 12–2. The matrix can include hourly rates or annual rates of pay, depending on whether the jobs are hourly or salary. Jobs are assigned to a particular pay grade, depending on the results of the job evaluation.

When job evaluation is completed, administrators must determine a final pay system to apply to jobs within

TABLE 12–2 A SAMPLE SCHEDULE OF HOURLY PAY GRADES AND STEPS

PAY GRADE	STEP 1	STEP 2	STEP 3	STEP 4	STEP 5	STEP 6	STEP 7
1	5.15	5.36	5.63	5.91	6.21	6.52	6.85
2	6.12	6.43	6.75	7.09	7.44	7.81	8.20
3	7.34	7.71	8.10	8.51	8.94	9.39	9.86
4	8.81	9.25	9.71	10.20	10.71	11.25	11.81
5	10.57	11.10	11.66	12.24	12.85	13.49	14.16
6	12.68	13.31	13.98	14.68	15.41	16.18	16.99
7	15.22	15.98	16.78	17.62	18.50	19.43	20.40
8	18.26	19.17	20.13	21.14	22.20	23.31	24.48
9	21.91	23.01	24.16	25.37	26.64	27.97	29.37

the organization. Their decisions involve establishing minimum and maximum pay levels for each pay grade and determining how individuals will advance in pay grades. A standardized pay system must be promulgated and documented in order to maintain internal as well as external *pay equity*. Also, management must be able to document and defend its pay system in court. Administrators have found it advantageous to develop pay grades and steps, or levels, which specify the annual amount paid salaried employees in a particular pay grade and step and to use a monthly or hourly basis for other jobs.

If the organization has undergone a point method of job evaluation, then the pay system can be illustrated on a *scatter diagram* by first plotting the wage rate and pay grade for each current employee. Each employee is then represented by one dot in the diagram. The scatter diagram in Figure 12–3 illustrates the use of equal-interval pay grades. That is, each pay grade has an equal number of points but has an unequal range in terms of the total pay within the pay grade. While the dollar figures in each pay range are not increased equally, the actual percent increase of pay for each step is 5 percent.

Number of Steps

In developing a compensation system, the number of steps within each **pay grade** must be decided. Figure 12–4 illustrates how pay grade 5 is divided into equal increases of approximately 5 percent. Thus employees receive a larger cents-per-hour increase with each step raise, and in the higher pay grades the increases become larger.

Deciding how many **steps** should be included within each pay grade is a difficult decision. If too many steps are included, employees' motivation for good performance may be less because the increase will be very

small. Having few steps in each pay grade creates larger increases and motivates employees to work for merit increases. Employees reach the top of their pay grades more quickly when grades have few steps. Once individuals have reached the top of their pay grades, the practice is usually to keep them at that highest step, to transfer them to jobs in a higher pay grade, or to promote them. Organizations with relatively few opportunities for promotion, or with turnover so low that many individuals stay within one pay grade for several years, find it wise to have many steps and, perhaps, even wider-ranging pay grades.

Figure 12–4 illustrates the practice of using two or more entry-level salaries for jobs within a particular pay grade. The reason for the practice is that while managers wish to be consistent and pay similar wages for similar jobs, allowances must be made for individual differences in job candidates who are hired. Candidates with more experience and skills can be hired in a higher step; a recruit who has just finished school and has no experience would logically be hired at step 1. In most situations this would not violate federal laws: Consistency within the pay system could be proved since similar wages were paid for similar work, making allowances for individual differences.

Red Circle Employees

Another decision to be made by the evaluation committee is illustrated in Figure 12–3. Seven individuals within the pay grade system have been frozen or hold **red circle jobs.** A red circle indicates that this individual is currently being paid more than the maximum for that pay grade. Through seniority or for some other reason, the individual is currently being paid more than the organization planned to pay any employee to perform jobs of

FIGURE 12–3   A SCATTER DIAGRAM

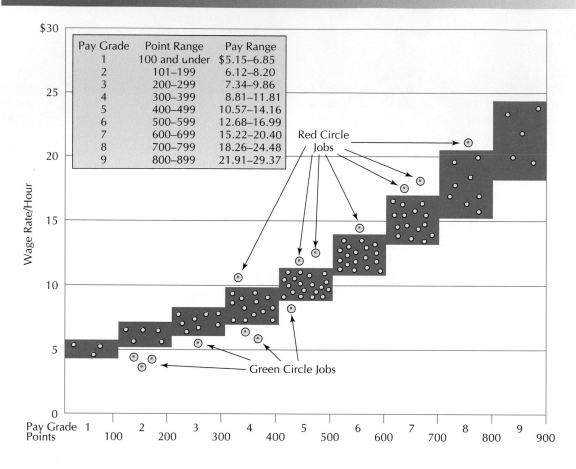

Pay Grade	Point Range	Pay Range
1	100 and under	$5.15–6.85
2	101–199	6.12–8.20
3	200–299	7.34–9.86
4	300–399	8.81–11.81
5	400–499	10.57–14.16
6	500–599	12.68–16.99
7	600–699	15.22–20.40
8	700–799	18.26–24.48
9	800–899	21.91–29.37

FIGURE 12–4   PAY GRADE 5 WITH INTERNAL STEPS

Step 7	$7.30	TOP LEVEL STEPS
Step 6	7.06	
Step 5	6.81	
Step 4	6.57	MIDPOINT
Step 3	6.32	ENTRY LEVEL STEPS
Step 2	6.08	
Step 1	5.84	

that pay grade. Red-circled individuals remain at the same pay level until either they are promoted to a higher pay grade or cost-of-living adjustments increase their pay grade salaries to equal or exceed the red-circle rate. The Equal Pay Act protects individuals from having their pay lowered through the job evaluation process related to a gender discrimination claim.

Those individuals who are currently paid below the minimum step of their pay grade are in **green circle jobs.** Normally when the pay system is finalized, their pay will be increased to the first step of the pay grade; otherwise, they would be paid less than the minimum worth of the job according to the pay system.

Overlap of Grades

The organization must also decide whether to overlap pay grades so that the maximum of one pay grade is higher than the minimum of the next higher pay grade. The compensation system in Figure 12–3 allows pay grades to overlap. One advantage is that employees can be transferred or promoted from one job to the next without necessarily being given pay increases. For example, an employee paid $10.71 per hour in pay grade 5 could be promoted to a job with a larger point total in pay grade 6 without a large increase in pay.

Management has the option of not paying individuals higher salaries immediately but of offering them higher salaries if they prove themselves and receive merit increases, thus moving up in the pay grade. Another advantage of overlapping pay grades is that this gives grades a greater range with more steps of a meaningful size. Thus, employees are rewarded with merit and seniority increases while they stay in the same job and pay grade.

One disadvantage of overlapping pay grades is that a promotion may not bring a pay increase and could even bring a cut in pay. Also, overlapping grades makes it possible for an individual in a higher pay grade to supervise employees in a lower pay grade who receive higher paychecks than the supervisor. For example, when a new supervisor is placed in a department in which an employee is at the highest step of the next lower pay grade, the employee will receive higher pay than the supervisor. In manufacturing and construction organizations this is not unusual.

PAY INCREASES

Primarily two types of pay increases are made: *across-the-board increases,* where everyone in the organization receives an equal pay increase, and *merit* or *seniority* increases given to selected individuals.

Across-the-Board Increases

These increase the employee's income due to the cost-of-living allowances or in order to make the organization's pay system compatible with the local labor market. An across-the-board **cost-of-living adjustment (COLA)** can be an equal percentage or equal dollars. Managers often prefer to give equal percentage increases because COLAs are related to the cost of living, which is measured in percentages. Hearing that the cost of living has

gone up a certain percentage, employees realize that their buying power has decreased. Therefore, they hope to receive a COLA at least equal to the increase in their cost of living.

An across-the-board percentage increase simply changes the dollar amounts for each grade and step in the compensation system; it does not move any employee or job within the system. Therefore, if a 3 percent cost-of-living pay increase were given to employees in the pay grades and steps in Table 12–2, all of the amounts would change but the pay grades and steps would not. In Figure 12–3, the pay grade configuration would become more sloped as the higher pay grades experienced greater dollar increases than the lower pay grades.

If an equal-dollar across-the-board increase is given as a COLA, the amounts in Table 12–2 would increase an equal dollar figure. In Figure 12–3, the scale on the left side would slide down because individuals in lower pay grades would get a larger percentage increase than individuals in higher pay grades.

Merit Increases

Time-based pay systems are not completely void of a relationship between pay and performance. Instead, many include **merit pay increases** to employees. After a performance appraisal of their work, employees receive increases in pay if their work record is judged meritorious. Merit raises are designed to motivate employees by tying at least part of their pay to their performance.

Merit pay systems rest heavily on three assumptions: (1) Employee differences in performance can be accurately measured, (2) employees can effectively perceive pay differences as relating to performance differences, and (3) individuals will improve their future performance to gain more merit increases.[15]

Critics of merit systems, however, point out their frequent problems: (1) There is only a slight relationship between performance appraisals and percentage pay increases, and employees are quick to realize it, (2) supervisor bias may be as important in the appraisal process than employee productivity, and (3) employees simply do not perceive that merit raises are linked to their performance, whether true or not. The *HR in the News:* "Remember When . . . ?" is typical of the anxiety that occurs when merit systems are eliminated and replaced with a variable-pay program.

Many managers believe that linking pay increases to performance is effective because behaviors that are rewarded are more likely to be repeated; behaviors that are punished are less likely to be repeated. Also, rewards that are obtained as a result of one's performance will

HR IN THE NEWS

REMEMBER WHEN. . . . ?

Remember vinyl records? Remember typewriters? Remember regular merit raises?

Routine salary increases for nonunion employees appear headed for extinction, overtaken by low inflation and an exploding array of variable-pay programs tied to individual, team, business-unit, and corporate performance. But the shift away from the annual merit raise could lower morale and lessen loyalty in an already anxious work force, compensation experts say.

"We are on the precipice of a very major change" in pay practices, says Sandra O'Neal, a principal at Towers Perrin consulting firm. She estimates that in the past two years, about 45 large- and medium-size employers in the United States have replaced some staffers' base pay with variable-pay programs. She foresees those numbers doubling by 1998.

While just a few companies have eliminated raises outright, many are trying to link rewards with results. About 61 percent of large- and medium-size companies now offer some kind of variable pay such as profit-sharing and bonus awards, up from 47 percent in 1990, say surveys by Hewitt Associates.

WWW.HEWITT.COM

And the raises that are left—which will show up in paychecks in coming weeks—seem to be losing their punch. Average increases for salaried employees sank to 3.9 percent in 1996 from 5 percent in 1990.

Bosses have been grumbling that regular merit raises, once a reward for top individual work, have come to be expected by all workers.

Dial, the big consumer-products maker, decided to do away with merit raises for its 1,400 nonunion staffers over the next three years. Instead, they will be eligible for an annual cash bonus, which primarily will reflect three measures of corporate financial performance: net revenue growth, operating margin, and asset turnover. Potential bonuses will rise as merit raises are phased out. To help ensure Dial can still attract workers after base salaries stop increasing, officials say they may further enlarge worker's potential bonuses.

These programs do create anxiety. At Dial, the new plan triggered a flurry of calls to a special hot line. Dawn Henson, a customer-service specialist, frets about the possibility "that I won't make any more money for the year. I may just get my base." She adds: "That's a very scary thing." She has collected raises averaging about 5 percent a year since joining Dial. She is reassured but nervous nevertheless.

If the company does well, she gets an 11.25 percent bonus. But she worries that management may set unrealistically tough targets. "For now, I will hang in there and take the risk," she says. If Dial skips her bonus after killing her merit raise, "I can bail out," she warns.

SOURCE: Joann Lublin, "Don't Count on That Merit Raise This Year," *The Wall Street Journal* (January 7, 1996): B1.

have greater value than rewards that are given to everyone. Thus, a 7 percent merit increase in an organization where the average is 5 percent will be more highly valued than if a 7 percent across-the-board increase was given.[16]

When employees receive merit increases, they do not change pay grades, since a pay grade is based on the point total of their jobs or their classifications. But employees who receive merit increases move up one or more steps within their pay grades. Administrators, for example, may give two-step increases to the top 5 percent of their employees and one-step increases to the next highest 20 percent.

Some organizations give seniority increases to employees who have successfully performed their jobs for a certain length of time. These increases move employees up one or more steps within their pay grades. If the organization of Table 12–2 has merit increases, the dollar amounts in each pay grade would stay the same but employees would move up one step. The same would be true for the organization in Figure 12–3.

Overall, merit pay disadvantages outweigh whatever gains may be possible. Merit pay systems undermine teamwork, encourage employees to focus on the short term, and lead people to link pay to political skills and in-gratiating personalities rather than to performance.

PERSON-BASED SYSTEMS

A contemporary compensation question that is often asked by HR professionals is: should organizations pay for the person or for the job? The latter approaches include performance-based programs, while the former introduce two relatively new ideas—broadbanding and skill-based pay. **Person-based pay** programs allow work-ers to increase their pay by taking on new or additional activities.

Broadbanding
What **broadbanding** does is to eliminate multiple salary grades in favor of just a few. The idea is to encourage flexibility in moving workers from one job to another without being constrained by narrow salary grades. According to the Hewitt Associates survey data, 60 percent of the participating companies that have implemented or considered bands did so in order to facilitate job transfers, encourage lateral job mobility, and pay for learning individual skills.[17]

Northern Telecom, the Canadian communications company, adopted a broadbanding plan in which 54 grades were compressed to 13. The fewer bands spanned the pay opportunities formerly covered by most of the old grades. But not all bands are alike. The most obvious differences occur between career bands and traditional bands. *Career bands* serve primarily as a management development compensation strategy. Their objective is to support the contemporary organization—new culture, fewer levels, lateral rather than vertical promotions, and movement away from relying on traditional merit increases. In contrast, *traditional bands* have wide salary ranges too, but the real objective may be a desire to alleviate the "topping-out" problem—a situation of having too many employees who are at, or near, the maximum of their range.

In theory, broadbanding makes sense. In practice, however, it does not address the question of how individuals progress in pay; all it does is make it easier to pay for skills and simplify the problem of putting people and/or jobs into a pay grade. It is easier because there are simply fewer grades in which to put employees or jobs. Broadbanding does not work well with traditional organizational hierarchies and may offer only a modest chance of success at companies attempting to support a new culture.

Skill-Based Pay
Skill-based pay is premised on the belief that employees who know more are more valuable to their employer and should be compensated accordingly. It is innovative and promotes workforce flexibility by rewarding individuals based on the number, type, and depth of skills mastered. It consists of cross-training, where the person actually acquires the skills other people use in the performance of other jobs

Traditional jobs were narrowly defined tasks, requiring an equally defined set of skills. Contemporary jobs are wider in scope and require a broader set of skills. Figure 12–5 depicts the differences between traditional and skill-based pay strategies.[18]

FIGURE 12–5   TRADITIONAL JOB-BASED SYSTEM

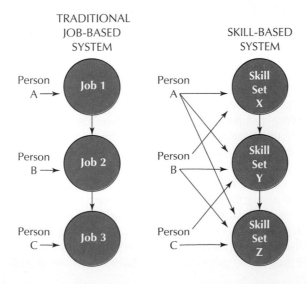

There are five types of skill-based plans:

❶ Vertical skill plans measure the acquisition of input/output skills (for example, a drill press operator mastering preventive maintenance and in-process inspection) within a single job.

❷ Horizontal skill plans reward the acquisition of complementary skills (for example, a clerk learns how to do both accounts payable and accounts receivable) across several jobs.

❸ Depth skill plans reward skill specialization (for example, a computer programmer specializing in database programming).

❹ Basic skill systems reward employees for developing expertise in the basic skill areas (four-function math; reading, writing, and speaking English).

❺ Combination plans reward any of the skills previously discussed.[19]

How does the process actually affect an employee? Assume a production worker, call her Betty, has been hired to fill a vacancy in an automotive factory. The physical plant is composed of interdependent operations. As an entry-level operator, she is paid a base rate and is initially responsible for the operation of machine *X*. After a combination of on-the-job and classroom education Betty demonstrates mastery of setup, inspection, and preventive maintenance (see Figure 12–5, Skill Set *X*). She receives a nominal pay increase and is rotated to operation *Y*. She repeats the same process but learns a new skill set with another adjustment in her pay. She continues until either all of the operations in the subassembly have been mastered or she "maxes" out (is unable to learn any additional skill sets and still maintain mastery on skill sets already certified).[20]

Skills-based pay is very different from traditional compensation strategies. A system must be created for training employees and helping them develop the required skills. A certification process must be established to ensure that they indeed have acquired those skills. Just as important, a decertification process is often necessary for employees who no longer have certain skills.[21]

The goal, or knowing what skills are really needed, and what the organization is paying for has to be thoughtfully conceived. Also, is the goal to produce more employees who are generalists—developing more, rather than higher, skills—or should they only acquire higher valued skills so that jobs actually become more valuable to the organization.[22] Teaching an engineer word processing, for example, may broaden his skills and allow elimination of some secretarial work, but it certainly won't make the engineer more valuable to the organization.

Over 50 percent of the Fortune 1000 companies have skill-based pay systems for at least part of their workforce.[23] Polaroid, Frito-Lay, and General Electric all have skill-based pay systems throughout most, if not all, of its workforce.

WWW.POLAROID.COM

Skill-based pay, in many ways, fits well with broadbanding when companies use the acquisition of skills to determine how an individual progresses through a particular pay band. It can work to support employees in choosing to make lateral moves—a frequent occurrence today—because the pay system has enough flexibility to reward individuals for this type of career move. Traditional pay systems tend to restrict, or penalize, an employee's decision to take a lateral move.

INCENTIVE-BASED SYSTEMS

As discussed earlier, people are likely to be more highly motivated, and thus to increase their productivity, if they perceive that there is a direct relationship between their level of performance and the rewards received. Most incentive pay systems provide employees with a base income and the opportunity to earn additional compensation if their productivity exceeds a predetermined standard.

Piece-Rate Systems

Piecework has been around longer than any other individual incentive system. Each worker is quoted a fixed, or standard, rate of pay for each unit of output produced. This is called the **straight piecework plan.** Jobs that are good candidates for piece-rate systems are typically found in manufacturing. Many computer chip manufacturers will pay workers a flat rate—for example, $2 per component. Production standards, usually set by industrial engineers, are stated in terms of expected output per hour or day. In the case of computer chips, a job evaluation may have indicated that 40 chips is the typical output over an eight-hour day. If the worker produced the expected output, the total compensation for the day would be $80. If the worker exceeded the standard output by 10, the day's compensation would jump to $100.

Variations of straight piecework plans include **rising and falling differentials.** With falling piece rates, any gain is shared between the employer and employee. Using the preceding example, instead of the worker collecting an extra $20 for exceeding the standard output by 10 chips, the worker and employer would split it according to a previously agreed-on standards. Plans that use a rising piece rate give workers even more incentive for exceeding the standard. Continuing with the example, instead of $2 per chip over 40, the employer agrees to increase it to $2.50 for every chip over 40, thus giving the worker a total daily compensation of $105 (40 × $2 = $80 plus 10 × $2.50 = $25). Why would management agree to a rising piece-rate system? If the higher hourly earnings are sufficiently motivational, the total cost per piece to the company could be lower.

Piece-rate systems have a number of advantages. They are easy to understand, simple to calculate, and effective motivational tools. Nevertheless, they are not implemented as often as one might think. One problem is that many jobs do not have output that can be objectively measured. Another problem is that jobs are becoming more interrelated, which means that one person's output is affected by the output of others. If the other person does not want to make an extra effort, that will destroy whatever motivational force piece-rate systems might have encouraged. But the most often heard complaint is how difficult it is for employers and workers to agree on what is a fair production standard. Unfortunately, some employers have arbitrarily and unilaterally reestablished standards after "concluding" that the old system was titled too favorably in the workers' direction.

Standard Hour Plans
Standard hour plans are similar in concept to piece-rate plans except that a standard amount of time is set to complete a particular job instead of paying the employee a price per piece. For example, an auto mechanic might be given a standard time of two hours to tune up an eight-cylinder car. If the worker's pay rate is $8.00 per hour and three eight-cylinder tune-ups are finished in six hours, then the employee earns $48.00. If a so-called Halsey 50/50 incentive plan is used, the worker and employer share equally in the time saved by the employee. Thus, if three tune-ups are completed in five hours, then the employee would be paid $52.00 ($48.00 + $4.00 [one-half hour saved at $8.00/hour]), and the employer has an additional hour's work time.

Commissions
An individual incentive system widely used in sales positions is the **commission.** Employees are given a percentage of sales (measured in units or dollars). The percentage may change at predetermined levels in a manner similar to falling or rising piece rates. Employees who are paid on commission generally receive either (1) *straight commission,* which means that their total pay is determined by the commission formula, or (2) *salary-plus-commission,* which combines a monthly salary base with a commission incentive. The salary-plus-commission method has the advantage of providing a minimum income level that employees can count on to pay their living expenses and provides stability against factors beyond the control of the employee that can affect sales, such as seasonal swings, increased competition, and inventory shortages.

How much of a salary-plus-commission total income should be commission? There is no easy or correct answer to this difficult question. In general, the commission portion is usually 20 to 40 percent of the total. The higher the percentage that is commission, one might argue, the more motivating to the employee. However, one problem with any commission system is determining what is a fair percentage of each sale. If the percentage is too low, employees may not find it motivating and may simply rely on their salary; if it is too high, the company may find that it has created some millionaire sales representatives. In one case, the new management of a regional television station substantially increased the commission percentage paid to its sales executives in an effort to increase commercial revenues. The plan worked; after the first quarter revenues were up 40 percent, and the top sales executive had earned more in commissions in one quarter than the station manager earned in a year!

TEAM-BASED INCENTIVE SYSTEMS

Organizations are recognizing that some individual incentive systems can do more harm than good, particularly in those situations where teamwork and coordination among workers are becoming more important. For interrelated tasks such as an assembly line, how one worker performs can influence the productivity of everyone else on the line. A pay system that encourages competitive behavior may find that the "competitor" is often a worker's colleague, not an external business competitor. When a situation such as too much competition begins to disrupt operations or when a new team-building program such as TQM is implemented, **team-based incentives** need to be considered.

Team incentive arrangements differ from traditional incentives in a many ways (see Figure 12–6). One difference is that goals and results are clarified and established for teams—not for individuals. Also, teams are evaluated on the degree to which performance targets are met. Goals must be clearly communicated and performance measurably defined—neither of which is an

FIGURE 12–6   TRADITIONAL VERSUS TEAM-BASED PAY

	TRADITIONAL COMPENSATION APPROACH		NEW APPROACH
DESIGN ELEMENT	HIERARCHICAL STRUCTURE	HOW IT AFFECTS TEAMS	WHAT TEAMS NEED
Job Evaluation	Based on *individual* job responsibilities.	Reinforces individual jobs and "specialist" nature of work. Creates unnecessary hierarchy on team. Weakens job market matches.	Flexible jobs that concentrate on results and work of the team. Less emphasis on individual jobs and fewer distinctions among individual team member jobs.
Pay Structure	Based on *individual* jobs plotted on a specialist/job hierarchy.	Focuses members on advancing through the job hierarchy.	A focus on common goals and results, not on hierarchy.
Base Pay Growth and Delivery	Merit increases based on *individual* performance with a fixed pool of available funds. Across-the-board increases based on market factors.	Individual merit increases cause competition among team members in a zero-sum game. Across-the-board increases create a feeling of entitlement.	Cooperation among team members. A focus on team objectives and results.
Performance Management	Top-down process with focus on *individual* performance.	Focuses team members on their own performance, perhaps to the detriment of team performance.	A focus on total team performance and team behavior. Assessment of individual performance in the context of team outcomes.
Career Development	*Individual* promotions to *individual* jobs—often to different jobs or up a ladder based on depth or breadth in a particular functional area.	Focuses team members on a hierarchical career path.	A focus on adding value and skills to the team. Advancement based on team success. Advancement defined, for example, as moving to a strategically more important team.
Recognition	Given for *individual* accomplishments—typically not a prominent part of rewards.	Reinforces individual "stars," potentially at the expense of teams.	Emphasis on team accomplishments. Recognition used more prominently.
Spot Awards (Large Discretionary Awards)	When used, often focused on *individual* performance and usually private (given to *individuals* with no public recognition).	Rewards individual "stars," resulting in jealousy or shutdown in communication.	A focus on team success. Teamwide or public awards to emphasize team accomplishments.

SOURCE: A. Saunier and E. Hawk, "Realizing the Potential of Teams through Team-Based Rewards," *Compensation and Benefits Review* (July–August 1994): 25.

FIGURE 12–6	(con't)		
	TRADITIONAL COMPENSATION APPROACH		NEW APPROACH
DESIGN ELEMENT	HIERARCHICAL STRUCTURE	HOW IT AFFECTS TEAMS	WHAT TEAMS NEED
Short-Term Incentives	Driven by large-scale measures, such as business unit or division performance, in addition to *individual* performance.	Overlooks contribution of the team and rewards individual performance, potentially at the expense of team performance.	Rewards for team performance. Reinforcement of team behavior. Reinforcement of individual contributions and behavior in context of team outcomes.
Long-Term Incentives	Driven by very large-scale measures of company performance; usually limited to upper levels and paid out based on an *individual's* level.	Does not apply to most teams.	Measurement of long-term contributions of the team. Extension of eligibility to all team members.

easy task to achieve. A prerequisite is the establishment of a solid communication system, both formal and informal, between management and the team and within the team as well. Ideally, teams should not be so large (more than 10) that communication and coordination suffer.[24]

A second difference from traditional systems is that team-based incentive awards are typically more comparable (but not necessarily equal) across participants. Members may be rewarded using a formula based on the final output of the team. Whether it is piece rate or standard hour does not really matter. Most of the evidence supports keeping incentive rewards approximately the same. What does seem to matter is when too much reward disparity occurs among the members. This may breed discontent and undermine cohesion.[25]

Yet it is hard to deny the strong—and particularly American—individualistic trait in so many high achievers. One problem with strong individualism within a team is the difficulty of putting the group's needs first. Team members who cannot put the good of the group before their own are called *social loafers* and *free riders* (see *HR in the News:* "Is the Free Ride Over for Free Riders?"). Other problems occur when members cannot make a psychological connection between their efforts and some positive team outcome. But it still may be possible for individual performance to play

some role. How to strike the right balance between individual performance rewards and team-based rewards is a challenge.[26]

An important measurement tool used in most team-based incentive systems is something called **360-degree feedback.** Pertinent sources for providing constructive feedback are approached and asked to complete an extensive questionnaire. Unlike traditional systems that rely primarily on superior feedback, 360-degree sources include peers, customers, suppliers, other managers, or anyone who is in a position to observe closely the team's or individual's performance. Self-appraisals are also performed. GE Appliances, in Louisville, Kentucky, has been gradually introducing this measurement tool into their teams. Participants are understandably apprehensive the first few times they get feedback from new sources, but they have found the feedback nonthreatening and constructive. One drawback is the time-consuming nature of the questionnaire and the reluctance of busy people to take time to fill it out and return it.

ORGANIZATIONAL INCENTIVE PLANS

The problems associated with individual incentive systems and the increased designing of more technical and

HR IN THE NEWS

IS THE FREE RIDE OVER FOR FREE RIDERS?

A small manufacturing company located in the upper Midwest and observed by one of the authors, which shall remain nameless, introduced a team-based incentive system. Production standards were established on the basis of historical averages. The monetary awards were generous. In fact, each team could conceivably earn approximately $500.

Anyone who has ever worked on a team has probably encountered a *social loafer.* These are the people who work and produce at less than their maximum capability. And when the loafer slacks off more than other team members, yet receives the full benefits of group membership, the member has become a **free rider.** Odd as it may seem at first, social loafing is more of a problem in the United States than in collectivistic societies like Japan and China. Most experts attribute it to our strong belief in individualism.

Soon after the new incentive system was implemented, however, a surprising phenomenon developed: the social pressure on free riders. The pressure was such that they usually quit. The need for supervision became superfluous; the employees essentially supervised themselves for maximum efficiency. Since the incentive reward went to the team, its members requested that those who quit not be replaced. The smaller the team, the greater the reward per member.

One other event worth noting occurred. Happy as the teams were with their monthly bonus, at one point their efforts began to level off—that is, until one worker noted, at a momentous morning meeting, that even better performance was possible if . . . "If what?" the manager demanded. "If management would guarantee that the basis for the incentive, the established standard, would not be raised," the worker blurted out.

Within an hour, the manager posted on the bulletin board and included in every paycheck a notice, signed by the CEO, that as long as he was there, under no circumstances, either now or in the future, would the historical rate on which the incentive bonus was based be changed. The only caveat would be the addition of new equipment or a new process. After that announcement appeared, the company's productivity continued to increase and profits hit all-time highs.

---

interdependent jobs have led to increased use of organizational incentive plans. Employers want employees to realize the link between a portion of their compensation and the performance of their group or the entire organization. In general, organizational incentive systems fall into two types: profit-sharing plans, which tie employee compensation to the bottom-line profits, and **gainsharing plans,** which tie compensation to specific productivity measures such as time, materials, or cost savings. Profit-sharing plans focus the incentive on the organization's ability to pay bonuses; obviously, bonuses are not paid when no profits are earned. Gainsharing plans focus on the contributions to specific productivity target goals.

GAINSHARING

The *Scanlon Plan* is a successful gainsharing program. The **Scanlon plan** was developed by Joseph Scanlon, an official of the United Steelworkers Union. It has since become a basis for labor–management cooperation above and beyond its use as a group incentive plan. The plan contains two primary features: (1) Departmental committees of union and management representatives meet together at least monthly to consider any cost-savings suggestions; and (2) documented costsavings are divided, with 75 percent going to the employees and 25 percent to the company.

The savings under a Scanlon plan are determined by comparing actual labor costs for a month to a standard productivity base, which is determined by reviewing past labor costs during normal operating periods. This formula is expressed as a percentage, and each month the labor costs as a percentage of sales are compared to the formula ratio. A reserve account is created to offset any deficit months, and at the end of the year the reserve account bonuses are paid out.

In Figure 12–7, for example, the standard ratio of labor costs to adjusted production is 30 percent; thus

FIGURE 12–7 BONUS STATEMENTS UNDER SCANLON, RUCKER, AND IMPROSHARE PLANS

SCANLON PLAN

Sales		$92,000
Inventory increase or decrease		10,000
Production at sales value		$102,000
Less returns and allowances		2,000
Adjusted production		$100,000
Allowed labor per ratio*		$30,000
Less actual labor		25,000
Savings or gain		$5,000
Less reserve for deficit—10%		500
For distribution		$4,500
Company share—25%		$1,125
Employee share—75%		$3,375
Participating payroll (adjusted for new employees, vacation pay, etc.)		$22,500

Bonus: $\dfrac{\$3,375}{\$22,500} = 15\%$ paid to each employee as a percentage of monthly wages

*Assumed ratio of labor costs to production

RUCKER PLAN

Sales		$100,000
Less materials, supplies, services		50,000
Value added		$ 50,000
Labor costs		$18,700
Other costs		$31,300
Rucker standard: $\dfrac{\text{Labor costs}}{\text{Value added}} = \dfrac{\$18,700}{\$50,000} = 37.4\%$		
Rucker standard—37.4%		$18,700
Less actual labor cost		16,700
Gain		$2,000
Balancing account		500
For distribution		$1,500
Participating payroll		$15,500

Bonus: $\dfrac{\$1,500}{\$15,500} = 9.7\%$ paid to participating employees on the basis of monthly earnings

IMPROSHARE

Base productivity factor = 1.80	
Production	20,000 units
Improshare hours earned: $20,000 \times 1.80 =$	36,000
Actual hours worked	30,000 hours
Savings	6,000 hours
Company share—50%	3,000 hours
Employee share—50%	3,000 hours
Bonus hours: $\dfrac{3,000}{30,000} = 10\%$	

Sample bonus calculation for one worker:

Hours worked	40
Pay rate	$8.12 per hour
Bonus hours (10%) 4.0 hours	
Bonus: 4.0 hours × $8.12 = $32.48	

SOURCE: Robert J. Doyle, *Gainsharing and Productivity* (New York: AMACOM, 1983), 10, 14, 15, 17. Used by permission.

when the actual labor costs were $25,000, a savings of $5000 was created and available for distribution. In comparison to the other gainsharing plans, the Scanlon plan emphasizes employee participation in developing plans to increase productivity.

Rucker Plan
The **Rucker plan** is similar to the Scanlon Plan except that an additional variable—the dollar value of all materials, supplies, and services used in the production process—is included in the formula. This difference from the Scanlon formula, however, allows workers to benefit from any reduction in materials, supplies, or services used in the production process and thus provides motivation to reduce those costs. The Rucker formula is:

$$\frac{\textbf{Labor costs}}{\textbf{Value added}}$$

(Production output—materials, supplies, and services)

The Rucker concept is often called *value added,* which refers to the difference in the value of the output and the value of the input (material, supplies, services) that has been added to the product by the employees. Employees earn an incentive or bonus in the Rucker plan by improving productivity through a reduction in materials and supplies, customer returns, hours of effort, or a combination of factors that leads to higher output. All savings, regardless of type, increase the value added, and thus a bonus results when the Rucker standard is exceeded (see Figure 12–7). If the Rucker standard is 37.4 percent, then labor receives 37.4 percent of value added. A portion of each monthly bonus is put into a balancing account to offset the deficits of negative months. The balancing account is then closed at the end of the year, with losses absorbed by the company and surpluses paid out as bonuses.[27]

Improshare
Improved productivity through sharing **(improshare)** plans are somewhat similar to piecework incentive plans, but with a standard and bonus system applied to all workers within the organization. In effect, improshare is an adaptation of the older individual incentive plans to the realities of today's integrated workplace. Improshare is a bonus system in which the productivity measurement is the labor hours, direct and indirect, needed to produce one unit of product. Gains are hours saved and are equally divided between the employees and the company. The employees' share is converted to a dollar bonus based on their number of hours worked during the period.

For example, as shown in Figure 12–7, the standard hours needed to produce a unit is calculated to be 1.80—

and this is the base productivity factor (BPF). A week's output is counted (20,000 units) and multiplied by the BPF. The result is the improshare hours earned $(36,000 = 20,0001 \times 1.80)$. The difference between the improshare hours and the actual hours worked $(36,000$ improshare hours $- 30,000$ actual hours $= 6,000$ hours) is the savings, which is shared 50/50.[28]

Can gainsharing plans work? At the Dana Spicer Heavy Axle Division's facility in Hilliard, Ohio, there are no supervisors or time clocks. After three years of gainsharing, the employees (all salaried) are very content, labor efficiency is up 45 percent, and quality problems are down 50 percent. During one six-month period, over 400 productivity ideas were contributed by the employees at Dana, and employees averaged monthly bonuses of 12 to 16 percent. The U.S. General Accounting Office estimates that over 1,000 American firms currently use gainsharing.[29]

One widely recognized example of gainsharing is that of the Nucor Corporation. The company reported a staggering growth of 600 percent in sales and 1500 percent in profits over ten years due to a production incentive program. The company actually developed four separate incentive programs: one each for production employees, department heads, professional employees, and senior officers. Their theory is that "money is the best motivation."[30]

PROFIT SHARING

In a **profit-sharing plan,** employees receive a share of the company's profits. The profit share is paid in addition to employees' regular wages and is generally intended to increase employees' incentive to work.

There are three major types of profit-sharing plans:[31]

❶ *Distribution plan.* Annual or quarterly payments are paid out in a cash bonus according to a predetermined formula. The payment is made on a quarterly or annual basis as soon as the profit-sharing pool is calculated. This is the most common type of profit-sharing plan.

❷ *Deferred plan.* Employees earn profit-sharing credits instead of cash payments, which are not distributed until disability, death, or retirement. This type of plan is similar to a deferred-income retirement plan.

❸ *Combination plan.* This type of plan allows employees to receive a portion of each period's profits in a cash bonus with the remainder put into a deferred plan.

Use of profit-sharing plans has increased in recent years because management prefers them to increases in salaries or wage rates, which become permanent increases in personnel costs. Profit-sharing bonuses, however, do not automatically carry over to future years. Instead they are paid only in those years in which the company earns a profit.

Profit-sharing plans have also increased in labor agreements.[32] Management favors replacing COLAs with profit sharing as a wage supplement for several reasons: (1) Payments are made only if the company makes a profit and thus is usually financially strong; (2) unlike COLAs, payments are not tied to inflation, which is not related to the company's financial status and may require increases during difficult times; (3) workers' pay is linked to their productivity, as well as to the number of hours they work, giving them a direct incentive to make the company more profitable; (4) workers may feel more a part of the company and develop increased interest in reducing waste and increasing efficiency in all areas, as well as in their own jobs.

Ford and Lincoln Electric feel that profit sharing is a strong inducement to increase performance. Indeed, the current rate of growth of these plans is significant.

EMPLOYEE STOCK OWNERSHIP PLANS (ESOPS)

Similar to profit sharing—with many of the same advantages and disadvantages—is stock ownership, sometimes called the **employee stock ownership plan (ESOP).** Millions of employees are becoming part owners of the companies they work for, and in the year 2000, 25 percent of all U.S. workers may have used an ESOP. The rapid increase is expected as a result of the 1984 Deficit Reduction Act passed by Congress, which provides lucrative tax incentives to employees. In fact, about 70 to 100 failing companies have used ESOPs to avoid hostile takeovers.

In one of the most visible cases, the employees at United Airlines (UAL) acquired ownership rather than see the company sold to a rival. It has become America's largest employee-owned company with 54,000 participants in its ESOP.

Although there have been problems, including union complaints that management is not sharing the wealth or treating employees as coequals, the partnership is still holding together. If the two sides fail to work out their disagreements, the airline could lose many of the gains from employees' enthusiastic attitudes.[33] Nevertheless, experts believe that employee-ownership plans will continue to grow, with many arrangements being configured more along the lines of participatory governance.

INCENTIVE GUIDELINES

A survey of some 1,600 American companies showed that about 10 percent of all employers reported using an incentive system and another 7 percent expect to add systems in the near future. The most popular incentive system was *profit sharing,* used by 32 percent of the respondents with an incentive system. *Lump-sum bonuses* not tied directly to profits were reported by 30 percent, individual incentive programs by 28 percent, and gain-sharing or small-group incentive plans by 14 percent. The new incentive plans appear to be replacing across-the-board increases.[34]

Just how much can a change from a time-based to a performance-based pay system affect the bottom line of a company? Victor Kiam, chairman of Remington Products, the shaver company, credits the profit-sharing plan he initiated shortly after purchasing the company with its turnaround from a $5 million-a-year loser to profits of over $10 million a year in 10 years. Kiam put "the whole company on incentive, from the maintenance guy to the chief financial officer." The average factory worker at Remington earns one-third of his income in bonuses based on company profits. Kiam also eliminated executive perks including separate washrooms, parking spaces, and dining rooms.[35]

Tom Peters states that American productivity and quality problems are directly linked to a failure to involve workers in their jobs and in the success of the organization. Incentive plans can provide that involvement if they follow these guidelines:[36]

- **Bold incentives.** Provide bold financial incentives to everyone, from the company president to the janitor. The ultimate recognition should be that their performance is linked to improved company performance. At least 10 percent of base pay should be attainable through incentives.
- **Emphasis on team performance.** Everyone in an incentive program must clearly perceive how they can influence the results. Therefore their additional effort, cost-saving suggestion, or emphasis on quality will affect the bottom line. Group incentive systems should focus on the 10- to 30-person work group and emphasize team performance. The facility, department, or division, which are the basic building blocks of the organization, should be used to structure the incentive system. See *HR In the News:* "Talent Agency Shows Stellar Teamwork . . ." for an example of this.
- **Quick feedback.** If possible, at least monthly feedback in terms of group or individual performance and

HR IN THE NEWS

TALENT AGENCY SHOWS STELLAR TEAMWORK—IN HOLLYWOOD, NO LESS

For 15 years, Deborah Miller hoarded Hollywood intelligence. She was a Hollywood agent. "Information was gold," she recalls.

Then, not long ago, she left a mammoth agency for the tiny Metropolitan Talent Agency, where the rules were radically different. Agents were actually sharing information! Even more unthinkable, they were eagerly collaborating on deals!

You hear a lot of platitudes about teamwork these days, even in Hollywood. But rarely will you see it practiced with the precision used at Metropolitan, thanks to its owner, Chris Barrett. The rules are simple: compensation that fosters collaborative efforts and data systems that make intelligence communal.

Talent agencies generally work on 10 percent of the client's pay. Individual agents, in turn, receive a fixed salary and a year-end bonus—often a massive bonus. Turf is sacrosanct. Everyone wants to be seen as a rainmaker.

At Metropolitan Talent, for each commission dollar coming in from a deal, 30 percent is scored for the agent who originally brought in the client, no matter how long ago. Another 30 percent goes to the employee currently representing that talent. The final 40 percent goes to whoever has landed the deal in question. The same employee frequently performs all these functions, but many deals link two, three, or more agents.

At bonus time, everyone receives a set percentage of the agency's revenue that has been attributed to him or her—usually about one-quarter of the sum, more in a few cases. The remaining revenue stays with the house, going toward overhead and, thereafter, to Mr. Barrett.

All this means that each of the firm's 10 agents represents every client. Any agent, moreover, has the power to veto any new client referred to the firm, ensuring that everyone works unreservedly for the entire client list.

The building is an old mansion, redesigned to encourage easy communication networks and no excuses for withholding intelligence. It is clear such a culture makes employees enthusiastic about their work.

SOURCE: Thomas Petzinger, Jr., "The Front Lines," *The Wall Street Journal* (January 26, 1996): B1.

---

the resulting bonus should be given. The bonus money should be distributed *separately* from the regular paycheck.

- **Above-average base.** In contrast to what may be assumed, base pay should be set above the norm for comparable jobs in the geographic area. With incentives added, total pay will be substantially above the norm.
- **Simple formula.** Keep the formula and process straightforward. People's motivation to increase productivity and profits will not improve if they do not understand the formula. Thus, use numbers like 5 percent instead of 7.33 percent.

PROBLEMS WITH INCENTIVE PLANS

Incentive or performance-based plans are not without their problems. Individual-based plans are limited to jobs in which the employee can directly increase his or her output without affecting the productivity of others and without having output affected by others. In addition, quality standards must be carefully maintained to ensure that quality is not sacrificed for quantity. In general, individual systems require employees to perform the same job every day or else their pay is adversely affected. Individual-based systems can also escalate rivalries among employees, which obviously can be counterproductive.

While organizational incentive plans can, if properly designed, avoid the limitations of individual-based plans, they also can cause problems. A major morale problem can occur if employees start to rely on their bonus checks and then receive smaller bonuses due to unanticipated declines in productivity or profits. Employees can also develop a short-term mentality and not make decisions that provide for maximum long-term profits. If plans are poorly designed, they can lead to employee apathy, or even a decrease in productivity if employees perceive that they are being used or mislead. The "peanut-butter approach" of spreading just a thin raise over everyone,[37] for example, can cause employees to believe that the incentive system is just another management program designed to get more work for the same rewards.

If all of the preceding limitations aren't enough, there is the additional problem of different cultural values and beliefs regarding the role of compensation. Performance-based pay is popular in North America and Europe but not in many other nations. In the Far East, for example, seniority, dedication, and loyalty are key compensation criteria. (See opening *International HR in the News:* "Global Dilemma").

EXECUTIVE COMPENSATION

In large, established companies, members of top management are paid differently from mid-level and lower-level managers. In general, **executive compensation** comes in four forms: (1) base salary, (2) annual bonus, (3) long-term incentives, and (4) benefits and perquisites ("perks").[38] Base salaries, at the center of executive pay, are generally determined through job evaluation and serve as the basis for the other types of benefits.

Annual bonuses for executives include both cash and stock payments. Bonuses are usually tied to the performance of the company as a whole for the previous year or, for division managers, to their particular area. Although most executive compensation plans design such bonuses to be pay for performance, to some extent executives have come to rely on them to maintain their standard of living.

Long-term incentives are designed to allow the executive to accumulate wealth. The basic philosophy is that these individuals should have a stake in the long-term future of the firm. It is expected that they will make decisions more in line with the company's long-term future if they have a personal stake in that future. Executive benefits and perks range from the traditional executive automobile and dining room to the more unusual country club membership, private use of company airplanes, and personal legal counseling.

GOLDEN PARACHUTES

A popular long-term incentive is the **golden parachute.** A parachute is a clause in the employment agreement that provides certain compensation if the executive is terminated for certain reasons such as acquisition, merger, or demotion. Termination due to normal retirement, resignation, or disability is not included in the provision. The compensation that is promised can provide, for example, five years of continued salary, even though the executive is no longer working. The parachute serves two major purposes—to retain key executives and to discourage the takeover of hostile organizations. **Golden handcuffs** are bonuses available only if the executive stays for a specified time period.

STOCK OPTIONS

Stock options are trickling down the corporate ladder to mid-level bosses and the rank and file. BankAmerica and NationsBank are two banks that recently started giving stock options to all employees. The gist of the **stock option** is that the employee is given the right to buy the company's stock at an option price up to a fixed future point in time, usually 10 years, by which time it must be exercised or it is lost.

Why are employers becoming more generous? Granting options is cheap. Companies can expand programs without having to take a charge against earnings. Options also are a powerful motivational tool. They boost morale, foster team spirit, and give workers an incentive to focus on increasing share value.[39]

COMPENSATION ISSUES

Several important issues face HR managers in the area of compensation. Inflation constantly decreases employees' disposable income. Social Security and income taxes are taking a bigger bite than ever before. No doubt, employers must be innovative in their approach to compensation problems.

WAGE COMPRESSION

Wage compression refers to decreasing the differentials between higher and lower pay grades. Faced with high turnover in low-paying jobs and with employees who cannot live within their means, employers have had to give greater increases to lower-paying positions than higher-paying positions. Pay differences between top- and middle-level jobs and between middle- and lower-level jobs are decreasing. With the graduated income tax, salary differences after taxes will probably become even lower in the future.

Compression, however, takes a number of forms. A manager may find that the salary difference after taxes between his or her salary and those of subordinates is insignificant. A similar form of compression occurs when a recent college graduate with no experience finds little difference between his or her pay and that of a qualified, successful graduate with ten years of experience.

When the results of compression are fully perceived, employees complain of pay inequity. Naturally, this results in a loss of morale and a tendency to work less effectively.

TWO-TIER WAGE SYSTEMS

A wage system that pays newly hired workers less than current employees performing the same or similar jobs is called a **two-tier wage system.** Following the institution of the historic first two-tier wage system in 1977 at General Motors' Packard Electric Division in Warren, Ohio, many more union-management negotiations have resulted in similar systems.[40] The basic concept is to provide continued higher wage levels for current employees if the union will accept reduced levels for future employees. Union leaders believe that they must accept the two-tier system or face greater layoffs in the future. Management usually claims that the system is needed to compete with nonunion and foreign competition. The airline, copper, trucking, auto, food, and aerospace industries have negotiated two-tier systems.[41]

While a two-tier system is contrary to the historic union doctrine of equal pay for equal work or pay equity, when the system is first negotiated, the union representatives can claim that they have avoided disaster and have saved the jobs and/or wage levels of current members (who must vote on the contract). It is relatively easy to sell such a concept since no workers at that point are accepting the lower tier. However, five or ten years later, when many workers are being paid lower wages for the same work as their fellow union members, it can become a source of conflict and resentment. In some cases, the lower-paid workers express their feelings with lower product quality and productivity records than their higher-paid counterparts. Thus, most two-tier systems merge the two tiers after a fixed time period. At Ford the low tier merges after 3 years.[42]

COMPARABLE WORTH

The concept of *comparable worth* requires that pay be equal not just for men and women performing the same job but for all jobs requiring comparable skill, effort responsibility, and working conditions. According to supporters, the doctrine represents the spirit, if not the letter, of the Equal Pay Act.

Opponents of the comparable worth concept argue that the large percentage of women in such lower-paying jobs as secretary, nurse, and elementary school teacher is a result of women's attraction to those jobs, and that their pay level is the result of the external marketplace, as verified by wage surveys. Furthermore, opponents argue, the demand for comparable worth is not a demand for equal opportunity but a demand to be protected against one's career choice.[43]

The debate on comparable worth may continue for many years. At stake are billions of dollars in employee wages. It is not an easy issue to decide: What is the worth of a secretary in comparison to a security guard?

EXPATRIATE PAY

As more organizations seek to do business abroad, more employees are becoming "expatriate" workers. Doing business internationally is increasing, including the small- and mid-size companies that historically focused on domestic markets now gearing up to export, engage in a joint venture, or perhaps establish a wholly owned subsidiary in a foreign country. It will be necessary in almost every case to send abroad people to impart some of the company's expertise or product knowledge, or, to bring people from abroad to the parent company for training. These "visits" can last from a few months to years and could cost hundreds of thousands of dollars per person.[44]

Differences in cost-of-living between home country and host country can be substantial. One year in Hong Kong, for example, can cost a half million dollars for one executive and a family of four. Not only is the company paying for the expatriate, but there is also the cost of housing—$250,000 in Hong Kong—transportation, food, essentials, paying for private schools, visits home, and medical costs.

There are three **expatriate pay** strategies: localization, semi-localization, or globalization. The first, *localization* simply means paying the same compensation as would be offered a local hire for an equivalent position. This strategy is rarely used; after all, the reason for sending an expat abroad was because there was no local available in the first place. Of course, localization makes sense for an expat who chooses to stay abroad after competent locals are available.

A *semi-localization* approach uses a base salary formulated along the lines of using locals, but with added allowances for inconvenience, cost-of-living adjustments, and some incentives. A "balance sheet" approach is used, in other words, a package that maintains the expat's home country standard of living. This is the most common compensation approach for expatriates.

The third strategy, *globalization,* includes a hefty premium and extras such as a luxury vehicle, private schooling for children, and similar perks. The expatriate who receives this package is usually going from one foreign assignment to another. Why such an incentive? The risk of losing connection with your home country and your home office comes at a steep price.[45]

SUMMARY POINTS

- In order to compete in a global economy, companies must look to control costs and to more closely tie performance to compensation through pay methods and benefits provision.

- Pay philosophy and business strategy alignment is crucial to long-term organizational success. There are three key compensation objectives: (1) Control labor costs, (2) attract and retain key personnel, and (3) motivate improved employee performance.

- Job evaluation is used to evaluate the design of work systematically. The objective is to create job classifications that employees view as equitable both internally and externally. The job is the focus, and compensation reflects more about the job than about the person.

- Pay systems are usually designed to compensate people for the amount of work they produce, the skills, they learn and use, or the time they spend on the job (hourly and salaried). Most employees in the United States are paid through time-based systems, but variable pay systems are increasing.

- Most merit-pay systems share two attributes: They absorb vast amounts of management time and make many employees unhappy.

- Pay method trends are moving away from concepts such as general pay increases and annual cost-of-living increases and toward such concepts as bonus systems, skill-based pay, gainsharing, team-based rewards, profit sharing, and stock options for all employees.

CASE STUDY

MERIT INCREASES

TASK

Break into small groups. Read the following incident and discuss each of the questions. Then as a class discuss each group's perceptions of the situation and how they would handle the problem.

INCIDENT: MERIT INCREASES

Dr. Carl Jones is chairperson of the Department of Management in the College of Business Administration at a large state university in the East. He has been a member of the department for 14 years and a full professor for five years. Last summer he was asked to assume the chair after a screening committee conducted interviews and reviewed resumés for him and three other candidates.

Carl was very excited about the new challenges and has begun several innovative projects to enhance faculty research and consulting. The teaching function in the department has always been first rate, while research has been somewhat weaker. Carl has continued to be very productive as a scholar, publishing three articles, two book chapters, and one proceedings article over the past year. He also made considerable progress on a management text which he is co-authoring. Finally, he has been active in his professional association, the Academy of Management, where he served as chair of one of the professional divisions.

The university's policy is that all salary increases are based only on merit. Carl had developed a very sophisticated performance appraisal system for his faculty to help him quantify salary recommendations. His point system considers and weighs different items in the areas of teaching, research, and service. Teaching and research were given weights of 40 percent each and service 20 percent. For the coming academic year, his recommended salary increases averaged 7 percent and ranged from 3 to 14 percent. Carl felt he had good documentation for all his recommendations.

Carl submitted his recommendations to Dean Edmund Smith and was pleased when all these recommendations were accepted. He then proceeded to schedule appointments to meet with each faculty member to discuss his recommendation, the reasons for the recommendation, and goals for the coming year. While a few of the faculty receiving lower increases indicated dissatisfaction with his weighting system, particularly the emphasis on research, these meetings generally went well.

Carl then submitted his own annual report detailing his accomplishments as chair, as well as his more personal accomplishments. From his perspective, he felt he deserved at least

CASE STUDY—cont'd

a 10 percent increase since his department had made major strides in a number of areas while the other departments had been standing still. Moreover, none of the other chairs were professionally active on the national level, and none had published in the past year. His teaching evaluations were also in the top 15 percent of faculty in the college.

Dean Smith sent out letters to all the department chairs in August. Carl was shocked to learn that his salary increase was just 7 percent. Information he received through the "grapevine" was that all the chairs had received the 7 percent increase. He also learned from one of the other chairs that the Dean always gave the chairs equal percentage increases each year. Contrary to the official university policy, there were no distinctions based on merit.

Carl was visibly upset about what he considered to be a major inequity. He then called the Dean's secretary to schedule an appointment to discuss the situation with Dean Smith.

QUESTIONS

1. Are "merit" salary increases always based on merit? Why or why not?

2. Why has Dean Smith had a policy of equal percentage salary increases for all department chairs despite the stated university's policy? Are all the chairs equally meritorious?

3. What should Dr. Jones say to Dean Smith at their meeting? What are the long-range benefits of a true merit program? What are the problems associated with the lack of such a merit system for department chairs? How likely is the discussion to change Dean Smith's decision and future behavior? Why? If the dean does not change his policy, what are the long-run implications for the college?

SOURCE: Stella M. Nkoma, Myron D. Fottler, and R. Bruce McAfee, *Applications in Personnel/Human Resource Management* (Boston: PWS-Kent Publishing Company, 1988), 139–140. Reprinted by permission.

EXPERIENTIAL EXERCISES

1. HOW SHOULD THESE EMPLOYEES BE PAID?

PURPOSE

To examine the various ways of compensating people using incentive plans.

INTRODUCTION

While most employees are paid a salary for the period of time worked, there is an increasing trend toward using *pay for performance,* whereby employees, in addition to their normal salary, are paid an incentive for high performance. The increasing use of incentive systems is primarily the result of organizational efforts to increase profits and competitiveness through increased employee productivity. Studies show that incentive plans, if well constructed and implemented, can have a dramatic effect on employee productivity.

CONDITIONS NECESSARY FOR USING INCENTIVE SYSTEMS

In reality, a relatively small percentage of the total labor force is paid on an incentive basis—about 15 percent. Why? Because an incentive pay system is impractical to administer unless certain key conditions can be met. Those conditions include the following:

1. The output must be measurable and suitable for standardization.

2. There must be a consistent relationship between the employee's skill and effort and the employee's output.

3. The output can be measured and credited to the proper individual or group.

4. The incentive system should lead to an increase in productivity.

5. The employees, the union (if one exists), and management must all support the incentive system.

TASK

Listed here are several jobs. For each job, complete the questions in the figure provided. Following this exercise, your instructor will lead a discussion on incentive compensation systems. Some jobs are appropriate for incentive compensation systems, while others are more appropriate for a wage or salary system.

VALERIE MCCLOUD—FORKLIFT DRIVER

Valerie McCloud drives a forklift for a small metals manufacturer. She picks up parts that have been boxed and loaded onto pallets and delivers them to the warehouse for shipping. She occasionally also performs odd jobs throughout the day at the request of her supervisor. McCloud is a member of the Teamsters' Union.

JILL PETERS—SEAMSTRESS

Jill Peters works as a seamstress for a large textile firm in South Carolina. She works independently, using an industrial sewing machine. All day, she sews sleeves and pockets to men's shirts. Her output is tallied twice a day by her supervisor.

WILLIAM GRANT—ASSEMBLY-LINE WORKER

William Grant is an assembly-line worker for a large home-appliance manufacturer. He attaches parts to washing machines as they reach his position on the line. Twenty-seven employees work on this particular assembly line in the plant. Daily output for the group is recorded by the employees' supervisor.

CLAIRE WALKER—DATA ENTRY OPERATOR

Claire Walker is a data entry operator for a large state government agency. Her work varies from day to day, although much of it is very similar in nature. Weekly, her supervisor receives a computer printout that details each keypuncher's production rate and quality index.

RICK FERNSTEIN—ACCOUNTING INSTRUCTOR

Rick Fernstein is an assistant professor for a large urban university. He is responsible for activities involving teaching, research, and community service. Annually, he prepares a performance report covering all activities for the year. This report includes summaries of student course evaluations, publica-

tions, committee work, and other school-related activities. Fernstein's department head closely reviews the report and assigns an overall performance evaluation of "excellent," "good," "satisfactory," "below satisfactory," or "unacceptable."

DENNIS CUESTICK—AUTOMOBILE SALESMAN

Dennis Cuestick is an automobile salesman for a Ford dealer in a midwestern town. Six days a week, he "works the floor." The company's sales personnel have an informal system for taking turns when customers enter the showroom or call to make inquiries about a car. Sales are recorded daily by the sales manager.

PAUL MCCLESKEY—ROUTE SALESMAN

Paul McCleskey is a route salesman for a large cola manufacturer. His route covers a large rural area in central Georgia and consists primarily of servicing small mom-and-pop grocery stores, lounges, and restaurants. At the end of each day, McCleskey turns in a report to his supervisor detailing his sales activity for each account.

CHARLEY BEDEMAN—FARM LABORER

Charley Bedeman is a farm laborer for the Jiffy Orange Juice Company in Orlando, Florida. He rises daily at 6:00 A.M. and is in the groves picking oranges by 7:00 A.M. Using a centuries-old technology, he carefully places each piece of ripe fruit in the

Employee	COMPENSATION PLAN					INCENTIVE PLAN	
	(A) Hourly only	(B) Hourly plus incentive	(C) Salary only	(D) Salary plus incentive	(E) Incentive only	1. If you checked B, D, or E, indicate the appropriate *form* of incentive (piecework, commission, merit increase, bonus, stock option, stock appreciation rights, performance shares, profit sharing, Scanlon plan).	2. If you have recommended some form of incentive, indicate the type of output (net sales, per item manufactured, per set of encyclopedias, etc.) that the incentive should be based on.
Valerie McCloud							
Jill Peters							
William Grant							
Claire Walker							
Rick Fernstein							
Dennis Cuestick							
Paul McCleskey							
Charley Bedeman							
Kathy Miller							
Sheldon Smedley							

deep "picking bag" slung over his shoulder. He dumps a full bag into a box and starts all over until quitting time at 5:00 P.M.

KATHY MILLER—SECRETARY

Kathy Miller is a secretary to the dean of the Arts and Sciences school at a small, private liberal arts college. She types correspondence and reports, takes dictation, files, maintains the dean's schedule, and so on. Miller's work is evaluated by the dean annually, using a performance appraisal form that includes quantity of work, quality of work, dependability, judgment, communication skills, ability to get along with others, and loyalty. For each of these traits, she is assigned a rating of "very good," "above average," "average,"

"below average," or "unsatisfactory." One of these ratings is also given to Miller to designate her overall performance for the year.

SHELDON SMEDLEY—ATTORNEY

Sheldon Smedley, a recent graduate of a prestigious eastern law school, works for a reputable Washington law firm specializing in corporate law. Smedley is assigned to the division that handles patent and trademark violations. He works directly with clients, researches cases, writes briefs, and represents clients in court. His performance is reviewed informally about every six months. No special forms are used to conduct these evaluations.

2. TESTING YOUR COMPENSATION IQ

Instructions: Your instructor will break you into groups. Each group should then read and discuss each of the following three scenarios. After approximately 30 minutes, each group should present to the class their take on each scenario and be able to defend their answer. The instructor will then share with the class the correct answers.

BACKGROUND

In general terms, compensation decisions come down to four questions:

1. How much to pay employees.

2. How much emphasis to place on financial compensation as a part of the total reward system.

3. How much emphasis to place on attempting to hold down the rate of pay.

4. Whether to implement a system of individual incentives to reward differences in performance and productivity and, if so, how much emphasis to place on these incentives.

Compensation strategy helps establish a company's culture by rewarding the business activities, behaviors, and values that senior managers choose and want to promote. It is also a fluid, dynamic field with new plans and concepts taking hold every month. In the scenarios described below, consider whether or not a strategy dependent upon low labor costs can create a sustainable competitive advantage.

SCENARIO 1

Consider two groups of steel minimills. One group pays an average hourly wage of $18.07. The second minimill pays an average of $21.52 an hour. Assume that other direct-employment costs such as benefits are the same for the two groups. Which group has the higher labor costs?

SCENARIO 2

An airline is seeking to compete in the low-cost, low-frills segment of the U.S. market where, for obvious reasons, labor productivity and efficiency are crucial for competitive success. The company pays virtually no one on the basis of individual merit or performance. Does it stand a chance of success?

SCENARIO 3

A company that operates in an intensely competitive segment of the software industry does not pay its salesforce commission. Nor does it pay individual bonuses or offer stock options or phantom stock, common incentives in an industry heavily dependent upon attracting and retaining scarce programming talent. Would you invest in this company?

SOURCE: Jeffrey Pfeffer, "Six Dangerous Myths About Pay," *Harvard Business Review* (May–June, 1998): 109–119.

Base compensation
Broadbanding
Commission
Compensatory time
Cost-of-living adjustment (COLA)

Employee stock ownership plan (ESOP)
Executive compensation
Exempt/nonexempt
Expatriate pay
Fair Labor Standards Act (FLSA)

KEY TERMS AND CONCEPTS—cont'd

Free rider
Gainsharing plans
Golden handcuffs
Golden parachute
Improshare
Incentives
Job evaluation
Merit pay increases
Pay mix
Pay grades and steps
Person-based pay
Prevailing wage
Profit-sharing plan

Red circle job/green circle job
Rising and falling differentials
Rucker plan
Scanlon plan
Skill-based pay
Stock option
Straight piecework plan
360-degree feedback
Team-based incentives
Two-tier wage system
Wage compression
Wage survey

REVIEW QUESTIONS

1. Describe three pay strategies and the organizations that use them. How important is pay compensation in each company's success?

2. Outline at least four reasons why an organization needs a compensation system.

3. Which jobs might effectively use performance-based pay systems?

4. What steps should an HR specialist take to maximize employee performance motivated by the organization?

5. What is the difference between employee evaluation and job evaluation?

6. What are the challenges in the design of team-based rewards?

7. Explain the difference between job-based and person-based compensation systems.

8. What are the reasons companies don't adopt variable pay plans?

9. What are the disadvantages of ESOPs?

DISCUSSION QUESTIONS

1. If you were working on an assembly line, would you prefer receiving COLAs or merit increases? Why? If you were a supervisor, would your decision be the same? If you were the owner of a manufacturing plant?

2. You are the head of the newly established HR department for a small company. The owner, who began the firm 50 years ago, refuses to allow employees to discuss their wages—and for good reason. The owner's relatives receive 10 percent more than other employees. Various employees have asked you why salaries have been kept secret, and you say . . . ?

3. Should federal and state governments be able to legislate minimum wages rather than adopting a laissez-faire

attitude that would allow employers operating on a slim profit margin to pay only what they could afford?

4. Which method of job evaluation would you prefer if you were implementing one? What factors would influence your decision?

5. What portion of an employee's annual pay should be due to the employer's profit-sharing plan—25 percent? 50 percent? 100 percent? Why?

6. In the move to reward teams what happens when people are on five or six teams?

ENDNOTES

Chapter 12

1. K. A. McNally, "Compensation as a Strategic Tool," *HRMagazine* 37, no. 7 (1992): 59–66. *See also*, E. F. Montemayor, "Congruence between Pay Policy and Competitive Strategy in High-Performance Firms," *Journal of*

Management, 22, no. 6 (1996): 889–908.

2. Montemayor, "Congruence between Pay Policy," 891.

3. Linda Bennett, "Compensation Fads, Custom Pay Plans, and Team Pay," *Compensation and Benefits Review* (March–April, 1996): 67–75.

4. E. W. Lawler III, *Strategic Pay: Aligning Organizational Strategies and Pay Systems* (San Francisco: Jossey–Bass, 1992), 12–32.

5. Edward E. Lawler III, *From the Ground Up* (San Francisco: Jossey-Bass, 1996), 199.

6. Ibid., 194–214.

7. J. Dittrich and M. R. Carrell, "Organizational Equity Perceptions, Employee Job Satisfaction, and Departmental Absence and Turnover Rates," *Organizational Behavior and Human Performance* 24 (1979): 29–40.

8. B. J. Dewey, "Changing to Skill-Based Pay," *Compensation and Benefits Review* (January–February, 1994): 38–43.

9. Christin Klingberg, "Violations of Child Labor Laws Up 250 Percent," *HR News* (March 1990): 9.

10. John A. Dantico, "Wage-hour Law Clarifies Exempt/Nonexempt," *HR News* (January 1990): 3.

11. Gina Ameci, "Bonuses and Commissions: Is Your Overtime Pay Legal?" *Personnel Journal* 66, no. 1 (January 1987): 107–110.

12. Ibid.

13. Bennett, "Compensation Fads," 67.

14. Hay Group Website: *http://www.havgroup.com/na/havnamer/nameric.htm*

15. William C. Mihal, "More Research Is Needed; Goals May Motivate Better," *Personnel Administrator* 28, no. 10 (October 1983): 61–67.

16. Richard E. Kapeleman, "Linking Pay to Performance Is a Proven Management Tool," *Personnel Administrator* 28, no. 10 (October 1983): 61–68.

17. Carol Braddick, Michael Jones, and Paul Shafer, "A Look at Broadbanding in Practice," *Journal of Compensation and Benefits* (July–August 1992): 28–32.

18. T. P. Flannery, D. Hofrichter, and P. Platten, *People, Performance, and Pay* (New York: The Free Press, 1996), 86–91.

19. R. J. Recardo and D. Pricone, "Is Skill-Based Pay For You?" *SAM Advanced Management Journal* (Autumn 1996): 16–23.

20. Ibid., 18.

21. Flannery, Hofrichter, and Platten, *People, Performance, and Pay,* 90.

22. Ibid.,

23. E. E. Lawler III, S. Mohrman, and G. Ledford, *Creating High Performance Organizations: Practices and Results of Employee Involvement and Quality Management in Fortune 1000 Companies* (San Francisco: Jossey-Bass, 1995), 159.

24. A. Saunier and E. Hawk, "Realizing the Potential of Teams through Team-based Rewards," *Compensation and Benefits Review* (July–August, 1994): 24–33.

25. Edward E. Lawler III, *From the Ground Up,* 211–213.

26. Edward E. Lawler III, "Tricky but Not Impossible," *Across the Board* (February 1997): 20–21.

27. Robert J. Doyle, *Gainsharing and Productivity* (New York: American Management Association, 1983), 11–19.

28. Ibid.

29. Larry Hatcher, Timothy L. Ross, and Ruth Ann Ross, "Gainsharing: Living Up to Its Name," *Personnel Administrator* 32, no. 6 (June 1987): 153–164.

30. John Savage, "Incentive Programs at Nucor Corporation Boost Productivity," *Personnel Administrator* 22 (August 1981): 33–36.

31. Gary W. Florkowski, "Analyzing Group Incentive Plans," *HR Magazine* 35, no. 1 (January 1990): 36–38.

32. *Basic Patterns in Union Contracts* (Washington, D.C.: Bureau of National Affairs, 1986), 122–123.

33. "United: The Dubious Joys of Ownership," *Business Week* (January 27, 1997): 33.

34. "Non-Traditional Pay Plans Gaining Popularity, Study Shows," *Resource* (December 1986): 1, 6.

35. Speech by Victor Kiam at the University of Louisville School of Business, February 26, 1987.

36. Tom Peters, *Thriving on Chaos* (New York: Harper Collins, 1991), 398–405.

37. D. Dolan, "Back to Piecework," *Wall Street Journal* (November 15, 1986): 1.

38. William J. Smith, "Executive Compensation After ERTA," *Personnel Administrator* (February 1983): 63–65.

39. Vanessa O'Connell, "Company Stock Options: Here's the Way to Exercise Properly, Without Sweating," *The Wall Street Journal* (December 6, 1996): C1.

40. "The Revolutionary Wage Deal at G.M.'s Packard Electric," *Business Week* (August 29, 1983): 54.

41. S. R. Premeaux, R. W. Mondy, and A. L. Bethke, "The Two-Tier Wage Systems," *Personnel Administrator* 31, no. 11 (November 1986): 93–100.

42. Michael R. Carrell and Christina Heavrin, *Collective Bargaining and Labor Relations,* 5th ed. (Englewood Cliffs, N.J.: Prentice-Hall, 1998) 249–51.

43. Robert D. Hershey, "The Wage Gap between Men and Women Faces a New Assault," *The Louisville Courier-Journal* (November 6, 1983): 1, 4.

44. M. L. O'Reilly, "Expatriate Pay: The State of the Art," *Compensation and Benefits Management* (Winter 1996): 54–59.

45. Ibid., 55.

CHAPTER 13

BENEFITS

CHAPTER OUTLINE

CHAPTER OBJECTIVES

1 To understand the growth of employee benefits and their organizational objectives.

2 To identify the benefits required by law.

3 To explain the major elements of pension systems.

4 To identify major paid time-off benefits.

5 To describe alternatives to traditional sick-leave policies.

6 To identify premium pay benefits.

7 To recognize the various methods of providing health care insurance.

8 To identify the various methods employers may utilize to provide child care.

9 To explain the advantages of flexible benefit plans.

10 To understand the employer's need to publicize the benefit program.

In 1906, "benefit" meant little more than working less than the standard 58 to 60-hour work week. Even then, 30 years before the 40-hour work week, NCR Corp. had instituted a progressive set of benefits which included an employee health club, on-site library, movies at lunch, and a smoke-free environment.[1] Today, **employee benefits** continue to expand in type and increase in importance in evaluating the entire compensation package.

The popularity of benefits among employers increased dramatically in the United States during World War II. The government imposed wage and price controls and so improving benefits was a way of increasing the overall compensation package. Once called *fringe benefits,* few employers consider something that costs 41 percent of total payroll costs (the current average cost of all benefits) "fringe." According to the U.S. Chamber of Commerce's most recent figures, the average cost of all benefits for each full-time worker totaled $14,086 in 1996, a slight drop from 1995. This unusual drop resulted from a reduction in expenses for retired and former employees in medium-sized and large companies. Medical costs and premiums actually continued to increase.[2] See *HR in the News:* "Health Care Costs Accelerating . . . Again" for more details on medical costs.

There have been three institutional driving forces behind changes in benefit costs in recent years: the large amount of corporate restructuring and downsizing, the shift to managed-care health plans, and the transfer of medical costs to employees (plan design).

Much of the manufacturing industry provides the most expensive benefits, while department stores, hospitals, banks, and publishing provide the least expensive.[3] See Table 13–1 to see a list of common benefits and the relative cost of each.

The general increase in benefits experienced by U.S. companies can be attributed to four causes[4]:

1 Federal wage ceilings during World War II and again in the 1970s caused unions and employers to look to benefits as a means of increasing compensation.

2 Companies use benefits to gain employee loyalty and improve retention.

3 Most employees' wages satisfy their basic needs; therefore, they have become interested in bargaining for more and greater benefits, especially in the areas of health care and pay for time not worked (vacations, holidays, and so on), which satisfy other needs.

4 The U.S. spends more on medical care and medical insurance than any other nation.

Government influences employee benefits through regulations concerning employment opportunities, safety, health care, retirement, unemployment compensation, and workers' compensation. Even greater federal governmental influence is expected. The government appears to be actively transferring the cost of welfare or social programs to private industries in the form of required employee benefits. To stem the tide of the rising costs of benefits, many HR administrators believe that

HEALTH CARE COSTS ACCELERATING . . . AGAIN

Annual health care costs for employers will increase 7 to 10 percent to an average cost of about $4,400 per employee in 1999, according to a study by Hewitt Associates. In 1998 health care costs increased about 4 percent.

"Employers are seeing some of the most dramatic health care cost increases in five years as managed-care plans try to recoup financial losses by raising prices," said Jack Bruner, national health care practice leader with Hewitt. "That, coupled with rising drug costs, an aging population, and a proliferation of health care legislation, is causing health care costs to escalate at a rapid pace."

"Unlike indemnity plans, managed-care plans have kept costs relatively flat in recent years by offering discounts through provider networks and, in some instances, significantly lowering rates to gain market share," Bruner said. Nearly 85 percent of insured employees are enrolled in some type of managed-care plan.

Regions of the nation often differ in the cost of medical care. "Some markets have experienced lower cost increases because of higher competition between managed-care plans and higher percentages of the population shifting into managed care," Bruner said. However, now that managed care is fairly prominent in most major markets, rising costs will affect markets more evenly."

To compensate for these increases, employers will have to shift costs to employees and shop for the most efficient networks in each community rather than just relying on national networks, according to Bruner. The Hewitt Health Value Initiative is the first community-based analysis of health plan costs, quality levels, and employee satisfaction. More than 2,000 health plans in 139 U.S. markets are evaluated.

SOURCE: Adapted from Stacy VanDerWall, "Health Care Costs to Accelerate in 1999, Hewitt Predicts," *HR News Online* (December 15, 1998). Used by permission of Society for Human Resource Management.

---

organizations must change their traditional approaches to employee benefits.

In an effort to contain benefit costs, many employers have instituted a *coordination of benefits (COB) program.* Such programs are primarily established to guard against having to pay duplicate claims when more than one medical policy covers a claimant. The dramatic increase in two-income households has made this type of coverage common. The national average in savings of COB programs is 4 to 5 percent of insurance costs. For example, Borden saved over $1,613,000 in the first two years of its COB program simply by self-administration of health care and major medical insurance.[5]

Flexible benefit plans, as discussed later in this chapter, have also been successfully used by employers to contain benefit costs. An employer can set any maximum benefit allowance per employee, requiring the employee to pay any additional costs.

TYPES OF BENEFITS

The various benefits offered by employers can be divided into six types: (1) those that are required by law, (2) retirement benefits, (3) pay for time not worked, (4) premium pay, (5) insurance, and (6) employee services. Each type presents a different challenge for the HR profession. High costs of insurance and retirement benefits have forced employers to reexamine the usefulness of those benefits. At the same time, employees are demanding more days away from the workplace with pay. Finally, employee services, which range from tuition reimbursement to outplacement counseling, have been increasing rapidly.

REQUIRED BENEFITS

Only certain employee benefits are required by federal or state law.

TABLE 13–1   ESTIMATED RELATIVE SHARE OF BENEFIT COSTS PER EMPLOYEE

BENEFIT	% OF TOTAL BENEFIT COSTS
Paid vacations, holidays, and sick leave	25.4%
Retirement and savings plans contributions	17.1
Medical insurance (current employees)	15.6
Old-age, survivors, disability, and health insurance (FICA)	15.4
Paid rest periods (coffee and lunch breaks, and so on)	8.6
Workers' compensation	2.7
Unemployment compensation	2.5
State sickness benefits insurance	2.1
Child care	1.5
Medical insurance (retirees)	1.5
Dental insurance	1.4
Short-term disability insurance	1.4
Life insurance and death benefits	1.2
Other medically related payments	.8
Discounts on goods and services	.6
Long-term or salary-continuation insurance	.5
Maternity and parental leave	.5
Miscellaneous	.5
Education expenditures	.4
Meals furnished	.2
Total annual benefits cost $14,086 (1996)	**100.0**

SOURCE: Adapted from various Chamber of Commerce and U.S. Department of Labor sources.

Unemployment insurance, Social Security, workers' compensation, and *family leave* represent important government-required benefits that are costly to management. **Unemployment insurance,** governed primarily by state laws, originated in 1938. Government economists say that unemployment insurance helps maintain the economy by stabilizing purchasing power and also helps workers bridge the gaps between jobs without having a significantly negative impact on their lives.[6] States are able to provide the unemployed employees with benefits by imposing payroll taxes on employers. Normally, the amount paid by employers varies according to the unemployment rate within the state. To receive benefits, unemployed workers must have worked for a certain period of time and must have registered for employment at a U.S. Employment Office.

In 1935 Congress established the **Social Security system** to provide supplemental income to retired workers. Initially, Social Security was to provide retirees with an income that, when added to their retirement savings, would enable them to live during their retirement years. The cost of the system is borne by both employers and employees; each group pays an equal amount of taxes into the system, which then uses the funds to pay benefits to currently retired individuals. Technically, Social Security taxes are Federal Insurance Contributions Act (FICA) taxes. It is often noted by management that employees pay half the cost of the system but receive all the benefits.

The Social Security system is actually two separate systems: one to provide retirement benefits and one to provide disability, survivors', and Medicare benefits. To become eligible, workers must have contributed for ten years or forty quarters in the system.

Since the Social Security Revision Act of 1972, the benefits paid to recipients who are eligible to receive the retirement income increase each year by a percentage equal to the increase in the consumer price index

(CPI) if the CPI increases by 3 percent or more. This automatic increase has been one of the causes of the periodic financial troubles of the Social Security system.[7] It also has given employers a strong argument not to provide for increases in employees' *private* pension dollars. The Social Security tax rate increased from 3.0 percent in 1960 to 7.65 percent in 1993 which means that the employee and the employer now each pay 7.65 percent, for a total of 15.3 percent.[8]

Laws requiring **workers' compensation** have been enacted by states to protect employees and their families against permanent loss of income and high medical bills in case of accidental injury or illness occurring on the job. The primary purpose of most state laws is to keep the question of the cause of the accident—whether the employer or employee was at fault—out of the debate. In most cases, the laws provide employees with assured payment for medical expenses and partial replacement of lost wages due to injury on the job. Workers' compensation funds are primarily provided through employer contributions to a statewide fund. A state board then reviews cases and determines eligibility for compensation. States may allow employers to purchase workers' compensation insurance from private insurance companies to augment state funds.

The **Family and Medical Leave Act (FMLA)** became law in 1993. The law requires employers with at least 50 employees to provide up to 12 weeks of family leave to employees for birth, adoption, or care of a family member who is ill. The law applies to private, not-for-profit, public employers, and to Congress, as well as state and federal workers.

The law guarantees the employee an opportunity to return to the same job or a job with equivalent status and pay. In addition, the employer must continue the employee's health benefits during the leave period. If the employee chooses not to return, other than for health reasons, the employer may recover employer-paid health care premiums.[9]

Up to 12 weeks of leave may be taken. The employer can require the employee to use up all paid vacation, personal, or family leave before taking unpaid leave. Employees planning to take the leave must give the employer 30 days' notice or, if this is not possible, as much notice as is practical. There is no reporting requirement, but records must be kept.

Research has found that the FMLA has proved valuable to workers without unduly burdening the companies they work for. About 75 percent of companies reported that implementing the FMLA cost them little or nothing financially, and 90 percent said the law had no noticeable affect on absenteeism, turnover, or productivity. Fewer than 4 percent of those eligible for leave actually used it. Of those who did take leave, 59 percent did so because of their *own* health problems.[10]

There is no law requiring employers to exclude part-time employees from receiving employer benefits. However, there has been an employer practice along these lines. Be cautious about labeling workers independent contractors (ICs) instead of employees. While the use of ICs allows you to avoid some of the legal risks of employment and reduce the cost of employee benefits, perhaps these gains can be lost if the classification of workers isn't legal. Microsoft learned in 1997 that merely rubber-stamping a temporary worker as an "independent contractor" isn't enough. Courts ruled that its hires were employees, and Microsoft's rich benefits programs had to be extended to this previously excluded group.[11]

People who work on the premises, under your general direction and control, are almost always so-called common-law employees. In another case, a partner in Ernst & Young was held to be an employee and protected under federal employment statutes. Employers must focus on the real attributes of the relationship, not the labels an employer may give them.

PENSIONS

In the United States, individuals are expected to provide for their retirement through the "three pillars": Social Security, a private pension, and personal savings. Together these three sources of income can replace an employee's preretirement disposable income, and thus can be considered to create the ideal pension system.[12] About 70 percent of workers have a pension plan.[13] But today, it is not unusual for someone to have several pensions, 401(k) money from a previous employer that has been rolled into an individual retirement account (IRA), other IRAs, personal savings, assorted annuities, Social Security, and perhaps executive deferred compensation. Planning for retirement can be a highly complicated process because there are so many more financial decisions, as Table 13–2 points out.

The consequences of poor retirement investments can be costly. Plans on how to handle various retirement funds should be prudently thought out and implemented (see *HR in the News:* "Unwise Retirement Choices …").

Unfortunately, in a mobile society such as ours, there are thousands of people whose lifestyles and careers involve moving from one job to another and from one company to another and who may reach the end of the trail prematurely (that is, via layoffs). For people in their

TABLE 13–2   RETIREMENT SAVINGS GLOSSARY

Ever wonder what the differences were between an IRA and an annuity? Don't feel alone; most people never give these alternatives a moment's thought—that is, until the inevitable point arrives and the decisions made early in their careers are the ones they have to live with for the rest of their lives.

RETIREMENT SAVINGS VEHICLE	TYPICAL PAYOUT OPTIONS AT RETIREMENT	DISTRIBUTION RULES AND TAX CONSEQUENCES
Profit-sharing or 401(k) plan from a recent employer	Lump sum Rollover to IRA* Deferred payout Installment	Withdrawals generally subject to regular income tax; 10% penalty under age $59^{1}/_{2}$; ceiling lowers to age 55 if the person is retiring; 50% penalty if withdrawals not begun by age $70^{1}/_{2}$.
Pension from current and former employers	Annuity Lump sum Rollover to IRA*	May have to begin taking payments at retirement; must begin by age $70^{1}/_{2}$; payments generally subject to regular income tax.
Nonqualified plans for top executives	Annuity Lump sum	Regular income tax on payouts. Must usually be taken at retirement; some allow wait of five years or so.
IRA	Withdrawals (various options)	Must begin by age 70. All deductible contributions and earnings subject to regular income tax; 10% penalty if money taken out before age $59^{1}/_{2}$.
Annuities	Withdrawals Annuity or installment	Surrender penalties may reduce payout. Payments subject to regular income tax; 10% penalty on money taken before age $59^{1}/_{2}$.
Social Security	Monthly check for life	No required date to begin taking payments; can begin at age 62, but monthly payments are greater the longer one waits, until age 70.

*Amounts rolled into IRAs can remain tax deferred until withdrawn

50s, finding a job is hard, and finding a job with a retirement plan in which they can participate is even harder. Most of these mobile professionals are wise enough to anticipate the dangers. For many, however, planning for retirement takes second place to paying for their children's education, home, etc. They anticipate having their 40s and 50s, usually the most financially rewarding years, to accrue a sufficient retirement cushion. Perhaps they never work long enough at one company to build vesting benefits, or maybe the company does not have a retirement plan in the first place. For people, who lose their jobs late in their careers and who do not have any private retirement plan, the penalties can be devastating. These are convincing reasons that employees must begin investing early, whether in a company retirement plan or independently and leave it there. A recent study identified six types of "savings personalities": deniers (10% of

the population), strugglers (9%), impulsives (20%), cautious savers (21%), planners (23%), and retiring savers (17%).[14]

When employees retire, they usually have lower living expenses than a working family because of the elimination or reduction of commuting costs, mortgage payments, and child-rearing costs. In addition, they gain eligibility for certain tax exemptions, for Medicare, and for other benefits made available to the aged.[15]

Private pension plans also normally provide for early retirement income to employees who lose their jobs because of disability. Approximately two-thirds of private employer pension plans provide immediate disability benefits; the remaining third defer benefits until retirement age. Employees under the latter plans are normally covered by disability insurance until they receive their pension payments.[16]

HR IN THE NEWS

UNWISE RETIREMENT CHOICES—401(K)S? MANY WORKERS LACK INVESTMENT SKILL, AND IT COULD HAUNT THEM

Millions of U.S. workers think they are saving for a cushy retirement through monthly contributions to company 401(k) plans. But evidence is mounting that poor investment decisions by many 401(k) participants may ultimately dim their golden years.

Many workers don't have the time, knowledge, or inclination to manage their 401(k) plans properly. Left by their employers to fend for themselves, some invest far too much in ultraconservative money market and bond funds, while others make risky moves into aggressive international and small-cap funds. As a result, a large number of Americans may find they haven't put away enough money to retire comfortably—with no traditional company pension plan to fall back on. One recent study of 401(k) plans found that participants' portfolios performed only half as well as the overall stock market.

"Trying to make all employees money managers is inherently flawed and will lead to disaster," warns Robert Markman, a Minneapolis money manager and retirement expert, who likens it to trying to make them all doctors or professional athletes.

Named after the relevant section of the *Internal Revenue Service code,* 401(k) plans were created by Congress in 1978 as a way for working Americans to save money for retirement. Plan participants can set aside up to 15 percent of their pretax income, investing it in a menu of options ranging from money market funds to more aggressive stock and bond mutual funds and, perhaps, the stock of the company they work for. No taxes are paid on the investment returns until the money is withdrawn during retirement, when the plan participant will presumably be in a lower tax bracket.

Today, there are more than 200,000 401(k) plans with about 25 million participants and assets of nearly $1 trillion. In many cases, company-sponsored 401(k) plans—known as *defined contribution plans*—have replaced traditional corporate pension programs. With old-style pensions (defined benefit) the money is contributed by the employer, who generally hires a money manager to invest the funds.

The crucial difference is that, under a defined benefit plan, the employee is promised a set amount of money during retirement, no matter how well the pension plan's investment portfolio performs. With a 401(k) plan, the employee is responsible for his own investment decisions. And if he makes the wrong choices, or if the stock market goes against him, the 401(k) account may not be able to finance a comfortable retirement or any retirement at all.

And therein lies the problem. Recent surveys show that significant numbers of investors don't know the difference between a money market fund and a stock fund or, in some cases, a stock from a bond. The situation is getting worse. A 1997 Merrill Lynch survey showed that 50 percent of investors considered themselves knowledgeable, compared with 67 percent in 1994. Michael A. Cantelme of Plano, Texas, a former AT&T employee and current regional vice president at Teligent Incorporation, probably speaks for a lot of 401(k) participants when he says he has done all right with his plan, "but I know I could have made a lot more money if it had been professionally managed."

SOURCE: Adapted from "Unwise Choices Affect Retirement: Many Workers Don't Have the Knowledge They Need to Manage Their Retirement Plans Effectively, and That Could Haunt Them Later," *The Orlando Sentinel* (December 20, 1998): H2. Used by permission of Sentinel Communications Co.

EARLY RETIREMENT

Employers sometimes offer an early-retirement *window.* This is usually characterized by the employer's offering for a specified period of time (usually two to six months) special benefits to eligible employees who choose to retire early. Thus, for a short period, employees have an alternative window to leave their employer. Employers have realized many benefits from early-retirement programs. They can reduce personnel costs and improve the organization's cash flow by replacing retiring employees with lower-paid junior employees. Employers may divide the retiree's duties among other remaining employees. During hard economic times, severe layoffs and pay cuts may be avoided with early retirements. Younger employees gain from early-retirement programs because new promotion opportunities may be created. Participation in an early-retirement program must be voluntary in order to comply with the Age Discrimination in Employment Act, as discussed in Chapters 4 and 11.

When do most employees choose to retire? This decision has been found to be largely determined by four variables.[17]

1 Changes in the Social Security system and the value of its benefits.

2 Personal health.

3 General economic conditions (people retire earlier during good times).

4 Mandatory retirement laws or policies.

Therefore, the passage of the Age Discrimination in Employment Act, which eliminated employer-mandatory retirement policies, combined with a generally healthier workforce and the change in the Social Security retirement age to 67 (with full benefits), may cause the average retirement age of employees to increase. However, a strong economic picture has led white males to retire at a younger age in recent years.

PENSION ELIGIBILITY

A 1949 decision by the Supreme Court, *Inland Steel Company* v. *NLRB,* brought more focus to pensions, when the Court declared pension plans to be mandatory collective bargaining subjects. In the early stages of the pension movement in the United States, this benefit was recognized as discretionary on the part of an employer and as a source of motivation for senior employees. Recently, the Bureau of Labor Statistics estimated that more than 60 percent of all nonfarm employees were covered by a private pension plan. Likewise, the number of private pension plans throughout the United States has increased dramatically since the 1949 decision. Fewer than 1000 private pension plans were in operation in 1940; over 700,000 are in operation today.[18]

Vesting   **Vesting** refers to an employee's right to receive retirement benefits paid into a plan by an employer. A vested employee can leave an employer and still collect a pension of some amount on attaining retirement age. Employees always have a right to the contributions they have made; vesting refers only to the employer's contributions.

The Tax Reform Act of 1986 requires most employers to choose one of two vesting options: (1) 100 percent vesting after five years of service or (2) 20 percent vesting after three years and an additional 20 percent each year, reaching 100 percent after seven years.[19]

Contributing to pension plans does not guarantee benefits. It is estimated that more than 10 million American workers who actively pay into pension plans will never collect from them. For example, one woman worked for more than 30 years for companies with private pension plans. But at the end of that time she was not eligible to receive a single penny in retirement benefits because she had never become vested with an employer for whom she worked.[20]

PENSION PLANS

Employer-provided pension plans are designed to supplement the employee's Social Security benefits. Pension benefits, when added to Social Security costs, represent the single most costly employee benefit. If an employer's pension plan qualifies under the Internal Revenue code, the employer may deduct pension costs as a business expense and must meet the standards set by the Employee Retirement Income Security Act of 1974 (ERISA). The nature of a pension plan, or how good a pension plan is for employees, is determined by how the plan addresses several basic pension issues.

Supplemental or Flat Rate   Supplemental pension plans are tied to Social Security benefits. A supplemental pension plan provides retirees with a fixed level of retirement dollars in addition to Social Security and a private pension. The intention is to have a guaranteed level of retirement benefits created by a pension that augments Social Security benefits. Therefore, as Social Security benefits increase each year, the amount employers must pay in pension benefits decreases.

Because Social Security benefits rose rapidly in the 1970s and 1980s, *flat-rate pension plans* are becoming more common. The flat-rate pension guarantees employees a certain pension payment based on years of service and level of pay. This amount is determined and paid by previous employers, regardless of any other income employees may receive in retirement. The flat-rate system is usually requested by unions.

Financing   Pension benefits received by employees are financed primarily through two plans. Under a

contributory plan the employee and employer share the cost of pension benefits. The percentage contributed by the employer changes according to the type of contributory plan. A **noncontributory plan** is financed entirely by the employer. Employers argue for a contributory plan because they feel that employees will value their pension plans more when they contribute something. Many small employers believe that they cannot afford to provide pension plans when they already must contribute to Social Security.

Funding Methods

There are four methods of funding pension plans. Each method provides a particular advantage to management; in general, the methods are: (1) trusted or funded plans, (2) current-expenditure plans, (3) insured plans, and (4) profit-sharing plans.

Trusted or **funded plans** are those for which employers have created a separate account for funds and invested dollars annually to provide the future retirement benefits for employees. Employers assume liability for the fund. The fund is usually administered by a bank or separate board, which makes decisions about the investment of the funds and the payment of retirement benefits. Usually, the fund is kept financially sound by an actuarial study of the estimated financial liability of the plan, as well as of its expected value of current assets. If the actuarial study, often done annually, determines that the fund does not have enough money to guarantee benefit payments to both present and past employees, the employer adds the additional money.

Current-expenditure plans treat the retirement benefits paid to previous employees as a current expense. Therefore, such a plan is known as a "nonfunded" or *pay-as-you-go* plan. Current-expenditure plans are not actuarially sound and guarantee no funds to be available to current employees for retirement benefits in later years. Yet, for many employers, the possibility of funding a trusted plan is very small because such plans usually require a large amount of capital to begin. In the current-expenditure plan, the employer simply meets the yearly retirement benefits due its previous employees as it meets other expenses. The largest non-funded plan in the world is the U.S. Social Security retirement system.

Insured plans are pension plans provided to employers by insurance companies. The insurance company usually treats the provisions of the pension plan for the employer as it would any other type of collective insurance. That is, the employer is required to pay a premium for which the insurance company administers the plan, pays out all benefits due, and assumes future payment liability.

Profit-sharing plans are funded pension plans, with the funds provided by a percentage of company profits. A profit-sharing plan is a compromise between a current-expenditure plan and a trusted plan. Management hopes employees will be more interested in the profitability of the company if their pensions share in the risk of doing business. Companies that experience stable profitability and growth will have little trouble funding a pension plan through a profit-sharing approach. But if profits decrease substantially or become nonexistent over several years, the plan may eventually become financially unsound.

Retirement Age

The age at which employees can begin collecting pension benefits is an important aspect of any pension plan. Many plans stipulate that a minimum age must be reached before collecting pension benefits; in most cases retirement age is 65, though sometimes this has been reduced to 60 or even 55. Some companies offer supplemental retirement benefits to encourage early retirement. Others do not set a retirement age but require a specific number of years of service, for example, "20 and out" or "30 and out." The advantage of pensions specifying a service requirement is that employees may collect one employer's pension while working for another employer and building up a second retirement income. For example, an employee who begins working for an employer at age 20 may be eligible to collect retirement benefits at age 40 and then begin a second career with a different employer. At retirement from the second job, this employee will receive two full pensions, in addition to Social Security, and is called a *double dipper.* However, employers with liberal "20 and out" policies should not feel as obligated to provide a dollar amount as high as more-conservative employers since a liberal plan, assumes you *will* have other retirement funds.

Benefit Formula

The many different private pension plans (see *HR in the News:* "Unwise Retirement Choices . . .") in use can be divided into two categories:

1 *Defined benefit retirement plans.* These provide a specific monthly benefit determined by a definite formula. The retirement benefit is usually a function of the employee's average earnings over a specific number of years multiplied by the number of years of service (see Figure 13–1).

2 *Defined contribution retirement plans.* In contrast to a defined benefit plan, which provides a known benefit, defined contribution plans provide a

FIGURE 13–1   DETERMINING RETIREMENT BENEFITS THROUGH A DEFINED BENEFIT PLAN.

Example I
Base pay = Average pay for last three years worked.
25 years service × $36,000 base pay × 2.0% = $18,000/year or $1500/month

Example II
Base pay = Average pay for total years worked.
25 years service × $16,000 base pay × 2.0% = $8,000/year or $667/month

Example III
Base pay = Average pay for total years worked.
35 years service × $12,000 base pay × 2.0% = $8,400/year or $700/month

---

fixed or known donation. The contribution is allocated annually to the employee's account, which accrues investment earnings. Employees have uncertain security because their future benefits are related to the employer's ability to continue making contributions and the fund investment results.

Defined contribution plans are always fully funded because they promise only to pay dollars that have accrued in the individual's account including investment gains or losses. Profit-sharing and stock-bonus plans are common examples of defined contribution plans. Defined benefit plans require actuarial calculations to determine what amount the employer needs to contribute to the account to meet promised benefits.

The defined benefit plan is the best means of satisfying the mutual needs of employers and employees, according to Kathleen P. Utzoff, executive director of the Pension Benefit Guarantee Corporation. The defined benefit plan provides employees a specific retirement income that is protected against the volatility of the investment market (like the stock market fall of October 19, 1987). Also, employees can easily understand and plan on a specified level of income on retirement. However, if the economic picture includes high levels of inflation like the 1970s, set-amount pension dollars are devalued.

Every defined benefit plan is based on a formula. The amount of benefits received by employees is usually determined by multiplying the average pay figure by the years of service and then multiplying that product by a stipulated benefit percentage, such as 2 or 3 percent. Normally, systems use an average of the last three or five years of the employee's career as the average pay figure because inflation substantially lowers the average pay figure and, therefore, retirement benefits. As the years of service increase, the benefit amount increases to a "cap" of perhaps 30 or 35 years of service.

Figure 13–1 illustrates how various average pay figures affect the determination of an individual's retirement benefits.

EMPLOYEE RETIREMENT INCOME SECURITY ACT

Prior to 1974, private pension systems were criticized because in too many cases they were not providing employees with sufficient funds to live comfortably in retirement. In addition, many systems were cheating employees out of pension dollars to which they were entitled. Finally, some mismanaged pension systems did not increase the value of their benefit portfolios. In response to these complaints, Congress approved the Pension Reform Act of 1974, officially designated the **Employee Retirement Income Security Act (ERISA).** Congress accomplished the most complete regulation of pension and benefit rules in U.S. history. ERISA affects virtually every pension and benefit plan. Responsibility for administering ERISA is shared by the U.S. Treasury Department and the U.S. Department of Labor.

The lengthy and complicated law primarily affects the following aspects of pension planning:

❶ Employers are required to count toward vesting all service from age 18 and to count toward earned benefits all earnings from age 21.

❷ Employers must choose between the two minimum vesting standards discussed earlier.

3 Each year, employers must file reports of their pension plans with the U.S. Secretary of Labor for approval. New plans must be submitted for approval within 120 days of enactment.

4 The Pension Benefit Guarantee Corporation (PBGC) was established within the Department of Labor to encourage voluntary employee pension continuance when changing employment. This is accomplished by providing voluntary **portability**—allowing an employee to transfer tax-free pension benefits from one employer to another. In addition, through employer premiums, the PBGC ensures that benefits are paid to participants should a pension plan terminate.

5 Pension plan members are permitted to leave the workforce for up to five consecutive years without losing service credit and are allowed up to one year of maternity or paternity leave without losing service credit.[21]

The law has been criticized by employers because it is quite complex and may have encouraged some employers to provide no retirement plan at all.[22]

UNISEX PENSIONS

In 1983, the U.S. Supreme Court, in a landmark decision, ruled that federal laws that prohibit sex discrimination in employment also prohibit sex discrimination in retirement plans. Pension plans must provide equal retirement payments to men and women. The ruling did soften the impact of the Court's decision on pension systems by denying retroactive relief and allowing for an August 1983 starting date for contributions to retirement plans to provide for equal payments. To comply with the decision, thousands of employers were faced with four options: (1) raise women's benefits to equal men's, (2) reduce men's benefits to equal women's, (3) strike an average between the two, or (4) eliminate lifetime annuities, which guarantee retirees a monthly income for as long as they live and instead give employees their benefits in a lump sum when they retire.

Why had employers previously paid men higher benefits than women? The life expectancy of female employees is longer than that of male employees. Therefore, the insurance companies must pay them retirement benefits for a longer period of time. If, then, male and female employees earn the same total dollar value of benefits, and if female employees will collect those benefits over a longer period of time, their monthly payments must be less.

SECTION 401(K) OF THE INTERNAL REVENUE CODE

Many small or medium-sized organizations offer **401(k) retirement plans.** Section 401(k) of the Internal Revenue code first became effective in 1980. It provides for company-sponsored IRS-qualified retirement plans. Usually such plans allow employees to defer a portion of their salary as a payroll deduction and thus reduce federal and state tax liabilities. In addition, most employers increase the incentive for employees to save in 401(k) plans by offering a matching contribution, commonly 50 cents for each employee dollar saved.[23]

The plans have become popular with employees because they can be tailored to meet individual needs. The employee decides how much is deposited in the plan and when to change the level of contributions. Younger employees can use the plan to save for a car or home, whereas older employees can use it as a retirement income supplement. In comparison to traditional savings plans, 401(k) plans allow employees to make pretax instead of after-tax contributions. But access to the funds is limited to age $59\frac{1}{2}$, separation from the employer, or to cover financial hardship.

Under the 1986 Tax Reform Act, the maximum salary deferral to a 401(k) plan is $7000 a year, to be increased as inflation increases. The act also requires 401(k) plans to meet a nondiscrimination test that prohibits highly paid employees from taking substantially greater advantage of this tax shelter than lower-paid employees. Employees' ability to make hardship withdrawals from 401(k) accounts is limited under the 1986 act to their own salary deferrals (not employer contributions), and withdrawals are subject to a 10 percent income tax.[24]

One successful 401(k) plan is in Phoenix, Arizona, at MeraBank. The previous pension plan had been voluntary, but virtually no one participated. The solution was Profit Plus, a new retirement plan. The new 401(k) plan provided quicker vesting, a guaranteed annual employer contribution of 2 percent of wages, an employer matching contribution of 50 percent of the first 6 percent of employee contribution, and a pretax 401(k) plan match. The 401(k) match was contingent on the firm's return on equity. The employees especially liked the guaranteed 2 percent employer contribution and the fact that they could increase the employer's contribution by increasing their own contribution. MeraBank used written materials, employee meetings, and a video presentation to communicate the new plan. More than 70 percent of the eligible employees enrolled in the new plan.[25]

PAID TIME OFF

Employees expect to be paid for holidays, vacations, and miscellaneous days they do not work—**paid time off work.** An examination of Table 13–1 shows that this category of benefits amounts to about 25.4 percent of all benefits. About 80 percent of workers receive holidays and vacations.[26] Employers' policies covering such benefits vary greatly. The most common examples of time off with pay are the following:

Holidays	Maternity leave
Vacations	Sick leave
Jury duty	Wellness leave
Election official	Time off to vote
Witness in court	Blood donation
Civic duty	Lunch, rest, and wash-up
Military duty	periods
Funeral leave	Personal leave
Family leave	Sabbatical leave
Marriage leave	

VACATIONS

Employers believe that vacations increase employees' productivity. Employees who take strenuous vacations may not receive physical rest from the job but usually receive a mental break from the workplace. Today virtually all organizations have a schedule of paid vacations based on years of service with the organization. A typical system is shown in Table 13–3.

Employers often require employees to stagger their vacation dates throughout the warmer months to provide the organization with a steady flow of goods or services. Manufacturing and production industries may shut down sometime during the summer, requiring all employees to take their vacations during the shutdown while the company retools or makes necessary repairs. The steel industry has utilized an unusual form of paid vacation termed a *sabbatical.* Sabbatical vacations are given to employees every five years to provide them with 13 weeks of continuous paid vacation. Employees may not take second jobs during their 13-week vacations. A sabbatical vacation gives employees in particularly unhealthful and tedious work environments time away for a complete rest.

HOLIDAYS

Following World War II, unions and employees increased their demands for paid holidays; previously, many holidays were unpaid. The average number of paid holidays in 1950 was three; 50 years later, employees in most organizations receive eight or nine holidays. Employees required to work on normal holidays are often given double pay. In the chemical, hotel, and restaurant industries, which operate every day, employees may get double pay for working on holidays, as well as another day off during the following week. Often when a holiday falls during an employee's paid vacation, the employee is scheduled for one extra day's vacation.

The *floating holiday,* which was first provided in the rubber industry, has increased in popularity as an employee demand. Floating holidays allow the selection of the day observed to be left to the discretion of the employee or to be mutually agreed on by management and the employee. Some employers prefer increasing holidays with a "floater" rather than shutting down the workplace an additional day.

The observance of Monday holidays is, in theory, designed to give employees more three-day weekends during the year for additional rest and relaxation. But in practice the Monday holiday has increased the chief administrative problem caused by paid holidays—absenteeism. Employees can easily see that being

TABLE13–3 A TYPICAL SCHEDULE OF PAID VACATIONS	
SERVICE	VACATION
1 year	1 week
2–5 years	2 weeks
6–10 years	3 weeks
11–15 years	4 weeks
16–20 years	5 weeks
Over 20 years	6 weeks

absent on Friday or Tuesday would provide them a four-day weekend, or almost a complete week's vacation. To minimize this problem and other holiday-related absenteeism problems, a written HR policy should provide for the following:

- **Eligibility.** Requiring employees to work the last working day before the holiday and the first scheduled working day after the holiday helps to minimize the problem of employees' stretching holiday periods.
- **Holiday rate.** If employees work on what is normally a paid holiday, they might receive some level of premium pay.
- **Paid holidays.** The days determined to be paid holidays should be specified in writing, in advance.
- **Holidays on nonwork days.** If a paid holiday falls on a nonwork day, such as Sunday, for example, will employees be given another day off? If so, which one?

PERSONAL ABSENCES

Employees may receive full pay for a number of personal absences, such as a summons by federal, state, or local courts to serve as jurors or witnesses. Employees may not be counted absent and are paid during the period covered by the summons. When a death occurs in the immediate family (spouse, child, parent, sister, brother, or in-laws), employees are generally eligible to receive three to five days of funeral leave. Usually employees are not charged with vacation or other paid leave, nor do they lose any pay during funeral leave. Policies should carefully define covered relationships (for example, step grandchild?).

MILITARY LEAVE

Military leave is provided for members of U.S. armed forces reserve units. While most employers do not charge leave time against vacation time, most also do not pay employees for military leave. Many employers pay the difference between the military pay and the employee's take-home pay. Often specific laws are passed protecting veterans of a specific military action.

SICK LEAVE

Sick leave may be given where days are accrued by employees at a specific rate, for example, one day per month from the first day of employment. Many employ-

ers allow unused sick leave to be accumulated without any maximum. A doctor's certificate is usually not necessary for short-term illnesses, but extended sick leave normally requires medical evidence. Sick leave pay provides income during personal or family illness. Providing "sick pay" may keep some employees from falsely claiming that they were hurt at work—just to draw worker's compensation.

Sick Leave Plan Alternatives   Reducing sick leave has become a high priority to most HR directors. Both the work disruption and the cost of sick leave can be of concern to top management and supervisors. The good intention of a typical sick leave program may become subject to abuse by employees. Paid sick leave is often used for nonillnesses such as weather, personal business, child care, hangover, and so on. The costs to the organization that are associated with sick leave abuse include money paid, extra work on others, loss of productivity, and low morale among resentful workers.

To deal with these abuses, employers have developed sick leave plan alternatives. One of the first published alternatives to the traditional sick leave plan was developed by a hospital. Their *paid-leave plan* combines the vacation days, holidays, and average number of sick days per employee into a total to be used at the discretion of the employee. The hospital's absenteeism was reduced considerably, and hospital employees preferred the paid-leave plan because they had increased control over their work schedules.[27]

Sick leave banks provide another alternative. This arrangement allows employees to pool some portion of their sick days into a common fund. For example, employees who currently receive ten sick days per year are given only seven days, with the remaining three days placed in a combined employee pool. The use of the pooled sick days is determined by a panel of employees who review requests from employees. Thus employees can be covered against long-term illnesses by the pool, whereas before they would likely have used up most of their personal sick days and been left without income. Peer pressure is used to control abuse by employees. The company benefits because the average number of sick days actually used by employees in a year decreases because the employee panel desires to build up the pool for legitimate needs.

Well-pay programs have become increasingly popular alternatives to the traditional sick leave plan. The concept is to provide positive reinforcement to employees for not being sick or absent. Employees are either given a bonus in dollars or paid time off for each week or month they are not absent.

Personal leave is an alternative that allows employees fewer days of leave without specifying why they miss work.

PREMIUM PAY

Many employers and virtually all labor agreements provide for special payments to employees for working under undesirable circumstances. The most common **premium pay** is for the Saturday or Sunday hours worked that are not part of the normally scheduled workweek. Other common examples of premium pay include *overtime* rates for time worked over eight hours per day and *shift differentials,* which provide higher hourly rates to employees who work the least desirable hours.

Dismissal pay, or *severance pay,* may be awarded to employees who have been permanently severed from their jobs through no fault of their own. Such premium pay is most common in manufacturing or unionized industries. Dismissal pay includes payments to workers who lose their jobs because of technological change, plant closings, plant mergers, or disability. Employees who quit their jobs or refuse to take other jobs within the company are often not covered. Nor does dismissal pay generally cover employees who are terminated for unsatisfactory performance. The amount of dismissal pay employees receive is often determined by their years of service and past salary. The purpose of dismissal pay is to cushion the loss of income of loyal employees. Details of premium pay are discussed in the Chapter 12, since this topic is not considered as a benefit by many employers.

INSURANCE

Many employers provide employees with life and medical insurance plans and pay part of the plans' costs. Health insurance packages normally cover group life, accident and illness, hospitalization, and accidental death or dismemberment. The health and life insurance programs are usually part of a **group insurance plan,** which permits the business and the employee to benefit from lower rates based on spreading the risk using the group policy. A majority of all health insurance plans are self-funded, usually employing an outside company, like BlueCross, to administer the plans.

HEALTH INSURANCE

In 1910, Montgomery Ward & Company offered its workers one of the first group health insurance plans—and helped launch a revolution. One of the most common employee benefits available, its purpose is to help covered employees maintain their standard of living when unexpected health-related problems occur. Today, employer-provided insurance dominates American medicine and the alternative, *socialized medicine,* has not been sufficiently attractive. See Table 13–4 for information on the fears of employees.

Companies are paying more than $200 billion a year for health care, and yet some statistics are shocking. Bureau of Labor Statistics (BLS) data indicates that about 55 percent of employees have employer-provided health insurance, and only 20 percent of the contingency workers have such coverage.[28]

There are so many different terms for the matrix of medical plan options that it is often as confusing to the health care providers as it is to the student. Some terms are currently getting less usage. For instance, it used to be a major discussion point to differentiate between *commercial insurance* and *fee-for-service plans.* Today, the focus is upon managed care and the three approaches to medical insurance: (1) point of service (POS/indemnity), (2) Health Maintenance Organizations (HMO/managed care), and (3) preferred provider organizations (PPO/managed care).

According to the Health Insurance Association of America, 70 percent of Americans whose health coverage is through their employer are enrolled in some type of managed-care plan. While the older **indemnity plans** (like POS's) simply reimburse enrollees/patients who use any doctor for most procedures, **managed care plans** (like HMO's and PPO's) allow the insurers and employers to control costs through a series of interventions and monitoring activities. In a managed-care plan, the employer or insurer contracts with the selected providers for a comprehensive set of services. Enrollees have a financial incentive to use the providers participating in the contract. Most managed-care plans also require the coordination of medical services through a primary care physician (PCP), in accordance with the modern system taught in most medical schools.

Point-of-service (POS) plans allow the enrollee to use any provider and hospital as long as the fee is "reasonable and customary" and is an approved medical procedure. Typically the enrollee/patient must pay a front-end deductible, perhaps $100 to $250 per person, then a copayment of perhaps 10 percent or 20 percent. Often the out-of-pocket expense to the enrollee has a cap of perhaps $1,000 or $2,500 per year. These indemnity plans are generally the most expensive option, have the highest premiums, but cost the enrollee the most money in terms of out-of-pocket expenses. However, POS plans incorporate many managed care

TABLE 13-4   1998 HEALTH CONFIDENCE SURVEY

Americans reveal a relatively low confidence level about the future of health care, and particularly in their ability to afford that care.

CONFIDENCE IN HEALTH CARE'S FUTURE IS LOW

- Americans are least confident that they will be able to afford medical care and that they will have adequate freedom to choose their own medical providers. Only about one-quarter express a high degree of confidence about these two aspects of care.
- About one-third of Americans are confident that they will be able to get the treatments they need and will have access to quality care over the next 10 years. However, significant proportions (around 40 percent) are only somewhat confident about these aspects.

ASPECT OF CARE OVER THE NEXT 10 YEARS	EXTREMELY OR VERY CONFIDENT	SOMEWHAT CONFIDENT	NOT CONFIDENT
Able to get the treatments you need	35%	42%	22%
Access to quality health care	33	40	25
Enough freedom to choose who provides your medical care	28	34	36
Able to afford health care without suffering financial hardship	22	34	41

CONFIDENCE VARIES BY AGE AND INCOME

Overall, middle-aged Americans (ages 35–54) are less confident than Americans ages 20–34 in health care over the next 10 years. In addition, low-income Americans (those earning less than $30,000) are less confident in the future of health care than higher income Americans ($50,000 or more).

ENROLLEES SATISFIED WITH CARE

The majority of Americans think the health care system needs major change (59 percent). At the same time, they are generally satisfied with the quality of the health care they are receiving today. Almost 60 percent (59 percent) report they are extremely satisfied or very satisfied with the quality of their current care. Those who are currently enrolled in private nonmanaged care plans are more satisfied with their quality of care (71 percent versus 57 percent of managed care participants).

SOURCE: 1998 Health Confidence Survey. The 1998 (HCS) was sponsored by the Employee Benefit Research Institute, a private,nonprofit, nonpartisan public policy research organization based in Washington, DC, and Mathew Greenwald & Associates, Inc., a full-service market research and consulting firm based Washington, DC. Used by permission.

elements, like negotiating fees and refusing certain procedures.

Health Maintenance Organizations (HMOs) are the only plans specifically created by a law. The HMO Act of 1973 saw the creation of HMO's as a way to improve health, health services, and control costs. HMO's must meet certain standards in administration and qualifications of providers. Local HMO's must be offered as an alternative by the employer, usually on an annual basis. The employer must pay at least the amount it pays toward any other medical insurance plan. These plans emphasize preventive care and often have no deductibles, no copays, and no forms to fill out. This insurance only covers participating health care providers, generally given to the enrollee as a list. HMO's usually only list doctors in general practice, pediatrics, and internal medicine, since all care must be coordinated through the primary care physician (PCP). Specialists are available to the enrollee, and the plan pays out-of-program specialists, once approved by the PCP, directly.

Stories about insurance plans refusing to approve needed surgery have often been directed toward HMO's, but HMO's are not alone in sometimes refusing to pay for emergency room visits, elective and "experimental" surgeries and therapies, and other procedures. Such stories should point out to consumers of health care and insurance that they must be knowledgeable and intelligent about their choices. The days of "dummying up" and saying "I don't understand anything about my insurance or what's wrong with me, I'll just do whatever Dr. X says," are over.

Preferred provider organizations (PPOs) vary widely, but may operate in ways similar to an HMO except the PPO *will* pay for an out-of-program doctor, generally paying only about 50 percent for out-of-program services. PPO's, like POS's, arrange for a discount, which is often invisible to the enrollee, on services with the provider. PPO's might either cost a little more (if coverage is similar) or a little less (if coverage is more limited) than HMO plans.

COBRA

The **Consolidated Omnibus Budget Reconciliation Act (COBRA)** was passed by Congress in 1986. The law provides for the continuation of medical and dental insurance for employees, spouses, and dependents in the event of termination of employment, death of the employee, divorce, legal separation, or reduction of hours, which results in the loss of health-plan eligibility. This coverage must be elected by the employee or dependents, and they must pay the full cost of the plan selected. The intent of this law is to alleviate gaps in health care coverage by allowing the employee or beneficiary to elect to continue medical and/or dental insurance.

Employers must notify employees and/or spouses of their COBRA rights within 60 days after their employment separation. The extended health coverage must be offered for a maximum of 18 or 36 months, depending on the qualifying circumstances (that is, reason for separation from employment). The same coverage that the employee and/or dependent received before the employment separation must be offered. If the individual chooses to take extended coverage, he or she must pay 102 percent (2 percent for administrative costs) of the costs.

An employer who fails to inform, in writing, an eligible person of his or her COBRA rights may be liable for resulting medical costs. In one such case, *Gardner* v. *Rainbow Lodge, Inc.* (D.C. Texas, 1990), a judge awarded $10,500 to a waiter who was not informed of his COBRA rights.

GROUP LIFE, DENTAL, LEGAL, AND VISION INSURANCE

For a way to offer employees more benefits inexpensively, W. Clarke Lindley has some advice. Lindley, president and CEO of Lindley Laboratories, a Gibsonville, North Carolina, manufacturer of chemicals for the textile industry, found a solution. He decided on a voluntary insurance program that allows his employees to buy life, disability, and dental coverage and have their premium payments deducted from their paychecks, all at minimal cost to Lindley Labs.

The employees decide the types and amounts of insurance they want, and they get the coverage at group rates which are often lower than the rates for individual policies. The only expense for Lindley Labs is the cost of administering the **Section 125** "pretax deduction" program, which involves deducting the premiums from the employees' paychecks and remitting the money to an insurer.

"It's a good way for us to keep good employees, and one of the main benefits is that the employees themselves choose where to spend their benefit dollars," says Lindley, "They have the say-so in the benefits they provide for themselves and their families—and they get the insurance at better rates than they would pay if they bought the coverage individually."[29]

Payroll-deduction insurance programs are highly popular. About one-third of U.S. employers offered payroll-deduction plans to their workers in 1994, according to a survey by LIMRA International, a Hartford, Connecticut, marketing and research organization funded by life insurers. Among companies employing 50 to 99 workers, 41 percent offered payroll-deduction insurance, according to LIMRA.

Life insurance is the most popular coverage. Insurers sell both term and universal life coverage through payroll-deduction programs. They also sell dental coverage and both short-term and long-term disability insurance. Some employers even offer automobile and homeowner's insurance via payroll-deduction programs.[30]

Comprehensive dental benefits have been developed to provide protection against the cost of basic types of dental care. Such plans include (1) schedule plans, (2) comprehensive plans, and (3) combination plans. *Schedule plans* have no deductible but provide only specific payments for each procedure covered. *Comprehensive plans* (or POS) require an initial deductible an then provide a fixed percentage payment of covered expenses. Most *combination plans* provide a fixed fee schedule for routine dental procedures and a deductible on other procedures, with a coinsurance clause requiring the covered employee to pay a percentage of the fee.[31]

The provision of full legal services through negotiated group plans is relatively new. During the early 1970s, prepaid legal services first became common through a Supreme Court decision that upheld such a plan and declared such legal expenses to be nontaxable. Two types of prepaid legal plans are commonly negotiated. One is so-called *open panel,* which allows the employee to select any attorney who will perform the service at a stated fee. The other type is a so-called *closed panel,* which requires employees to use specific attorneys. Most plans require the employee to pay part of the annual fee. Employees usually prefer the open panel because they can use their own attorneys. Companies, however, prefer closed panels, which can be more easily administered.

Routine eye examinations, glasses, and contact lenses are usually included in provisions for *vision care.* Employees may be given the choice of doctors or may be limited to certain ones who are retained under contract.

EMPLOYEE SERVICES

Employee services include a variety of employee benefits. Organizations vary greatly in the services they offer and the service costs they pay.

A recent study of large employers finds them increasingly likely to offer programs that help workers balance work and family responsibilities. Although benefits aimed at child care abound, the vast majority (97 percent) of firms restrict their offering to dependent care spending accounts that allow employees to earmark pretax dollars for child care. Four in 10 major companies offer resource and referral services that can help with child care, but only about one in 20 provides a subsidized on-site center.

From 1991 to 1996, a study by Hewitt Associates shows, *elder-care programs* have doubled. Resource and referral services are the most popular offering, provided by eight in 10 respondents, but one in four firms now offers (but probably does not pay for) *long-term care insurance.*

Nearly three out of four large employers allow flextime. Compressed scheduling, in which employees squeeze a full week's work into, say, four very long days, is far less common: Just over one in five firms surveyed allows it.

Three out of four companies help pay legal fees associated with adoptions, with most capping expenditures at $2,000.[32]

CHILD CARE PROGRAMS

The recent growth of employee interest in employer-provided **child care programs** is enhanced by Sections 125 and 129 of the Internal Revenue Service code. Under these sections, employers may provide employees the ability to pay for child care with pretax dollars. This enables employees to save up to 40 percent of their childcare expenses.

The history of employer-sponsored child care (or day care) in the United States began in the 19th century. As early as 1854 there was some employer involvement in child care. The textile industry in the early to mid-1900s sponsored many centers as it greatly expanded its largely female workforce.[33]

By 1985, more than half of women with a child under age six were working, and the number of employer-sponsored child care programs grow to meet the demand.

At least five different approaches to child care are offered by employers. Each offers certain advantages and varying costs:

1 *On-site programs.* Large employers, particularly in the healthcare industry, can offer to build a facility on the premises, or nearby, which allows employees to bring their children to work and visit them during lunch.

2 *Flexible benefits.* Employers will provide, as one flexible benefit option, money to employees to reimburse (voucher systems) existing child care programs. Employers who do not need child care can spend their dollars on other benefits. This is the fastest-growing approach to child care.

3 *Referral centers.* The employer contracts with a firm that maintains information on child care facilities and assists employees in finding suitable service. While employers often pay the referral fee, they usually do not pay any of the child care expenses.

4 *Consortium of employers.* Several organizations located together (in an industrial park or shopping center) pool their resources to purchase and manage a child care center for their employees. The advantages are similar to those of an on-site facility.

5 *Public-private partnership.* Cities and counties have used a wide variety of approaches to the provision of child care but usually require private-sector involvement. For instance, San Francisco requires office building and hotel developers either to provide facilities for their employees or contribute to a city fund.

The U.S. Department of Labor estimates that women and minorities will fill 80 percent of the 21 million *new* jobs that will be created by the year 2000. Employers, however, have been slow to realize that this new workforce will demand family care benefits—primarily maternity/paternity leave and day care. "They have been reluctant to venture into this area because family care changes the whole atmosphere at work—forever," claims Dana Friedman, senior research fellow at the Work and Family Life Center of the Department of Labor.[34]

ELDER-CARE PROGRAMS

Older Americans represent the fastest-growing segment of the population. Today's workers are increasingly faced with care problems at both ends of the age spectrum. They might be called the "sandwich generation," according to Robert Beck, executive vice president for corporate human resources at Bank of America. The care issue of the future, according to Beck, will be **elder-care.** Research by several large employers, including IBM, Merck, and Corning Glass, indicates that employees with elder-care responsibilities experience work-related problems similar to those of employees with child care responsibilities. Higher turnover, absenteeism, and health problems, as well as lower productivity, are common problems for employees who must care for older relatives.[35]

A pioneering elder-care program is IBM's Elder-Care Project Development Fund. The program provides assistance to employees with elder-care responsibilities. Services include respite-care development, recruitment and training of in-home health and social service workers, and support programs. According to IBM representative Jim Smith, the program represents IBM's continuing response to the changing social environment that affects employees.[36]

A study by Hewitt Associates, benefit consultants, found that only 43 percent of employers offered elder care. That compares to 74 percent of the respondents offering some kind of child care assistance.[37]

CREDIT UNIONS

Company credit unions are a long-established employee service that are provided by many organizations. Employees become members by purchasing shares of stock for a small fee. They may then deposit savings that accrue interest at rates higher than those provided by local financial institutions. Employees may apply for loans from their credit union at lower rates than those charged by many financial institutions. Normally administered by a separate board of directors, the credit union is an entity independent of the organization.

FOOD SERVICES

Most companies provide some type of food facility to minimize the time taken for breaks and lunch periods. Food services vary: some organizations only provide vending machines and a few tables; others provide complete cafeteria services underwritten by the company. To minimize the time employees spend on coffee breaks, companies have experimented by placing coffee and soft drink stands in each department or by providing mobile coffee stands to bring doughnuts and coffee to individual employees.

EDUCATION EXPENSES

Many organizations offer employees partial or total tuition reimbursement. Employees often use this highly sought benefit to prepare themselves for promotion opportunities. The portion of tuition that organizations reimburse may depend on the grades received. For example, the organization may pay 100 percent of the tuition costs for an A, 80 percent for a B, and 50 percent for a C. Employers may also require that employees take career-related courses to receive tuition reimbursement.

TRANSPORTATION PROGRAMS

Higher energy costs have caused employers to consider methods of helping employees get to work. Ride sharing, in use since World War II, is probably still the most common employee transportation program. The HR department can assist employees who want to share rides by providing them the names of other employees who live nearby or by working with other employers to involve their employees.

CONCIERGE, SPIRITUAL BENEFITS, AND OTHER FEATURES

Lots of employers are offering so-called **soft benefits** which add comfort and flexibility to the life of their employees. America Online adds a flexible work schedule and a casual dress code to more common benefit elements like child and elder-care referral services, a choice of three health plans, and a 3 percent match on a

401(k) retirement plan. AOL offers something now referred to as **concierge services**—like drop-off and pick-up of dry cleaning. film developing, a campus store, and a Starbuck's coffee shop—all at the workplace.[38] Other concierge-type services include on-site haircuts, manicures, and massages; shoe repair; and on-site delivery pickup for the pizza or other food which you called for and can now pick up on your way to your car.

"When I have a problem that is far larger than what I can discuss with our own staff," Dwight Smith, president of Sophisticated Systems says, "I often turn to other Christian business people. It's wonderful to have other spiritual business people to talk to."[39] Marketplace Ministries (MM), founded in Dallas in 1984, makes chaplains available to companies that want to extend **spiritual benefits** to their workers. MM is available in 176 cities in 35 states and had 585 chaplains on staff serving 156 companies in 1998. "Our services are voluntary," Art Stricklin, director of ministry relations says. "We go into a workplace and no one has to acknowledge us; nobody has to come to us. It's another benefit that a company will offer its employees."

Chaplains are available to counsel employees with family or spiritual concerns and visit the sick. Pilgrim's Pride, a chicken producer, has 64 full-time chaplains representing 28 Christian denominations serving 11,000 employees. These chaplains performed over 500 free weddings in the reported year. "The average non-Christian will simply say, 'These are the values of the company,' but they are values (integrity, honesty, caring about people, and so on) that are congruent with biblical principles," says Jonathan Hanks, leader of the Environment Control Company.[40]

"There are plenty of very good places to work," says Ray Baumruk, consultant with Hewitt Associates, "But the best organizations are taking a differentiation tack, much as a brand would do in a consumer market. The message has to be 'We stand for something that others don't. We're special. We're relevant.'"[41]

Working Mother, Business Week, and *Fortune* all publish lists which identify the best places to work in the U.S. and employee benefits is near the top of the list of requirements to be so recognized. For more information see *HR in the News:* "Top Places to Work."

TOTAL BENEFIT PLANNING

With benefit costs requiring to up to 40 percent of total payroll costs, employers are reevaluating their total benefit packages. Many benefit packages have little effect on employee motivation and performance. Since many costly and expensive benefits such as vacation and retirement income are tied to seniority, employers seldom link benefits to level of performance. Some HR specialists believe that most employees do not truly understand the nature of their benefit packages nor do they appreciate the total cost of providing them with benefits. When given the choice between additional benefits or disposable income, employees overwhelmingly choose additional disposable income. The organization may find it less expensive and more popular to offer employees fewer benefits and higher wages.

FLEXIBLE BENEFIT PLANS

An alternative to providing employees with a fixed combination of employer-provided benefits is a flexible benefit package. In a typical **flexible benefit plan,** employees are allowed to choose the benefits they believe will best meet their needs from a wide range of benefits. Generally, their choices are limited to the total cost the employer is willing to assume. Thus, for example, employees may be given a monthly benefit-dollar figure and told that they can allocate the dollars to the benefits they select from a list of benefits, each of which is a cost to the employees. In many programs, employees may exceed their benefit limit, but they pay the difference. If employees choose to allocate fewer dollars than their maximum, they may be allowed to keep part of the savings as additional monthly income, but this is a rare policy among employers.

Flexible benefit plans have had an on-again–off-again–on-again life. *Cafeteria plans* which allowed employees to choose some benefits from a "menu" of benefits became popular. However, the cafeteria approach ran into problems. Employees found it confusing and difficult to make decisions, and employers found the administration of the programs expensive and difficult.

Recently, employers have increasingly implemented flexible benefit plans. A survey of the top 150 *Fortune* 500 companies found that 45 percent either had flexible benefit plans or were considering implementing them.[43] The primary reason employers are switching from fixed to flexible plans, in addition to better meeting employee needs, is to contain their medical costs. In fact, flexible benefit plans may be the most effective means employers have of containing medical costs. A survey of 330 employers with flexible plans found that almost half (49 percent) had achieved their medical cost target, an additional 43 percent reported that it

HR IN THE NEWS

TOP PLACES TO WORK: THE TOP 12 COMPANIES ACCORDING TO *FORTUNE*

Fortune magazine reviews over 1,000 large and mid-size firms and polls over 25,000 employees to identify the best places to work. "Compensation is still certainly key," says Milton Moskowitz, a compiler of the list, "but the list also reflects the level of trust, pride, and camaraderie that employees share with management and their peers, as well as what practices the company has in place to support those things." Here's the top 12, starting with the best.[42]

1 *Synovus Financial,* Columbus, GA—A "culture of the heart"; 3,000 employees' names appear on bricks in their building; free banking, stock options, lots of awards.

2 *TD Industries,* Dallas, TX—Managers must respect the interests and preferences of their subordinates; management subscribes to guru Robert Greenleaf's philosophy of "servant leadership"; democratic management; ESOP.

3 *SAS Institute,* Cary, NC—"If you do right by people, they'll do right by you," says founder James Goodnight; 35 hour work week; child care at $250/month; free on-site medical clinic; 12 paid holidays plus Christmas week holiday.

4 *Southwest Airlines,* Dallas, TX—Morale so high that flight attendants crack jokes, yet the ground crew races to get aircraft ready; ringmaster CEO Herb Kelleher sings and dances on ads and training films; love for Southwest include 85 percent of the workforce which is unionized.

5 *SCITOR,* Sunnyvale, CA—Employees rated this workplace the highest; "If we had an organization chart, it would be an inverted triangle, with the employees at the top and the president at the bottom."

6 *PeopleSoft,* Pleasanton, CA—Annual take-your-*parents*-to work day; "best place to have a bad day."

7 *Goldman Sachs,* New York, NY—Smart people abound, but egomaniacs are told to hit the road; pay is at the top of the scale. Executive secretaries start at $50K.

8 *Deloitte & Touche,* Wilton, CT—Leads the Big 5 accounting firms in keeping professional women; excellent work–family policies include flextime and telecommuting; employees expected to do community volunteering and are recognized for it.

9 *MBNA,* Wilmington, DE—Beautiful facilities with on-site day care, dry cleaning, shoe repair, and a beautician; $15K goes to best suggestion of the year; $2,500 goes into an education fund for every child born or adopted.

10 *Hewlett-Packard,* Palo Alto, CA—The "HP way" is respect for people, avoidance of layoffs, and commitment to professional growth; top pay and benefits.

11 *Edward Jones,* St. Louis, MO—Spends $50K per broker on training and 27 percent of employees are partners, earning returns on capital from 20 to 25%.

12 *Finova Group,* Phoenix, AZ—Wide range of benefits includes $3K per year for child's college tuition, 500 stock-option shares when hired, concierge service with free on-site massages, birthday card signed from Chairman Sam (Eichenfield).

was too soon to tell whether their targets would be met, and only 8 percent reported that they could not meet their target. The survey also reported that more than 87 percent of employers met employees' needs.[44]

American Can was one of the early major employers to implement a serious flexible benefit plan, starting with 700 participating employees. A survey of the company's participating employees disclosed that 92 percent thought they had substantially improved their benefits by producing the proper mix of benefits. Pepsi Cola and North American Van Lines were among major firms that followed with their own successful plans. Small firms (8 to 20 employees) have also reported employee and employer satisfaction with flexible plans.[45]

An important feature of a cafeteria plan is the opportunity for each employee to spend employer dollars as personally desired. By contrast, many so-called flexible plans are fixed, offering the employee the opportu-

nity to choose among limited alternatives or offering a "take-it-or-leave-it" approach. For example, the employer offers to pay a portion of an employee's medical insurance if the employee pays the balance. But if the employee does not choose medical insurance (possibly because of a spouse's coverage), then the employer's contribution is lost. A true flexible plan credits the employee with the employer's share which could be applied to another benefit.

Types of Flexible Plans   There are at least three major types of flexible benefit plans. First, there is the *core cafeteria plan*, which provides employees "core" (minimum) coverage in several areas and allows them to choose either additional benefits or cash, up to a maximum total cost to the employer. In the core cafeteria plan shown in Figure 13–2, the employee has a choice of items 1 through 6 and cash. This plan strikes a

---

FIGURE13–2   FLEXIBLE EMPLOYEE BENEFITS PLANS

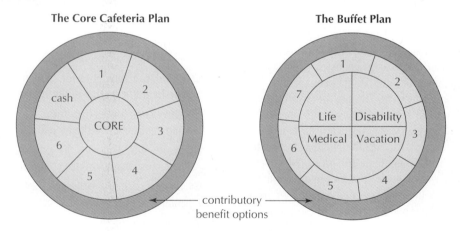

The Core Cafeteria Plan

The Buffet Plan

contributory benefit options

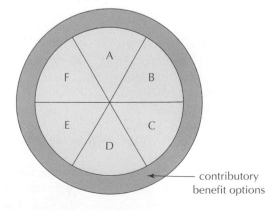

The Alternative Dinners Plan

contributory benefit options

balance between giving the employee complete freedom to choose among benefits and the employer's need to protect employees against poor decisions. Second is the *buffet plan*, which starts employees with their exact current benefit coverage and allows them to decrease coverage in some areas (life insurance, medical insurance, and so on) in order to earn credits for other benefits (dental care, day care, and so on). Third is the *alternative dinners plan*, which provides a number of packages ("dinners") to choose from. For example, one package might be aimed at the employee with a non-working spouse and children, another at the single employee, and a third at an employee with a working spouse and no children. The total cost of each dinner would be approximately the same.[46]

Advantages of Flexible Plans

Originally created as a means of better meeting the needs of employees, flexible plans can often provide a growing number of advantages:

- *Meet diverse needs of employees.* As our workforce changes, with an increasing number of single working parents, dual-career couples, second-career retirees, and so forth, flexible plans become increasingly effective as a means of matching employees' needs with their benefit plan.
- *Control benefit costs.* Of employers with flexible plans, 78 percent reported that a major objective in their initiating a plan was to contain rising health-care costs.[47] With health-care costs continuing to rise, this method is likely to continue to spread. Why does it work? Employers can set the maximum amount of benefit dollars they will spend on employees' benefits as part of their budget process. As the costs of individual health care options rise, the employee can choose one of several medical plans with varying levels of coverage and different premiums. Employers can avoid automatically absorbing the cost increases.
- *Improve benefits offered.* Employers can better meet the needs of their employees by expanding the variety of benefits offered. Since the total cost of all benefits is set by the employer, the cost of adding a new benefit to the package can be minimal. Child care is a good example; employers can pay a portion or all of the cost of providing child care at an off-site facility through a voucher system. In choosing the coverage, employees must either reduce the coverage of another benefit in their plan or have the increased cost deducted from their pay (Section 125).
- *Attract and retain employees.* The changing workforce is causing employers in some industries to consider flexible benefits as a tool in the recruitment and retention of employees. Just as flexible work schedules can be utilized to attract and keep employees, flexible benefit plans can be included in recruitment advertising.
- *Avoid unions.* A flexible benefit plan can provide an effective tool against union organizers. It is far more difficult for a union to promise to increase one or two benefits if employees already have the ability to choose the benefits in a flexible plan.
- *Avoid duplicate coverage.* Another aspect of the changing labor force is the increased number of working married couples with duplicate benefit coverage from separate employers. Flexible benefit plans may allow a married couple to save thousands of dollars in wasted duplicate coverage.

Implementation of Flexible Plans

Companies that have experienced success with flexible benefit plans have begun by "dreaming big but starting small." A small start can be successful if top management is aggressive in adopting the plan and is willing to involve employees.[48] Recommended steps in adopting a cafeteria approach are as follows:

- Review employees' total compensation needs and obtain top management support for the program.
- Develop a timetable for implementation within the benefits section of the HR department.
- Survey employees to determine what their needs and desires are in the benefits area.
- Review the plan with the IRS, appropriate state agencies, and insurance companies.
- Design or buy a program (like PeopleSoft) to minimize paperwork and cost.
- Communicate to employees the need for core coverage which guarantees certain benefits such as life insurance and hospitalization that all employees need, unless they have similar coverage elsewhere.
- Implement the program through employee selection, but only after extensive communications through meetings, brochures, and the like, to ensure that employees can make informed choices.

PUBLICIZING BENEFITS

As employers reexamine benefit programs and question if they are cost-effective, they should determine whether there is a lack of communication with employees concerning the benefit programs. Without such communication, some employees cannot visualize the entire benefit program and its value to them. Since employers must report their pension program to employees under ERISA, the entire benefit program should be communicated.

Studies have demonstrated that employees who give little thought to their benefits may not be able to recall 15 percent of the benefits they receive.

An example of one method of providing employees with this information is an **employee earnings and benefits letter,** as shown in Figure 13–3. This letter keeps employees informed and aware of what the company does in terms of benefits. Any benefit that does not

---

FIGURE13–3 A SAMPLE EMPLOYEE EARNINGS AND BENEFITS LETTER

Jackson Steel Co.

Employee's Name: William A. Hailey
Address: 1500 North Lake Circle
Erie, PA

Dear Mr. Hailey:

Enclosed are your W-2 forms showing the amount of taxable income that you received during 1999. Listed below in Section A are your gross wages and a cost breakdown of various fringe benefit programs that you enjoy. In addition to the money you received as wages, the company paid benefits for you which are not included in your W-2 statement. These are fringe benefits that are sometimes overlooked. In an easy-to-read form, here's what was paid to you in 1999.

SECTION A—PAID TO YOU IN YOUR W-2 EARNINGS

Cost-of-living Adjustment	$ 1,875.
Shift Premium	3,125.
Suggestion Award(s)	0.
Service Award(s)	1,200.
Vacation Pay	2,400.
Holiday Pay	825.
Funeral Pay	0.
Jury-Duty Pay	0.
Military Pay	0.
Accident & Sickness Benefits	1,956.
Regular Earnings	42,000.
Overtime Earnings	2,450.
Allowances	150.
Gross Wages	**56,481.**

SECTION B—PAID FOR YOU AND NOT INCLUDED IN YOUR W-2 EARNINGS

Company Contribution to Stock Purchase & Savings Plan	$ 2,125.
Company Contribution to Pension Plan	2,975.
Company Cost of Your Hospitalization Payments	2,400.
Company Cost of Your Life & Accidental Death Insurance	250.
Company Cost for Social Security Tax on Your Wages	3,251.
Company Cost of the Premium for Your Workers Compensation	300.
Company Cost for the Tax on Your Wages for Unemployment Compensation	150.
Company Cost for Tuition Refund	0.
Company Cost for Safety Glasses	75.
Total Cost of Benefits not Included in W-2 Earnings	**$11,526.**
Total (A & B) Paid	
for Your Services in 1999	**$68,007.**

You have earned the amount on the bottom line, but we wanted to give you a clearer idea of the total cost of your services to the company and the protection and benefits that are being purchased for you and your family.

Melanie Fitzpatrick
HR Director

show up on an employee's paycheck should be included to make the employee aware of benefit costs.

Benefits administration is a detail-filled process that has long required the HR benefits professionals to be constantly monitoring details to avoid errors. A tiny mistake could result in an employee not receiving the benefits for which they signed or the employee being charged incorrectly for their selected benefits. Employees can modify their benefits plans throughout the year to reflect changes in address, addition of a spouse or birth of a child. Employee changes to benefit packages are allowed once a year during the "open enrollment" period. With several health insurance plans and other benefit choices there are many places where minor data errors can occur.

To see the complexity of this task, think about a mid-size Florida based company with 500 employees where each employee may make 20 or more decisions about their benefit package during open enrollment. This means that the HR professional(s) running benefits open enrollment may need to complete 10,000 or more error free transactions during the open enrollment period. This task grows more complex as the number of employees grows or the company has a business pres-

ence in additional states or countries. Failure of employees to respond during open enrollment creates another problem. Many HR professionals now have help managing complex benefits administration tasks from their HR Information Systems (HRIS). PeopleSoft, one of the leaders in enterprise-wide information systems, integrates the traditional functional areas of HR (benefits, compensation, recruiting, training, labor relations, legal compliance). PeopleSoft enables the benefits professional to define its own default rules about benefit selections, benefit changing events, and benefit package combinations.

Mike Bedell has been recently transferred from his position as regional manager in Iowa to the corporate headquarters in Ohio. The benefit program offered to employees in Ohio is different. When Mike's transfer to his new job is entered into the database, the HRIS automatically notifies the HR professional that Mike is eligible for a different set of benefit options because of his transfer and location change. Mike can then select new benefits or the PeopleSoft Event Rules will default him into appropriate elections. A properly implemented HRIS benefits module can provide enormous efficiencies in the ever changing world of the modern organization.

Summary Points

- Employee benefits are not just a fringe cost to employers; they represent a substantial percentage of the total payroll. Benefits are usually awarded equally to all workers or on a seniority basis.

- Certain benefits are required by law, including Social Security, workers' compensation, and unemployment insurance.

- Retirement income is provided through Social Security, private pension plans, and personal savings. Employers believe that they directly or indirectly provide all of these sources—which constitute the single most expensive benefit area.

- Insurance programs provided by employers have expanded to include life insurance, dental, legal, and vision

care, as well as health care. Employers are looking to self-funding, HMOs, and PPOs to minimize health insurance rate increases.

- Paid time off from work represents the largest category of benefit costs.

- Flexible benefit plans have received great interest from employers because they help contain benefit costs and provide employees with more individualized benefit programs.

- Changing employee demographics and social pressures have caused employers to become "family friendly" and offer child care, elder care, and other programs to help employees meet their family needs.

Case Study

Family Health Insurance

Laura Gains is a confused employee. Washington Electric Company, her employer, is offering a local HMO as an alternative to the company's POS health insurance plan. Gains attended the employees' meeting, where an HMO official

explained the medical services and costs. The official outlined many services, such as dental checkups and flu shots, which would be provided at little cost. Gains knows she spends over $400 a year in these areas alone. The HMO is located about

CASE STUDY—cont'd

two miles from Gains's home and is always open—something Gains thinks would add to her use of the services. The company will provide the same dollars for the HMO as it currently does for the employees' health insurance plan (a requirement of the HMO Act). Gains, however, is bothered by the lack of choice of physicians and dentists, though she is not really attached to the ones she is going to now. During this month, Gains must decide whether to change to the HMO for at least a year or else wait until next year's sign-up period.

A widow, Gains is the sole support of her three daughters—Shari, age nine; Amber, age seven; and Tracy, age four. In the past, her annual medical expenses have often exceeded $5000. Whereas the company's health insurance plan does not cover most of her medical expenses, the HMO would

cover almost all of them; however, this very high quality HMO plan would cost Gains $20 per month more in premiums (this is unusual). Gains's salary is about $42,000 per year. She prepares her own tax forms and always itemizes deductions.

QUESTIONS

1 How should Gains compare the plans? What quantitative criteria should be considered?

2 What additional information would help Gains make her decision?

3 What would you decide? Why?

EXPERIENTIAL EXERCISES

1. FLEXIBLE BENEFIT DECISIONS

The purpose of this exercise is to help you gain an understanding of the philosophy behind flexible benefit plans and the individual decision making involved. Management is increasingly striving to negotiate flexible benefit plans as a means of controlling the total cost of employer-paid employee benefits.

If *today* you were given $600 per month in benefit dollars

to allocate among the following, what package of benefits would you choose? Complete the following chart by placing a dollar amount for each benefit you choose in the left column. If your total benefit cost is less than $600 per month, you will keep one-third of the difference as a monthly cash bonus. You pay any amount over $600 per month.

BENEFIT PLAN   BENEFIT

_____   Pension plan (matched by employer 50/50 up to $500/month)
_____   Paid vacations ($50/mo. for 2 weeks/year)
_____   Paid holidays ($50/mo. for 10 days/year)
_____   Paid sick leave ($50/mo. for 10 days/year)
_____   Guaranteed maternity or paternity leave ($50/month)
_____   POS-Medical insurance ($250/employee, $450/family/month)
_____   Health maintenance organization health-care option ($200/employee, $400/family/month)
_____   Legal insurance ($50/mo. for 100% legal needs)
_____   Vision care ($50/month for routine checkups and one pair of glasses or contact lenses/year)
_____   Partially Subsidized child care ($100/month per child for on-site care)
_____   Credit union ($25/month)
_____   Subsidized company cafeteria ($50/month for free hot lunches)
_____   Tuition reimbursement ($50/month for 100% tuition)
_____   Funeral leave ($50/month; 3 days/death)
_____   Company-sponsored social events (annual picnic, parties, etc. $25/month)
_____   Life insurance ($50/mo. for $250,000)
_____   Disability insurance ($100/month)
_____   Dental insurance ($50/month for routine checkup and all required care)
_____   Free parking ($50/month—local lots charge $65/month)

_____   Total cost

EXPERIENTIAL EXERCISES—cont'd

2. BENEFITS SURVEY: FIELD RESEARCH

PURPOSE

To identify, design, and implement benefit programs

TASK

Break into small groups. Each group is to interview or call the head of a benefits department or a person who would be responsible for designing and administering the benefits programs. The instructor will inform the class regarding when the project is due.

Each group should plan on giving a short classroom presentation that summarizes their findings.

In preparing their questions, the group should consider the following:

- What demographic changes within the company have influenced the choice of benefit programs?

- What tax changes have taken place that influence specific programs?
- How did the company identify employees' needs?
- How does the company communicate benefit programs?
- Does the company depend on contract workers? If so, what if any benefits are available to them?
- Assess the company's pension program. How many years does it take to become vested? Is there an employee contribution? What type of plan is it?
- Does the company offer tuition reimbursement?
- Which of the three types of medical plans are offered (HMO, PPO, POS)? How much does an employee have to pay each month?
- What future benefits are being considered?
- How does the company measure the effectiveness of their benefit programs?

KEY TERMS AND CONCEPTS

Child care programs
Concierge services
Consolidated Omnibus Budget Reconciliation Act (COBRA)
Contributory/noncontributory plan
Current-expenditure plans
Dismissal pay
Elder care
Employee benefits
Employee earnings and benefits letter
Employee Retirement Income Security Act (ERISA)
Family and Medical Leave Act (FMLA)
Flexible benefit plan
Funded plans
401(k) retirement plans
Health maintenance organizations (HMOs)
Group insurance plan
Indemnity plans

Insured plans
Managed care plans
Paid time off work
Point-of-service (POS) plans
Portability
Preferred provider organizations (PPOs)
Premium pay
Profit-sharing plans
Section 125
Sick leave banks
Social Security system
Soft benefits
Spiritual benefits
Unemployment insurance
Vesting
Workers' compensation
Well-pay programs

REVIEW QUESTIONS

① How can employee benefits attract, retain, and motivate employees?

② About how much of the total payroll cost consists of benefits?

③ What factors are important in determining the size of an employee's retirement benefit?

④ Why do some states require employers to pay more unemployment insurance taxes than others?

⑤ What are the traditional problems with paid sick leave? Solutions?

⑥ What are the advantages of health insurance self-funding? What are the relative advantages of POSs? HMOs? PPOs medical plans?

DISCUSSION QUESTIONS

1. If you were establishing your own business, which benefits would you be legally required to pay and which would you voluntarily offer?

2. Prove that the cost of living for retired individuals increases as much as or less than the CPI increases. Should Social Security increase as the CPI rises?

3. In view of the fact that fewer persons are now working to provide benefits for the Social Security system, would you agree that all state, federal, and local government employees and nonprofit association employees should enter the Social Security system?

4. Do you believe that the government should transfer support of welfare or social programs to private industries in the form of required benefits or allow the public funds be invested in the stock market?

5. Periodically, pension fund frauds involving the loss of retirement funds for thousands of employees are reported. How can persons and companies that have contributed to the pension fund safeguard their contribution to the future?

6. Should employers provide child care? Elder-care? Why?

7. Do you think a national government health insurance (socialized medicine) system is needed?

ENDNOTES

Chapter 13

1. Jan Goldberg, "Benefits Basics: These 'Perks' Can Represent Thousands of Dollars in Annual Compensation," *Equal Employment Opportunity Career Journal* (June 30, 1994): 30.

2. Stephen Blakely, "Company-Paid Costs Decline Slightly (Statistics on Employee Benefit Costs in 1996)," *Nation's Business* 86 (February 1, 1998): 40.

3. *The Consumer Price Index,* U.S. Department of Labor, 1987–1990.

4. Richard I. Henderson, *Compensation Management* (Reston, VA: Reston, 1979), 321–322.

5. Thomas N. and Teresa N. Fannin, "Coordination of Benefits: Uncovering Buried Treasure," *Personnel Journal* 62, no. 5 (May 1983): 386–389.

6. Evan Claque and Leo Kramer, *Manpower Policies and Programs: A Review* 1935–1975 (Kalamazoo, MI: Upjohn, 1976), 82–83.

7. Jerry Flint, "The Old Folks," *Forbes* (February 18, 1980): 51–56.

8. Dale Detlefs, *1984 Guide to Social Security* (Louisville, KY: Meidinger and Associates, 1985), 6–9.

9. "Family and Medical Leave Act of 1993," Society for Human Resource Management (Alexandria, VA: 1993), Report.

10. Michael P. Littea and James E. Inman, *The Legal Environment of Business: Text, Cases and Readings* (Columbus, OH: Grid, 1980), 464–465.

11. Milton Bordwin, "The Courts Get You Coming and Going," *Management Review* 87 (November 1998):51–53.

12. Kenneth P. Shapiro, "An Ideal Pension System," *Personnel Journal* 60, no. 4 (April 1981): 294–297.

13. "Studies Reveal Ever-Widening Wage Gap; Detailed Work Data Point to Disparity That Extends to Benefits," *Minneapolis Star Tribune* (June 14, 1998): 8A.

14. "What Is Your Savings Personality? The 1998 Retirement Confidence Survey," *EBRI Issue Brief* no. 200 (August 1998).

15. Vincent M. Tobin, "What Goes Into a Retirement Income Policy?" *Personnel* 61, no. 4 (July–August 1984): 60–66.

16. Donald Bell and William Wiatrowski, "Disability Benefits for Employees in Private Pension Plans," *Monthly Labor Review* 105, no. 8 (August 1982): 36–40.

17. Kathryn H. Anderson, Richard V. Burkhauser, and Joseph F. Quinn, "Do Retirement Dreams Come True? The Effect of Unanticipated Events on Retirement Plans," *Industrial and Labor Relations Review* 39, no. 4 (July 1986): 518–526.

18. *Basic Patterns in Union Contracts,* 12th ed. (Washington, DC: Bureau of National Affairs, 1989), 27.

19. Fredrick I. Schick, "Tax Reform's Impact on Benefit Programs," *Personnel Administrator* 32, no. 1 (January 1987): 80–88.

20. Lawrence Meyer, "Many Workers Lose Retirement Benefits Despite Reform Laws," *Washington Post* (September 7, 1982): 1.

21. The Retirement Equity Act of 1984, an Amendment to the Employee Retirement Income Security Act of 1974 (ERISA).

22. "When Pension Liabilities Dampen Profits," *Business Week* (June 16, 1983): 80–81.

23. Trisha Brambley, "The 401(k) Solution to Retirement Planning," *Personnel Journal* 63, no. 12 (December 1984): 66–67.

24. William M. Mercer-Meidinger, Inc., "How Will Reform Tax Your Benefits?" *Personnel Journal* 65, no. 12 (December 1986): 49–57.

25. Adapted from Carroll Roartz, "How MeraBank Lowered Pension Costs Without Lowering Morale," *Personnel Journal* (November 1987): 63–71.

26. "Studies reveal ever-widening wage gap," *Minneapolis Star Tribune.*

27. F. C. Joran, "A Fair System for Time Off the Job: Combine Sick Days,

Vacation Days and Holidays into Paid Days," *Modern Business Practice* (June, 1974): 113–114.

28. "Women, Family, Future trends—A Selective Research Overview," *Contemporary Women's Issues Database* (January 1, 1997), from a National Committee on Pay Equity news release.

29. Juan Hovey, "A Minimum-Cost Insurance Plan for Employees," *Nation's Business* 87 (January 1999):24.

30. Ibid.

31. Henderson, *Compensation Management*, 323.

32. "Big Gains in Family-Friendly Benefits," *Business and Health* 15 (June 1997): 16.

33. Sandra E. La Marre and Kate Thompson, "Industry-Sponsored Day Care," *Personnel Administrator* 29, no. 2 (February 1984): 53–65.

34. James Fraze, "Preparing for a Different Future," *Resource* 7, no. 1 (January 1988): 1, 10.

35. Sue Shellenbarger, "Firms Try Harder, But Often Fail, to Help Workers Cope with Elder-Care Problems," *The Wall Street Journal* (June 23, 1993): B1.

36. Anne Ritter, "Dependent Care Proves Profitable," *Personnel* 67, no. 3 (March 1990): 12–16.

37. Sue Shellenbarger, "Firms Try Harder, but Often Fail."

38. Susanna Duff, "AOL Takes Its Employees to the Cleaners," *Employee Benefit News* 12 (July 1998): 20.

39. Brian Williams, "Finding Fulfillment: Companies Encouraging Workers' Spirituality." *The Columbus Dispatch* (December 21, 1998): 5.

40. Ibid.

41. Shelly Branch, "The 100 best companies," *Fortune* (January 11, 1999): 118.

42. Ibid. Freely adapted.

43. Robert B. Cockrum, "Has the Time Come for Employee Cafeteria Plans?" *Personnel Administrator* 27, no. 7 (July 1982): 66–69.

44. Albert Cole Jr., "Flexible Benefits Are a Key to Better Employee Relations," *Personnel Journal* 62, no. 1 (January 1983): 49–53.

45. Ibid., 51–53.

46. Elisabeth K. Ryland and Benson Rosen, "Attracting Job Applicants with Flexible Benefits," *Personnel* (March 1988): 71–73.

47. "Flex Plans Lower Health Costs: Hewitt Study," *Employee Benefit Plan Review* (July 1989): 19–20.

48. David Thompson, "Introducing Cafeteria Compensation in Your Company," *Personnel Journal* (March 1977): 126–128.

CHAPTER

14

HEALTH AND SAFETY

CHAPTER OUTLINE

CHAPTER OBJECTIVES

1 To understand the recent investment of employers in employee wellness programs.

2 To reveal the problems caused by employee alcohol and drug abuse.

3 To discuss policy issues surrounding AIDS in the work place.

4 To identify the purposes of employee assistance programs.

5 To understand the general provisions of the Occupational Safety and Health Act.

6 To identify the points needed in a comprehensive drug testing policy and the requirements of the Drug-free Workplace Act.

7 To describe the federal right-to-know regulations.

8 To identify job stress warning signs and methods of care.

9 To discuss effective accident prevention programs.

EYE INJURIES: 400,000 CASES EACH YEAR

Did you know that 400,000 cases of occupationally related eye injuries occur annually? That's more than 1,000 eye injuries in the American work place each day! Some 70 percent of serious injuries are the result of flying or falling objects. Approximately 60 percent of those objects are smaller than the head of a pin.

More than 77,000 eye injuries (19 percent) result in lost time, defined as one full day or more out of work. The financial impact to employers in lost time and workers' compensation annually is estimated to be in excess of $300 million.

But eye injuries don't stop at the plant gates. According to Prevent Blindness America, 41 percent of eye injuries occur after hours in or around the home. Shrub and tree trimming, lawn care, woodworking projects, and chopping wood are just a few examples of how home activities can result in eye injuries.

Any injury to the human eye can have serious consequences, no matter where it occurs, warns Anne Chambers, marketing manager for safety eyewear for Uvex Safety Incorporated, the Smithfield, Rhode Island–based manufacturer of safety eyewear. Whether it is on the job or in the home, an eye injury can cause an employee to lose time from work and suffer temporary or permanently impaired vision. There can be significant consequences for the employer. Employee injuries result in sick or disability leave, lost productivity, higher workers' compensation costs, and increased medical insurance costs. Everyone loses.

WWW.UVEX.COM

During the past two decades, much attention has been given to establishing stricter guidelines and implementing precautionary measures to reduce the incidence of work-related eye injuries. Some employers have implemented ongoing eye safety training and hazard assessment programs. Snapper, Gulfstream, and Toyota all provide spectacles at no cost, and required employees to wear them—no exceptions, no excuses.

Despite these efforts, the most recent statistics do not reflect a significant reduction in the number of annual eye injuries. According to OSHA, 90 percent of occupationally related injuries could have been avoided through the use of proper protective eyewear. In addition, a 1995 market study conducted by Future Technology Surveys Incorporated estimates that of the 20 million workers required to wear eye and face protection, only 60 percent are actually in compliance.

Unfortunately, many workers who suffered eye injuries believed protective eyewear was not required in their particular situation. This points out, says Chambers, that employee eyewear training must be ongoing. Employees need to know how and when to use protective eyewear. An excellent source of training materials for preventing eye injuries is Prevent Blindness America, Schaumburg, Illinois (847/847–2020).

SOURCE: "Achieving Safe Sight 24 Hours a Day", *Occupational Hazards* (April 1998): 71–72.

Whether it happens to executives or to a minimum-wage employee working during the hectic Christmas rush season, stress and burnout are real problems. Some work place analysts are telling employers that offices, factories, and stores could become "stress pools" unless management helps workers cope.

But the employees' mental health is just one set of problems. Organizations are also responsible for creating and maintaining a healthy and safe work environment free from unnecessary hazards that can lead to injury, illness, or death. One thing is certain: ignoring the problems will only lead to increased absenteeism, disability claims, health care costs, additional recruiting, and training costs. These employee HR health and safety - issues are explained in this chapter.

STRESS

Job stress is considered to be a major concern in many organizations. The possible causes include increased domestic and foreign competition, which has led to a substantial number of downsizing, layoff, and merger activities; rapidly changing technology; tension among diverse groups of employees; and increased demands for higher quality and better service. Organizational managers are interested in maintaining a lower level of job stress for good reasons: high levels of stress can result in low productivity, increased absenteeism and turnover, and an assortment of other employee problems including alcoholism, drug abuse, hypertension, and a host of cardiovascular problems.

Another reason for concern over job stress is that stress-related workers' compensation claims have risen dramatically. About 14 percent of occupational disease claims are stress-related. Stress-related claims, on average, are estimated at $15,000, twice as much as those for employees with physical injuries.[1] But what exactly is job stress?

A comprehensive definition based on the integration of many definitions is as follows:[2]

> Stress is a discrepancy between an employee's perceived state and desired state, when such a discrepancy is considered important by the employee. Stress influences two behaviors—(1) the employee's psychological and physical well-being, and (2) the employee's efforts to cope with the stress by preventing or reducing it.

Just how common is job stress in the United States? Consider the statistics in Figure 14–1. Over two-thirds of workers in the United States report that their jobs are either extremely or highly stressful. In addition, one-third seriously consider quitting their jobs each year due to stress. The major factors reported that causes these high stress levels are "too much work," "lack of time for self," and "little control over their jobs."[3]

Just how stressful is your position? Some jobs, such as those in Figure 14–2, consistently have high stress levels due to the nature of the work. Individuals who cannot cope with continuous stress are probably best advised to avoid these careers. The level of stress that exists in any job or organization is not easily determined. The outcomes in high-stress situations are usually high levels of absenteeism, turnover, grievances, accidents, and chemical dependency. Accurately measuring stress levels, however, is not easy. The most common measurement techniques employ paper-and-pencil tests that ask employees about the existence of stressors in their job environment.

The measurement of employee stress may enable an organization to change its cultural environment and thus lower the level of stress. A good example is the Armstrong Transfer and Storage Company in Memphis, Tennessee. Armstrong suffered a serious problem with stress-related workers' compensation claims and saw its claims rise from $93,000 to $272,000 in just two years. To determine the extent of work place stress, Armstrong administered questionnaires to its 500 employees. The results showed, for example, that employees were worried about worn-out loading equipment but failed to report it for fear that they would have to pay for it. In response to the survey results, Armstrong's management repaired or replaced broken equipment and held weekly meetings to allow employees to air their grievances. Following the stress-reduction program, accidents fell from 65 to 10 per year, and a follow-up survey showed that perceived stress had dropped significantly.[4]

CONTROLLING STRESS

Job stress caused by factors in the work place is a serious, growing aspect of organizational culture. In general, strategies to control stress focus on organizational-level HR policies and individual-based efforts.

FIGURE 14–1   EXTENT OF JOB STRESS IN THE UNITED STATES

PERCENT	STRESS ISSUE
66	Employees who report that their jobs are extremely or highly stressful.
34	Employees who seriously thought about quitting their jobs due to stress.
25	Employees reporting stress-related illnesses.
90	Workers who think their employers should act to reduce stress.
40	Workers who feel more stress due to the recession.

DOLLARS	STRESS ISSUE
$73,270	Average amount corporations sets aside for stress-related disabilities.
$1,925	Average cost of rehabilitating a stressed employee.

SOURCE: Adapted from Jennifer J. Laabs, "Job Stress," *Personnel Journal* (April 1992): 43.

FIGURE 14-2   HIGH-STRESS JOBS, WARNING SIGNS, AND WAYS TO COPE

Only recently have consultants and psychologists begun to study work place tension in depth. They've discovered the most trying professions are those involving danger and extreme pressure—or that carry responsibility without control. The symptoms of stress have been found to range from frequent illness to nervous tics and mental lapses. The most common tips for dealing with it focus on relaxation. But sometimes the only answer is to fight back—or walk away.

10 TOUGH JOBS	WARNING SIGNS	WAYS TO COPE
Inner-city high-school teacher	Intestinal distress	Maintain a sense of humor
Police officer	Rapid pulse	Meditate
Miner	Frequent illness	Get a massage
Air-traffic controller	Insomnia	Exercise regularly
Medical intern	Persistent fatigue	Eat more sensibly
Stockbroker	Irritability	Limit alcohol and caffeine
Journalist	Nail biting	Take refuge in family and friends
Customer service/complaint department worker	Lack of concentration	Delegate responsibility
Waitress	Increased use of alcohol and drugs	Quit
Secretary	Hunger for sweets	

SOURCE: Annetta Miller et al., "Stress on the Job," *Newsweek* (April 25, 1988). Copyright 1988, Newsweek, Inc. All rights reserved. Reprinted by permission.

Organizational strategies include the following:

- **Preventive management.** With this approach, managers identify potential problems that may become serious stressors and take steps to reduce or eliminate them. Surveys and employee/group interviews are important tools in this process.
- **Maintaining a productive culture.** The development of, and adherence to, a mission statement that includes the maintenance of a positive organizational environment and satisfied employees sets the right direction. However, following through with programs that actually create and maintain a positive culture is the most important facet of a stress-reduction strategy.
- **Management by objectives.** A management by objectives or similar performance appraisal technique that identifies employees' goals, clarifies roles and responsibilities, and strengthens communication can reduce stress by eliminating uncertainty in critical aspects of employees' jobs.
- **Controlling the physical environment.** Reducing stress in the physical environment requires that management undertake one or two different strategies (or both). The first strategy is to alter the physical environment (reduce noise, institute better control of temperature, and so on). The second

strategy is to protect employees from the environment (with improved safety equipment).
- **Employee fitness facilities.** An increasing number of organizations provide physical fitness facilities to improve employee health and morale and to reduce stress. Many such facilities include exercise equipment and programs such as aerobics, weight training, racquet sports, and running. More sophisticated wellness programs include health testing and counseling by medical professionals.

Personal strategies include the following:

- **Meditation.** While many forms of meditation exist, one of the more popular is transcendental meditation (TM). Using TM, the participant silently utters a mantra—a word or sound that the meditator concentrates on—to enter a state of mental and physical relaxation. While detractors of TM are easily found, research shows that meditation can reduce anxiety and improve work performance and job satisfaction.
- **Exercise.** One of the least expensive and potentially most effective stress-reduction strategies is exercise—jogging, racquet sports, fitness classes, bicycling, and swimming. Research shows that a sound program of physical fitness can improve mental health as well as physical well-being.

- **Entertainment.** Many people find that watching a favorite movie or listening to music can relieve stress.
- **Removing the cause of stress.** Sometimes one can easily identify the major cause of stress—a confrontational supervisor, difficult support staff, no possibility for advancement, and so on. Thus the key is to remove or lessen the cause. One of the authors of this textbook recalls working with a woman who, year after year, drove away the best people in her office by making their lives miserable; he avoided all contact with her and, when it was necessary to communicate with her, used written forms to avoid a conversation. This provided a tolerable environment until a new manager finally removed her and brought peace to the office.
- **Becoming a mentor.** When one has mastered one's own job, helping a junior person learn the job and the organization's culture can reduce excessive stress.
- **Seeking counseling.** Stress is a common psychological problem. Counselors can offer helpful insights and stress-reduction techniques that may alleviate problems. Counseling is also far less expensive than quitting one's job.[5]
- **Extended leave.** Sometimes one can put stress-causing problems into a larger perspective by taking extended leave—such as an extended vacation, sabbatical, or personal leave. On returning, the worker often finds that some problems have resolved themselves and that others simply don't cause the same high levels of stress they did before.

BURNOUT

Job stress and *job burnout* are sometimes used interchangeably or are confused. **Job burnout,** however, is more than job stress; it occurs when a person believes that he or she cannot or will not continue to do the job.[6] The difference, according to a physician who has treated both, is that a person who is stressed can take an extended vacation and return rested and ready to get back to work. If that person has experienced burnout, however, within a few days after returning to work he or she will feel as miserable as before the vacation. While stress usually contributes to burnout, it does not explain the whole phenomenon. Burnout, in essence, is the overall perception that one is giving more than one is receiving—in monetary rewards, recognition, support, or advancement. It can occur at all organizational levels, at all pay levels, and in all age groups.[7]

A good example of burnout is Rochelle Ruane, an HR professional. Ms. Ruane, fresh out of college, was hired by a biotechnology company to build its HR department from scratch. It was a job she enjoyed. "I liked the people, I liked the company. It was that wonderful start-up feeling and everybody was working together, and it was a really good atmosphere—a positive culture." The stress and eventual burnout occurred because the more Ruane did, the more she was expected to contribute. "A lot of it was my own fault. . . . It's the classic situation that if the work is getting done, why should they give you any more help? . . . I did far too much and I burned out."[8]

Managers who want to maintain the positive culture Rochelle Ruane mentioned and help employees avoid burnout should first admit that it can and does occur in all organizations—with all levels of employees. Then they should learn to recognize the personal traits or characteristics that may indicate that a person is experiencing burnout (see Figure 14–3).

If one suspects that another person may be experiencing burnout (see Figure 14–4), one can help determine if that may be the situation by asking the person to answer three questions:

1 What do you want from your job?

2 What do you have to do to get what you want?

3 Is it worth it to you to do what is necessary to get what you want?

If the troubled person can answer these questions honestly and is able to get what he or she wants from the job, the person may be rehabilitated. The employee must develop a program of setting and working toward the goals—a key to preventing burnout. These goals provide a reason to continue with the career and an important sense of direction.[9]

EMPLOYER HEALTH CARE PROGRAMS

Employee assistance programs designed to help employees overcome personal crises such as alcoholism, job burnout, or family problems are offered by many large employers. Such programs have proven that valuable, skilled employees who experience problems can be helped. Once they have dealt with their problems, those employees often provide many more productive years of service. In fact, employees may be particularly grateful to employers who have lent them assistance during a time of personal or financial crisis.

FIGURE 14–3   SYMPTOMS OF EMPLOYEE BURNOUT

PHYSICAL

A change in physical appearance; decline in grooming or wardrobe.
Complaints such as headaches, backaches, or gastrointestinal problems.
Increased absenteeism for health reasons.
Signs and symptoms of depression such as a change in weight or eating habits or chronic fatigue.
Frequent infections, especially respiratory infections.

EMOTIONAL

Depressed appearance, such as sad expression, slumped posture, or rounded shoulders.
Appearing bored or speaking of boredom.
Attitudes of cynicism, resentfulness, apathy, or anxiety.
Expressions of frustration and hopelessness.

BEHAVIORAL

Decreased productivity, inability to focus on the job or complete a task.
Tardiness.
More frequent absenteeism.
Withdrawal or listlessness.
Expressions of irritability or hostility.
Overworking.
Abuse of drugs, alcohol, or caffeine; increased smoking.
Excessive exercise, often to the point of injury.

SOURCE: Hugh F. Stallworth, "Realistic Goals Help Avid Burnout," *HRMagazine* (June 1990): 171. Used by permission.

FIGURE 14–4   ARE YOU BURNED OUT?

JOB BURNOUT: FIVE WARNING SIGNS

Employees are vulnerable if they have:

1 Little say about how to do the job.

2 Feelings of never being caught up.

3 Frequent sickness.

4 A desire to quit but fear of doing so.

5 Major changes in the work place.

SOURCE: Northwestern National Life's Research Report, *Employee Burnout: America's Newest Epidemic* (1993).

The top source of such employee problems is *clinical depression.* A national survey of employee assistance professionals cited depression as the root cause for the increase in medical claims, work place injuries/accidents, and illnesses. About 71 percent cited it as the "top problem" in the work place.[10]

WELLNESS PROGRAMS

Employers have tried a number of approaches to address rising health costs and the poor fitness and health of employees. One approach is the establishment of **wellness programs.** The Health Insurance

Association of America defines *wellness* as a "freely chosen lifestyle aimed at achieving and maintaining an individual's good health."[11]

Today, about 20 percent of U.S. employers offer some wellness activity, and the number is growing. Why? "Back surgery can cost a half million dollars and carpal tunnel treatment a quarter million," explains Ken Ditzian, a New York director of a corporate wellness program. Preventive wellness programs can cut insurance premiums up to 30 percent. The most common wellness activities include:[12]

- Smoking cessation.
- Healthy eating.
- Cardiovascular risk profile.
- Stress/time management.
- Cancer prevention.
- Aerobic and stretching exercise.
- Ergonomic worksite assessment.

These classes are usually voluntary and free of charge to employees.

Adolph Coors Company in Golden, Colorado, has carefully developed a wellness program that has saved $1.9 million annually in documented savings. Coors estimates that for each dollar spent on their program, the company saves $6.15 in reduced medical costs, reduced sick leaves, reduced workers' compensation stress claims, and increased productivity.[13]

The Coors wellness program has received two national awards and is considered a model program. How does the Coors program work? "By making wellness a part of the corporate culture," says William Coors, chairman and CEO, who pushed the board of directors to build a 25,000-square-foot wellness facility. The facility offers aerobics, strength training, cardiovascular equipment, and an indoor running track. The program is far more than just a facility, however; employees and their spouses can participate in health-risk assessments, nutritional counseling, stress management, smoking cessation programs, on-site mammography and blood pressure screenings, family counseling, and pre- and postnatal education. Each of these components follows the Coors model to achieve behavioral change.[14]

- ***Awareness.*** The health hazard appraisal (HHA) gives each employee and spouse personal information about their potential for premature death or disease.

- ***Education.*** The HHA counselor describes the variety of on-site fitness activities, as well as programs that can help change employees' behavior. Education is also achieved through brochures, luncheon lectures, and elevator posters such as one describing the early warning signs of a heart attack.

- ***Incentives.*** The company provides the financial incentive of refunding the cost of a program if participants achieve and maintain their personal goals. The programs are held on site.

- ***Programs.*** A range of programs is offered, and employees are given a choice of one that interests them and meets their needs. In addition, the company cafeteria provides low-calorie and low-fat food choices.

- ***Self-action.*** Programs are made available to all employees and their dependents since they are included in all medical benefits. On-site and off-site exercise facilities are also made available, and participants are encouraged to continue a personal exercise program. It is believed that for the program to succeed in the long run, employees must take responsibility for their health.

- ***Follow-up and support.*** Follow-up information, such as direct-mail reminders of blood pressure screenings and mammograms are provided. Periodic follow-up classes are also conducted.

Company Physical-Fitness Programs   One major employer-sponsored method of increasing employees' health is the company **physical fitness program (PFP).** The National Industrial Recreation Association estimates that more than 50,000 firms have PFPs. Such programs are relatively new; more than 70 percent of company PFPs have been started since 1975.[15] A leading authority on PFPs believes that all HR departments should initiate such programs to develop employees mentally and physically. Most employees need up to three years to realize the full benefits from a program.[16]

PFPs vary greatly, from a basketball hoop in the employee parking lot to the Kimberly Clark Company's $2.5 million physical fitness center. According to a survey of 226 program directors, 41 percent of PFPs have gymnasiums and exercise rooms, 34 percent have an entire building used exclusively for physical fitness, 10 percent have company-sponsored teams, and 6 percent use YMCA facilities. In most programs, employees are encouraged to use the facilities and participation is voluntary. In 67 percent of programs, facilities, are used on employees' own time; in 33 percent, on company time.[17]

Organizations that support PFPs generally expect them to be attractive to employees, to reduce the impact of stress, and to increase employee productivity. In addition, they are often expected to decrease absenteeism and turnover, as well as accidents and medical claims.[18] Documented improvements by employees who actively participate in a PFP include the following:

- Improved cardiovascular function, decreased body weight, and fat reduction.[19]
- Lower medical claims.[20]
- Smoking reduction and blood pressure normalization.[21]
- General physical fitness.[22]

Today, more employers develop PFPs because many believe that they positively affect both the employees and the organization. Table 14–1 shows the benefits thought to accrue from the establishment of such programs.

EMPLOYEE ASSISTANCE PROGRAMS

Employee assistance programs (EAPs) began 40 years ago when employers first began recognizing the work place-related problems associated with alcohol abuse. Today, however, EAPs have a much broader and more comprehensive approach to helping employees identify and solve their personal problems, regardless of the cause. The general philosophy of an EAP is the belief that while the employer has no right to interfere in an employee's personal life, it does have the right to set performance standards and to establish sanctions when those standards are not met. A major cause of the increasing number of EAPs is their success. The recovery rate of participants in EAPs is three times that of the general public. This is likely due to (1) identifying problems early in their development; (2) the use of positive and negative employer reinforcement to motivate EAP patients to continue treatment; and (3) EAP follow-up monitoring to minimize relapse problems.[23]

But the primary reason company-sponsored EAPs have increased is that they may enhance a company's profitability by reducing absenteeism, turnover, tardiness, accidents, and medical claims. It is estimated that a troubled employee costs the employer at least 5 percent of that employee's annual salary.[24]

A milestone in the growth of EAPs occurred in 1987. More than 800 EAP practitioners applied to take their first professional certification test. The test was developed and sponsored by the Association of Labor—Management Administrators and Consultants on Alcoholism (ALMACA). The certification program was designed to legitimize the EAP profession through standardization. Eventually state or federal laws as well as insurance companies may require EAP certification similar to that required by other professions.[25]

The typical program addresses psychological and physical problems including job stress, chemical dependency (alcohol and drugs), depression, marital and family problems, financial problems, health, anxiety, and even job boredom. The procedure in virtually all EAPs consists of (1) problem identification, (2) intervention, and (3) treatment and recovery. Program operations generally fall into two categories: *internal programs* that use a full-time staff of counselors and other employees,

TABLE 14–1 BENEFITS OF PHYSICAL FITNESS PROGRAMS		
PHYSIOLOGICAL IMPROVEMENTS	**BEHAVIOR CHANGES**	**BENEFITS TO THE ORGANIZATION**
Weight and body fat loss	Less absenteeism	Lower medical claims and insurance premiums
Greater strength and endurance	Fewer fatigue-related accidents	Fewer disability claims
Better nutritional habits	Higher productivity	Fewer losses due to accidents
Less smoking	Enhanced mental alertness	Lower workers' compensation costs
Improved blood pressure and cardiovascular function		Higher employee morale and productivity
Stress reduction		Lower overtime and temporary-worker salaries due to absenteeism reduction

and *external referral centers* that use a full-time specialist who identifies the problem and refers the employee to a community agency for treatment.

An example of a successful referral program is the EAP at the Bechtel Power Corporation in San Francisco. When a supervisor believes that an employee's performance has been adversely affected by personal problems, the supervisor phones the EAP office.[26] (An alternative first step is employee self-referral.) Once the supervisor and the EAP specialist discuss the particulars of the situation—such as the employee's performance record, absenteeism, and so on—the supervisor is normally advised to suggest that the employee use the EAP. It is carefully explained to the employee that participation is voluntary and does not affect the discipline process, which may be implemented if required by poor work. Strict confidentiality is guaranteed. At some point, the employee may be given the choice of termination or using the EAP.

This critical first step—getting the employee to voluntarily seek assistance from the EAP—can be a difficult process for the supervisor. In general, the supervisor in approaching the employee should do the following:[27]

- Be specific about why the employee's behavior is unacceptable. Do not criticize the person; address only his or her job performance.

- Get a commitment from the employee to meet certain specific work standards that address the performance problem.

- Be consistent and firm in requiring the employee to meet the work standards.

- Resist the urge to diagnose the problem.

- Be prepared to cope with the employee's resistance, defensiveness, and hostility.

- Try to get the employee to acknowledge the problem and then suggest the EAP service, but emphasize that seeking assistance is voluntary.

- Emphasize that if the employee does not seek help, continued employment will depend on the employee's improving his or her performance without help.

When the employee calls the EAP office, a specialist then performs *triage*—the determination of the relative urgency of the case. A case may be (1) a life-threatening emergency such as a suicide attempt; (2) an urgent need such as extreme anxiety or crying; or (3) a routine need. In the first case, the counselor responds immediately; in the second, within hours; in the third, a counseling session is set up within days. At the counseling session,

a referral to a local agency is made and the follow-up process is started. Follow-up by the agency is continued for as long as is needed, with particular attention given to the continuance and frequency of the employee's sessions.[28]

Internal programs are usually more expensive and therefore found mostly in larger organizations. Such programs provide a sense of security because the employee is not given a quick diagnosis and sent to an outside source. Instead, sessions with in-house counselors provide the needed treatment in most cases. Exceptions include cases of chemical abuse and various physical problems.[29]

EAP professionals generally agree on what components are essential for a successful program. Essentials for an effective EAP include the following:[30]

- **Confidentiality.** Employees must believe that all information about their problems will be kept confidential by the counselor. Supervisors should only be informed that the employee is continuing to receive assistance.

- **Normal disciplinary procedures.** No employee should receive lenient or harsh treatment due to participation (or lack of it) in an EAP. Some programs allow the suspension of discipline as an incentive to enter the program. Even in such cases, the employee's work must improve and the problem eventually resolved.

- **Voluntary participation.** Supervisors can strongly urge an employee to participate and even give termination as the alternative, but the employee must seek help voluntarily for any chance of success.

- **Job security.** No employee will be affected by disciplinary or other actions because he or she participated in the program.

- **Insurance coverage.** Both inpatient and outpatient treatment must be covered by insurance.

- **Management support.** Management must provide written assurance that the company is committed to the process.

- **Accessibility.** Employees must know how and for what types of problems they can receive assistance. A broad range of assistance ensures a better image and greater use.

- **Follow-up.** Some problems will take years to correct, though most can be rectified in a number of months. Periodic follow-up whether by in-house counselors or outside agencies, is critical to a high recovery rate.

- **Separate location.** The program should be located away from the work place to help ensure privacy.

SUBSTANCE ABUSE IN THE WORK PLACE

Almost every major change in our society affects the work place sooner or later. Substance abuse is certainly not an exception. Drug and alcohol abuse in the United States is currently a major contributor to many of society's problems, including the breakup of families, crime, and students' dropping out of school.

The annual cost to employers of substance-abusing employees is about $100 billion, in the form of higher absenteeism, accidents, medical liability, and health expenses. EAP programs can significantly help, but many employers can't afford them.[31]

ALCOHOL ABUSE

One of society's most persistent and devastating ills, alcoholism often leads to severe marital problems, family abuse, estrangement between parents and children, the loss of close friends and acquaintances, emotional illness, and ostracism by society. Statistics show that alcohol and other mood-altering substances increase violent crimes and traffic accidents that result in death. The societal burdens of alcoholism have long been of major concern to professionals in social work, medicine, and psychiatry.

Alcoholism has received a great deal of attention from both management academicians and HR practitioners. Much of this interest has been created by the publication of data that show that (1) a high percentage of American workers are alcoholics and (2) the alcoholic worker has many more work-related problems than a nonalcoholic worker.

What causes alcoholism? There is little agreement about the specific causes. Predicting precisely who will or will not become an alcoholic is impossible. Alcoholism does not discriminate against any particular social or economic class; this disease is as likely to victimize the middle manager as the assembly-line worker.

Nonetheless, researchers have isolated a mix of circumstances that greatly influence problem drinkers. The National Council on Alcoholism (NCA) suggests that the **problem drinker** is one who has the following characteristics:

- Experiences intense relief and relaxation from alcohol.
- Has difficulty in dealing with and overcoming depression, anxiety, and frustration.

- Is a member of a culture in which there is pressure to drink, as well as culturally induced guilt and confusion regarding appropriate drinking behavior.

According to the NCA, when these persons encounter problems with their families, spouses, jobs, loneliness, old age, and so on, their probability of becoming alcoholics increases significantly.

Even though alcoholism may be difficult to measure quantitatively, persons may determine if they have the symptoms of the problem. Both the NCA and Alcoholics Anonymous (AA) have developed checklists to help individuals decide if they may need help in combating alcohol. Although a checklist may not be useful for research purposes, it may be part of an organization's alcoholism education program given to employees who inquire about the organization's rehabilitation services. The AA checklist is shown in Figure 14–5.

Because alcoholism is difficult to measure in an organizational setting, research will be limited. For example, it may be impossible to analyze which employees have the highest rates of alcoholism or what work conditions and environmental settings tend to aggravate the problem.

Reducing Alcoholism   Because employee alcoholism may stem from both personal and work factors, the most effective strategy for combating alcoholism is to minimize the potential for alcoholism by keeping stress and anxiety at the lowest possible levels. Rehabilitation programs for employees who are currently suffering from alcoholism should be implemented.

Programs to minimize alcoholism in the work place may be most difficult for the HR administrator to implement and control. Challenge, stress, and conflict seem to be inevitable in the jobs of many modern managers and administrators. Further, the HR administrator has only moderate control over the work climate and goal-setting process for employees outside of the HR department. Nonetheless, the HR staff can educate top and middle managers about the potentially harmful effects of excessive job stress and anxiety. Through training and development activities, the HR staff can make executives aware that the way people are managed and how their jobs are designed may significantly affect their mental and physical health.

The second strategy to fight alcoholism—the implementation of rehabilitation policies and programs—has become an important personnel responsibility in many larger organizations today. As management and labor continue to accept employee rehabilitation efforts, such programs will, no doubt, continue to expand.

FIGURE 14–5   12 QUESTIONS ONLY YOU CAN ANSWER

Yes   No

1 *Have you ever decided to stop drink-ing for a week or so, but only lasted for a couple of days?*

Most of us in A.A. made all kinds of prom-ises to ourselves and to our families. We could not keep them. Then we came to A.A. A.A. said: *"Just try not to drink today."* (If you do not drink today, you cannot get drunk today.)

2 *Do you wish people would mind their own business about your drinking— stop telling you what to do?*

In A.A. we do not *tell* anyone to do any-thing. We just talk about our own drinking, the trouble we got into, and how we stopped. We will be glad to help you, if you want us to.

3 *Have you ever switched from one kind of drink to another in the hope that this would keep you from getting drunk?*

We tried all kinds of ways. We made our drinks weak. Or just drank beer. Or we did not drink cocktails. Or only drank on weekends. You name it, we tried it. But if we drank *anything* with alcohol in it, we usually got drunk eventually.

4 *Have you had to have an eye-opener upon awakening during the past year?*

Do you need a drink to get started, or to stop shaking? This is a pretty sure sign that you are not drinking "socially."

5 *Do you envy people who can drink without getting into trouble?*

At one time or another, most of us have wondered why we were not like most people, who really can take it or leave it.

6 *Have you had problems connected with drinking during the past year?*

Be honest! Doctors say that if you have a problem with alcohol and keep on drinking, it will get worse—never better. Eventu-ally, you will die, or end up in an institution for the rest of your life. The only hope is to stop drinking.

Yes   No

7 *Has your drinking caused trouble at home?*

Before we came into A.A., most of us said that it was the people or problems at home that made us drink. We could not see that our drinking just made everything worse. It never solved problems anywhere or anytime.

8 *Do you ever try to get "extra" drinks at a party because you do not get enough?*

Most of us used to have a "few" before we started out if we thought it was going to be that kind of party. And if drinks were not served fast enough, we would go some place else to get more.

9 *Do you tell yourself you can stop drinking any time you want to, even though you keep getting drunk when you don't mean to?*

Many of us kidded ourselves into thinking that we drank because we wanted to. After we came into A.A., we found out that once we started to drink, we couldn't stop.

10 *Have you missed days of work or school because of drinking?*

Many of us admit now that we "called in sick" lots of times when the truth was that we were hung-over or on a drunk.

11 *Do you have "blackouts"?*

A "blackout" is when we have been drink-ing hours or days which we cannot remem-ber. When we came to A.A., we found out that this is a pretty sure sign of alcoholic drinking.

12 *Have you ever felt that your life would be better if you did not drink?*

Many of us started to drink because drink-ing made life seem better, at least for a while. By the time we got into A.A., we felt trapped. We were drinking to live and living to drink. We were sick and tired of being sick and tired.

What's your score?

Did you answer YES four or more times? If so, you are probably in trouble with alcohol. Why do we say this? Because thousands of people in A.A. have said so for many years. They found out the truth about themselves – the hard way.

But again, only *you* can decide whether you think A.A. is for you. Try to keep an open mind on the subject. If the answer is YES, we will be glad to show you how we stopped drinking ourselves. Just call.

A.A. does not promise to solve your life's problems. But we can show you how we are learning to live without drinking "one day at a time." We stay away from that "first drink." If there is no first one, there cannot be a tenth one. And when we got rid of alco-hol, we found that life became much more manage-able.

SOURCE: "Is AA for You? 12 Questions Only You Can Answer," A.A. World Services, Inc. (New York: 1973). www.alcoholics-anonymous.org/index.html

Kemper Insurance Companies, one of the first or-ganizations to implement a formal employee assistance program, has outlined its approach to employee reha-bilitation in a pamphlet titled ***Management Guide on Alcoholism.***[32] Kemper's policies are shown in Fig-ure 14–6.

DRUG ABUSE

Employers are increasingly concerned over the rise of drug abuse in the work place. As a result, testing has moved into almost every industry. In 1987 President Reagan's Commission on Organized Crime requested that all U.S. companies test their employees for drug use. Employee testing, the commission believed, can create a safer work environment and reduce society's demand for illegal drugs. How serious are the problems created by a drug user? One company estimated, based on employee records, that the typical drug user, com-pared to the norm for the work unit:[33]

- Functions at about 67 percent of potential capacity.
- Is 360 percent more likely to be involved in an accident.
- Requires three times the average use of sick leave and benefits.

FIGURE 14–6   KEMPER'S POLICIES ON EMPLOYEE ALCOHOLISM

Alcoholism Policy. In accordance with our general personnel policies, whose underlying concept is regard for the employee as an individual as well as a worker:

① We believe alcoholism, or problem drinking, is an illness and should be treated as such.

② We believe the majority of employees who develop alcoholism can be helped to recover, and the company should offer appropriate assistance.

③ We believe the decision to seek diagnosis and accept treatment for any suspected illness is the responsibility of the employee. However, continued refusal of an employee to seek treatment when it appears that substandard performance may be caused by any illness is not tolerated. We believe that alcoholism should not be made an exception to this commonly accepted principle.

④ We believe that it is in the best interest of employees and the company that alcoholism be diagnosed and treated at the earliest possible stage.

⑤ We believe that the company's concern for individual drinking practices begins only when they result in unsatisfactory job performance.

⑥ We believe that confidential handling of the diagnosis and treatment of alcoholism is essential.

The objective of this policy is to retain employees who may develop alcoholism by helping them to arrest its further advance before the condition renders them unemployable. . . .

Supervisory Practices. Supervisors are instructed that they should *not* attempt to identify alcoholic employees. Further, supervisors should not discuss "drinking problems" with their employees, except where drinking on the job or an intoxicated employee is observed (the diagnosis of alcoholism is the job of trained professionals). Rather, the supervisor's responsibility is to closely and accurately monitor employee *performance* and *work habits* and confront the employee whose performance problems persist with the warning that continued poor performance will lead to disciplinary action. . . .

Treatment Facilities. Kemper, as do most companies which conduct employee assistance programs, uses a variety of alcoholism treatment sources. These include both private alcoholism consulting and treatment firms and not-for-profit organizations such as AA and Al-Anon, which provides support and assistance to the family members of an alcoholic.

SOURCE: *Management Guide on Alcoholism* (Long Grove, IL: Kemper Insurance Companies, undated), 6–11. Used by permission

● Is five times more likely to file a workers' compensation claim.

● Is absent 10 more workdays per year.

● Is more likely to file a grievance complaint.

The Drug-Free Workplace Act of 1988

Under the 1988 federal **Drug-Free Workplace Act,** federal contractors and grantees who receive more than $25,000 in federal grants or contracts must certify that they will maintain a drug-free work place. Companies must ensure that drug use by employees does not occur in the work place if they continue to do business with the federal government. The act does not include the use of tobacco or alcohol by employees. The act does require employers to take the following steps to ensure they operate a drug-free work place:[34]

① *Policy statement.* Establish and notify all employees of a policy prohibiting the illegal use, possession, manufacture, or distribution of controlled substances in the work place. Warn employees of action that will be taken against violators.

② *Awareness programs.* Provide a drug-awareness program that educates employees on the dangers of drug abuse. Inform employees of available drug counseling, rehabilitation, and employee assistance programs.

❸ Conditions of employment. Notify employees that the drug-abuse policy is a condition of employment. Employees must agree to inform the employer of any criminal conviction for a drug-abuse statute violation within five days.

❹ Agency notifications. The employer must notify the federal contracting agency within 10 days of receiving the notice of a conviction from an employee.

❺ Good-faith effort. The employer must make a goodfaith effort to maintain a drug-free work place.

Supporters of the 1988 act believe that it provides employers with a good incentive to initiate a drug-free program without being subjected to negative public and employee reactions. Every company that has instituted drug programs has recorded steep drops in drug incidents. When Pfizer, Incorporated, the New York based pharmaceutical company, started testing job applicants in 1987, 9.9 percent turned up with evidence of having recently used drugs. But by last year, the percentage had fallen to 3.2.

Hoffmann-Laroche, the big pharmaceutical company, with its U.S. headquarters in New Jersey, and Mobil Corporation, which has major offices in New York and New Jersey, found about 7 percent of their job applicants were using drugs when they began testing in the early and mid-1980s. Now, both companies say fewer than 1 percent are testing positive. Many companies offer counseling and treatment to employees found using drugs and give them a second chance, sometimes even a third. But applicants get no help. They are simply not hired, and many never learn why.[35]

Employee Drug Testing   Many employers question what key policy and legal issues should be considered when developing a comprehensive drug policy. According to an American Management Association survey of more than 1000 companies, 48 percent test employees for drug use, compared to only 21 percent two years earlier (just prior to the commission's report). The survey found that drug-testing programs generally fall into two areas: preemployment testing of new hires and post-employment testing of current employees.[36]

Applicant Testing   Employers may require any applicant to submit to a drug-screening test, unless limited by

HR IN THE NEWS

IS WORK PLACE DRUG-TESTING EFFECTIVE?

YES!—J. Michael Walsh, former executive director of the Presidents Drug Advisory Council

Since the widespread implementation of work place programs in the mid-80s, there has been a significant decline in the use of drugs according to the National Household Survey. In 1985, reported use was over 12 percent—but only about 6 percent in 1995. Employee drug testing has become a standard business practice. The American Management Association estimates 80 percent of firms test for drugs. Over 30 million employee are tested on an annual basis. HR professionals have witnessed the success stories, and how programs have changed habits.

NO!—Lewis L. Maltby, director, American Civil Liberties Union's National Taskforce on Civil Liberties in the Work Place

The most important evidence comes from a National Academy of Sciences report which casts doubts on testing. The critical assumption is that those who use drugs are less productive than other employees. While that is true for hard-core drug users, most people who use drugs are not addicts, just as most who use alcohol are not alcoholics. The critical question is, "Are casual users less safe, productive, etc." The academy found no such relationship.

The American Management Association has also questioned the cost-effectiveness of programs, noting many were dropped or reduced due to costs.

SOURCE: "Is Workplace Drug-Testing Effective?" *HR News* (April 1996): S–6.

a state law. Employers, in a statement of policy, can express their desire to hire only qualified applicants. Since drug use may adversely affect job performance, they can choose to hire only applicants who pass a drug-screening test.

This concept was generally upheld by a U.S. Supreme Court decision in *New York City Transit Authority* v. *Baeger.*[37] The Court ruled that the safety and efficiency of the public transportation system constituted a valid business necessity and was a justifiable reason to require drug testing of bus driver applicants.

In a landmark 1989 decision, the National Labor Relations Board (NLRB) upheld an employer's right to require applicants to pass a drug test without negotiating the issue with their union. In the case, the *Star Tribune,* a Minneapolis newspaper, denied employment to job applicants who tested positive or refused to take the drug test.[38] The union demanded that the *Star Tribune* bargain over the policy. When management denied the demand, the union filed an unfair labor practice charge based on the refusal to bargain.

The need for drug screening for all job candidates may increase in the future due to several factors:

- Increased drug use in all segments of society.
- Reluctance of previous employers to report suspected or known drug use by former employees for fear of litigation.
- Employer liability for the negligent hiring of employees.

Preemployment drug testing requires the careful consideration of several issues. The following points are contained in the policy developed by the International Business Machine (IBM) Corporation:[39]

- *Notification.* Notify applicants of the screening on the physical examination questionnaire to minimize claims of invasion of privacy.
- *No rescheduling of the test.* Do not allow an applicant to reschedule a test after he or she appears at the doctor's office and realizes that it is part of the physical examination. The person may be a substance abuser who could refrain from illegal substance use before the next exam.
- *Test validity.* In the event of a positive test result, repeat the test using the same sample in order to ensure validity. Ensure that test samples are kept by the doctor's office for 180 days in case of litigation.
- *Confidentiality.* Maintain confidentiality by recording positive test results only on the doctor's records. On personnel records, use a code if an individual fails the test. Only the applicant should be aware of the test results, and the person can simply be informed that his or her test result was unsatisfactory. This policy holds true for current employees also.

Testing of Current Employees   The testing of current employees raises more difficult policy issues, as well as the need to keep up-to-date with court arbitration decisions. Employers usually test employees according to one of three policies:

- *Random testing.* All employees are tested at random, periodic intervals or randomly selected employees are tested on predetermined dates.
- *Probable cause.* An employee is tested only when his or her behavior causes a reasonable suspicion on the part of supervisors.
- *After accidents.* All employees involved are tested after any accident or major incident.

Of the three policies, the use of random testing has raised the strongest criticisms, largely based on an employee's perceived right to privacy. Random testing has been initiated, however, for federal employees.

By Executive Order 12564 (1988), President Reagan provided that federal employees who used illegal drugs—off or on duty—were unfit for federal employment. The executive order provided that random drug testing would be initiated in those federal agencies where the employees' duties involved public safety or law enforcement.

Private-sector employees not involved in public safety should probably not be randomly tested. Instead, there should be a reasonable basis for probable cause before an employee is tested. An important jury decision sent a strong message to employers with random-testing policies. A computer programmer for the Southern Pacific Transportation Company was awarded $485,000 after she was fired for refusing to take a random urinalysis. Her case relied on the general right-of-privacy provisions of the California constitution, which were similar to those found in many states.[40] In general, a random-testing policy will most likely be upheld by a court or arbitrator if it is related to public safety.

Probable Cause   A policy of testing employees for drug usage only when there is probable cause will be more readily accepted by employees. Probable-cause testing has also received support from the courts and from arbitrators if the test is given based on a reasonable suspicion of drug use. A supervisor's reasonable suspicion based on an employee's absenteeism, erratic behavior, poor work performance, and the like can generally be accepted as a reason to test.

A major accident involving employees can be considered an immediate probable-cause situation and thus can invoke required testing of all employees involved. The federal government's regulation requiring railroads to test all crew members after major train accidents was upheld by the U.S. Supreme Court in the 1989 *Skinner* case.[41] The Court held that private railroads subject to federal regulations must test all members of a train crew following a major train accident. Both blood and urine tests are required.[42]

There are several policy considerations regarding the probable-cause testing process and the use of test results:

- ***Valid testing procedure.*** The burden of proof is clearly on management regarding the use of confidential, fair, and valid testing procedures. Proper testing procedures include the use of an approved, certified laboratory with state-of-the-art tests. To guard against false-positive results that may lead to unfair discipline or other actions, a second, confirming test should be required.
- ***On-the-job-impairment.*** In cases involving discipline as a result of a positive drug test, an employee or union may contend that the tests prove the presence of a drug in the employee's body but not on-the-job use or impairment. Indeed, in a court case, *Shelby County Health Care Center,* the

---

FIGURE 14–7   HOW MOTOROLA ENFORCES ITS DRUG-FREE POLICY

Motorola's drug policy is stated simply: "No use of illegal drugs; no use of legal drugs illegally." To enforce the policy, Motorola instituted a universal drug-testing program on January 1, 1991. HR professionals administer the program.

Every employee becomes a part of the database, including the CEO and contractors. A specially designed computer program selects from each Motorola site employee names to be tested each day. The computer program ensures that every employee is selected at least once in three years. for a drug test. It's possible, however, for some employees to be selected more than once during that period. This is designed to prevent an employee's feeling safe from testing after taking one test.

The HR department informs the employees' supervisors, who are responsible for relaying the information to the employees. The supervisor then has time to plan for the employee's absence. Failure of an employee to report to a designated location may result in disciplinary action.

The collection area prepares *split samples* for the Motorola employees, allowing for analyses from two different labs if the employees request it. If an employee's test comes out positive, the company's medical-review officer discusses the situation with the employee to determine if there's some legitimate reason—such as a prescription drug that the employee forgot to mention—for a positive result.

If it's determined that a drug-abuse problem exists, the next step for the employee is to report to HR to set up a meeting with an EAP advisor and plan rehabilitation methods. The company pays for the employee's rehabilitation. In the meantime, unless it is some safety-sensitive or security-clearance position, the employee continues working on the job.

After employees complete their rehabilitation programs, their names go into a special random pool. Motorola tests these employees once every 120 days for a one-year period. If during this one-year period an employee again tests positive, the organization terminates him or her. If, however, all tests following rehabilitation come out negative, the employees name goes back into the three-year pool, and he or she begins the testing process again.

SOURCE: Adapted from Dawn Gunsch, "Training Prepares Workers for Drug Testing, *Personnel Journal* (May 1993): 54.

relevant provision of the contract limited drug- or alcohol-related "major" offenses to drug or alcohol use on the employer's premises or being "under the influence." A fired employee was reinstated because, while his drug test was positive, there was no on-the-job impairment.[43]

There is concern that positive drug tests involving illegal drugs might be used to discipline an employee for the illegal activity involved in obtaining and possessing the drug—regardless of the on-the-job effect. The employer's position is that an employee who engages in such illegal activity is not a fit employee. To date, however, arbitrators and courts have often required a link between the employee's drug use and behavior in the work place before just cause for discipline is found. Such a relationship should not be difficult to establish in most cases.

- **Refusal to be tested.** An employer can usually sustain the termination of an employee for failure to take a drug test in cases of probable cause. However, just as with other offenses that can lead to termination, the employee should be warned that failure to submit to testing will result in discharge.
- **Supervisor training.** A policy that includes the training of all supervisors to recognize the typical signs of employee drug use is important if probable cause is the basis of testing. The reasonableness of a supervisor's request for a test is more likely to be upheld if the supervisor has participated in an appropriate training program.[44] While many supervisors may be able to detect alcoholic intoxication, behavior caused by drug abuse is more difficult to recognize without training.

SMOKING IN THE WORK PLACE

A report of the U.S. Surgeon General concluded that sidestream or passive smoking, the involuntary inhaling by nonsmokers of tobacco smoke, is dangerous to their health. The report stated that environmental tobacco smoke (ETS) causes 2,400 to 4,000 lung cancer deaths annually among nonsmokers. ETS is the combination of sidestream smoke, which comes from burning cigarettes between puffs, and mainstream smoke, which is exhaled by a smoker.[45] Tobacco smoke is also a severe problem for allergy sufferers. Legal restrictions on smoking in the work place are mostly found at the state and local levels. Some states had enacted laws regulating smoking in the private sector work place. Many local governments have also passed restrictions. The 1973 federal Vocational Rehabilitation Act was applied to work place smoking in a 1982 court case when an employee successfully claimed that he was handicapped as a result of inhaling the smoke of fellow employees.[46] The court found, however, that the employer only had to make "reasonable accommodations" for the employee and was not required to ban work place smoking.

Balancing the rights of smokers and nonsmokers is a difficult HR policy issue. However, more employers have continued to develop new policies: In addition to the health considerations of nonsmokers, employers must consider that the employee who smokes costs the employer an average of $400 to $1,000 per year more than the nonsmoker in health insurance claims, absenteeism, maintenance, and productivity.[47] But there are conflicting opinions on the specific effects of employee smoking in the work place. A nonaffiliated research group has published research results indicating that smokers are high achievers and among the most productive employees.[48] Employers have developed a number of **policies on work place smoking:**

- **Total ban.** In 1984, the Boeing Company in Seattle announced its intention to provide a smoke-free environment for all employees. With over 85,000 employees, Boeing became the largest U.S. company to ban smoking in the work place. According to the company's president, Malcolm Stamper, developing a smoke-free environment is an essential ingredient in providing a clean, safe, and healthy working environment.[49]
- **Workstation ban.** Restrict smoking to separate, ventilated smoking lounges.
- **Encouragement of no smoking.** A bonus or award may be given to employees who do not smoke. The City Federal Savings and Loan Association of Birmingham, Alabama, for example, awards $20 per month to employees who do not smoke at work.[50]
- **Dangerous area ban.** Allow smoking in all areas except near combustible materials or in other hazardous situations. This policy meets minimum federal Occupational Health and Safety Administration (OSHA) standards.
- **Reasonable accommodation.** Separate employees who complain of smoke from adjacent co-workers who smoke, and improve ventilation.

Before establishing one of these policies, an employer should consider the following:

① All employees, from the president down, must be included in formulating the policy.

2 Disciplinary actions to be invoked when violations occur should be included in any policy.

3 Allow a transition period of several months between the announcement and implementation of the policy. This will give smokers who must quit the time to adjust.

4 Provide smoking cessation classes for smokers if a total ban is imposed.

5 Inform new employees of the policy during the interview process.

"Once adopted, a smoking policy that is properly communicated and fairly enforced can greatly assist employers in protecting the rights of nonsmokers. Such a policy can also help avoid the many legal liabilities which may result from tobacco smoke in the work place."[51]

The courts have upheld the legal right of employers to prohibit smoking in the work place, as well as to require job applicants to be nonsmokers. But the U.S. Supreme Court has not yet addressed the issue in a precedent-setting case. HR policymakers have many issues to consider—the rights of smokers and nonsmokers, the health and safety problems that may be caused by smoking in the work place, and a variety of policy options. The issue will likely continue to be one of the most controversial in the area of employee health and safety.

AIDS IN THE WORK PLACE

The U.S. Center for Disease Control and Prevention (CDC) released a national survey on employer policies and programs on AIDS, acquired immune deficiency syndrome, control. The survey results of 2,200 businesses indicate that almost half of U.S. employers have implemented AIDS work place policies, and nearly 20 percent have HIV and AIDS education programs. One of the objectives of the survey was to determine the adoption of the CDC-sponsored Business Responds to AIDS (BRTA) work place program, which contains five core elements. The survey found that 41 percent of large firms have adopted at least two of the HIV/AIDS work place program elements recommended by CDC. The Business Responds to AIDS Program was designed to prevent the spread of HIV through a comprehensive work place education program. The BRTA Program recommends businesses establish comprehensive HIV and AIDS prevention programs comprising the following five components:[52]

- Development of an HIV/AIDS policy.
- Training of supervisors in the policy.
- HIV/AIDS education for employees.
- HIV/AIDS education for employees' families.
- Encouragement of employee volunteerism, community service, and corporate philanthropy.

Almost an unknown issue before the 1980s, by 1995 AIDS, had become the leading cause of death among Americans ages 25 to 44—a group which is more than half the nations workforce, and the reason employers have increased their awareness programs.[53]

Employees with AIDS are covered under the 1990 Americans with Disabilities Act (see Chapter 4). The act considers being HIV-positive a physical disability; thus employers cannot discriminate against employees with AIDS with regard to employment decisions or compensation. In addition, the act requires an employer to make "reasonable accommodation" for disabled employees, which may include changes in facilities, hours, and nonessential job duties. The act does not, however, require an employer to hire or continue to employ individuals who cannot perform the essential duties of their jobs.

Generally, AIDS educational programs should address the following:

- Utilize guest speakers who possess an expertise in AIDS education and in providing care for people with AIDS.[54]
- Make brochures, printed facts, and videos regarding AIDS available. A majority of AIDS information is free or available at low cost.
- Provide hotline, community health consultants, and support group phone numbers. This allows for anonymity.
- Utilize the occupational health nurse to counsel, promote a safe work place, and influence attitudes and behaviors.[55] The nurse is a vital part of the education and referral system.

Research was done on corporate AIDS educational programs and revealed that knowledge increased, attitudes were improved, and risk behaviors reduced.[56] AIDS education reduces tension between infected and uninfected employees and creates a more positive atmosphere in the work place.[57]

The American Association of Occupational Health Nurses has issued guidelines about what *it* believes should be the ethical treatment of workers with AIDS:[58]

- Each person has the right to respect for human dignity. Managers must provide equality without prejudice of individual attributes, value systems, and lifestyles.

- The employee is entitled to privacy and confidentiality as an inalienable right. Only employees with a "need to know" should be informed of a co-worker's with HIV or AIDS condition.

- Disclosure of positive HIV test results or announcement of persons with AIDS could have disastrous social consequences and affect job performance and productivity. Approximately half the states in the United States have laws that protect workers against unnecessary disclosure of AIDS information.

- Employees with AIDS should be allowed to work as long as they are able. However, AIDS may cause a decrease in productivity, workers might be allowed to transfer to less physically demanding jobs or part-time work.

A difficult employment issue is the rights of co-workers of AIDS victims. The Occupational Health and Safety Administration (OSHA) requires every employer to provide a safe and healthy work place. The Secretary of Labor may take action against employers who fail to provide a safe working environment. Co-workers of a person with AIDS who might seek such action, however, would need to prove that they are at risk of contracting the disease, a difficult task given current medical evidence. Federal OSHA regulations do provide that an employee may refuse to work if "a reasonable person would conclude [that] he faced an immediate risk of death or serious injury." Such action may not be considered reasonable by the Labor Department unless direct contact with blood or other body fluids were required by the job.[59]

SAFETY PROGRAMS

It is estimated that 70 to 95 percent of injuries resulting from work place accidents can be attributed directly to employees' engaging in unsafe acts. Therefore, **safety programs** are most effective when they are oriented toward training and motivating employees to adopt safe work habits. Most programs include the logical steps of identifying from safety records the most common unsafe acts that lead to accidents, training employees in proper and safe methods, and then designing a motivational

strategy that combines goal setting with feedback or incentives for safe behavior. Employers with safety incentive programs average about $33,000 per year in incentive costs.[60]

Making safety programs and recognition awards work often involves changing the culture of a work place. The solution is to create a safety culture that focuses on the behaviors and attitudes of the workers. A safety culture is a process that has many components, takes time, and requires a collective effort. The benefits of safety recognition awards reach far beneath the surface and have dramatic effects: (1) they make a loud and clear statement that the management of a company is recognizing individuals for their part in contributing to the achievement of the overall goals of the company, (2) they show that the company is serious about worker safety and is willing to invest in safety achievement as an expression of its commitment to the safety culture.

The question is often asked, "Why should employees be awarded for not having accidents? They're expected to work safely." Although this is to some extent true, the fact is that on an average day, 17 working Americans are killed and 16,000 are injured in work-related accidents, costing business and industry more than $110 billion annually.[61] One reason for the increase in some accidents is the aging American workforce. According to the Bureau of Labor Statistics, older workers are four times more likely to die from job-related causes. Also, older workers take twice as long to recover from accidents.[62] The most dangerous industries in America are listed in Figure 14–8.

The reasons for safety recognition programs are clear: Not only is a company legally and financially liable if employees are injured on the job, but it also loses business for every hour, and every day, that workers can't perform their jobs. That's why recognizing employees for good safety practices is a crucial business strategy, and why human resources and safety professionals are becoming more savvy in what motivates employees to be safe at work. Although the number of lost workday cases due to injury has steadily decreased from a high of 4.3 per 100 full-time workers in 1979 to 3.8 cases per 100 full-time workers in 1994 (the most recent figures available from the U.S. Department of Labor Occupational Safety and Health Administration—OSHA), keeping people safe on the job has remained an important business issue for human resources and safety professionals. The good news is that it also indicates safety programs, for the most part, are working.[63]

Safety-incentive programs usually provide cash rewards or prizes to employees in teams or individuals, (see *HR in the News:* "UPS, Ford Safety Programs"), for

FIGURE 14–8 THE MOST DANGEROUS INDUSTRIES IN AMERICA

INDUSTRY	RATE
Meat-products processing	27.6
Motor-vehicles manufacturing	24.0
Nursing-care facilities	17.3
Office-furniture manufacturing	15.5
Trucking services	14.0
Logging	13.8
Construction	12.2
Department stores	10.8
Coal mining	10.3
Eating and drinking places	8.5

Industry rate per 100 workers, by industry.

SOURCE: Bureau of Labor Statistics   NOTE: Numbers only include nonfatal injuries and illnesses for industries with at least 100,000 cases. 1993 figures.

each week or month on the job without an accident. Even the most successful incentive programs report eventual loss of interest on the part of workers and thus must constantly be replaced with new incentives.

The cost of an effective incentive program, however, will be greatly outweighed by the benefits of a successful program, which includes (1) reduction in insurance premiums; (2) reduction in related legal expenses; (3) savings in wages and benefits paid to injured workers; (4) less overtime and training of new workers to replace injured employees; and (5) greater productivity.[64]

The National Safety Council advises employers to use the **three E's of safety** to prevent accidents: *engineering, education,* and *enforcement* of safety rules.[65]

Designing safe working conditions is the task of safety engineers, who, for example, design a workstation to include adequate lighting, the right tools or equipment for the job, required safety guards and proper electrical grounding for tools and equipment, adequate ventilation, safe storage and usage of chemicals, paints, and so on, and the wearing of safety shoes, clothing, or goggles when necessary. The proper safety training of new employees or all employees given new tools, chemicals, or equipment is a critical part of accident prevention. An employee who has never been shown the safe method of operating a machine or pouring a dangerous liquid cannot be expected to avoid an accident. Safety programs for employees can effectively reduce accidents. Such programs often offer monetary rewards, prizes, or paid leave for employees or departments that work without an accident for a specified

number of days. The enforcement of safety rules is a critical aspect of accident prevention. Yet, unfortunately, supervisors may be hesitant to discipline employees for not wearing safety goggles or for storing chemicals carelessly. Strong top-management commitment to daily emphasis on employee safety can effectively reinforce strong safety discipline.

Safety engineers encourage the following five steps in designing and maintaining a safe work place:[66]

1 Eliminate hazards.

2 Use safeguards on equipment.

3 Post warning signs near dangerous chemicals or machinery.

4 Train workers.

5 Require protective clothing, shoes, goggles, hats, and so on.

PARTICIPATIVE SAFETY MANAGEMENT PROGRAMS

In recent years, employers have increasingly given employees greater authority and responsibility in job design, work procedures, and decision making concerning their jobs. Generally, as employees have become more self-directed, their motivation has increased, and the

HR IN THE NEWS

UPS, FORD SAFETY PROGRAMS

UPS: REWARDING INDIVIDUALS

UPS rewards individual drivers for safety. United Parcel Service (UPS), based in Atlanta, Georgia, primarily rewards individuals rather than teams for safe work practices That's because UPS's workforce is chiefly its 70,000 drivers nationwide. And those drivers perform their jobs as individuals, rather than in teams.

UPS has been rewarding its drivers for safety since 1923. In 1985 the organization launched a special recognition program which honors UPS drivers who achieve 25 years of continuous safe driving (defined as having no avoidable accidents). Every year, all of the drivers who achieve a twenty five-year safety record participate in a celebration dinner and are inducted into the company's Circle of Honor. As Circle of Honor members, employees receive a camel-hair jacket (with a detachable Circle of Honor patch), which the company purchases from Rodes Professional Apparel in Louisville, Kentucky, (approximate cost is $200). Members also receive a special plaque commemorating their achievement.

So far, 2,700 drivers have reached Circle of Honor status. And for the past three years, UPS has recognized those individuals by publishing all their names in *The Wall Street Journal* and *USA Today*.

FORD

A team approach to safety. At Ford Motor Company, based in Dearborn, Michigan, safety is a corporate-wide priority. "Safety is a critical element of the workforce relationship," says Greg Anderson, manager of health and safety programs with responsibility for joint programs and union affairs for Ford's U.S. divisions. "It's the responsibility of the employee to perform his or her tasks in a safe manner and of the supervisor to provide the necessary instruction and equipment." The automotive giant has safety professionals at each level of the organization, culminating with a safety committee at the headquarters site that Anderson and another union official oversee. Both union and company management professionals are responsible for safety at every level.

At Ford, there's an emphasis on teams. So that's how the company trains *and rewards* employees for safe work practices—at the team level. Every quarter, the company gives a RISE (Recognition of Innovation Support in Excellence) award (a crystal memento) to the team that has demonstrated the greatest improvement in safe work practices or the most innovative approach to getting employees to be safe on the job. At year's-end, the company holds a safety conference, and one of the four teams that wins a quarterly RISE award then wins an annual award. The team that wins the annual award also wins a $1,500 grant.

Anderson says Ford doesn't reward individual team members for safety for this reason: "We don't want to make health and safety a competitive exercise because it's something that's a person's right—to [have] a safe work environment, to be able to go home healthy," he explains.

SOURCE: Jennifer Laabs, "Cashing in on Safety," *Workforce* (August 1997): 53–57.

---

result has been improved productivity with lower turnover and absenteeism.

At many places, like the General Electric plant in Columbia, Maryland, the concept of greater employee involvement was extended to safety. Management had witnessed the positive effects of General Electric's participative safety management program in the manufacturing operations and decided that the same principles could be applied to promote safety in the work place.

The General Electric plant manufactures electric ranges, thus injuries range from sheet-metal cuts and slivers of metal in the eye to carpal tunnel syndrome (repetitive motion trauma). In the past, General Electric had developed an extensive safety program that taught employees how to use tools and equipment properly and designed workstations to fit the person, rather than force the employee to fit the job. It was clear, however, that if employees realized that safety procedures were for their own protection and actively participated in designing the safety program, the program could be improved.[67]

The General Electric participative safety management system began with informal meetings, with staff delivering pep talks and providing safety information and statistics. To encourage workers to take an active role in safety and depend less on supervisory discipline, unique "safety warning cards" were distributed (see Figure 14–9). If an employee witnesses another worker doing something unsafe, the worker silently hands the person the card and walks away. The cards are effective reminders to employees that they are responsible not only for their own safety, but also for the safety of their co-workers. The next step was to create safety management teams in each section of the plant. Each team selected its own leader and conducted complete walk-through inspections similar to OSHA inspections. The team noted safety problems, listed corrective actions needed, and assigned the responsibility for those actions to specific individuals. The team monitored the list of items until all have been corrected. The benefits of the program included the following: (1) workers increased their awareness of responsibility for safety and were encouraged by management's willingness to pay for the changes their safety teams requested; (2) a worker MASH (Make Accidents Stop Happening) team reduced the weekly average number of accidents from about 8 to 2.4; and (3) safety team statistics pointed out that the same workers were getting injured each month, fewer than 5 percent of all employees. The safety teams developed a new safety performance policy that includes mandatory training after three injuries in a 12-month period and a written plan (by the employee) to end the problem. After one additional injury, the "unsafe" employee is placed on "lack of suitable work" status. While the safety team did not call the action termination, it did remove the worker from the work place, with normal layoff benefits and no hope of returning to work.[68]

OCCUPATIONAL SAFETY AND HEALTH ADMINISTRATION

In 1970 Congress passed the Williams-Steiger Occupational Safety and Health Act (Public Law 91-596). The Williams-Steiger Act was the culmination of years of effort by employee groups, unions, and the National Safety Council to provide safety in the work place. The act established the **Occupational Safety and Health Administration (OSHA),** within the U.S. Department of Labor and the **National Institute for Occupational Safety and Health (NIOSH)** within the U.S. Department of Health, Education, and Welfare (now Health and Human Services). NIOSH conducts research and gathers data and statistics relating to the occupational safety and health of employees; it helps determine standards for safety within the work place by working closely with OSHA.

FIGURE 14–9   SAFETY AWARENESS CARD

Caras & associates, inc.
EMPLOYEE RELATIONS CONSULTANTS

SAFETY AWARENESS
THE BEST ACCIDENT PREVENTION

I JUST NOTICED YOU DOING SOMETHING THAT COULD HAVE CAUSED AN ACCIDENT. THINK ABOUT WHAT YOU'VE DONE IN THE LAST FEW MINUTES AND YOU WILL PROBABLY RECALL WHAT I SAW.

I AM GIVING YOU THIS CARD AS PART OF OUR CAMPAIGN TO MAKE ALL OF US SAFETY CONSCIOUS. KEEP IT UNTIL YOU SEE SOMEONE DOING SOMETHING IN AN UNSAFE WAY AND THEN PASS IT ON.

P.S. I HOPE I DON'T GET IT BACK!

SOURCE: Caras & Associate Inc. Used by permission.

The Williams-Steiger Act (the OSHA act) is unique because it not only provides federal occupational safety standards through OSHA but also allows states to administer their own occupational safety and health programs. That provision was a compromise between those who believe that employee safety is a national concern and those who believe that the federal government is infringing on states' rights. A state-run OSHA program must receive federal approval and include federal safety requirements.

The 1970 act requires employers to furnish working environments free from *recognized hazards that may cause injury or illness to employees.* Employers are required to comply with safety and health standards created by the act and by states that administer their own programs. Employees are also required to comply with health and safety standards and regulations and submit a **log and summary of occupational injuries and illnesses.** Laws are enforced through the U.S. Department of Labor or state labor OSHA agencies or both. Regulations cover the use of toxic chemicals; levels of dust, fumes, and noise; the safe use of equipment and tools; and safe work procedures.

Enforcement is provided by inspectors entering the work place and determining whether employers have violated safety standards. Employers are required to allow the inspectors to enter their work places, answer questions, and provide requested data. If the inspector finds a violation of a safety standard, a written citation is issued; inspectors have the authority to determine whether the employer should be fined or warned and given time to correct the unsafe situation. Employers may be assessed a civil penalty of up to $10,000, a criminal penalty of up to $20,000, or a maximum of one year in prison. In most states, however, inspectors try to work with employers to correct the unsafe conditions rather than using penalties. Inspectors may find as many as 30 or 40 violations, *serious* and or *non-serious,* within a worksite that has not previously been checked. Thus, the inspector could issue several thousand dollars in fines or instruct the employer to make alterations in order that the standards be met within a reasonable amount of time. Returning to the worksite, often without warning, inspectors make sure that those changes have been made. Employers have the right to appeal a citation or fine.

OSHA Cooperative Compliance Program.

In 1997, OSHA introduced a new program based on a Maine pilot program. The program targets the "most dangerous" work places in a state and removes OSHA inspectors from employers with credible safety programs.

OSHA Penalties

Employers in various industries know that OSHA means business. As an example, in 1979 Texaco agreed to pay an OSHA penalty that was a record at the time. Texaco, OSHA, and the Chemical and Atomic Workers Union agreed on a payment of $169,400 as a penalty for OSHA citations issued at Texaco's Port Arthur, Texas, refinery. OSHA had originally recommended penalties totaling $394,000. The citations included 6 willful, 99 serious, and 7 repeated serious violations. A Texaco official stated that payment of the fine was not admission of negligence or a violation of the law in regard to a fire in which eight workers died.[69]

RIGHT-TO-KNOW REGULATIONS

In 1986, OSHA began enforcement of a new set of rules formally termed *hazard communication* but popularly known as **right-to-know regulations.** Unlike most OSHA regulations, right-to-know only requires that employers provide employees with information. Specifically, workers are given the right to know what hazardous substances they may encounter on the job. Common examples of over 1000 hazardous substances include asbestos, cyanide, polychlorinated biphenyls (PCBs), gasoline, acetone, and rosin core solder. The regulations do not require employer testing or study of hazardous substances. Nor do they include "mixed articles," such as automobile tires or vinyl upholstery, which contain hazardous substances that are not released in normal use. The regulations generally apply only when hazardous substances are known to be present in the work place and employees can be exposed due to routine operations or a foreseeable emergency. Federal and state hazard communication standards generally require:[70]

- Material safety data sheets (MSDSs) must be maintained for every hazardous substance that employees may be exposed to or handle.

- MSDSs must be kept readily accessible by all affected employees. Many employers keep the MSDSs in three-ring binders and include them in standard operating procedures.

- Labeling must be provided for all types of containers of hazardous substances including barrels, bags, boxes, cans, cylinders, drums, and tanks.

- A written hazard communication program for employee information and training must be developed. The program should begin with a list of all known hazardous substances in the work place. Employees should receive training in safe procedures, as well as methods of exposure detection such as distinctive odors, gases, and appearances.

ERGONOMIC STANDARDS

Work place injuries from repetitive motions—such as striking computer keys, fileting fish, and checking out groceries—are the most common occupational hazards. All repetitive motion injuries and illnesses taken together account for 48 percent of employee illnesses and injuries. The industry with the highest rate of cumulative trauma disorders caused by repetitive motions is the meat processing industry, where cutting, trimming, and preparing are performed by hand, much the same as they were 50 years ago.

Recent recognition of the extent of cumulative trauma disorders led the U.S. Department of Labor to develop voluntary employer guidelines to reduce their occurrence. Research shows that **repetitive-motion problems** can be minimized through work place engineering and job design. The voluntary OSHA guidelines concentrate on four related elements:[71]

1 *Worksite analysis.* Review existing plan layout and identify problems and hazards.

2 *Tools.* Improve the design of the assembly process and tools utilized to minimize hazards.

3 *Medical treatment.* Improve treatment of repetitive-motion ergonomic problems.

4 *Training.* Provide employees with the training needed so that they can protect themselves from repetitive-motion problems.

SHIFT WORK AND SAFETY

More and more companies are operating on a 24-hour-a-day, seven-days-a-week schedule. For many organizations, it is simply good economic sense. A manufacturing facility could increase production without the major expenditure of building a new plant. GM, for example, is going to 24 hours-a-day operations at its Ontario, Canada, truck plant. It hopes to hold down investment costs while boosting production of popular models.[72]

While equipment and buildings do not care whether they work 24 hours a day, people do. For some workers, adjusting to a new work schedule can be an enormous problem. At GM, workers have complained of disorientation because they work different hours and days each week. People typically do not perform as well at night as they do during the day. Rotating and fixed night-shift workers are not as alert and ready to meet the demands of their job as day workers.

There are numerous difficulties with **shift work,** but the most serious concerns are worker health and safety. The natural rhythms of the body must either be adjusted or ignored. Consequently, shift workers have a harder time maintaining good health. One study reported that women regularly working an evening or a night shift while pregnant are more likely to have a miscarriage than women who work the day shift.[73] Eating habits are disrupted, and the food they do eat is not always the healthiest. Regular exercise is a problem, and regular sleep is almost impossible. The odd hours cause friction at home too, where shift workers feel irritable and guilty for having to choose between rest and spending time with their families—and without family support, it is hard to cope effectively with shift work.[74]

While shift work will always pose problems, there are a few steps that HR professionals can take to make life more palatable. Poor shift scheduling design is often part of the problem. Improving shift schedules by offering more flexibility is one option. The most common shift schedule is the 8-hour rotating shift, where workers work five days, evenings, or nights and then take two days off. However, many employers are moving toward a 10- or 12-hour shift. Longer shifts require workers to "bite the bullet" and just work, eat, and sleep for three or four days, but then they get three or four days off to spend with their families. Another step that can improve workers' shift lives is to provide counseling—on family-related, work-related, or personal matters.[75] Offering employees and their families more flexibility and counseling is necessary for any long-term shift routines.

SUMMARY POINTS

● Job stress is a pervasive problem in our society. It may result in low productivity, increased absenteeism and turnover, and other employee problems including substance abuse, mental health problems, and cardiovascular illnesses. Strategies to control stress include: fitness programs, meditation, counseling, and leaves.

● EAPs can help employees overcome serious problems that affect productivity. Employers can retain highly skilled and valuable employees who suffer from alcoholism, drug abuse, depression, family problems, or other common crises. But normal disciplinary procedures should be followed when an EAP is provided. Employee participation

SUMMARY POINTS—cont'd

may be strongly encouraged, but ultimately the employee must voluntarily seek help.

● OSHA regulations require employees to keep records of employee injuries and illnesses. Employers should ensure that relevant OSHA regulations are met. Organizations can benefit from a safe work place through reduced insurance premiums, fewer lost worker hours, and fewer accident claims.

● Policies on smoking in the work place, drug usage, and AIDS are being developed by many employers as these issues generate greater concern in our society. However, while more employers are adopting a smoking ban and testing employees for illegal drugs, fewer are adopting an AIDS policy.

● Employers today are developing and implementing drug-free work place programs and drug-testing policies. Courts have upheld policies that require all job applicants to submit to testing. Preemployment testing policies should cover the issues of applicant notification, test validation, rescheduling, and confidentiality.

● The use of random post-employment drug testing has generally been upheld only in cases in which the employer can demonstrate an overwhelming need to protect public safety. Otherwise, the employee's right of privacy may require the employer to demonstrate probable cause before requiring a test. A probable-cause testing policy should provide a valid and confidential testing procedure, job impairment provision, warning of termination for failure to submit to testing, and supervisor training.

CASE STUDY

DESIGNING A SAFETY PROGRAM

Jay Vahaly is the training director of a 1,200-employee agricultural products company located in Albuquerque, New Mexico. In the past few months, new equipment has been installed that is expected to increase productivity substantially by minimizing the manual handling of food products in the cleaning, sorting, and packaging processes. The owners, Robert and Juanita Hillard, are concerned about employee safety. In the past, the plant utilized almost no machinery that could pose safety problems for the largely poor and uneducated workforce. The Hillards care deeply about their employees; they provide a generous wage-and-benefit package including a substantial profit-sharing plan. The 50-year-old firm has had successful employee relations including high productivity and low absenteeism and turnover.

In the process of evaluating the impact of the new equipment, the Hillards learned that other employers had encountered many start-up accidents because their employees simply did not take seriously the training program in equipment safety that the manufacturer of the new equipment had provided. Several had suffered permanently disabling accidents. The Hillards have contracted with the equipment manufacturer for a six-month extensive employee training

program, but they believe that a permanent safety incentive program is needed to keep safety in the minds and actions of their employees. From the anticipated increased revenues, the Hillards have pledged $100,000 annually for prizes and/or cash to be awarded in the safety program. Vahaly has been instructed to have the new program ready in six months, when the training program ends.

QUESTIONS

1 Do you agree with the Hillards' decision? Consider that the firm has already spent millions of dollars on OSHA-approved equipment that includes state-of-the-art safety mechanisms and that the manufacturer has provided a six-month extensive training program.

2 Describe in detail the safety program you would recommend Vahaly implement.

3 Would you anticipate any specific problems that might occur with a safety incentive program that uses prizes or cash as a motivation for safe practices?

4 How should Vahaly evaluate the success of his program?

EXPERIENTIAL EXERCISES

1. WHAT DO YOU REALLY KNOW ABOUT DRUG AND ALCOHOL ABUSE?

PURPOSE

To determine what you know and do not know about the use of alcohol and illegal drugs.

TASK

Complete the following Security Pacific Corporation drug-and-alcohol awareness survey. Your instructor will lead a class discussion about the issue.

EXPERIENTIAL EXERCISES—cont'd

Drug and Alcohol Awareness Survey

1 What percentage of alcoholics do you believe can return to stable moderate drinking after treatment?
2% [ ]   12% [ ]   20% [ ]   66% [ ]
Note: Moderate drinking is less than 7 drinks 4 times a month, and freedom from alcohol related social, legal, or health problems.

2 What is the fastest growing group of new drug users in America?
Women [ ]   Men [ ]   Age: 18-34 [ ]   35–44 [ ]   45–54 [ ]

3 Compared to others, what risk do children of alcoholics or drug-abusing parents have to become alcoholic or drug abusing themselves?
Twice as much [ ]   Three times as much [ ]   Four times as much [ ]

4 Prolonged use of heroin is less toxic than comparable use of cocaine (as evidenced by lab studies of animals).
True [ ]   False [ ]

5 How many of your friends', family's or co-workers' lives do you feel have been affected by alcohol or drugs?
1 in 3 [ ]   1 in 5 [ ]   1 in 7 [ ]   1 in 10 [ ]

6 As a commuter, I have probably seen more alcoholics while traveling to work on the highway than on the streets of skid row.
Yes [ ]   No [ ]

7 What do you think is the estimate of the percentage of the workforce that abuses alcohol, drugs, or both?
5–10% [ ]   15–25% [ ]   30–35% [ ]   40–45% [ ]

8 Absenteeism, medical expenses, and lost productivity as a result of substance abuse are costing employers, on average, what percentage of their total payroll?
2% [ ]   3% [ ]   4% [ ]   5% [ ]

9 As a manager/supervisor do you feel you can positively impact an alcoholic or substance abuser if he/she is unwilling to listen?
Yes [ ]   No [ ]

10 Either job-performance failure or lowered job responsibility always happens before an alcoholic or substance abusing employee is terminated.
True [ ]   False [ ]

SOURCE: Anthony Kramer, *The Security Pacific Drug and Alcohol Awareness Survey,* Security Pacific Corporation. Used by permission.

2. ARE YOU BURNED OUT?

PURPOSE

Everyone at some time feels burned out on the job or with life in general. Sometimes a variation, such as a new car, hobby, promotion, or even a serious illness, will revitalize a person and lessen the feeling of burnout.

This exercise can give you an objective appraisal of your degree of burnout if you answer it honestly. There are no right or wrong answers, and only you know if your answers are accurate. Once you determine your burnout score, consult the general discussion of what different scores may indicate and decide if any behavioral change is needed in your life, but don't make any major decisions based solely on this test; talk with family, friends, co-workers, or even a counselor first. Wait a week and take the test again if you contemplate any substantial action.

TASK

Compute your burnout score by completing the following questionnaire. You can use it to determine how you feel about your work or your life, either today or in general.

WHAT THE SCORE MEANS

Of the thousands who responded to this self-diagnosis instrument, none scored either 1 or 7. The reason is obvious. It is unlikely that anyone would be in a state of eternal euphoria implied by the score 1, and it is unlikely that someone who scored 7 would be able to cope with the world well enough to participate in a burnout workshop or a research project.

EXPERIENTIAL EXERCISES—cont'd

How Often Do You Have Any of the Following Experiences?

Please use the scale:

1	2	3	4	5	6	7
Never	Once in a great while	Rarely	Sometimes	Often	Usually	Always

_____ 1. Being tired.
_____ 2. Feeling depressed.
_____ 3. Having a good day.
_____ 4. Being physically exhausted.
_____ 5. Being emotionally exhausted.
_____ 6. Being happy.
_____ 7. Being "wiped out."
_____ 8. "Can't take it anymore."
_____ 9. Being unhappy.
_____ 10. Feeling rundown.
_____ 11. Feeling trapped.
_____ 12. Feeling worthless.
_____ 13. Being weary.
_____ 14. Being troubled.
_____ 15. Feeling disillusioned and resentful.
_____ 16. Being weak and susceptible to illness.
_____ 17. Feeling hopeless.
_____ 18. Feeling rejected.
_____ 19. Feeling optimistic.
_____ 20. Feeling energetic.
_____ 21. Feeling anxious.

Computation of score:
Add the values you wrote next to the following items:
1, 2, 4, 5, 7, 8, 9, 10, 11, 12, 13, 14, 15, 16, 17, 18, 21(A) _____.

Add the values you wrote next to the following items:
3, 6, 19, 20(B) _____, subtract B from 32(C) _____.

Add A and C (D) _____.

Divide D by 21 _____. This is your burnout score.

If your score is between 2 and 3, you are doing well. The only suggestion we make is that you go over your score sheet to be sure you have been honest in your responses. If your score is between 3 and 4, it would be wise for you to examine your work life, evaluate your priorities, and consider possible changes. If your score is higher than 4, you are experiencing burnout to the extent that it is mandatory that you do something about it. A score of higher than 5 indicates an acute state and a need for immediate help.

SOURCE: Adapted from Ayala Pines, Ph.D. and Elliot Aronson, Ph.D., "Why Managers Burn Out," _Sales & Marketing Management_ 4 (February 1989): 38.

KEY TERMS AND CONCEPTS

Drug-Free Workplace Act
Employee assistance programs (EAPs)
Job burnout
Job stress

National Institute for Occupational Safety and Health (NIOSH)
Occupational Safety and Health Administration (OSHA)
Physical fitness program (PFP)
Problem drinker

KEY TERMS AND CONCEPTS—cont'd

Repetitive-motion problems
Right-to-know regulations
Safety programs

Shift work
Three *E*'s of safety
Wellness programs

REVIEW QUESTIONS

1. Should an employer have an EAP? How should it be established?

2. How can wellness programs be cost-effective?

3. What actions are required of an employer under the Drug-Free Workplace Act?

4. How can an employer meet OSHA right-to-know regulations?

5. When is the problem drinker cured?

6. How does the performance of a typical drug user differ from that of other workers?

DISCUSSION QUESTIONS

1. An increasing number of employees are turning to a variety of mood-altering substances to help them get through each day. In most instances, union workers can be dismissed for drinking or taking drugs on the job. If your nonunion company has a pleasant, nonstressful environment, would it be justified in dismissing substance abusers rather than spending the money necessary for rehabilitation?

2. What is a fair and responsible policy on smoking in the work place?

3. Which common wellness program activities should small employers consider offering to employees? Why?

4. Government officials frequently waver in their enforcement of OSHA. What influences have caused government officials to relax safety rules at times and to create more stringent regulations at others?

5. If supervisors warn their employees about the possible health hazards connected with their jobs and supply safety equipment to the employees, is the company responsible if employees do not use the required safety equipment?

6. How can an employer minimize job stress in the work place?

7. Is employee drug testing an invasion of privacy? What do you consider a fair and effective drug-testing policy?

ENDNOTES

Chapter 14

1. C. Hymowitz, "Which Corporate Culture Fits You?" *The Wall Street Journal* (July 17, 1989): B1.

2. Jeffrey R. Edwards, "A Cybernetic Theory of Stress, Coping, and Well-Being in Organization," *Academy of Management Review* 17, no. 2 (1992): 238–274.

3. Jennifer J. Laabs, "Job Stress," *Personnel Journal* (April 1992): 43.

4. Ibid.

5. Thomas L. Brown, "Are You Living in 'Quiet Desperation'?" *Industry Week* (March 16, 1992): 17.

6. Ibid.

7. Harry Levinson, "When Executives Burn Out," *Harvard Business Review* 68 (March–April 1990): 69.

8. Hugh F. Stallworth, "Realistic Goals Help Avoid Burnout," *HRMagazine* (June 1990): 169–171.

9. Jennifer J. Laabs, "Surviving HR Burnout," *Personnel Journal* (April 1992): 82–85.

10. "Depression More Prevalent at Work Than Drugs: EAPA," *Alcoholism Report* 24, no. 12 (December 1996): 5.

11. *Your Guide to Wellness at the Worksite* (Washington, D.C.: Health Insurance Association of America, 1983), 3.

12. Valerie Frazee, "Employee Wellness Generates Corporate Wellness," *Personnel Journal* 75, no. 5 (May 1976): 26.

13. "Cost-benefit Analysis of the Coors' Wellness Program," University of Oregon Graduate School of Management, Eugene, OR (December 1988).

14. Shari Caudran, "The Wellness Payoff," *Personnel Journal* 69, no. 7 (July 1990): 55–60.

15. Jack N. Kondrasuk, "Corporate Physical Fitness Programs: The Role of the Personnel Department," *Personnel Administrator* 29, no. 12 (December 1984): 75–80.

16. R. L. Pyle, "Corporate Fitness Programs—How Do They Shape Up?" *Management Review* 68 (December 1979).

17. Kondrasuk, "Corporate Physical Fitness Programs," 78–79.

18. Loren E. Falkenberg, "Employee Fitness Programs: Their Impact on the Employee and the Organization," *Academy of Management Review* 12, no. 3 (July 1987): 511–522.

19. A. M. Paolone et al., "Results of Two Years of Exercise Training in Middle-Aged Men," *Physicians and Sports Medicine* 4 (December 1976): 77.

20. M. L. Collis, *Employee Fitness* (Ottawa, Canada: Minister of Supplies and Services, 1977), 81.

21. L. M. Catheart, "A Four-Year Study of Executive Health Risk," *Journal of Occupational Medicine* (May 1977): 357.

22. Sandra E. Edwards and Larry K. Gettmans, "The Effects of Employee Physical Fitness on Job Performance," *Personnel Administrator* 25, no. 11 (November 1980): 41–44, 60–61.

23. Steven H. Appelbaum and Barbara T. Shapiro, "The ABCs of EAPs," *Personnel* 7 (July 1989): 33–46.

24. William G. Wagner, "Assisting Employees with Personal Problems," *Personnel Administrator* 27, no. 11 (November 1982): 59–64.

25. Virginia K. Tyler, "Growth of EAPs Brings Certification," *Employee Benefit News* 1, no. 4 (May–June 1987): 1.

26. Fred Dickman and William G. Emener, "Employee Assistance Programs: Basic Concepts, Attributes and an Evaluation," *Personnel Administrator* (August 1982): 55–62.

27. Appelbaum and Shapiro, "The ABCs of EAPs," 43–45.

28. Roger K. Good, "What Bechtel Learned Creating an Employee Assistance Program," *Personnel Journal* 63, no. 9 (September 1984): 80–86.

29. Wagner, "Assisting Employees with Personal Problems," 59–64.

30. Donald V. Forrest, "Employee Assistance Programs in the 1980s: Expanding Career Options for Counselors," *Personnel and Guidance Journal* 62 (October 1983): 105–108.

31. "Experts Demand More Attention to Workplace Treatment," *Alcoholism & Drug Abuse* 8, no. 39 (October 1996): 3.

32. The Kemper Insurance Companies publish a number of excellent guidebooks on alcoholism and drug abuse. For information on obtaining these guides, write Public Relations, Kemper Insurance Companies, Long Grove, IL 60049.

33. Ian A. Miners, Nick Nykodym, and Diane M. Samerdyke-Traband, "Put Drug Detection to the Test," *Personnel Journal* 66, no. 8 (August 1987): 92–97.

34. Janet Deming, "Drug-Free Workplace Is Good Business," *HR Magazine* 35, no. 4 (April 1990): 61–62.

35. Joseph B. Treasfer, *The New York Times*, as reprinted in the *Omaha World-Herald* (November 21, 1993): 11-G.

36. Michael R. Carrell and Christina Heavrin, "Before You Drug Test . . ." *HR Magazine* 35, no. 6 (June 1990): 64-68.

37. *New York City Transit Authority* v. *Beazer*, 440 U.S. 568, 99 S. Ct. 1355, 59L. Ed. 2d 598 (1979).

38. *Minneapolis Star Tribune*, 295, NLRB 63 (1989).

39. David D. Schein, "How to Prepare Company Policy on Substance Abuse Control," *Personnel Journal* 65 (July 1986): 30–38.

40. Katie Hafner and Susan Garland, "Testing for Drug Use: Handle with Care," *Business Week* (March 28, 1988): 65.

41. *Skinner* v. *Railway Labor Executives Association*, 109 D. Vy. 1902 (1989).

42. Ibid.

43. *Shelby County Health Care Center*, 90 LA 1225 (1988).

44. *Consolidated Coal Co.*, 87 LA 111 (1986).

45. *Report of the U.S. Surgeon General* (Washington, DC: Office of the U.S. Surgeon General, 1986).

46. *Vickers* v. *Veterans Administration*, 29 FEP Cases 1197 (1982).

47. Philip R. Voluck, "Burning Legal Issues of Smoking in the Workplace," *Personnel Journal* 66, no. 6 (June 1987): 140–143.

48. Alfred Vogel, *Smoking and Productivity in the Workplace* (Washington, D.C.: Tobacco Institute, 1985).

49. William L. Weis, "No Smoking," *Personnel Journal* 63, no. 9 (September 1984): 53–58.

50. George Munchus, "An Update on Smoking: Employees' Rights and Employers' Responsibilities," *Personnel* 64 (August 1987): 46–56.

51. R. Craig Scott, "The Smoking Controversy Goes to Court," *Management World* 17, no. 1 (January–February 1988): 14.

52. Keith Key, "AIDS in the Workplace Survey: Wake-Up Call for American Businesses," *AIDS Weekly* (July 29, 1996): 18.

53. Ibid.

54. R. Riccio, and D. Zaenger, "Educating Employees about AIDS," *Personnel Management* 5 (1989): 28–30.

55. A. Nyamathi, and J. H. Flasherua, "Effectiveness of an AIDS Education Program on Knowledge, Attitudes, and Practices of State Employees, *American Association Occupational Health Nurses Journal* 37, no. 10 (1989): 403.

56. Ibid.

57. Jane Eshleman, R.N., M.S., "AIDS in the Workplace: Implementing an AIDS Policy," *Health Care Supervision* 13, no. 2 (1994): 51–57.

58. Ibid.

59. Lawrence Z. Lorber and J. Robert Kirk, *Fear Itself: A Legal and Personnel Analysis of Drug Testing, AIDS, Secondary Smoke, VDTs* (Washington, DC: ASPA Foundation, 1987), 25–33.

60. Robert A. Reber, Jerry A. Wallin, and David L. Duhan, "Safety Programs That Work," *Personnel Administrator* 34, no. 9 (September 1989): 66–69.

61. Jim Barr, "Cultivating Culture," *Occupational Health and Safety* 67, no. 1 (January 1998): 32.

62. Michael Moss, "Gray Area," *The Wall Street Journal* (June 17, 1997): A1, 10.

63. Jennifer Laabs, "Cashing in on Safety," *Workforce* (August 1997): 53–57.

64. D. S. Thelan et al., "Health and Safety in the Workplace: A New Challenge for Business Schools," *Personnel Administrator* 30, no. 10 (October 1985): 38.

65. Lester Bittel, *What Every Supervisor Should Know* (New York: McGraw Hill, 1974), 97.

66. R. L. Barnett and D. B. Breckman, "Safety Hierarchy," *Journal of Safety Research* 17 (1986): 50.

67. John A. Jenkins, "Self-Directed Workforce Promotes Safety," *HRMagazine* 35, no. 2 (February 1990): 54–56.

68. Ibid.

69. American Society for Personnel Administration, *Occupational Safety and Health Review* (Berea, OH: March 1979), 7.

70. Bruce D. May, "Hazardous Substances: OSHA Mandates the Right to Know," *Personnel Journal* 65, no. 8 (August 1986): 128–130.

71. Oswald Johnston and Bob Baker, "U.S. Takes Initial Steps On Ergonomic Standards," *The Los Angeles Times* (September 1, 1990): D1, 12.

72. Neal Templin, "GM Hopes to Awaken Profits by Operating Plants 24 Hours a Day," *The Wall Street Journal,* (October 6, 1993): A1.

73. Jerry Bishop, "Study Finds Night-Shift Workers More Likely to Have Miscarriages," *The Wall Street Journal* (January 11, 1993): A5.

74. Stephenie Overman, "Not the Usual 9 to 5," *HR Magazine* (January 1993): 47.

75. Jon Pierce and Randall Dunham, "The 12-Hour Work Day: A 48-Hour, Eight-Day Week," *Academy of Management Journal,* 35, no. 5 (1992): 1086–1098.

PART

V

EMPLOYEE RELATIONS

CHAPTER 15

EMPLOYEES AND LABOR UNIONS

CHAPTER OUTLINE

CHAPTER OBJECTIVES

(1) To identify and discuss the legislation that pertains to labor–management relationships, with emphasis on the legal rights of both unions and management.

(2) To describe how unions and their federation—the AFL-CIO—are organized and structured.

(3) To understand what takes place during a union organizing drive, with emphasis on the legal dos and don'ts for both labor and management.

(4) To explain how management may remain nonunion if it wishes to do so.

(5) To discuss why employees may work more effectively in teams and the union response to teams.

(6) To identify the stages of the collective bargaining process.

(7) To describe the major power tactics used by labor and management.

(8) To explain grievance procedures.

(9) To cite methods used to end an impasse.

(10) To identify the subject areas of labor contracts.

HR IN THE NEWS

UNION "SUMMER CAMP" FOR COLLEGE STUDENTS

The "in-your-face" confrontation style of the 1960s is being taught to a new breed of union organizers—college interns. The interns, called *summeristas,* are trained at 34 sites across the United States by the AFL–CIO. They attend a three-week intensive program that includes an overview of union history, current working conditions, and organizing techniques.

One intern, Ron Eldridge, a sophomore at Wichita State University, spent his summer organizing health care workers in St. Louis. He returned encouraged that "people are beginning to see the light" but surprised at the number of workers who were not receptive to his message, which had focused on the benefits of unionization.

A major goal of the program is to recruit union organizers to be trained at the AFL–CIO's Organizing Institute and return them to the field as full-time *organizers*. About 20 percent of the interns have signed up in past years. Even those who do not sign up may end up working for unions as lawyers or officers. At least, they "won't cross picket lines," and they will "look at power relationships and know that employees don't have real power unless they have their own [union] organization," according to Andrew Levin, a Williams College and Harvard Law School graduate who directed the Summeristas program.

Adapted from Robert Grossman, "AFL-CIO 'Summeristas' Fan Out to Sow Seeds for Unions' Future," *HR News* (September 1996): 1, 10–12.

There are many reasons why the study of unions is important for any student of HR management. Some students may even become union organizers as discussed in the chapter opening *HR in the News.* All students need to be aware of collective bargaining rights and the labor-relations process. The presence of a union has significant implications for the structure of an organization and for the management of human resources. For union employees, HR procedures and policies are largely shaped by a written agreement between management and the union. A labor administrator's job in a unionized firm will be markedly different from that same job in a nonunionized firm. Beyond the confines of one organization, the tone of an area's labor relations—whether they are perceived to be good or bad—can have significant impact on the economic health of that area.

A **union** is an organization of workers formed to further the economic and social interests of its members. There are three kinds of unions: industrial unions, trade unions, and employee associations. An **industrial union** is a union composed primarily of semiskilled blue-collar employees in the manufacturing industries such as automobiles, chemicals, and utilities. A **trade union** (sometimes called a *craft union)* generally includes among its membership skilled employees in a single trade, such as electricians, carpenters, and machinists. An **employee association** (or *fraternal order)* is generally composed of white-collar or professional employees such as teachers; police officers; and clerical, administrative, technical, and health care employees. **Collective bargaining** is a continuous process which includes contract administration and negotiation in good faith between the employer and the union on wages, benefits, hours of work, and other terms and conditions of employment. The result of negotiation is a written contract specifying the agreements that management and the union have been able to reach.

Why did workers in many manufacturing industries choose to unionize after the passage of the 1935 *Wagner Act?* At that time, many of the manufacturing plants were oppressive places of employment. Each morning, men lined up at the gate. If there was no work, they were sent home; if they were hired, it was for that day, not continuous employment. They never knew when their workday ended until the whistle blew. One autoworker recalls that some foremen were so intimidating that workers had to do the foremen's yardwork on the weekends and had to bring along their daughters to provide sexual services. The foremen managed by terror and hired prizefighters to keep control. Workers could not talk during lunch and had to raise their hands to go to the bathroom. The bathrooms did not have doors, and foremen followed workers who took a bathroom break to make sure the break was needed. Such indignities, as well as poor wages and unsafe working conditions, made workers ready to join unions.[1]

Today it is unlikely that many managers would consider using the intimidating tactics of the 1930s. In general, however, when workers today choose to unionize, it is due to the same frustration with management over issues such as wages, benefits, or fair treatment that caused their grandfathers to unionize. The labor union developed as a means by which individuals could unite and have the collective power to accomplish goals that could not be accomplished alone. Whether that power is used to increase take-home wages, to ensure job protection, to improve working conditions, or simply to sit across the bargaining table as an equal with the employer, members believe that *in union there is strength!*[2] The most common union means of demonstrating strength has been the strike.

A great deal of time and effort have been devoted to the question "Why do employees choose to join a union?" Studies have failed to find a list of reasons that apply to all organizing efforts. But there is general agreement among labor experts that certain issues are likely to lead to an organizing drive by employees. Among them are the following.[3] The *HR in the News* on the 1997–1999 UAW–GM, Ford, Chrysler Agreements illustrates the fact that job security remains a top union objective.

- ***Job security.*** Employees need to have a sense of job security and want to believe that management will not make unfair and arbitrary decisions about their employment. Further, they wish to be protected against layoffs and may look to the union to ensure that jobs are protected against such technological advances as automation and robotics. For example, the union could request that any employee displaced by an industrial robot be retrained and placed in another job. The most important element in job security is *seniority,* or the length of an employee's service. It is a common practice for HR decisions affecting the union employee—such as layoffs, recall, and promotions—to be made according to seniority.
- ***Wages and benefits.*** Bread-and-butter economic issues have always been an important concern for employees and are always important in unionization. Specifically, employees want to be paid fairly and receive wages on par with those of other workers in the community. Such benefits as hospitalization insurance, pensions, paid sick leave, vacations, and holidays are also significant issues in employees' decisions to organize. They may think that the union, with its collective power, will be able to achieve a higher level of wages and benefits than could employees acting individually.
- ***Working conditions.*** Employees want a healthy and safe working environment. Although federal legislation exists to protect health and safety in the

HR IN THE NEWS

HISTORIC UAW–GM, FORD, CHRYSLER 1997–1999 AGREEMENTS

A historic round of negotiations between the Big 3 automobile makers—General Motors, Ford, and Chrysler—and the United Automobile Aerospace and Agricultural Implement Workers of America (UAW) set a new precedent in the automobile industry. Negotiations in 1996 occurred with no "strike target" being declared by the UAW. In past years the UAW's designation of a strike target had always led to bitter strikes. But the cooperative negotiations of 1996 led to agreements that met all of the UAW's top concerns:

1. *Job security.* A guarantee that union employment will not fall below 95 percent of the level at the time of the signing.
2. *Outsourcing.* The automakers agreed to replace any jobs lost to outside suppliers, with a few exceptions for GM.
3. *Bonuses and wage hikes.* A lump-sum $2,000 bonus to eligible workers, with 3 percent wage increases in the last two years.
4. *Retirees.* Rare cost-of-living protection was provided to inactive members.
5. *Employee tuition plans.* First-time assistance up to $3,800 per year for high school, college, and other targeted courses of study.
6. *Veterans holiday.* The new holiday increases the annual paid holiday total to 16.

Adapted from *UAW–Chrysler Newsgram*, October 1996.

work place, employees may feel more secure knowing that a union is directly involved in safety and health issues.

- **Fair and just supervision.** The day is long gone when supervisors could rule their employees with an iron fist. A significant reason for the general shift in leadership styles from autocratic to people-oriented patterns is the insistence by unions that supervisors treat their employees fairly, justly, and respectfully. Most contracts specify that employees can only be disciplined for "just cause." A union employee who thinks he or she has been mistreated may file a written *grievance* against the employer, initiating a formal procedure through which the complaint will be heard by both union and management representatives.
- **Mechanism to be heard.** Employees often complain that they have little or no say in matters that affect their work. They often feel powerless to bring about changes that will benefit them. Through unionization, employees have a powerful collective voice that may be used to communicate to management their dissatisfactions and frustrations. The collective bargaining and grievance procedures ensure that union employees will have their wants, needs, and concerns brought before management without retaliation.

- **Need to belong.** The need to belong is strong in all human beings in both their personal and work lives. The union provides a mechanism for bringing people together not only to promote common job-related interests but also to provide programs, activities, and social events that create a strong bond among union members.

Overall, management's failure to include employees as part of the team, involve them in decision making, or even inform them of the business's status motivates employees to organize. The increase in Japanese owned and operated businesses in the United States, primarily in the highly unionized automotive industry, has shown a marked contrast in management styles. To increase productivity, Japanese managers cultivate workers' loyalty by shortening or eliminating the distance between them, by giving employees a voice in management, and by minimizing layoffs. Allowing workers to participate in job-related decisions has increased efficiency. Training workers for more than one job cultivates flexibility, job pride, and ultimately more productivity. The relationship at these plants between management and employees represented by a union is good; and at unorganized plants, unions are having difficulties convincing workers that they need a union.[4]

VIEW OF UNION MEMBERS

How do union members believe they benefit from union representation? To answer that question, the Louis Harris Organization conducted a national survey of 1,500 union and nonunion workers (see Table 15–1). The following basic questions were asked of individuals of both groups: What conditions in the workplace would change if workers lost their unions? Would conditions get better, worse, or stay the same? The results showed a substantial difference between union and nonunion workers. Union workers responded that conditions would get worse. Of the 10 workplace conditions in the survey, they expected the following to worsen: benefits (67 percent of those responding); pay (62 percent); job security (56 percent); treatment by supervisors (46 percent); worker participation in decision making (38 percent); and health and safety conditions (38 percent). Nonunion workers, however, predicted that if they became unionized, they would see pay and benefits "get better" (43 percent) but predicted no change in any nonwage conditions. Therefore, workers who are union members believe unions help them to improve a variety of important economic and noneconomic conditions, while nonunion workers seem unaware of any noneconomic benefit to union representation.[5]

UNION MEMBERSHIP

Union membership has declined since the 1970s, and this fall can be traced to several factors. (See Table 15–2.) The number of new workers included in organizational elections each year has declined significantly, as has the success rate of unions trying to win those new workers in organizational elections. Unions have also lost existing members by losing decertification elections.

In the traditional union stronghold, production jobs in metropolitan areas, the proportion of union to nonunion employees declined from 73 to 42 percent from 1961 to 1997. This substantial drop in the nation's large cities was not limited to production workers; nonsupervisory office clerical workers in unions also declined.[6]

The construction industry, once one of the strongholds of unions in the United States, has had a decline in union membership from about one-half in 1966 to less than 30 percent today. Possible reasons for the continued decline include (1) the rising number of union members working for nonunion contractors; (2) the gradual narrowing of the union–nonunion wage gap; and (3) the disappearance of the union sector's productivity advantage, which had enabled union contractors to pay higher union salaries and still compete with nonunion contractors. The *union productivity advantage* had been built on the successful recruitment, screening, and training programs in the construction unions. The perceived lack of a productivity advantage in union workers has given owners and contractors a strong incentive to switch from union to less costly nonunion labor in the construction industry.[7]

Avoiding unionization has become a major task of HR managers in such traditional nonunion areas as health care, financial planning, and insurance companies. But these white-collar workers are obvious targets for organizational campaigns. Their responsibilities and

TABLE 15–1	WHAT UNION EMPLOYEES BELIEVE THEIR UNIONS PROVIDE BETTER COMPARED TO NONUNION EMPLOYEES

ITEM	PERCENT RESPONDING
Better benefits	67
Better pay	62
Better job security	56
Better fair treatment by supervisors	46
Better participation in decision making	38
Better health and safety conditions	38

SOURCE: Adapted from Carol Keegan, "How Union Members and Nonunion View the Role of Unions," *Monthly Labor Review* 110, no. 8 (August 1987): 50–51.

TABLE 15–2   UNION MEMBERSHIP, 1935–1996

| | | PERCENTAGE OF LABOR FORCE | |
YEAR	TOTAL MEMBERSHIP (THOUSANDS)	TOTAL	NONAGRICULTURAL
1935	3,728	6.7	13.2
1940	8,944	15.5	26.9
1945	14,796	21.9	35.5
1950	15,000	22.3	31.5
1955	17,749	**24.7**	**33.2**
1960	18,177	23.6	31.4
1965	18,519	22.4	28.4
1970	20,751	22.6	27.3
1975	**21,090**	20.7	25.5
1980	20,100	18.8	23.0
1985	17,400	17.8	19.1
1990	17,000	16.8	18.5
1996	16,200	15.0	16.4

SOURCE: U.S. Department of Labor.

education cause their expectations for respect and participation at their workplace to be higher even than those of assembly-line workers.[8] Clerical employees, the majority of whom are women, may be increasingly attracted to organizing, especially when the union organization is a young one geared to their demographic arrangement.[9]

What union in North America has the most members? The Teamsters? The Steelworkers? AFSCME? No! The National Education Association (NEA) is the largest (see Table 15–3). The NEA is largely made up of elementary and secondary school teachers. Although the teachers' union may not be as well-known as some others, it is extremely well organized, very political, and consistently keeps its 2.2 million members informed on important issues and elections. In fact, at the 1996 Democratic National Convention in Chicago, roughly 10 percent—more than 400 delegates—were members of the NEA. Indeed, some people believe that the teachers' unions (including the American Federation of Teachers, with 850,000 members) are the core of the Democratic Party. In addition to a sizable budget of over $200 million, the NEA has a strong political asset in its 2.2 million members, most of whom are college-educated and politically aware. Their summer break provides an excellent time to become active in teachers' causes.[10]

UNION GOALS

The goals of unions have not changed significantly in almost 200 years. In a broad sense, the primary goal of any union is to promote the interests of its membership. Through collective bargaining and lobbying for labor legislation, union leaders enhance their members' standard of living and improve many conditions that surround their work.

UNION SECURITY

Union security, or the ability to grow and prosper in either good or poor economic times, is organized labor's foremost goal. Labor legislation has created the following **union security provisions** (except the closed shop) that organized labor may collectively bargain for:

- *Union shop.* All new employees in a union shop must join the union within a specified time, usually 30 days. About 20 states have passed *right-to-work* laws which prohibit compulsory union membership but allow other forms of unions. Most collective bargaining agreements provide for a union shop.

TABLE 15–3   LARGEST NORTH AMERICAN UNIONS

ORGANIZATION	NUMBER OF ACTIVE MEMBERS
National Education Association	2,200,000
International Brotherhood of Teamsters, Chauffeurs, Warehousemen and Helpers of America	1,300,000
American Federation of State, County, and Municipal Employees	1,200,000
United Food and Commercial Workers International	1,200,000
Service Employees International Union	950,000
American Federation of Teachers	850,000
United Automobile, Aerospace and Agriculture Implement Workers of America	800,000
International Brotherhood of Electrical Workers	750,000
United Steelworkers of America	700,000
Communications Workers of America	700,000
Laborers and International Union of North America	700,000
International Association of Machinists and Aerospace Workers	500,000
Carpenters and Joiners of America	500,000

SOURCE: *The World Almanac and Book of Facts 1995.* © 1994 by K-III Reference Corporated, Mahwan, NJ.

- *Agency shop.* No employee is required to join a union. However, all nonunion employees must give the union an amount equal to union dues to provide their share of the union's expenses. This arrangement is believed to be reasonable since all employees within the bargaining unit (union and nonunion) receive the same negotiated wages and benefits and must be represented by the union in grievance cases.

  A landmark 1992 court decision, however, provided that dues collected from nonunion members can only be spent on collective bargaining activities, and not union activities such as political campaigns or lobbying efforts. The National Right to Work Foundation cheered the court decision because it forbids unions to use funds provided by nonunion employees for pro-union political activities.[11]
- *Maintenance-of-membership shop (M-O-M).* Employees are not required to join the union in a *maintenance-of-membership shop.* However, employees who do join must remain in the union until the contract expires or until a designated "escape" period occurs.
- *Closed shop.* The new employee must be a union member at the time of hiring. While the closed shop is illegal, it exists in practice, particularly in the con-

struction and printing industries. The practice is promoted by hiring through the union's own placement services and by management's desire to avoid the trouble that may accompany the hiring of nonunion employees.
- *Open shop.* No employee is required to join or contribute money to a labor organization as a condition for employment in an open shop.

JOB SECURITY

Job security is one of the primary goals of unions. Without jobs, union goals of higher wages and greater benefits are meaningless. Unions provide for job security by negotiating for any of the following contract clauses:

Seniority System   A set of rules governing promotion and layoff/recall opportunities on the basis of service with an employer is called a **seniority system.** It is by far the most commonly negotiated means of measuring service and comparing employees for promotion and employment decisions.

Seniority is perhaps the most important measure of job security to employees, and the issue of seniority is popular among unions and viewed as critical to job security. Seniority is highly visible because it is so easy to define and measure. Normally, it is calculated in terms of days, beginning with the employee's date of hire and, with a few exceptions, continues over the years during the employee's tenure. Union negotiators will vehemently claim that management, in the absence of a job seniority system, will make promotion, layoff, and other decisions based solely on possible short-run cost savings or individual biases rather than the objective criteria that seniority easily provides.

Subcontracting (or outsourcing)

What is subcontracting? It has been termed the "twilight zone" of management rights in collective bargaining, and is considered a headache by both labor and management. Basically, **subcontracting** or **outsourcing** may be defined as arranging to make goods or perform services with another firm that could be accomplished by the bargaining unit employees within the company's current facilities.[12]

An example of a contract clause limiting the ability of management to subcontract is provided in Figure 15–1. In this example, management may only subcontract work to another employer if the second employer also has a contract with the union.

Retraining Rights

The need to stay competitive with nonunion and foreign businesses has caused union leaders to accept technology changes as necessary and normal conditions of work. Today, rather than oppose technological change, negotiators anticipate it and bargain for advance notice, **retaining rights,** and outplacement assistance for affected workers.

SOCIAL ACTION

Today many unions advocate goals that affect society as a whole. These goals are not achieved through the normal collective bargaining process, but by lobbying for federal and state legislation and government-sponsored programs and policies. As the major voice of labor, the AFL–CIO takes a firm stand on certain social, political, and economic goals. Consider which of the goals shown in Figure 15–2 are political and which are simply contractural.

LABOR– MANAGEMENT LEGISLATION

Beginning in the early 1930s, labor–management relations have been heavily regulated by federal and state legislation. Prior to this period, lawmakers took a laissez-faire attitude toward unions and management and relied primarily on common law to govern labor–management relations. *Common law*, a heritage of the English legal system, is the body of law based on court decisions, custom, and precedent. In contrast, *statute law* is the body of laws established by legislative acts. When enacting the various statutes, Congress was reacting to public opinion and the special needs of labor and management.[13]

FIGURE 15–1   SUBCONTRACTING PROVISION

ARTICLE 6—SUBCONTRACTING

SECTION A: The Employer agrees that where portions of the Employer's contracts for construction, repair, or alteration are sublet or assigned to subcontractors, the subcontractor shall be required by the Employer to conform to all of the terms and conditions of this Agreement. The Union will not recognize a contractor's manpower request without first having a signed Agreement.

The Employer will not subcontract any work within the jurisdiction of the Union which is to be performed at the job site except to a subcontractor who holds an Agreement with the Union, or who agrees in writing, prior to or at the time of the execution of his sub-contract, to be bound by the terms of this Agreement.

SECTION B: A contractor, company, or Employer acting in the capacity of a Construction Manager agrees that it, or any of its subcontractors, will not contract or subcontract carpenter work to be done at the site of construction, alteration, repair of a building, or structure except to a person, firm, or corporation party to a current Labor Agreement with the Union.

SOURCE: *Agreement* between the Kentucky State District Council of Carpenters, Local Union 472 and Tri-State Contractors Association, 1995–1998.

FIGURE 15–2   SOCIAL, POLITICAL, AND ECONOMIC GOALS OF THE AFL–CIO

8-hour Day
Paid Sick Leave
Higher Wages
Health Insurance
Overtime Pay
Pensions
Safer Working Conditions
Paid Holidays
Job Security
Severance Pay
Paid Vacations
Maternity Leave

The preceding was brought to you by the men and women of the Unions of the AFL-CIO who won these benefits at the bargaining table and set the standard for all working Americans.

The new Union Yes "Benefits" commercial premiered nationwide on Solidarity Day, 1991.

SOURCE: AFL–CIO.

RAILWAY LABOR ACT (1926)

In 1926, the Railway Labor Act gave railroad workers the right to organize and bargain collectively. It prohibited interference by employers. The act was amended in 1934 to include the airline industry. The provisions of the act foreshadowed those of the Wagner Act of 1935.

NORRIS-LAGUARDIA ACT (1932)

Throughout organized labor's early history, union power was often undercut by *injunctions,* court orders requiring performance or restraint of a particular act. Management frequently obtained a temporary or permanent injunction prohibiting a strike or picketing. In 1932, the Norris-LaGuardia Act expressly forbade the federal courts from issuing injunctions in labor disputes, except to maintain law and order during a union activity. The act also forbade employers from enforcing a *yellow dog contract.* Such a contract stipulated as a condition of employment that an employee was not a union member and would not join a union. (Labor believed only a "yellow dog" would accept a job under such terms.)

NATIONAL LABOR RELATIONS ACT (1935)

The 1929 stock market crash plunged the United States into a major depression, the worst in its history. The impact of the Great Depression on workers was devastating. One-third of the country's workforce was unemployed. The labor movement made more emphatic efforts to organize and demand recognition and became more politically active. The severity of conditions led to public sympathy for its problems.

Senator Robert Wagner, a champion of labor who had President Roosevelt's support, proposed an act that recognized employees' rights to organize and bargain collectively. A quasi-judicial tribunal with the power and authority to enforce its own orders would be created. While the act purported to protect the public from the disruption of interstate commerce resulting from labor disputes, Senator Wagner stated that it would also give the employee freedom. Labor–management relations generally improved after the passage of this historic act, and union membership rapidly grew to levels previously undreamed of by labor leaders.

The original National Labor Relations Act of 1935 is more widely known as the **Wagner Act** because it was sponsored by New York Senator Wagner. The Wagner Act is often called the Magna Carta of organized labor. In essence, the act protects a worker's right to join a union without the employer's interference. Bringing broad powers and sweeping reform to the labor movement, the act encouraged the movement's spectacular growth between 1935 and the early 1950s. Important provisions of the act include the following:

1 The employer may not interfere with, restrain, or coerce employees in the exercise of their right to join unions and bargain collectively through representatives of their own choosing.

2 The employer may not dominate or interfere with the formation or administration of labor unions.

3 The employer may not discriminate against the employee in any condition of employment for taking part in legal union activities.

4 The employer may not fire or discriminate against the employee in any condition of employment for taking part in legal union activities.

5 The employer may not fire or discriminate against the employee for charging an unfair labor practice against the company.

6 The employer may not refuse to bargain collectively with employee representatives in good faith.

National Labor Relations Board The **National Labor Relations Board (NLRB)** was created to administer and enforce the Wagner Act. The National Labor Relations Board is an independent agency of the federal government; members are presidential appointees. The first of the NLRB's two main functions is to investigate charges of **unfair labor practices (ULPs).** Basically, an unfair labor practice exists when either the employer or the union violates any provision of labor law. For example, a union will likely charge the employer with an unfair labor practice if the employer bribes employees to vote against the union or discriminates against employees who hold prounion sentiments. Examples of activities that may result in a charge of unfair labor practice against a union include instigating violence on a picket line, refusing to bargain in good faith with the employer, charging union employees excessive initiation fees or dues, and featherbedding. If the NLRB finds an employer guilty of a violation and the employer fails to alter certain practices, the board will seek legal action through the U.S. Court of Appeals. Employers may appeal the decisions of the board.

A second function of the board is to conduct certification elections by secret ballot to determine whether employees will be represented by a union. The election process will be discussed later in this chapter.

LABOR–MANAGEMENT RELATIONS ACT (1947)

While the Wagner Act may be appropriately called pro-labor, the Labor–Management Relations Act—more commonly known as the **Taft-Hartley Act**—is decidedly pro-management. Its purpose was to create a balance of power between unions and employers. During the decade following the passage of the Wagner Act in 1935, a feeling developed that unions had grown too big and too influential, that their escalating power had to be brought under control. The act that was sponsored by Senator Robert Taft and Representative Frederick Hartley actually amends the Wagner Act. Important provisions of the Taft-Hartley Act include the following:

● The union may not coerce or restrain employees from exercising their bargaining rights. For example, the union may not make false statements to employees during organizing drives.

● The union may not cause an employer to discriminate against an employee in order to encourage or discourage union membership.

● The union may not refuse to bargain in good faith with the employer.

● The union may not engage in **featherbedding.** The U.S. Supreme Court has decided that it is lawful to require employers to pay for make-work activities even though they may be inefficient or ineffective.

Section 14b From labor's perspective, a particularly troublesome provision in labor law is Section 14b of the Taft-Hartley Act. This section allows individual states to pass legislation that bars any form of compulsory union membership (union shops); such states are known as **right-to-work** states. Only 21 states, mostly located in the South and Southwest (see Figure 15–3), have passed such legislation.

Section 14b has long been a battleground between organized labor and right-to-work advocates. Labor leaders have for years attempted to repeal it. On the other side is the National Right-to-Work Committee, which works to advance the right-to-work movement and presses for federal right-to-work legislation.

FIGURE 15–3   RIGHT-TO-WORK STATES

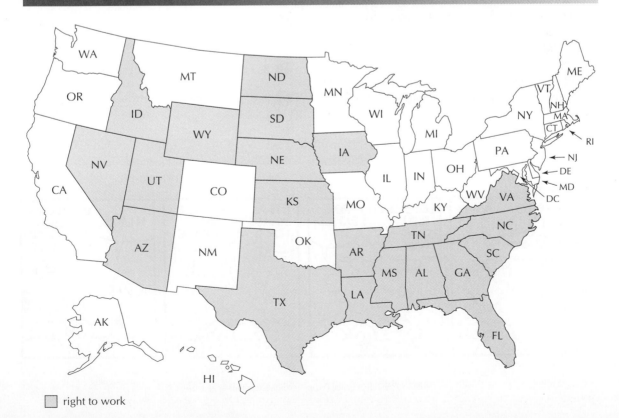

☐ right to work

Opponents contend that right-to-work legislation is an attempt to change the bargaining power at the negotiating table in management's favor. In addition, "right-to-work" as a slogan is misleading. Such laws guarantee no one a job and, in their opinion, confer rights only on employers.[14] The phrase implies the union's concomitant right to prevent a person from working. According to union advocates, the requirement of union membership as a condition of employment is no more restrictive of an individual's freedom than the requirement of specific hours of work. Union members contend that employees should support the union primarily because all union and nonunion employees alike receive benefits through collective bargaining agreements and unions are required to represent both union and nonunion employees in open shops.[15]

A 1986 right-to-work referendum election was held in Idaho. Both sides waged extensive media campaigns and focused the debate on the issues of lower wages and growth in the Idaho economy. Whether someone should be forced to join a union became a peripheral issue in the campaign. The voters chose to keep the new right-to-work law by a narrow margin—50.2 percent. Idaho had been targeted by the National Right-to-Work Committee since 1976, when it successfully pushed passage of the Louisiana right-to-work law.[16] Right-to-work states have several characteristics that differ from union-shop states. These characteristics include (1) low union membership, (2) little heavy industry, and (3) a high level of agriculture. Idaho shared these characteristics with the 20 right-to-work states.[17]

Section 10(j): Court Injunctions Section 10(j) of the NLRA permits the NLRB to seek a federal court injunction in situations in which the action of the union or employer might cause substantial harm to the other side. The court in response can then order either party to resume or desist from a certain action. In general, the NLRB must demonstrate that the unfair labor practice, if left alone, will irreparably harm the other side before a final NLRB decision can be administered, or "justice delayed is justice denied." In the 1994–1996 baseball strike, for example, players would have found their abilities slipping with increasing age, so a U.S. District Court ordered the owners to abide by the old contract and to "play ball" until a new one was reached. Some baseball fans believed that the NLRB saved the game (see Figure 15–4). Most Section 10(j) cases fall within the following 13 categories:[18]

1. Union organizing campaign interference.

2. Subcontracting work to outside employers.

3. Withdrawing recognition of the union.

4. Undermining or denigrating the members of the union's bargaining team.

5. Granting exclusive representation to a minority union.

6. Successor employer refusing to recognize and bargain.

7. Bad faith conduct during negotiations.

8. Picketing violence.

FIGURE 15–4   DRABBLE

SOURCE: DRABBLE © United Feature Syndicate, reprinted by permission.

⑨ Strike or picketing notice or waiting period violations.

⑩ Employer refusal to allow protected activity on private property.

⑪ Retaliation for NLRB processes.

⑫ Shut down of operations during litigation.

⑬ Union coercion to achieve unlawful object.

Today we refer to the combination of the Taft-Hartley and Wagner Acts as the **National Labor Relations Act (NLRA).**

LABOR–MANAGEMENT REPORTING AND DISCLOSURE ACT (1959)

During the 1950s, unionism's reputation was tarnished considerably when a series of exposés uncovered corruption and racketeering in unions, particularly in the Teamsters Union. During 1952 and 1953, the state of New York found widespread racketeering on the New York City waterfront involving the International Longshoremen's Union. The investigation, which uncovered gross mismanagement of the union pension fund, was a principal factor underlying the passage of the Welfare and Pension Plans Disclosure Act of 1958.

The most widely publicized account of union corruption was the investigation held by the McClellan Committee in the U.S. Senate. The committee heard 1526 witnesses in 270 days of hearings. Over half of the testimony was devoted to racketeering and corruption in the Teamsters Union. The committee hearings ultimately led to the expulsion from the AFL–CIO of the Teamsters Union and the Laundry and Bakery and Confectionery Workers Union. The committee hearings influenced the passage of the Labor–Management Reporting and Disclosure Act of 1959, more commonly known as the **Landrum-Griffin Act.** Important provisions of the act include the following:

- **Creation of a "bill of rights" for union members.** The act provided equal rights for union members to attend, participate, and vote in meetings; the right to meet and express any views or opinions about union business and candidates; the right to be free of unreasonably high dues, fees, and assessments; the right to testify against and sue the union for violation of their rights; and the right to inspect copies of collective bargaining agreements.
- **Reporting requirements.** The act requires unions to submit an annual financial report covering assets, liabilities, income, expenses, and so on to the Secretary of Labor, who must approve the report.
- **Election safeguards.** The act set forth the ground rules for proper union conduct during elections. For example, ballots must be secret and every member in good standing must be allowed a vote.
- **Restrictions on officers.** The act disallows convicted felons from holding union office for five years after conviction. The act also requires union officials to be bonded.

UNION STRUCTURE AND ORGANIZATION

There are approximately 100 national and international unions in America. *National unions* have collective bargaining agreements with different employers in two or more states; *international unions* are headquartered in the United States but have members in Canada.

A union is a private, nonprofit organization whose primary purpose is to advance the interests of its members. In many respects, a union closely resembles the structure and operation of a business firm. Union leaders must plan and organize activities, recruit and hire for union positions, create and manage a budget, influence and motivate other union officials and the rank-and-file membership, see that union goals are met, and be sure that union policies, procedures, and rules are followed. In particular, they must be able to influence and persuade management representatives when a new union contract is being negotiated. A union's function contains basic elements common to all organizations: Union goals must be created, jobs must be defined, leaders must be given responsibilities and authority, and departments must be formed.

LOCAL UNIONS

Most local unions are affiliated with national or international unions. Local unions receive their charters from the national union, which may disband or suspend the local. Less than 2 percent of all local unions are completely independent; these generally serve a single employer or small geographical territory.

Local union leaders are elected by their members, usually for a one- or three-year term. While local union leadership varies by size and union, a typical leadership group consists of a president, vice president, secretary, and treasurer. In very large locals, union officials work full time for the local union. More often, however, the officials have a full-time job and conduct union affairs on their own time and on time allowed by a company during working hours.

Perhaps the local union's most critical function is to negotiate a contract with employers. The contract is most frequently negotiated by either the president of the local or the business agent; sometimes the contract is negotiated by representatives from the national union. A *business agent* is an elected, full-time, salaried official who represents a *local union.* The agent may also be heavily involved in handling employee grievances or leading union members during a strike.

Another important local union member is the *shop steward,* sometimes referred to as a *committeeman* or *grievance person.* As the last term suggests, the steward acts as the union representative in processing grievances against management. The handling of grievances will be discussed in detail later in the chapter.

NATIONAL AND INTERNATIONAL UNIONS

Like a corporate headquarters with plants and offices scattered throughout the United States, national or international unions direct and support local unions. Direction and support are achieved by creating major policies and maintaining important functions and programs. Some of those policies, functions, and programs include the following:

- Creating uniform contract provisions regarding wages or seniority for local unions in a given area or industry.

- Assisting the local union in contract negotiations.

- Training local union officials in union management and administration.

- Creating and administering strike funds to support local union members on strike.

- Providing data collection services for cost-of-living data, wage data, and so on.

- Increasing union membership by organizing non-union employees.

National or international unions often employ elected officials and staff specialists appointed by top union leaders. Economists, lawyers, and public relations specialists are among those who provide valuable services in promoting the union effort.

INDEPENDENT UNIONS

The majority of national or international unions are affiliated with the AFL–CIO. Some unions decided at their inception to remain autonomous and thus never joined the AFL or the CIO; they are called **independent unions.** Others, such as the Teamsters in 1957, were expelled from the AFL for corruption; 11 unions were expelled from the CIO. In 1987 the Teamsters rejoined the AFL–CIO, ending one of the deepest rifts in the labor movement.

THE AFL–CIO

A single federation of autonomous labor unions, the **American Federation of Labor–Congress of Industrial Organizations (AFL–CIO)** influences the activities of its member unions and the labor movement as a whole. Eighty-nine of the national and international unions in the United States are AFL–CIO affiliates. The structure of the AFL–CIO is shown in Figure 15–5.

The national and international affiliates operate autonomously, retaining decentralized decision-making authority over their own affairs. AFL–CIO officials are not authorized to call strikes, influence the negotiating process, or control the behavior of affiliate leaders.

THE ORGANIZING DRIVE

The impetus to organize employees may come from two sources. First, the workers may be dissatisfied with their pay or work conditions and initiate contact with the union. Such is typically the case. Second, workers may be contacted by a *union organizer,* a fulltime, salaried staff member who generally represents a national union. As the job title suggests, the union organizer increases union membership and strength by organizing groups of workers who are not presently unionized. An organizing drive usually follows the series of events shown in Figure 15–6.

The union's goal is to organize workers and bring them into the union. Labor's strategy is to convince the workers that union membership will bring them benefits they do not presently enjoy. Union organizers may suggest that union representation will result in higher pay, more benefits, better working conditions, and greater fairness in promotions, job transfers, and layoffs. Speaking proudly of the benefits and work improvements they have achieved for other workers, union organizers often cite impressive and convincing statistics about wage gains achieved through collective bargaining. To tell the union side of the story, labor advocates hold formal meetings at the local union hall and encourage supporters to spread the word informally about the

FIGURE 15–5 THE STRUCTURE OF THE AFL–CIO

AMERICAN FEDERATION OF LABOR AND CONGRESS OF INDUSTRIAL ORGANIZATIONS

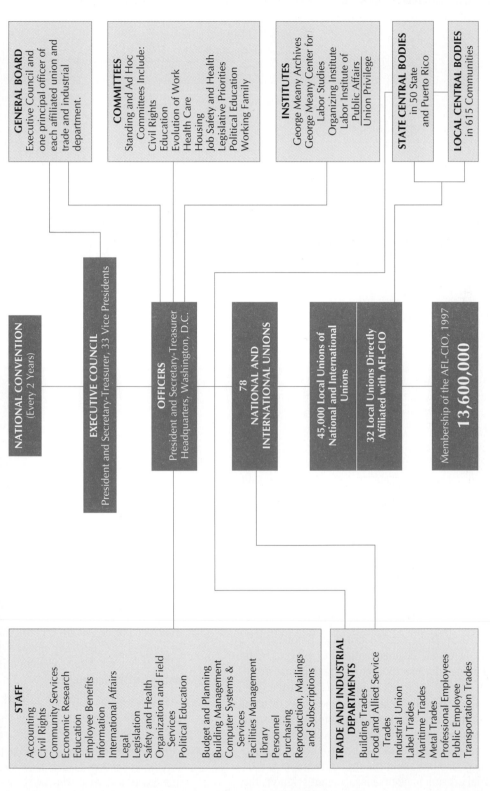

SOURCE: Labor Net, AFL–CIO Home Page, 1997.

FIGURE 15–6   THE ORGANIZING PROCESS

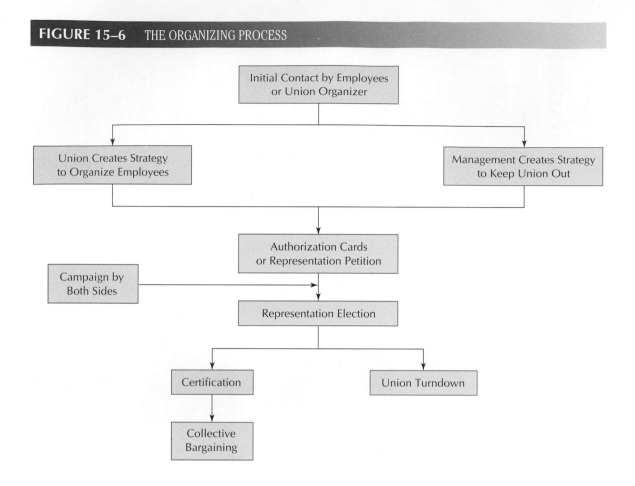

benefits a union would bring to the employees' place of work. A new breed of organizers today is largely female and minority. Labor has also targeted industries and even cities. (see *HR in the News:* "Big Labor's Next Target"). Pro-union handbills and flyers are often passed to workers as they leave work or go to lunch.

Management's goal is simply to keep the union out of the work place. Their strategy is to convince the workers that unionization will do them more harm than good. Management may attempt to assure workers that their present pay and benefits are competitive and may show data to prove it. Emphasizing a philosophy of fair dealings with all employees, management may discuss the union's involvement in violent or corrupt activities if such has been the case. Management will also enumerate the costs of union membership, which include initiation fees, dues, and other assessments. The workers will be reminded that wages will be lost should a strike occur. Management may also talk about the loss of freedom and the potential erosion in labor–management relations that unionization might bring.

ILLEGAL ORGANIZATIONAL ACTIVITIES

Throughout the **organizing drive,** emotions often run high on both sides, and both union and management supporters often make passionate and dramatic arguments to further their causes. To ensure that both labor and management play fair during the organizing drive, labor legislation has spelled out in detail illegal campaign tactics. During the organizing drive, union representatives or pro-labor employees cannot do the following:[19]

- Solicit employees where they are working unless employees are normally allowed to converse while they work. Oral solicitation is acceptable during breaks and lunch.

- Distribute union literature in work areas; non-work areas typically include lunch rooms and break areas.

- Offer an employee free union membership before the election unless free membership is granted to everyone who joins the union up to the time the first contract is negotiated.

BIG LABOR'S NEXT TARGET: LAS VEGAS

The AFL–CIO decided in 1997 to mount its largest organizing campaign in decades. The target is not a single manufacturing or service industry, but the city of Las Vegas. If the campaign is successful, Las Vegas will become the symbol of a "revitalized labor movement" according to labor expert, Harley Shaiken. The organizational effort is focusing on three industries that are prominent in the town: hotels, hospitals, and construction.

At first glance, Las Vegas might appear to be an unlikely target because it is in a very conservative right-to-work state. But as Mark Smith, president of the Chamber of Commerce notes, it has a booming economy—and employers tend to not fight as hard in boom times; its jobs cannot be moved elsewhere; and it is a very "visible" city, which should give the AFL-CIO a great deal of free publicity if it is successful. The AFL–CIO plans on spending at least $6 million on paid organizers with the materials unions, which are involved spending millions more. The unions involved include the Hotel and Restaurant Employees Union, the Service Employees International Union, and the Building Trades Council. The AFL–CIO money "allows us to do things on a scale we couldn't do before," says Mark Kay Hewiz, a union organizer. The final result—which will not be known for years—could be a good indication of the future rate of union growth in the United States.

Adapted from G. Pascal Zachary, "AFL–CIO Mounts Organizing Drive in Las Vegas," *The Wall Street Journal* (January 27, 1997): A1, 4.

- Offer excessive attendance prizes to employees who attend a campaign rally. Payment of a sum of money to each participant is an obvious infraction of the rule.

- Make substantial misrepresentations. While both management and labor are allowed a generous amount of puffing (promises and propaganda), the *Hollywood Ceramics* rule forces the election to be set aside if either side makes a "substantial misrepresentation on a material fact made at a time when the other party has inadequate time to respond and correct the misrepresentation."

During the organizing drive, representatives of employers cannot do the following:[20]

- Discipline or threaten employees who engage in lawful solicitation or distribution of union material.

- Prohibit existing employees from legal solicitation and distribution activities at work. Management can, if it desires, prohibit outside union organizers from entering the premises.

- Engage in anti-union rhetoric before a mass audience 24 hours before an election. However, the 24 hours rule does not forbid talks to individuals and small groups.

- Speak to employees about organizing in "areas of management authority" such as the bosses' offices or management conference rooms. Such a setting is thought by the NLRB to be overly intimidating.

- Tell employees that absolutely no good will come if the union gets in. Called the *futility doctrine,* this prohibits the employer from making statements suggesting that it is futile for the employees to unionize.

- Promise certain benefits if the union loses. Further, a raise in pay or an increase in benefits cannot be given during the drive unless the increase was planned before the election. Similarly, existing benefits or a planned increase in benefits cannot be rescinded because of the union campaign.

- Keep track of employees' union activities or give the impression that pro-union employees are under surveillance.

REPRESENTATION ELECTION

Before an election is called by the NLRB, the union must provide a "showing of support" by getting at least 30 percent of the employees to sign **authorization cards** or a *representation petition.* The card, as shown in Figure 15–7, states that the employee designates the union as

FIGURE 15–7   A UNION AUTHORIZATION CARD

University of Louisville
American Association of University Professors

I, _Frank E. Kuzmits_, hereby designate the University of Louisville Chapter of the American Association of University Professors to represent my professional and economic interests in collective bargaining.

Date: 8/1/99 _____
Signature

Management _____
Department

the bargaining agent. If more than 50 percent of the employees sign authorization cards, the union may formally request the employer to recognize it as the employees' bargaining agent. The employer still generally refuses to recognize the union; thus the union must then formally petition the NLRB to hold an election.

The NLRB oversees the **representation election** to ensure that at least 30 percent of the employees in the bargaining unit have signed authorization cards and that no illegal campaign activities have taken place. At this time, the NLRB investigator also defines the **bargaining unit.** The bargaining unit is the group of employees the union will represent and bargain for if the election favors the union. Although the NLRB considers several factors in deciding the makeup of the bargaining unit, the most important is the *community of interest principle;* that is, the more employees have in common, the more likely the board is to find that they constitute a valid bargaining unit. Specific factors examined by the board include similarity of work performed, geographical proximity of workers, job integration, similarity of working conditions, prevailing wage rates and benefits, and whether employees work under a common management group. If the union wins the election, all employees within the bargaining unit—both union and nonunion employees—will be represented by the union. Management cannot treat the union employee any differently than the nonunion employee.

CERTIFICATION AND DECERTIFICATION

The union becomes the official bargaining agent for the employees if it receives over 50 percent of the votes cast in a secret election. If the union does not receive at least 50 percent of the votes cast, it is not allowed to petition the NLRB for another representation election for at least a year.

Under the provisions of the Taft-Hartley Act, an NLRB **certification** is valid only for a one-year period. After that time, employees (but not the employer) within the bargaining unit may petition the NLRB for a **decertification election.** In a process similar to the representation election, the NLRB will conduct a vote if at least 30 percent of the employees sign the petition. If labor fails to receive a majority vote, it loses its bargaining rights, and no additional elections within the bargaining unit may be held for one year. The purpose of the decertification election is to allow employees to rid themselves of a union in which they no longer have faith or confidence. As would be expected, employers will campaign strongly for the defeat of a union, and they may use any lawful method to achieve that end.

Until the 1970s, about 95 percent of elections were certification—and unions won over 50 percent of elections. Today, however, decertification elections represent 25 percent of elections—and unions win only 38 percent of elections. The combined effects of more elections being decertification (thus unions must win just to keep current membership) and their sliding percentage of victories has had a double-barreled effect on union membership.[21]

THE COLLECTIVE BARGAINING PROCESS

Collective bargaining comprises two broad and highly related processes: contract negotiations and contract administration (the day-to-day enforcement of the contract). Grievance handling is part of contract administration. The first process involves activities associated with the creation of the labor–management contract. In essence, the contract spells out the rules of the game: seniority rights, wages and benefits, work rules (see *HR in the News:* "Job Security and Cooperation: The Negotiation Philosophy of the 1990s"), disciplinary procedures, and so on. But rules need interpretation and enforcement; therefore, the collective bargaining process includes a "judicial" mechanism for handling what are believed to be violations of the labor agreement. These steps, referred to as the **grievance procedure,** are an important part of most modern labor–management contracts. The first part of this section discusses the steps involved and the issues related to contract negotiations; the second part examines grievance handling, with attention devoted to how grievances may be kept to a minimum.

CONTRACT NEGOTIATIONS

Unions and employers may conduct contract negotiations within two basic structures: single-employer bar-

gaining and multiple-employer bargaining. Most labor agreements involve a single employer and a single union. Should a single employer have several plants in various parts of the country, the union may represent employees at all plants with one *master agreement* or only represent a single plant if it is the bargaining unit. Certain issues (normally a small number) are left to local negotiation. For example, a basic agreement between the United Auto Workers (UAW) and General Motors covers employees at all GM plants, and each plant negotiates a *supplemental agreement* with the local union.

A large single employer with diverse activities and manufacturing processes will generally negotiate contracts with more than one union. For example the publishers of the *Louisville Courier-Journal* have in the past contracted with six unions: the Electrical Workers, Graphic Arts, Mailers, Machinists, Printing and Graphic Communications, and Typographical workers. The structures involved in *single-employer bargaining* are shown in Figure 15–8.

In *multiple-employer bargaining,* two or more employers join together to bargain with one or more unions. Two types of multiple-employer bargaining are

HR IN THE NEWS

JOB SECURITY AND COOPERATION: THE NEGOTIATION PHILOSOPHY OF THE 1990S

For a period of about 50 years from World War II to the 1990s, the U.S. automobile industry was subjected to strikes and hard times each time labor agreements with the United Auto Workers Union (UAW) expired. In the 1970s and 1980s, especially, the UAW announced which automaker was the "strike target." In most cases, it was the most profitable of the "Big 3" (GM, Ford, Chrysler). After the agreement expired, a costly strike would idle hundreds of thousands workers and disrupt production. Then, once a new agreement had been reached, the UAW would demand similar agreements from the other automakers—to follow the "pattern" set by the first. The year 1996, however, proved to be a historic turning point in UAW–automaker negotiations. In that year, a "no-strike" philosophy was followed in several related industries.

Ford Motor Company was chosen as the "negotiation target"—not the *strike* target. The UAW wanted it to be clearly known that no strikes were planned. Instead, a historic agreement with Ford was reached in record time. The agreement provided the UAW with its top priority: *95 percent* of the 105,025 UAW–Ford jobs were *guaranteed* to be maintained, with no layoffs, downsizing, or shutdowns during the three-year agreement. Another historic precedent in the Ford–UAW agreement was the wage package: 3 percent raises in years two and three with a $2,000 *lump-sum* payment in the first year, thus no first-year wage raise. Chrysler Corporation followed the Ford pattern within weeks. Chrysler Chairman Robert Eaton noted the historic changes in the negotiations: "These negotiations were very different. . . . We never faced a strike deadline. . . . They produced very, very good results for both sides. It was very professional on both sides."

Adapted from "Chrysler, UAW Forge Agreement," Associated Press as reported in the *Omaha World-Herald* (September 30, 1996): 12.

FIGURE 15–8   THE STRUCTURES INVOLVED IN SINGLE-EMPLOYER BARGAINING

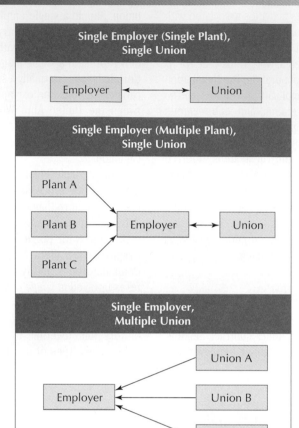

common today. One involves contract negotiations be-tween an association of two or more employers and a union council representing a group of craft or industrial unions. This bargaining arrangement is common in the construction industry, in which all unionized contractors in a given area will bargain with a variety of craft unions through their building trades council. A second type in-volves industry-wide bargaining, whereby several com-panies in a given industry bargain with a union through an employers' association. For example, the Interna-tional Woodworkers of America bargains with the West-ern States Wood Products Employers' Association, which represents the Crown Zellerbach Corporation, the Georgia-Pacific Corporation, and the Weyerhaeuser Company, among others. The structures involved in multiple-employer bargaining are shown in Figure 15–9.

Both the union and the employer cite advantages to multiple-employer bargaining. Bargaining with an em-ployers' association is less costly for unions than bar-gaining individually with several employers. Further, the union favors the creation of uniform wages and work conditions (such as grievance procedures) among unionized firms within a particular industry.

A common wage-and-benefits package is also advan-tageous to employers, because it eliminates inter-company wage competition and the threat of employees' leaving to work for competitors for higher wages or ben-efits. Multiple-employer bargaining has also enabled employers to increase bargaining strength and has, per-haps, enabled them to achieve agreements more attrac-tive than those that would be negotiated individually.

PRENEGOTIATION

According to the Wagner Act, an employer must recog-nize and bargain with a union that has been certified by the National Labor Relations Board (NLRB) following a representation election. An employer is also required to bargain with an existing union for a new or modified agreement in order to replace a labor contract about to

FIGURE 15–9   THE STRUCTURES INVOLVED IN MULTIPLE-EMPLOYER BARGAINING

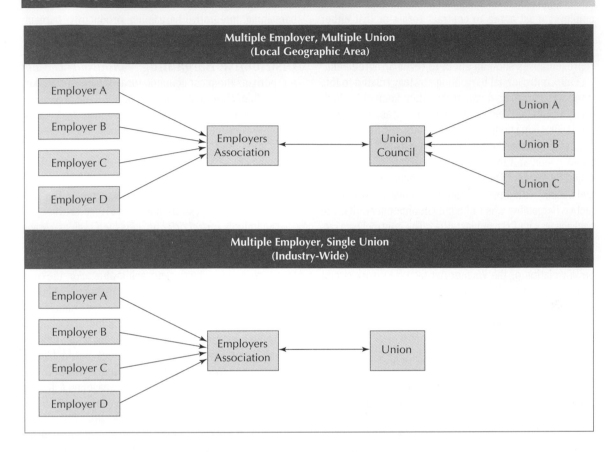

expire. Both parties are required by law to bargain in good faith, but neither party is compelled to agree or to conclude the negotiation with a contract. In the case of either a newly certified union or an existing union, the collective bargaining process follows three distinct phases: the first is prenegotiation, the second is negotiation, and the third is administering the labor–management agreement.

Labor and management representatives are involved in a great deal of preparation long before they actually sit down at the bargaining table. Local union officials meet with the rank and file to learn what they consider to be major contract issues and problem areas. A questionnaire may be used to help collect information on employee needs. Union officials study the gains made by other unions and familiarize themselves with trends in new benefits packages, shorter workweeks, cost-of-living adjustments, profit-sharing plans, job security methods, and so on. They also carefully study the employers financial condition.

The employer also prepares for the bargaining sessions. Responsibility for doing prenegotiation home-

work often falls on the HR or industrial relations director and staff. They scrutinize the existing contract, looking for vague contract language and anticipate union proposals.

NEGOTIATION

To begin the actual negotiation process, both management and labor send a team of representatives to bargain at a neutral site—often a hotel suite. Labor representatives may include the local union president, the business agent, local officers, or perhaps an official from the national union. The employer is typically represented by one or two top manufacturing executives, the HR director, the company's labor attorney (or specialist), and line managers. A company's chief executive will rarely participate in labor negotiations, except when a small firm is involved.

Good Faith   Both sides are legally bound to bargain in good faith, which simply means that labor and management must negotiate with each other and make every reasonable effort to enter into an agreement. *Good-faith bargaining* does not mean that either labor or the employer must agree to contract terms or that either must make concessions. The stronger party may use its power to obtain a favorable agreement, as long as its representatives show an intent to reach an agreement.

One controversial bargaining strategy related to this issue was known as *boulwarism,* after Lemuel R. Boulware, a General Electric Company vice president during the 1950s. Using boulwarism, GE canvassed first-line supervisors to determine employee needs and integrated those needs and managerial considerations into a so-called "package." The package was publicly announced and backed with a public relations campaign. When collective bargaining was to begin, GE announced that the package was its first and last offer. The contract was ratified but the union later protested this practice as a gesture of bad faith, and in 1969 boulwarism was found to be in violation of the Wagner Act by a New York circuit court. In essence, the practice was found to constitute bad faith because there was no give-and-take in management's negotiations.[22]

BARGAINING STRATEGIES

The actual bargaining process and the events that take place during negotiation depend to a great degree on the relationship between management and the union. Depending on the strength of the employer and the union and on the degree of cooperation that character-izes their relationship, a number of different bargaining strategies may be employed. They include distributive bargaining, integrative bargaining, productivity bargaining, and concession bargaining.

Distributive Bargaining   *Distributive bargaining,* perhaps the most common form of bargaining, takes place when labor and management are in disagreement over the issues in the proposed contract, such as wages, benefits, work rules, and so on. This form of bargaining is sometimes referred to as *win–lose* bargaining, because the gains of one side are achieved at the expense of the other (for example, a wage increase won by labor may be considered a loss suffered by management). The mechanics of this process are shown in Figure 15–10.

The union's *initial offer* on an issue (such as a wage rate) is generally higher than it expects to receive; the *resistance point* is the minimally acceptable level; the *target point* is realistic and achievable. For the employer, these points are basically reversed. Management's resistance point is a ceiling, or upper limit, on a particular issue; its initial point is the low end of an issue to be used to begin negotiations; its target point is in the general area that management would like to achieve. The *settlement range* lies somewhere between the resistance points of labor and management. If both sides are unable to come to terms on a particular issue or issues, a bargaining impasse results. The consequences and possible actions taken by both sides during an impasse will be discussed later in this chapter.

FIGURE 15–10   THE MECHANICS OF DISTRIBUTIVE BARGAINING (INCREASE IN BASE WAGE RATE PERCENTAGE, FIRST YEAR OF NEW CONTRACT)

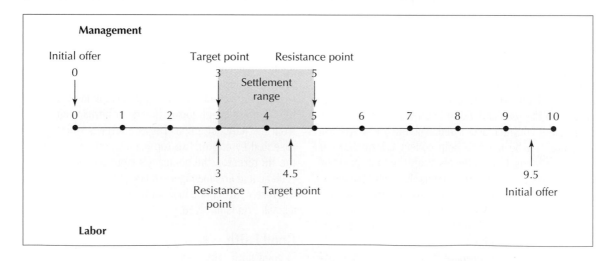

SOURCE: Michael R. Carrell and Christina Heavrin, *Collective Bargaining and Labor Relations,* 5th ed. (Columbus, OH: Merrill, 1998), 201. Used by permission.

Integrative Bargaining

The purpose of *integrative bargaining* is to create a cooperative negotiating relationship that benefits both parties. In this situation, both labor and management win rather than face a win–lose situation. Although integrative bargaining is not nearly as common as the distributive process, signs seem to indicate a steadily growing trend toward this cooperative form of bargaining.

One popular form of integrative bargaining is a jointly sponsored, labor–management quality of working life (QWL) program. An example is the Ford Motor Company–UAW program called *Employee Involvement (EI)*, a QWL program designed to strengthen plant productivity and quality through enhanced job satisfaction and cooperative labor–management relationships. At the heart of the EI program are quality circles. By using quality circles, Ford scored a number of impressive improvements in quality and productivity. Some examples of improvements made through EI at the Dearborn plant are shown in Figure 15–11. The improvements in Ford's

---

FIGURE 15–11   THE EI PROGRAM WAS A JOINT EFFORT BETWEEN FORD'S
DEARBORN ENGINE PLANT AND UAW LOCAL 600

The Employee Involvement Program

The Dearborn Engine Plant's joint steering committee was formed in March, and employee volunteers were chosen by lottery. Problem-solving training started in May, and the first employee problem-solving group presentation to the joint steering committee was made in June. Following are some examples of the problems addressed—and the fixes implemented—at this location:

Problem: *Excessive scrap and tool breakage on cylinder head milling machines caused by broken timing belts.*

Solution: Install limit switch to automatically stop the head feed when timing belts break.

Payoff: Reduced scrap and tool breakage . . . improved quality and reduced tool cost.

Problem: *Lack of information about EI activities for employees not participating in problem-solving groups.*

Solution: Install bulletin boards in the plant for posting of EI information. Devote part of the plant newspaper to EI news.

Payoff: Better communication . . . better-informed employees.

Problem: *Coolant dripping from parts hung on an overhead conveyor.*

Solution: Install drip pans.

Payoff: Better housekeeping . . . improved work environment.

Problem: *Quality problems and excessive tool breakage on cylinder head transfer machine.*

Solution: Redesign fixture to include set screws to secure locating pins and bushings.

Payoff: Reduced tool breakage and downtime . . . better product quality.

Problem: *Inefficient dust collection on a cutter grinder.*

Solution: Replace fixed exhaust duct with flexible duct to permit operator to adjust duct to most effective position.

Payoff: Improved working conditions . . . better observation of the work in process.

SOURCE: "Employee Involvement . . . It Works." UAW–Ford Committee on Employee Involvement (April 1981).

productivity, partly as a result of the program's effort, have strengthened their competitive position in the national and international automobile and truck markets. The benefits to the UAW membership at Ford are stable employment, job security, and a more satisfying work environment.[23]

When the EI program first began, many union leaders and members were against it because they believed that in the long run it would diminish the role of the UAW. The EI program at Ford, however, has been a success and is now supported by most workers. The reasons for the change in attitudes toward the program can be found in the words of a veteran UAW member: "In my new department there was a strong EI group. People met for an hour on Wednesday afternoons after work in the conference room, and we got paid for it. We talked about all kinds of problems—anything from oil coming out of hoists to bolts not going in, case nuts coming off, bad clips, bad metal. We discussed how the company could improve quality and improve our jobs. In the past, nobody was taking care of these problems. It was dog-eat-dog. You came in, you hated your foreman, and your foreman hated you, you did your job, and you hoped they didn't mess with you. . . . Those days are gone, and EI helped get rid of them. You don't see people these days deliberately trying to make life miserable for their foreman. When I'm running EI meetings, I make sure we stay away from contractual issues. EI is not supposed to touch anything that's in the contract. . . . EI is supposed to deal with quality issues—bad parts, bad stock, and other things that get swept under the rug in the rush to keep up production. We're seeing a lot of improvement in the plants today because of EI and because of profit sharing."[24]

Productivity Bargaining   One of the primary purposes of productivity bargaining is to improve the effectiveness of the organization by eliminating work rules and inefficient work methods that inhibit productivity. Getting labor's agreement to eliminate old, ineffective work habits is not easy. Some unions fear that this form of bargaining will eventually lead to unemployment and a weakening of the union's power base. A primary reason for a union's acceptance of new, improved work methods is a feeling that jobs will become more secure as the employer's productivity strengthens.

An excellent example of labor–management cooperation on the elimination of restrictive work rules in exchange for job security involves GE's "factory of the future" in Lynn, Massachusetts. The factory, which employs only about half as many workers as a conventional factory, builds aircraft engine parts and uses robot carts to move engine parts between computer-controlled work centers. GE promised the Electrical Workers that it would maintain a minimum level of jobs for a specified time. GE also promised to spend $450 million to add plant capacity over a period of several years. In return, the Electrical Workers Union agreed to the following work rules:[25]

- To enable the factory to operate 24 hours a day, the union agreed that employees will work 7 12-hour shifts every fourteen days, with four hours' overtime pay for each shift.

- The number of job classifications was to shrink from 12 to 3 to enable the plant to operate with only 100 employees, who perform a variety of tasks.

- For the first time, the union agreed to let GE set production goals.

BARGAINING CATEGORIES

The NLRB identifies three broad categories of bargaining subjects: mandatory, permissive, and illegal. The parties must negotiate mandatory items if either party requests to do so. Typical *mandatory subjects* include provisions concerning wages, benefits, and working conditions.

Permissive subjects (voluntary) include those not directly related to wages, benefits, conditions of work. If one party desires to bargain over a permissive subject, the other party may agree or refuse to do so. For example, the union may wish to bargain for an increase in the size of the bargaining unit, but the employer could refuse to negotiate this permissive subject if it so desires. Neither side can refuse to sign a contract because the other refuses to discuss a permissive subject.

The inclusion of *illegal subjects* renders an agreement invalid and unenforceable. One example of an illegal item is a provision that permits discrimination on the basis of religion, sex, or national origin or a provision that establishes a closed shop. Any subject that violates any federal, state, or local law is an unlawful bargaining item.

CONTRACT AGREEMENT

After both sides have arrived at an informal agreement, the agreement is taken back to their representatives for final and formal approval. For the employer, top management—often the board of directors—may be required to approve the contract (although often the employer's chief negotiator may be empowered to give approval); for labor, the rank and file normally must ratify the contract by a majority vote. Failure to ratify the contract sends union representatives back to the bargaining table to negotiate a revised agreement. Most contracts, however, are ratified on the first vote.

The agreement becomes official once approved, ratified, and signed by labor and management representatives. Once signed, labor and management meet with their respective members to go over the details of the contract. Generally, union members and members of management all receive copies of the agreement. Supervisors and union stewards who have the day-to-day responsibility for contract administration should be intimately familiar with the agreement so that they may avoid any activity or decision that violates it.

CONTRACT FORMAT

Labor contracts may vary considerably in length and content. Some agreements contain 10 or 15 pages; others, hundreds of pages. The more mandatory and permissive subjects that are negotiated, the lengthier the contract. The order of topics may also vary somewhat, but the following list is fairly representative of most agreements:

- *Union recognition and scope of the bargaining unit.* This section reflects the employer's recognition of the union as the sole bargaining agency for its employees and defines specifically which employees are included within the bargaining unit.
- *Management rights.* This section reflects the union's recognition of the employer's sole and exclusive right to determine the way in which the business shall be managed. Management rights include determining production methods, which products and services to produce, and how products and services should be marketed.
- *Union security.* This section defines the type of union security (union shop, maintenance-of-membership shop, etc.).
- *Strikes and lockouts.* This section outlines the approach each side will take toward strikes and lockouts (a **lockout** is management's refusal to allow employees to work). Typically, this section includes a statement such as "there will be no strikes or lockouts during the term of this agreement" (although a strike may be permitted over certain specific items detailed in the agreement).
- *Job rights and seniority.* This section defines how transfers, promotions, layoffs, and recalls are to be made. Generally, the contract will stipulate that these decisions are to be made on the basis of seniority and experience.

- *Wages.* This section outlines the wage structures and related provisions such as wage adjustments, wage incentives, shift differentials, and bonuses.
- *Benefits and paid time off.* This section lists the employee benefits such as hospitalization, pensions, holidays, vacations, sick leave, and rest periods.
- *Safety and health.* This section normally includes statements that underscore both the union's and the employer's desire to maintain safe and healthy working conditions. Many contracts include provisions for the creation of a labor–management safety committee and the administration of a health-and-safety program.
- *Discipline, suspension, and discharge.* This section outlines the procedures an employer must follow to discipline, suspend, or discharge an employee. Many contracts include provisions for progressive disciplinary systems, whereby additional infractions of a work policy, standards, rules, or regulations result in increasingly serious disciplinary action leading to discharge. Some contracts include a very detailed list of violations and resulting penalties. For example, working under the influence of illegal drugs may result in immediate dismissal, while horseplay may result in a verbal warning, and so on.
- *Grievance handling and arbitration.* This section normally details (1) the steps an employee follows to lodge a formal grievance against the employer and (2) the procedure for bringing in an outside arbitrator if the union and employer are unable to settle the grievance.

BARGAINING IMPASSE

Historically, collective bargaining has proven to be an effective method for settling differences between labor and management. Most negotiations (about 98 percent) end in a signed contract that is agreeable—although not necessarily favorable—to both sides. Management and labor generally recognize that continuous, dispute-free operations are important to preserve harmonious labor relations and maximize the goals of the employee and employer alike.

Serious conflicts do sometimes occur, however, during the course of negotiations. Labor and management may simply be unable to reach accord over certain issues dealing with wages or other contract provisions. When negotiations break down or when the existing contract expires and the union and employer have been unable to reach an agreement, a bargaining **impasse** results. Should this occur, there are three options. One, the parties may ask for assistance in settling the dispute from an impartial third party called a *mediator.* Two, the union may exert a show of force so that their demands will be accepted. Three, the employer may also show force through one of several pressure techniques. Let us first explore common union strategies for ending the bargaining impasse on their terms.

UNION POWER TACTICS

A union's primary power tactics include calling a strike, waging a corporate campaign, setting up a picket line, or imposing a boycott.

Strike   Officially termed a *work stoppage,* the strike is the refusal of union members to work and is recognized as a basic union right. Strike tactics and procedures, however, are subject to considerable regulation by a variety of labor statutes. Various types of strikes include the following:

Economic Strike   An **economic strike** is a strike to gain an economic goal—such as better working conditions, wages, or benefits (see *HR in the News:* "The 1997 UPS Strike"). The employer is free to maintain operations and hire *permanent replacements* for economic strikes. An employee who is not replaced is entitled to reemployment if the labor dispute is settled.

Often, however, when a strike ends there are only a few jobs left for returning workers. An employer can, therefore, in effect, fire striking workers by hiring permanent replacements during the economic strike. This practice by American employers sharply increased after the 1981 air traffic controllers strike, when President Reagan fired the strikers and hired replacement workers. Prior to 1981, it was more common for employers to hire only short-term strikebreakers and then bring back striking union members after a settlement was reached.

Before Reagan permanently replaced the striking workers, most large U.S. employers relied on supervisors and temporary workers to keep operating during a strike and then brought back all striking workers once the strike was settled. Since then, however, employers have hired permanent replacement workers with increasing frequency—thus breaking the union. This use of permanent replacement workers has caused a major change in American labor relations, according to U.S. Labor Secretary Robert Reich. The number of major strikes has steadily declined since the 1981 air traffic controllers strike, from a peak in 1974 of 424 to a 50 year low of 38 in 1997 (see Figure 15–12).[26]

Thus today economic strikes are likely to occur only in cases of severe worker discontent, such as the American Transit Union (ATU) strike. In 1990, 9,000 ATU Greyhound drivers struck after hearing of wage-freeze demands by the new owner, Fred Currey. This demand followed sharp wage cuts in their previous two contracts. Greyhound hired replacement drivers as well as several hundred union drivers who crossed the picket lines. Within a year, ridership was 95 percent of the pre-strike level. Greyhound was forced to file for bankruptcy, however, to stay in business.[27]

Unfair-Labor-Practice Strike (ULP)   An *unfair-labor-practice strike* protests an action by the employer, for example, discrimination against union members because of union activity. A worker who strikes because of an unfair labor practice specified in the NLRA cannot be permanently replaced.

Sympathy Strike   A strike in which other unions agree to a work stoppage, not because of actions by their own employer but to support other union members striking other firms, is called a *sympathy strike.* A

HR IN THE NEWS

THE 1997 UPS STRIKE

In 1997 the Teamsters Union strike against the United Parcel Service received national media coverage as it idled over 180,000 workers worldwide. The central economic issue was part-time versus full-time jobs. The union wanted more full-time jobs for its part-time members to move into as an incentive. Ron Carey, Chair of the Teamsters' national negotiating team had posted a bargaining survey on the Teamsters' Web page and member responses let the leadership know the issue was critical to any proposed new contract. UPS ended the strike by agreeing to 10,000 new full-time positions in the new labor agreement.

FIGURE 15–12   NUMBER OF MAJOR U.S. STRIKES (WORK STOPPAGES), 1960–1997

YEAR	NO. OF STRIKES
1960	222
1965	268
1969	412
1974	424
1979	235
1981	145
1984	62
1989	51
1990	44
1997	38

SOURCE: U.S. Bureau of Labor Statistics, *Compensation and Working Conditions* (Washington, D.C.: Department of Labor, 1997).

common example of the sympathy strike is the refusal of truck drivers to cross a picket line and make deliveries to an employer whose employees are on strike. Legally, the sympathy striker is in violation of a no-strike clause in the agreement unless the contract specifically permits this form of strike activity.

Wildcat Strike   An unauthorized work stoppage, the *wildcat strike* is an unlawful activity if the contract contains a no-strike clause; therefore, wildcat strikers must not be sanctioned by union leadership. If a wildcat strike does occur, the union must disavow it or risk being charged with violation of the contract and federal law. The employer may generally take disciplinary action, including suspension and discharge, against wildcat strikers.

Other forms of union pressure include a *sit-down strike*, in which employees strike but remain at their jobs and refuse to work; a *sick out*, in which employees call in sick en masse; and a *slowdown*, in which workers remain at work but cut back their output significantly. Unions, however, usually disapprove of individual worker pressures and support a work stoppage only if it has been formally approved by union leadership. For example, the national union must usually approve a strike by a local affiliate, even after a majority of the local members have approved it.

Picket   The *picket*, a line of strikers who patrol the employer's place of business, can be a powerful union pressure tactic. Picketing can help keep a plant or building site closed during a strike. Applicants who cross the picket line to apply for the jobs of striking workers must often confront the jeers and taunts of the picketers.

Such strikebreakers, often disparagingly labeled *scabs* because they "close the wound," are held in great contempt by union members and union sympathizers. The courts allow picketing at the primary employer's place of business, or *primary situs picketing*, as long as laws are observed. The picketers must avoid violence, must not mass in large numbers, and must not create physical barriers to the employer's entrance.

Boycott   A boycott is the refusal to purchase an employer's goods or services. An important distinction must be made between primary and secondary boycotts. A *primary boycott* involves only those parties directly involved in a dispute, such as a large appliance manufacturer and the electrical workers' union. In a primary boycott, the union pressures members (and often the public) to avoid patronizing an employer, even going as far as to levy fines against members who do. Primary boycotts are generally legal. A *secondary boycott* involves a third party not directly involved in a dispute, such as an electrician's union persuading retailers not to buy the manufacturer's products. A secondary boycott is an attempt to increase the power and strength of the union so that the employer is more likely to give in to union demands. Under the Taft-Hartley Act, secondary boycotts are illegal, except in the construction and clothing industries.

One of the longest successful boycotts was waged by the AFL–CIO against Coors, the Golden, Colorado, beer company. The 10-year boycott ended in 1987 when Coors allowed its employees to seek union representation. The historic boycott began in 1977 when 1,500 union workers struck—and Coors hired replacement workers. During the long boycott, Coors lost substantial market share to Budweiser while it started selling in eastern states for the first time.

EMPLOYER POWER TACTICS

Employers use a number of methods designed to end a bargaining impasse on terms favorable to management. These include the lockout of employees, hiring temporary nonunion employees during a strike, hiring permanent replacement workers, contracting out work, and filing for bankruptcy.[28]

Replacement Workers   The most successful but controversial strike tactic is to hire permanent *replacement workers* for strikers. According to labor law, an employer may hire permanent replacements for economic strikers but only temporary replacements for unfair-labor-practice strikers. This strategy is not without problems. First, many workers may be extremely hesitant to cross picket lines to be ridiculed by picketers and union sympathizers as scabs. Second, in the case of an unfair-labor-practice dispute, workers may hesitate to accept what is likely to be only short-term employment. Third, this practice is almost sure to seriously damage labor–management relations and lower worker morale if a settlement is reached.

Hiring permanent replacement workers, or threatening to do so, however, has become the employer's most effective power tactic. While the problems just discussed still exist, they are often far outweighed by the advantages. The 1981 air traffic controllers strike, in which President Reagan hired replacement air traffic controllers, began a new era in labor–management relations. Following the strike, employers quickly realized that public support for the strikers was minimal and that if highly technical air traffic controllers can be effectively replaced, then almost any strike can be broken by hiring replacement employees. Qualified workers no longer appear to be hesitant to cross the picket lines of striking union workers. A series of strikes, including those of Eastern Air Lines pilots, machinists, and flight attendants (1989), Greyhound bus drivers (1990), Kroger Company supermarket employees (1992), and Caterpillar industrial workers (1992) (see *HR in the News:* "Both Sides of 'Replacement Workers' Issue.") were successfully broken when management hired replacement employees. The hiring of replacement workers has been so successful that unions have called far fewer strikes in recent years (see Figure 15–12) and blame the tactic, in part, for their continuing membership decline.

Lockout   Another tactic, a *lockout,* is the refusal to allow employees to work until an agreement is signed. Because an employer must normally halt operations with this tactic, the lockout sees only limited use (like the NBA in 1998–99). In addition, most contracts contain a no-lockout clause prohibiting a lockout while a contract is in force.

Temporary Nonunion Workers   Should a union strike, the employer may still attempt to maintain operations. One way is for supervisors and other nonunion employees to perform the duties of striking employees. This strategy may be successful where operations are highly automated or routine and where little training is required to perform the strikers' jobs. During a 1989 strike against American Telephone and Telegraph by the Communications Workers of America Union, for example, supervisors and administrators were able to keep phone lines open and force strikers back to work with no pay increase.[29]

Contracting Out   Another technique for maintaining business is to contract out or arrange for another company to handle the employer's business during a strike. This may be a useful strategy for firms in very competitive fields or those that fear that a strike would damage customer relations. For example, a janitorial service that cleans office buildings may contract out their work until the strike is over. If the subcontractor is unionized, however, its employees may legally refuse to perform work for the struck firm. Courts have ruled that this "not cargo" action does not constitute an illegal secondary boycott.

Bankruptcy   In the past, an organization was bound to the terms of the labor agreement, including the level of wages and benefits, until the agreement expired. A Supreme Court decision has changed that interpretation of the law, enabling organizations to use Chapter 11 of the bankruptcy laws to cancel a union contract, cut wages, and lay-off workers. In addition, an organization may do this without having to prove that the labor pact would cause the company to go completely broke. The company must only show that "the labor contract burdens its prospects for recovery and that it has made reasonable attempts to bargain with the union for deferred or smaller wage increases or other money saving measures."[30]

Two major corporations, Wilson Foods and Continental Airlines, chose bankruptcy to void labor contracts and slash wages and benefits. In the case of Wilson Foods, top management decided to file Chapter 11 because of massive losses from sliding revenues

HR IN THE NEWS

BOTH SIDES OF "REPLACEMENT WORKERS" ISSUE

Historically, unions have counted on their ability to put on a successful strike as a means of gaining new wages and benefits at the negotiation table. Employers feared that a lengthy strike could cost them substantial market share or even put them out of business if customers supported the union or simply changed to competitors' products.

The 1981 air traffic controllers strike, however, in which President Reagan permanently replaced striking workers with nonunion employees, began a new era in labor relations. Many employers began hiring replacement workers as soon as a strike was called—often forcing the union to agree to their demands. In 1992, the United Auto Workers (UAW) became the victim of such a strategy when it staged a strike against Caterpillar, the last unionized U.S. manufacturer of heavy equipment. When the UAW called the strike, Caterpillar advertised for replacement workers, and thousands of would-be-strikebreakers responded. UAW quickly canceled the strike without gaining a concession at the negotiating table and after losing thousands of union jobs.

In contrast to the experience of UAW, a 1993 strike by American Airline flight attendants negated the use of permanent strike replacements by utilizing a limited-duration strike. Having been engaged in very difficult negotiations, the Association of Professional Flight Attendants and the management of American Airlines reached an impasse in early November 1993 over pay, medical benefits, staffing, and work rules. Management refused to continue the meetings until the union agreed to certain concessions. The union decided to go on strike. A strategic decision was made to start the strike a week before Thanksgiving, thereby disrupting the holiday travel plans of millions of customers. In addition, the union announced that the strike would be a limited-duration strike to last only 10 days. The timing of the strike was guaranteed to cripple one of the nation's largest airlines during one of its busiest times of the year, and the short duration of the strike ensured that no replacement workers for the strike period could be hired.

On Sunday, November 21, four days into the strike, President Bill Clinton intervened and convinced the president of American Airlines that it was in his company's and the country's best interest to cut the strike short. President Clinton persuaded both sides to agree to binding interest arbitration on the issues still in dispute. Labor leaders praised the union's strike strategy as a way to reshape the traditional strike tactic to make it, once again, an effective weapon to use in a labor dispute.

In 1997, a declared strike by American Airlines pilots was only hours away when President Clinton invoked a seldom-used section of the 1926 Railway Labor Act to halt the strike in the interest of avoiding an interruption of commerce.

Adapted from Dana Milbank, "Unions' Woes Suggest How the Labor Force in U.S. Is Shifting," *The Wall Street Journal* (May 5, 1992): A1, 4; and "Clinton's Intervention Halts American Strike: Flight Attendants' Union and Airline Agree to Arbitration in 4-Day-Old Work Stoppage," *Louisville Courier-Journal* (November 23, 1993): D1.

and what it claimed was an excessively costly labor contract. Wilson's estimated net worth was $67 million, but the company estimated its losses at $1 million a week. Shortly after filing for bankruptcy, the company terminated its labor contract and cut almost in half the wages for its 6,000 union employees. Nonunion employees also faced similar pay cuts. At Continental Airlines, many workers were laid off, and pilots' and other staff members' pay was cut by as much as 50 percent after the airline filed Chapter 11.[31]

Successorship   Management can decide to sell out to a new owner as a means of ending a labor dispute or ending an existing contract. When there is a change in the ownership of the organization or the union, the courts refer to the collective bargaining situation as a matter of *successorship.* Corporate mergers and acquisitions have occurred much more frequently in recent years and have posed a new threat to the effectiveness of labor unions.

The U.S. Supreme Court in a landmark decision reaffirmed that when a genuine change of employer occurs, the new employer is required to recognize (and negotiate with) the union as the representative bargaining unit of the employees. However, the new employer is not bound by the conditions of any existing labor agreement (even if unexpired).[32] Thus, the new employer may be free to negotiate an entirely new contract with the existing labor unions.

BREAKING THE IMPASSE

When a bargaining impasse occurs and negotiations stall, labor and management may implement certain techniques to ward off an impending strike or lockout. These techniques, which keep both parties communicating, negotiating, and examining each other's positions, may lead to an eventual resolution of their differences. Each of these methods—mediation, fact-finding, and interest arbitration—requires the involvement of a third party.

Mediation

The **mediation** process, in which a neutral third party attempts to bring the union and employer into agreement, follows no particular format. Mediation may, in fact, take place before an impasse occurs. In such cases, labor and management practice *preventive mediation*, requesting that a mediator participate in the negotiations during the early stages. The presence of a mediator during collective bargaining is often instrumental in keeping both parties working toward an agreement and thus avoiding an impasse. In other cases, an impasse may have been reached and a mediator may be called in after negotiations have completely broken off.

The primary role of a mediator is to lead the parties to an agreement by acting as a go-between for the union and the employer. The mediator does not have the authority to impose a decision. After feeling out the parties, the mediator determines which demands are actually firm and which may still be negotiated. The mediator must have the confidence of both sides and be perceived as truly unbiased and impartial.

After an initial joint session with all three parties, labor and management teams are often assembled in separate meeting rooms. The mediator then presents proposals and counterproposals to each side. Although the mediator avoids injecting public opinion or personal feelings into the proceedings, it may become necessary to criticize an extreme demand or unworkable solution presented by either side.

Mediators are often full-time employees of the Federal Mediation and Conciliation Service (FMCS), which

was created by the Taft-Hartley Act to help solve labor disputes. Before becoming mediators, most have had experience in labor relations. After formal training in Washington, D.C., mediators are assigned to a regional office to work with experienced mediators.

Fact-Finding

Compared to the mediation process, *fact-finding* is rarely used in the private sector. This public sector process is commonly used to settle disputes involving police officers, teachers, and public-health employees. The fact-finding board, often composed of three nonpartisan individuals, holds a hearing in which each side presents its views regarding the disputed issues. After studying each party's position and arguments, the board publicly repeats the evidence or announces a recommended settlement, putting pressure on both sides to accept the pact.

Fact-finding appears to be successful in resolving an impasse. It is estimated that 90 percent of the disputes going to fact-finding are resolved and that the fact-finder's reports are responsible for the resolution in 60 to 70 percent of the cases.[33]

Interest Arbitration

This process occurs when an arbitrator (or panel) is called to solve a possible dispute involving issues in a future contract. *Interest arbitration* has seen relatively greater use in the private sector. Unlike mediation and fact-finding, the arbitrator not only studies the dispute but also determines the terms of agreement, which is final and binding on both parties.

Interest arbitration received considerable publicity in labor circles when the United Steelworkers and an employers' association of 10 steel companies agreed to submit unresolved issues to an interest arbitration panel in order to avoid a strike or lockout. Although differences were resolved and the panel was not called, the inclusion of the interest arbitration provision in the negotiation agreement (formally termed an *experimental negotiating agreement)* may have helped the parties reach agreement.

Final-Offer Arbitration

The *final-offer arbitration* method requires both parties to submit their final offer to the three-member panel that has the authority to select one of the proposals. Final-offer arbitration gives the parties the motivation to make their final offers reasonable. Both parties realize that an unreasonable offer will have a lower chance of selection. Therefore, they strive to make their offer appear as fair and reasonable as possible. In 1987, Detroit Tiger Jack

Morris won a $1.85 million contract dispute through final-offer arbitration. The baseball players' union and major league owners had agreed to begin using the impasse-resolution technique in 1974 to settle salary disputes. When the Tigers and their star pitcher could not reach a salary agreement, they each presented their final offer to an arbitrator, who could only choose one of the two offers and could not choose a compromise. The Tigers' last offer was $1.35 million—$500,000 larger than the previous largest final-offer arbitration award. Morris proposed $1.85 million based on his 123–81 record (most wins in the 1980s) and his performance in the 1984 World Series.[34]

Mediation-Arbitration   Using this combination method, both parties agree to bring in a mediator with authority to arbitrate *any* unresolved issues. Since the parties must agree to abide by the mediator-arbitrator's decision, they will likely agree on the substantive issues as well.

CONTRACT ADMINISTRATION

The signing of the contract spells a new relationship between management and labor, because the agreement often reflects significant changes in wages, benefits, work regulations, and other conditions of employment. In effect, the agreement constitutes a new set of work rules, and both management and labor are bound to abide by the new rules. Implementation and enforcement of the agreement, referred to as *contract administration*, represents a critical responsibility for the HR or industrial relations director.

A contract must run for a specific term. Most contracts contain renewal provisions, with prior notice of termination or of a time for reopening negotiations. Contracts can have *openers*—clauses that allow for negotiations to proceed during the terms of the contract on one or more items, generally wages.

A majority of contracts (about 82 percent) contain three-year or longer terms. A movement from one-year to three-year terms was aided by the NLRB in a general ruling that extended the *contract bar* rule (see the next section) to a three-year period.[35] In recent years, the number of contracts with periods extended to four or five years has increased. The desire by both labor and management to provide greater long-term stability in labor relations has greatly motivated negotiators to work out longer multi-year agreements.[36]

MANAGEMENT RIGHTS

The area of contract administration known as *management rights* has evoked more emotion and controversy than any other single issue. At the core of the debate is the concept of management's right to run the operation versus the union's quest for job security and other protections for its members. Generally, these provisions are found in almost all contracts in a section labeled *management rights;* union rights, however, are usually scattered throughout a contract according to subject matter.[37]

Unquestionably, the question of who controls the workplace is of great interest to both management and labor. **Management rights** generally include decisions governing the working environment of employees, including supervising the workforce, controlling production, setting work rules and procedures, assigning duties, and the use of plant and equipment. Management generally believes that if it is to operate efficiently, it must have control over all decision-making factors of the business. Management also contends that any union involvement in the area is an intrusion on its inherent right to manage. Union advocates respond that where the right to manage involves wages, hours, or working conditions, labor has a legal interest under federal law.[38] Arthur Goldberg, former Secretary of the U.S. Department of Labor and U.S. Supreme Court justice, summarizes the management rights issue:

> . . . Somebody must be boss; somebody has to run the plant. People can't be wandering around at loose ends, each deciding what to do next. Management decides what the employee is to do. However, right to direct or to initiate action does not imply a second-class role for the union. The union has the right to pursue its role of representing the interest of the employee with the same stature accorded it as is accorded management. To assure order, there is a clear procedural line drawn: The company directs and the union grieves when it objects.[39]

A management rights clause often appears at the beginning of a contract following the union recognition and security clauses. An example of a common management rights clause appears in Figure 15–13.

THE GRIEVANCE PROCEDURE

Regardless of how clearly and objectively a contract is written, disputes will generally arise during its enforcement. Rarely does any agreement run its term completely void of any dispute. For this reason, most contracts contain a contract administration process to

FIGURE 15–13   MANAGEMENT RIGHTS PROVISION

ARTICLE III
Management
The management of the plant and the direction of its working force are vested exclusively in the Company. These functions are broad in nature and include such things as the right to schedule work and shift starting and stopping time, to hire and to discharge for just cause, to transfer or lay off because of work load distribution or lack of work. In the fulfillment of these functions the Company agrees not to violate the following Articles or the intent and purpose of this Contract, or to discrimiante against any member of the Union.

SOURCE: Anaconda Company and United Steel Workers of America *Agreement* (Local Union 4612, AFL–CIO, 1980).

solve conflicts. If, for example, management finds that an employee has violated work rules or some aspect of the contract, it may discipline the employee. The employee may be disciplined for any one of many causes: excessive absenteeism, fighting, drinking on the job, verbal abuse, deliberate work slowdown, or disregard for the safety of others. Most disciplinary systems are progressive and contain several separate disciplinary steps beginning with an oral warning and ending in discharge. The employee may feel that the discipline was unjust and may therefore file a grievance. This sets in motion the contract procedure designed to settle the difference known as the *grievance procedure*.

Exactly what is a grievance? A *grievance* is a formal complaint by an employee concerning a possible violation of the labor contract, an employer's past practice, or a local, state, or federal law. A grievance is not a *gripe*, which is generally defined as a complaint by an employee concerning an action by management that does not violate the contract, past practice, or law. As an example, an employee may only have a gripe if his supervisor speaks to him in a harsh tone, but when the supervisor assigns him work outside of his job classification, he may have a grievance.

Procedural Steps

The procedure for handling grievances varies from agreement to agreement, but most involve four steps.

Step One   In the initial step, the employee generally discusses the grievance with the shop steward. Experienced in grievance matters and familiar with contract terms and provisions, the steward probably has a good idea of how the contract language should be interpreted. In effect, the shop steward screens complaints and often persuades employees to drop

those that are insignificant or invalid, but the steward will encourage an employee to pursue a legitimate grievance.

The steward normally investigates the grievance to provide documented facts on the case. The pertinent facts are written on a grievance form such as the one in Figure 15–14. A good rule for remembering the crucial facts in a grievance is the "5 *W*'s":

1. What happened?

2. When did the event take place?

3. Who was involved? (Were there witnesses?)

4. Where did it happen?

5. Why is the complaint a grievance?

The written grievance is delivered to the supervisor, and a meeting of the three parties is held (the shop steward is occasionally accompanied by an HR or industrial relations representative). In discussing the grievance, all the parties make an attempt to settle the matter at that point. Research shows that most grievances are settled at the first step. If the grievance cannot be resolved there, the employee and union may appeal the decision to step two of the process. Figure 15–14 shows that the disposition resulted in management's rejecting the employee's grievance and that the union has decided to refer the grievance to step two.

Step Two   The format for step two is basically the same as for step one: Both sides meet to discuss the grievance, with labor representing the employee.

FIGURE 15–14   A STANDARD GRIEVANCE RECORD FORM, STEP 1

GRIEVANCE NUMBER *82-003*   DATE FILED *4/23/97*   UNION *Local 1233*

NAME OF GRIEVANT(S) *Flacko, George*   CLOCK # *0379*

DATE CAUSE OF GRIEVANCE OCCURRED *4/20/82*

CONTRACTUAL PROVISIONS CITED *Articles III, VII, and others*

STATEMENT OF THE GRIEVANCE:

On April 20, Foreman Pat Zajac asked George Flacko to go temporarily to the Rolling Mill for the rest of the turn. Flacko said he preferred not to, and that he was more senior to others who were available. The foreman never ordered Flacko to take the temporary assignment. He only requested that Flacko do so.

Flacko was improperly charged with insubordination and suspended for three days. The foreman did not have just cause for the discipline.

RELIEF SOUGHT

Reinstatement with full back pay and seniority.

GRIEVANT'S SIGNATURE *George Flacko*_____ DATE **4/22/97**

STEWARD'S SIGNATURE *Paul Smith*_____ DATE **4/23/97**

STEP 1

DISPOSITION:

Foreman Zajac gave Flacko clear instructions to report temporarily to the Rolling Mill for the remainder of the shift. Flacko refused to do so and was warned that it could result in discipline. When he again refused the foreman's directive, he was disciplined.

The discipline was for just cause. The grievance is rejected.

SIGNATURE OF EMPLOYER REPRESENTATIVE *J. K. Ellis*_____ DATE *4/26/97*

_____ Grievance Withdrawn   or   ✔ Referred to Step 2

SIGNATURE OF UNION REPRESENTATIVE *Paul Smith*_____ DATE **4/28/97**

SOURCE: Donald S. McPherson, *Resolving Grievances: A Practical Approach* (Englewood Cliffs, NJ: Prentice-Hall, 1983), 55. Reprinted by permission.

Higher-level union and management officials are involved at this step. The union representative may be the steward or business agent; the management representative is often the plant superintendent or plant manager. If the employee and union representatives are not satisfied with management's decision, they may appeal to the next step.

Step Three   At this step, the employee is often represented by a plantwide union grievance committee. The plant manager and the industrial-relations director often represent management. Again, management hears the union's case and arguments and then issues its rul-

ing on the matter. If the employee and union are still unsatisfied with the results, they may appeal to a fourth and final step: arbitration.

Step Four   The negotiated procedure in which the parties agree to submit an unresolved grievance to a neutral third party for binding settlement is **grievance arbitration.** During the arbitration process, the arbitrator studies the evidence, listens to the arguments on both sides, and renders a decision. The arbitrator's decision, an *award* to one of the sides, is *binding* in that it must be accepted by both sides and cannot be appealed further.

Each arbitration case is unique, and arbitrators can and do vary in their approach to cases. Two national studies of arbitrators concluded that the following eight elements carry the most weight (in order of influence, from most to least critical) in determining the final decision:[40]

1 *Labor contract language.* If the agreement provides clear, specific directives concerning the questions, it is applied.

2 *Past practice.* If the employer and union developed their own interpretation of the contract via a lengthy and consistent past practice, it is accepted.

3 *Judgment of fairness.* The merits of the case, given the grievant's record and the circumstances of the incident, should lead to a fair and reasonable decision.

4 *Future labor relations.* The decision may affect future labor relations between the employer and the union.

5 *State and federal laws.* While often not a factor, if an action violated a law, it becomes a very important factor.

6 *Outside precedent.* The decisions of other arbitrators in similar cases, while not legally binding, may carry some weight.

7 *Social mores and customs.* Changes in society may be integrated into a decision.

8 *Industry practice.* While the parties involved may not have developed a practice relating to the issues, others in the industry may have, which can provide a reasonable guideline.

SUMMARY POINTS

● Collective bargaining provides a way for employees to negotiate terms of employment with an employer. Those terms usually include wages, benefits, working conditions, and discipline. When employees desire such a negotiated relationship with their employer, they can petition the NLRB and begin an organizing drive. If a majority votes for a union to represent them, then the NLRB certifies the union as their bargaining agent for purposes of collective bargaining.

● The union and employer usually then begin to negotiate a labor contract which will specify wages, benefits, seniority, and so on for a period of time, usually three years.

● If negotiations break down, the parties may declare an impasse—which can lead to an economic strike, lockout, or the hiring of permanent replacement workers by the employer. However, 98 percent of negotiations end in a new contract and peaceful labor relations between the employees and the employer.

CASE STUDY

UNFAIR LABOR PRACTICE BY AN EMPLOYER

Facts

The employer manufactures automobile parts and supplies those parts to major auto manufacturers. The UAW filed a representation petition to unionize the employer's workforce. Between November 14, 1994, when the petition was filed, and January 12, 1995, when the election was held, the employer did the following:

1 The human resource director distributed a letter to employees asserting that two-thirds of the 600 plants that had closed in their state over the past 20 years had been unionized.

2 The employer distributed an article concerning Ford's decision to move a parts contract from a supplier whose workforce had gone out on strike, emphasizing that the striking union was the UAW.

3 Around Christmas, the employer relocated production of a Ford part to another one of its plants at a location not subject to the pending election petition. The employer offered no explanation for the move.

4 The employer told the employees that negotiations on a renewal contract with a customer were being held in abeyance until the outcome of the union election, although the customer also had issues of quality and delivery to discuss.

5 The employer displayed large photo posters of closed manufacturing plants and distributed a letter noting that all of the plants had been unionized.

CASE STUDY—cont'd

6 On January 9, 1995, the president of the company sent a letter to employees telling of his concern that its manufacturing partners would become nervous and go elsewhere if the company developed "a reputation for not being dependable because of labor problems, a UAW-led strike, or even the possibility of a strike every time the contract comes up for renewal."

7 On January 10, 1995, the division manager told employees that the employer was concerned about the impact of the union vote on its manufacturing customers. On January 9 and 10, one such customer did a very visible "walk-through" inspection of the facility accompanied by numerous managers.

When the ballots were counted, the union lost 196 to 154. The union filed an unfair labor charge against the employer, charging that its campaign tactics had violated the NLRA and invalidated the results.

QUESTIONS

1 Which, if any, of the employer's actions might the court find violated the National Labor Relations Act and therefore might cause the election to be set aside?

2 Recognizing that this election took place in 1995, do you think the court might find that the employees could have seen through the employer's tactics and vote the way they wanted despite the employer's actions?

3 Would *you* have been swayed by the employer's actions to the point you could not have voted with "freedom of choice"?

SOURCE: Adapted from *SPX Corporation*, 151 LRRM 1300 (1995), by Michael R. Carrell and Christina Heavrin in *Collective Bargaining and Labor Relations*, 5th ed. (Upper Saddle Creek, NJ: Prentice-Hall, 1998), 176.

EXPERIENTIAL EXERCISES

1. ATTITUDES TOWARD UNIONS

PURPOSE

To examine your attitudes toward unions and to recognize the underlying reasons for them.

TASK

Complete the following survey. Score it by summing the scores for all items. Following the completion of the survey, your instructor will lead the class in a discussion of attitudes toward unions and labor–management relations.

DIRECTIONS

The statements in this survey are listed in pairs. Put an "X" next to the statement that you agree with more firmly. If you *strongly* agree with the statement, put *two* "X's" next to it. You may not entirely agree with either of them, but be sure to mark one of the statements. *Do not omit any statement.*

1. **a.** Unions are an important, positive force in our society.
   b. The country would be much better off without unions.

2. **a.** Without unions, the state of personnel management would be set back 100 years.
   b. Management is largely responsible for introducing humanistic programs and practices in organizations today.

3. **a.** Unions help organizations become more productive.
   b. Unions make it difficult for management to produce a product or service efficiently.

4. **a.** Today's standard of living is largely due to the efforts of the labor movement.
   b. The wealth that people are able to enjoy is largely the result of creativity, ingenuity, and risk taking by management decision makers.

5. **a.** Most unions are moral and ethical institutions.
   b. Most unions are as corrupt as the mafia.

6. **a.** Unions afford the worker protection against arbitrary and unjust management practices.
   b. Managers will treat their employees fairly regardless of whether a union exists.

7. **a.** Unions want their members to be hardworking, productive employees.
   b. Unions promote job security rather than worker productivity.

8. **a.** Unions promote liberty and freedom for the individual employee.
   b. With the union, employees lose their individual freedoms.

9. **a.** Section 14b of the Taft-Hartley Act (which allows individual states to pass right-to-work laws) should be repealed.
   b. Congress should pass federal right-to-work legislation.

10. **a.** Unions are instrumental in implementing new, efficient work methods and techniques.
    b. Unions resist management efforts to adopt new, labor-saving technology.

EXPERIENTIAL EXERCISES—cont'd

11. a. Without unions, employees would not have a voice with management.
b. Labor–management communication is strengthened with the absence of a union.

12. a. Unions make sure that decisions about pay increases and promotions are fair.
b. Union politics often play a role in deciding which union employee gets a raise or gets promoted.

13. a. The monetary benefits that unions bargain for are far greater than the dues the member must pay to the union.
b. Union dues are usually too high for what the members get through collective bargaining.

14. a. Employee discipline is administered fairly if the organization is unionized.
b. Union procedures generally make the disciplinary process slow, cumbersome, and costly.

15. a. Without the union, the employee would have no one with whom to discuss work-related problems.
b. The best and most accessible person for the employee to discuss personal problems with is the immediate supervisor.

16. a. Union officers at all levels carry out their jobs in a competent and professional manner.
b. Union officers are basically political figures who are primarily interested in their own welfare.

17. a. Most unions seek change through peaceful means.
b. Most unions are prone to use violence to get what they want.

18. a. Unions are truly democratic institutions with full participation of the rank and file.
b. Unions are controlled by the top leadership rather than by the rank and file.

19. a. Union members do the real work in our society and form the backbone of our country.
b. Union employees are basically manual laborers who would flounder without management's direction and guidance.

20. a. Unions are necessary to balance the power and authority of management.
b. The power and authority of management, guaranteed by the Constitution and the right to own private property, are severely eroded by the union.

2. BASEBALL UMPIRES STRIKE, 1996

PURPOSE

For students to gain an appreciation of the dynamics of a work stoppage through role playing.

TASK

The instructor will assign to five people the roles of (1) Roberto Alomar of the Baltimore Orioles; (2) Baseball Commissioner Bud Selig; (3) Umpires Union President Richie Phillips; (4) American League President Gene Budig; and (5) Baltimore Oriole CEO, Peter Angelos. Each student should then study the following fact situation and assume the identity of his or her assigned role. In a round-table discussion format, the instructor will ask each student to respond to the three questions at the end.

FACTS

On September 30, 1996, the Major League Baseball umpires unanimously voted to begin an unprecedented strike the next day—the first day of the playoffs. The strike vote was a response to the decision by American League President Gene Budig. The disputed decision was to allow Baltimore Oriole second baseman Roberto Alomar to play in postseason games. Alomar had been given a five-game suspension by Budig only days earlier for intentionally spitting in the face of umpire John Hirschbeck, who had ejected him from the game for arguing a called third strike. Alomar later apologized to

Hirschbeck publicly and donated $50,000 to a medical charity. Alomar served two days of the suspension but then appealed the decision, and Budig allowed the final three days of the suspension to be the first three days of the 1997 season.

The strike called by the umpires union was a historical first and came at a critical moment in major league baseball. The previous two seasons had been marred by a players' union strike that canceled the 1994 World Series. After the players' strike, attendance at ball parks and the ratings of televised games dropped significantly. But as the season ended in 1996, fan interest was beginning to rebound as several favorite big-city teams made it to the playoffs, including the Yankees, Dodgers, Indians, Padres, Cardinals, Braves, Rangers, and Orioles. Then the Alomar incident and umpires' decision to strike suddenly cast a dark, strike-related cloud over baseball. It was a very difficult decision for the umpires, who had much to lose in terms of fan support and postseason earnings. But union President Richie Phillips provided the basis for the strike decision: "Deferring the imposition of a penalty until next season is an unmistakable signal that the American League is willing to tolerate this type of behavior from its players."

American League President Budig responded to the umpires decision to strike by noting that the umpires contract contained a "no strike" clause that prohibited them from a work stoppage. The umpires' contract also provided a grievance mechanism to resolve disputes. Thus the umpires were contractually obligated to work during the playoffs.

EXPERIENTIAL EXERCISES—cont'd

QUESTIONS

1. Did the umpires act reasonably in calling a strike over the Alomar incident?

2. How should American League President Budig and Base-ball Commissioner Bud Selig have responded to the union's announced strike?

3. What could the Baltimore Orioles organization have done to avert the strike?

SOURCE: Hal Bodley, "Umps: Alomar Plays, We Sit," *USA Today* (October 1, 1996): C1, adapted by Michael R. Carrell and Christina Heavrin in *Collective Bargaining and Labor Relations,* 5th ed. (Upper Saddle Creek, NJ: Prentice-Hall, 1998), 112–113.

KEY TERMS AND CONCEPTS

American Federation of Labor–Congress of Industrial Organizations (AFL–CIO)
Arbitration
Authorization card
Bargaining unit
Certification/decertification election
Collective bargaining
Contract administration
Economic strike
Employee association
Featherbedding/Make-work activities
Grievance arbitration
Grievance procedure
Independent unions
Industrial union
Impasse
Landrum-Griffin Act
Lockout

Management rights
Mediation
National labor relations act (NLRA)
National Labor Relations Board (NLRB)
Organizing drive
Representation election
Retraining rights
Right to work
Seniority system
Subcontracting/outsourcing
Taft-Hartley Act
Trade union
Unfair labor practices
Union
Union security provisions
Union, agency, M-O-M, closed, and open shop
Wagner Act

REVIEW QUESTIONS

1. Why do workers vote to unionize? Why do they stay unionized?

2. How has union membership changed since the 1950s?

3. What are the primary goals of unions?

4. What are the major labor laws, and what are their key provisions?

5. What are the functions and duties of the national and local unions? What is the AFL–CIO, and what are its functions?

6. What are the major bargaining strategies utilized by negotiations?

7. What are the primary events in a union organizing drive?

8. How may a firm remain nonunion if it chooses to do so?

9. Why has the number of major strikes declined in recent years?

10. How can a union provide job security to its members?

11. What does collective bargaining include besides negotiation?

DISCUSSION QUESTIONS

1. Assume that you are a recent graduate applying for a job as foreman trainee. During a series of interviews, the plant manager says, "Tell me your philosophy toward unions. We are nonunion, and I would specifically like to know how you would feel about this company becoming unionized." How would you respond?

2. Would you prefer to manage union or nonunion workers? Why?

DISCUSSION QUESTIONS—cont'd

(3) Why has organized labor failed to increase its membership significantly in the past two decades? What do you believe must be done to increase union membership?

(4) Comment on the following statement: "We live in an age of professional management. The average worker has a safe job, fair wages, good benefits, and competent supervision. Therefore, unions have outlived their purpose."

(5) Many organizing campaigns are taking place at colleges and universities to bring their faculties into a union. Do you think that professors should organize? Why or why not?

(6) One of the most controversial parts of the Taft-Hartley Act is Section 14b, which enables individual states to ban union and agency shops. Since the passage of the act, labor has lobbied long and hard to repeal Section 14b. On the other hand, many employers feel that a federal right-to-work law should be passed banning union and agency shops throughout the country. Do you believe society would benefit most from the repeal of Section 14b or the passage of a federal right-to-work law? Discuss.

(7) Should an employer be legally allowed to hire permanent replacement workers during a strike?

(8) If you represented a newly unionized employer, would you agree to binding arbitration of grievances as a provision in your first contract?

ENDNOTES

Chapter 15

1. Richard Feldman and Michael Betzold, *End of the Line: Autoworkers and the American Dream* (New York: Weidenfeld & Nicolson, 1988), 6.

2. Albert Rees, *The Economics of Trade Unions* (Chicago: University of Chicago Press, 1977), 30.

3. See D. H. Rosenbloom and Jay M. Shafritz, *Essentials of Labor Relations* (Reston, VA: Reston, 1985); P. L. Martin, *Contemporary Labor Relations* (Belmont, CA: Wadsworth, 1979); and J. M. Brett, "Why Employees Want Unions," *Organizational Dynamics* 6 (Spring 1980): 56–67.

4. Aaron Bernstein, "The Difference Japanese Management Makes," *Business Week* (July 14, 1986): 47–50.

5. Carol Keegan, "How Union Members and Nonunion View the Role of Unions," *Monthly Labor Review* 110, no. 8 (August 1987): 50–51.

6. U.S. Bureau of Labor Statistics.

7. Steven G. Allen, "Declining Unionization in Construction: The Facts and the Reasons," *Industrial and Labor Relations Review* 41, no. 3 (April 1988): 343–359.

8. Daniel C. Stove, Jr, "Can Unions Pick up the Pieces?" *Personnel Journal* 65, no. 2 (February 1986): 37–40.

9. Amos N. Okafor, "White-Collar Unionization," *Personnel* 62, no. 8 (August 1985): 17–21.

10. Glenn Barkins and Glenn Simpson, "As Democrats Meet, the Teachers' Unions Will Show Their Clout," *The Wall Street Journal* (August 23, 1996): A1, 2.

11. Scott Foster, "Court: VFW Member Dues Cannot Fund Non-Union Work," *The Bakersfield Californian* (May 5, 1992): B1.

12. Bureau of National Affairs, *Grievance Guide*, 9th ed. (Washington, D.C.: Bureau of National Affairs, 1995), 278–285.

13. For a detailed treatment of labor legislation, see Kenneth L. Sovereign, *Personnel Law*, 2d ed. (Englewood Cliffs, NJ: Prentice-Hall, 1989), chaps. 15 and 16; and Theodore Kheel, *Labor Law* (New York: Matthew Bender, 1988).

14. Norman Hill, "The Double-Speak of Right-to-Work," *AFL–CIO American Federationist* 87 (October 1980): 13–16.

15. Barry T. Hirsch, "The Determinants of Unionization: An Analysis of Interarea Differences," *Industrial and Labor Relations Review* 33, no. 227 (January 1980): 147–161.

16. William A. Wines, "An Analysis of the 1986 'Right-to-Work Referendum in Idaho,'" *Labor Law Journal* 39, no. 9 (September 1988): 622–628.

17. Thomas M. Carroll, "Right-to-Work Laws Do Matter," *Southern Economic Journal* 5, no. 2 (October 1983): 494–509.

18. Clifford M. Coen, Sandra J. Hartman, Dinah M. Payne, "NLRB Wields a Rejuvenated Weapon," *Personnel Journal* (December 1996): 85–87.

19. Roy J. Lewicki, David M. Saunders, and John W. Minton, *Essentials of Negotiation* (Chicago: Irwin, 1997).

20. Ibid.

21. Martin T. Levine, "Double-Digit Decertification Election Activity: Union Organizational Weakness in the 1980s," *Labor Law Journal* 40, no. 5 (May 1989): 311–319.

22. Rosenbloom and Shafritz, *Essentials of Labor Relations*, 140–141.

23. Similar benefits were achieved by the Jones & Laughlin Steel Corporation and the United Steel Workers. See "Steel Listens to Workers and Likes What It Hears," *Business Week* (December 19, 1983): 92–95.

24. Richard Feldman and Michael Betzold, *End of the Line: Autoworkers and the American Dream* (New

York: Weidenfeld & Nicolson, 1988), 17–21.

25. "Swapping Work Rules for Jobs at GE's 'Factory of the Future,'" *Business Week* (September 10, 1984): 43.

26. "Reagan Action Altered Landscape," *The Chicago Tribune* (July 11, 1993): 1, 6.

27. Bob Baker, "Workers Fear Losing Jobs to Replacements in Strikes," *The Los Angeles Times* (June 7, 1990): A5; and Scott Forter, "Effects of Strike Overcome, Greyhound Claims," *The Bakersfield Californian* (March 2, 1991): B1, 2.

28. R. S. Greenberger, "More Firms Get Tough and Keep Operating in Spite of Walkouts," *The Wall Street Journal* (October 11, 1983): 1.

29. R. S. Greenberger, "AT&T's Managers Weather Strike Despite Long Hours, Tedious Work," *The*

Wall Street Journal (August 17, 1983): 26.

30. "Bankruptcy as an Escape Hatch," *Time* (March 5, 1984): 14.

31. J. S. Lublin, "Conservative Pilots' Union Turns Militant in Response to Fight at Continental Airlines," *The Wall Street Journal* (November 22, 1983): 35.

32. *Fall River Dyeing and Finishing Corp.* v. *NLRB,* No. 85–1208 (1987).

33. Rosenbloom and Shafritz, *Essentials of Labor Relations,* 163.

34. Carrell and Heavrin, *Collective Bargaining and Labor Relations: Cases, Practice, and Law* 5th ed. (Upper Saddle River, NJ: Prentice-Hall, 1998), 142.

35. *Basic Patterns in Union Contracts,* 14th ed. (Washington, D.C.: Bureau of National Affairs, 1995), 1–3.

36. Harold S. Roberts, *Roberts' Dictionary of Industrial Relations,* 3rd ed. (Washington, D.C.: Bureau of National Affairs, 1986), 396.

37. Marvin Hill, Jr., and Anthony V. Sinicrope, *Management Rights* (Washington, D.C.: Bureau of National Affairs, 1986), 3; and *Basic Patterns in Union Contracts,* 1995, 79–81.

38. Hill and Sinicrope, *Management Rights,* 4–5.

39. Arthur J. Goldberg, "Management's Reserved Rights: A Labor View," *Proceedings of the 9th Annual Meeting of the National Arbitration Association,* 118 (1956): 120–121.

40. Daniel Jennings and A. Dale Allen, Jr., "How Arbitrators View the Process of Labor Arbitration: A Longitudinal Analysis," *Labor Studies Journal* 31 (Winter 1993): 41–50.

DISCIPLINE AND COUNSELING

CHAPTER OUTLINE

CHAPTER OBJECTIVES

1. To recognize the various sources of poor performance through the illustration and discussion of an unsatisfactory performance model.

2. To explain both good and poor ways to discipline employees, with emphasis on effective disciplinary techniques.

3. To discuss how organizations can manage employees in such a way as to keep disciplinary problems to a minimum.

4. To illustrate a model of positive discipline and describe the procedures for ensuring that discipline achieves its goals.

5. To identify the procedures for carrying out the discharge decision humanely and tactfully.

6. To recognize how the erosion of the employment-at-will concept affects the HR function.

7. To understand what constitutes a defamation action and to identify how employers can minimize their exposure to such cases.

Even in the best organizations—those blessed with high-quality HR programs and competent supervisors—a small percentage of employees will be unwilling or unable to achieve a satisfactory level of performance. No level of the organization can be considered immune to the problems of incompetence. Managers who view the employee as a resource rather than simply a factor of production will take positive steps to maintain high levels of job satisfaction and productivity. But those who view the worker as a necessary evil will, more than likely, show little attention to employee needs and suffer "people problems" and performance shortfalls.

PERFORMANCE PROBLEMS

Mikhail Bedelov is an assistant manager at a chain department store. His sales are consistently below goals, and customer complaints are high. Mikhail is also absent too often. Mikhail is an unsatisfactory performer. Why? Is he high on drugs or alcohol? Is his boss unfairly giving him a hard time? Has he been promoted beyond his abilities? Perhaps he is simply lazy and shiftless?

Determining *why* an employee is performing at an unsatisfactory level is important, because a problem cannot be corrected unless the main causes are known. Managers must be alert for employee performance problems and realize that such problems stem from a variety of causes. The effective manager identifies performance problems and seeks solutions (See *HR in the News:* "When Workers Seek Pastoral Advice . . .").

PERFORMANCE ANALYSIS

The proper analysis of a performance problem is a critical managerial skill. The model in Figure 16–1 shows the major causes of unsatisfactory performance and the approaches available for solving them. Examination of the components of the model is helpful in understanding how managers should treat problems of poor performance.

Step 1: Define Expectations   Managers often assume that employees know what good performance is and think it unnecessary to state management's expectations. For the new employee or the employee who receives a new job assignment, the manager may describe performance standards in vague or subjective terms, leaving the employee to decipher the job standards on his or her own. The problem is that an employee's perception of good performance may differ markedly from

that of the manager. One of the manager's major responsibilities is to define clearly and precisely what good performance means.

Step 2: Identify Causes   Recognizing that a gap exists between expected and actual performance brings the supervisor to another issue: What is the cause of the performance gap? Without proper analysis of the problem, any solution that is implemented will probably be ineffective. Effective management of unsatisfactory performance greatly depends on identifying the correct causes of the problem. Four major causes can be identified:

1 *Lack of skills.* On too many occasions, organizations place an employee in a job for which he or she is unsuited. This difficult problem for management (and for the employee) can normally be remedied in only one of three basic ways: (a) train the employee; (b) transfer the employee to a job that utilizes the skills he or she does possess; or (c) terminate the employee.

2 *Lack of motivation.* A multitude of theories and approaches to employee motivation exists, but most motivational strategies boil down to one seemingly simple axiom: *Determine what the employee needs and offer it as a reward for good performance.* Yet, as most students of management know, determining the needs of an employee and creating an environment in which those needs are satisfied is one of the manager's most challenging tasks. In addressing that challenge, decision makers must know the common techniques for motivating the unmotivated.

- Create meaningful goals which are challenging but attainable.
- Invite and use employee participation in decision making.
- Keep employees informed on "where they stand."
- Reward good work; be generous with praise.
- Treat employees fairly.
- Make work as interesting and fulfilling as possible.
- Be sensitive to individual and cultural differences.
- Help employees grow and develop.

3 *Lack of respect for rules.* A third cause of unsatisfactory performance is associated with rule breaking. An example of the rule breaker is the employee who is occasionally absent or late to work, violates the dress code, swears at the manager, and/or drinks excessively during

WHEN WORKERS SEEK PASTORAL ADVICE—*HOW* WILL YOU ANSWER THEM?

"Yes, I know my work hasn't been up to standards. But I'm having a very hard time concentrating. I hate to say this, but my child may be involved in local gang activity, and I can't decide whether to turn her in. My other child needs better child care, and I can't find it. I can't cope anymore. What do you think I should do?"

You've just heard an explanation of diminished job performance. What should you do? There is a work-related (professional) problem, but the employee has framed it as an urgent moral issue requiring spiritual guidance or (pastoral) care, rather than management intervention. This is private family business which, as employer, you have no real need to know. To top it off, the employee wants your help.

Employee problems that seem to cross the lines between the spiritual, personal, and professional are knocking more frequently at HR's door. In this more secular age, in a more diverse workplace, HR faces complex personal issues increased by the waves of downsizing and intense work hours for the survivors. Lisa Carp, director of HR for Talbot Agencies Incorporated in Riverside, California, says, "The number of people having problems has escalated. Job loss, single-parent families, taking care of elderly parents, drug abuse . . . 'Leave it at home' is the old school of thought, and it doesn't work now."

Carp suggests two guides: the Golden Rule and a mentoring system. She helped the employee state the problems in manageable terms, then negotiated a one-week leave so the employee could find better child-care arrangements. That piece worked. The other problem was pastoral and needed a referral.

Here are some other guidelines:

1. Accept that for some people, there is a greater level of community and intimacy at the work place than in any other place—respond accordingly.

2. Be a sounding board, but don't try to solve a pastoral problem.

3. Learn your limitations (once again, refer).

4. Develop a database of referrals that includes well-regarded spiritual leaders or organizations in the faiths represented among your employees. Under duress, employees who haven't been active in their faith of choice since childhood may derive great benefit from reconnecting with their spiritual roots.

5. Present employees with alternatives (or pros and cons), then encourage them to make their own decisions.

SOURCE: Adapted from Nancy L. Breuer, "When Workers Seek Pastoral Advice—How Will You Answer Them?" *Workforce* 76 (April 1997): 44–51.

---

lunch. This employee has the necessary skills and normally does a fair day's work but nevertheless disregards the policies, rules, and regulations of the workplace.

Although the situation of each rule breaker is different, the most effective approach for dealing with this form of unsatisfactory performance is to apply positive discipline, a technique discussed later in this chapter.

4 *Personal problems.* A final cause of unsatisfactory performance is associated with the *troubled employee.* A troubled employee is one whose personal problems are so significant that they prevent the employee from performing satisfactorily at work. Although the troubled employee may suffer from a variety of

problems such as emotional illness, financial crises, drug dependency, chronic physical problems, and family problems. By far the most common ailment of the troubled employee is the abuse of alcohol. Because of the significance and severity of this problem in business and industry today (alcoholism is estimated to cost billions of dollars a year in lost productivity and other expenses), many organizations have created employee assistance programs, a topic discussed in Chapter 14.

Step 3: Select Corrective Approach   This
model suggests that there are a host of possible tactics the manager may take to solve performance problems. The best approach will be one which is based upon the

FIGURE 16–1   A MODEL FOR ANALYZING AND CORRECTING UNSATISFACTORY PERFORMANCE

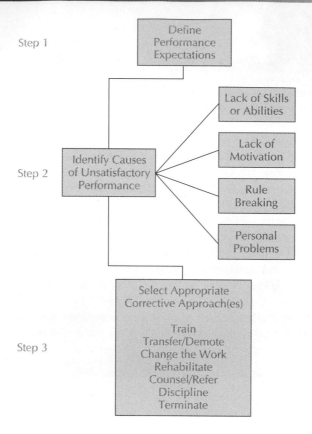

proper analysis of the cause of the performance problem (step two). Training, transferring/demoting, work design, and rehabilitation are discussed in earlier chapters. This chapter focuses upon counseling, disciplining, and the "capital punishment of the workplace"—termination.

DISCIPLINE

The primary objective of discipline is to motivate an employee to comply with the company's performance standards. An employee receives discipline after failing to meet some obligation of the job. The failure to perform as expected could be directly related to the tasks performed by the employee or to the rules and regulations that define proper conduct at work.

A second objective of discipline is to create or maintain mutual respect and trust between the supervisor and employee. Improperly administered, discipline can create such problems as low morale, resentment, and ill will between the supervisor and the employee. In such

cases, any improvement in the employee's behavior will be relatively short-lived, and the supervisor will need to discipline the employee again in the near future. The proper administration of discipline will not only improve employee behavior but will also minimize future disciplinary problems through a positive supervisor–subordinate relationship.

In effect, discipline is management's last resort to improve the performance of employees. Generally, discipline for poor task performance should not be applied while employees are being trained and are learning the job. Nor should employees be disciplined for problems beyond their control. Discipline should be applied only when it has been determined that the employee is the cause of unsatisfactory performance.

INEFFECTIVE DISCIPLINE

Just as ineffective disciplinary techniques are sometimes applied by parents in long lines in discount stores, they are also applied by managers in organizations. Some of the mistakes associated with the disciplinary process in the work setting include the following:

- **Punitive discipline.** Punitive discipline, sometimes referred to as *negative discipline,* is discipline through fear. Punitive discipline often involves threats, harassment, intimidation, and browbeating. Widespread in the industries of the early 20th century, punitive discipline is still found among supervisors who prefer to do things the "old way."
- **Retaliation.** It is not unnatural to be tempted to retaliate against an employee who has posed problems. Retaliation charges have doubled in recent years according to the EEOC. "Getting even" for problems caused by employees who assert their rights under the various nondiscrimination laws discussed in Chapter 4 is illegal. EEOC has issued an internal directive which can guide employer discipline. Employees engaged in protected activities (filing a charge, giving evidence, protesting discrimination, or requesting accommodation) may not be retaliated against as long as their conduct is reasonable and based on a good faith belief that the challenged practices are unlawful. The employee does not have to be a member of a protected class and is not required to ultimately win on the complaint. Companies and individual supervisors can be held liable for unlawful retaliation.[1]

For example, a senior manager was assigned a computer previously used by the HR department. As he was deleting old HR files, he discovered two documents: one addressed the need to promote young employees; the other targeted a group of over 40 managers, including himself, for outplacement. He complained about these memos and was told to return the documents. He refused and gave the documents to his attorney instead. After his firing for insubordination, the ex-manager filed an age bias and a retaliation claim. While the lower court found that keeping the memos was not a "protected activity," the federal appeals court reinstated both the age and retaliation suits.[2]

Retaliation is an inappropriate motive even outside discrimination laws. For instance, Bull Moose Tube Company recently was ordered to pay three former executives about $9 million in compensation. The employer claimed the men were fired for performance reasons—"misconduct and neglect of duties." But a federal judge ruled that the men were actually fired in retaliation for exercising their rights under a phantom-stock plan. They had asked for their stock distribution which angered the owner, who then fired them.[3]
- **Negative feedback.** Some supervisors give employees feedback only when poor performance occurs

and fail to provide positive reinforcement when performance improves or when a job is done well. Feedback should be both positive and negative.
- **Late intervention.** Perhaps best labeled *procrastination discipline,* this form of discipline takes place when supervisors allow a problem to drag on until it reaches a serious level.
- **Inadequate definition.** During counseling, a supervisor may tell an employee that he or she is "uncooperative" or not a "team player." Couching a performance problem in such vague and ambiguous terms may confuse and frustrate the employee.
- **Labeling employees, not behavior.** Unsatisfactory performance may result in an employee's being labeled "lazy" or a "goof-off" by the supervisor. Such labeling has two major problems. First, the employee may carry the label over to other jobs and work units, and the label may serve as a self-fulfilling prophecy. Second, such descriptions focus on the employee and not on the act of unsatisfactory performance—which is what must be addressed.
- **Misplaced responsibility.** Supervisors often have to realize that they, themselves, or the organization, sometimes contribute to the performance problems of their employees.

PREVENTIVE DISCIPLINE

Of all the approaches to discipline, preventive discipline is the most desirable. By **preventive discipline,** people are managed in a way that prevents behaviors that need to be disciplined. Much like the person who eats nutritious food and exercises regularly to avoid health problems, managers and supervisors who practice preventive discipline create an organizational climate conducive to high levels of both job satisfaction and productivity. In such cases, the need to discipline will be minimal. To create a working environment that supports a preventive discipline approach, managers must do the following:

- Match the employee with the job through effective selection and testing, realistic job preview, and placement procedures.
- Properly orient the employee to the job and provide necessary training.
- Clarify proper employee behavior.
- Provide frequent and constructive feedback to employees on their performance.
- Enable employees to address their problems to management through techniques such as an

open-door policy and management—employee group meetings.

POSITIVE DISCIPLINE APPROACH

Positive discipline corrects unsatisfactory behavior through support, respect, and people-oriented leadership. The purpose of positive discipline is to help rather than harass. Positive discipline is not an attempt to soft-pedal or sidestep a problem. Rather, it is a management philosophy that assumes that improved employee behavior is most likely to be long-lived when discipline is administered without revenge, abuse, or vindictiveness. Positive discipline is a Theory Y philosophy which assumes that most employees are willing to accept personal responsibility for their work problems and, with management's confidence and support, will reverse their unsatisfactory performance. While positive discipline is not a panacea, this process offers a number of advantages over the punitive approach.

Positive discipline is much more than the simple act of a supervisor discussing performance problems with an employee. Rather, it is a process that comprises a series of policies and procedures. Important steps in that process are shown in Figure 16–2.

Clarify Responsibility   The question of who should administer discipline is subject to some debate. In theory, the responsibility for discipline should fall on an employee's immediate supervisor. Because the immediate supervisor is responsible for the employee's output, that supervisor should possess the authority to correct the employee's performance problems. Some managers, however, think that decentralizing the responsibility for discipline will result in the inconsistent application of discipline throughout the organization.

To overcome the problem of where to place the responsibility for discipline, many organizations give the supervisor authority to administer less-severe forms of discipline such as an oral warning or a written notice. For situations involving suspension or discharge, the supervisor is often required to consult with an HR representative; in some cases the decision is made by an upper-level line manager or HR executive. With this type of approach, consistency in the application of discipline can be achieved while the supervisor retains authority and control over employee behavior.

Define Performance Expectations   A central part of every disciplinary process is the definition of behavior that management expects from its employees. Disciplining an employee for unsatisfactory performance is imprudent unless management has clearly defined good performance.

It is not only fair to employees but is also a prudent HR practice to provide employees with written principles of behavior such as those in the Lens Lab Company Policy Manual (Figure 16–3).

Communicate Disciplinary Policies, Procedures, and Rules   Management is responsible for telling employees precisely what is expected of them

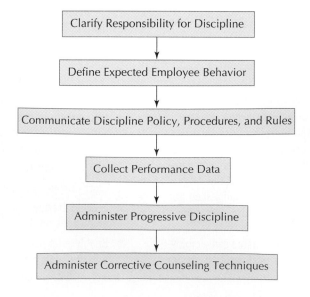

FIGURE 16–2   STEPS IN THE PROCESS OF POSITIVE DISCIPLINE

Clarify Responsibility for Discipline

↓

Define Expected Employee Behavior

↓

Communicate Discipline Policy, Procedures, and Rules

↓

Collect Performance Data

↓

Administer Progressive Discipline

↓

Administer Corrective Counseling Techniques

FIGURE 16–3 AN EXPECTED BEHAVIOR POLICY

Lens Lab, Inc.
Personnel Policies
Discipline and Investigations

PRINCIPLES OF BEHAVIOR

It is expected that employees shall be mindful of the following principles in their conduct and behavior. Violations of these principles may constitute grounds for disciplinary action or termination.

11.1(1)   Employees, in conducting the business of Lens Lab-Paris Miki, Inc., shall deal with co-workers and the public in a respectful and courteous manner and act in a manner consistent with the trust inherent in employment relationships.

11.1(2)   Employees shall strive to perform their work at a consistently high level of quality.

11.1(3)   Employees shall obey and uphold the laws of the United States and the political subdivisions and jurisdictions thereof.

11.1(4)   Employees shall follow and promote general standards of safety and health on the job. In keeping with these standards, all employees are required to wear seatbelts while operating licensed vehicles owned, leased, or rented by Lens Lab-Paris Miki, Inc. and when operating personal vehicles for work-related assignments. Employees are required to carry a valid driver's license when operating any vehicles owned, leased, or rented by Lens Lab-Paris Miki, Inc.

11.1(5)   Employees shall follow all the rules and regulations established for the department or store in which they have been assigned so long as those rules and regulations do not conflict with Lens Lab-Paris Miki, Inc. Personnel Policies.

11.1(6)   Employees shall conduct themselves off the job in a manner which does not cause discredit to Lens Lab-Paris Miki, Inc.

11.1(7)   Employees shall report any illegal activity of co-workers or supervisors to their Department Executive or Store Manager.

11.1(8)   Employees shall cooperate fully in all hearings and investigations conducted by or authorized by Lens Lab-Paris Miki, Inc.

11.1(9)   Employees shall not possess, consume, distribute, or be under the influence of alcohol or illegal drugs while on the premises of Lens Lab-Paris Miki, Inc. Further, employees shall not engage in activities related to these substances which might reflect negatively on Lens Lab-Paris Miki, Inc.

SOURCE: Randy Coe, Lens Lab, Inc., Louisville, Kentucky. Used by permission.

and for ensuring that all standards, rules, and regulations are clearly communicated. These expectations may be communicated by methods such as employee handbooks, orientation programs, union contracts, rules and regulations distributed in writing to employees or posted on bulletin boards, and employee meetings on job standards and company policies and procedures.

Some administrators avoid publishing rules and regulations, feeling that such a list is demeaning and condescending to employees. As one executive put it, "We have resisted publishing the whole painful list on the theory that it is more insulting than useful and that there is going to be some rule overlooked, and if everything is spelled out, then you have no recourse and are in trouble. I speak particularly of the nonunion situation, as evidently unionized companies feel that the contract must be all-inclusive in the matter of behavior."[4] Most firms do formalize their rules for employee conduct. A Bureau of National Affairs survey of 218 companies found that 79 percent put their rules and regulations in writing for nonunion workers. The figure increased to 85 percent for 97 union companies sampled.[5]

Collect Performance Data Before an employee is disciplined, there must be indisputable proof that some standard, rule, or regulation was violated.

Discipline should not be a gut reaction by a supervisor. There must be no doubt that unsatisfactory performance has taken place, and the collection of information clearly indicating an employee's wrongdoing makes discipline more effective and easier to administer.[6]

Some performance data are easy to collect; others are difficult. For example, absenteeism is routinely recorded and rarely subject to misinterpretation. Many companies with computerized absenteeism records furnish their supervisors with weekly or biweekly printouts so that employees requiring discipline for unsatisfactory attendance can be pinpointed. Sales, production, and quality statistics are routinely collected in many companies. Other measures of performance, however, are somewhat subjective and difficult to record. For example, many firms have specific rules against "horseplay," "insubordination," and "abusive or threatening language to supervisors." Inexperienced supervisors may ask, "How do I know when an employee is 'insubordinate'?" Although describing all possible occasions of unsatisfactory performance is impossible, management should ensure that supervisors are trained to recognize and record unsatisfactory performance in difficult areas.

Concrete, indisputable records of unsatisfactory performance are important for three reasons. First, the burden of proof lies with the employer: A person is innocent until proven guilty. Second, an employee is more likely to improve his or her behavior if presented with facts about poor performance. Third, if the unionized employee files a grievance indicating that discipline was unjustly administered, and the grievance then reaches arbitration, the arbitrator will look very closely at the data management has collected.

Work Place Searches and Surveillance

Employers increasingly concerned about employee misconduct, loafing, theft, and other workplace discipline problems are utilizing sophisticated technology to collect information on employees' performance. **Work place searches and surveillance** of employee workstations, electronic surveillance of employee telephone calls, and closed-circuit television monitoring of workstations are common examples. Employees, however, concerned about their perceived "right of privacy," are challenging such HR practices. The U.S. Supreme Court has indicated that in the case of work place searches, employees' privacy rights are limited to what are "normal" employer practices. Thus, what would otherwise constitute an illegal invasion of privacy by the *government* at home is probably permissible when conducted by an *employer* at work. For example, if it is common practice for others to open employees' desks or files to find needed items or information, employees should not expect the contents of their desk and files to be private. Employers generally retain control over lockers, toolboxes, desks, computer files, and the like by maintaining master keys and access codes. Employers who utilize work place searches are advised by the Society for Human Resource Management to consider the following:[7]

- **Written statement.** Publish a policy in an employee handbook (or other format) stating the search policy and the conditions that would instigate a work place search.
- **Retain access.** Indicate in the policy that desks, files, lockers, computer files, and so on are subject to search, and retain master keys and access codes. Do not permit employee locks.
- **Conduct random searches.** If the stated policy includes random searches, then do so regularly or lose the right.
- **No wrongdoing.** Clarify that areas and employees included in a search are not accused of any wrongdoing.
- **Search process.** Do not allow personnel to touch or search an employee during a search. Also, do not prevent an employee from leaving the premises if it would normally be permitted.

Electronic devices give employers increased abilities in work place searches. The use of closed-circuit television monitoring of work place activities is generally not limited by law. The Omnibus Crime Control and Safe Streets Act, however, does prohibit eavesdropping on employee telephone calls with electronic devices. Individuals violating the law can receive a maximum fine of $250,000 and five years in prison. The organization may receive a $500,000 fine as well. Employers can, however, use telephone-monitoring devices for purposes of training employees, evaluating their performance, investigating misconduct, or ensuring the quality of customer service. In practice it may be difficult to separate monitoring for legitimate business purposes from eavesdropping on personal telephone calls. Employers should consider the following steps if telephone monitoring devices are used.[8]

- **Inform employees.** Provide written notice to employees, in advance, that calls will be monitored and state the purposes for the monitoring.
- **Restrict monitoring.** Use monitoring only for business purposes. Provide separate, unmonitored lines for personal calls if any are allowed.
- **Announce monitoring.** A beep tone or verbal announcement of monitoring is required in some states.

Administer Progressive Discipline Most companies follow a procedure of progressive discipline for many employee problems, such as poor performance, minor rule violations, and absenteeism/tardiness. The critical element of a **progressive discipline** system is that it strengthens the punishment when offenses are repeated or shortcomings are not corrected. A typical progressive discipline procedure, found in most union contracts and handbooks for medium and large employers, has from three to perhaps seven "steps" like the following:

Step One—Verbal warning (or the first written warning)
Step Two—Written warning (or the second written warning)
Step Three—Suspension (with or without pay)
Step Four—Termination

The **suspension** step serves two purposes: giving the offending employees one last chance, and providing any neutral party who may review the termination (arbitrator, agency, or judge) with convincing proof that the employees had clear warning that they would be fired upon the next offense.

Can you imagine giving an employee a verbal warning for shooting his pistol over the heads of his co-workers and saying, "Next time that will be a written warning!"? Even within progressive discipline systems, some infractions fall into the *nonprogressive discipline* category. Employers routinely fire employees upon the first work place offense of stealing, lying, violence, insubordination (undermining the authority of supervision by refusing an order), and WUI (working under the influence of drugs or alcohol).

Administer Corrective Counseling The final step in the process of positive discipline is **corrective counseling.** The purpose of positive discipline is to solve an employee's problems rather than simply to administer penalties and punishment. For corrective counseling to be effective, a supervisor must be genuinely interested in helping an employee overcome problems and must offer support, encouragement, and assistance. Each counseling session will differ somewhat, but there are a number of steps common to every corrective-counseling interview. Figure 16–4 lists the steps and gives examples of how a supervisor might handle an employee being disciplined for excessive absenteeism.

One important way that corrective counseling differs from traditional techniques is that a supervisor avoids telling employees how to solve problems. Supervisors tend to tell employees the "right thing to do." With corrective counseling, however, a supervisor helps employees find solutions. Thus, employees are responsible for determining the most effective way to overcome the problem.

Successful Process General Electric implemented positive discipline in a plant with the goal of creating an adult-to-adult problem-solving method. The program used supervisor training, employee discussions about good performance, and nondisciplinary counseling sessions to bring attention to problems and prevent the need for formal discipline. The first year required the investment of 3,565 informal counseling sessions to discuss the performance improvements needed in the first year. Success was obvious when there were only 90 cases of the first level of formal discipline—a success rate calculated as 97.5 percent.[9]

CSX Transportation was known for a military culture of command-and-control that meted out punishment for even minor indiscretions. The top safety and labor relations managers started emphasizing teamwork, trust, and mutual respect but realized that their discipline system was out of step with their new philosophy. Now, violations of the detailed and confusing railroad rules are dealt with through nonpunitive collaboration among the offender, CSXT management, and the union. The rail industry's terrible labor environment has been created in part by a distrust of employees. The labor relations manager said, "Now, when rules are violated, the unions will choose who will talk to violators." In most cases, there will be no records and no discipline unless violations are repetitive.[10]

THE HOT-STOVE RULE

One effective way to approach the disciplinary process is to follow what is popularly known as the **hot-stove rule,** which suggests that applying discipline is much like touching a hot stove:

- The burn is *immediate;* the cause is clearcut.
- The person had a *warning;* knowing that the stove was hot, the person should have known what would happen if it was touched.
- The burn is *consistent;* those who touch the stove are burned every time it is touched.
- The burn is *impersonal;* the stove will burn anyone, regardless of who he or she is.

Like touching a hot stove, the application of discipline should also be immediate, with warning, consistent, and impersonal. These guidelines are consistent

FIGURE 16–4 STEPS IN A CORRECTIVE-COUNSELING INTERVIEW— EXAMPLE: *ABSENTEEISM*

1 **Get the facts first**—Make sure you understand the attendance policy; review the employee's attendance records; and have copies of both at hand.

2 **Counsel in private**—Leave the employee's work area; halt interruptions; meet as soon as possible.

3 **Put the employee at ease, but get to the point**—Offer the employee a comfortable seat; keep cool and don't show anger, disgust, or resentment.

4 **Describe the problems using facts**—Emphasize the act, not the employee; identify the problems caused by employee absences.

> Good attendance is really important to use to produce a quality product. Two weeks ago, we couldn't start the line because of absenteeism—it took us over an hour to get people shifted and the line going. This upset employees and hurt production. When I have to replace you the work is not as good.

Be specific—Talk number and dates.

> Yolanda, you were absent on Monday, July 26; Friday, August 20; Monday, August 30; and again Friday, September 24. Therefore, according to our policy, I must apply the first disciplinary step . . .

State the consequences of failing to perform properly.

> For four occurrences, you are given this written warning. Seven and nine occurrences within the rolling 12-month period will result in suspension and discharge, respectively.

5 **Get agreement on the problem**—Make sure the employee understands the policy, disciplinary system, and the facts (even though he or she may not like the facts).

6 **Involve the employee in the problem solving**—Listen; get the employee to talk about the problem *("What can you do to avoid another absence?");* avoid offering your own suggestions; discuss until the employee reaches a satisfactory approach or solution.

7 **Have the employee sum up the problems and the solution.**

> OK, Dwight, now I would like for you to sum up the problem and tell how you're going to ensure we don't go to the next discipline step . . .

8 **State the goal and end on a positive note.**

> Mary, as you know, a month of perfect attendance will remove one of your occurrences. Will you shoot for this?

> Bob, when you are here you do a great job. Keep in mind I'm here to help you. If there's a work problem, let's talk about it. I believe you can conquer your "Monday–Friday-itis" and I look forward to a continued positive relationship.

with the positive approach to discipline. Supervisors who follow these guidelines should experience less tension and anxiety when applying discipline and should learn to view discipline as a supervisory responsibility rather than as a personal dilemma.

EMPLOYEE TURNOVER AND DISCIPLINARY DISCHARGE

Turnover refers to employees separating from a work place and ceasing employment there. This occurs for a number of reasons, leading to several turnover terms. *Functional turnover* refers to the fact that turnover in certain positions or situations provides an opportunity for the organization to hire better employees or employees with fresh ideas. *Dysfunctional turnover* refers to harm created when a valued employee quits to work for a competitor. *Voluntary turn-over* is an employee-directed action such as when an employee quits or retires. *Involuntary turnover* is a management-directed action such as discharge for theft or layoff due to workload.

Employers generally calculate their overall turnover rate as follows:

$$\text{Overall Turnover Rate} = \frac{\text{Separations}}{\text{Average Number of Employees}} \times 100$$

Employers and other research organizations like the Bureau of National Affairs (BNA) calculate quit and discharge and other rates (substitute *quits* or *discharges* for *separations* in the formula above) as well as industry rates. The turnover rate among U.S. corporations is often calculated at 6 percent. However, a recent William Mercer Incorporated study found the median rate to be 13 percent in a survey of medium and large employers.[11] The cost associated with the 6 percent turnover is about $18 million a year for an employer with 50,000 employees.[12] These costs are so high that in 1998 over half of surveyed employers took steps to improve professional- and executive-level retention, and these employers found that raising salaries was insufficient to lower turnover.[13] In fact, recently just 9 percent of employers said that their retention efforts had been highly successful though only 15 percent categorized their results as unsuccessful.[14] Employers realize that turnover, almost any turnover, is expensive and needs to be minimized.

Disciplinary discharge is one of the four categories of turnover, which also includes quits/resignations, retirement, and layoffs. Some employees call all involuntary separations "terminations," but most employers reserve the word *termination* for disciplinary discharges. Research has recently shown that there are separate and independent reasons for each of the four types of separations. For instance, in a recent study of turnover in the trucking industry, quit rates were predicted by lower pay and benefits, higher use of electronic monitoring, and longer time on the road. Discharge rates were predicted by less-valid selection techniques and disfavorable (high) selection rates.[15]

A great deal of colorful jargon describes the act of discharge. Employees talk about getting canned, sacked, booted, axed, pink-slipped, and so on. Perhaps the most common lament of the discharged employee is "I got fired."

A disciplinary discharge occurs when an employee has committed a serious offense, has repeatedly violated rules and regulations, or has shown a consistent inability to meet performance expectations. In many disciplinary systems, the first infraction involving "nonprogressive discipline" or serious offenses—intoxication at work, insubordination, theft, willful damage to company property, or falsifying work records—will result in discharge.

Any discharge should be carried out fairly and legally. At worst, a botched discharge can lead to a highly publicized, costly lawsuit and significant damage to the firm's reputation. At best, the disgruntled employee will probably bring disrepute to the company whenever the opportunity arises.

The following are examples of disciplinary steps which may precede discharge.[16] Note that some of these carry consequences almost as severe as discharge (see *HR in the News:* "Police Officer Demoted For Sex . . .").

verbal warning	retraining
angry reprimand	loss of privileges
increased monitoring by boss	probationary status
	suspension
withholding of praise	change of job duties
unfavorable appraisal	reduced responsibility
written warning	delay of raise or promotion
exclusion from awards	demotion

DEFAMATION IN EMPLOYMENT

More than one million employees are disciplined and discharged each year. In almost every case, other employees want to know why. They will ask questions and rumors will spread—on fact or fiction.[17] In some cases, the employer will want to publicize the case—either to make a point about strict enforcement of policy or to notify employees of new policies. The press or potential new employers may also ask exactly why an employee was terminated.

Discharged employees, however, have a right to privacy. They may disagree with the discharge decision and are often angry. Their anger can quickly turn into a **defamation** lawsuit—which is actually rare but occurring with greater frequency in the American work place (see Preface).[18]

In substance, defamation is an invasion of your interest in your reputation and your good name. In order for a statement to be considered defamatory, it must: (1) have been communicated to someone other than the person in question, (2) be false, and (3) tend to harm that person's reputation and to lower him or her in the estimation of the community.[19]

In 1990, the U.S. Supreme Court ruling in *Milkovich* v. *Lorain Journal Co.*[20] substantially altered the scope of defamation cases. "Opinion statements" had been protected under the First Amendment. Thus a person who stated, "John Jones is a liar" would be viewed differently from one who said, "In my opinion, John Jones is a liar," the first being stated as a fact, the second as an opinion. In *Milkovich*, however, the Supreme Court ruled that "simply prefacing such statements in terms of an opinion does not negate the underlying implications . . . and can cause much damage to [a] reputation."

HR IN THE NEWS

POLICE OFFICER DEMOTED FOR SEX WITH DRUG FELON; TAXPAYERS STUCK WITH BILL

If you think lawsuits and lottery-like verdicts are reserved for *discharge* cases only . . .

Jeffery Anadon was a lieutenant with the Pleasanton Police Department (PD) narcotics division when he started a six-month affair with a woman he met when he arrested her for a felony drug charge. She later became a paid police informant. In 1989, the police chief received information about the affair and confronted Anadon. He confessed, promised to stop the liaison, and agreed to forfeit 56 hours of vacation leave as punishment. He gladly agreed to this punishment, because his wife didn't know about the affair. Two months later the affair resumed.

Four years later Anadon informed the chief that he was facing criminal charges for molesting the informant's child. The chief kept him on the payroll through the trial; however, as punishment for "conduct unbecoming an officer," Anadon was demoted to patrol officer.

A year later, Anadon filed a federal complaint claiming that the Pleasanton PD demoted him because he is Mexican-Filipino and married. He claims that Pleasanton didn't demote non-Mexican-Filipinos who had adulterous affairs. His attorney says that the PD's code of conduct did not specifically prohibit sex with a snitch. He cheats on his wife, then sues the PD citing his marital status.

In 1998, a local jury found that his demotion was not discriminatory (was not based on national origin) yet awarded Anadon $525,000 in economic damages and $100,000 for pain and suffering, because they found that the PD retaliated against Anadon *after* he filed his civil-rights claim.

SOURCE: Adapted from Debra Saunders, "Taxpayers Stuck with Bill for an Officer's Misconduct," *Denver Rocky Mountain News* (August 6, 1998): 52A. Reprinted with permission.

In employment situations, employers are entitled to receive information about both the achievements and shortcomings of an employee under what is known as a *qualified privilege*—both the person making the statement and the third party receiving it had a legitimate interest in the subject matter. Thus, communications that arise out of normal employer–employee relationships are easily defended under the qualified privilege principle. In such situations, however, an employee may win a defamation case if he or she can prove that the employer exceeded the qualified privilege by making a statement with *malice* (knowledge that the statement was false) or by communicating it to those who had *no need to know the information.*[21]

The most common defamation claims involve publication of the reasons for an employee's termination. Such cases involve company newsletters or bulletin boards; statements to prospective employers, employment agencies, and outplacement firms; and statements to the press. Generally, employers may communicate (under the need-to-know principle) to managers, supervisors, union officials, and employees who work in the same unit as the terminated employee. However, employees who do not work in the same unit and other people outside the organization generally do not need to know why an employee was terminated.[22]

Examples of defamation cases include the following:[23]

- Procter & Gamble was forced to pay $15.6 million in damages to an employee it accused of stealing a $35 company telephone. The company posted notices accusing him of the theft on company bulletin boards to make an example of him. The telephone was found to be the personal property of the employee.
- John Hancock Mutual Life Insurance Company was ordered by a jury to pay $26 million to a former employee whose termination was discussed in a company newsletter. The newsletter stated that the employee was under investigation for giving a client bad advice and for "shady dealings," yet neither claim could be substantiated during the trial.[24]

To minimize the risk of losing in a rare but expensive defamation suit when dealing with employment references, managers and HR professionals should observe the following guidelines:

① Limit communication to those who have a "need to know," realizing there is a difference between another employer (a qualified privilege) and a bank verifying loan information (no privilege).

2 Make the statements as neutral as possible and avoid any stigma-creating statements, name-calling, or other evidence of *malice* (the only thing that destroys the "truth" defense).

3 Make sure your opinion sets forth the underlying facts on which it is based.

4 Demonstrate that you made it in an official (that is, not casual) context and that it comes from the designated source (usually HR).

5 Document that it was requested by the employee and/or prospective employer (a "volunteered" reference enjoys no qualified privilege).

6 Remember that releases may not be successful, but may be evidence of good faith.[25]

NEGLIGENT MISREPRESENTATION

The fear of defamation might lead employers to a "no reference" policy or, at least, to a "name, rank, and serial number" response. However, the legal system has also removed these options. The failure to warn about an employee's particular propensity may open the possibility for an action of negligent misrepresentation. An HR department following a "no reference" policy may be held liable for the unintentional failure to communicate an important fact, regardless of its policy. Employers are filing their own suits as they may become liable for "negligent hiring."

For example, when the local YMCA hires a swimming instructor, it would expect to be told if the applicant was terminated for molesting swimmers at a previous job. If the YMCA knew—but hired—and there was a new molestation, the YMCA might be found guilty of **negligent hiring.** But if the old employer, realizing the job for which the employment verification was being processed, mislead or failed to accurately warn the YMCA, the old employer might be found guilty of negligent misrepresentation.

The elements required for an action for **negligent misrepresentation** are: (1) knowledge that the information is required for a serious purpose; (2) knowledge that the party to whom it is given intends to rely and act upon it; (3) there is injury to person or property because of such reliance; and (4) due to the relationship of the parties, and according to morals and good con-

science, one party has the right to rely upon the other for information, and the other owed a duty to give it with care.[26]

The best approach to avoid the twin horns of defamation and negligent misrepresentation is to carefully work out a reference letter which is factual (can you prove each statement in court?) but neutral in tone. This letter would then only be given to those who have a need to know.

ADMINISTERING THE DISCHARGE DECISION

Companies approach the problem of unsatisfactory performance in different ways. Many firms do everything they possibly can to avoid firing employees. Other employers think that the best interests of the company and the employee necessitate a direct approach in discharging an employee who has a minimal or nonexistent chance to perform up to current expectations.

Carrying out the discharge decision should involve tact, maturity, and careful planning. The discharge should be administered so that ill feelings between the employee and the company are minimized. As with the administration of any step in a disciplinary procedure, the discharge should be conducted unemotionally and without vindictiveness, revenge, or malice.

The final alternative to firing is to **dehire** the employee. A dehired employee is encouraged to quit before being fired. For example, at the end of a performance appraisal session, the employee may be told: "The job isn't right for you. . . . Have you considered other employment? I think it would be in your best interests to find employment more suited to your particular skills and abilities. . . ."

Why dehire, rather than fire, an employee? Perhaps the primary advantage of dehiring is that the employee saves face by leaving the company before being fired. The supervisor may even allow the dehired employee to seek other employment on company time.

EMPLOYMENT-AT-WILL

Historically, employers and employees have enjoyed mirror-imaged rights: Employees are free to quit their job at any time for any reason at all, and employers have similarly been free to terminate employees for "good reason, bad reason, or no reason at all".[27] The rights of the employers has, since the Civil War, been referred to as the doctrine of *employment-at-will* (or *termination at will*). Therefore, perhaps 85 percent of employees are "at will" as are the employers of those employees (see *HR in the News:* "Dear Annie . . .").

Since the 1960s, there has been increasing discussion of the erosions of this doctrine. Unfortunately this, and perhaps the outrageous lawsuits we see in the evening news (that's why such stories *are* news), has deluded many to believe that employees cannot be fired. A senior labor negotiator once described how to pick an arbitrator for a termination case. "Management should pick arbitrators with union backgrounds, because it is their experience that employers get away with firing anyone they please. Personnel and management types see it the opposite; they feel like you can't fire anyone unless you have all your ducks in a row." Consider the following cases cited in a recent *Fortune* article titled "Yes, They Can Fire You."

Carlos Gomariz, a New Yorker, claimed that his employer fired him simply because he had reported for jury duty. A 1996 appeals court upheld the dismissal observing that even assuming his claims were true, Gomariz was "an at-will employee whose employment may be freely terminated at any time."[28]

Michael Bullard worked for a real estate company that allegedly discriminated against blacks and allegedly fired Bullard for saying to a co-worker that "blacks have rights too." A 1995 Nevada Supreme Court decision threw out Bullard's *wrongful-termination* award, pointing out that his boss had "the right to fire Bullard because she did not like people like him, people who are sympathetic to African Americans."[29]

As unfair as these cases may seem, they demonstrate that in a nontotalitarian nation, employees and private employers generally remain free to quit and fire as fits their personal interests. There *are* erosions

HR IN THE NEWS

"DEAR ANNIE: I WAS FIRED RECENTLY IN A MANNER THAT I THINK WAS UNFAIR . . .," SIGNED *CONFUSED*

DEAR ANNIE: I was fired recently in a manner that I think was unreasonable and unfair, and I'm trying to decide whether to sue. But most of the reading I have done seems to indicate that an employer can terminate someone "at will." If that is true, then what exactly does the phrase "wrongful termination" mean?

CONFUSED

DEAR CONFUSED: I talked to several lawyers for you, and I doubt you're going to like what they said, but here goes. "Employment at will" is indeed the dominant principle of U.S. labor law, meaning that your employer can sack you anytime for any reason. "Most Americans just don't buy this," notes James Nagle, a partner in Goodwin Procter & Hoar in Boston. "They think any firing that isn't 'fair' should be called 'wrongful.'" Juries often agree, which is why it is sometimes (though rarely) worth suing even when the law is against you.

But a great deal depends on the circumstances in which you were fired, which, alas, you haven't told me. First, there are some exceptions to employment-at-will, notably if you were covered by an employment contract or a union agreement that spelled out how and why you could be canned. Another exception: If your employer fired you in violation of public policy, i.e., in contravention of antidiscrimination laws (age, race, sex) or because you fulfilled some civic responsibility like serving on a jury.

Public policy is a standard that varies widely from state to state—for instance, you can't be fired for smoking in the office in Kentucky, but you could be dismissed for the same offense in California—and, says employment lawyer David Skidmore from the firm Frost & Jacobs in Cincinnati, "'public policy' sometimes gets used as a catchall for situations that fall outside the other exceptions."

In other words, talk to an attorney in your state and explain what happened. "Be honest with your lawyer," urges Skidmore. "Don't try to make your story fit one of the exceptions to employment-at-will if it really didn't, because nothing is worse for your career—or your bank account—than a fabricated case that unravels in the courtroom." He's seen a few of these, and they are not pretty.

SOURCE: Annie Fisher, "Ask Annie," *Fortune* 137 (April 13, 1998): 172. Reprinted with permission.

to this at-will doctrine, all of which have a public policy element:

❶ *Civil rights laws.* These laws create protected classes which cannot be fired for the mere reason of their protected-class status. For instance, employers can fire older employees, but not just *because* they are older.

❷ *Contracts.* Formal employment contracts fall into two major categories: collective bargaining contracts and individual contracts. Collective bargaining contracts or "labor agreements" almost all have a "just cause" requirement which limits terminations to those with good reasons—often as determined by an arbitrator. Individual contracts generally specify "just cause" or in some other way limit the employer's right to discharge.

❸ *Whistle-blower provisions or public policy.* Most laws which provide a forum for employees to complain against their employers contain a **whistle-blower** provision which specifically says that the employer cannot fire or discriminate against the "whistle-blower." OSHA, the National Labor Relations Act, worker's compensation laws, civil rights acts, the Age Discrimination in Employment Act, the Americans with Disabilities Act, and other such acts all contain a provision generally protecting the complaining employee and employees who provide testimony or cooperate in agency investigations. Indeed, employees cannot be terminated for refusing to break a law. Sometimes this erosion is referred to as "public policy," but the cases almost always link to whistle-blowing.

❹ *Public sector protections.* Hundreds of federal, state, and local laws specifically require "just cause" before any of the millions of government workers can be terminated. For instance, the Civil Service Reform Act requires that discharges of government employees be for cause.

At this point in the list, it is clear that significant millions of employees cannot be fired for "bad cause or no cause at all" or simply because of their race, religion, or gender. However, there are two smaller or limited erosions which should be discussed.

❺ *Good faith and fair dealing.* California and a small number of other states have a law which states that there is an implied contract of good faith and fair dealing between employers and employees. In essence, this allows the courts in those states to substitute their own judgment about good faith and fair dealing for the judgment of employers and employees. In one case, the standard for the employer became to "treat employees in a fair and reasonable manner." An example of violating this implied standard was firing an employee to avoid paying a Christmas bonus.[30]

❻ *Implied contract.* This erosion worries employers. An implied contract is one which is not formal nor is it written in the form of a contract. These cases are few and far between, but open windows for judges to have a final say in termination cases. Most implied contracts are based upon *other* written employer documents. For instance, Blue Cross–Blue Shield of Michigan claimed employees were at-will, but the company lawyers must have forgotten to tell HR, because the company's personnel manual stated that employees would be discharged for cause. Not surprisingly, the court found that Blue Cross needed cause to fire employees. The few cases where employees were fired for failing to violate a law (like OSHA or tax laws) might also be interpreted as implied-contract cases since certainly there are written documents at each work place claiming to comply with laws.

There are numerous cases which attempt to abolish the employment-at-will doctrine entirely. Some of these cite the Civil Rights Act of 1871 and attempt to require a "just cause" requirement if the employee has been "injured in his person or property" by the termination.[31] Others argue that an employee's discharge constitutes an actual legal injury. For instance, the Ninth Federal Circuit Court has ruled that under U.S. Code, Section 1985(2) of Title 42, at-will employees can sue their employers when terminated, but most other circuits disagree. Section 1985(2) is more generally considered a whistle-blower protection for those giving testimony in court.[32]

Many employers are changing HR policies and practices to minimize any implied contract. Some of the steps employers are taking to minimize their risk include the following:

- ***At-will policy.*** Maintain, in writing, a strict at-will policy that states that employees may leave at any time of their own will and that the employer may ask them to leave under the same conditions.[33]
- ***At-will statements.*** Many employers have added at-will statements to their employment application forms. Applicants are required to sign the statements to be considered for a position. A survey of statements used by employers indicates that they vary in level of assertion, some being "strong," others "moderate" or "soft" (see Figure 16–5). All

FIGURE 16–5   EXAMPLES OF EMPLOYMENT-AT-WILL STATEMENTS

Strong

I understand that if I am employed by "XYZ" Company that my employment and compensation can be terminated, with or without cause, and with or without notice at any time, at the option of either the company or myself. I also understand that neither this application for employment nor any present or future employee handbook or personnel policy manual is an employment agreement, either expressed or implied, and that no employee or manager of "XYZ" company except the vice president of human resources has any authority to enter into any agreement for employment for any specified period of time, or to make any agreement contrary to the foregoing.

Moderate

I understand that my employment is not governed by any written or oral contract and is considered an "at-will" arrangement. This means that I am free, as is the company, to terminate the employment relationship at any time for any reason, so long as there is no violation of applicable federal or state law.

In the event of employment, I understand that my employment is not for any definite period or succession of periods and is considered an "at-will" arrangement. That means I am free to terminate my employment at any time for any reason, as is the company, so long as there is no violation of applicable federal or state law.

Soft

I understand that, if employed, I may end my employment at any time and that the employer has the same right with any employees. I understand my employment is "at-will," as it is not the practice of the company to enter into employment contracts, express or implied.

I understand that no representative of the company is authorized to state or imply that a contract for permanent employment shall exist between the company and me.

SOURCE: Raymond L. Hilgert, "Employers Protected by At-Will Statements," *HRMagazine* (March 1991): 57–60. Used by permission.

three levels of at-will statements provide (1) that *both* the employee and the employer have the right, at any time, to terminate the employment contract; (2) that the employment situation is for no definite period of time; and (3) that the employment is defined to be at will. Many other employers, however, responded that they decided not to require such statements because they "conflicted with the organization's approach to managing its personnel."[34]

- **Standard revision.** State that the at-will standard can only be modified in writing by the CEO of the company.
- **Termination conduct.** List examples of conduct that may result in immediate termination. Specify, however, that the list is not definitive, but only a list of examples.
- **Progressive discipline.** Utilize progressive discipline and document all steps taken. Do not, however, guarantee continued employment until all steps have been exhausted. Reserve the right to discharge an employee without completing all steps.

- **Probationary periods.** Do not establish probationary periods for a specific length of time, such as 90 days, which may guarantee the employee 90 days of work.[35]
- **Employee handbooks.** Employers are revising employee handbooks for the purpose of removing any reference to "just cause," "fairness," "permanent employee," or "job security." The employee-based book can be considered an implied contract; thus, any policies or procedures that are included must be followed by an employer.

OUTSIDE MISCONDUCT

When an employer learns that an employee has been involved in a crime outside the work place, it may be faced with a difficult decision. If the employee is fired, the employer may face a legal suit involving wrongful discharge, discrimination, or defamation—and may lose. However, if no action is taken, and the employee commits a wrongful act against a customer or co-worker, the employer may face a legal suit for negligent inaction. Thus, such situations must be handled carefully. The first factor to consider in such a case is whether it is an arrest or a conviction. If an employee is arrested and jailed, he or she can be put on a leave of absence until the outcome is known. If the employee is arrested but is not jailed, the employer may allow the employee to return to work until the issue is resolved. The logical exceptions to this policy involve employees accused of assault, child abuse, rape, or other serious crimes of violence where the effect on co-workers must be considered. Thus, the employee may be put on leave or suspension until the case is settled. Once a case is settled, before deciding on a disciplinary action or discharge, the employer should consider several factors:[36]

1 **The relationship between the job and the misconduct.** This is probably the most critical factor. Many employers would be on shaky grounds for firing an employee for drunken and disorderly conduct or off-duty use of marijuana, while termination for a crime of violence would usually be on firm ground.

2 **Tenure.** A 20-year veteran may be given a second chance if a lesser crime was committed, while a new hire might be terminated.

3 **Public interaction.** Employees who must work with the public—on the employer's premises or elsewhere—can be dismissed if they have committed a crime that indicates that their continued employment might endanger the public or affect the employer's ability to operate the business effectively.

Before finalizing a decision in such a case, the employer should make sure that the decision is consistent with the way others were treated in the past. In addition, the employer should consider that if what occurred outside the work place has no relationship to the job, then it probably should not be the basis for a disciplinary action.

ARBITRATION OF DISCRIMINATION COMPLAINTS

The recent Supreme Court decision, in **Gilmer v. Interstate/Johnson Lane Corp.,** upheld an agreement written by the employer which required an employee to use binding arbitration for his employment discrimination complaint concerning his termination. Many employers are now using this approach, requiring the use of neutral ad hoc arbitrators, to handle discrimination claims. Federal government agencies and personal-injury plaintiff lawyers are outraged, and legislation to reverse *Gilmer* is being considered. However, extrajudicial binding arbitration has been used successfully for a century, is insisted upon by unions in all union contracts, and is encouraged by the 1925 Federal Arbitration Act (FAA) to settle commercial disagreements.

These *"mandatory arbitration"* (the term used by detractors) approaches divert employee (and commercial) complaints away from politicized government agencies and courts and into formal arbitration hearings where the parties themselves pick a specific arbitrator(s) to hear their case. According to the *Steelworkers Trilogy* of 1960 Supreme Court cases, labor arbitration is actually superior to courts because it is faster, less expensive, and more focused upon the actual complaint. In the 1983 *Alexander Trilogy* of cases, the Court said that arbitrators were not equipped enough to be the *final* disposition of all discrimination cases, but can hear such complaints. For instance, in *Alexander* v. *Gardner-Denver,* the Court said that a black union employee has the right to have his termination case heard both by the labor arbitrator *and* EEOC, since there was an element of race discrimination. In the 1985 *Mitsubishi Trilogy,* the Court again upheld the presumption favoring arbitrability and lessened the criticism of arbitration which some saw in the *Alexander* cases. For instance, in *Mitsubishi Motors Corp.* v. *Soler Chrysler Plymouth Inc.,* the Court said "by agreeing to arbitrate a statutory claim, a party does not forgo the substantive rights afforded by the statute [but] submits to their resolution in an arbitral, rather than judicial, forum."[37]

When Gilmer registered as a securities representative of the New York Stock Exchange (NYSE), his application said that he was required to arbitrate "any dispute, claim, or controversy . . . required to be arbitrated under the rules (which include termination complaints)" of the NYSE. Gilmer was fired at age 62 and later filed an Age Discrimination in Employment Act (ADEA) complaint with the EEOC and later the federal court. The court ruled that Gilmer's ADEA claim was arbitrable under the required arbitration agreement and that Gilmer could *not* litigate the claim. Gilmer's decision disagrees with *Alexander,* and follows *Steelworkers* and *Mitsubishi*—favoring arbitration. The court said the FAA "reflects a liberal federal policy favoring arbitration agreements."[38]

Gilmer has since been extended to all forms of statutory discrimination (race, sex, religion, and so on) by every U.S. Court of Appeals.

- Many reasons may cause an employee to perform unsatisfactorily. Some of these reasons may be directly attributable to management's shortcomings or to some other problem of the organization.

- Discipline should be applied only when it has been determined that the employee is the cause of the unsatisfactory performance. There are different approaches to the disciplinary process; the most effective technique involves administration of *preventive discipline*.

- Corrective counseling is a particularly important part of the *positive discipline approach*. It helps build respect and trust between the supervisor and subordinate and encourages the employee to find his or her own solutions to problems. The more the employee participates in the problem-solving process, the greater the chances for a permanent improvement in employee behavior.

- Supervisors should be trained to follow the *hot-stove rule*. With this technique, discipline is administered immediately, with warning, consistently, and impersonally.

- *Turnover* should be calculated at each workplace. Costs associated with turnover are high, but some turnover is considered functional.

- Discharge can be traumatic and costly for both the dismissed employee and the organization. The discharge should be thoroughly planned and carried out in a professional manner.

- The doctrine of employment-at-will has eroded in recent years because court decisions have supported employees' claims of unfair and unjust treatment. HR rules, policies, and procedures must be closely examined to ensure that they comply with federal and state laws.

- Employees who are disciplined or terminated may file defamation suits against their former employers. HR policies should limit the communication of such actions and only provide information that is factual, on a confidential basis, to those who have a true need to know.

Defamation Claim at Milbrae Window Co.

Alexis Rojas was terminated by her supervisor, Colleen Wilson, on Friday, December 23, at 4:30 P.M. She was just putting on her coat when Wilson asked her to step into the office of President Synhorst. She was given no explanation. Rojas had been employed by the Milbrae Window Company for 12 years as an outside sales representative. She had won the company's highest annual sales award in four of the past six years and was generally considered one of the most loyal employees. Thus, her abrupt termination came as a shock to her and everyone else. She drove home in a daze but decided to telephone her best friends, Shari Mendoza and Juan Estaban, as soon as possible to ask if they knew what had caused her dismissal. Neither of the two had heard a word from anyone and were as puzzled as Rojas.

President Synhorst had made the decision to terminate Rojas on Thursday after receiving substantial evidence from local law enforcement officials and two representatives of major clients that Rojas had accepted kickbacks on large sales orders. Synhorst's attorney recommended the immediate dismissal.

By Monday all of the 300 employees at Milbrae Window Company had heard of the termination. Many were angry and demanded an explanation, but Synhorst refused to comment. Then at 1:00 P.M. almost all of the production and sales employees refused to leave the cafeteria and return to work until Synhorst answered their questions. They began talking about unionizing. Synhorst decided that the situation could become violent and would at least cause major morale problems for several days, and thus walked to the cafeteria at about 1:50 P.M. The employees demanded an explanation, and the following exchange occurred:

Synhorst: Ms. Rojas was terminated for just cause.

Mendoza: And what was the cause?

Synhorst: I can't say.

Mendoza: Why wasn't even Rojas given a reason?

Synhorst: She knows why . . .

Estaban: She says she doesn't!

Synhorst: She knows.

Estaban: She has been a good friend to many of us for years, and she was a good employee. She says she has *no* idea why she was let go . . . and we believe her!

Mendoza: We demand an explanation; is this a racial thing?

Synhorst: *(pause)* No, she was let go because she took kickbacks, pure and simple. Now get back to work, or I'll start docking your pay!

QUESTIONS

1. Rojas, after hearing what occurred, is considering suing Synhorst for defamation. Do you think she has a case? Explain.

2. Would you change your answer to the first question if you knew she was guilty of accepting kickbacks?

3. What could Synhorst have done to possibly avoid the confrontation with the employees?

4. If Rojas was guilty, should she have been terminated for a first offense or given a different disciplinary action?

1. COUNSELING THE TROUBLED EMPLOYEE

PURPOSE

To show the importance of using correct counseling techniques with troubled employees.

INTRODUCTION

Disciplining and counseling the troubled employee—the employee who suffers from a personal problem such as alcoholism to the extent that he or she is unable to perform effectively—presents a special challenge to supervisors.

For example, it may not be appropriate for the supervisor to discuss drinking or a suspicion of drinking because diagnosis is the job of trained professionals. What is the job of the supervisor?

The supervisor's job is to focus on *job performance* during counseling. The supervisor should confront the employee with specific performance problems in an attempt to motivate the employee to seek treatment and rehabilitation. The supervisor will only aggravate the problem by accusing the employee of having a personal problem such as alcoholism, drug abuse, or emotional instability. In addition, it is the supervisor's job to make it clear to the employee what will happen if the unsatisfactory performance continues. Usually, that means discipline, including the possibility of discharge.

The theory behind this method is simple: If the employee's job is on the line, he or she will likely seek treatment rather than face being fired.

TASK

Listed below are several statements that a supervisor made to an employee suspected of excessive drinking. These are actual statements that have been collected anonymously from employees through surveys. Your job is to evaluate the supervisor's statements and, if necessary, to write what the supervisor *should* have said. After you have completed the exercise, your instructor will lead a discussion on discipline and the troubled employee.

Effective counseling depends very much on saying the right thing to the employee who is suspected of being troubled. Saying the wrong thing will do little to motivate the employee to overcome the problem and could well make matters worse.

Kim, the supervisor of a large group of computer personnel, suspects that Skip, a computer operator, is suffering from alcoholism. At one time, Skip was an excellent employee, but he has recently begun to perform erratically and demonstrates behavioral problems. For example, Skip has made many errors in operating the computer and has experienced several interpersonal problems with Kim and other co-workers. Kim has just begun to talk to Skip in her office. All of Kim's statements are poor and represent the use of improper counseling techniques. Your job is to decide what Kim should have said.

WHAT KIM SAID

1. "Skip, I've really been troubled by your performance lately. You've made a lot of computer errors, and you haven't gotten along well with the other employees."

2. "Skip, I strongly suspect that problems stem from excessive drinking. It's no secret that you've had drinking problems for some time."

3. "If your performance does not improve, you'll be digging your own grave."

4. *(With a heated voice)* "Don't disagree with me, Skip. I can back up everything I say. Like it or not, these are the facts."

5. "I have decided that the best thing for you to do is attend AA meetings once a week until your problem clears up."

6. "The company has special programs available for alcoholic employees."

WHAT KIM SHOULD HAVE SAID

_____
_____
_____

_____
_____
_____

_____
_____
_____

_____
_____
_____

_____
_____
_____

_____
_____
_____

EXPERIENTIAL EXERCISES—cont'd

7. "I heard you were drinking in the men's room this morning. Is that true?"

_____
_____
_____

8. "Look, don't disagree with me. You've got a drinking problem and you know it. All the facts point to it."

_____
_____
_____

9. "You have a real attendance problem and I think I know why. You're on some kind of drug, aren't you? Aren't those needle marks on your arms?"

_____
_____
_____

10. "I know what your problem is, but don't worry; we're not going to fire you if you attend the special program the personnel department has for alcoholics."

_____
_____
_____

SOURCE: Adapted from F. Kuzmits, R. Herden, and L. Sussman, _Managing the Unsatisfactory Employee_ (Homewood, IL: Dow Jones-Irwin, 1984), 82–83.

2. CAUSE FOR TERMINATION?

PURPOSE

An employee's right to privacy outside the work place is generally protected by law in the United States. However, when an employee's outside activity makes the news, the employer is faced with a difficult decision. In some cases, an employee's criminal activity outside the work place warrants suspension or termination. In others, it may not affect their job at all, and thus no disciplinary action is warranted.

TASK

You are the HR director for a 2,000-employee retail sales organization. In each of the situations described below, you must choose one of five courses of action: (1) termination; (2) temporary suspension; (3) written warning; (4) notification to the employee that he or she is not allowed to return to work (without pay) until the issue is resolved; (5) no disciplinary action.

SITUATION

1. A sales clerk is convicted of sexually molesting a child.

2. A supervisor is arrested for theft while working on a second job.

3. A janitor is one of 56 people arrested in a political demonstration.

4. A sales supervisor is convicted of tax evasion.

5. A window dresser is convicted of drunk driving.

6. A maintenance person is arrested in a massage parlor.

7. A shift supervisor is given a three-day jail sentence for failing to pay child support.

8. A security guard is convicted on charges of grand auto theft.

COURSE OF ACTION

_____
_____
_____
_____
_____
_____
_____
_____
_____
_____
_____
_____
_____
_____
_____
_____
_____
_____
_____

EXPERIENTIAL EXERCISES—cont'd

9. A computer technician is arrested in a bar fight.   _____

10. A stock clerk is convicted of assaulting a neighbor.   _____

KEY TERMS AND CONCEPTS

Corrective counseling

Defamation

Dehire

Disciplinary discharge

Employment-at-will

Gilmer v. *Interstate/Johnson Lane Corp.*

Hot-stove rule

Negligent hiring

Negligent misrepresentation

Positive discipline

Preventive discipline

Progressive discipline

Suspension

Turnover

Whistle-blower

Work place searches and surveillance

REVIEW QUESTIONS

1. What are the four general causes of unsatisfactory employee performance?

2. Compare and contrast punitive, preventive, and positive discipline.

3. What are the steps involved in the process of positive discipline?

4. How can an employer legally and fairly utilize work place searches or surveillance of employees?

5. Define turnover and discuss when it is that a work place should decide it has too much.

6. How can employers avoid rare defamation claims? Negligent hiring claims? Negligent representation claims?

7. What is the concept of employment at will, and how can organizations avoid legal problems involving this doctrine?

8. Can employers require employees to sign agreements to take discrimination complaints to arbitration instead of agencies like the EEOC or Federal Courts?

9. When should an employee be disciplined for actions outside the work place?

DISCUSSION QUESTIONS

1. In the past, supervisors often used punitive discipline against their employees. What reasons might account for this?

2. With corrective counseling, the supervisor encourages the employee to find solutions to his or her problems. Why might this method be more effective than having the supervisor tell employees how to solve their problems?

3. Assume that you were recently appointed to the job of HR director for a small bank. How would you communicate the company's rules and regulations to employees?

4. If an employee shows up at work intoxicated, what action should the supervisor take? Should the supervisor counsel the employee about the evils of drinking?

5. An employee has repeatedly caused problems with peers and has flaunted his disobedience of work rules until he is terminated through a progressive discipline system. Should the other employees be made aware of this?

6. As HR director you read in the morning newspaper that one of your 20-year employees was arrested for mail fraud. What should you do?

7. Your company spent $200,000 in legal fees last year to settle three EEOC complaints from fired employees. Is there any strategy or tactic you might apply to lessen this burden?

ENDNOTES

Chapter 16

1. Mary Kathryn Zachary, "EEOC Issues Guidance on Retaliation," *Supervision* 59 (October 1998): 21.

2. Lynn Atkinson, "Employer Sees Insubordination: Court Suspects Retaliation," *HR Focus* 75 (April 1998): 15.

3. "Bull Moose Managers Wrongfully Fired, Judge Says," *Iron Age New Steel* 14 (September 1998): 22.

4. *Employee Conduct and Discipline* (Washington, D.C.: Bureau of National Affairs, 1973), 4.

5. *Employee Discipline and Discharge* (Washington, D.C.: Bureau of National Affairs, 1985), 4.

6. I. Asherman and S. Vance, "Documentation: A Tool for Effective Management," *Personnel Journal* 60 (August 1981): 641–643.

7. Georgeanna Henshaw and Kernwood C. Youmans, "Employee Privacy in the Workplace and an Employer's Right to Conduct Workplace Searches and Surveillance," SHRM *Legal Report* (Spring 1990): 1–5.

8. Ibid.

9. A. Bryant, "Replacing Punitive Discipline with a Positive Approach," *Personnel Administrator* 10 (February 1984): 79–87.

10. Frank N. Wilner, "Labor relations: How CSXT Is Leaving Past Practices Behind," *Railway Age* 199 (November 1998): 72.

11. Leon Rubis, "HR Update," *HRMagazine* 43 (May 1998): 2.

12. Barbara Ettorre, "How Are Companies Keeping the Employees They Want?" *Management Review* 86 (May 1, 1997): 2.

13. Cheryl Comeau-Kirchner, "Reducing Turnover Is a Tough Job," *Management Review* 88 (January 1999): 9.

14. "Traditional Retention Methods Aren't Deterring Employee Turnover," *HRMagazine* 43 (August 1998): 20.

15. Jason D. Shaw, John E. Delery, G. Douglas Jenkins Jr., and Nina Gupta, "An organization-level analysis of voluntary and involuntary turnover," *Academy of Management Journal* 41 (October 1998), 511. *See also* Gary A. Adams and Terry A. Beehr, "Turnover and Retirement: A Comparison of Their Similarities and Differences," *Personnel Psychology* 51 (Autumn 1998), 643–665 for a discussion of similar findings comparing quits with retirements.

16. "Examples of Common Punishments," *Occupational Hazards* 60 (October 1998), 113.

17. Marty Denis and Jon Andes, "Defamation—Do You Tell Employees Why a Coworker Was Discharged?" *Employee Relations Law Journal* 16, no. 4 (Spring 1991): 469–479.

18. Ibid.

19. Robert J. Posch, Jr., "Your Personal Exposure for Interoffice Communications," *Direct Marketing* 61 (August 1998), 64.

20. *Milkovich* v. *Lorain Journal Co.,* 110 S. Ct. 2695, 111 L. Ed. 2d. 1 (1990).

21. Robert S. Soderstrom and James R. Murray, "Defamation in employment: Suits by at-will employees," *FICC Quarterly* (Summer 1992): 395–426.

22. Ibid., p. 410.

23. Gabriella Stern, "Companies Discover That Some Firings Backfire into Costly Defamation Suits," *The Wall Street Journal* (May 5, 1993): B1.

24. Soderstrom and Murray, "Defamation in Employment," 395.

25. Robert J. Posch, Jr., "Your personal exposure for interoffice communications," 66.

26. Ibid.

27. *Payne* v. *Western Atlantic R.R.,* 81 Tenn. 507, 519–520 (1884).

28. "Matt Siegel, "Yes, they can fire you," *Fortune* 138 (October 26, 1998), 301.

29. Ibid., 302.

30. Alan B. Krueger, "The Evolution of Unjust-Dismissal Legislation in the United States," *Industrial and Labor Relations Review* 44, no. 4 (July 1991): 644–649.

31. *Michael A. Haddle* vs *Jeanetter G. Garrison et al.* 1998 case in which the Washington State Supreme Court followed this reasoning, cited in "Right to Sue Expanded," *Business Insurance Updates* (December 21, 1998).

32. Charles J. Muhl, "Constitutional protection for "at-will" employees?" *Monthly Labor Review* 121 (October 1998), 32.

33. Debbie Keary, "Minimize the Risk of Wrongful Discharge," *HR News* (June 1990): 7.

34. Raymond L. Hilgert, "Employers Protected by At-Will Statements," *HRMagazine* (March 1991): 57–60.

35. Keary, "Minimize the Risk of Wrongful Discharge," 7.

36. Steve Bergsman, "Employee Conduct Outside the Workplace," *HRMagazine* (March 1991): 62–64.

37. Andrea Fitz, "The Debate Over Mandatory Arbitration in Employment Disputes," *Dispute Resolution Journal* 54 (February 1999), 36.

38. Ibid., 39.

Appendix

APPENDIX OUTLINE

HR IN THE NEWS

RESEARCH: USING ATTITUDE SURVEYS TO EVALUATE NEW INCENTIVE PAY PLAN

Simcom is a young, small, privately held, rapid-growth company with locations in Orlando and Phoenix. It builds flight simulators and trains pilots on small aircraft. The 80 employees work in teams based on functional units. In 1992, senior management asked a consultant to assess the need for an incentive pay plan. The current plan was based upon the market and had seniority-based increases. The company's new president wanted associates to act like owners and wanted to examine the possibility of incentive pay to help bring this about.

In response to this situation, Simcom and the consultant implemented a three-phase project. In phase one, a survey was developed to assess the need for incentive pay. In phase two, it developed and implemented an incentive pay system in 1997. In phase three, management assessed the effectiveness of the incentive pay system by comparing the survey results prior to the pay system change with survey results after the change. Each time surveys were used, focus group discussions were also held with employees. The consultant explored whether "soft" data, such as satisfaction scores, might be helpful in gauging pay system effectiveness.

Several statistically significant correlations were found when comparing the pre- and post-change employee attitudes about pay. Attitudes about pay improved, and extrinsic satisfaction was also more positive. More research is needed since performance slackened somewhat after the change, but could not be attributed solely to the incentive plan because there was significant turnover among employees. "Soft" data proved to be useful in this case.[1]

In the past, research may have had the connotation of manipulating useless details using difficult math and statistics. However, we know that managers and HR professionals collect information, make sense of it, then carefully diagnose and solve problems. From a scientific standpoint, this is *research*. In this information age, and era of high education levels, organizations demand more-sophisticated research. A front-line supervisor can now control and manipulate more information today than an entire HR department could 10 years ago—and is expected to. Problems managing people continue to be some of the hardest yet most important problems to solve.

In this Appendix, we define key terms in organizational research, identify *who* does *what kind* of business research, list and discuss common research techniques, and list helpful Web sites for conducting HR, management and Internet research. We hope that this will prepare the student to engage in research both at work and in student projects.

HR AND MANAGEMENT RESEARCH

HR and management research is the collection and investigation of facts related to HR and management

problems in order to eliminate or reduce those problems. Using research, managers can substitute facts about human behavior for their hunches, guesses, and gut reactions. Specific uses of this research include:

- Measurement and evaluation of present work conditions.
- Prediction of future conditions, events, and behavior patterns.
- Appraisal of current employer policies, programs, and activities.
- Discovery of rational bases for revising current policies, programs, and activities.
- Evaluation of proposed or new policies, programs, and activities.
- Examination and identification of best practices across employers.

TYPES OF RESEARCH

Many books have been written about research. Here's some basic information to get you started. There are basically two types of research: basic and applied. *Basic research* (or *pure research*) is undertaken simply to advance knowledge in a particular field—gaining knowledge for its own sake. Pure or basic research has no immediate application at the work place (or anywhere else). For example, if a researcher discovers something new about brain chemistry and sleep patterns, it may take years before someone is able to apply this knowledge to managing people at the work place.

Applied organizational research is conducted to solve a particular work problem and can immediately be put to use at the work place. Applied researchers may be interested in the new *basic* knowledge about sleep patterns and discover its relationship to evening shift workers. Building upon basic research, applied research might identify a preemployment test which selects people who will perform better on evening shifts—something many employers can use immediately. Other applied research can start without building upon basic research. The famous Hawthorne studies are applied research as are the national studies on turnover rates. Common applied research areas include examination of training effectiveness, validation of selection systems, performance appraisal, compensation systems and pay levels, benefit systems, absenteeism and turnover, job satisfaction, and job design.

THE RESEARCHERS

A generation ago, 39 percent of HR research was done by private research organizations, 34 percent by colleges and universities, 22 percent by government agencies, and 5 percent by business firms.[2] Since that study, the shift has been toward businesses doing their own research in cooperation with consulting partners. Government agencies, professional groups (for instance the Society for Human Resource Management [SHRM]), libraries, and other groups have made the Internet an information-packed resource for preparing research.

An example of combining research participants would be the Hatfield Hat Company who keeps its own turnover records and computes various turnover rates (for example, quit and discharge rates), comparing them to regional and manufacturing industry rates for employers of HHC's size—available through SHRM membership at its Web site—from Bureau of National Affairs (BNA), and then meeting with a HR consultant from State University to write up an analysis and plan for improvement of retention.

A list of helpful research sites on the World Wide Web is found inside the cover of this book. A list of the categories of available researchers includes the following.

Federal Government
Fifteen federal agencies spend $500,000 or more per year on statistical research

(see *www.fedstats.gov*). Several of these are helpful in HR research—Bureau of Labor Statistics, Bureau of Economic Analysis, Bureau of the Census, Economic Research Service, IRS's Statistics of Income Division, National Center for Education Statistics, and National Center for Health Statistics. Many other federal agencies offer helpful statistics, including Veterans Affairs, Employment Standards, Employment and Training, EEOC, Health Care Financing, OSHA, Small Business Administration, and Institutes on Aging, Alcohol Abuse, and Health.

HR Associations
Large national and international personnel/HR associations conduct and publish applied research of concern to their members. The Society for Human Resource Management (SHRM) is the largest U.S. HR organization (*www.shrm.org*), and was formerly named American Society for Personnel Administration (ASPA). (See Figure A-1.)

The World Federation of Personnel Management Associations (WFPMA) was founded in 1976 during the annual conference of the SHRM. WFPMA *(www.wfpma. com)* membership now represents about 50 national personnel associations and nearly 400,000 personnel professionals worldwide. The founding members of the WFPMA were:

- European Association for Personnel Management (EAPM)
- Interamerican Federation of Personnel Administration (FIDAP)
- Society for Human Resource Management (SHRM)

WFPMA now also includes:

- Canadian Council of Human Resources Associations (CCHRA)
- North American Human Resource Management Association (NAHRMA) which includes Canada, the United States, and Mexico
- Institute of Personnel Management/IPM South Africa
- Asia Pacific Federation of Human Resource Management (APFHRM)

There are other organizations concerned with functional areas within HR. In the United States these include the American Society for Training and Development (ASTD), American Compensation Association (ACA), American Association for Affirmative Action, Employee Benefit Research Institute (EBRI), The American Safety

FIGURE A–1

& Health Institute, American Arbitration Association (AAA), and the International Association of Business Communicators (IABC).

Private Research Organizations

Many private organizations have been formed with the purpose of conducting research in HR and management. Some of these include the Bureau of National Affairs, the Conference Board, and Commerce Clearing House. Other broader consulting companies perform HR research, including William M. Mercer Companies and Ernst and Young. Some of the larger HR information technology firms like PeopleSoft *(www.peoplesoft.com)* also perform dynamic HR research.

Colleges and Universities

Schools are a great source for research in the HR and management fields. Many faculty members regularly conduct research as a normal part of their job and often consult with employers on management problems. Many universities also operate research centers which focus upon specific areas. For instance, the University of Michigan operates the Survey Research Center which maintains one of the most sophisticated databases on attitudes of employees.

Business Firms

All firms maintain data and perform analysis. Several of the largest companies, like General Electric, IBM, and AT&T, operate full-scale departments of behavioral research. HR professionals often receive requests from management to conduct special ad hoc studies of HR problems in addition to regular periodic analytical reports. Specific research requests may include investigating a very high number of employee grievances at one location; examining absenteeism and recommending a program to control the level; justifying a pay increase; developing a team performance appraisal instrument; or developing a better, valid, employee selection process using the Internet.

HR RESEARCH PUBLICATIONS

The results of HR research may be found in a variety of printed media. The prudent manager and staff member should keep up-to-date on major research results and use the findings to promote managerial effectiveness, employee productivity, and effective HR management.

The most practical and expedient way for HR professionals to keep on top of the research is by regularly reading a selected group of HR journals and magazines, subscribing to one of many electronic services, and joining one or more professional news on interest groups. For instance, Cornell University hosts the *HRNet* which is sponsored by the Academy of Management and has an open subscription policy for all HR professionals, consultants and academicians.

Figure A-2 contains a list of journals that frequently report research results in a variety of personnel areas. Journals written primarily for the academician are heavy on technical discussions of research techniques and normally report the results of a research undertaking. Journals written primarily for managers and professionals focus on the application of research and are often written in a "how to" format.

FIGURE A–2   JOURNALS USEFUL TO THE MANAGER AND HR PROFESSIONAL

Primarily for the Academician
Academy of Management Journal
Academy of Management Review
Administrative Science Quarterly
Industrial and Labor Relations Review
Journal of Applied Behavioral Science
Journal of Applied Psychology
Organizational Behavior and Human Decision
    Processes
Personnel Psychology

Primarily for the Manager or Administrator
Academy of Management Executive
Advanced Management Journal
Business Horizons

California Management Review
Harvard Business Review
HRMagazine
Human Resource Management
Labor Law Journal
Management Review
Monthly Labor Review
Organizational Dynamics
Personnel
Personnel Journal
Public Personnel Management
Supervisory Management
Training
Training and Development

RESEARCH TECHNIQUES

Many different research techniques exist, and the choice of a particular one depends on the purpose of the research and the type of problem under study. Familiarity with various research techniques is important for two reasons. First, practitioners encounter a variety of HR problems in the work place, and the appropriate research technique must be applied. Second, a broad knowledge of research techniques is necessary in order to read and understand the studies reported by other employers and researchers. The research techniques most often used to conduct HR studies include the survey, interview, historical study, and controlled experiment.

SURVEYS

The employee survey is the most widely used research technique among HR professionals. The most common surveys include the wage survey and the job satisfaction (or attitude) survey.

Job Satisfaction Survey   Although job dissatisfaction has been linked with absenteeism and turnover in many studies, the relationship between job satisfaction and productivity remains controversial and weak. Since morale and job satisfaction have been thought to be important determinants of employee productivity, absenteeism, and turnover, managers have systematically used *job satisfaction surveys* to analyze employee attitudes on important topics.

Many factors contribute to employee job satisfaction. However, the following are the four elements that most surveyed employees reported they like best about their jobs:

1 *The job itself.* Perhaps the most important factor in job satisfaction is the kind of work employees perform (especially when it is challenging or interesting) and the freedom they have to determine how the work is done.

2 *Co-worker relations.* The quality of relationships within the workgroup is very important to employees.

3 *Good supervision.* Job satisfaction is considerably improved when supervisors are perceived to be fair, helpful, competent, and effective.

4 *Opportunity to grow.* Employees derive a great deal of satisfaction from learning and developing new skills. Promotion opportunity is also very important.

On the other hand, the most frequently reported factors that detract from job satisfaction are the following:

1 *Poor supervision.* Insensitive, incompetent, unfair, and uncaring supervisors seem to have the most negative effect on employee job satisfaction.

2 *Interpersonal conflicts.* Interpersonal conflicts, lack of teamwork, unfriendliness among co-workers, and rivalries among managers and supervisors have a major negative effect.

3 *Poor work environment.* Dirty, noisy, unsafe, and unhealthy work conditions also are leading detractors from job satisfaction.

4 *Poor pay.* Possibly symptomatic of other problems, low, uncompetitive pay is nonetheless often reported as one of the things that detracted from overall job satisfaction.

On such surveys, pay and promotions are generally the lowest-ranked items in terms of job satisfaction, while supervision and co-workers, are rated highest.

One of the most widely used job satisfaction surveys is the *Job Descriptive Index (JDI)*. Sample questions on the JDI are shown in Figure A-3.

Specific-Use Questionnaire

HR researchers often find it useful to gather employees' opinions about specific job-related issues at the work place. For example, employees may be asked to evaluate the organization's T&D function, orientation program, a proposed flextime, or a job enrichment program. Because these *specific-use questionnaires* focus on an organization's particular problems or issues, they are generally custommade by members of the HR staff or an outside consultant. Site-specific, or specific-use, questions are often added to another questionnaire.

Survey Administration

The total process of planning, implementing, and analyzing employee surveys and questionnaires includes a number of important elements. Regardless of the type of survey implemented, the following issues should be considered.

Objectives As an initial step, management must identify the objectives of the survey. Common objectives of surveys include the identification of communication problems, excessive turnover, concerns about pay and benefits, T&D needs, and predicting unionization efforts.

Top Management Commitment The interest of top management is critical if the survey is to be of benefit to the organization. In particular, management must be willing to share and frankly discuss the outcomes of the survey with the employees.

Survey Development Surveys may either be developed internally or prepared by an outside consulting firm. While management may be inclined to prepare the survey itself, research indicates several advantages to outside development. The consultant brings experience and objectivity, and there is an art to writing questions. Employees are also apt to have more faith in the process when they see the company pay an outside firm to objectively develop and administer the survey.

Announcing the Survey

Practitioners differ on whether or not a survey administration should be announced in advance. If the survey is a regularly scheduled event at the workplace, there may be benefit in sending a letter to employees explaining what is and is not the purpose of the survey.

In other circumstances, prior announcements about an upcoming survey can stimulate political or group behavior dysfunctional to the survey. The author of this appendix discovered that union officials had "suggested" that employees should respond to the questions by giving the same (negative) prearranged answers. This kind of "marshalling" of responses can happen in other circumstances. In such cases, particularly for a first survey at a work place, an announcement should be made just before the administration of the survey (for example, on the same day). This approach should elicit more honest responses than those marshalled by informal leaders.

Implementation Some important considerations for administering the survey are the following: (1) Allow employees time to complete the survey, (2) administer the survey (if possible) to all employees at the same time, and (3) administer the survey on company premises (research shows that only about one-third of the employees who take a survey home will complete and return it).

Analysis Survey results can reflect total organizational results in comparison to individual employee groups (e.g., older versus younger, male versus female, long length of service versus short length of service). Remember, employees are cautious about identifying themselves on surveys (this author color-coded surveys). Based on the results, problem areas may be identified, and recommendations to overcome these problems might later be developed.

Feedback Survey results should be communicated to the employees soon after they have been tabulated and reviewed by top management. Face-to-face meetings between supervisors and employees are usually most effective for providing survey feedback.

Follow-up Most surveys are *general* in nature— such as the JDI—and do *not* call on management directly to do anything particular in response, other than listen and discuss. Other surveys can operate like a referendum and ask employees what they think should be done. The advisability of such surveys is questionable.

FIGURE A–3   SAMPLE QUESTIONS FROM THE JDI

Think of the work you do at present. How well does each of the following words or phrases describe your work? **In the blank beside each word below, write**

___Y___ for "Yes" if it describes your work
___N___ for "No" if it does NOT describe it
___?___ if you cannot decide

Work on present job

_____ Routine
_____ Satisfying
_____ Good

Think of the kind of supervision that you get on your job. How well does each of the following words or phrases describe this? **In the blank beside each word below, write**

___Y___ for "Yes" if it describes the supervision you get on your job
___N___ for "No" if it does NOT describe it
___?___ if you cannot decide

Supervision

_____ Impolite
_____ Praises good work
_____ Doesn't supervise enough

Think of the pay you get now. How well does each of the following words or phrases describe your present pay" **In the blank beside each word below, write**

___Y___ for "Yes" if it describes your pay
___N___ for "No" if it does NOT describe it
___?___ if you cannot decide

Present pay

_____ Income adequate for normal expenses
_____ Insecure
_____ Less than I deserve

SOURCE: The Job Descriptive Index is copyrighted by Bowling Green State University. The complete forms, scoring key, instructions, and norms can be obtained from Dr. Patricia C. Smith, Department of Psychology, Bowling Green State University, Bowling Green, OH 43403. Used by permission.

Caution   Survey statistics gain meaning only by virtue of relevant comparisons. Survey results can be much more useful if there is a large comparative database collected over a period of time. A one-time survey of worker attitudes, while somewhat useful, can be open to wide interpretation. Surveys gathered over time permit the HR analyst to note trends and comparisons or determine if the results are simply related to specific one-time events.

EXIT INTERVIEWS

Organizations often conduct *exit interviews* with employees who have voluntarily decided to leave. These employees can provide valuable information about the work environment that might not be available through any other source.

The success of the exit interview depends largely on the employees' belief that their responses will not affect the employer's response to future reference requests. Personnel interviewers generally agree that to obtain the employee's cooperation, the interviewer should be someone from the HR department and definitely not the immediate supervisor. The subject matter of the structured interview usually includes the reason for leaving, perceptions of the supervisor, salary, benefits, training, the job, and opportunities for advancement. The employee may provide more candid responses if the interviewer's interest in improving conditions for his or her co-workers is emphasized.

HISTORICAL STUDIES

HR researchers often find that tracking certain data over time helps them gain greater insight into human behavior. By isolating a small number of variables, a *historical study* analyzes patterns over weeks, months, or years. For example, many organizations analyze absenteeism and turnover data to assess whether these problems are increasing, decreasing, or remaining unchanged. One example of a long-standing historical (or longitudinal) study is a project mentioned earlier—the University of Michigan's Survey Research Center Job Satisfaction Survey. Since 1958, the center has tracked a large sample of employee attitudes concerning overall satisfaction with work. The research indicates that most employees are satisfied in general with their jobs and that workers' attitudes have changed only in certain ways since the study began.

One of the most fascinating—yet frustrating—longitudinal studies on job satisfaction is a study by Barry Staw. His study followed individuals for 30 years, starting with collecting their mood or satisfaction level in high school (cheerful, irritable, congenial) as assessed by counselors. These scores were found to be highly correlated with job satisfaction scores collected years later. The score from an adolescent at school was one of the best predictors of how that same person would respond on a job satisfaction survey 10, 20, and 30 years later.[3] This stability of satisfaction may be very frustrating to a manager who believes that his or her highest duty should be trying to create satisfaction at work.

CONTROLLED EXPERIMENTS

Compared to surveys and interviews, *controlled experiments* are seldom conducted at actual worksites. Unlike the scientist's laboratory or classroom, where variables are created and controlled, the HR researcher in an organization has little such control. Ma-

nipulating human or technological factors simply for the sake of experimentation is impractical. But there are some occasions when this technique is feasible and may help a research effort. To illustrate the steps involved, a job enrichment pilot study in a large manufacturing plant will be used.[4]

- *Define the problem.* Poor productivity, excessive rejects and so on.
- *Evaluate alternatives and select an alternative.* Possible alternatives: Implement an incentive pay system, introduce new technology, tighten up through closer supervision, and job enrichment. Select job enrichment.
- *State the hypothesis.* Six months after the implementation of job enrichment, average employee productivity will have increased by 20 percent and the average rejects per employee will have decreased by 25 percent.
- *Select experimental and control groups.* Implement job enrichment in one area; select a similar area with no job enrichment to serve as a control group.
- *Measure experimental and control groups prior to the experiment.* Collect productivity and quality data for both groups before the experiment begins.
- *Conduct the experiment.* Implement job enrichment (experimental group only).
- *Measure experimental and control groups after the experiment.* Collect productivity and quality data for six months after the implementation of job enrichment.
- *Analyze data, draw conclusions, report results.* Compare before-and-after data, determine the impact of the program, report conclusions to top management.

COST-BENEFIT ANALYSIS

HR activities such as recruiting, selection, training, and labor relations are increasingly being measured and evaluated in economic terms. By attaching dollars-and-cents criteria to HR programs and problems—what is called *cost-benefit analysis*—HR professionals are able to generate support and confidence from top management, who ultimately decide on the size of the HR budget. By analyzing HR activities and problems by cost, HR professionals not only can evaluate proposed programs but also can identify costly personnel problems that require immediate attention.

ENDNOTES

Appendix

1. Robert L. Heneman, Don E. Eskew, and Julie A. Fox, "Using Employee Attitude Surveys to Evaluate a New Incentive Pay Program," *Compensation and Benefits Review* 30 (January 19, 1998): 13.

2. William C. Byham, *The Uses of Personnel Research,* Research Study 91 (New York: American Management Association, 1968), 8.

3. B. M. Staw, N. E. Bell, and J. A. Clausen, "The Dispositional Approach to Job Attitudes: A Lifetime Longitudinal Test," *Administrative Science Quarterly* 31 (1986): 56–77.

4. For details of the various forms of experimental design, see D. T. Campbell and J. C. Stanley, *Experimental and Quasi-Experimental Designs for Research* (Chicago: Rand-McNally, 1963); T. S. Bateman and G. R. Ferris, *Method and Analysis in Organizational Research* (Reston, VA: Reston, 1984); and William G. Cochran and Gertrude M. Cox, *Experimental designs,* 2d ed. (New York: Wiley, 1992).

NAMES INDEX

CORPORATIONS AND ORGANIZATIONS INDEX

Subject Index

CREDITS

Management, vol. 4, February 1989. Copyright © 1989 by Bill Communications.

Business & Economic Review: From "Hiring the Best" by Carol Lyles and Alisa Mosley from *Business & Economic Review,* vol. 44, no. 1, October 1,1997. Published by The Darla Moore School of Business, The University of South Carolina.

Caras & Associates: Card, "Safety Awareness."

Catalyst, Inc.: From "Two Careers, One Marriage: Making It Work in the Workplace." Copyright © 1998 by Catalyst, Inc.

CCH Inc.: From "1993 SHRM/CCH Survey" from *Human Resources Management,* May 26, 1993. Copyright © 1993 by CCH Inc. From "Preferential Affirmative Action in Employment" by John A. Gray from *Labor Law Journal,* January 1999. Copyright © 1993 by CCH Inc. From "Defining Workforce Diversity Programs and Practices in Organizations" by Michael R. Carrell and Everett E. Mann from *Labor Law Journal,* no. 12, December 1993. Copyright © 1993 by CCH Inc.

Randy Coe: "Lens Lab Inc.: Personnel Policies: Discipline and Investigations."

The Dallas Morning News: From "401Ks fall short for many workers" by Bill Deener from *The Dallas Morning News,* November 15, 1998, p. 1H. Copyright © 1998 by The Dallas Morning News. Reprinted by permission of The Dallas Morning News.

Dow Jones, Inc.: From "Mergers Entail Human Costs, a Study Shows" from *Dow Jones Newswires,* December 21, 1998. Copyright © 1998 by Dow Jones and Company, Inc. From "Auto Plants, Hiring Again, Are Demanding Higher-Skilled Labor" by Neal Templson from *The Wall Street Journal,* March 11, 1994. Copyright © 1994 by Dow Jones and Company, Inc. From " A Foot in the door" by Robert Rose from *The Wall Street Journal,* February 27, 1995. Copyright © 1995 by Dow Jones and Company, Inc. From "Don't Count on That Merit Raise This Year" by JoAnn Lublin from *The Wall Street Journal,* January 7, 1996. Copyright © 1996 by Dow Jones and Company, Inc. From "The Front Lines" by Thomas Petziner, Jr., from *The Wall Street Journal,* January 26, 1996. Copyright © 1996 by Dow Jones and Company, Inc. From "AFL-CIO Mounts Organizing Drive in Las Vegas" by G. Pascal Zachary from *The Wall Street Journal,* January 27, 1997. Copyright © 1997 by Dow Jones and Company, Inc. From "Side Effects:

Cross-border Merger Results in Headaches for Drug Company" by R. Frank and T. Burton from *The Wal Street Journal,* February 4, 1997. From "CIGNA Directors Diversity Challenge Hits a Dead End" by JoAnn Leblin from *The Wall Street Journal,* June 4, 1998. Copyright © 1998 by Dow Jones and Company, Inc. From "College Recruiting Becomes Lavash" by Carl Quintanilla from *The Wall Street Journal,* June 4, 1998. Copyright © 1998 by Dow Jones and Company, Inc. From *Wall Street Journal,* Asian Edition, December 11, 1998. Copyright © 1998 by Dow Jones and Company, Inc. From "Sign of Changed Times: Japan's Jobless Rates Rises to the U.S. Level" by Yumiko Ono and Jacob Schlesinger from *The Wall Street Journal,* December 28, 1998. Copyright © 1998 by Dow Jones and Company, Inc. All Rights Reserved Worldwide. Reprinted by permission of Dow Jones, Inc. via Copyright Clearance Center, Inc.

Employee Benefit Research Institute: From the 1998 Health Confidence Survey. Copyright © 1998 by the Employee Benefit Research Institute.

GE Appliances: From "Sexual Harassment: A Spectrum of Behavior Patterns" from *Sexual Harassment Manual.*

Harvard Business Review: From "Six Dangerous Myths About Pay" by Jeffrey Pfeffer from *Harvard Business Review,* May-June 1998, p. 109. Copyright © 1998 by the President and Fellows of Harvard College. All rights reserved. Reprinted by permission of *Harvard Business Review.*

HR Magazine: From "Realistic Goals Help Avoid Burnout" by Hugh F. Stallworth from *HR Magazine,* June 1990. Copyright © 1990 by the Society for Human Resource Management. From "Employers Protected by At-will Statements" by Raymond L. Hilgert from *HR Magazine,* March 1991. Copyright © 1991 by the Society for Human Resource Management. From "Piecing Together the Diversity Puzzle" by Benson Rose and Kay Lovelace from *HR Magazine,* vol. 36, June 1991. Copyright © 1991 by the Society for Human Resource Management. From "Employment Law Lingo" by Jode-Trager Planer from *HR Magazine,* May 1992. Copyright © 1992 by the Society for Human Resource Management. From "Look at Who's Talking" by K. Michele Kacman from *HR Magazine,* February 1993. Copyright © 1993 by the Society for Human Resource Management. From "McDonald's Focuses on Similarities" from *HR Magazine,* vol. 42, no. 7, July 1997. Copyright © 1997 by the Society for Human Resource Management. Published by the Society for Human Resource Management, Alexandria, VA.

HR News: From "Is Workplace Drug-Testing Effective?" from *HR News,* April 1996. Copyright © 1996 by the Society for Human Resource Management. From "AFL-CIO 'Summeristas' Fan Out to Sow Seeds for Unions' Future" by Robert Grossman from *HR News,* September 1996. Copyright © 1996 by the Society for Human Resource Management. From "Health Care Costs to Accelerate in 1999, Hewitt Predicts" by Stacy VanDerWall from *HR News Online,* December 15, 1998. Copyright © 1998 by the Society for Human Resource Management. Published by the Society for Human Resource Management, Alexandria, VA.

Hudson Institute: From *Workforce 2000: Work and Workers for the 21st Century* by William B. Johnston and Arnold H. Packer. Copyright © 1987 by the Hudson Institute.

Indiana State Department of Training: State Form 45910 (4-93) "Evaluation for Training."

Jossey-Bass Inc., Publishers: From *Empowered Teams* by Richard S. Wellins, William C. Byham, and Jeanne M. Wilson. Copyright © 1991 by Jossey-Bass Inc.

Kemper Insurance Companies: From *Management Guide on Alcoholism.*

Knight-Ridder/Tribune Information Services: From "Arbitration Rules Force Debate" from *The Dallas Morning News,* July 20, 1998. Copyright © 1998 by Knight-Ridder/Tribune Information Services. Reprinted with permission.

The Lexington Herald-Leader: From "Truth or Consequences" by Jim Jordan from *The Lexington Herald-Leader,* May 4, 1998. Copyright © 1998 by The Lexington Herald-Leader.

Los Angeles Times Syndicate: From "Battling to Climb the Ladder" by Barry Siegel from *Los Angeles Times,* February 7, 1990. Copyright © 1990 by the Los Angeles Times.

The Louisville Courier-Journal: From "Resumania" by Byron Crawford from *The Louisville Courier-Journal*, February 25, 1985. Copyright © 1985 by The Courier-Journal & Louisville Times Co. Reprinted with permission.

The McGraw-Hill Companies: From "What's a Team" by Aaron Bernstein from *Business Week,* May 4, 1992. Copyright © 1992 by The McGraw-Hill Companies. Reprinted by special permission. From *Managing the*

HR WEB SITES

HR PUBLICATIONS

HR Magazine
www.shrm.org/docs/HRmagazine.html

Workforce Online (Personnel Journal)
www.workforceonline.com

NewsEdge NewsPage
www.newspage.com

HR Live
www.hrlive.com

HR/PC (from HRWorld)
www.hrworld.com/pages/dgm/dgm_hrpc.htm

Asia Pacific Management Forum
www.mcb.co.uk/apmforum/nethome.htm

HR Today
www.hrtoday.com

Up-To-Date Library
www.utdlibrary.com

Benefits and Compensation Solutions
www.bcsolutionsmag.com

HRFocus
www.amanet.org/periodicals/hrf/hrf.htm

Center for HRM (public sector)
www.hrm.napawash.org

Employment Law Central
www.employmentlawcentral.com

JOB BANKS

CareerNet
www.careernet.com

EmploymentSpot
www.employmentspot.com

Wall Street Journal–Careers
careers.wsj.com

CareerMosaic
www.careermosaic.com

What Color Is Your Parachute: Job Hunt Online
www.tenspeedpress.com/parachute/front.htm

America's Employers
www.americasemployers.com

Yahoo Employment Listings
www.yahoo.com/business_and_
economy/employment/jobs

Monster Board
dir.yahoo.com/Business_and_Economy/
Employment/Jobs/Monster_Board/

Career Resource Center
www.careers.org

American Management Association International
www.amanet.org

International HR Information Management Assoc.
www.ihrim.org

International Personnel Management
www.ipma-hr.org

Training Forum
www.trainingforum.com

International Foundation of Employee Benefit Plans
www.ifebp.org

College and University Personnel Association
www.cupa.org

American Arbitration Association
www.adr.org

National Business & Disability Council
www.business-disability.com/home.asp

AFL-CIO
www.aflcio.org/front.htm

Families and Work Institute
www.familiesandwork.org

Commerce Clearing House
www.cch.com

The Conference Board
www.conference-board.org

William M. Mercer Companies
www.wmmercer.com

Andersen Consulting
www.ac.com

The Clayton Wallis Company
www.claytonwallis.com

Ernst and Young
www.ey.com

Towers Perrin
www.towers.com

ERI Economic Research Institute
www.erieri.com/

PeopleSoft
www.peoplesoft.com

Best Practices, LLC
www.best-in-class.com

Work & Family Connection
www.workfamily.com/resource.htm

PRIVATE RESEARCH AND CONSULTING COMPANIES
Bureau of National Affairs
www.bna.com